SEA FORCES
OF THE WORLD

This 1990 edition is published by Crescent Books
Distributed by Crown Publishers, Inc.

Copyright © Brian Trodd Publishing House Limited 1990

ISBN 0-517-69129-9

hgfedcba

Printed in Italy

SEA FORCES
OF THE WORLD

CHRISTOPHER CHANT

CRESCENT BOOKS
New York

CONTENTS

HMS *Norfolk*, lead of the Type 23 frigates, under the impulsion of its two Rolls-Royce Spey gas turbines.

'Delta I' class SSBN

(USSR)

Type: nuclear-powered ballistic missile submarine
Displacement: 8,750 tons surfaced and 10,200 tons dived
Dimensions: length 137·0 m (449·5 ft); beam 12·0 m (39·4 ft); draught 8·7 m (28·5 ft)
Gun armament: none
Missile armament: 12 vertical launch tubes for 12 SS-N-8 'Sawfly' underwater-launched ballistic missiles
Torpedo armament: six 533-mm (21-in) tubes (all bow), two of them with 406-mm (16-in) liners, for a typical load of 18 533-mm (21-in) Type 53 dual-role torpedoes or 12 533-mm (21-in) Type 53 dual-role and 10 406-mm (16-in) Type 40 anti-submarine torpedoes
Anti-submarine armament: torpedoes (see above)
Electronics: one 'Snoop Tray' surface-search and navigation radar, one low-frequency active/passive bow sonar, one medium-frequency torpedo fire-control sonar, one 'Brick Group' ESM system, one SINS, one 'Pert Spring' satellite navigation system, one 'Park Lamp' direction-finder, and extensive communications systems
Propulsion: two pressurized water-cooled reactors supplying steam to two sets of geared turbines delivering 37,300 kW (50,025 hp) to two shafts
Performance: maximum speed 20 kt surfaced and 26 kt dived; diving depth 400 m (1,315 ft) operational and 600 m (1,970 ft) maximum
Complement: 120

The main external difference between the 'Yankee' and 'Delta I' class SSBNs is the higher casing over the latter's SS-N-8 'Sawfly' SLBM compartment.

Class
1. USSR
18 boats
Note: Successor to the 'Yankee' class, the 'Delta I' class began to come off the slips at Severodvinsk in 1972, and was then produced in parallel at Severodvinsk (10 boats) and Komsomolsk (eight boats). The missile section was revised to accommodate the longer and larger-diameter SS-N-8 missile, whose greater capabilities meant that the missile complement could be reduced from 16 to 12.

'Delta II' class SSBN

(USSR)

Type: nuclear-powered ballistic missile submarine
Displacement: 9,750 tons surfaced and 11,300 tons dived
Dimensions: length 155·0 m (508·5 ft); beam 12·0 m (39·4 ft); draught 8·7 m (28·5 ft)
Gun armament: none
Missile armament: 16 vertical launch tubes for 16 SS-N-8 'Sawfly' underwater-launched ballistic missiles
Torpedo armament: six 533-mm (21-in) tubes (all bow), two of them with 406-mm (16-in) liners, for a typical load of 18 533-mm (21-in) Type 53 dual-role torpedoes or 12 533-mm (21-in) Type 53 dual-role and 10 406-mm (16-in) Type 40 anti-submarine torpedoes
Anti-submarine armament: torpedoes (see above)
Electronics: one 'Snoop Tray' surface-search and navigation radar, one low-frequency active/passive bow sonar, one medium-frequency torpedo fire-control sonar, one 'Brick Group' ESM system, one SINS, one 'Pert Spring' satellite navigation system, one 'Park Lamp' direction-finder, and extensive communications systems
Propulsion: two pressurized water-cooled reactors supplying steam to two sets of geared turbines delivering 37,300 kW (50,025 hp) to two shafts
Performance: maximum speed 20 kt surfaced and 25 kt dived; diving depth 400 m (1,315 ft) operational and 600 m (1,970 ft) maximum
Complement: 130

By comparison with the boats of the 'Delta I' class, those of the 'Delta II' class have a longer missile compartment that slopes down onto the after casing without the kink of the earlier boats. This allows an increase in the SLBM complement from 12 to 16, a one-third boost in offensive capability with only slight degradation of underwater performance.

Class
1. USSR
4 boats
Note: Built only at Severodvinsk, and appearing from 1974, the 'Delta II' class is a simple extension of the 'Delta I' design with a lengthened missile section to accommodate 16 rather than 12 missiles.

'Delta III' class SSBN

(USSR)

Type: nuclear-powered ballistic missile submarine
Displacement: 9,750 tons surfaced and 11,700 tons dived
Dimensions: length 160·0 m (524·9 ft); beam 12·0 m (39·4 ft); draught 8·7 m (28·5 ft)
Gun armament: none
Missile armament: 16 vertical launch tubes for 16 SS-N-18 'Stingray' underwater-launched ballistic missiles
Torpedo armament: six 533-mm (21-in) tubes (all bow), two of them with 406-mm (16-in) liners, for a typical load of 18 533-mm (21-in) Type 53 dual-role torpedoes or 12 533-mm (21-in) Type 53 dual-role and 10 406-mm (16-in) Type 40 anti-submarine torpedoes
Anti-submarine armament: torpedoes (see above)
Electronics: one 'Snoop Tray' surface-search and navigation radar, one low-frequency active/passive bow sonar, one medium-frequency torpedo fire-control sonar, one 'Brick Group' ESM system, one SINS, one 'Pert Spring' satellite navigation system, and extensive communications systems

Propulsion: two pressurized water-cooled reactors supplying steam to two sets of geared turbines delivering 37,300 kW (50,025 hp) to two shafts
Performance: maximum speed 20 kt surfaced and 24 kt dived; diving depth 400 m (1,315 ft) operational and 600 m (1,970 ft) maximum
Complement: 130

Class
1. USSR
14 boats
Note: Built only at Severodvinsk from 1974 to 1982, the 'Delta III' design is a fairly straightforward revision of the basic 'Delta' concept to carry liquid-fuelled SS-N-18 rather than solid-fuelled SS-N-8 missiles. The SS-N-18 is of the same diameter as the SS-N-8, but somewhat longer and fitted with a MIRVed warhead system. This entailed a further enlargement of the missile compartment aft of the sail: in the two earlier 'Delta' classes the decking above this compartment is some 7·75 m (25·4 ft) above the waterline, but in the 'Delta III' it is 9·0 m (29·5 ft) above the waterline to provide the longer tubes needed by the newer missile.

'Delta IV' class SSBN

(USSR)

Type: nuclear-powered ballistic missile submarine
Displacement: 10,100 tons surfaced and 12,150 tons dived
Dimensions: length 166·0 m (544·6 ft); beam 12·0 m (39·4 ft); draught: 8·7 m (28·5 ft)
Gun armament: none
Missile armament: 16 vertical launch tubes for 16 SS-N-23 'Skiff' underwater-launched ballistic missiles
Torpedo armament: six 533-mm (21-in) tubes (all bow), two of them with 406-mm (16-in) liners, for a typical load of 18 533-mm (21-in) Type 53 dual-role torpedoes or 12 533-mm (21-in) Type 53 dual-role torpedoes and 10 406-mm (16-in) Type 40 anti-submarine torpedoes
Anti-submarine armament: torpedoes (see above)
Electronics: one 'Snoop Tray' surface-search radar, one low-frequency active/passive bow sonar, one medium-frequency torpedo fire-control sonar, one 'Brick Group' ESM system, one SINS, one 'Pert Spring' satellite navigation system, one 'Park Lamp' direction-finder, one 'Cod Eye' navigation system, and extensive communication and navigation equipment

Propulsion: two pressurized water-cooled reactors supplying steam to four sets of geared steam turbines delivering 45,000 kW (60,355 hp) to two shafts
Performance: maximum speed 20 kt surfaced and 23·5 kt dived; diving depth 400 m (1,315 ft) operational and 600 m (1,970 ft) maximum
Complement: 150

Class

1. USSR
5 boats plus 1 more boat building
Note: The 'Delta IV' is in essence the 'Delta III' revised to carry the newer SS-N-23, which combines the range of the SS-N-8 with the MIRVed warhead capability of the SS-N-18. Instead of the cruciform tail surfaces of the earlier 'Delta' classes, the 'Delta IV' has the angled rudder/fin arrangement first seen on the second 'Oscar' class unit, complete with a tubular housing for a towed VLF or ELF communications system. Like the other 'Delta' variants, the 'Delta IV' class boats have a continuous outer acoustic coating. The first of the class was launched in February 1984 after building at Severodvinsk.

As well as a new SLBM type, the 'Delta IV' class boats have a revised fin/rudder unit housing the towed portion of a new communications system.

'Hotel III' class SSBN

(USSR)

Type: nuclear-powered ballistic missile submarine
Displacement: 5,000 tons surfaced and 6,350 tons dived
Dimensions: length 130·0 m (426·4 ft); beam 9·2 m (30·2 ft); draught 7·6 m (25·0 ft)
Gun armament: none
Missile armament: six vertical launch tubes for six SS-N-8 'Sawfly' underwater-launched ballistic missiles
Torpedo armament: six 533-mm (21-in) tubes (all bow) for a maximum of 16 533-mm (21-in) Type 53 dual-role torpedoes
Anti-submarine armament: two 406-mm (16-in) tubes (both stern) for four 406-mm (16-in) Type 40 anti-submarine torpedoes
Electronics: one 'Snoop Tray' surface-search and navigation radar, one 'Herkules' high-frequency active/passive bow sonar, one 'Feniks' bow

sonar, one 'Stop Light' ESM system, one 'Quad Loop' direction-finder, one SINS, one satellite navigation system, one 'Cod Eye' navigation system, and various communication systems
Propulsion: two pressurized water-cooled reactors supplying steam to two sets of geared turbines delivering 22,500 kW (30,175 hp) to two shafts
Performance: maximum speed 20 kt surfaced and 26 kt dived
Complement: 90

Class

1. USSR
1 boat
Note: One of eight 'Hotel I' class built at Severodvinsk between 1958 and 1962 with three surface-launched SS-N-4 missiles, this is the only unit left in its original SSBN form after being modified between 1963 and 1970 as a 'Hotel II' with underwater-launched SS-N-5 missiles and then between 1969 and 1970 as the sole 'Hotel III' as evaluation platform for the SS-N-8.

'Lafayette' and 'Benjamin Franklin' class SSBNs

(USA)

Type: nuclear-powered ballistic missile submarine

Displacement: 7,250 tons surfaced and 8,250 tons dived

Dimensions: length 425·0 ft (129·5 m); beam 33·0 ft (10·1 m); draught 31·5 ft (9·6 m)

Gun armament: none

Missile armament: 16 vertical launch tubes for 16 underwater-launched ballistic missiles (UGM-96A Trident I C4 in the modernized SSBN627, 629, 630, 632, 633, 634, 640, 641, 643, 655, 657 and 658, and UGM-73A Poseidon C3 in the unmodernized other boats)

Torpedo armament: four 21-in (533-mm) Mk 65 tubes (all bow) for 12 Mk 48 dual-role wire-guided torpedoes

Anti-submarine armament: UUM-44A SUBROC tube-launched missiles, and torpedoes (see above)

Electronics: one BPS-11A or BPS-15 surface-search and navigation radar, one BQR-7 passive detection sonar, one BQR-15 passive detection towed-array sonar, one BQR-19 short-range rapid-scanning active navigation sonar, one BQR-21 passive detection sonar, one BQS-4 active/passive search and classification sonar, three Mk 2 Mod 4 SINS, one Mk 88 (Poseidon) or Mk 98 (Trident) SLBM fire-control system, one Mk 113 underwater weapons fire-control system, Emerson Electric Mk 2 torpedo decoys, one WLR-8 ESM system with intercept element, one WSC-3 satellite communications transceiver, and one satellite navigation receiver

Propulsion: one Westinghouse S5W pressurized water-cooled reactor supplying steam to two sets of geared turbines delivering 15,000 hp (11,185 kW) to one shaft

Performance: maximum speed 20 kt surfaced and about 25 kt dived; diving depth 1,150 ft (350 m) operational and 1,525 ft (465 m) maximum

Complement: 13 + 130

The Lafayette is the lead boat of this impressive class, and is typical of American SSBN design practices in being considerably 'cleaner' in the hydrodynamic sense than comparable Soviet boats. This derives mainly from the full incorporation of the SLBM compartment into the basic structure rather than as a semi-external addition.

Class
1. USA

Name	No.	Builder	Laid down	Commissioned
Lafayette	SSBN616	GD (EB Div)	Jan 1961	Apr 1963
Alexander Hamilton	SSBN617	GD (EB Div)	Jun 1961	Jun 1963
John Adams	SSBN620	Portsmouth NY	May 1961	May 1964
James Monroe	SSBN622	Newport News	Jul 1961	Dec 1963
Woodrow Wilson	SSBN624	Mare Island NY	Sep 1961	Dec 1963
Henry Clay	SSBN625	Newport News	Oct 1961	Feb 1964
Daniel Webster	SSBN626	GD (EB Div)	Dec 1961	Apr 1964
James Madison	SSBN627	Newport News	Mar 1962	Jul 1964
Tecumseh	SSBN628	GD (EB Div)	Jun 1962	May 1964
Daniel Boone	SSBN629	Mare Island NY	Feb 1962	Apr 1964
John C. Calhoun	SSBN630	Newport News	Jun 1962	Sep 1964
Ulysses S. Grant	SSBN631	GD (EB Div)	Aug 1962	Jul 1964
Von Steuben	SSBN632	Newport News	Sep 1962	Sep 1964
Casimir Pulaski	SSBN633	GD (EB Div)	Jan 1963	Aug 1964
Stonewall Jackson	SSBN634	Mare Island NY	Jul 1962	Aug 1964
Benjamin Franklin	SSBN640	GD (EB Div)	May 1963	Oct 1965
Simon Bolivar	SSBN641	Newport News	Apr 1963	Oct 1965
Kamehameha	SSBN642	Mare Island NY	May 1963	Dec 1965
George Bancroft	SSBN643	GD (EB Div)	Aug 1963	Jan 1966
Lewis & Clark	SSBN644	Newport News	Jul 1963	Dec 1965
James K. Polk	SSBN645	GD (EB Div)	Nov 1963	Apr 1966
George C. Marshall	SSBN654	Newport News	Mar 1964	Apr 1966
Henry L. Stimson	SSBN655	GD (EB Div)	Apr 1964	Aug 1966
George Washington Carver	SSBN656	GD (EB Div)	Aug 1964	Jun 1966
Francis Scott Key	SSBN657	GD (EB Div)	Dec 1964	Dec 1966
Mariano G. Vallejo	SSBN658	Mare Island NY	Jul 1964	Dec 1966
Will Rogers	SSBN659	GD (EB Div)	Mar 1966	Apr 1967

Note: The *Benjamin Franklin* and later boats are fitted with quieter machinery and are thus regarded as a separate class. The two classes remain the numerical mainstay of the USA's SLBM capability pending delivery of larger numbers of the 'Ohio' class boats. As the 'Ohio' class boats become available in larger numbers, some of these boats have been decommissioned or converted to other roles such as a moored reactor training submarine.

'L'Inflexible' class SSBN

(France)

Type: nuclear-powered ballistic missile submarine

Displacement: 8,080 tons surfaced and 8,920 tons dived

Dimensions: length 128·7 m (422·2 ft); beam 10·6 m (34·7 ft); draught 10·0 m (32·8 ft)

Gun armament: none

Missile armament: 16 vertical launch tubes for 16 MSBS M-4/TN-71 underwater-launched ballistic missiles, and four SM.39 Exocet tube-launched anti-ship missiles carried in place of an equal number of torpedoes

Torpedo armament: four 533-mm (21-in) tubes (all bow) for 18 L5 dual-role wire-guided anti-ship torpedoes

Anti-submarine armament: torpedoes (see above)

Electronics: one DRUA 33 surface-search and navigation radar, one DSUX 21 multi-function active/passive bow/flank sonar, one DUUX 2 passive ranging and intercept sonar, one DSUV 61 towed-array sonar, one ESM system with warning element, one SINS, one missile fire-control system, one DLT D3 torpedo fire-control system, two SINSs. and other systems

Propulsion: one pressurized water-cooled reactor supplying steam to two sets of geared turbines powering two turbo-alternators/one electric motor delivering 11,925 kW (15,990 hp) to one shaft

Performance: maximum speed 18 kt surfaced and 25 kt dived; diving depth 250 m (820 ft) operational and 330 m (1,085 ft) maximum

Complement: 15 + 112

Class
1. France

Name	No.	Builder	Laid down	Commissioned
L'Inflexible	S615	Cherbourg ND	Mar 1979	Apr 1985

Note: This was France's sixth SSBN, a type intermediate between the five boats of the 'Le Redoutable' and the planned 'Le Triomphant' classes to

***L'Inflexible* bridges the operational gap between the 'Le Redoutable' and 'Le Triomphant' classes, combining the former's hull and propulsion (the latter in quietened form) with some of the latter's features.**

provide for a constant patrol availability of three boats. The boat is similar to the 'Le Redoutable' class boats apart from its quieter machinery. The type also has a diesel-electric auxiliary propulsion system that provides a range of 9250 km (5,750 miles) at 4 kt.

'Le Redoutable' class SSBN

(France)

Type: nuclear-powered ballistic missile submarine

Displacement: 8,045 tons surfaced and 8,940 tons dived

Dimensions: length 128·7 m (422·1 ft); beam 10·6 m (34·8 ft); draught 10·0 m (32·8 ft)

Gun armament: none

Missile armament: 16 vertical launch tubes for 16 MSBS M-20 (being replaced by M-4/TN-71 in all but S611) underwater-launched ballistic missiles, and four SM.39 Exocet tube-launched anti-ship missiles carried in place of torpedoes

Torpedo armament: four 533-mm (21-in) tubes (all bow) for 18 L5 dual-role and F17 wire-guided anti-ship torpedoes

Anti-submarine armament: torpedoes (see above)

Electronics: one Calypso surface-search and navigation radar, one DUUV 23 active/passive bow sonar (to be replaced by DSUX 21 multi-function bow/flank sonar), one DUUX 2 passive ranging and intercept sonar, one ESM system with warning element, one missile fire-control system, one DLT D3 torpedo fire-control system, one SINS, and various communication systems

Propulsion: one pressurized water-cooled reactor supplying steam to two sets of geared turbines powering two turbo-alternators/one electric motor delivering 11,925 kW (15,990 hp) to one shaft

Performance: maximum speed 20 + kt surfaced and 25 kt dived; diving depth 250 m (820 ft) operational and 330 m (1,085 ft) maximum

Complement: 15 + 120

Class
1. France

Name	No.	Builder	Laid down	Commissioned
Le Foudroyant	S610	Cherbourg ND	Dec 1969	Jun 1974
Le Redoutable	S611	Cherbourg ND	Mar 1964	Dec 1971
Le Terrible	S612	Cherbourg ND	Jun 1967	Dec 1973
L'Indomptable	S613	Cherbourg ND	Dec 1971	Dec 1976
Le Tonnant	S614	Cherbourg ND	Oct 1974	May 1980

Note: These boats form the main strength of France's nuclear deterrent force, and though they are first-generation types they have been usefully modernized in terms of their equipment and missiles. Like other nuclear-powered submarines, the boats of this class are fitted with an auxiliary propulsion system for use should the primary propulsion suffer a breakdown, this auxiliary system comprising two diesels delivering 975 kW (1,307 hp) for a range of 9250 km (5,750 miles) at 4 kt.

***Le Redoutable* is one of the five boats that constitute France's first generation of SSBNs.**

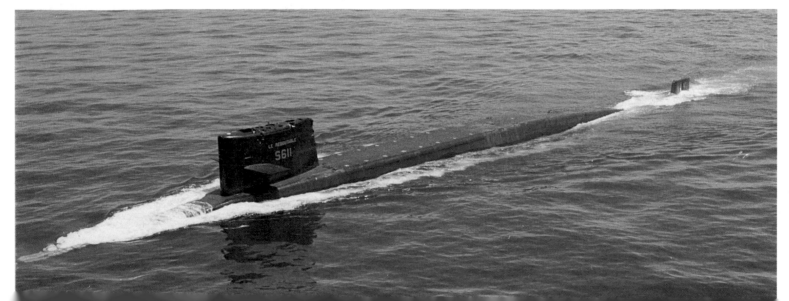

'Le Triomphant' class SSBN

(France)

Type: nuclear-powered ballistic missile submarine

Displacement: 12,700 tons surfaced and 14,200 tons dived

Dimensions: length 138·0 m (452·75 ft); beam 12·5 m (41·0 ft); draught not revealed

Gun armament: none

Missile armament: 16 vertical launch tubes for 16 MSBS M-4/TN-71 (to be replaced by M-5/TN-75) underwater-launched ballistic missiles, and four SM.39 Exocet tube-launched anti-ship missiles in place of torpedoes

Torpedo armament: four 533-mm (21-in) tubes (all bow) for wire-guided anti-ship and Murène anti-submarine torpedoes

Anti-submarine armament: torpedoes (see above)

Electronics: one surface-search and navigation radar, various active/passive sonars, one ESM system, one missile fire-control system, one DLT D3 torpedo fire-control system, one SINS, and various communication systems

Propulsion: one Type K15 pressurized water-cooled reactor supplying steam to two sets of geared turbines powering two turbo-alternators/one electric motor delivering 30,500 kW (40,905 hp) to one shaft

Performance: maximum speed 20+ kt surfaced and 25 kt dived; diving depth 300+ m (985+ ft) operational

Complement: 110

Class

1. France

Name	No.	Builder	Laid down	Commissioned
Le Triomphant		Cherbourg ND	1988	1994

Note: Designed to enter service at two/three-year intervals, the six boats of the 'Le Triomphant' class are planned as replacement for the boats of the 'Le Redoutable' class. The later boats of the new class may be longer, at 170·0 m (557·7 ft).

'Ohio' class SSBN

(USA)

Type: nuclear-powered ballistic missile submarine

Displacement: 16,600 tons surfaced and 18,700 tons dived

Dimensions: length 560·0 ft (170·7 m); beam 42·0 ft (12·8 m); draught 36·5 ft (11·1 m)

Gun armament: none

Missile armament: 24 vertical launch tubes for 24 UGM-96A Trident I C4 (Trident II D5 from SSBN734 onward) underwater-launched ballistic missiles

Torpedo armament: four 21-in (533-mm) Mk 68 tubes (all bow) for Mk 48 dual-role wire-guided torpedoes

Anti-submarine armament: torpedoes (see above)

Electronics: one BPS-15A surface-search radar, one BQQ-6 multi-function sonar suite including one BQS-13 active/passive bow sonar, one BQS-15 active/passive close-range sonar, one BQR-19 short-range rapid-scanning active navigation sonar, one BQR-15 passive towed-array sonar, one BQS-19 active/passive detection towed-array sonar, one Mk 98 SLBM fire-control system, one Mk 118 underwater weapons fire-control system, two Mk 2 SINS, one WLR-8(V)5 ESM system with warning element, Emerson Electric Mk 2 torpedo decoys, one WSC-3 satellite communications transceiver, and various communication and navigation systems

Propulsion: one General Electric S8G pressurized water-cooled reactor supplying steam to two sets of General Electric geared turbines delivering 60,000 hp (44,740 kW) to one shaft

Performance: maximum speed 28 kt surfaced and 30 kt dived; diving depth 985 ft (300 m) operational and 1,640 ft (500 m) maximum

Complement: 15+140

Class

1. USA

Name	No.	Builder	Launched	Com-missioned
Ohio	SSBN726	GD (EB Div)	Apr 1979	Nov 1981
Michigan	SSBN727	GD (EB Div)	Apr 1980	Sep 1982
Florida	SSBN728	GD (EB Div)	Nov 1981	Jun 1983
Georgia	SSBN729	GD (EB Div)	Nov 1982	Feb 1984
Henry M. Jackson	SSBN730	GD (EB Div)	Oct 1983	Oct 1984
Alabama	SSBN731	GD (EB Div)	May 1984	May 1985
Alaska	SSBN732	GD (EB Div)	Jan 1985	Jan 1986
Nevada	SSBN733	GD (EB Div)	Sep 1985	Aug 1986
Tennessee	SSBN734	GD (EB Div)	Dec 1986	Dec 1988
Pennsylvania	SSBN735	GD (EB Div)	Apr 1988	Aug 1989
West Virginia	SSBN736	GD (EB Div)	Apr 1989	Apr 1990
Kentucky	SSBN737	GD (EB Div)	Apr 1990	Dec 1990
Maryland	SSBN738	GD (EB Div)	Apr 1991	Dec 1991
Nebraska	SSBN739	GD (EB Div)	Nov 1991	Dec 1992
	SSBN740	GD (EB Div)	Nov 1992	Jan 1994
	SSBN741	GD (EB Div)		
	SSBN742	GD (EB Div)		

Note: These boats, eventually to total 17, are becoming the mainstay of the US Navy's SLBM force with the potent Trident missile types. A 'Launched' date is quoted instead of the standard 'Laid down' because the extensive prefabrication of these boats makes the latter irrelevant.

The *Florida* is the third boat of the strategically vital 'Ohio' class.

'Resolution' class SSBN

(UK)

Type: nuclear-powered ballistic missile submarine
Displacement: 7,600 tons surfaced and 8,500 tons dived
Dimensions: length 425·0 ft (129·5 m); beam 33·0 ft (10·1 m); draught 30·0 ft (9·1 m)
Gun armament: none
Missile armament: 16 vertical launch tubes for 16 UGM-27C Polaris A3TK underwater-launched ballistic missiles
Torpedo armament: six 21-in (533-mm) tubes (all bow) for Mk 24 Tigerfish dual-role wire-guided torpedoes
Anti-submarine armament: torpedoes (see above)
Electronics: one Type 1006 surface-search and navigation radar, one Type 2001 long-range active/passive hull sonar, one Type 2007 long-range passive hull/flank sonar, one Type 2046 retractable towed-array passive sonar, one Type 2019 passive intercept and ranging sonar, one SLBM fire-control system, one underwater weapons fire-control system, one ESM system with UA-11/12 intercept elements, one SINS, and various communication and navigation systems
Propulsion: one Rolls-Royce PWR-1 pressurized water-cooled reactor supplying steam to one set of English Electric geared turbines delivering 15,000 hp (11,185 kW) to one shaft
Performance: maximum speed 20 kt surfaced and 25 kt dived; diving depth 1,150 ft (350 m) operational and 1,525 ft (465 m) maximum
Complement: 13 + 130

The four boats of the UK's first-generation 'Resolution' class are to be phased out of service as the altogether more capable boats of the new 'Vanguard' class are commissioned.

Class
1. UK

Name	No.	Builder	Laid down	Commissioned
Resolution	S22	Vickers	Feb 1964	Oct 1967
Repulse	S23	Vickers	Mar 1965	Sep 1968
Renown	S26	Cammell Laird	Jun 1964	Nov 1968
Revenge	S27	Cammell Laird	May 1965	Dec 1969

Note: These boats are the mainstay of the UK's nuclear deterrent force, but despite major improvements their Polaris SLBMs are obsolescent and the boats will be phased out of service as the 'Vanguard' class of Trident-equipped boats is introduced in the 1990s.

'Typhoon' class SSBN

(USSR)

Type: nuclear-powered ballistic missile submarine
Displacement: 18,500 tons surfaced and 26,500 tons dived
Dimensions: length 171·5 m (562·7 ft); beam 24·6 m (80·7 ft); draught 13·0 m (42·7 ft)
Gun armament: none
Missile armament: 20 vertical launch tubes for 20 SS-N-20 'Sturgeon' underwater-launched ballistic missiles and, according to some sources, surface-to-air missiles
Torpedo armament: four 650-mm (25·6-in) and two 533-mm (21-in) tubes (all bow) for a maximum load of 36 650-mm (25·6-in) Type 65 and 533-mm (21-in) Type 53 torpedoes
Anti-submarine armament: torpedoes and, instead of some of the maximum torpedo complement, SS-N-15 'Starfish' and SS-N-16 'Stallion' missiles fired from the 533-mm (21-in) and 650-mm (25·6-in) tubes respectively
Mines: can be carried in place of torpedoes and/or anti-submarine missiles
Electronics: one 'Snoop Pair' surface-search and navigation radar, one air-search radar (only if SAMs are carried), one low-frequency active/passive bow sonar, one medium-frequency torpedo fire-control sonar, one 'Rim Hat' ESM system, one or two SINS, one 'Pert Spring' satellite communications system, one 'Shot Gun' VHF communications antenna, one 'Park Lamp' direction-finder, one 'Cod Eye' navigation system, and other communications and navigation systems
Propulsion: two pressurized water-cooled reactors supplying steam to two sets of geared turbines delivering 60,000 kW (80,460 hp) to two shafts
Performance: maximum speed 20 kt surfaced and 30 kt dived; diving depth 400 m (1,315 ft) operational and 600 m (1,970 ft) maximum
Complement: 150

Class
1. USSR
5 boats plus 2 more building and ? more planned
Note: Built at Severodvinsk since 1977, this is the world's largest type of submarine, with truly prodigious performance based on high power and control of the boundary layer. The hull consists of two side-by-side major pressure vessels and separate central and forward pressure compartments inside an outer casing fitted with 'Cluster Guard' anechoic tiling.

The 'Typhoon' class SSBN is the Soviet equivalent to the American 'Ohio' class, but the Soviet boats are very considerably beamier and carry 20 rather than 24 SLBMs.

'Vanguard' class SSBN

(UK)

Type: nuclear-powered ballistic missile submarine
Displacement: 5,000 tons dived
Dimensions: length 486·4 ft (148·3 m); beam 42·0 ft (12·8 m); draught 39·4 ft (12·0 m)
Gun armament: none
Missile armament: 16 vertical launch tubes for 16 Trident II D5 underwater-launched ballistic missiles
Torpedo armament: four 21-in (533-mm) tubes (all bow) for Spearfish and Mk 24 Tigerfish dual-role wire-guided torpedoes
Anti-submarine armament: torpedoes (see above)
Electronics: one Type 1007 surface-search and navigation radar, one Type 2054 hull-mounted active/passive intercept sonar, one Type 2046 passive search towed-array sonar, one SLBM fire-control system, one underwater weapons fire-control system, one UAC-3 ESM system with warning element, one or two SINS, and various communication and navigation systems
Propulsion: one Rolls-Royce PWR-2 pressurized water-cooled reactor supplying steam to one set of English Electric geared turbines delivering 27,500 hp (20,505 kW) to one shaft
Performance: maximum speed 20 kt surfaced and 25 kt dived; diving depth 1,150 ft (350 m) operational and 1,525 ft (465 m) maximum
Complement: 135

An artist's impression of the UK's new 'Vanguard' class SSBN, which offers much higher levels of survivability with very considerably enhanced offensive capability through its Trident II D5 SLBMs.

Class
1. UK

Name	No.	Builder	Laid down	Commissioned
Vanguard		VSEL	Sep 1986	1992
Victorious		VSEL	Dec 1987	
		VSEL		
		VSEL		

Note: These four boats are designed as one-for-one replacements for the obsolete 'Resolution' class SSBNs, far superior operational capability being offered by greater underwater performance and quietness combined with the new Trident II D5 SLBM.

'Xia' or 'Type 09' class SSBN

(China)

Type: nuclear-powered ballistic missile submarine
Displacement: 8,000 tons dived
Dimensions: length 120·0 m (393·7 ft); beam 10·0 m (32·8 ft); draught 8·0 m (26·25 ft)
Gun armament: none
Missile armament: 12 vertical launch tubes for 12 JL-1 (CSS-N-3) or JL-2 (CSS-N-4) underwater-launched ballistic missiles
Torpedo armament: probably four 533-mm (21-in) tubes (all bow) for Type 53 dual-role torpedoes
Anti-submarine armament: torpedoes (see above)
Electronics: one surface-search and navigation radar, several sonar systems, one SINS, and communications and navigation systems

Propulsion: one pressurized water-cooled reactor supplying steam to a turbo-electric drive system delivering unknown power to two shafts
Performance: maximum speed 18 kt surfaced and 22 kt dived; diving depth about 300 m (985 ft) operational
Complement: 84

Class
1. China
1 boat plus 3 more building and (possibly) 8 more planned
Note: The first 'Xia' class SSBN was laid down in 1978 at Huludao and launched in 1981, and the programme is notable for the slow pace apparently imposed by difficulties with the nuclear propulsion system. A total of 12 boats is expected, and it is possible that the last 10 may be stretched in the hull to accommodate 16 rather than 12 missile tubes, though the Chinese claim that all the boats have 20 tubes.

'Yankee I' and 'Yankee II' class SSBNs

(USSR)

Type: nuclear-powered ballistic missile submarine
Displacement: 7,800 tons surfaced and 9,600 tons dived
Dimensions: length 129·5 m (424·9 ft); beam 11·6 m (38·0 ft); draught 7·8 m (25·6 ft)
Gun armament: none
Missile armament: ('Yankee I' class) 16 vertical launch tubes for 16 SS-N-6 'Serb' underwater-launched ballistic missiles, or ('Yankee II' class) 12 vertical launch tubes for 12 SS-N-17 'Snipe' underwater-launched ballistic missiles
Torpedo armament: six 533-mm (21-in) tubes (all bow), two of them with 406-mm (16-in) liners, for a typical load of 18 533-mm (21-in) Type 53 dual-role torpedoes or 12 533-mm (21-in) Type 53 dual-role and 10 406-mm (16-in) Type 40 anti-submarine torpedoes
Anti-submarine armament: torpedoes (see above)
Electronics: one 'Snoop Tray' surface-search and navigation radar, one low-frequency active/passive bow sonar, one medium-frequency torpedo fire-control sonar, one 'Brick Group' ESM system, one SINS, one 'Pert Spring' satellite navigation system, one 'Cod Eye' navigation system, one 'Park Lamp' direction-finder, and various communication and navigation systems
Propulsion: two pressurized water-cooled reactors supplying steam to two sets of geared turbines delivering 37,300 kW (50,025 hp) to two shafts
Performance: maximum speed 20 kt surfaced and 27 kt dived; diving depth 400 m (1,315 ft) operational and 600 m (1,970 ft) maximum
Complement: 120

Class
1. USSR
15 'Yankee I' class boats
1 'Yankee II' class boat
Note: The 'Yankee' class was the USSR's first series-produced type of SSBN, and the original 34 boats were produced in parallel at the Severodvinsk 402 and Komsomolsk shipyards between 1963 and 1972. The type entered service in 1967, and its production peaked in the 1969-72 period, when 25 units were completed. The 'Yankee' class design has after compartments 30% longer and a missile compartment 30% shorter than those of the contemporary 'Lafayette' class in US Navy service, indicating a less efficient (and thus bulkier) nuclear powerplant, and shorter range for the smaller-diameter missiles. The class is being reduced in number as newer 'Delta' and 'Typhoon' class SSBNs enter service. The single 'Yankee II' class unit was converted between 1971 and 1975 for the SS-N-17 SLBM.

The obsolete 'Yankee I' class boats are being withdrawn from SSBN service.

'Golf II' class SSB

(USSR)

Type: ballistic missile submarine
Displacement: 2,400 tons surfaced and 2,950 tons dived
Dimensions: length 98·0 m (321·5 ft); beam 8·6 m (28·2 ft); draught 6·6 m (21·7 ft)
Gun armament: none
Missile armament: three vertical launch tubes for three SS-N-5 'Serb' submarine-launched ballistic missiles
Torpedo armament: 10 533-mm (21-in) tubes (six bow and four stern) for a maximum load of 16 Type 53 dual-role torpedoes
Anti-submarine armament: torpedoes (see above)
Electronics: one 'Snoop Tray' or 'Snoop Plate' surface-search and navigation radar, one 'Herkules' high-frequency active/passive hull sonar, one 'Feniks' bow sonar, one 'Stop Light' ESM system with warning element, and various communication and navigation systems
Propulsion: diesel-electric arrangement, with three diesels delivering 4500 kW (6,035 hp) and three electric motors delivering 4125 kW (5,530 hp) to three shafts

Performance: maximum speed 17 kt surfaced and 14 kt dived; range 11,125 km (6,915 miles) at 14 kt surfaced
Complement: 12 + 75

Class
1. USSR
12 'Golf II' class boats

Note: Built between 1958 and 1962 at Severodvinsk (15 boats) and Komsomolsk (eight boats), the original 'Golf I' class numbered 23 units. Between 1963 and 1968 13 units were converted (eight at Severodvinsk and five at Komsomolsk) to 'Golf II' standard with the underwater-launched SS-N-5 SLBM system in place of the surface-launched SS-N-4 system. The single 'Golf III' class SSB was a conversion with its hull lengthened by 20·0 m (65·6 ft) to allow the incorporation of six launch tubes for the SS-N-8 SLBM system, but this unit was scrapped in 1987. The sole 'Golf III' class SSB was converted at Severodvinsk between 1974 and 1975 as a trials boat for use in the SS-N-20 SLBM programme.

'Wuhan' class SSB

(USSR/China)

Type: ballistic missile submarine
Displacement: 2,350 tons surfaced and 2,950 tons dived
Dimensions: length 98·0 m (321·4 ft); beam 8·5 m (27·9 ft); draught 6·4 m (21·0 ft)
Gun armament: none
Missile armament: two vertical launch tubes for two JL-1 (CCS-N-3) submarine-launched ballistic missiles
Torpedo armament: six 533-mm (21-in) tubes (all bow) for 12 Type 53 dual-role torpedoes
Anti-submarine armament: torpedoes (see above)
Electronics: one 'Snoop Plate' surface-search and navigation radar, various sonar systems, and various communication and navigation systems
Propulsion: diesel-electric arrangement, with three diesels delivering 4500 kW (6,035 hp) and three electric motors delivering 9000 kW (12,070 hp) to three shafts
Performance: maximum speed 17 kt surfaced and 14 kt dived; range 26,000 km (16,155 miles) at 14 kt surfaced
Complement: 12 + 74

Class
1. China
1 boat
Note: Built at Dalian and launched in 1964, this is a Chinese development of the Soviet 'Golf' class design, and is used mainly for trials work in connection with the CSS-N-3 SLBM programme.

'Charlie I' class SSGN

(USSR)

Type: nuclear-powered cruise missile submarine
Displacement: 4,200 tons surfaced and 5,000 tons dived
Dimensions: length 94·0 m (308·3 ft); beam 9·9 m (32·5 ft); draught 7·5 m (24·6 ft)
Gun armament: none
Missile armament: eight launch tubes for eight SS-N-7 'Starbright' underwater-launched anti-ship missiles
Torpedo armament: six 533-mm (21-in) tubes (all bow), two of them with 406-mm (16-in) liners, for a maximum load of 12 533-mm (21-in) Type 53 dual-role torpedoes and four 406-mm (16-in) Type 40 anti-submarine torpedoes
Anti-submarine armament: torpedoes (see above) and two SS-N-15 'Starfish' tube-launched missiles carried in place of two Type 53 torpedoes
Mines: up to 24 AMD-1000 mines instead of torpedoes
Electronics: one 'Snoop Tray' surface-search and navigation radar, one low-frequency active/passive bow sonar, one medium-frequency underwater weapons fire-control sonar, one combined 'Stop Light' and 'Brick Group' ESM system with warning element, one 'Park Lamp' direction-finder, one SINS, and various communication and navigation equipment
Propulsion: one pressurized water-cooled reactor supplying steam to one set of geared turbines delivering 11,250 kW (15,090 hp) to one shaft
Performance: maximum speed 20 kt surfaced and 27 kt dived; diving depth 400 m (1,325 ft) operational and 600 m (1,970 ft) maximum
Complement: 100

Class
1. USSR
10 boats
2. India

Name	No.	Builder	Laid down	Commissioned
Chakra		Gorky		Jan 1988
Chitra		Gorky		1990

Note: These boats were built at Gorky between 1967 and 1972, and were the world's first SSGNs able to fire their primary missiles whilst submerged. It is thought that the Indian boats, of which an unknown number are being procured, differ only in detail from their Soviet counterparts.

Despite their age, the boats of the 'Charlie I' class still provide the Soviet Navy with a potent capability against US battle groups.

'Charlie II' and 'Charlie III' class SSGNs

(USSR)

Type: nuclear-powered cruise missile submarine
Displacement: 4,400 tons surfaced and 5,500 tons dived
Dimensions: length 102·0 m (334·6 ft); beam 9·9 m (32·5 ft); draught 7·8 m (25·6 ft)
Gun armament: none
Missile armament: eight launch tubes for ('Charlie II' class) eight SS-N-9 'Siren' underwater-launched anti-ship missiles or ('Charlie III' class) eight SS-N-22 'Sunburn' underwater-launched anti-ship missiles
Torpedo armament: six 533-mm (21-in) tubes (all bow), two of them with 406-mm (16-in) liners, for a maximum load of 10 533-mm (21-in) Type 53 dual-role torpedoes and six 406-mm (16-in) Type 40 anti-submarine torpedoes
Anti-submarine armament: torpedoes (see above) and two SS-N-15 'Starfish' tube-launched missiles carried in place of two Type 53 torpedoes
Mines: up to 24 AMD-1000 mines instead of torpedoes
Electronics: one 'Snoop Tray' surface-search and navigation radar, one low-frequency active/passive bow sonar, one medium-frequency underwater weapons fire-control sonar, one combined 'Stop Light' and 'Brick Group' ESM system with warning element, one SINS, and various communication and navigation systems
Propulsion: one pressurized water-cooled reactor supplying steam to one set of geared turbines delivering 11,250 kW (15,090 hp) to two shafts
Performance: maximum speed 20 kt surfaced and 26 kt dived; diving depth 400 m (1,325 ft) operational and 600 m (1,970 ft) maximum
Complement: 90

Class
1. USSR
6 'Charlie II' class boats
5 'Charlie III' class boats

Note: Built at Gorky between 1973 and 1980, these are similar to the 'Charlie I' class SSGNs apart from their primary missile armament, whose longer range requires a more advanced fire-control system that was the main reason for the lengthening of the hull.

'Echo II' class SSGN

(USSR)

Type: nuclear-powered cruise missile submarine
Displacement: 4,900 tons surfaced and 5,800 tons dived
Dimensions: length 119·0 m (390·4 ft); beam 9·2 m (30·2 ft); draught 6·9 m (22·6 ft)
Gun armament: none
Missile armament: eight launch tubes for eight SS-N-3A or SS-N-3C 'Shaddock' or (in 10+ boats) SS-N-12 'Sandbox' surface-launched anti-ship missiles
Torpedo armament: six 533-mm (21-in) tubes (all bow) for a typical load of 16 Type 53 dual-role torpedoes
Anti-submarine armament: four 406-mm (16-in) tubes (both stern) for four Type 40 torpedoes, and Type 53 torpedoes (see above)
Mines: up to 40 AMD-1000 mines instead of 533-mm (21-in) torpedoes
Electronics: one 'Snoop Slab' (SS-N-3A) or 'Snoop Tray' (SS-N-12) surface-search and navigation radar, one 'Front Piece/Front Door' (SS-N-3) or 'Punch Bowl' (SS-N-12) midcourse guidance radar, one 'Herkules' high-frequency active/passive hull sonar, one 'Feniks' bow sonar, one combined 'Stop Light' and 'Brick Pulp' or 'Squid Head' ESM system, one 'Quad Loop' direction-finder, one SINS, and various communication and navigation systems
Propulsion: two pressurized water-cooled reactors supplying steam to two sets of geared turbines delivering 22,500 kW (30,175 hp) to two shafts
Performance: maximum speed 20 kt surfaced and 25 kt dived; diving depth 300 m (985 ft) operational and 500 m (1,640 ft) maximum
Complement: 90

Class
1. USSR
29 boats

Note: Built at Severodvinsk and Komsomolsk between 1961 and 1967, these boats offer a useful capability against surface battle groups. They were probably built not to satisfy any particular operational requirement, but rather to exploit slipway availability between the building of the 'Hotel' and 'Yankee' class SSBNs.

'Oscar I' and 'Oscar II' class SSGNs

(USSR)

Type: nuclear-powered cruise missile submarine
Displacement: 7,500 tons or ('Oscar II' class) 8,400 tons surfaced and 12,500 tons or ('Oscar II' class) 13,400 tons dived
Dimensions: length 143·0 m (469·2 ft) for 'Oscar I' and 154·0 m (505·2 ft) for 'Oscar II'; beam 18·2 m (59·7 ft); draught 9·0 m (29·5 ft)
Gun armament: none
Missile armament: 12 two-round launchers for 24 SS-N-19 'Shipwreck' underwater-launched anti-ship missiles
Torpedo armament: four 650-mm (25·6-in) and four 533-mm (21-in) tubes (all bow), for a maximum load of 12 650-mm (25·6-in) Type 65 and 12 533-mm (21-in) Type 53 dual-role torpedoes
Anti-submarine armament: torpedoes (see above) and two SS-N-15 'Starfish' and two SS-N-16 'Stallion' missiles launched through the 533- and 650-mm (21- and 25·6-in) tubes respectively
Mines: up to 48 AMD-1000 mines instead of 533-mm (21-in) torpedoes
Electronics: one 'Snoop Head' surface-search and navigation radar, one low-frequency active/passive bow sonar, one medium-frequency underwater weapons fire-control sonar, one 'Rim Hat' ESM system with warning element, one 'Park Lamp' direction-finder, one SINS, one 'Pert Spring' satellite communications system, and various communication and navigation systems
Propulsion: two pressurized water-cooled reactors supplying steam to two sets of geared turbines delivering about 67,000 kW (89,860 hp) to two shafts
Performance: maximum speed 20 kt surfaced and 30 kt or ('Oscar II' class) 28 kt dived; diving depth 500 m (1,640 ft) operational and 830 m (2,725 ft) maximum
Complement: 130

Although they are large and comparatively noisy, the boats of the 'Oscar' classes provide high underwater performance combined with a very powerful anti-ship missile capability. This makes them a distinct long-range threat to surface battle groups of the US Navy.

Class
1. USSR
2 'Oscar I' boats
3 'Oscar II' boats plus 1 more building and ? more planned

Note: These boats have been built at Severodvinsk since 1978, and the missile tubes are arranged in banks of 12 on each side: the tubes are angled to fire forward and upward at an angle of 40°, and are located in pairs with a single hatch over each pair. The greater length of the 'Oscar II' variant is devoted to a new noise-suppression system for the propulsion arrangement, and these boats also have upgraded electronic suites.

'Papa' class SSGN

(USSR)

Type: nuclear-powered cruise missile submarine
Displacement: 6,100 tons surfaced and 7,000 tons dived
Dimensions: length 109·0 m (357·5 ft); beam 11·6 m (38·1 ft); draught 7·8 m (25·6 ft)
Gun armament: none
Missile armament: 10 launch tubes for 10 SS-N-9 'Siren' underwater-launched anti-ship missiles
Torpedo armament: four 533-mm (21-in) tubes (all bow), for a maximum load of 12 Type 53 dual-role torpedoes
Anti-submarine armament: torpedoes (see above) and two SS-N-15 'Starfish' tube-launched missiles carried in place of Type 53 torpedoes
Mines: up to 24 AMD-1000 mines instead of torpedoes
Electronics: one 'Snoop Tray' surface-search and navigation radar, one low-frequency active/passive bow sonar, one medium-frequency underwater weapons fire-control sonar, one combined 'Stop Light' and 'Brick Group' ESM system with warning element, one SINS, one 'Pert Spring' satellite communications system, and various communication and navigation systems
Propulsion: two pressurized water-cooled reactors supplying steam to two sets of geared turbines delivering 44,750 kW (60,020 hp) to two shafts
Performance: maximum speed 20 kt surfaced and 40 kt dived; diving depth 400 m (1,325 ft) operational and 600 m (1,970 ft) maximum
Complement: 85

Class
1. USSR
1 boat

Note: This singleton boat was built at Severodvinsk between 1969 and 1971, and is probably a trials type developed from the 'Charlie' class SSGN with some features of the 'Alfa' class SSN. The type has undergone three major refits and has seldom operated away from the USSR, confirming that experimental work for the development of the 'Oscar' class SSGN was its main task.

'Yankee' class SSGN

(USSR)

Type: nuclear-powered cruise missile submarine
Displacement: 13,650 tons dived
Dimensions: length 153·0 m (501·8 ft); beam 15·0 m (49·2 ft); draught 8·0 m (26·2 ft)
Gun armament: none
Missile armament: 12 launch tubes for 12 SS-N-24 anti-ship cruise missiles
Torpedo armament: six 533-mm (21-in) tubes (all bow), for a maximum load of 12 Type 53 dual-role torpedoes
Anti-submarine armament: torpedoes (see above)
Mines: up to 24 AMD-1000 mines instead of torpedoes
Electronics: one 'Snoop Tray' surface-search and navigation radar, one low-frequency active/passive bow sonar, one medium-frequency underwater weapons fire-control sonar, one combined 'Brick Spit' and 'Brick Pulp' ESM system with warning element, one SINS, and various communication and navigation systems
Propulsion: two pressurized water-cooled reactors supplying steam to two sets of geared turbines delivering 37,300 kW (50,025 hp) to two shafts
Performance: maximum speed 15 kt surfaced and 23 kt dived; diving depth 400 m (1,325 ft) operational and 600 m (1,970 ft) maximum
Complement: 120

Class
1. USSR
1 boat

Note: This single conversion from 'Yankee' class SSBN was completed in 1983 as a trials boat for the new SS-N-24 underwater-launched anti-ship cruise missile. The conversion involved a 23-m (75·5-ft) lengthening of the hull in the area of the erstwhile SLBM section, and the addition of two six-tube external missile banks outside the pressure hull abaft the sail.

'Juliett' class SSG

(USSR)

Type: cruise missile submarine
Displacement: 3,150 tons surfaced and 3,850 tons dived
Dimensions: length 87·0 m (285·4 ft); beam 10·0 m (32·8 ft); draught 7·0 m (22·9 ft)
Gun armament: none
Missile armament: four launch tubes for four SS-N-3A or SS-N-3C 'Shaddock' or four SS-N-12 'Sandbox' surface-launched anti-ship missiles
Torpedo armament: six 533-mm (21-in) tubes (all bow) for a maximum load of 18 Type 53 dual-role torpedoes
Anti-submarine armament: torpedoes (see above)
Electronics: one 'Snoop Tray' or 'Snoop Slab' surface-search and navigation radar, one 'Front Piece/Front Door' or (SS-N-12 boats) 'Punch Bowl' midcourse guidance radar, one 'Herkules' high-frequency active/passive hull sonar, one 'Feniks' bow sonar, one 'Stop Light' ESM system with warning element, one 'Quad Loop' direction-finder, and various communication and navigation systems
Propulsion: diesel-electric arrangement, with three diesels delivering 3375 kW (4,525 hp) and two electric motors delivering 2600 kW (3,485 hp) to two shafts
Performance: maximum speed 19 kt surfaced and 14 kt dived; range 16,675 km (10,360 miles) at 8 kt snorting
Complement: 79

Class
1. USSR
16 boats

Note: Completed between 1961 and 1968 at Gorky, the 'Juliett' class was designed as a conventionally powered interim type of missile-armed attack submarine pending the development of more potent nuclear-powered types. The primary armament of four SS-N-3A 'Shaddock' missiles (replaced in refitted boats by four SS-N-12 'Sandbox' missiles) is carried in elevating launchers, one pair forward of the sail and the other pair aft of it. The missiles are launched after the boat has surfaced and the launchers have been elevated to 20°.

'Wuhan (Modified)' or 'ES5G' class SSG

(USSR/China)

Type: cruise missile submarine
Displacement: 1,650 tons surfaced and 2,100 tons dived
Dimensions: length 76·8 m (251·9 ft); beam 7·3 m (23·9 ft); draught 5·5 m (18·0 ft)
Gun armament: none
Missile armament: six launchers for six C-801 surface-launched anti-ship missiles
Torpedo armament: eight 533-mm (21-in) tubes (all bow) for 16 Type 53 dual-role torpedoes
Anti-submarine armament: torpedoes (see above)
Mines: up to 20 in place of torpedoes
Electronics: one 'Snoop Plate' and 'one 'Snoop Tray' surface-search and navigation radar, one 'Herkules' or 'Tamir 5' active/passive search and attack hull sonar, and various communication and navigation systems
Propulsion: diesel-electric arrangement, with two diesels delivering 3000 kW (4,025 hp) and two electric motors delivering unknown power to two shafts
Performance: maximum speed 15 kt surfaced, 13 kt dived and 10 kt snorting
Complement: 10 + 44

Class
1. China
1 boat

Note: This boat was converted as a trials platform, and appears to have been so successful that other boats may be rebuilt to a similar standard.

'Akula' class SSN

(USSR)

Type: nuclear-powered attack (fleet) submarine
Displacement: 9,100 tons dived
Dimensions: length 115·0 m (377·3 ft); beam 14·0 m (45·9 ft); draught 10·4 m (34·1 ft)
Gun armament: none
Missile armament: SS-N-21 'Sampson' tube-launched land-attack cruise missiles in place of torpedoes
Torpedo armament: two 650-mm (25·6-in) and four 533-mm (21-in) tubes (all bow) for six 650-mm (25·6-in) Type 65 and 12 533-mm (21-in) Type 53 dual-role torpedoes
Anti-submarine armament: torpedoes (see above) plus two SS-N-15 'Starfish' and two SS-N-16 'Stallion' missiles fired from the 533- and 650-mm (21- and 25·6-in) tubes respectively
Electronics: one 'Snoop Pair' surface-search and navigation radar, active and passive sonars (possibly including a towed-array type with its sensor cable in a fintop housing), various under- and over-water fire-control sys-

tems including a 'Punch Bowl' midcourse guidance antenna for the SSMs, one 'Rim Hat' ESM system with warning element, one 'Park Lamp' direction-finder, one SINS, one 'Pert Spring' satellite communications system, and extensive communication and navigation systems
Propulsion: two pressurized water-cooled nuclear reactors supplying steam to two sets of geared turbines delivering unknown power to one shaft
Performance: maximum speed 42+ kt dived
Complement: not revealed

Class
1. USSR
4 boats plus 1 more building and ? more planned
Note: Production of about one unit per year has been undertaken from 1983 at Komsomolsk, and the class offers very high capabilities in the multi-role SSN task as successor to the 'Victor III' class boats.

The 'Akula' class is in production as successor to the 'Victor III' class, and offers much improved overall capabilities as well as quieter operation.

'Alfa' class SSN

(USSR)

Type: nuclear-powered attack (fleet) submarine
Displacement: 2,800 tons surfaced and 3,680 tons dived
Dimensions: length 81·5 m (267·4 ft); beam 9·5 m (31·2 ft); draught 7·5 m (24·6 ft)
Gun armament: none
Missile armament: none
Torpedo armament: six 533-mm (21-in) tubes (all bow) for 20 Type 53 dual-role torpedoes
Anti-submarine armament: torpedoes (see above) and two SS-N-15 'Starfish' tube-launched missiles in place of torpedoes
Mines: up to 40 in place of torpedoes
Electronics: one 'Snoop Head' surface-search and navigation radar, one low-frequency passive bow sonar, one medium-frequency active/passive underwater weapons fire-control sonar, one combined 'Bald Head' and 'Brick Group' ESM system with warning element, one 'Park Lamp' direction-finder, one SINS, one satellite navigation system, and extensive communication and navigation systems
Propulsion: two liquid metal-cooled reactors supplying steam to two sets of turbo-alternators supplying current to one electric motor delivering 35,000 kW (46,940 hp) to one shaft
Performance: maximum speed 20 kt surfaced and 45 kt dived; diving depth 600 m (1,970 ft) operational and 1000 m (3,280 ft) maximum
Complement: 40

Use of titanium as the primary structural material and a reactor with liquid metal cooling gives the 'Alfa' class prodigious deep diving capability and exceptionally high underwater performance.

Class
1. USSR
6 boats
Note: Laid down in the mid-1960s and completed during 1970 at the Sudomekh Yard in Leningrad, the first 'Alfa' class boat marked a new departure in SSN design through its use of a liquid metal-cooled reactor and titanium hull for very high underwater speed and very great diving depth respectively: both these factors combine to present any foes with extreme difficulty in effective torpedo attack. This first boat was essentially a prototype, and was scrapped in 1974, experience in its design and operation being incorporated in the succeeding six production-standard boats built between 1979 and 1983 at Sudomekh and Severodvinsk. The small crew suggests a very high level of automation. Each boat is fitted with an auxiliary diesel-electric propulsion system delivering power to a pair of dedicated auxiliary shafts.

'Churchill' and 'Valiant' class SSNs

(UK)

Type: nuclear-powered fleet (attack) submarine

Displacement: 4,300 tons standard and 4,800 tons dived

Dimensions: length 285·0 ft (86·9 m); beam 33·2 ft (10·1 m); draught 27·0 ft (8·2 m)

Gun armament: none

Missile armament: six UGM-84 Sub-Harpoon tube-launched anti-ship missiles in place of torpedoes

Torpedo armament: six 21-in (533-mm) tubes (all bow) for 32 Mk 24 Tigerfish wire-guided dual-role torpedoes

Anti-submarine armament: torpedoes (see above)

Mines: up to 64 Mk 5 Stonefish or Mk 6 Sea Urchin mines instead of torpedoes

Electronics: one Type 1006 surface-search and navigation radar, one Type 2020 active/passive search and attack chin sonar, one Type 2046 passive search towed-array sonar, one Type 2007 long-range passive sonar, one Type 2019 active/passive range and intercept sonar, one Type 197 passive ranging sonar, one DCB torpedo fire-control system, one Type UAL ESM system with warning element, one SINS, and extensive communication and navigation systems

Propulsion: one Rolls-Royce PWR-1 pressurized water-cooled reactor supplying steam to two sets of English Electric geared turbines delivering 15,000 hp (11,185 kW) to one shaft

Performance: maximum speed 20 kt surfaced and 28 kt dived; diving depth 985 ft (300 m) operational and 1,640 ft (500 m) maximum

Complement: 13 + 103

Class
1. UK ('Churchill' class)

Name	No.	Builder	Laid down	Com-missioned
Churchill	S46	Vickers	Jun 1967	Jul 1970
Conqueror	S48	Cammell Laird	Dec 1967	Nov 1971
Courageous	S50	Vickers	May 1968	Oct 1971

The two 'Valiant' class SSNs are similar to the three 'Churchill' class boats apart from their slightly noisier propulsion machinery. The boats are being modernized, but are nonetheless beginning to approach the end of their effective lives.

2. UK ('Valiant' class)

Name	No.	Builder	Laid down	Com-missioned
Valiant	S102	Vickers	Jan 1962	Jul 1966
Warspite	S103	Vickers	Dec 1963	Oct 1971

Note: These were the UK's first production-standard SSNs following the semi-experimental *Dreadnought*, and originally carried Type 2001 chin sonar but no Type 2026 towed-array sonar. The two subclasses are similar in most respects, though the later 'Churchill' variant is quieter than the 'Valiant' type.

'Echo I' class SSN

(USSR)

Type: nuclear-powered attack (fleet) submarine

Displacement: 4,200 tons surfaced and 5,200 tons dived

Dimensions: length 114·0 m (374·0 ft); beam 9·2 m (30·2 ft); draught 6·9 m (22·6 ft)

Gun armament: none

Missile armament: none

Torpedo armament: six 533-mm (21-in) tubes (all bow) for 16 Type 53 dual-role torpedoes

Anti-submarine armament: four 406-mm (16-in) tubes (both stern) for four Type 40 torpedoes

Mines: up to 28 in place of 533-mm (21-in) torpedoes

Electronics: one 'Snoop Tray' surface-search and navigation radar, one 'Herkules' high-frequency active/passive sonar, one 'Feniks' bow sonar, one 'Stop Light' ESM system with warning element, one 'Quad Loop' direction-finder, one SINS, and extensive communications and navigation systems

Propulsion: two pressurized water-cooled reactors supplying steam to two sets of geared turbines delivering 22,500 kW (30,175 hp) to two shafts

Performance: maximum speed 20 kt surfaced and 28 kt dived; diving depth 300 m (985 ft) operational and 500 m (1,640 ft) maximum

Complement: 12 + 80

Class
1. USSR
5 boats

Note: These boats were delivered between 1960 and 1962 from Komsomolsk as SSGNs with a primary armament of SS-N-3 anti ship missiles in launchers under the after casing. The advent of the 'Yankee' class boats made the 'Echo I' class boats superfluous, and between 1969 and 1974 the boats were converted into SSNs. All are due for deletion in the near future.

The 'Echo I' class design is essentially that of a conventional submarine converted to nuclear propulsion, and is totally obsolete.

'Ethan Allen' class SSN

(USA)

Type: nuclear-powered attack (fleet) and special forces insertion/extraction submarine

Displacement: 6,955 tons surfaced and 7,880 tons dived

Dimensions: length 410·5 ft (125·2 m); beam 33·0 ft (10·1 m); draught 32·0 ft (9·8 m)

Gun armament: none

Missile armament: none

Torpedo armament: four 21-in (533-mm) Mk 65 tubes (all bow) for eight Mk 48 dual-role wire-guided torpedoes

Anti-submarine armament: torpedoes (see above)

Electronics: one BPS-15 surface-search and navigation sonar, one BQS-4 multi-function active/passive search and attack sonar, one BQR-7 passive search sonar, one BQR-15 passive search towed-array sonar, one BQR-19 active close-range detection hull sonar, one Mk 112 torpedo fire-control system, one ESM system with warning element, one SINS, one WSC-3 satellite communications transceiver, and extensive communication and navigation systems

Propulsion: one Westinghouse S5W pressurized water-cooled reactor supplying steam to two sets of General Electric geared turbines delivering

15,000 hp (11,185 kW) to one shaft

Performance: maximum speed 20 kt surfaced and 25 kt dived; diving depth 985 ft (300 m) operational

Complement: 12 + 120, plus berthing, equipment stowage and airlock equipment for 67 special-force troops delivered for clandestine missions

Class				
1. USA				**Com-**
Name	**No.**	**Builder**	**Laid down**	**missioned**
Sam Houston	SSN609	Newport News	Dec 1959	Mar 1962
John Marshall	SSN611	Newport News	Apr 1960	May 1962

Note: These are the only survivors of the five-strong 'Ethan Allen' class of SSBNs built in the late 1950s and early 1960s with 16 UGM-27 Polaris SLBMs. Though now classified as SSNs, their real task is the carriage and insertion of special forces teams. It is expected that these elderly boats will remain in service in this role until the late 1990s.

There are only two survivors of this once five-strong class (illustrated by the now-deleted *Ethan Allen*) which were built as SSBNs but have now been revised as delivery and extraction vehicles for special forces teams.

'Glenard P. Lipscomb' class SSN

(USA)

Type: nuclear-powered attack (fleet) submarine

Displacement: 5,815 tons standard and 6,480 tons dived

Dimensions: length 365·0 ft (111·3 m); beam 31·7 ft (9·7 m); draught 31·0 ft (9·5 m)

Gun armament: none

Missile armament: four UGM-84 Sub-Harpoon tube-launched anti-ship missiles carried in place of torpedoes

Torpedo armament: four 21-in (533-mm) Mk 63 tubes (all amidships) for 15 Mk 48 wire-guided dual-role torpedoes

Anti-submarine armament: torpedoes (see above) and four UUM-44A SUBROC tube-launched missiles carried in place of torpedoes

Electronics: one BPS-15 surface-search and navigation radar, one BQQ-5 active/passive search and attack sonar, one BQS-14 under-ice and close-range attack sonar, one passive search towed-array sonar, one Mk 117 underwater weapons fire-control system, Emerson Electric Mk 2 torpedo

decoys, one WLR-4 ESM system with warning element, one Mk 2 SINS, one WSC-3 satellite communications transceiver, and extensive communication and navigation equipment

Propulsion: one Westinghouse S5Wa pressurized water-cooled reactor supplying steam to one General Electric turbo-electric drive delivering unrevealed power to one shaft

Performance: maximum speed 18 kt surfaced and 25+ kt dived; diving depth 1,315 ft (400 m) operational and 1,970 ft (600 m) maximum

Complement: 14 + 115

Class				
1. USA			**Laid**	**Com-**
Name	**No.**	**Builder**	**down**	**missioned**
Glenard P. Lipscomb	SSN685	GD (EB Div)	Jun 1971	Dec 1974

Note: This singleton unit is an operational SSN, but was designed principally to test a number of quietening features as well as the turbo-electric propulsion system that has been adopted for no other SSN.

'Han' class SSN

(China)
Type: nuclear-powered attack (fleet) submarine
Displacement: 4,300 tons surfaced and 5,000 tons dived
Dimensions: (estimated) length 100·0 m (328·1 ft); beam 11·0 m (36·1 ft); draught 8·5 m (27·9 ft)
Gun armament: none
Missile armament: none
Torpedo armament: six 533-mm (21-in) tubes (all bow) for 12 Type 53 torpedoes
Anti-submarine armament: torpedoes (see above)
Mines: between 24 and 28 in place of torpedoes
Electronics: not known, but certainly including one surface-search and navigation radar, several sonar systems (possibly including the French

DUUX 5), one SINS, and various items of communication and navigation equipment
Propulsion: one pressurized water-cooled reactor supplying steam to one turbo-electric system delivering unrevealed power to one shaft
Performance: maximum speed 18 kt surfaced and 25 kt dived; diving depth 300 m (985 ft) operational
Complement: about 100

Class
1. China
3 boats with 1 more building and ? more planned
Note: Building since 1968 at Huludao, these boats are taking about 10 years each to complete, and are of an obsolescent design based on the US-developed 'albacore' hull. Later units may have launchers for C-801 anti-ship missile located aft of the sail.

'Hotel II' class SSN

(USSR)
Type: nuclear-powered attack (fleet) submarine
Displacement: 4,500 tons surfaced and 5,500 tons dived
Dimensions: length 130·0 m (426·4 ft); beam 9·1 m (29·8 ft); draught 7·6 m (25·0 ft)
Gun armament: none
Missile armament: none
Torpedo armament: six 533-mm (21-in) tubes (all bow) for 16 Type 53 dual-role torpedoes
Anti-submarine armament: two 406-mm (16-in) tubes (both stern) for four Type 40 anti-submarine torpedoes
Electronics: one 'Snoop Tray' surface-search and navigation radar, one 'Herkules' high-frequency active/passive hull sonar, one 'Feniks' bow sonar, one 'Stop Light' ESM system with warning element, one 'Quad Loop' direction-finder, one SINS, and various communication systems

Propulsion: two pressurized water-cooled reactors supplying steam to two sets of geared turbines delivering 22,500 kW (30,175 hp) to two shafts
Performance: maximum speed 20 kt surfaced and 26 kt dived
Complement: 90

Class
1. USSR
6 boats

Note: These six boats were built at Severodvinsk between 1958 and 1962 as first-generation 'Hotel I' class SSBNs using a hull and propulsion system derived from those of the 'Echo' and 'November' class SSNs. The type originally had three SS-N-4 surface-launched missiles, an arrangement modified between 1963 and 1970 for three SS-N-5 underwater-launched missiles. Of the original eight boats, these six were converted into second-line and training SSNs during the early 1980s, while a seventh was modified into a 'communications submarine'.

'Los Angeles' class SSN

(USA)
Type: nuclear-powered attack (fleet) submarine
Displacement: 6,000 tons standard and 6,925 tons dived
Dimensions: length 360·0 ft (109·7 m); beam 33·0 ft (10·1 m); draught 32·3 ft (9·9 m)
Gun armament: none
Missile armament: four UGM-84 Sub-Harpoon tube-launched anti-ship missiles carried in place of torpedoes, and 12 BGM-109 Tomahawk underwater-launched land-attack cruise missiles (tube-launched weapons in place of Mk 48 torpedoes in SSBN712/718, and vertically launched from two six-tube Vertical Launch System banks in the remaining boats)
Torpedo armament: four 21-in (533-mm) Mk 67 tubes (all amidships) for 26 Mk 48 wire-guided dual-role torpedoes
Anti-submarine armament: torpedoes (see above) and four tube-launched UUM-44A SUBROC missiles (in place of torpedoes in boats with the Mk 113 fire-control system)
Mines: up to 78 Mk 57, Mk 60 and Mk 67 mines in place of other tube-launched weapons
Electronics: one BPS-15A surface-search and navigation radar, one BQQ-5A(V)1 (being updated to BQQ-5D) multi-function active/passive search and attack bow sonar with BQR-7 passive and BQS-13 active/passive search elements, one BQS-15 under-ice and close-range active sonar, one BQR-23/25 (being replaced by OK 276) passive search towed-array sonar, one Mine and Ice Detection Avoidance System (from SSN751 onwards), one Mk 113 or (from SSN712 onwards and being retrofitted in SSN699 onwards), one Mk 117 underwater weapons fire-control system with UYK-7 tactical computers, one BSY-1 (SUBACS) action data automation system (from SSN751 onwards), one ESM system with BRD-7 direction-finding, WLR-12 threat-warning and WLR-9A intercept elements, Emerson Electric Mk 2 torpedo decoys, one SINS, one WSC-3 satellite communications transceiver, and extensive communication and navigation systems
Propulsion: one General Electric S6G pressurized water-cooled reactor supplying steam to two sets of geared turbines delivering about 35,000 hp (26,100 kW) to one shaft
Performance: maximum speed 18 kt surfaced and 31 kt dived; diving depth 1,475 ft (450 m) operational and 2,460 ft (750 m) maximum
Complement: 13 + 120

At speed on the surface, this 'Los Angeles' class SSN provides striking evidence of the power that gives these boats such underwater performance.

Note: This is the largest SSN class yet planned, the total being postulated at 66 boats up to SSN777 that is to be ordered under the FY1992 programme. Some criticism has been voiced about the type's comparative lack of underwater speed and its relatively limited diving depth by comparison with Soviet types, but on the other side of the coin are the advanced and diverse weapon options of the boats, and their electronic sophistication. From SSN721 the forward diving planes are located on the forward hull rather than the sail to provide a genuine ice-penetration capability, and from SSN751 anechoic tile cladding is being fitted as part of the intensive effort to reduce the sound signature of these important boats.

Name	No.	Builder	Laid down	Commissioned
Los Angeles	SSN688	Newport News	Jan 1972	Nov 1976
Baton Rouge	SSN689	Newport News	Nov 1972	Jun 1977
Philadelphia	SSN690	GD (EB Div)	Aug 1972	Jun 1977
Memphis	SSN691	Newport News	Jun 1973	Dec 1977
Omaha	SSN692	GD (EB Div)	Jan 1973	Mar 1978
Cincinatti	SSN693	Newport News	Apr 1974	Jun 1978
Groton	SSN694	GD (EB Div)	Aug 1973	Jul 1978
Birmingham	SSN695	Newport News	Apr 1975	Dec 1978
New York City	SSN696	GD (EB Div)	Dec 1973	Mar 1979
Indianapolis	SSN697	GD (EB Div)	Oct 1974	Jan 1980
Bremerton	SSN698	GD (EB Div)	May 1976	Mar 1981
Jacksonville	SSN699	GD (EB Div)	Feb 1976	May 1981
Dallas	SSN700	GD (EB Div)	Oct 1976	Jul 1981
La Jolla	SSN701	GD (EB Div)	Oct 1976	Oct 1981
Phoenix	SSN702	GD (EB Div)	Jul 1977	Dec 1981
Boston	SSN703	GD (EB Div)	Aug 1978	Jan 1982
Baltimore	SSN704	GD (EB Div)	May 1979	Jul 1982
City of Corpus Christi	SSN705	GD (EB Div)	Sep 1979	Jan 1983
Albuquerque	SSN706	GD (EB Div)	Dec 1979	May 1983
Portsmouth	SSN707	GD (EB Div)	May 1980	Oct 1983
Minneapolis-St Paul	SSN708	GD (EB Div)	Jan 1981	Mar 1984
Hyman G. Rickover	SSN709	GD (EB Div)	Jul 1981	Jul 1984
Augusta	SSN710	GD (EB Div)	Mar 1982	Jan 1985
San Francisco	SSN711	Newport News	May 1977	Apr 1981
Atlanta	SSN712	Newport News	Aug 1978	Feb 1982
Houston	SSN713	Newport News	Jan 1979	Sep 1982
Norfolk	SSN714	Newport News	Aug 1979	May 1983
Buffalo	SSN715	Newport News	Jan 1980	Nov 1983
Salt Lake City	SSN716	Newport News	Aug 1980	May 1984
Olympia	SSN717	Newport News	Mar 1981	Nov 1984
Honolulu	SSN718	Newport News	Nov 1981	Jul 1985
Providence	SSN719	GD (EB Div)	Oct 1982	Jul 1985
Pittsburgh	SSN720	GD (EB Div)	Apr 1983	Nov 1985
Chicago	SSN721	Newport News	Jan 1983	Dec 1985
Key West	SSN722	Newport News	Jul 1983	Sep 1987
Oklahoma City	SSN723	Newport News	Jan 1984	May 1988
Louisville	SSN724	GD (EB Div)	Sep 1984	Nov 1986
Helena	SSN725	GD (EB Div)	Mar 1985	Jul 1987
Newport News	SSN750	Newport News	Mar 1984	Jan 1989
San Juan	SSN751	GD (EB Div)	Aug 1985	Aug 1988
Pasadena	SSN752	GD (EB Div)	Dec 1985	Feb 1989
Albany	SSN753	Newport News	Apr 1985	Dec 1989
Topeka	SSN754	GD (EB Div)	May 1986	Apr 1989
Miami	SSN755	GD (EB Div)	Oct 1986	Oct 1989
Scranton	SSN756	Newport News	Jun 1986	Aug 1990
Alexandria	SSN757	Newport News	Jun 1987	Apr 1990
Asheville	SSN758	GD (EB Div)	Jan 1987	Dec 1990
Jefferson City	SSN759	Newport News	Jul 1987	Apr 1991
Annapolis	SSN760	GD (EB Div)	Jun 1988	1991
Springfield	SSN761	GD (EB Div)	Nov 1988	1992
Columbus	SSN762	GD (EB Div)	Mar 1989	1992
Santa Fe	SSN763	GD (EB Div)	Jul 1989	1992
Boise	SSN764	Newport News	Aug 1988	Nov 1991
Montpelier	SSN765	Newport News		Mar 1992
Charlotte	SSN766	Newport News	Jun 1989	Jul 1992
Hampton	SSN767	Newport News	Apr 1989	Nov 1992
Hartford	SSN768	GD (EB Div)		
Toledo	SSN769	Newport News		
Tucson	SSN770	Newport News		
	SSN771			
	SSN772			
	SSN773			
	SSN774			
	SSN775			
	SSN776			
	SSN777			

The white markings toward the stern of this 'Los Angeles' class SSN provide docking cues for the deep-submergence rescue vehicles that would be used to evacuate the crew (or crew survivors) should the submarine be stranded on the bottom for any reason.

'Narwhal' class SSN

(USA)

Type: nuclear-powered attack (fleet) submarine
Displacement: 5,285 tons standard and 5,830 tons dived
Dimensions: length 314·6 ft (95·9 m); beam 37·7 ft (11·5 m); draught 27·0 ft (8·2 m):
Gun armament: none
Missile armament: UGM-84 Sub-Harpoon tube-launched anti-ship missiles in place of torpedoes, and being fitted for eight BGM-109 Tomahawk underwater-launched land-attack cruise missiles
Torpedo armament: four 21-in (533-mm) Mk 63 tubes (all amidships) for 15 Mk 48 wire-guided dual-role torpedoes
Anti-submarine armament: torpedoes (see above)
Mines: up to 46 Mk 57, Mk 60 and Mk 67 mines in place of torpedoes
Electronics: one BPS-14 surface-search and navigation radar, one BQQ-5 active/passive search and attack bow sonar with BQS-6 active and BQR-7 passive elements, one BQS-8 under-ice sonar, one Mk 117 underwater weapons fire-control system, Emerson Electric Mk 2 torpedo decoys, one ESM system with WLR-4 warning element, one SINS, one WSC-3 satellite communications transceiver, and extensive communication and navigation systems
Propulsion: one General Electric S5G pressurized water-cooled reactor supplying steam to two sets of General Electric geared turbines delivering 17,000 hp (12,675 kW) to one shaft
Performance: maximum speed 20 + kt surfaced and 30 + kt dived; diving depth 1,315 ft (400 m) operational and 1,970 ft (600 m) maximum
Complement: 13 + 116

Class

1. USA

Name	No.	Builder	Laid down	Com-missioned
Narwhal	SSN671	GD (EB Div)	Jan 1966	Jul 1969

Note: This is basically a version of the 'Sturgeon' class SSN fitted with a natural-circulation nuclear propulsion system.

The *Narwhal* uses a pumpless natural-circulation cooling system.

'November' class SSN

(USSR)

Type: nuclear-powered attack (fleet) submarine
Displacement: 4,200 tons surfaced and 5,000 tons dived
Dimensions: length 109·7 m (359·8 ft); beam 9·1 m (29·8 ft); draught 6·7 m (21·9 ft)
Gun armament: none
Missile armament: none
Torpedo armament: eight 533-mm (21-in) tubes (all bow) for 24 Type 53 dual-role torpedoes
Anti-submarine armament: torpedoes (see above)
Mines: up to 48 AMD-1000 mines in place of 533-mm (21-in) torpedoes
Electronics: one 'Snoop Tray' surface-search and navigation radar, one 'Herkules' high-frequency active/passive search and attack hull sonar, one 'Feniks' bow sonar, one 'Stop Light' ESM system with warning element, one 'Park Lamp' direction-finder, one SINS, and various communication and navigation systems
Propulsion: two pressurized water-cooled reactors supplying steam to two sets of geared turbines delivering 22,500 kW (30,175 hp) to two shafts
Performance: maximum speed 20 kt surfaced and 30 kt dived; diving depth 300 m (985 ft) operational and 500 m (1,640 ft) maximum
Complement: 86

Class

1. USSR

12 boats

Note: Delivered between 1958 and 1963 from Severodvinsk, these were the USSR's first nuclear-powered submarines. The type is obsolete because of its very high levels of radiated underwater noise, and there have also been severe problems with the nuclear propulsion system and its radiation shielding. One boat sank and another was apparently scrapped, and the serviceability of others is suspect.

'Rubis' or 'SNA 72' class SSN

(France)

Type: nuclear-powered attack (fleet) submarine

Displacement: 2,385 tons or (S605 onwards) 2,400 tons surfaced and 2,670 tons dived

Dimensions: length 72·1 m (236·5 ft) or (S605 onwards) 73·6 m (241·5 ft); beam 7·6 m (25·0 ft); draught 6·4 m (21·0 ft)

Gun armament: none

Missile armament: four tube-launched SM.39 Exocet anti-ship missiles in place of torpedoes

Torpedo armament: four 533-mm (21-in) tubes (all bow) for a maximum of 18 F17 wire-guided anti-ship and L5 dual-role torpedoes

Anti-submarine armament: torpedoes (see above)

Mines: up to 32 in place of torpedoes

Electronics: one DRUA 23 surface-search and navigation radar, one DSUV 22 passive search sonar, one DUUA 2B active search sonar, one DUUX 2 or DUUX 5 passive detection and ranging sonar, one DSUV 62 passive search towed-array sonar (to be fitted in all boats by 1991), one TUUM 1 underwater telephone, one ESM system with ARUD warning and ARUR intercept elements, one SADE tactical data-handling system, one DLT-D3 underwater weapons fire-control system, one SINS, one Syracuse satellite communications system (from S605), and various communication and navigation systems

Propulsion: one CAS pressurized water-cooled reactor supplying steam to two turbo-alternators/one electric motor delivering 7100 kW (9,525 hp) to one shaft

Performance: maximum speed 18 kt surfaced and 25 kt dived; diving depth 300 m (985 ft) operational and 500 m (1,640 ft) maximum for the first four units, and deeper for the last two units

Complement: 9 + 57

Class

1. France

Name	No.	Builder	Laid down	Com-missioned
Rubis	S601	Cherbourg ND	Dec 1976	Feb 1983
Saphir	S602	Cherbourg ND	Sep 1979	Jul 1984
Casabianca	S603	Cherbourg ND	Sep 1979	Apr 1987
Emeraude	S604	Cherbourg ND	Mar 1981	Nov 1988
Amethyste	S605	Cherbourg ND	Oct 1984	1991
CQ270	S606	Cherbourg ND	Mar 1987	1993
	S607	Cherbourg ND	Jun 1988	1995
	S608	Cherbourg ND		

Note: These are the world's smallest operational SSNs, and may be regarded as nuclear-powered derivatives of the 'Agosta' class SS with improved versions of that class's armament, sensor and fire-control systems. *Amethyste* is the lead vessel of a proposed four-strong subclass with improved silencing (to be retrofitted on the first four boats), better streamlining of the bow and superstructure, the Syracuse satellite communications system, a new tactical data-processing system, and more sensitive sonar including new low-frequency sonars and the DSUV 62 very low-frequency towed-array sonar that is also to be retrofitted on the earlier boats. There also are to be at least another two boats to a radically improved design, displacing 4,000 tons and having a vertical-launch system for anti-ship missiles, and the first of these is due to enter service in about 2000.

Lead boat of its class, the *Rubis* is based on the design of the 'Agosta' class SS revised for a nuclear powerplant, and carries a modern system of sensors and weapons while remaining the world's smallest type of SSN.

'Seawolf' class SSN

(USA)

Type: nuclear-powered attack (fleet) submarine

Displacement: 9,150 tons dived

Dimensions: length 326·1 ft (99·4 m); beam 42·3 ft (12·9 m); draught 35·8 ft (10·9 m)

Gun armament: none

Missile armament: UGM-84 Sub-Harpoon tube-launched anti-ship missiles in place of torpedoes, and 12 BGM-109 Tomahawk underwater-launched land-attack cruise missiles

Torpedo armament: eight 30-in (762-mm) tubes (all bow) for 50 tube-launched weapons including Mk 48 ADCAP dual-role wire-guided torpedoes

Anti-submarine armament: torpedoes (see above) and (as a retrofit) Sea Lance tube-launched missiles

Mines: Mk 57, Mk 60 and Mk 67 mines in place of other tube-launched weapons

Electronics: one BPS-15A surface-search and navigation radar, one BQQ-5D multi-function active/passive search and attack bow sonar with BQR-7 passive and BQS-13 active/passive search elements, one BQS-15 under-ice and close-range active sonar, one TB-16 passive search towed-array sonar, one TB-23 passive search towed-array sonar, one Mk 117 underwater weapons fire-control system with UYK-7 tactical computers, one

BSY-2(V) action data automation and fire-control system, one BRD-7 ESM system with WLQ-4(V)1 intercept, WLR-9A warning and WLR-12 warning elements, Emerson Electric Mk 2 torpedo decoys, one SINS, one WSC-3 satellite communications transceiver, and extensive communication and navigation systems

Propulsion: one Westinghouse S6W pressurized water-cooled reactor supplying steam to two sets of geared turbines delivering about 60,000 hp (49,210 kW) to one pump-jet propulsor

Performance: maximum speed 22 kt surfaced and 35 kt dived

Complement: 12 + 118

Class

1.USA

Name	No.	Builder	Laid down	Com-missioned
Seawolf		GD (EB Div)	1989	1995

Note: This class is eventually to total 29 boats, and is planned as a complement to the 'Los Angeles' class with greater optimization for the anti-submarine role with improved machinery (including a pump-jet propulsor rather than a propeller), greater underwater agility, additional quietening features for a 'silent' speed of 20 kt, and better combat capability through improved sensors and more weapons. The units of the class will each have eight 30-in (762-mm) rather than 21-in (533-mm) torpedo tubes for a new and considerably more potent anti-submarine torpedo type.

'Sierra' class SSN

(USSR)

Type: nuclear-powered attack (fleet) submarine
Displacement: 8,100 tons dived
Dimensions: length 107·0 m (351·0 ft); beam 12·0 m (39·4 ft); draught 8·8 m (28·9 ft)
Gun armament: none
Missile armament: SS-N-21 'Sampson' tube-launched land-attack cruise missiles in place of Type 53 torpedoes
Torpedo armament: four 650-mm (25·6-in) and two 533-mm (21-in) tubes (all bow) for 12 650-mm (25·6-in) Type 65 and 10 533-mm (21-in) Type 53 dual-roled torpedoes
Anti-submarine armament: torpedoes (see above), and two SS-N-15 'Starfish' and two SS-N-16 'Stallion' missiles fired through the 533- and 650-mm (21- and 25·6-in) tubes respectively
Mines: between 50 and 60 in place of torpedoes
Electronics: one 'Snoop Pair' surface-search and navigation radar, various active and passive sonars including a towed-array type, various fire-control systems, one 'Rim Hat' ESM system with warning element, one SINS, one 'Pert Spring' satellite communications system, and extensive communication and navigation systems
Propulsion: two reactors (probably with liquid metal cooling) supplying steam to one set of turbo-alternators delivering 30,000 kW (40,235 hp) to one shaft
Performance: maximum speed 34 kt dived; diving depth about 550 m (1,805 ft) operational
Complement: about 100

Class

1. USSR

2 boats plus 1 more building and ? more planned
Note: Delivered since 1984 from Severodvinsk, this may be the production boat evolved after experience with the 'Mike' class SSN, and production appears to be proceeding at the rate of some two units per year. The hull is of steel rather than titanium construction.

It is thought that the 'Sierra' class may have resulted from the USSR's experience with the sole 'Mike' class SSN that sank north of Norway in 1989. The use of a reactor system with liquid metal cooling provides high performance, and while a steel rather than titanium primary structure reduces diving depth it also allows cheaper and more rapid construction.

'Skipjack' class SSN

(USA)

Type: nuclear-powered attack (fleet) submarine
Displacement: 3,075 tons surfaced and 3,515 tons dived
Dimensions: length 251·7 ft (76·7 m); beam 31·5 ft (9·6 m); draught 29·4 ft (8·9 m)
Gun armament: none
Missile armament: none
Torpedo armament: six 21-in (533-mm) Mk 59 tubes (all bow) for 24 Mk 48 wire-guided dual-role torpedoes
Anti-submarine armament: torpedoes (see above)
Mines: up to 48 Mk 57 mines in place of torpedoes
Electronics: one BPS-12 surface-search and navigation radar, one BQS-4 active/passive search and attack bow sonar, one BQR-2 passive search sonar, one Mk 101 torpedo fire-control system, one SINS, and various communication and navigation systems
Propulsion: one Westinghouse S5W pressurized water-cooled reactor supplying steam to two sets of geared turbines (Westinghouse in SSN585 and General Electric in the others) delivering 15,000 hp (11,185 kW) to one shaft
Performance: maximum speed 18 kt surfaced and 30 kt dived; diving depth 985 ft (300 m) operational and 1,640 ft (500 m) maximum
Complement: 9 + 85

Class

1. USA

Name	No.	Builder	Laid down	Commissioned
Skipjack	SSN585	GD (EB Div)	May 1956	Apr 1959
Sculpin	SSN590	Ingalls	Feb 1958	Jun 1961
Shark	SSN591	Newport News	Feb 1958	Feb 1961

Note: These were the US Navy's first SSNs with a teardrop hull, single propeller and hydroplanes mounted on the sail. The class was originally six strong: *Scorpion* was lost in May 1968 and two others were decommissioned in 1986 and 1988. The three surviving units are due for deletion in the near future.

The *Shark* is one of three survivors from this originally six-strong SSN class, which introduced a teardrop hull form, sail-mounted hydroplanes and a single propeller for high underwater performance. Later US boats can dive deeper, are quieter and have superior sonar, but have fewer torpedo tubes and, until the advent of the 'Los Angeles' class boats, are slower.

'Sturgeon' class SSN

(USA)

Type: nuclear-powered attack (fleet) submarine

Displacement: 4,460 tons standard and 4,780 tons or (SSN678/684, 686 and 687) 4,960 tons dived

Dimensions: length 292·2 ft (89·0 m) or (SSN678/684, 686 and 687) 302·2 ft (92·1 m); beam 31·7 ft (9·5 m); draught 28·9 ft (8·8 m)

Gun armament: none

Missile armament: four UGM-84 Sub-Harpoon tube-launched anti-ship missiles in place of torpedoes (in SSN638, 639, 646, 652, 660, 662, 665, 667/670, 679, 684, 686 and 687), and provision for eight tube-launched BGM-109 Tomahawk land-attack and/or anti-ship cruise missiles in place of torpedoes (in all but SSN637, 647, 650, 651, 653, 661, 664, 666, 674/678, 680 and 683)

Torpedo armament: four 21-in (533-mm) Mk 63 tubes (all amidships) for 23 Mk 48 dual-role wire-guided torpedoes

Anti-submarine armament: torpedoes (see above), and four tube-launched UUM-44A SUBROC anti-submarine missiles in place of torpedoes in boats fitted with the Mk 113 fire-control system

Mines: up to 46 Mk 57, Mk 60 or Mk 67 mines in place of torpedoes

Electronics: one BPS-14 or BPS-15 surface-search and navigation radar, one BQQ-2 active/passive search and attack bow sonar with BQS-6 active and BQR-7 passive elements or (SSN678 onwards) one BQQ-5 active/passive search and attack bow sonar, one BQS-8 or BQS-14A under-ice sonar, one BQS-12 (SSN637/639, 646/653 and 660/664) or BQS-13 (other boats) active/passive bow search sonar, one BQR-15 passive search towed-array sonar, one Mk 113 (SSN637, 650, 653, 661, 672, 675/678, 683 and 687) or Mk 117 (other boats) underwater weapons fire-control system, Emerson Electric Mk 2 torpedo decoys, one ESM system with WLR-4 warning element, one SINS, one WSC-3 satellite communications transceiver, and extensive communication and navigation systems

Propulsion: one Westinghouse S5W pressurized water-cooled reactor supplying steam to two sets of geared turbines delivering 15,000 hp (11,185 kW) to one shaft

Performance: maximum speed 20+ kt surfaced and 30+ kt dived; diving depth 1,325 ft (400 m) operational and 1,970 ft (600 m) maximum

Complement: 13+116, or 14+126 in longer boats (see above)

Note: These boats are essentially improved versions of the 'Permit/Thresher' class SSNs, and their sail-mounted hydroplanes can be turned to the vertical position to permit under-ice operations. The longer boats carry additional sonar and electronic equipment for clandestine reconnaissance purposes, and thus have additional crew men for this equipment. Several of the class have been modified for additional roles such as swimmer delivery (SSN684) and rescue (SSN666, 672 and 680).

Class 1.USA Name	No.	Builder	Laid down	Com-missioned
Sturgeon	SSN637	GD (Quincy)	Aug 1963	Mar 1967
Whale	SSN638	GD (Quincy)	May 1964	Oct 1968
Tautog	SSN639	Ingalls	Jan 1964	Aug 1968
Grayling	SSN646	Portsmouth NY	May 1964	Oct 1969
Pogy	SSN647	Ingalls	May 1964	May 1971
Aspro	SSN648	Ingalls	Nov 1964	Feb 1969
Sunfish	SSN649	GD (Quincy)	Jan 1965	Mar 1969
Pargo	SSN650	GD (Quincy)	Jun 1964	Jan 1968
Queenfish	SSN651	Newport News	May 1964	Dec 1966
Puffer	SSN652	Ingalls	Feb 1965	Aug 1969
Ray	SSN653	Newport News	Apr 1965	Apr 1967
Sand Lance	SSN660	Portsmouth NY	Jan 1965	Sep 1971
Lapon	SSN661	Newport News	Jul 1965	Dec 1967
Gurnard	SSN662	Mare Island NY	Dec 1964	Dec 1968
Hammerhead	SSN663	Newport News	Nov 1965	Jun 1968
Sea Devil	SSN664	Newport News	Apr 1966	Jan 1969
Guitarro	SSN665	Mare Island NY	Dec 1965	Sep 1972
Hawkbill	SSN666	Mare Island NY	Sep 1966	Feb 1971
Bergall	SSN667	GD (Quincy)	Apr 1966	Jun 1969
Spadefish	SSN668	Newport News	Dec 1966	Aug 1969
Seahorse	SSN669	GD (Quincy)	Aug 1966	Sep 1969
Finback	SSN670	Newport News	Jun 1967	Feb 1970
Pintado	SSN672	Mare Island NY	Oct 1967	Sep 1971
Flying Fish	SSN673	GD (Quincy)	Jun 1967	Apr 1970
Trepang	SSN674	GD (Quincy)	Oct 1967	Aug 1970
Bluefish	SSN675	GD (Quincy)	Mar 1968	Jan 1971
Billfish	SSN676	GD (Quincy)	Sep 1968	Mar 1971
Drum	SSN677	Mare Island NY	Aug 1968	Apr 1972
Archerfish	SSN678	GD (Quincy)	Jun 1969	Dec 1971
Silversides	SSN679	GD (Quincy)	Oct 1969	May 1972
William H. Bates	SSN680	Ingalls	Aug 1969	May 1973
Batfish	SSN681	GD (Quincy)	Feb 1970	Sep 1972
Tunny	SSN682	Ingalls	May 1970	Jan 1974
Parche	SSN683	Ingalls	Dec 1970	Aug 1974
Cavalla	SSN684	GD (Quincy)	Jun 1970	Feb 1973
L. Mendel Rivers	SSN686	Newport News	Jun 1971	Feb 1975
Richard B. Russell	SSN687	Newport News	Oct 1971	Aug 1975

The *Richard B. Russell* was the last of the large 'Sturgeon' class to be commissioned. The design was evolved from that of the 'Thresher/Permit' class with an improved electronic suite, a taller sail for more mast volume, and the capability for operations under the polar ice cap.

'Swiftsure' class SSN

(UK)

Type: nuclear-powered fleet (attack) submarine

Displacement: 4,400 tons standard and 4,900 tons dived

Dimensions: length 272·0 ft (82·9 m); beam 32·3 ft (9·8 m); draught 28·0 ft (8·5 m)

Gun armament: none

Missile armament: five UGM-84 Sub-Harpoon tube-launched anti-ship missiles in place of torpedoes

Torpedo armament: five 21-in (533-mm) tubes (all bow) for 25 Mk 24 Tiger-fish wire-guided dual-role torpedoes

Anti-submarine armament: torpedoes (see above)

Mines: up to 50 Mk 5 Stonefish or Mk 6 Sea Urchin mines in place of torpedoes

Electronics: one Type 1006 surface-search and navigation radar, one Type 2001 long-range active/passive search and attack chin sonar being replaced by Type 2020 active/passive search and attack bow sonar (to be replaced by Type 2074 active/passive search and attack sonar), one Type 2007 passive search flank sonar, one Type 2046 clip-on passive search towed-array sonar, one Type 2019 long-range passive intercept and ranging sonar, one Type 197 passive ranging sonar, one KAFS tactical data-handling system, one DCB underwater weapons fire-control system, one decoy system, one Type UAC ESM system with warning element, one SINS, and extensive communication and navigation systems

Propulsion: one Rolls-Royce PWR-1 pressurized water-cooled reactor supplying steam to two sets of General Electric geared turbines delivering 15,000 hp (11,185 kW) to one shaft

Performance: maximum speed 20 kt surfaced and 30+ kt dived; diving depth 1,325 ft (400 m) operational and 1,970 ft (600 m) maximum

Complement: 13 + 103

Class

1.UK Name	No.	Builder	Laid down	Com-missioned
Swiftsure	S126	Vickers	Jun 1969	Apr 1973
Sovereign	S108	Vickers	Sep 1970	Jul 1974
Superb	S109	Vickers	Mar 1972	Nov 1976
Sceptre	S104	Vickers	Feb 1974	Feb 1978
Spartan	S105	Vickers	Apr 1976	Sep 1979
Splendid	S106	Vickers	Nov 1977	Mar 1981

Note: Though based on the design of the 'Valiant' class, these boats have a slightly fuller form for higher underwater speed and diving depth. The torpedo armament is reduced by one tube, but this is balanced by an improved and considerably faster torpedo reloading system. The type is quieter than the 'Valiant' class, a fact aided by a covering of anechoic tiles, and has a 4,000-hp (2982-kW) auxiliary propulsion system of the diesel-electric type with Paxman diesel engines.

The 'Swiftsure' class of SSNs has a fuller hull form to offer superior but quieter underwater operation than the preceding 'Churchill/Valiant' class, and, as indicated by this illustration of the *Sovereign*, has the ability to operate in the Arctic ice cap.

'Thresher' or 'Permit' class SSN

(USA)

Type: nuclear-powered attack (fleet) submarine

Displacement: 3,750 tons or (SSN613/615) 3,800 tons standard and 4,470 tons or (SSN613/615) 4,245 tons dived

Dimensions: length 278·5 ft (84·9 m) or (SSN605) 297·4 ft (90·7 m) or (SSN613/615) 292·2 ft (89·1 m); beam 31·7 ft (9·6 m); draught 28·4 ft (8·7 m)

Gun armament: none

Missile armament: four UGM-84 Sub-Harpoon tube-launched anti-ship missiles in place of torpedoes

Torpedo armament: four 21-in (533-mm) Mk 63 tubes (all amidships) for 22 Mk 48 dual-role wire-guided torpedoes

Anti-submarine armament: torpedoes (see above) and four tube-launched UUM-44A SUBROC anti-submarine missiles in place of torpedoes in boats fitted with the Mk 113 fire-control system

Mines: up to 46 Mk 57, Mk 60 and Mk 67 mines in place of torpedoes

Electronics: one BPS-11 or BPS-15 surface-search and navigation radar, one BQQ-3 active/passive search and attack bow sonar with BQS-6 active and BQR-7 passive elements (being replaced by BQQ-5 active/passive search and attack sonar), one BQS-14 active/passive bow search sonar, one Mk 113 (SSN604-606 and SSN612-615) or Mk 117 (other boats) underwater weapons fire-control system, one ESM system with WLR-1 warning element, Emerson Electric Mk 2 torpedo decoys, one SINS, one WSC-3 satellite communications transceiver, and extensive communication and navigation systems

Propulsion: one Westinghouse S5W pressurized water-cooled reactor supplying steam to two sets of geared turbines delivering 15,000 hp (11,185 kW) to one shaft, except SSN605 which has an ungeared contra-rotating turbine driving co-axial contra-rotating propellers

Performance: maximum speed 18 kt surfaced and 30 kt dived; diving depth 1,325 ft (400 m) operational and 1,970 ft (600 m) maximum

Complement: 13 + 114 (more in boats used for 'Holy Stone' reconnaissance work)

Class
1. USA

Name	No.	Builder	Laid down	Commissioned
Permit	SSN594	Mare Island NY	Jul 1959	May 1962
Plunger	SSN595	Mare Island NY	Mar 1960	Nov 1962
Barb	SSN596	Ingalls	Nov 1959	Aug 1963
Haddo	SSN604	New York SB	Sep 1960	Dec 1964
Jack	SSN605	Portsmouth NY	Sep 1960	Dec 1964
Tinosa	SSN606	Portsmouth NY	Nov 1959	Oct 1964
Dace	SSB607	Ingalls	Jun 1960	Apr 1964
Guardfish	SSN612	New York SB	Feb 1961	Dec 1966
Flasher	SSN613	GD (EB Div)	Apr 1961	Jul 1966
Greenling	SSN614	GD (EB Div)	Aug 1961	Nov 1967
Gato	SSN615	GD (EB Div)	Dec 1961	Jan 1968
Haddock	SSN621	Ingalls	Apr 1961	Dec 1967

Note: These boats are of a modified teardrop design with the bows devoted to sonar and the torpedo tubes relocated to an amidships position. The lead boat, *Thresher*, sank in April 1963 and the 'Thresher' class was later redesignated the 'Permit' class. The class is to be decommissioned as the later 'Los Angeles' class boats enter service, the first 'Permit' class boat to be deleted being the *Pollack*, which was decommissioned in January 1989.

The *Plunger* is one of 12 surviving 'Permit' class SSNs.

'Trafalgar' class SSN

(UK)
Type: nuclear-powered fleet (attack) submarine
Displacement: 4,700 tons surfaced and 5,210 tons dived
Dimensions: length 280·1 ft (85·4 m); beam 32·1 ft (9·8 m); draught 26·9 ft (8·2 m)
Gun armament: none
Missile armament: five UGM-84 Sub-Harpoon tube-launched anti-ship missiles in place of torpedoes
Torpedo armament: five 21-in (533-mm) tubes (all bow) for 25 Spearfish and Mk 24 Tigerfish wire-guided dual-role torpedoes
Anti-submarine armament: torpedoes (see above)
Mines: up to 50 Mk 5 Stonefish or Mk 6 Sea Urchin mines in place of torpedoes
Electronics: one Type 1006 surface-search and navigation radar (to be replaced by Type 1007 radar), one Type 2020 multi-function active/passive search and attack chin sonar, one Type 2007 long-range passive search flank sonar, one Type 2026 or Type 2046 passive search towed-array flank sonar, one Type 2019 active/passive ranging and intercept sonar, one Type 197 passive ranging sonar, one KAFS action data system, one DCB underwater weapons fire-control system, one Type UAC ESM system with CXA warning element, one SINS, and extensive communication and navigation systems
Propulsion: one Rolls-Royce PWR-1 pressurized water-cooled reactor supplying steam to two sets of General Electric geared turbines delivering 15,000 hp (11,185 kW) to one pump-jet propulsor
Performance: maximum speed 20 kt surfaced and 32 kt dived; diving depth 1,315 ft (400 m) operational and 1,970 ft (600 m) maximum
Complement: 12 + 85

Class

1. UK				Com-
Name	No.	Builder	Laid down	missioned
Trafalgar	S107	VSEL	1978	May 1983
Turbulent	S87	VSEL	1979	Apr 1984
Tireless	S88	VSEL	1981	Oct 1985
Torbay	S90	VSEL	Dec 1982	Feb 1987
Trenchant	S91	VSEL	Apr 1984	Jan 1989
Talent	S92	VSEL	Apr 1986	May 1990
Triumph	S93	VSEL	1987	1991

Note: Designed to complement the boats of the 'Swiftsure' class, these vessels have much reduced radiated noise levels because of their pump-jet propulsion and wraparound anechoic tiling. The boats also possess a 4,000-hp (2982-kW) auxiliary propulsion system of the diesel-electric type using Paxman diesels.

The *Turbulent* was the second unit of the 'Trafalgar' class to be commissioned, the pump-jet propulsion of these seven boats offering lower noise levels than in the companion boats of the 'Swiftsure' class.

'Victor I' class SSN

(USSR)
Type: nuclear-powered attack (fleet) submarine
Displacement: 4,400 tons surfaced and 5,300 tons dived
Dimensions: length 94·0 m (308·4 ft); beam 10·5 m (34·4 ft); draught 7·3 m (23·9 ft)
Gun armament: none
Missile armament: none
Torpedo armament: six 533-mm (21-in) tubes (all bow) for 18 Type 53 dual-role torpedoes
Anti-submarine armament: torpedoes (see above) and two SS-N-15 'Starfish' tube-launched missiles in place of torpedoes
Mines: up to 36 AMD-1000 mines in place of torpedoes
Electronics: one 'Snoop Tray' surface-search and navigation radar, one low-frequency active/passive bow sonar, one medium-frequency underwater weapons fire-control sonar, one combined 'Brick Spit' and 'Brick Pulp' ESM system with warning element, one 'Park Lamp' direction-finder, one SINS, and extensive communication and navigation systems
Propulsion: two pressurized water-cooled reactors supplying steam to one set of geared turbines delivering 22,500 kW (30,175 hp) to one main and two auxiliary shafts
Performance: maximum speed 20 kt surfaced and 32 kt dived; diving depth 400 m (1,325 ft) operational and 600 m (1,970 ft) maximum
Complement: 90

Class
1.USSR
16 boats
Note: Built between 1964 and 1974 at the Admiralty Yard in Leningrad, these were the USSR's first albacore-hulled submarines. The type has recently suffered a spate of problems, and must be regarded as increasingly unreliable.

'Victor II' class SSN

(USSR)

Type: nuclear-powered attack (fleet) submarine
Displacement: 4,900 tons surfaced and 5,800 tons dived
Dimensions: length 103·0 m (337·9 ft); beam 10·6 m (34·8 ft); draught 7·4 m (24·3 ft)
Gun armament: none
Missile armament: none
Torpedo armament: six 533-mm (21-in) tubes (all bow) for 21 Type 53 dual-role torpedoes
Anti-submarine armament: torpedoes (see above) and two SS-N-15 'Starfish' tube-launched missiles in place of torpedoes
Mines: up to 36 AMD-1000 mines in place of torpedoes
Electronics: one 'Snoop Tray' surface-search and navigation radar, one low-frequency active/passive bow sonar, one medium-frequency underwater weapons fire-control sonar, one combined 'Brick Spit' and 'Brick Pulp'

ESM system with warning element, one 'Park Lamp' direction-finder, one SINS, one satellite navigation system, and extensive communication and navigation systems
Propulsion: two pressurized water-cooled reactors supplying steam to one set of geared turbines delivering 22,500 kW (30,175 hp) to one main and two auxiliary shafts
Performance: maximum speed 20 kt surfaced and 31 kt dived; diving depth 400 m (1,325 ft) operational and 600 m (1,970 ft) maximum
Complement: 100

Class
1. USSR
7 boats
Note: Successor to the 'Victor I' class, this type began delivery from the Admiralty Yard in Leningrad and from Gorky during 1972, and is mainly distinguishable by its longer hull, in which the additional volume is used for improved equipment and habitability.

'Victor III' class SSN

(USSR)

Type: nuclear-powered attack (fleet) submarine
Displacement: 5,000 tons surfaced and 6,000 tons dived
Dimensions: length 107·0 m (351·0 ft); beam 10·6 m (34·8 ft); draught 7·4 m (24·3 ft)
Gun armament: none
Missile armament: SS-N-21 'Sampson' tubed-launched land-attack cruise missiles in place of torpedoes
Torpedo armament: four 650-mm (25·6-in) and two 533-mm (21-in) tubes (all bow) for 18 650-mm (25·6-in) Type 65 and 533-mm (21-in) Type 53 dual-role torpedoes
Anti-submarine armament: torpedoes (see above), and two SS-N-15 'Starfish' and two SS-N-16 'Stallion' missiles launched from 533- and 650-mm (21- and 25·6-in) tubes respectively
Mines: up to 36 AMD-1000 mines in place of torpedoes
Electronics: one 'Snoop Tray' surface-search and navigation radar, one low-frequency active/passive bow sonar, one low-frequency towed-array sonar, various fire-control systems including one medium-frequency underwater weapons fire-control sonar, one combined 'Brick Spit' and 'Brick Pulp' ESM system with warning element, one 'Park Lamp' direction-

finder, one SINS, one 'Pert Spring' satellite communications system, one satellite navigation system, and extensive communication and navigation systems
Propulsion: two pressurized water-cooled reactors supplying steam to one set of geared turbines delivering 22,500 kW (30,175 hp) to two contra-rotating propellers (some boats) or one main and two auxiliary shafts
Performance: maximum speed 20 kt surfaced and 30 kt dived; diving depth 400 m (1,325 ft) operational and 600 m (1,970 ft) maximum
Complement: 100

Class
1. USSR
23 boats plus 1 more building
Note: This much quietened version of the 'Victor II' class SSN with more versatile armament first appeared from Komsomolsk during 1978, and then entered an extremely rapid production programme at Komsomolsk and the Admiralty Yard in Leningrad that has seen each builder deliver about one boat per year.

Availability in large numbers makes the 'Victor III' class the USSR's most potent single asset for the protection of its own SSBNs and the destruction of enemy surface and (more importantly) underwater craft.

'Yankee Notch' class SSN

(USSR)

Type: nuclear-powered attack (fleet) submarine
Displacement: 10,300 tons dived
Dimensions: length 142·0 m (465·9 ft); beam 11·6 m (38·0 ft); draught 8·1 m (26·6 ft)
Gun armament: none
Missile armament: possibly SS-N-21 'Sampson' tube-launched land-attack cruise missiles (see Note below)
Torpedo armament: probably two 650-mm (25·6-in) and four 533-mm (21-in) tubes (all bow) for 18 650-mm (25·6-in) Type 65 and 533-mm (21-in) Type 53 dual-role torpedoes
Anti-submarine armament: torpedoes (see above) and probably SS-N-16 'Stallion' missiles fired from the 650-mm (25·6-in) tubes
Electronics: one 'Snoop Tray' surface-search and navigation radar, one low-frequency bow sonar, one medium-frequency torpedo fire-control sonar, one 'Brick Group' ESM system with warning element, one 'Park Lamp' direction-finder, one SINS, one 'Pert Spring' satellite communications system, and various communication and navigation systems
Propulsion: two pressurized water-cooled reactors supplying steam to two sets of geared turbines delivering 37,300 kW (50,025 hp) to two shafts
Performance: maximum speed 22 kt surfaced and 26 kt dived; diving depth 400 m (1,315 ft) operational and 600 m (1,970 ft) maximum
Complement: 120

Class

1. USSR

3 boats plus 13 more being converted

Note: The 'Yankee' class was the USSR's first series-produced type of SSBN, and the original 34 boats were produced in parallel at the Severodvinsk 402 and Komsomolsk shipyards between 1963 and 1972. Since the signing of the SALT I treaty limiting the USSR to 62 SSBNs carrying 950 SLBMs, several 'Yankee' class boats have been taken in hand for conversion to 'Yankee Notch' SSN standard: in each such conversion the whole SLBM section is replaced by a 'notch-waisted' section, increasing overall length and perhaps boosting performance by a slight degree, while adding what are thought to be launch tubes for an unknown number of SS-N-21 cruise missiles, while the armament is upgraded towards current Soviet SSN standards by the replacement of at least two 533-mm (21-in) tubes by 650-mm (25·6-in) tubes; it is also possible that such tubes have been added in addition to, rather than as replacement for, the original tubes. It is likely that the 'Yankee Notch' class SSNs share the deployment areas of the 'Yankee' class SSBNs off the eastern and western seaboards of the USA to provide a dual forward-deployed deterrent with nuclear-armed SS-N-21 and SS-N-17 missiles respectively.

The 'Yankee Notch' conversion of obsolescent 'Yankee' class SSBNs provides the USSR with a useful force of second-line SSNs which can also be used for training and other subsidiary tasks.

'Abtao' class SS

(USA)

Type: patrol (attack) submarine
Displacement: 825 tons surfaced and 1,400 tons dived
Dimensions: length 243·0 ft (74·1 m); beam 22·0 ft (6·7 m); draught 14·0 ft (4·3 m)
Gun armament: one 5-in (127-mm) L/25 (SS41 and 42 only)
Missile armament: none
Torpedo armament: six 21-in (533-mm) tubes (four bow and two stern) for Mk 37 torpedoes
Anti-submarine armament: none
Electronics: one surface-search and navigation radar, one Eledone active/passive search and attack sonar, one torpedo fire-control system, one ESM system with warning element, and various communication and navigation systems
Propulsion: diesel-electric arrangement, with two General Motors 12-278A diesels delivering 2,400 hp (1790 kW) and two electric motors delivering unrevealed power to two shafts
Performance: maximum speed 16 kt surfaced and 10 kt dived; range 5,750 miles (9255 km) at 10 kt surfaced
Complement: 40

Class

1. Peru ('Dos de Mayo' class)

Name	No.	Builder	Laid down	Com-missioned
Dos de Mayo	SS41	GD (EB Div)	May 1952	Jun 1954
Abtao	SS42	GD (EB Div)	May 1952	Feb 1954
Angamos	SS43	GD (EB Div)	Oct 1955	Jul 1957
Iquique	SS44	GD (EB Div)	Oct 1955	Oct 1957

Note: These are modified 'Mackerel' class boats, and now of little if any operational value.

'Agosta' class SS

(France)
Type: patrol (attack) submarine
Displacement: 1,230 tons standard, 1,490 tons surfaced and 1,740 tons dived
Dimensions: length 67·6 m (221·8 ft); beam 6·8 m (22·3 ft); draught 5·4 m (17·7 ft)
Gun armament: none
Missile armament: SM.39 Exocet tube-launched anti-ship missiles in place of torpedoes
Torpedo armament: four 533-mm (21-in) tubes (all bow) for 20 L5 dual-purpose and F17 wire-guided anti-ship torpedoes
Anti-submarine armament: torpedoes (see above)
Mines: up to 36 TSM3510 (MCC23) mines in place of torpedoes
Electronics: one DRUA 33 surface-search and navigation radar, one DSUV 22 passive search sonar, one DUUA 1D active search sonar, one DUUA 2D active search and attack sonar, one DUUX 2A passive ranging sonar, one DSUV 62 passive search towed-array sonar (to be fitted on all boats by 1991), one DLT-D3 action information and underwater weapons fire-control system, one ESM system with ARUD warning and ARUR intercept elements, and various communication and navigation systems
Propulsion: diesel-electric arrangement, with two SEMT-Pielstick 16 PA4 185VG main diesels delivering 2700 kW (3,620 hp) and one electric motor delivering 3500 kW (4,695 hp) to one shaft; there is also one 23-kW (31-hp) cruising diesel
Performance: maximum speed 12 kt surfaced and 20 kt dived; diving depth 300 m (985 ft) operational and 500 m (1,640 ft) maximum; range 15,750 km (9,785 miles) at 9 kt snorting and 400 km (249 miles) at 3·5 kt dived; endurance 45 days
Complement: 7 + 47

***La Praya* is one of the French navy's 'Agosta' class boats, which were the service's first with 533-mm (21-in) rather than 550-mm (21·7-in) tubes.**

Class

1. France

Name	No.	Builder	Laid down	Com-missioned
Agosta	S620	Cherbourg ND	Nov 1972	Jul 1977
Bévéziers	S621	Cherbourg ND	May 1973	Sep 1977
La Praya	S622	Cherbourg ND	1974	Mar 1978
Ouessant	S623	Cherbourg ND	1974	Jul 1978

(These were the French navy's first submarines to be fitted with 533-mm/21-in torpedo tubes. In recent years the service has made considerable efforts to improve the type's operational capabilities by a reduction of acoustic signature through damping of internal noise and cleaning up the casing.)

2. Pakistan

Name	No.	Builder	Laid down	Com-missioned
Hashmat	S135	Dubigeon	Sep 1976	Feb 1979
Hurmat	S136	Dubigeon		Feb 1980

(These Pakistani boats carry at least four UGM-84 Sub-Harpoon missiles instead of Exocets, but are otherwise similar to the French submarines.)

3. Spain ('S70' or 'Galerna' class)

Name	No.	Builder	Laid down	Com-missioned
Galerna	S71	Bazan	Sep 1977	Jun 1982
Siroco	S72	Bazan	Nov 1978	May 1983
Mistral	S73	Bazan	May 1980	Jun 1985
Tramontana	S74	Bazan	Dec 1981	Jun 1985

(The Spanish boats have a different electronics fit compared with the French units, with DRUA 33C radar, two DUAA 2 active sonars, one DSUV 22 passive sonar, Eledone intercept sonar, and one DUUX 2A [first pair] or DUUX-5 [second pair] ranging sonar. The boats may be fitted for UGM-84 Sub-Harpoon rather than Exocet missiles.)

'Barbel' class SS

(USA)
Type: patrol (attack) submarine
Displacement: 1,740 tons standard, 2,145 tons surfaced and 2,895 tons dived
Dimensions: length 219·1 ft (66·8 m); beam 29·0 ft (8·8 m); draught 28·0 ft (8·5 m)
Gun armament: none
Missile armament: none
Torpedo armament: six 21-in (533-mm) Mk 58 tubes (all bow) for Mk 48 dual-role wire-guided torpedoes
Anti-submarine armament: torpedoes (see above)
Electronics: one BPS-12 surface-search and navigation radar, one BQS-2 active/passive search and attack sonar, one Mk 101 torpedo fire-control system, one ESM system with WLR-1 warning element, and various communication and navigation systems
Propulsion: diesel-electric arrangement, with three Fairbanks-Morse 38D8 diesels delivering 4,800 hp (3580 kW) and two General Electric electric motors delivering 3,150 hp (2350 kW) to one shaft
Performance: maximum speed 15 kt surfaced and 21 kt dived
Complement: 8 + 77

Barbell class patrol submarine surfaced in ice field.

Class

1. USA

Name	No.	Builder	Laid down	Com-missioned
Barbel	SS580	Portsmouth NY	May 1956	Jan 1959
Blueback	SS581	Ingalls	Apr 1957	Oct 1959

Note: These were the US Navy's last operational submarines of the non-nuclear type, and amongst their advanced features are a teardrop hull and centralized sensor/fire-control suite. As built, the boats had bow-mounted forward hydroplanes, but these were later moved to the sail. The *Bonefish* suffered a battery fire and explosion in April 1988 and was scrapped.

'Daphné' class SS

(France)

Type: patrol (attack) submarine
Displacement: 700 tons standard, 860 tons surfaced and 1,040 tons dived
Dimensions: length 57·75 m (189·5 ft); beam 6·76 m (22·2 ft); draught 4·62 m (15·2 ft)
Gun armament: none
Missile armament: none
Torpedo armament: 12 550-mm (21·65-in) tubes (eight bow and four stern) for 12 E15 torpedoes
Anti-submarine armament: torpedoes (see above)
Mines: up to 24 TSM3510 (MCC23) mines instead of torpedoes
Electronics: one DRUA 31F surface-search and navigation radar, one DSUV 2 passive search sonar, one DUUA 1 (S641) or DUUA 2A active/passive search and attack sonar, one DUUX 2 passive ranging sonar, one DLT-D3 action information and torpedo fire-control system, and various communication and navigation systems
Propulsion: diesel-electric arrangement, with two 1820-kW (2,440-hp) SEMT-Pielstick/Jeumont Schneider diesel generators supplying current to two electric motors delivering 1940 kW (2,600 hp) to two shafts
Performance: maximum speed 13·5 kt surfaced and 16 kt dived; diving depth 300 m (985 ft) operational and 575 m (1,885 ft) maximum; range 18,500 km (11,495 miles) at 7 kt surfaced or 5560 km (3,455 miles) at 7 kt snorting
Complement: 6 + 39

Class

1. France

Name	No.	Builder	Laid down	Com-missioned
Daphné	S641	Dubigeon	Mar 1958	Jun 1964
Diane	S642	Dubigeon	Jul 1958	Jun 1964
Doris	S643	Cherbourg ND	Sep 1958	Aug 1964
Flore	S645	Cherbourg ND	Sep 1958	May 1964
Galatée	S646	Cherbourg ND	Sep 1958	Jul 1964
Junon	S648	Cherbourg ND	Jul 1961	Feb 1966
Vénus	S649	Cherbourg ND	Aug 1961	Jan 1966
Psyché	S650	Brest ND	May 1965	Jul 1969
Sirène	S651	Brest ND	May 1965	Mar 1970

(These small boats are still of operational utility, having been modernized between 1971 and 1981. They are based at Lorient and Toulon, and are best employed in coastal operations.)

2. Pakistan

Name	No.	Builder	Laid down	Com-missioned
Hangor	S131	Brest Arsenal	Dec 1967	Jan 1970
Shushuk	S132	CN Ciotat	Dec 1967	Jan 1970
Mangro	S133	CN Ciotat	Jul 1968	Aug 1970
Ghazi	S134	Dubigeon	May 1967	Oct 1969

(These boats differ only marginally from the French norm.)

3. Portugal

Name	No.	Builder	Laid down	Com-missioned
Albacora	S163	Dubigeon	Sep 1965	Oct 1967
Barracuda	S164	Dubigeon	Oct 1965	May 1968
Delfim	S166	Dubigeon	May 1967	Oct 1969

(These boats differ only marginally from the French norm with Calypso II radar and an ESM system with ARUR intercept element.)

4. South Africa

Name	No.	Builder	Laid down	Com-missioned
Maria van Riebeeck	S97	Dubigeon	Mar 1968	Jun 1970
Emily Hobhouse	S98	Dubigeon	Nov 1968	Jan 1971
Johanna van der Merwe	S99	Dubigeon	Apr 1969	Jul 1971

(These boats differ only marginally from the French norm, but have been provided with improved weapon/fire-control systems and habitability features during a mid-life update.)

5. Spain ('S60' class)

Name	No.	Builder	Laid down	Com-missioned
Delfin	S61	Bazan	Aug 1968	May 1973
Tonina	S62	Bazan	Mar 1970	Jul 1973
Marsopa	S63	Bazan	Mar 1971	Apr 1975
Narval	S64	Bazan	Apr 1972	Nov 1975

(These boats differ from the French standard only in their armament and sensor fits, the former comprising L5, F17 and E18 torpedoes, and the latter comprising DRUA 31 or DRUA 33 radar with ECM equipment, and DUUA 2A sonar in place of the original DUUA 1, resulting in a more bulged bow housing for the transducer arrays.)

The **Junon** and her nine sister boats of the 'Daphne' class are small vessels designed largely for coastal operations, and carry no reload torpedoes for their 12 tubes (eight bow and four stern).

'Delfinen' class SS

(Denmark)

Type: patrol (attack) submarine
Displacement: 595 tons surfaced and 645 tons dived
Dimensions: length 54·0 m (177·2 ft); beam 4·7 m (15·4 ft); draught 4·2 m (13·8 ft)
Gun armament: none
Missile armament: none
Torpedo armament: four 533-mm (21-in) tubes (all bow) for four Tp 41 anti-submarine and Tp 61 wire-guided anti-ship torpedoes
Anti-submarine armament: torpedoes (see above)
Electronics: one surface-search and navigation radar, one active/passive search and attack sonar, one passive sonar, one torpedo fire-control system, and various communication and navigation systems
Propulsion: diesel-electric arrangement, with two Burmeister & Wain diesels delivering 900 kW (1,205 hp) and two electric motors delivering 900 kW (1,205 hp) to two shafts
Performance: maximum speed 16 kt surfaced and 16 kt dived; diving depth 100 m (330 ft) operational; range 7400 km (4,600 miles) at 8 kt surfaced
Complement: 31

Class

1. Denmark

Name	No.	Builder	Laid down	Com-missioned
Spaekhuggeren	S327	Royal Dockyard	Nov 1954	Jun 1959
Springeren	S328	Royal Dockyard	Jan 1961	Oct 1964

Note: These small coastal boats are reaching the end of their operational lives, and are to be replaced by ex-Norwegian 'Kobben' class boats.

'Dolfijn' and 'Potvis' class SSs

(Netherlands)
Type: patrol (attack) submarine
Displacement: 1,140 tons standard, 1,520 tons or ('Potvis' class) 1,510 tons surfaced and 1,830 tons or ('Potvis' class) 1,835 tons dived
Dimensions: length 79·5 m (260·9 ft) or ('Potvis' class) 78·3 m (256·9 ft); beam 7·8 m (25·8 ft); draught 5·0 m (16·4 ft)
Gun armament: none
Missile armament: none
Torpedo armament: eight 21-in (533-mm) tubes (four bow and four stern) for 20 NT 37C/E dual-role wire-guided torpedoes
Anti-submarine armament: torpedoes (see above)
Electronics: one Type 1001 surface-search and navigation radar, one active/passive search and attack sonar, one WM-8 torpedo fire-control system, one ESM system with warning element, and various communication and navigation systems
Propulsion: diesel-electric arrangement, with two MAN 12-V6V 22/30 diesels delivering 2300 kW (3,085 shp) and two electric motors delivering 3120 kW (4,185 hp) to two shafts ('Potvis' class) or two SEMT-Pielstick PA4 diesels delivering 2300 kW (3,085 hp) and two electric motors delivering 3280 kW (4,400 hp) to two shafts
Performance: maximum speed 14·5 kt surfaced and 17 kt dived; diving depth 300 m (985 ft) operational

Complement: 8 + 59

Class

1. Netherlands ('Dolfijn' class)

Name	No.	Builder	Laid down	Com-missioned
Zeehond	S809	Rotterdamse DD	Dec 1954	Mar 1961

2. Netherlands ('Potvis' class)

Name	No.	Builder	Laid down	Com-missioned
Potvis	S804	Wilton-Fijenoord	Sep 1962	Nov 1965
Tonijn	S805	Wilton-Fijenoord	Nov 1962	Feb 1966

Note: These basically similar triple-hulled designs each comprise a triangular arrangement of three pressure hulls, the upper unit accommodating the crew and weapon/sensor systems, and the side-by-side lower units containing the propulsion system and stores. The boats are obsolescent and in the process of being phased out of service, the lead unit *Dolfijn* having been deleted in 1985.

The boats of the closely related 'Dolfijn' and 'Potvis' classes are obsolete and are being phased out of service. This is the *Potvis* moving at modest speed on the surface.

'Draken' class SS

(Sweden)
Type: patrol (attack) submarine
Displacement: 770 tons standard, 835 tons surfaced and 1,110 tons dived
Dimensions: length 69·0 m (226·4 ft); beam 5·1 m (16·7 ft); draught 4·6 m (15·1 ft)
Gun armament: none
Missile armament: none
Torpedo armament: four 533-mm (21-in) tubes (all bow) for 12 Tp 61 wire-guided torpedoes
Anti-submarine armament: torpedoes (see above)
Mines: up to 24 in place of torpedoes
Electronics: one Subfar 100 surface-search and navigation radar, one active/passive search and attack sonar, one torpedo fire-control system, and various communication and navigation systems
Propulsion: diesel-electric arrangement, with two Hedemora/Pielstick 16V 12PA diesels and one electric motor delivering 1250 kW (1,675 hp) to one shaft
Performance: maximum speed 17 kt surfaced and 20 kt dived
Complement: 36

Class

1. Sweden

Name	No.	Builder	Laid down	Com-missioned
Delfinen	Del	Karlskrona	1959	Jun 1962
Nordkaparen	Nor	Kockums	1959	Apr 1962
Springaren	Spr	Kockums	1960	Nov 1962
Vargen	Vgn	Kockums	1958	Nov 1961

Note: These coastal boats are obsolescent, and in the process of being laid up in reserve as they are replaced by the 'Västergotland' class submarines.

The 'Draken' class was derived from the twin-shaft 'Hajen' class based on Germany's 'Type XXI' design of World War II, and originally numbered eight boats. One of those which has been deleted is the *Gripen*.

'Foxtrot' class SS

(USSR)

Type: patrol (attack) submarine

Displacement: 1,950 tons surfaced and 2,500 tons dived

Dimensions: length 91·5 m (300·1 ft); beam 8·0 m (26·2 ft); draught 6·1 m (20·0 ft)

Gun armament: none

Missile armament: none

Torpedo armament: 10 533-mm (21-in) tubes (six bow and four stern) for 22 Type 53 torpedoes

Anti-submarine armament: torpedoes (see above)

Mines: up to 44 AMD-100 mines in place of torpedoes

Electronics: one 'Snoop Tray' or 'Snoop Plate' surface-search and navigation radar, one 'Herkules' high-frequency active/passive hull sonar, one 'Feniks' bow sonar, one torpedo fire-control system, one 'Stop Light' ESM system with warning element, one 'Quad Loop' direction-finder, and various communication and navigation systems

Propulsion: diesel-electric arrangement, with three diesels delivering 4500 kW (6,035 hp) and three electric motors delivering 3900 kW (5,230 hp) to three shafts

Performance: maximum speed 18 kt surfaced and 16 kt dived; diving depth 300 m (985 ft) operational and 500 m (1,640 ft) maximum; range 29,650 km (18,425 miles) at 8 kt surfaced; endurance 70 days

Complement: 8 + 67

Class

1. Cuba

3 boats

A soviet 'Foxtrot' class conventional submarine is pictured on the surface in Mediterranean company with a 'Kashin' class guided-missile destroyer.

(These boats are identical to the Soviet units in all essential respects, and were delivered in February 1979, March 1980 and February 1984.)

2. India

Name	No.
Kursura	S20
Karanj	S21
Kanderi	S22
Kalvari	S23
Vela	S40
Vagir	S41
Vagli	S42
Vagsheer	S43

(These boats are identical to the Soviet units in all essential respects, and were delivered between July 1968 and December 1975. It is thought that two boats are in reserve, with the others to follow as newer submarines enter service.)

3. Libya

Name	No.
Al Badr	311
Al Fateh	312
Al Ahad	313
Al Matrega	314
Al Khyber	315
Al Hunain	316

(These boats are identical to the Soviet units in all essential respects, and were delivered between December 1976 and February 1983.)

4. USSR

55 boats including 10 in reserve

Note: These boats were built at Sudomekh between 1958 and 1971 for the Soviet navy, with production continuing to 1984 for export deliveries. Total production was 62 boats out of a planned 180, the successful development of nuclear-powered boats persuading the Soviet navy to curtail production.

'Guppy IA' class SS

(USA)

Type: patrol (attack) submarine

Displacement: 1,870 tons surfaced and 2,440 tons dived

Dimensions: length 308·0 ft (93·8 m); beam 27·0 ft (8·2 m); draught 17·0 ft (5·2 m)

Gun armament: none

Missile armament: none

Torpedo armament: 10 21-in (533-mm) tubes (six bow and four stern) for 24 Mk 37 torpedoes

Anti-submarine armament: none

Electronics: one surface-search and navigation radar, one BQR-2B passive search and attack sonar with active capability added by one BQS-4 sonar, one torpedo fire-control system, one ESM system with warning element, and various communication and navigation systems

Propulsion: diesel-electric arrangement, with three Fairbanks-Morse 38D8 diesels delivering 4,800 hp (3580 kW) and two Elliot Motor electric motors delivering 5,400 hp (4025 kW) to two shafts

Performance: maximum speed 17 kt surfaced and 15 kt dived; diving depth 400 ft (120 m) operational; range 9,200 miles (14,805 km) at 12 kt surfaced

Complement: 85

Class

1. Peru

Name	No.	Builder	Laid down	Com-missioned
La Pedrera	S49	Portsmouth NY	Feb 1944	Jul 1944

Note: This World War II American boat was modernized under the 1951 GUPPY programme, but can now be regarded only as obsolescent. Its sister boat Pacocha sank in September 1988 after colliding with a fishing vessel.

'Guppy II' class SS

(USA/Brazil)

Type: patrol (attack) submarine
Displacement: 1,870 tons surfaced and 2,420 tons dived
Dimensions: length 307·5 ft (93·6 m); beam 27·2 ft (8·3 m); draught 18·0 ft (5·5 m)
Gun armament: none
Missile armament: none
Torpedo armament: 10 21-in (533-mm) tubes (six bow and four stern) for 24 Mk 37 wire-guided multi-role torpedoes
Anti-submarine armament: torpedoes (see above)
Electronics: one SPS-2A surface-search and navigation radar, one BQR-2 active/passive search and attack hull sonar, one BQG-4 PUFFS passive ranging sonar, one torpedo fire-control system, and various communication and navigation systems
Propulsion: diesel-electric arrangement, with three Fairbanks-Morse 38D8 diesels delivering 4,800 hp (3580 kW) and two Elliot Motor electric motors delivering 5,400 hp (4025 kW) to two shafts
Performance: maximum speed 18 kt surfaced and 15 kt dived; diving depth 400 ft (120 m) operational; range 13,800 miles (22,210 km) at 10 kt surfaced
Complement: 82

Class

1. Brazil ('Guanabara' class)

Name	No.	Builder	Laid down	Com-missioned
Bahia	S12	Portsmouth NY	Nov 1944	Jun 1945

(The 'Guppy II' class is essentially a modernization of the 'Tench' class and is the only Brazilian survivor of three boats transferred from the US Navy in 1973. The boat is due for deletion.)

2. Taiwan

Name	No.	Builder	Laid down	Com-missioned
Hai Shih	736	Portsmouth NY	Jul 1944	Mar 1945
Hai Pao	794	Federal SB	Aug 1943	Apr 1946

(The Taiwanese boats differ from the norm in having SS 2 surface-search and navigation radar, BQR-2B passive search and attack sonar with active capability added by a BQS-4C subsystem, DUUG 1B passive ranging sonar, and an ESM system with WLR-1 and WLR-3 warning elements.)

3. Venezuela

Name	No.	Builder	Laid down	Com-missioned
Picua	S22	Boston NY	Feb 1944	Feb 1951

(This Venezuelan boat is essentially similar to the Brazilian unit in everything but its torpedo armament, which includes Mk 14 in addition to Mk 37 weapons. The boat is used only for alongside training.)

'Guppy IIA' class SS

(USA/Turkey)

Type: patrol (attack) submarine
Displacement: 1,850 tons surfaced and 2,440 tons dived
Dimensions: length 306·0 ft (93·2 m); beam 27·0 ft (8·2 m); draught 17·0 ft (5·2 m)
Gun armament: none
Missile armament: none
Torpedo armament: 10 21-in (533-mm) tubes (six bow and four stern) for 24 torpedoes
Anti-submarine armament: none'
Mines: up to 40 inplace of torpedoes
Electronics: one SS 2A surface-search and navigation radar, one BQR-2B passive search and attack sonar with active capability added by a BQS-4 subsystem, one BQG-3 passive ranging sonar, one Mk 106 torpedo fire-control system, and various communication and navigation systems
Propulsion: diesel-electric arrangement, with three Fairbanks-Morse 38D8 or (S345) three General Motors 16-278A diesels delivering 5,400 hp (4025 kW) to two electric motors delivering 5,400 hp (4025 kW) to two shafts
Performance: maximum speed 17 kt surfaced and 15 kt dived; diving depth 400 ft (120 m) operational; range 13,800 miles (22,210 km) at 10 kt surfaced
Complement: 8 + 74

Class

1. Greece

Name	No.	Builder	Laid down	Com-missioned
Papanikolis	S114	Manitowoc SB	Jul 1943	Apr 1944

(This obsolescent boat is generally similar to the Turkish 'Guppy IIA' units but has Mk 37 wire-guided dual-role torpedoes and an ESM system with WLR-1 warning element.)

2. Turkey

Name	No.	Builder	Laid down	Com-missioned
Burakreis	S335	Portsmouth NY	Nov 1943	Jun 1944
Muratreis	S336	Portsmouth NY	Sep 1943	Apr 1944
Ulucalireis	S338	Portsmouth NY	Apr 1944	Oct 1944
Cerbe	S340	Portsmouth NY	Dec 1943	Nov 1944
Birinci Inonu	S346	Portsmouth NY	Mar 1944	Aug 1944

(These modernized boats were transferred by the US Navy during the early 1970s, and being obsolescent they are being phased out of first-line service as Turkey's new 'Type 209' boats are delivered.)

Depicted below is a 'Balao' class submarine externally identical to the 'Guppy II' class boats. Operated by Brazil this boat was not upgraded to 'Guppy II' fit.

'Guppy III' class SS

(USA/Turkey)

Type: patrol (attack) submarine

Displacement: 1,975 tons surfaced and 2,450 tons dived

Dimensions: length 326·5 ft (99·4 m); beam 27·0 ft (8·2 m); draught 17·0 ft (5·2 m)

Gun armament: none

Missile armament: none

Torpedo armament: 10 21-in (533-mm) tubes (six bow and four stern) for 24 torpedoes

Anti-submarine armament: none

Mines: up to 40 in place of torpedoes

Electronics: one SS 2A surface-search and navigation radar, one BQR-2B passive search and attack sonar with active capability added by a BQS-2 subsystem, one BQG-4 PUFFS passive fire-control sonar, one Mk 106 torpedo fire-control system, and various communication and navigation systems

Propulsion: diesel-electric arrangement, with four General Motors 16-278A diesels delivering 6,400 hp (4770 kW) and two General Electric electric motors delivering 5,400 hp (4025 kW) to two shafts

Performance: maximum speed 17·5 kt surfaced and 15 kt dived; diving depth 400 ft (120 m); range 11,500 miles (18,505 km) at 10 kt surfaced and 110 miles (177 km) at 9 kt dived

Complement: 8 + 78

Class

1. Brazil

Name	No.	Builder	Laid down	Com- missioned
Goias	S15	Cramp SB	Aug 1943	Jan 1946
Amazonas	S16	Electric Boat	Jun 1944	Jun 1946

(These Brazilian boats were transferred in 1973, and are being phased out of service as the Brazilian navy's new 'Type 209' class boats are brought into commission. They are generally similar to the Turkish boats but have Mk 37 torpedoes, SPS-2A radar and an ESM system with warning element.)

2. Greece

Name	No.	Builder	Laid down	Com- missioned
Katsonis	S115	Portsmouth NY	Mar 1945	Jan 1946

(This Greek boat is similar to the Turkish units and was procured in 1973. The boat has Mk 37 torpedoes and an ESM system with WLR-1 warning element, and is used mainly for training.)

3. Turkey

Name	No.	Builder	Laid down	Com- missioned
Canakkale	S341	Electric Boat	Apr 1944	Aug 1945
Ikinci Inonu	S333	Electric Boat	Apr 1944	Nov 1945

(These Turkish boats were transferred in 1973, and as they are obsolescent are used mainly for training. It is probable that their diving limit is periscope depth.)

'Heroj' class SS

(Yugoslavia)

Type: patrol (attack) submarine

Displacement: 1,070 tons standard, 1,170 tons surfaced and 1,350 tons dived

Dimensions: length 64·0 m (210·0 ft); beam 7·2 m (23·6 ft); draught 5·0 m (16·4 ft)

Gun armament: none

Missile armament: none

Torpedo armament: six 533-mm (21-in) tubes (all bow) for Swedish or Type 53 dual-role torpedoes

Anti-submarine armament: torpedoes (see above))

Mines: can be carried in place of torpedoes

Electronics: one 'Snoop' series surface-search and navigation radar, Soviet active sonar system, one Krupp-Atlas PRS 3 passive ranging sonar, one Swedish torpedo fire-control system, and various communication and navigation systems

Propulsion: diesel-electric arrangement, with two Sulzer diesels and two electric motors delivering 1800 kW (2,415 hp) to one shaft

Performance: maximum speed 16 kt surfaced and 10 kt dived; range 11,175 km (6,945 miles) at 10 kt surfaced

Complement: 55

Class

1. Yugoslavia

Name	No.	Builder	Laid down	Com- missioned
Heroj	821	Uljanik SY	1964	1968
Junak	822	S & DE Factory	1965	1969
Uskok	823	Uljanik SY	1966	1970

Note: These Yugoslav boats are an interesting combination of Soviet-bloc and Western equipment, and are well suited to Adriatic operations.)

'Kilo' class SS

(USSR)

Type: patrol (attack) submarine

Displacement: 2,400 tons surfaced and 3,000 tons dived

Dimensions: length 73·0 m (239·5 ft); beam 10·0 m (32·8 ft); draught 6·5 m (21·3 ft)

Gun armament: none

Missile armament: none

Torpedo armament: eight 533-mm (21-in) tubes (all bow) for 18 Type 53 dual-role torpedoes

Anti-submarine armament: torpedoes (see above)

Mines: up to 36 AMD-1000 mines in place of torpedoes

Electronics: one 'Snoop Tray' surface-search and navigation radar, one low-frequency active/passive bow sonar, one medium-frequency torpedo fire-control sonar, one action information system, one 'Squid Head' ESM system with warning element, and various communication and navigation systems

Propulsion: diesel-electric arrangement, with two diesel generators supplying current to one electric motor delivering 3000 kW (4,025 hp) to one shaft

Performance: maximum speed 11 kt surfaced and 18 kt dived; diving depth 450 m (1,475 ft) operational and 650 m (2,135 ft) maximum

Complement: 45

Class

1. Algeria

2 boats

(These were delivered in October 1987 and January 1988 to allow the Algerian navy to begin the creation of an effective submarine force after the Algerian navy had gained initial experience on a pair of 'Romeo' class boats. The boats are identical with their Soviet counterparts.)

2. India

Name	No.	Builder	Commissioned
Sindhughosh	S55	Sudomekh, Leningrad	Apr 1986
Sindhudhvaj	S56	Sudomekh, Leningrad	Jun 1987
Sindhuraj	S57	Sudomekh, Leningrad	Oct 1987
Sindhuvir	S58	Sudomekh, Leningrad	Jul 1988
Sindhuratna	S59	Sudomekh, Leningrad	Feb 1989
Sindhukesari	S60	Sudomekh, Leningrad	Mar 1989

(These Indian boats are similar in all essential respects to their Soviet counterparts, but have a crew of 12 + 41.)

3. Poland

Name	No.	Builder	Commissioned
Orzel	291	Sudomekh, Leningrad	Jun 1986
	292	Sudomekh, Leningrad	
	293	Sudomekh, Leningrad	
	294	Sudomekh, Leningrad	

(These Polish boats are identical to the Soviet units, and the delivery of the later units has been delayed because of the USSR's transfer of two boats to Algeria.)

4. Romania

1 boat plus ? more planned

(This first unit was transferred in 1986.)

5. USSR

12 boats plus 2 more building and ? more planned

(Building at three yards since the delivery of the first boat from Komsomolsk in 1979, these capable patrol boats are being produced in Leningrad for the important export market as well as at Gorky and Komsomolsk for the Soviet navy. There are persistent reports that the type carries a lightweight surface-to-air missile system in the after part of the sail, but this fact remains unconfirmed.)

'Ming' or 'Type 035' class SS

(China)
Type: patrol (attack) submarine
Displacement: 1,585 tons surfaced and 2,115 tons dived
Dimensions: length 76·0 m (251·9 ft); beam 7·6 m (24·9 ft); draught 5·1 m (16·7 ft)
Gun armament: none
Missile armament: none
Torpedo armament: eight 533-mm (21-in) tubes (six bow and two stern) for 14 Type 53 dual-role torpedoes
Anti-submarine armament: torpedoes (see above)
Mines: up to 28 in place of torpedoes
Electronics: one 'Snoop Plate' or 'Snoop Tray' surface-search and navigation radar, active and passive sonars, one torpedo fire-control system, and various communication and navigation systems
Propulsion: diesel-electric arrangement, with two diesels delivering 1850 kW (2,480 hp) and two electric motors delivering unrevealed power to two shafts
Performance: maximum speed 15 kt surfaced, 10 kt snorting and 18 kt dived; diving depth 250 m (820 ft) operational; range 15,750 km (9,785 miles) at 10 kt surfaced, 14,285 km (9,210 miles) at 8 kt snorting and 610 km (380 milers) at 4 kt dived
Complement: 8 + 48

Class
1. China
3 boats

Note: These boats were built from 1971, and are believed to be of a design developed from that of the Soviet 'Romeo' class built in China as the 'Type 033' class. It is probable that the capabilities of the design fell far short of those required, explaining why construction of only three units has been completed.

'Näcken' or 'A14' class SS

(Sweden)
Type: patrol (attack) submarine
Displacement: 1,015 tons surfaced and 1,085 tons dived
Dimensions: length 49·5 m (162·4 ft) or (*Näcken*) 55·5 m (182·1 ft); beam 5·6 m (18·4 ft); draught 5·6 m (18·4 ft)
Gun armament: none
Missile armament: none
Torpedo armament: six 533-mm (21-in) tubes (all bow) for eight Tp 613 wire-guided dual-role torpedoeŝ
Anti-submarine armament: 533-mm (21-in) torpedoes (see above), and two 400-mm (15·75-in) tubes (both bow) for four Tp 423 (to be replaced by Tp 431) wire-guided torpedoes
Mines: up to 20 in place of 533-mm (21-in) torpedoes
Electronics: one Subfar 100 surface-search and navigation radar, one Krupp-Atlas CSU 83 active/passive search and attack sonar, one ESM system with Argo warning element, one AI-FCS torpedo fire-control system, and various communication and navigation systems
Propulsion: diesel-electric arrangement, with one MTU 16V 652 diesel delivering 1575 kW (2,110 hp) to one Jeumont Schneider generator supplying current to one electric motor delivering 1350 kW (1,810 hp) to one shaft
Performance: maximum speed 20 kt surfaced and 25 kt dived; diving depth 300 m (985 ft) operational
Complement: 5 + 14

Class
1. Sweden

Name	No.	Builder	Laid down	Com-missioned
Näcken	Näk	Kockums	Nov 1972	Apr 1980
Najad	Nad	Kockums	Sep 1973	Jun 1981
Neptun	Nep	Kockums	Mar 1974	Dec 1980

Note: These are very capable coastal boats optimized for the defence of the Swedish coastline from naval and amphibious assault. *Näcken* has been converted to evaluate a non-nuclear closed cycle propulsion system (a Tilma Sterling diesel system) to obviate the need for surfacing: this increases length by 6·0 m (19·7 ft).

'Narhvalen' class SS

(Denmark)
Type: patrol (attack) submarine
Displacement: 420 tons surfaced and 450 tons dived
Dimensions: length 44·3 m (145·3 ft); beam 4·6 m (15·0 ft); draught 4·2 m (13·8 ft)
Gun armament: none
Missile armament: none
Torpedo armament: eight 533-mm (21-in) tubes (all bow) for eight Tp 41 anti-submarine and Tp 61 wire-guided dual-role torpedoes
Anti-submarine armament: torpedoes (see above)
Mines: up to 16 in place of torpedoes
Electronics: one Subfar 100 surface-search and navigation radar, one Krupp-Atlas CSU 3-2 active/passive search and attack sonar, one Krupp-Atlas& PRS 3-4 passive ranging sonar, one torpedo fire-control system, and various communication and navigation systems
Propulsion: diesel-electric arrangement, with two MTU 820 Db diesels delivering 900 kW (1,205 hp) and one electric motor delivering 900 kW (1,205 hp) to one shaft
Performance: maximum speed 12 kt surfaced and 17 kt dived
Complement: 4 + 17

Class
1. Denmark

Name	No.	Builder	Laid down	Com-missioned
Narhvalen	S320	Royal Dockyard	Feb 1965	Feb 1970
Nordkaperen	S321	Royal Dockyard	Mar 1966	Dec 1970

Note: These boats are a development of the West German 'Type 205' class with modifications suiting them to Denmark's particular coastal requirements.

This cutaway view of a 'Nacken' class submarine reveals details of the notably compact accommodation, command, machinery and propulsion spaces, but fails to reveal details of the weapon space in the bow, where there are six large and two small tubes for eight large dual-role and four small anti-submarines torpedoes, all of the modern wire-guided type.

'Oberon' and 'Porpoise' class SSs

(UK)

Type: patrol (attack) submarine

Displacement: 1,610 tons standard, 2,030 tons surfaced and 2,410 tons dived

Dimensions: length 295·2 ft (90·0 m); beam 26·5 ft (8·1 m); draught 18·0 ft (5·5 m)

Gun armament: none

Missile armament: none

Torpedo armament: six 21-in (533-mm) tubes (all bow) for 20 Mk 24 Tigerfish wire-guided dual-role torpedoes

Anti-submarine armament: torpedoes (see above)

Mines: up to 50 Mk 5 Stonefish and Mk 6 Sea Urchin mines in place of torpedoes

Electronics: one Type 1006 surface-search and navigation radar, one Type 2051 Triton active/passive search and attack hull sonar or (unmodified boats) Type 187 active/passive search and attack hull sonar, one Type 2007 long-range passive flank sonar, one Type 186 sonar, one Type 2024 passive search clip-on towed-array sonar, one DCH action information and fire-control system, one Manta UAL or UA4 ESM system with warning element, and various communication and navigation systems

Propulsion: diesel-electric arrangement, with two Admiralty Standard Range 116VMS diesels delivering 3,680 hp (2745 kW) and two electric motors delivering 6,000 hp (4475 kW) to two shafts''

Performance: maximum speed 12 kt surfaced and 17 kt dived; diving depth 650 ft (200 m) operational and 1,115 ft (340 m) maximum; range 10,350 miles (16,655 km) at 12 kt surfaced

Complement: 7 + 62

Class

1. Australia ('RAN Oberon' class)

Name	No.	Builder	Laid down	Com-missioned
Oxley	S57	Scotts SB	Jul 1964	Apr 1967
Otway	S59	Scotts SB	Jun 1965	Apr 1968
Onslow	S60	Scotts SB	Dec 1967	Dec 1969
Orion	S61	Scotts SB	Oct 1972	Jun 1977
Otama	S62	Scotts SB	May 1973	Apr 1978
Ovens	S70	Scotts SB	Jun 1966	Apr 1969

(These Australian boats have been upgraded with Sperry Micropuffs passive ranging sonar, Krupp-Atlas CSU 3-41 attack sonar, Singer Librascope SFCS-RAN-Mk 1 fire-control system, Mk 48 wire-guided torpedoes, and UGM-84 Sub-Harpoon underwater-launched anti-ship missiles. A later retrofit may add the Kariwara towed-array sonar.)

2. Brazil ('Humaita' class)

Name	No.	Builder	Laid down	Com-missioned
Humaita	S20	Vickers	Nov 1970	Jun 1973
Tonelero	S21	Vickers	Nov 1971	Dec 1977
Riachuelo	S22	Vickers	May 1973	Mar 1977

(The Brazilian boats are similar to the unmodified British submarines except that they have the Vickers TIOS-B action information and fire-control system, and are being updated with the Mk 24 Mod 1 Tigerfish heavyweight torpedo.)

The 'Oberon' class boats are obsolescent, but were built so well that there is a demand for secondhand boats as they are phased from British service.

3. Canada

Name	No.	Builder	Laid down	Com-missioned
Ojibwa	72	Chatham DY	Sep 1962	Sep 1965
Onondaga	73	Chatham DY	Jun 1964	Jun 1967
Okanagan	74	Chatham DY	Mar 1965	Jun 1968

(The Canadian boats are similar to the British boats, but have better air-conditioning and a high level of Canadian equipment; the Submarine Operational Update Project has added Sperry BQG-501 Micropuffs passive ranging sonar, Singer Librascope fire-control and provision for at least four UGM-84A Sub-Harpoon submarine-launched anti-ship missiles; the main torpedo armament comprises Mk 37C anti-submarine weapons, being replaced in the SOUP modernization by the Mk 48 Mod 4 wire-guided heavyweight torpedo. Canada has also bought the ex-British *Olympus* [S12 laid down by Vickers in March 1960 and commissioned in July 1962] as an alongside-training submarine, freeing her three boats for operational tasks.)

4. Chile

Name	No.	Builder	Laid down	Com-missioned
O'Brien	22	Scott-Lithgow	Jan 1971	Apr 1976
Hyatt	23	Scott-Lithgow	Jan 1972	Sep 1976

(The Chilean boats are similar to the original British standard with the Type 187 main sonar, but carry the West German SUT wire-guided heavyweight torpedo.)

5. Egypt

Name	No.	Builder	Laid down	Com-missioned
ex-Oberon		Chatham DY	Nov 1957	Feb 1961
ex-Walrus		Scotts SB	Feb 1958	Feb 1961

(These two ex-British boats, the first of the 'Oberon' class and the second of the 'Porpoise' class, were to have been sold to Malaysia, but problems with the after-sales package have led to their purchase by Egypt in part replacement for that country's force of elderly 'Romeo' and 'Whiskey' class submarines. As purchased, the boats lack a combat control system, and after purchase in 1989 are to be refitted in a two-year programme to full British standard with the Triton sonar and Ferranti DCH tactical data-handling system; the weapons fit may be American, possibly including UGM-84 Sub-Harpoon tube-launched missiles and Mk 48 heavyweight wire-guided torpedoes, the latter for use possibly with a clip-on towed-array sonar of US origin. It is expected that the total Egyptian purchase of ex-British boats will be eight units, all to be refitted before delivery in a programme that will ensure a hull life of another 15 to 20 years.)

6. UK ('Oberon' class)

Name	No.	Builder	Laid down	Com-missioned
Odin	S10	Cammell Laird	Apr 1959	May 1962
Osiris	S13	Vickers	Jan 1962	Jan 1964
Onslaught	S14	Chatham DY	Apr 1959	Aug 1962
Otter	S15	Scotts SB	Jan 1960	Aug 1962
Oracle	S16	Cammell Laird	Apr 1960	Feb 1963
Ocelot	S17	Chatham DY	Nov 1960	Jan 1964
Otus	S18	Scotts SB	May 1961	Oct 1963
Opossum	S19	Cammell Laird	Dec 1961	Jun 1964
Opportune	S20	Scotts SB	Oct 1962	Dec 1964
Onyx	S21	Cammell Laird	Nov 1964	Nov 1967

(This important patrol submarine class is being reduced in number rapidly in expectation of the arrival of the new 'Upholder' class, and the closely similar 'Porpoise' class boats have already been deleted.)

'Romeo' class SS

(USSR)

Type: patrol (attack) submarine
Displacement: 1,400 tons surfaced and 1,700 tons dived
Dimensions: length 76·8 m (251·9 ft); beam 7·3 m (23·9 ft); draught 5·5 m (18·0 ft)
Gun armament: none
Missile armament: none
Torpedo armament: eight 533-mm (21-in) tubes (six bow and two stern) for 14 Type 53 dual-role torpedoes
Anti-submarine armament: torpedoes (see above)
Mines: up to 28 AMD-1000 mines in place of torpedoes
Electronics: one 'Snoop Plate' surface-search and navigation radar, one 'Herkules' high-frequency active/passive hull sonar, one 'Feniks' bow sonar, one torpedo fire-control system, one 'Stop Light' ESM system with warning element, and various communication and navigation systems
Propulsion: diesel-electric arrangement, with two Type 37D diesels delivering 3000 kW (4,025 hp) and two electric motors delivering 2000 kW (2,680 hp) to two shafts
Performance: maximum speed 17 kt surfaced and 14 kt dived; diving depth 300 m (985 ft) operational and 500 m (1,640 ft) maximum; range 29,650 km (18,425 miles) at 10 kt surfaced; endurance 45 days
Complement: 54

Class

1. Algeria
2 boats
(These boats were transferred in January 1982 and February 1983 so that Algeria could start the development of a submarine arm, and the original five-year loan has been extended.)

2. Bulgaria

Name	No.
Pobeda	81
Slava	82
	83
	84

(The first two boats were transferred in 1972 and 1973, and are the unnamed boats now used for alongside training. The two operational boats are the named units transferred in 1985 and 1986.)

3. China
84 boats
(These Chinese boats are ex-Soviet units and Chinese-built craft constructed at Jiangnan yard in Shanghai between 1962 and 1984 with the Chinese designations **'Type 031'**, **'Type 032'** and **'Type 033'** (**ES3B** to **ES3E**). It is thought that up to 50 of the boats are currently inoperative for a variety of reasons.)

4. Egypt

Name	No.
	831
	834
	837
	840
	843
	846
	849*
	852*
	855*
	858*

* Chinese-built boats
(These obsolete submarines are to be replaced by ex-British 'Oberon' class boats in the 1990s, but are undergoing a limited upgrade: two of the boats are being reserved for cannibalization, the six ex-Soviet boats have received a modest update and refit, and the four ex-Chinese boats are to be upgraded more substantially by Tacoma Boatbuilding of the USA with improved electronic and sensor systems as well as provision for the UGM-84 Sub-Harpoon tube-launched missile and Mk 37 torpedo.)

5. North Korea
7 ex-Chinese boats
10 North Korean boats with ? more building and ? more planned
(China transferred two boats in 1973, another two in 1974 and three in 1975. North Korean production delivered its first boat in 1975, and production appears to be continuing at the rate of one boat every two years.)

6. Syria
3 ex-Soviet boats
(The first two boats were transferred in July 1986, the third following in December of the same year. It is likely that after Syria has laid the foundations for a submarine service with these boats, they will be replaced with more modern equipment, probably 'Kilo' class submarines.)

7. USSR
4 boats
(The 'Romeo' class design was a development of the 'Whiskey' class design. All Soviet boats were built at Gorky between 1957 and 1962, only 20 out of a planned 550 units being completed because of the advent of nuclear-powered submarines. It is likely that these last four units are about to be scrapped.)

'Sauro' or 'Tipo 1081' class SS

(Italy)

Type: patrol (attack) submarine
Displacement: 1,455 tons surfaced and 1,630 tons dived
Dimensions: length 63·9 m (210·0 ft); beam 6·8 m (22·5 ft); draught 5·7 m (18·9 ft)
Gun armament: none
Missile armament: none
Torpedo armament: six 533-mm (21-in) tubes (all bow) for 12 A 184 wire-guided dual-role torpedoes
Anti-submarine armament: torpedoes (see above)
Mines: up to 24 in place of torpedoes
Electronics: one BPS 704 surface-search and navigation radar, one IPD 70/S active/passive search and attack bow/flank sonar, one MD100 Mk 1 passive ranging sonar, one SACTIS action data system, one CCRG torpedo fire-control system, one ESM system with BLD 727 warning element, and various communication and navigation systems
Propulsion: diesel-electric arrangement, with three 905-kW (1,215-hp) Fiat/GMT A 210·16 NM diesel generators supplying current to one electric motor delivering 2400 kW (3,220 hp) to one shaft
Performance: maximum speed 11 kt surfaced, 12 kt snorting and 20 kt dived; diving depth 250 m (820 ft) operational and 410 m (1,345 ft) maximum; range 13,000 km (6,080 miles) at surfaced cruising speed, 23,150 km (14,385 miles) at 4 kt snorting, and 750 km (465 miles) at 4 kt or 38 km (24 miles) at 20 kt dived; endurance 45 days
Complement: 7 + 38 plus provision for 4 trainees

Fecia di Cossato is one of the four 'Sauro Batch 1/2' class boats that is to be upgraded to the more capable 'Sauro Batch 3/4' class standard.

Class

1. Italy ('Tipo 1081' or 'Sauro Batch 1/2' class)

Name	No.	Builder	Laid down	Commissioned
Nazario Sauro	S518	Italcantieri	Jun 1974	Feb 1980
Fecia di Cossato	S519	Italcantieri	Nov 1975	Nov 1979
Leonardo da Vinci	S520	Italcantieri	Jun 1978	Oct 1981
Guglielmo Marconi	S521	Italcantieri	Oct 1979	Sep 1982

Note: These are useful boats for Mediterranean operations, and are to be upgraded in due course to 'Sauro Batch 3/4' class standard.

'Sauro Batch 3/4' or 'Sauro (Improved)' class SS

(Italy)
Type: patrol (attack) submarine
Displacement: 1,475 tons surfaced and 1,660 tons dived
Dimensions: length 64·4 m (211·2 ft); beam 6·8 m (22·5 ft); draught 5·6 m (18·9 ft)
Gun armament: none
Missile armament: none
Torpedo armament: six 533-mm (21-in) tubes (all bow) for 12 A 184 wire-guided dual-role torpedoes
Anti-submarine armament: torpedoes (see above)
Mines: up to 24 in place of torpedoes
Electronics: one BPS 704 surface-search and navigation radar, one IPD 70/S active/passive search and attack bow/flank sonar, one MD100/S passive ranging sonar, one BSN 716 action data system, one CCRG Mk 2 torpedo fire-control system, one ESM system with BLD 727 warning element, and various communication and navigation systems
Propulsion: diesel-electric arrangement, with three 905-kW (1,215-hp) Fiat/GMT A 210.16 NM diesel generators supplying current to one electric motor delivering 3200 kW (4,290 hp) to one shaft

Performance: maximum speed 11 kt surfaced, 12 kt snorting, and 20 kt dived; diving depth 300 m (985 ft) operational and 600 m (1,970 ft) maximum; range 20,500 km (12,740 miles) at 11 kt surfaced and 460 km (285 miles) at 4 kt dived; endurance 45 days
Complement: 7 + 38

Class
1. Italy

Name	No.	Builder	Laid down	Com-missioned
Salvatore Pelosi	S522	Fincantieri	Aug 1985	Jul 1988
Giuliano Prini	S523	Fincantieri	Jul 1986	Apr 1989
	S524	Fincantieri	1989	1993
	S525	Fincantieri	1989	1993

Note: Based on the original 'Sauro' class but built from pre-assembled sections [hence 'Started' rather than 'Laid down' in the section above], this closely related subtype has a hull of stronger steel for increased diving depths as well as enhanced weapons (later versions of the A 184 wire-guided torpedo and possibly UGM-84 Sub-Harpoon underwater-launched anti-ship missiles) and more advanced sensors/electronics. The two boats of the 'Sauro Batch 4' subclass will each be 66·4 m (217·4 ft) long for a dived displacement of 1,760 tons, and will have the SEPA Mk 3 fire-control system.

'Sava' class SS

(Yugoslavia)
Type: patrol (attack) submarine
Displacement: 500 tons standard, 770 tons surfaced and 965 tons dived
Dimensions: length 65·8 m (215·8 ft); beam 7·0 m (22·9 ft); draught 5·5 m (18·0 ft)
Gun armament: none
Missile armament: none
Torpedo armament: six 533-mm (21-in) tubes (all bow) for 16 Type 53 dual-role torpedoes
Anti-submarine armament: torpedoes (see above)
Mines: up to 20 in place of torpedoes
Electronics: one 'Snoop' series surface-search and navigation radar, Soviet active sonar, Krupp-Atlas PRS 3 passive ranging sonar, one torpedo fire-control system, one ESM system with warning element, and various communication and navigation systems

Propulsion: diesel-electric arrangement, with two diesels and two electric motors delivering 1800 kW (2,415 hp) to one shaft
Performance: maximum speed 16 kt dived; diving depth 300 m (985 ft) operational; endurance 28 days
Complement: 35

Class
1. Yugoslavia

Name	No.	Builder	Laid down	Com-missioned
Sava	831	S & DE Factory	1975	1978
Drava	832	S & DE Factory	1978	1981

Note: These small submarines are designed for use in Yugoslavia's tortuous coastal waters, with emphasis on agility rather than outright performance and deep diving.

'Sjöormen' or 'A12' class SS

(Sweden)
Type: patrol (attack) submarine
Displacement: 1,125 tons surfaced and 1,215 tons dived
Dimensions: length 51·0 m (167·3 ft); beam 6·1 m (20·0 ft); draught 5·8 m (19·0 ft)
Gun armament: none
Missile armament: none
Torpedo armament: four 533-mm (21-in) tubes (all bow) for 10 Tp 61 wire-guided dual-role torpedoes
Anti-submarine armament: two 400-mm (15·75-in) tubes (both bow) for four Tp 42 (to be replaced by Tp 431) wire-guided torpedoes, and 533-mm (21-in) torpedoes (see above)
Mines: up to 16 in place of 533-mm (21-in) torpedoes
Electronics: one Terma surface-search and navigation radar, one Hydra active/passive search and attack hull sonar, one AI-FCS action information and torpedo fire-control system, one ESM system with warning element, and various communication and navigation systems
Propulsion: diesel-electric arrangement, with four Hedemora/SEMT-Pielstick V12 A2 diesels delivering 1660 kW (2,225 hp) and one ASEA electric motor delivering 1640 kW (2,200 hp) to one shaft
Performance: maximum speed 15 kt surfaced and 20 kt dived; diving depth 150 m (485 ft) operational and 250 m (820 ft) maximum; endurance 21 days
Complement: 7 + 16
Note: This is an albacore-hulled design with twin decks. Two of the boats are being modernized with the sensor/electronic fit of the 'Näcken' class for continued operational capability into the 1990s, and all of the class are being fitted with Plessey sonar in place of the original Krupp-Atlas CSU 3 sonar.

Like other Swedish submarines, the *Sjoormen* is notably compact for agility in coastal waters, but sacrifices nothing in electronics and weapons.

Class
1. Sweden

Name	No.	Builder	Laid down	Com-missioned
Sjöormen	Sör	Kockums	1965	Jul 1968
Sjölejonet	Sle	Kockums	1966	Dec 1968
Sjöhunden	Shu	Kockums	1966	Jun 1969
Sjöbjörnen	Sbj	Karlskrona	1967	Feb 1969
Sjöhästen	Shä	Karlskrona	1966	Sep 1969

'Tango' class SS

(USSR)

Type: patrol (attack) submarine
Displacement: 3,000 tons surfaced and 3,800 tons dived
Dimensions: length 92·0 m (301·8 ft); beam 9·5 m (31·2 ft); draught 7·2 m (23·6 ft)
Gun armament: none
Missile armament: none
Torpedo armament: 10 533-mm (21-in) tubes (six bow and four stern) for 24 Type 53 dual-role torpedoes
Anti-submarine armament: torpedoes (see above) and two SS-N-15 'Starfish' tube-launched missiles in place of torpedoes
Mines: up to 48 AMD-1000 mines in place of torpedoes
Electronics: one 'Snoop Tray' surface-search and navigation radar, one low-frequency active/passive bow sonar, one medium-frequency underwater weapons fire-control sonar, one action information system, one 'Stop Light' ESM system with warning element, and extensive communication and navigation systems
Propulsion: diesel-electric arrangement, with three 1500-kW (2,010-hp) diesel generators and three electric motors delivering 3900 kW (5,230 hp) to three shafts
Performance: maximum speed 20 kt surfaced and 16 kt dived; diving depth 300 m (985 ft) operational and 500 m (1,640 ft) maximum
Complement: 62

Class
1. USSR
18 boats
Note: These 18 boats were built from about 1971 at Gorky, and the construction programme is now complete. By comparison with other Soviet patrol submarine classes, the 'Tango' class is notable for its large internal volume and comparatively long range.

The existence of the small but effective 'Tango' class is good evidence of the Soviets' continued belief in the conventionally powered patrol boat.

'Tipo S 90' class SS

(Italy)

Type: patrol (attack) submarine
Displacement: 2,230 tons surfaced and 2,475 tons dived
Dimensions: length 74·6 m (244·8 ft); beam 7·4 m (24·3 ft); draught 6·3 m (20·1 ft)
Gun armament: none
Missile armament: UGM-84 Sub-Harpoon anti-ship missiles in place of torpedoes
Torpedo armament: six 533-mm (21-in) tubes (all bow) for 24 free-running and wire-guided dual-role torpedoes
Anti-submarine armament: torpedoes (see above)
Mines: up to 48 in place of torpedoes
Electronics: one surface-search and navigation radar, one active/passive search and attack bow/flank sonar, one passive ranging sonar, one action information system, one torpedo fire-control system, one ESM system with warning element, and various communication and navigation systems
Propulsion: diesel-electric arrangement, with three Fincantieri SMA 210·16 diesel generators supplying current to one electric motor delivering 4500 kW (6,035 hp) to one shaft
Performance: maximum speed 11 kt surfaced and 20 kt dived; diving depth 400 m (1,315 ft) operational; range 1125 km (700 miles) at 4 kt dived
Complement: 8 + 42

Class
| 1. Italy | | | | Com- |
Name	No.	Builder	Started	missioned
		Fincantieri, Monfalcone		

Note: The details of this class, which should total four boats to replace the obsolescent 'Toti' class, are still uncertain. The design may be revised to accommodate oxygen storage in toroidal hull sections to extend underwater endurance, and the first of the class should enter service in the mid-1990s.

'Toti' or 'Tipo 1075' class SS

(Italy)

Type: patrol (attack) submarine
Displacement: 460 tons standard, 525 tons surfaced and 585 tons dived
Dimensions: length 46·2 m (151·5 ft); beam 4·7 m (15·4 ft); draught 4·0 m (13·1 ft)
Gun armament: none
Missile armament: none
Torpedo armament: four 533-mm (21-in) tubes (all bow) for six A 184 wire-guided dual-role torpedoes
Anti-submarine armament: torpedoes (see above)
Mines: up to 12 in place of torpedoes
Electronics: one BPS 704 surface-search and navigation radar, one IPD 64 active/passive search and attack sonar, one MD 64 passive search sonar, one Velox M5 passive ranging sonar, one IPD 64 torpedo fire-control system, one ESM system with warning element, and various communication and navigation systems
Propulsion: diesel-electric arrangement, with two Fiat/Mercedes-Benz 820 N/I diesels delivering unrevealed power and one electric motor delivering 1640 kW (2,200 hp) to one shaft
Performance: maximum speed 14 kt surfaced and 15 kt dived; diving depth 180 m (590 ft) operational and 300 m (985 ft) maximum; range 5550 km (3,450 miles) at 5 kt surfaced
Complement: 4 + 22

Class
| 1. Italy | | | | Com- |
Name	No.	Builder	Laid down	missioned
Attilio Bagnolino	S505	Italcantieri	Apr 1965	Jun 1968
Enrico Toti	S506	Italcantieri	Apr 1965	Jan 1968
Enrico Dandolo	S513	Italcantieri	Mar 1967	Sep 1968
Lazzaro Mocenigo	S514	Italcantieri	Jun 1967	Jan 1969

Note: These were the first submarines built in Italy after World War II, and are small boats suitable only for coastal operations.

S514 is the *Lazzaro Mocenigo*, fourth and last of the Italian navy's 'Toti' class of small submarines for coastal operations in the Mediterranean.

'TR 1700' class SS

(West Germany/Argentina)
Type: patrol (attack) submarine
Displacement: 2,115 tons surfaced and 2,265 tons dived
Dimensions: length 66·0 m (216·5 ft); beam 7·3 m (23·9 ft); draught 6·5 m (21·3 ft)
Gun armament: none
Missile armament: none
Torpedo armament: six 533-mm (21-in) tubes (all bow) for 22 SST4 wire-guided dual-role torpedoes
Anti-submarine armament: torpedoes (see above)
Mines: up to 44 in place of torpedoes
Electronics: one surface-search and navigation radar, one Krupp-Atlas CSU 3 active/passive search and attack sonar, one DUUX 2A passive ranging sonar, one Sinbads torpedo fire-control system, one ESM system with warning element, and various communication and navigation systems
Propulsion: diesel-electric arrangement, with four MTU 16V 652 MB80 diesels delivering 5000 kW (6,710 kW) and one electric motor delivering 6000 kW (8,050 hp) to one shaft

Performance: maximum speed 13 kt surfaced, 15 kt snorting and 25 kt dived; diving depth 300 m (985 ft) operational and 500 m (1,640 ft) maximum; range 27,800 km (17,275 miles) at 5 kt surfaced, and 200 km (125 miles) at 15 kt or 37 km (23 miles) at 25 kt dived; endurance 70 days
Complement: 26 plus 6 spare berths

Class

1. Argentina				Com-
Name	No.	Builder	Laid down	missioned
Santa Cruz	S41	Thyssen	Dec 1980	Oct 1984
San Juan	S42	Thyssen	Mar 1982	Nov 1985
Santiago del Estero	S43	Astilleros	Oct 1983	
Santa Fe	S44	Astilleros	Aug 1985	
	S45	Astilleros		
	S46	Astilleros		

Note: These are advanced patrol submarines featuring a high level of automation to reduce crew requirements without any sacrifice of armament and electronic capability. Argentina's poor economic situation has led to a slowing of the local production programme for the last four boats, of which the last two may have to be cancelled.

'Type 205' class SS

(West Germany)
Type: patrol (attack) submarine
Displacement: 420 tons surfaced and 450 tons dived
Dimensions: length 43·9 m (144·0 ft); beam 4·6 m (15·1 ft); draught 4·3 m (14·1 ft)
Gun armament: none
Missile armament: none
Torpedo armament: eight 533-mm (21-in) tubes (all bow) for eight Seal wire-guided dual-role torpedoes
Anti-submarine armament: torpedoes (see above)
Mines: up to 16 in place of torpedoes
Electronics: one Calypso II surface-search and navigation radar, one Krupp-Atlas SRS M1H active/passive search and attack sonar, one WM-7/8 torpedo fire-control system, one ESM system with warning element, and various communication and navigation systems
Propulsion: diesel-electric arrangement, with two MTU 12V 493Az diesels delivering 1700 kW (2,280 hp) and one Siemens electric motor delivering 1125 kW (1,510 hp) to one shaft
Performance: maximum speed 10 kt surfaced and 17 kt dived; diving depth

150 m (490 ft) operational
Complement: 4 + 18

Class

1. West Germany				Com-
Name	No.	Builder	Laid down	missioned
U 1	S180	Howaldtswerke	Feb 1965	Jun 1967
U 2	S181	Howaldtswerke	Sep 1964	Oct 1966
U 9	S188	Howaldtswerke	Dec 1964	Apr 1967
U 10	S189	Howaldtswerke	Jul 1965	Nov 1967
U 11	S190	Howaldtswerke	Apr 1966	Jun 1968
U 12	S191	Howaldtswerke	Sep 1966	Jan 1969

Note: These were the first submarines built in West Germany after World War II, and are coastal boats now considered obsolescent at best. They are confined to operations in the North Sea and the Baltic, and will be replaced from 1995 by the new 'Type 212' class boats. *U 1* has been lengthened by 3·8 m (12·5 ft) to permit the trial installation of an air-independent (fuel cell) propulsion system, and began trials in 1987. *U 11* and *U 12* have also been modified, in this instance for weapon trials and 'special tasks'.

West Germany's 'Type 205' class boats are useful only for coastal work.

'Type 206' class SS

(West Germany)
Type: patrol (attack) submarine
Displacement: 450 tons surfaced and 500 tons dived
Dimensions: length 48·6 m (159·4 ft); beam 4·6 m (15·1 ft); draught 4·5 m (14·8 ft)
Gun armament: none
Missile armament: none
Torpedo armament: eight 533-mm (21-in) tubes (all bow) for eight Seeschlange wire-guided dual-role torpedoes
Anti-submarine armament: torpedoes (see above)
Mines: up to 16 mines in place of torpedoes, plus another 24 in two external strap-on containers
Electronics: one Calypso II surface-search and navigation radar, one Krupp-Atlas 410 A4 active/passive search and attack hull sonar, one DUUX 2 passive ranging sonar, one WM-8/8 torpedo fire-control system, one ESM system with warning element, and various communications and navigation systems
Propulsion: diesel-electric arrangement, with two MTU 12V 493Az diesels delivering 1700 kW (2,280 hp) and one Siemens electric motor delivering 1125 kW (1,510 hp) to one shaft
Performance: maximum speed 10 kt surfaced and 17 kt dived; diving depth 150 m (490 ft) operational and 250 m (820 ft) maximum; range 8350 km (5,190 miles) at 5 kt surfaced
Complement: 4 + 18

Note: Twelve of these boats are being upgraded by 1992 to **'Type 206A' class** standard with the Krupp-Atlas SLW 83 combat information system (based on the CSU 83 [DBQS-21D] active sonar) and the Seal 3 wire-guided heavyweight dual-role torpedo version of the SST4. The class is confined to operations in the North Sea and the Baltic, and the six unmodernized boats will be replaced from 1995 by six of the new 'Type 212' class boats.

Seen during its trials, _U 13_ was the lead boat of the 'Type 206' class that provided the West German navy with a considerably improved capability against surface vessels from the mid-1970s.

Class
1. West Germany

Name	No.	Builder	Laid down	Com-missioned
_U 13_	S192	Howaldtswerke	Nov 1969	Apr 1973
_U 14_	S193	Rheinstahl	Sep 1970	Apr 1973
_U 15*_	S194	Howaldtswerke	May 1970	Apr 1974
_U 16*_	S195	Rheinstahl	Apr 1970	Nov 1973
_U 17*_	S196	Howaldtswerke	Oct 1970	Nov 1973
_U 18*_	S197	Rheinstahl	Jul 1971	Dec 1973
_U 19_	S198	Howaldtswerke	Jan 1971	Nov 1973
_U 20_	S199	Rheinstahl	Feb 1972	May 1974
_U 21_	S170	Howaldtswerke	Apr 1971	Aug 1974
_U 22*_	S171	Rheinstahl	May 1972	Jul 1974
_U 23*_	S172	Howaldtswerke	Aug 1972	May 1975
_U 24_	S173	Rheinstahl	Jul 1972	Oct 1974
_U 25*_	S174	Howaldtswerke	Oct 1971	Jun 1974
_U 26*_	S175	Rheinstahl	Nov 1972	Mar 1975
_U 27*_	S176	Howaldtswerke	Jan 1972	Oct 1974
_U 28*_	S177	Rheinstahl	Jan 1972	Dec 1974
_U 29*_	S178	Howaldtswerke	Feb 1972	Nov 1974
_U 30*_	S179	Rheinstahl	Apr 1973	Mar 1975

* 'Type 206A' class boats

'Type 207' or 'Kobben' class SS

(West Germany/Norway)
Type: patrol (attack) submarine
Displacement: 370 tons surfaced and 435 tons dived
Dimensions: length 45·4 m (149·0 ft); beam 4·6 m (15·1 ft); draught 4·3 m (14·1 ft)
Gun armament: none
Missile armament: none
Torpedo armament: eight 533-mm (21-in) tubes (all bow) for eight Tp 61 wire-guided anti-ship and NT 37C wire-guided anti-submarine torpedoes
Anti-submarine armament: torpedoes (see above)
Mines: up to 16 mines in place of torpedoes
Electronics: one Subfar 100 surface-search and navigation radar, one Krupp-Atlas active/passive search and attack sonar, one WM-8/10 (being replaced by MSI-70U or MSI 90U) action information and torpedo fire-control system, one ESM system with warning element, and various communication and navigation systems
Propulsion: diesel-electric arrangement, with two MTU 12V 493Az diesels delivering 900 kW (1,210 hp) and one Siemens electric motor delivering 1275 kW (1,710 hp) to one shaft
Performance: maximum speed 12 kt surfaced and 18 kt dived; diving depth 200 m (655 ft) operational; range 9250 km (5,750 miles) at 8 kt snorting
Complement: 5 + 13

Class
1. Denmark

Name	No.	Builder	Laid down	Com-missioned
Tumleren	S322	Rheinstahl	Mar 1965	Dec 1965
Saelen	S323	Rheinstahl	May 1965	Feb 1966
Springaren	S324	Rheinstahl	May 1963	Jan 1964

(These three ex-Norwegian boats are to enter Danish service in 1990 after a modernization programme that lengthens the hull to 47·0 m/154·2 ft and adds new communication, fire-control and navigation systems.)

The Norwegian _Kya_ is now one of three Danish 'Type 207' class boats.

2. Norway

Name	No.	Builder	Laid down	Com-missioned
Utsira	S301	Rheinstahl	Oct 1964	Jul 1965
Utstein	S302	Rheinstahl	Jan 1965	Sep 1965
Sklinna*	S314	Rheinstahl	Aug 1965	May 1966
Skolpen*	S306	Rheinstahl	Nov 1965	Aug 1966
Stord*	S308	Rheinstahl	Apr 1966	Feb 1967
Svenner	S309	Rheinstahl	Sep 1966	Jun 1967
Kaura*	S315	Rheinstahl	May 1964	Feb 1965
Kinn*	S316	Rheinstahl	Aug 1964	May 1965
Kobben	S318	Rheinstahl	Dec 1963	Aug 1964
Kunna	S319	Rheinstahl	Mar 1964	Oct 1964

*modernized boats

(These boats were built with Norwegian and US financing to a design developed from that of the West German 'Type 205' class. _Stadt_ was scrapped in 1986 after hitting the bottom. Of the surviving Norwegian boats six are to be updated to a standard comparable with that of the Danish boats, the other four being scrapped or handed over to the US Navy for trial purposes.)

'Type 209/0' or 'Type 1100' class SS

(West Germany/Greece)
Type: patrol (attack) submarine
Displacement: 990 tons standard, 1,100 tons surfaced and 1,210 tons dived
Dimensions: length 54·4 m (178·4 ft); beam 6·2 m (20·3 ft); draught 5·5 m (18·0 ft)
Gun armament: none
Missile armament: none
Torpedo armament: eight 533-mm (21-in) tubes (all bow) for 14 SST4 wire-guided dual-role torpedoes
Anti-submarine armament: torpedoes (see above)
Mines: up to 28 in place of torpedoes
Electronics: one Calypso II surface-search and navigation radar, one Krupp-Atlas CSU 3-2 active/passive search and attack hull sonar, one Krupp-Atlas PRS 3-4 passive ranging hull sonar, one Kanaris torpedo fire-control system, one ESM system with warning element, and various communications and navigation systems
Propulsion: diesel-electric arrangement, with four MTU 12V 493 TY60 diesels delivering 7040 kW (9,440 hp) and one Siemens electric motor delivering 3700 kW (4,960 hp) to one shaft

Performance: maximum speed 11 kt surfaced and 22 kt dived; diving depth 300 m (985 ft) operational and 500 m (1,640 ft) maximum; endurance 50 days
Complement: 6 + 25

Class

1. Greece ('Glavkos' class)

Name	No.	Builder	Laid down	Com-missioned
Glavkos	S110	Howaldtswerke	Sep 1968	Nov 1971
Nereus	S111	Howaldtswerke	Jan 1969	Feb 1972
Triton	S112	Howaldtswerke	Jun 1969	Nov 1972
Proteus	S113	Howaldtswerke	Oct 1969	Aug 1972

Note: A comparatively simple design with modest automation, this is a capable short-range patrol submarine. S110 is to be fitted for UGM-84 Sub-Harpoon tube-launched anti-ship missiles in place of some of its torpedoes, and all four boats are to have their electronic systems upgraded.

Overleaf: *Glavkos* is lead boat of the Greek navy's 'Type 1100' subclass of eight 'Type 209' conventionally powered attack submarines. The boats have very high-capacity batteries for long submerged endurance.

'Type 209/1' or 'Type 1200' class SS

(West Germany/Greece)
Type: patrol (attack) submarine
Displacement: 1,185 tons surfaced and 1,285 tons dived
Dimensions: length 55·9 m (183·4 ft); beam 6·3 m (20·5 ft); draught 5·5 m (17·9 ft)
Gun armament: none
Missile armament: none
Torpedo armament: eight 533-mm (21-in) tubes (all bow) for 14 SST4 wire-guided dual-role torpedoes
Anti-submarine armament: torpedoes (see above)
Mines: up to 28 in place of torpedoes
Electronics: one Calypso II surface-search and navigation radar, one Krupp-Atlas CSU 3-4 active/passive search and attack hull sonar, one DUUX 2 passive ranging hull sonar, one WM-series torpedo fire-control system, one ESM system with warning element, and various communication and navigation systems
Propulsion: diesel-electric arrangement, with four MTU 12V 493 TY60 diesels delivering 7040 kW (9,440 hp) and one Siemens electric motor delivering 3700 kW (4,960 hp) to one shaft
Performance: maximum speed 10 kt surfaced and 22 kt dived; diving depth 300 m (985 ft) operational and 500 m (1,640 ft) maximum; endurance 50 days
Complement: 6 + 25

Class

1. Argentina ('Salta' class)

Name	No.	Builder	Laid down	Com-missioned
Salta	S31	Howaldtswerke	Apr 1970	Mar 1974
San Luis	S32	Howaldtswerke	Oct 1970	May 1974

(These Argentine boats are similar in all vital respects to the Greek units.)

2. Colombia

Name	No.	Builder	Laid down	Com-missioned
Pijao	SS28	Howaldtswerke	Apr 1972	Apr 1975
Tayrona	SS29	Howaldtswerke	May 1972	Jul 1975

(These Colombian boats are similar to the Greek units, but have separate Krupp-Atlas CSU 3-2 active and PRS 3-4 passive sonars, the WM-8/24 combat system and SUT torpedoes.)

3. Greece ('Glavkos' class)

Name	No.	Builder	Laid down	Com-missioned
Posydon	S116	Howaldtswerke	Jan 1976	Mar 1979
Amphitrite	S117	Howaldtswerke	Apr 1976	Jul 1979
Okeanos	S118	Howaldtswerke	Oct 1976	Nov 1979
Pontos	S119	Howaldtswerke	Jan 1977	Apr 1980

(These are generally similar to the 'Glavkos' class boats, and the lead sub-marine is to be fitted for tube-launched UGM-84 Sub-Harpoon anti-ship missiles in place of some of its torpedo load.)

4. Peru ('Casma' class)

Name	No.	Builder	Laid down	Com-missioned
Casma	S31	Howaldtswerke	Jul 1977	Dec 1980
Antofagasta	S32	Howaldtswerke	Oct 1977	Feb 1981
Pisagua	S33	Howaldtswerke	Aug 1978	Jul 1983
Chipana	S34	Howaldtswerke	Nov 1978	Sep 1982
Islay	S45	Howaldtswerke	May 1971	Aug 1974
Arica	S46	Howaldtswerke	Nov 1971	Jan 1975

(Similar to the Greek boats, these Peruvian boats fall into two subclasses, S45 and S46 having the WM-8/24 combat system with separate CSU 3-2 active and PRS 3-4 passive sonars, and the four later boats having the Sinbads combat system and integrated CSU 3-4 active/passive sonar. The boats carry Mk 37C and SST4 torpedoes, though a recent purchase has been the Italian A 184 torpedo to be interfaced with the SEPA Mk 3 combat system, which can also handle the SST4 torpedo.)

5. South Korea

Name	No.	Builder	Laid down	Com-missioned
		Howaldtswerke	1988	
		Howaldtswerke		
		Howaldtswerke		
		Howaldtswerke		
		Howaldtswerke		
		Howaldtswerke		

(South Korea ordered its first three 'Type 1200' submarines in 1988 and the second three in 1989 as part of a programme probably intended to produce a total of at least nine boats, with an upper figure of 18 such submarines possible. It is as yet unknown how these boats will differ from those of other operators of the same basic type, but it is known that South Korea would like to produce the type at Daewoo's Okpo yard rather than import all the boats from West Germany.)

6. Turkey

Name	No.	Builder	Laid down	Com-missioned
Atilay	S347	Howaldtswerke	Dec 1972	Jul 1975
Saldiray	S348	Howaldtswerke	Jan 1973	Oct 1976
Batiray	S349	Howaldtswerke	Jun 1975	Jul 1978
Yildiray	S350	Golcuk NY	May 1976	Jul 1981
Doganay	S351	Golcuk NY	Mar 1980	Nov 1985
Dolunay	S352	Golcuk NY	Mar 1981	Aug 1989

(Turkey had planned to build 12 of this class, the last six to a slightly enlarged design, but has now decided to build its next six boats to a more advanced West German design, the 'Type 209/3'. The radar is the S 63B, and the combat system is either the WM-8/24 [S347 and S348] or Sinbads [other boats] interfaced with Krupp-Atlas CSU 3-4 active/passive search and attack sonar. The crew is 6 + 27.)

'Type 209/2' or 'Type 1300' class SS

(West Germany/Ecuador)

Type: patrol (attack) submarine

Displacement: 1,285 tons surfaced and 1,390 tons dived

Dimensions: length 59·5 m (195·1 ft); beam 6·3 m (20·5 ft); beam 5·4 m (17·9 ft)

Gun armament: none

Missile armament: none

Torpedo armament: eight 533-mm (21-in) tubes (all bow) for 16 SUT wire-guided dual-role torpedoes

Anti-submarine armament: torpedoes (see above)

Mines: up to 32 in place of torpedoes

Electronics: one Calypso surface-search and navigation radar, one Krupp-Atlas CSU 3-4 active/passive search and attack hull sonar, one DUUX 2 passive ranging hull sonar, one WM-8/24 torpedo fire-control system, one ESM system with warning element, and various communication and navigation systems

Propulsion: diesel-electric arrangement, with four MTU 12V 493 TY60 diesels delivering 7040 kW (9,440 hp) and one Siemens electric motor delivering 3700 kW (4,960 hp) to one shaft

Performance: maximum speed 11 kt surfaced, 11 kt snorting and 21·5 kt dived; diving depth 300 m (985 ft) operational and 500 m (1,640 ft) maximum; range 13,900 km (8,635 miles) at 10 kt surfaced

Complement: 5 + 28

Class

1. Ecuador

Name	No.	Builder	Laid down	Com-missioned
Shyri	S11	Howaldtswerke	Aug 1974	Nov 1977
Huancavilca	S12	Howaldtswerke	Jan 1975	Mar 1978

(These Ecuadorean boats are clearly very similar to the earlier 'Type 209' variants, differing only in details of electronics and armament. Key features of the design are remote-control machinery, very high-capacity batteries and a slow-turning propeller.)

2. Indonesia

Name	No.	Builder	Laid down	Com-missioned
Cakra	401	Howaldtswerke	Nov 1977	Mar 1981
Nanggala	402	Howaldtswerke	Mar 1978	Jul 1981

(The Indonesian boats have the Sinbads combat system with separate Krupp-Atlas CSU 3-2 active and PRS 3-4 passive sonars. A total of four or even six boats is planned if the financing can be arranged.)

3. Venezuela

Name	No.	Builder	Laid down	Com-missioned
Sabalo	S31	Howaldtswerke	May 1973	Aug 1976
Caribe	S32	Howaldtswerke	Aug 1973	Mar 1977

(The Venezuelan boats carry 14 SST4 heavy-weight and Mk 37 medium-weight wire-guided torpedoes, which are fired with the aid of the WM-8/24 combat system and associated Krupp-Atlas CSU 3-4 active/passive sonar.)

'Type 209/3' or 'Type 1400' class SS

(West Germany/Chile)
Type: patrol (attack) submarine
Displacement: 1,260 tons surfaced and 1,390 tons dived
Dimensions: length 59·5 m (195·1 ft); beam 6·2 m (20·3 ft); draught 5·5 m (18·0 ft)
Gun armament: none
Missile armament: none
Torpedo armament: eight 533-mm (21-in) tubes (all bow) for 14 SUT wire-guided dual-role torpedoes
Anti-submarine armament: torpedoes (see above)
Mines: up to 28 in place of torpedoes
Electronics: one Calypso II surface-search and navigation radar, one Krupp-Atlas CSU 3-4 active/passive search and attack hull sonar, one WM-8/24 underwater weapons fire-control system, one Porpoise ESM system with warning element, and various communication and navigation systems
Propulsion: diesel-electric arrangement, with four MTU 12V 493 A280 diesels delivering 7040 kW (9,440 hp) and one Siemens electric motor delivering 3750 kW (5,030 hp) to one shaft
Performance: speed 11 kt surfaced and 21·5 kt dived; diving depth 250 m (820 ft) operational; range 15,200 km (9,445 miles) at 8 kt snorting and 740 km (460 miles) at 4 kt or 30 km (18·6 miles) at 21·5 kt dived; endurance 50 days
Complement: 5 + 27

Class
1. Brazil ('Tupi' class)

Name	No.	Builder	Laid down	Com-missioned
Tupi	S30	Howaldtswerke	Mar 1985	1989
Tamoio	S31	Arsenal	Jul 1986	1991
Timbira	S32	Arsenal	Sep 1987	
Tapajos	S33	Arsenal		

A 'Type 209/2' class submarine on trials before delivery to its purchaser.

(These Brazilian boats are close to the Chilean units in displacement, dimensions, propulsion and performance, but the armament fit is optimized for the Mk 24 Mod 1 Tigerfish wire-guided torpedo used in conjunction with the Ferranti KAFS action information and fire-control system; the boats also have the Krupp-Atlas CSU 83/1 sonar and Thomson-CSF DR-4000 ESM systems. The crew is 30, and it is possible that another two boats will be built to an updated and stretched **'S-NAC 1'** class version of the same basic design. With the aid of the West Germany design consultancy IKL, Brazil is working on a nuclear-powered submarine using a reactor design currently under development in Brazil, and this **'S-NAC 2'** class design may be a derivative of the 'S-NAC 1' design with a displacement of between 2,700 and 3,000 tons, a submerged speed in the order of 25/30 kts and a main armament of six 533-mm/21-in tubes with 12 torpedoes. More likely, however, is a derivative of the Dutch 'Walrus' class design.)

2. Chile

Name	No.	Builder	Laid down	Com-missioned
Thompson	20	Howaldtswerke	Nov 1980	Sep 1984
Simpson	21	Howaldtswerke	Feb 1982	Jan 1985

(These Chilean boats differ from the 'Type 209' norm in having a sail and masts lengthened by 0·5 m/1·64 ft to cope with the increased height of the waves off the Chilean coast. Another two boats of the same design are to be procured when finance permits.)

3. Turkey

Name	No.	Builder	Laid down	Com-missioned
Titiray	S353	Golcuk NY	Aug 1989	1993
	S354	Golcuk NY	Aug 1989	1993

(The contract for these boats was signed in February 1988, and it is planned that six of the type will be built in Turkey. The boats will have a displacement of 1,440 tons dived, a Krupp-Atlas active/passive search and attack hull sonar and a Krupp-Atlas torpedo fire-control system.)

'Type 209/4' or 'Type 1500' class SS

(West Germany/India)
Type: patrol (attack) submarine
Displacement: 1,450 tons standard, 1,660 tons surfaced and 1,850 tons dived
Dimensions: length 64·4 m (211·3 ft); beam 6·5 m (21·3 ft); draught 6·0 m (19·7 ft)
Gun armament: none
Missile armament: none
Torpedo armament: eight 533-mm (21-in) tubes (all bow) for 14 SUT wire-guided dual-role torpedoes
Anti-submarine armament: torpedoes (see above)
Mines: strap-on external containers can be fitted
Electronics: one Calypso surface-search and navigation radar, one Krupp-Atlas CSU 83 active/passive search and attack hull sonar, one DUUX 5 passive ranging and intercept hull sonar, one Librascope Mk 1 underwater weapons fire-control system, one Phoenix II ESM system with warning element, and various communication and navigation systems

Propulsion: diesel-electric arrangement, with four MTU 12V 493 TY60 diesels delivering 1800 kW (2,415 hp) and one Siemens electric motor delivering 3750 kW (5,030 hp) to one shaft
Performance: speed 11 kt surfaced and 22 kt dived; diving depth 260 m (855 ft) operational; range 14,825 km (9,210 miles) at 8 kt surfaced
Complement: 8 + 32

Class

1.India				Com-
Name	No.	Builder	Laid down	missioned
Shishumar	S44	Howaldtswerke	May 1982	Sep 1986
Shankush	S45	Howaldtswerke	Sep 1982	Nov 1986
	S46	Mazagon	Jun 1984	1990
	S47	Mazagon		1991

Note: The 'Type 1500' is derived closely from the basic 'Type 209' series, but has an integral 40-man rescue system, provision for external mine containers and a number of operational modifications. India planned to build the last four boats at Mazagon, but problems have led to the cancellation of the last two units.

'Type 210' or 'Ula' class SS

(West Germany/Norway)
Type: patrol (attack) submarine
Displacement: 940 tons standard, 1,040 tons surfaced and 1,150 tons dived
Dimensions: length 59·0 m (193·6 ft); beam 5·4 m (17·7 ft); draught 4·6 m (15·1 ft)
Gun armament: none
Missile armament: none
Torpedo armament: eight 533-mm (21-in) tubes (all bow) for 14 Seal 3 wire-guided dual-role torpedoes
Anti-submarine armament: torpedoes (see above)
Electronics: one Calypso III surface-search and navigation radar, one Krupp-Atlas CSU 83 (DBQS-21F) active/passive search and attack hull sonar, one Thomson Sintra passive flank-array sonar, one MSI-90U underwater weapons fire-control system, one ESM system with warning element, and various communication and navigation systems
Propulsion: diesel-electric arrangement, with two MTU 16V 652 TB91 diesels delivering 4100 kW (5,500 hp) and one Siemens electric motor delivering 4475 kW (6,000 hp) to one shaft

Performance: maximum speed 11 kt surfaced and 23 kt dived; diving depth 250 m (820 ft) operational; range 9250 km (5,750 miles) at 8 kt surfaced
Complement: 3 + 15/17

Class

1. Norway ('Type P 6071' class, ex-'Type 210' class)				Com-
Name	No.	Builder	Laid down	missioned
Ula	S300	Thyssen Nordseewerke	Jan 1987	May 1989
Utsira	S301	Thyssen Nordseewerke		Apr 1992
Utstein	S302	Thyssen Nordseewerke		Oct 1991
Utvaer	S303	Thyssen Nordseewerke		Nov 1990
Uthaug	S304	Thyssen Nordseewerke		Apr 1991
Uredd	S305	Thyssen Nordseewerke	Jun 1988	Apr 1990

Note: This is an advanced type of coastal submarine combining the best of French, West German and Norwegian technologies.

'Type 212' class SS

(West Germany)
Type: patrol (attack) submarine
Displacement: 1,200 tons dived
Dimensions: not revealed
Gun armament: none
Missile armament: none
Torpedo armament: eight 533-mm (21-in) tubes (all bow) for 14 Seal 3 wire-guided dual-role torpedoes
Anti-submarine armament: torpedoes (see above)
Electronics: one surface-search and navigation radar, one Krupp-Atlas active/passive search and attack hull sonar, one towed-array sonar, one Kongsberg underwater weapons fire-control system, one ESM system with warning element, and various communication and navigation systems
Propulsion: hybrid fuel cell/electric arrangement, with one Siemens electric motor delivering unrevealed power to one shaft
Performance: not revealed
Complement: not revealed

Class
1. Norway
6 boats
2. West Germany
12 boats
Note: This advanced class is to have a hybrid propulsion system of the type being trialled in the 'Type 205' class boat *U 1*. In Norwegian service the class is eventually to number six boats replacing the six modernized 'Kobben' class submarines. In West German service the class is to number 12 boats replacing the six 'Type 205' class and six unmodernized 'Type 206' class boats from 1995. The superior capabilities of the class are recognized by the West Germans for the likelihood of German submarine operations in support of NATO in the North Atlantic and the Norwegian Sea.

'Type 471' class SS

(Sweden/Australia)
Type: patrol (attack) submarine
Displacement: 2,450 tons surfaced and 2,700 tons dived
Dimensions: length 75·0 m (246·1 ft); beam 7·8 m (25·6 ft); draught 6·8 m (22·3 ft)
Gun armament: none
Missile armament: UGM-84 Sub-Harpoon anti-ship missiles in place of torpedoes
Torpedo armament: six 21-in (533-mm) tubes (all bow) for 23 Mk 48 wire-guided dual-role torpedoes
Anti-submarine armament: torpedoes (see above)
Electronics: one surface-search and navigation radar, one Scylla active/passive search and attack bow/flank, one Kariwara passive search towed-array sonar, one Librascope Mk 3 action information and torpedo fire-control system, one Phoenix ESM system with warning element, and various communication and navigation systems
Propulsion: diesel-electric arrangement, with three Hedemora diesels delivering unrevealed power and one Jeumont-Schneider electric motor delivering 4700 kW (6,305 hp) to one shaft
Performance: maximum speed 10+ kt surfaced and 20+ kt dived; range 16,675 km (10,360 miles) at 10 kt surfaced
Complement: 42 plus provision for 5 trainees

Class

1. Australia				Com-
Name	No.	Builder	Laid down	missioned
		ASC, Adelaide	1989	1995

Note: This design by Kockums is based on that of the Swedish 'A17' or 'Västergotland' class. The initial programme for this Swedish-designed submarine covers six boats, with the possibility of a further two boats under consideration. It is conceivable that later boats will have a Stirling closed-cycle propulsion system for much improved underwater endurance.

'Type 540' class SS

(West Germany/Israel)
Type: patrol (attack) submarine
Displacement: 420 tons surfaced and 600 tons dived
Dimensions: length 45·0 m (146·7 ft); beam 4·7 m (15·4 ft); draught 3·7 m (12·0 ft)
Gun armament: none
Missile armament: UGM-84 Sub-Harpoon tube-launched anti-ship missiles in place of torpedoes, and possibly one SLAM launcher for Blowpipe surface-to-air missiles
Torpedo armament: eight 533-mm (21-in) tubes (all bow) for 10 NT 37E wire-guided dual-role torpedoes
Anti-submarine armament: torpedoes (see above)
Mines: up to 20 in place of torpedoes
Electronics: one Plessey surface-search and navigation radar, one Plessey active/passive search and attack hull sonar, one TIOS torpedo fire-control system, one ESM system with warning element, and extensive communications and navigation systems
Propulsion: diesel-electric arrangement, with two MTU 12V 493 TY60 die-

sels delivering 3520 kW (4,720 hp) and one electric motor delivering 1350 kW (1,810 hp) to one shaft
Performance: maximum speed 11 kt surfaced and 17 kt dived; diving depth 300 m (985 ft) operational and 500 m (1,640 ft) maximum
Complement: 22

Class

1. Israel Name	No.	Builder	Laid down	Com- missioned
Gal		Vickers	1973	Jan 1977
Tanin		Vickers	1974	Jun 1977
Rahav		Vickers	1974	Dec 1977

Note: For political reasons these West German-designed coastal submarines were built in the UK. Capability for the UGM-84 Sub-Harpoon was added in 1983, with the NT 37E replacing the Mk 37C torpedo in 1987. Israel is currently examining the possibility of replacing these obsolescent boats with newer boats, probably of West German design.

'Upholder' or 'Type 2400' class SS

(UK)
Type: patrol (attack) submarine
Displacement: 2,160 tons surfaced and 2,455 tons dived
Dimensions: length 230·6 ft (70·3 m); beam 25·0 ft (7·6 m); draught 17·7 ft (5·5 m)
Gun armament: none
Missile armament: at least four UGM-84 Sub-Harpoon tube-launched anti-ship missiles in place of torpedoes
Torpedo armament: six 21-in (533-mm) tubes (all bow) for 18 Spearfish and Mk 24 Tigerfish and Spearfish wire-guided dual-role torpedoes
Anti-submarine armament: torpedoes (see above)
Mines: up to 44 Mk 5 Stonefish and Mk 6 Sea Urchin mines in place of torpedoes
Electronics: one Type 1007 surface-search and navigation radar, one Type 2040 or (second batch) Type 2075 passive search and intercept hull sonar, one Type 2007 passive search flank sonar, one Type 2019 passive intercept and ranging sonar, one Type 2026 towed-array passive sonar, one DCC action information and underwater weapons fire-control system, one Type UAC ESM system with warning element, and extensive communication and navigation systems

Propulsion: diesel-electric arrangement, with two Paxman/GEC Valenta 1600 RPA-200 SZ diesel generators supplying current to one GEC electric motor delivering 5,400 hp (4030 kW) to one shaft
Performance: maximum speed 12 kt surfaced, 12 kt snorting and 20 kt dived; diving depth 985 ft (300 m) operational and 1,640 ft (500 m) maximum; range 9,200 + miles (14,805 + km) at 8 kt snorting and 310 miles (195 km) at 3 kt dived; endurance 49 days
Complement: 7 + 37

Class

1. UK Name	No.	Builder	Laid down	Com- missioned
Upholder	S40	VSEL	Nov 1983	Dec 1989
Unseen	S41	Cammell Laird	Jan 1986	1990
Ursula	S42	Cammell Laird	Aug 1987	1991
Unicorn	S43	Cammell Laird	Feb 1989	1993

Note: This class has been designed as successor to the 'Oberon' class with very advanced systems and weapons in a hull/machinery arrangement optimized for very quiet operation. A total of at least nine boats is planned.

Upholder, lead boat of the new 'Type 2400' class of British patrol submarines, reveals the substantial hull that yields large internal volume.

'Uzushio' or 'Type 566' class SS

(Japan)

Type: patrol (attack) submarine

Displacement: 1,850 tons standard, 1,900 tons surfaced and 2,430 tons dived

Dimensions: length 72·0 m (236·2 ft); beam 9·9 m (32·5 ft); draught 7·5 m (24·6 ft)

Gun armament: none

Missile armament: none

Torpedo armament: six 533-mm (21-in) tubes (all amidships) for GRX-2 wire-guided dual-role torpedoes

Anti-submarine armament: torpedoes (see above)

Mines: can be carried in place of torpedoes

Electronics: one ZPS-4 surface-search and navigation radar, one ZQQ-2 or (SS572) ZQQ-3 active/passive search and attack bow sonar, one SQS-36(J) or (SS568/570) SQS-4 active search fin sonar, one torpedo fire-control system, one ESM system with warning element, and various communication and navigation systems

Propulsion: diesel-electric arrangement, with two Kawasaki/MAN V8/V24-30 AMTL diesels delivering 2550 kW (3,420 hp) and one electric motor delivering 5375 kW (7,210 hp) to one shaft

Performance: maximum speed 12 kt surfaced and 20 kt dived; diving depth 200 m (655 ft) operational

Complement: 10 + 70

The 'Uzushio' class has a teardrop hull for high underwater performance. This is the lead boat of the class, _Uzushio_, which with _Makishio_ (SS567) has now been deleted in favour of more modern and capable construction.

Class

1. Japan

Name	No.	Builder	Laid down	Com-missioned
Isoshio	SS568	Kawasaki	Jul 1970	Nov 1972
Narushio	SS569	Mitsubishi	May 1971	Sep 1973
Kuroshio	SS570	Kawasaki	Jul 1972	Nov 1974
Takashio	SS571	Mitsubishi	Jul 1973	Jan 1976
Yaeshio	SS572	Kawasaki	Apr 1975	Mar 1978

Note: These are teardrop-hulled boats with only modest diving depth in accordance with Japan's constitutionally-limited role of local defence only, which dictates operations over the islands' continental shelf regions. The boats are being relegated to secondary tasks as newer submarines enter service, _Isoshio_ becoming a training boat in March 1989.

'Västergotland' or 'A17' class SS

(Sweden)

Type: patrol (attack) submarine

Displacement: 1,070 tons surfaced and 1,145 tons dived

Dimensions: length 48·5 m (159·1 ft); beam 6·1 m (20·0 ft); draught 5·6 m (18·4 ft)

Gun armament: none

Missile armament: none

Torpedo armament: six 533-mm (21-in) tubes (all bow) for 12 Tp 613 wire-guided dual-role torpedoes

Anti-submarine armament: three 400-mm (15·75-in) tubes (all stern) for Tp 42 (to be replaced by Tp 431) wire-guided torpedoes, and 533-mm (21-in) torpedoes (see above)

Mines: up to 22 in disposable external containers

Electronics: one Terma surface-search and navigation radar, one Krupp-Atlas CSU 83 active/passive search and attack hull sonar, one IPS 17 action information and underwater weapons fire-control system, one ESM system with Argo warning element, and various communication and navigation systems

Propulsion: diesel-electric arrangement, with two Hedemora VRA/1546 diesels delivering unrevealed power and one Jeumont-Schneider electric motor delivering 1350 kW (1,810 hp) to one shaft

Performance: maximum speed 11 kt surfaced and 20 kt dived; diving depth 300 m (985 ft) operational and 500 m (1,640 ft) maximum

Complement: 21

Class

1. Sweden

Name	No.	Builder	Laid down	Com-missioned
Västergötland	Vgd	Karlskrona	Jan 1983	Mar 1988
Hälsingland	Hgd	Karlskrona	Jan 1984	1989
Södermanland	Söd	Karlskrona	1985	1989
Östergötland	Ögd	Karlskrona	1986	1990

Note: This is a coastal-defence submarine class with high levels of automation to reduce crew requirements, and a combination of advanced electronics and weapons for optimum operational capability.

A notable feature of the 'Vastergotland' class submarine is its extensive automation for compact overall design and reduced manning levels.

'Walrus' class SS

(Netherlands)

Type: patrol (attack) submarine
Displacement: 1,900 tons standard, 2,450 tons surfaced and 2,800 tons dived
Dimensions: length 67·7 m (222·1 ft); beam 8·4 m (27·6 ft); draught 6·6 m (21·6 ft)
Gun armament: none
Missile armament: at least four UGM-84 Sub-Harpoon tube-launched anti-ship missiles in place of torpedoes
Torpedo armament: four 533-mm (21-in) tubes (all bow) for 20 Mk 48 Mod 4 wire-guided dual-role and NT 37C/E wire-guided anti-submarine torpedoes
Anti-submarine armament: torpedoes (see above)
Mines: up to 40 in place of torpedoes
Electronics: one ZW-07 surface-search and navigation radar, one Eledone Octopus active/passive search and attack hull sonar, one Type 2026 passive search towed-array sonar, one Fenelon passive ranging sonar, one SEWACO VIII action information system, one Gipsy III underwater weapons fire-control system, one ESM system with warning element, and extensive communication and navigation systems
Propulsion: diesel-electric arrangement, with three SEMT-Pielstick 12 PA4-V200 diesels delivering 5175 kW (6,940 hp) and one Holec electric motor delivering 4100 kW (5,500 hp) to one shaft
Performance: maximum speed 12 kt surfaced and 20 kt dived; diving deptha 450 m (1,475 ft) operational and 650 m (2,135 ft) maximum; range 18,500 km (11,495 miles) at 9 kt snorting
Complement: 7 + 42

Class

1. Netherlands

Name	No.	Builder	Laid down	Com-missioned
Walrus	S802	Rotterdamse DD	Oct 1979	1991
Zeeleeuw	S803	Rotterdamse DD	Sep 1981	1989
Dolfijn	S804	Rotterdamse DD	Jun 1986	1992
Bruinvis	S805	Rotterdamse DD	Jun 1987	1993

Note: This is in essence a version of the 'Zwaardvis' class design with greater diving depth and improved systems. Plans for another two units have been cancelled in favour of the first two units of the 'Moray' class, a smaller design intended to replace the 'Zwaardvis' class boats.

'Whiskey' class SS

(USSR)

Type: patrol (attack) submarine
Displacement: 1,080 tons surfaced and 1,350 tons dived
Dimensions: length 76·0 m (249·3 ft); beam 6·5 m (21·3 ft); draught 4·9 m (16·1 ft)
Gun armament: none
Missile armament: none
Torpedo armament: six 533-mm (21-in) tubes (four bow and two stern) for a maximum of 14 Type 53 dual-role torpedoes
Anti-submarine armament: torpedoes (see above)
Mines: up to 28 AMD-1000 mines in place of torpedoes
Electronics: one 'Snoop Plate' surface-search and navigation radar, one 'Tamir 5L' high-frequency active bow sonar, one torpedo fire-control system, one 'Stop Light' ESM system with warning element, and various communication and navigation systems
Propulsion: diesel-electric arrangement, with two Type 37D diesels delivering 3000 kW (4,025 hp) and two electric motors delivering 2000 kW (2,680 hp) to two shafts
Performance: maximum speed 18 kt surfaced and 14 kt dived; diving depth 300 m (985 ft) operational and 500 m (1,640 ft) maximum; range 15,750 km (9,785 miles) at 10 kt surfaced
Complement: 54

Class

1. Albania

Name	No.
	512
	514
	516

(These are the survivors of four boats received in the early 1960s. Only two boats are operational, the third being used only for harbour training and battery charging.)

2. China
15 boats
(These submarines were built in the 1960s in China, and although they are generally similar to the Soviet units some have two 25-mm AA guns in a twin mounting at the base of the sail. Most of the boats are now in reserve.)

3. Egypt

Name	No.
	810
	816

(These are the survivors of eight boats supplied between 1958 and 1962.)

4. North Korea
4 boats
(These are 1974 replacements for pairs of boats originally transferred in 1960 and 1962.)

5. Poland

Name	No.
Sokol	293
Bielik	295

(These boats were transferred from the USSR in 1962 and 1964.)

6. USSR
105 'Whiskey' class boats including 60 in reserve
(This was the USSR's first submarine design after World War II, and was built to the extent of some 340 units in five subvariants, of which all surviving examples have been standardized to the 'Whiskey Type V' standard described above.)

Based largely on German designs of World War II, the 'Whiskey' class boat is obsolete and has largely disappeared from service with advanced navies.

'Yuushio' or 'Type 573' class SS

(Japan)
Type: patrol (attack) submarine
Displacement: 2,200 tons or (SS574 and SS577/582) 2,250 tons surfaced and 2,450 tons dived
Dimensions: length 76·0 m (249·3 ft); beam 9·9 m (32·5 ft); draught 7·5 m (24·6 ft)
Gun armament: none
Missile armament: at least four UGM-84 Sub-Harpoon tube-launched anti-ship missiles in place of torpedoes (SS574 and 577/582 only)
Torpedo armament: six 533-mm (21-in) tubes (all amidships) for 18 GRX-2 and Mk 37C wire-guided dual-role torpedoes
Anti-submarine armament: torpedoes (see above)
Mines: up to 44 in place of torpedoes
Electronics: one ZPS-6 surface-search and navigation radar, one ZQQ-4 (BQS-4) active/passive search and attack bow sonar, one SQS-36(J) active attack fin sonar, one action information and underwater weapons fire-control system, one ESM system with warning element, and various communication and navigation systems
Propulsion: diesel-electric arrangement, with two Kawasaki/MAN V8/V24-30 AMTL diesels delivering 2500 kW (3,355 hp) and one Fuji electric motor delivering 5375 kW (7,210 hp) to one shaft
Performance: maximum speed 12 kt surfaced and 20+ kt dived; diving depth 300 m (985 ft) operational and 500 m (1,640 ft) maximum
Complement: 10 + 65

Class
1. Japan

Name	No.	Builder	Laid down	Com-missioned
Yuushio	SS573	Mitsubishi	Dec 1976	Feb 1980
Mochishio	SS574	Kawasaki	May 1978	Mar 1981
Setoshio	SS575	Mitsubishi	Apr 1979	Mar 1982
Okishio	SS576	Kasawaki	Apr 1980	Mar 1983
Nadashio	SS577	Mitsubishi	Apr 1981	Mar 1984
Hamashio	SS578	Kawasaki	Apr 1982	Mar 1985
Akishio	SS579	Mitsubishi	Apr 1983	Mar 1986
Takeshio	SS580	Kawasaki	Apr 1984	Mar 1987
Yukishio	SS581	Mitsubishi	Apr 1985	Mar 1988
Sachishio	SS582	Kawasaki	Apr 1986	Mar 1989

Note: This is essentially an enlarged and modernized version of the 'Uzushio' class with greater diving depth.

'Yuushio (Improved)' class SS

(Japan)
Type: patrol (attack) submarine
Displacement: 2,400 tons standard and 2,750 tons dived
Dimensions: length 80·0 m (262·5 ft); beam 10·8 m (35·4 ft); draught 10·5 m (34·5 ft)
Gun armament: none
Missile armament: at least four UGM-84 Sub-Harpoon tube-launched anti-ship missiles in place of torpedoes
Torpedo armament: six 533-mm (21-in) tubes (all amidships) for 18 GRX-2 wire-guided dual-role torpedoes
Anti-submarine armament: torpedoes (see above)
Mines: up to 36 in place of torpedoes
Electronics: one ZPS-6 surface-search and navigation radar, one ZQQ-5 active/passive search and attack bow sonar, one action information and underwater weapons fire-control system, one ESM system with warning element, and various communication and navigation systems
Propulsion: diesel-electric arrangement, with two Kawasaki/MAN V8/V24-30 AMTL diesels delivering 3730 kW (5,005 hp) and one Fuji electric motor delivering 5375 kW (7,210 hp) to one shaft
Performance: maximum speed 12 kt surfaced and 20+ kt dived; diving depth 300 m (985 ft) operational and 500 m (1,640 ft) maximum
Complement: 10 + 65

Class
1. Japan

Name	No.	Builder	Laid down	Com-missioned
	SS583	Mitsubishi	Apr 1987	Dec 1990
	SS584	Kawasaki	Apr 1988	Mar 1991
	SS585	Mitsubishi	Apr 1989	1992
	SS586	Kawasaki		

Note: This is a deeper-draught version of the 'Yuushio' class with more advanced sensors and electronics, the object apparently being the commissioning of one boat per year against requirement for possibly six boats.

'Zwaardvis' class SS

(Netherlands)
Type: patrol (attack) submarine
Displacement: 2,350 tons surfaced and 2,640 tons dived
Dimensions: length 66·2 m (217·2 ft); beam 10·3 m (33·8 ft); draught 7·1 m (23·3 ft)
Gun armament: none
Missile armament: at least four UGM-84 Sub-Harpoon tube-launched anti-ship missiles in place of torpedoes
Torpedo armament: six 533-mm (21-in) tubes (all bow) for 20 Mk 48 wire-guided dual-role and NT 37C/E wire-guided anti-submarine torpedoes
Anti-submarine armament: torpedoes (see above)
Mines: up to 40 in place of torpedoes
Electronics: one Type 1001 surface-search and navigation radar, one Krupp-Atlas DSQS-21 active/passive search and attack bow sonar (being replaced by Eledone active/passive search and attack hull sonar), one Krupp-Atlas passive ranging sonar, one Type 2026 passive search towed-array sonar, one SEWACO VIII action information system, one ESM system, one WM-8/7 underwater weapons fire-control system, one ESM system with warning element, and several communications and navigation systems
Propulsion: diesel-electric arrangement, with three 1050-kW (1,410-hp) Werkspoor RUB 215-12 diesel generators supplying current to one Holec electric motor delivering 3150 kW (4,225 hp) to one shaft
Performance: maximum speed 13 kt surfaced and 20 kt dived; diving depth 300 m (985 ft) operational and 500 m (1,640 ft) maximum; range 18,500 km (11,500 miles) at 9 kt snorting
Complement: 8 + 59

Class
1. Netherlands

Name	No.	Builder	Laid down	Com-missioned
Zwaardvis	S806	Rotterdamse DD	Jul 1966	Aug 1972
Tijgerhaai	S807	Rotterdamse DD	Jul 1966	Oct 1972

(These are highly capable submarines with a teardrop hull shape.)

2. Taiwan ('Zwaardvis Mk 2' or 'Hai Lung' class)

Name	No.	Builder	Laid down	Com-missioned
Hai Lung	793	Wilton-Fijenoord	1982	Oct 1987
Hai Hu	794	Wilton-Fijenoord	1982	Apr 1988

(These Taiwanese boats have surfaced and submerged displacements of 2,375 and 2,560 tons, and a diesel-electric propulsion system with Bronswerk D-RUB 215-12 diesels, and the armament is thought to comprise 'waterslug' torpedo tubes for NT 37E and possibly Mk 24 Tigerfish torpedoes [a maximum of 28 weapons used in conjunction with the Sinbads-M fire-control system and associated SIASS-Z sonar] as well as submarine-launched anti-ship missiles [possibly a variant of Taiwan's Hsiung Feng II ship-launched missile]. Another alteration from the Dutch norm is the Rapids ESM system. The Dutch government has refused a Taiwanese request that additional boats be built in the Netherlands, and it is likely that Taiwan will therefore embark on the construction of another two, and possibly four, boats in Taiwan.)

The Zwaardvis attack submarine of the Royal Netherlands navy.

The other unit of the Dutch 'Zwaardvis' class is the *Tijgerhaai*, seen here on the surface in choppy conditions.

'Charles de Gaulle' class CVN

(France)

Type: nuclear-powered multi-role aircraft-carrier
Displacement: 34,000 tons standard and 36,000 tons full load
Dimensions: length 261·5 m (857·7 ft); beam 31·8 m (104·3 ft); draught 8·5 m (27·8 ft); flightdeck length 261·5 m (857·7 ft) and width 62·0 m (203·4 ft)
Gun armament: none
Missile armament: seven SAAM octuple vertical-launch system launchers for 56 SAN 90 Aster SAMs, and two SADRAL sextuple launchers for Mistral SAMs
Torpedo armament: none
Anti-submarine armament: aircraft and helicopters (see below)
Aircraft: 40 fixed-wing and an undetermined number of rotary-wing
Electronics: one DRBJ 11B 3D surveillance radar, one DRBV 27 air-search radar, one DRBV 15 air/surface-search radar, two Arabel 3D air-search and Aster fire-control radars, two Decca 1226 navigation radars, one NRBA-series landing radar, one Syracuse satellite navigation system, one torpedo-warning sonar, one SENIT 6 action information system, one ESM system with one ARBR 17 warning and two ARBB 33 jamming elements, one DIBV 10 Vampir IR detector, four Sagaie chaff/flare launchers, and SRN-6 TACAN

Propulsion: two Type K15 pressurized water-cooled reactors supplying steam to two sets of geared turbines delivering 61,150 kW (82,015 hp) to two shafts
Performance: maximum speed 27 kt
Complement: 1,150 plus an air group of 550, with accommodation for 1,950 possible

Class

1. France

Name	No.	Builder	Laid down	Com-missioned
Charles de Gaulle	R91	Brest ND	Apr 1989	1996
Richelieu	R92	Brest ND		2004

Note: Designed to replace the two 'Clemenceau' carriers at about the turn of the century, these carriers will each have a flightdeck angled at 8·5°, and fitted with two 75-m (246-ft) steam catapults and two lifts each measuring 19 m (62·3 ft) by 12·5 m (41·0 ft). The ships use a reactor design derived from that of the French SSBN force, and the comparatively low power thus imposed makes these ships the slowest aircraft-carriers in the world other than the Spanish *Principe de Asturias*.

'Clemenceau' class CV

(France)

Type: multi-role aircraft-carrier
Displacement: 27,310 tons standard and 32,780 tons full load
Dimensions: length 265·0 m (869·4 ft); beam 51·2 m (168·0 ft); draught 8·6 m (28·2 ft); flightdeck length 265·5 m (871·1 ft) and width 29·5 m (96·8 ft)
Gun armament: four 100-mm (3·9-in) Creusot Loire L/55 DP in Modèle 1953 single mountings
Missile armament: two Naval Crotale octuple launchers for 36 Matra R.440 SAMs
Torpedo armament: none
Anti-submarine armament: aircraft and helicopters (see below)
Aircraft: 36 fixed-wing (16 Dassault-Breguet Super Etendards, 3 Dassault-Breguet Etendard IVPs, 10 Vought F-8 Crusaders and 7 Dassault-Breguet Alizes) and two rotary-wing (Aérospatiale SA 319B Alouette IIIs, to be replaced by two Aérospatiale SA 365F Dauphin 2s)
Armour: flightdeck, hull sides and bulkheads (magazine and engine room areas) and island
Electronics: one DRBV 23B surveillance radar, two DRBI 10 air/surface-search radars, one DRBV 15 air-warning radar, two DRBC 32 fire-control radars, one Decca 1226 navigation radar, one NRBA 51 landing radar, one SQS-505 active search hull sonar, one SENIT 2 action information system, one

ESM system with ARBR 16 warning and ARBX 10 jamming elements, two Sagaie chaff/flare launchers, and SRN-6 TACAN
Propulsion: six boilers supplying steam to two sets of Parsons geared turbines delivering 126,000 hp (93,960 kW) to two shafts
Performance: maximum speed 32 kt; range 13,900 km (8,635 miles) at 18 kt or 6500 km (4,040 miles) at 32 kt
Complement: 64 + 1,274

Class

1. France

Name	No.	Builder	Laid down	Com-missioned
Clemenceau	R98	Brest ND	Nov 1955	Nov 1961
Foch	R99	Ch. de l'Atlantique	Feb 1957	Jul 1963

Note: These were the first French aircraft-carriers designed as such, and are moderately advanced ships. A mixed complement of aircraft is carried for the 8° angled flightdeck, which is fitted with steam catapults and two lifts, the latter each measuring 16·0 m (52·5 ft) by 11·0 m (36·1 ft). The two units are due to be replaced in 1996 (*Clemenceau*) and 2004 (*Foch*) when the nuclear-powered *Charles de Gaulle* and *Richelieu* enter service.

A Vought F-8E(FN) Crusader air-defence fighter is lined up for take-off on the flightdeck of the French navy's multi-role aircraft-carrier *Clemenceau*.

'Colossus' class CVLS

(UK/Brazil)

Type: light anti-submarine aircraft-carrier
Displacement: 15,890 tons standard, 17,500 tons normal and 19,890 tons full load
Dimensions: length 695·0 ft (211·8 m); beam 80·0 ft (24·4 m); draught 24·5 ft (7·5 m); flightdeck length 690·0 ft (210·3 m) and width 119·6 ft (36·4 m)
Gun armament: 10 40-mm Bofors L/60 AA in two Mk 2 quadruple mountings and one Mk 1 twin mounting
Missile armament: none
Anti-submarine armament: aircraft and helicopters (see below)
Aircraft: generally six fixed-wing (Grumman S-2E Trackers) and 11 rotary-wing (six Sikorsky SH-3D Sea Kings, three Aérospatiale AS 332F Super Pumas and two Aérospatiale AS 355F Ecureuil 2s)
Electronics: one SPS-40B air-search radar, one SPS-4 surface-search radar, one SPS-8A combat-control radar, one Raytheon MP 1402 navigation radar, two SPG-34 40-mm fire-control radars, two Mk 63 gun fire-control systems, one Mk 51 gun fire-control system, and one SLR-2 ESM system with warning element
Propulsion: four Admiralty boilers supplying steam to two sets of Parsons geared turbines delivering 40,000 hp (29,830 kW) to two shafts
Performance: maximum speed 24 kt; range 13,800 miles (22,210 km) at 14 kt or 7,140 miles (11,490 km) at 23 kt
Complement: 1,000 plus an air group of about 300

Class
1. Argentina

Name	No.	Builder	Laid down	Com- missioned
Veinticinco de Mayo	V2	Cammell Laird	Dec 1942	Jan 1945

(This Argentine ship differs considerably in appearance and equipment from the Brazilian aircraft-carrier, and normally operates with 18 fixed-wing [12 Dassault-Breguet Super Etendards and six Grumman S-2E Trackers, although the McDonnell Douglas A-4P/Q Skyhawk can also be embarked] and five rotary-wing [four Sikorsky SH-3D Sea King and one Aérospatiale SA 319B Alouette III] aircraft. The electronic fit comprises one LW-08 surveillance radar, one DA-08 air/surface-search radar, one VI/SGR-109 height-finding radar, one DA-02 surface-search radar, one ZW-01 navigation radar, one SPN 720 landing radar, URN-20 TACAN, and one CAAIS action information system. The armament comprises nine 40-mm Bofors L/70 AA in single mountings. In the late 1980s the ship was taken in hand for revision with diesel engines in place of the elderly Parsons steam turbines: this will ease maintenance and improve reliability, but its main advantage will be a higher speed so that the ship is more compatible with its Super Etendard strike fighters, which have often been forced to operate from shore bases.)

2. Brazil

Name	No.	Builder	Laid down	Com- missioned
Minas Gerais	A11	Swan Hunter	Nov 1942	Jan 1945

(This Brazilian unit is operated mainly in the anti-submarine role, and the flightdeck includes an 8·25° angled section, a single catapult and two lifts, the latter each measuring 45·0 ft/13·7 m by 34·0 ft/10·4 m.)

'Enterprise' class CVN

(USA)

Type: nuclear-powered multi-role aircraft-carrier
Displacement: 73,500 tons light, 75,700 tons standard and 90,970 tons full load
Dimensions: length 1,088·0 ft (331·6 m); beam 133·0 ft (40·5 m); draught 39·0 ft (11·9 m); flightdeck length 1,088·0 ft (331·6 m) and width 252·0 ft (76·8 m)
Gun armament: three 20-mm Phalanx Mk 15 CIWS mountings, and three 20-mm AA in Mk 68 single mountings
Missile armament: three Mk 29 octuple launchers for RIM-7 NATO Sea Sparrow SAMs
Torpedo armament: none
Anti-submarine armament: aircraft and helicopters (see below)
Aircraft: typically 90 in a multi-role carrier air wing with 20 Grumman F-14 Tomcat, 20 McDonnell Douglas F/A-18 Hornet, 5 Grumman EA-6B Prowler, 20 Grumman A-6E Intruder, 4 Grumman KA-6D Intruder, 5 Grumman E-2C Hawkeye and 10 Lockheed S-3A Viking fixed-wing aircraft, and six Sikorsky SH-3G/H Sea King helicopters
Electronics: one SPS-48C 3D radar, one SPS-49 air-search radar, one SPS-65 threat-warning radar, one SPS-58 low-level threat-warning radar, one SPS-67 surface-search radar, one SPN-64 navigation radar, four SPN-series aircraft landing radars, one Mk 23 and six Mk 57 radars used in conjunction with three Mk 91 SAM fire-control systems, one Naval Tactical Data System, Link 11 and 14 data-links, one SLQ-32(V) ESM system with intercept element, one SLQ-29(V)5 ECM system with WLR-8 warning and SLQ-17AV jamming elements, four Mk 36 Super RBOC chaff/flare launchers, one OE-82 satellite communications system, one SSR-1 satellite communications receiver, and URN-25 TACAN
Propulsion: eight Westinghouse A2W pressurized water-cooled reactors supplying steam to four sets of Westinghouse geared turbines delivering 280,000 hp (208,795 kW) to four shafts
Performance: maximum speed 35 kt; range 460,000 miles (741,245 km) at 20 kt
Complement: 180 + 3,139 plus an air group of 310 + 2,010

Class
1. USA

Name	No.	Builder	Laid down	Com- missioned
Enterprise	CVN65	Newport News	Feb 1958	Nov 1961

Note: This was the world's first nuclear-powered aircraft-carrier, and is in essence a development of the 'Forrestal' class design. The massive flight-deck is served by four 295-ft (89·9-m) steam catapults and four deck-edge lifts (two forward and one on each side abaft the island), and the ship carries aviation consumables (fuel and weapons) for 12 days of sustained operations.

A multi-role carrier air wing (including the McDonnell Douglas A-4 Skyhawk, Grumman E-2 Hawkeye and Lockheed S-3 Viking aircraft visible here) gives the *Enterprise* great offensive punch as well as defensive capability. The ship is also notable for its highly distinctive island, whose appearance alters as the primary sensors are updated and/or replaced with newer items.

'Forrestal' class CV

(USA)
Type: multi-role aircraft-carrier
Displacement: 59,650 tons or (CV61/62) or 60,000 tons standard and 79,250 tons (CV59), 80,385 tons (CV60), 81,165 tons (CV61) or 80,645 tons (CV62) full load
Dimensions: length (CV59) 1,086·0 ft (331·0 m) or (others) 1,071·0 ft (326·4 m); beam 129·5 ft (39·5 m); draught 37·0 ft (11·3 m); flightdeck length 1,047·0 ft (319·1 m) and width 252·0 ft (76·8 m)
Gun armament: three 20-mm Phalanx Mk 15 CIWS mountings
Missile armament: three Mk 29 octuple launchers for RIM-7 NATO Sea Sparrow SAMs
Anti-submarine armament: aircraft and helicopters (see below)
Aircraft: typically 90 in a multi-role carrier air wing with 20 Grumman F-14 Tomcat, 20 McDonnell Douglas F/A-18 Hornet, 20 Grumman A-6E Intruder, 4 Grumman KA-6D Intruder, 5 Grumman EA-6B Prowler, 10 Lockheed S-3A Viking and 5 Grumman E-2C Hawkeye fixed-wing aircraft, and six Sikorsky S-3G/H Sea King helicopters
Electronics: one SPS-48C 3D radar, one SPS-49 air-search radar, one SPS-67 surface-search radar, one SPS-58 low-level threat-warning radar, one SPN-64 navigation radar, four SPN-series carrier landing radars, one Mk 23 and four or six Mk 91 radars used in conjunction with two (CV59 and 62) or three (others) Mk 91 SAM fire-control systems, one Naval Tactical Data System, Link 11 and 14 data-links, one SLQ-29(V)3 ESM system, one SLQ-26 ECM system with WLR-1, WLR-3 and WLR-11 warning elements, four Mk 36 Super RBOC chaff/flare launchers, one OE-82 satellite communications system, one WSC-3 satellite communications transceiver, one SSR-1 satellite communications receiver, and URN-25 TACAN
Propulsion: eight Babcock & Wilcox boilers supplying steam to four sets of Westinghouse geared turbines delivering 260,000 hp (193,855 kW) in CV59 or 280,000 hp (208,795 kW) in the others to four shafts
Performance: maximum speed 33 kt (CV59) or 34 kt (others); range 9,200 miles (14,805 km) at 20 kt or 4,600 miles (7400 km) at 30 kt
Complement: 148 + 2,810 (CV59), 136 + 2,760 (CV60), 161 + 2,728 (CV61) or 150 + 2,643 (CV62) plus an air group of 290 + 2,190

Class
1. USA

Name	No.	Builder	Laid down	Com-missioned
Forrestal	CV59	Newport News	Jul 1952	Oct 1955
Saratoga	CV60	New York NY	Dec 1952	Apr 1956
Ranger	CV61	Newport News	Aug 1954	Aug 1957
Independence	CV62	New York NY	Jul 1955	Jan 1959

Note: These were the first aircraft-carriers built after World War II, and were also the world's first aircraft-carriers designed specifically for the operation of jet aircraft. The design for the lead ship drew heavily on the US Navy's experience with the proposed *United States* (CVA58), and the ships were initially designated as CVBs (heavy aircraft-carriers) but subsequently redesignated as CVAs (attack aircraft-carriers) and finally as CVs (multi-purpose aircraft-carriers). Though designed from the start with enclosed

The *Forrestal* was the first American aircraft-carrier produced after the implications of World War II carrier warfare had been fully digested.

bows for improved seaworthiness, as well as the British-developed angled flightdeck (served by four steam catapults and four deck-edge lifts, the latter each measuring 72·0 ft/21·9 m by 50·0 ft/15·2 m), the ships have been considerably upgraded over the years with improved electronics and medium-calibre guns replaced by surface-to-air missile systems. CV59 has a less advanced propulsion arrangement with boilers working at lower pressure and at a higher fuel consumption.

'Garibaldi' class CVLS

(Italy)
Type: light anti-submarine aircraft-carrier
Displacement: 10,000 tons standard and 13,850 tons full load
Dimensions: length 180·0 m (590·4 ft); beam 33·4 m (110·2 ft); draught 6·7 m (22·0 ft); flightdeck length 173·8 m (570·2 ft) and width 30·4 m (99·7 ft)
Gun armament: six 40-mm Breda L/70 AA in three Dardo twin mountings
Missile armament: four Teseo container-launchers for 10 Otomat Mk 2 anti-ship missiles, and two Albatros octuple launchers for 48 Aspide SAMs
Anti-submarine armament: two triple ILAS 3 tube mountings for 324-mm (12·75-in) A 244/S torpedoes, and helicopter-launched weapons (see below)
Aircraft: up to 16 Agusta (Sikorsky) ASH-3D Sea King helicopters
Electronics: one SPS 52C 3D radar, one RAN 3L air-search radar, one RAN 10S air/surface-search radar, one SPS 702 surface-search and target designation radar, one SPN 728 air-control radar, one SPN 703 navigation radar, two RTN 30X radars and two NA 30 optronic directors used in conjunction with two Argo NA30 Albatros fire-control systems with optronic back-ups, three RTN 20X radars used in conjunction with three Dardo fire-control systems, one IPN 20 (SADOC 2) action information system, Link 11 and 16 data-links, one Raytheon DE 1164 active search bow sonar, one Nettuno ESM system with warning and jamming elements, one SLQ-25 Nixie towed

Right: The Italian Navy's flagship *Garibaldi*.

torpedo-decoy system, two Breda SCLAR-D chaff/flare launchers, one satellite communication and navigation system, and URN-25 TACAN
Propulsion: COGAG arrangement, with four Fiat/General Electric LM2500 gas turbines delivering 59,655 kW (80,000 hp) to two shafts
Performance: maximum speed 30 kt; range 13,000 km (8,080 miles) at 20 kt
Complement: 550 plus an air group of 230 and provision for a flag staff of 45

Class
1. Italy

Name	No.	Builder	Laid down	Com-missioned
Giuseppe Garibaldi	C551	Italcantieri	Jun 1981	Jul 1985

Note: This modern ship is admirably suited to Mediterranean anti-submarine operations with its advanced sensors and electronics complemented by a potent but well-balanced array of weapons. The type has two lifts, each measuring 18·0 m (59·0 ft) by 10·0 m (32·8 ft) and a 6·5° 'ski-jump' to allow embarkation of STOVL aircraft (BAe Sea Harriers or McDonnell Douglas AV-8B Harrier IIs) in the multi-purpose role once Italian law permits: the law was changed in 1988 and the Italian navy started the process of evaluating the two possible types. The ship can also carry two 250-man fast personnel launches for use in disaster relief or amphibious operations.

'Hermes' class CV

(UK/India)
Type: multi-role aircraft-carrier
Displacement: 23,900 tons standard and 28,700 tons full load
Dimensions: length 744·3 ft (226·9 m); beam 90·0 ft (27·4 m); draught 28·5 ft (8·7 m); flightdeck length 744·3 ft (226·9 m) and width 160·0 ft (48·8 m)
Gun armament: none
Missile armament: probably to be fitted with a Soviet SAM system
Torpedo armament: none
Anti-submarine armament: helicopter-launched weapons (see below)
Aircraft: normally six BAe Sea Harrier FRS.Mk 51 STOVL fighters and seven Westland Sea King Mk 42 helicopters, with a maximum of 37 aircraft possible
Armour: belt 1/2 in (25·4/50·8 mm) over machinery spaces and magazines; deck 0·75 in (19 mm)
Electronics: one Type 965 air-search radar, one Type 993 air/surface-search radar, one Type 1006 navigation radar, Soviet fire-control radars to be fitted to complement the two Type 904 fire-control radars retained for the GWS 22 fire-control system left aboard despite the removal of its associated Sea Cat SAM launchers, one CAAIS action information system (perhaps to be replaced by a Soviet system), Link 10 data-link, one Type 184M active search and attack hull sonar, one UAA-1 Abbey Hill ESM system with warning and jamming elements, two Corvus chaff launchers, and FT 13-S/M TACAN
Propulsion: four Admiralty boilers supplying steam to two sets of Parsons geared turbines delivering 76,000 hp (56,675 kW) to two shafts
Performance: maximum speed 28 kt
Complement: 143 + 1,207 including air group

Note: Originally the British *Hermes*, this ship was sold to India in 1985 and is fitted with a 7·5° ' ski-jump' for the launching of Sea Harrier aircraft.

The Indian Navy's *Viraat*, the former HMS *Hermes*.

'Invincible' class CVSA

(UK)
Type: light multi-role aircraft-carrier
Displacement: 19,500 tons or (R07) 20,000 tons standard
Dimensions: length 677·0 ft (206·6 m) or (R07) 685·8 ft (209·1 m); beam 90·0 ft (27·5 m) and width 105·0 ft (31·9 m) or (R07) 118·0 ft (36·0 m); draught 26·0 ft (7·9 m); flightdeck length 550·0 ft (167·8 m) and width 44·3 ft (13·5 m) with fore and aft lateral extensions to the maximum width of each ship
Gun armament: two or (R09) three 20-mm Phalanx Mk 15 CIWS mountings (replaced from 1989 by three 30-mm Goalkeeper CIWS mountings), two 20-mm Oerlikon AA in GAM-B01 single mountings, and (R07) two 30-mm Oerlikon AA in one GCM-A03 twin mounting
Missile armament: one twin launcher for 36 Sea Dart SAMs and (to be retrofitted from 1991) four GWS 26 Mod 2 Lightweight Sea Wolf launchers for Sea Wolf SAMs
Torpedo armament: none
Anti-submarine armament: helicopter-launched weapons (see below)
Aircraft: since 1988 the ships have been upgraded to CVSA (Carrier Vessel Submarine Attack) configuration with a normal air group of 12 Westland Sea King helicopters (three AEW.Mk 2s and nine HAS.Mk 5s) and nine BAe Sea Harrier FRS.Mk 1/2 fixed-wing aircraft, with the possibility that European Helicopter Industries EH.101 Merlin helicopters may replace the Sea Kings during the 1990s
Electronics: one Type 1022 air-search radar, one Type 992R surface-search radar, two Type 1006 navigation radars, two Type 909 radars used in conjunction with two GWS 30 Sea Dart SAM fire-control systems, two Type 911(3) radars used in conjunction with four GWS 26 fire-control systems (when Sea Wolf SAMs are retrofitted), one ADAWS 6 or (R07) ADAWS 10 action information system, Link 10, 11 and 14 data-links, one Type 2016 active search and attack hull sonar (R07 only), one UAA-1 Abbey Hill ESM system with warning and jamming elements, two Corvus chaff launchers, two Mk 36 Super RBOC chaff/flare launchers, two Sea Gnat chaff launchers (R07 only), one OE-82 satellite communications system, one SCOT-2 satellite communications system, and one SCOT-1 satellite communications system
Propulsion: COGAG arrangement, with four Rolls-Royce Olympus TM3B gas turbines delivering 94,000 hp (70,085 kW) to two shafts
Performance: maximum speed 28 kt; range 5,750 miles (9250 km) at 18 kt
Complement: 57 + 609 plus an air group of 84 + 318, the post-1988 update adding a further 120 men

Note: Though conceived originally as anti-submarine ships, these vessels are now useful multi-role types as a result of an embarked complement of Sea Harrier STOVL aircraft. The first two units were completed with 7° 'ski-jumps' but have been retrofitted with the 12° jump fitted to R07 from the beginning of her life. Considerable effort is being made to improve the close-range defence of these ships with more capable SAM and CIWS systems, as well as enhanced decoy measures, and during refits accommodation is being provided for an additional 120 aircrew and flag staff.

Right: HMS *Invincible* following its major 1988/89 refit.

'Jeanne d'Arc' class CVLS

(France)

Type: light anti-submarine aircraft-carrier/assault ship

Displacement: 10,000 tons standard and 12,365 tons full load

Dimensions: length 182·0 m (597·1 ft); beam 24·0 m (78·7 ft); draught 7·3 m (24·0 ft); flightdeck length 62·0 m (203·4 ft) and width 21·0 m (68·9 ft)

Gun armament: four 100-mm (3·9-in) Creusot Loire L/55 DP in Modèle 1953 single mountings

Missile armament: two triple container-launchers for six MM.38 Exocet anti-ship missiles

Torpedo armament: none

Anti-submarine armament: helicopter-launched weapons (see below)

Aircraft: up to eight Westland Lynx Mk 2/3 helicopters, or when used as a commando carrier 14 Aérospatiale SA 321 Super Frelon helicopters

Capacity: in the assault role the ship has accommodation for a 700-man commando battalion and its associated equipment

Electronics: one DRBV 22D air-search radar, one DRBV 50 air/surface-search radar, one DRBN 32 navigation radar, three DRBC 32A fire-control radars, one DUBV 24 active search hull sonar, one SENIT 2 action information system, one ESM system with ARBR 16 warning element, two Syllex chaff launchers, and SRN-6 TACAN

Propulsion: four boilers supplying steam to two sets of Rateau-Bretagne geared turbines delivering 30,000 kW (40,230 hp) to two shafts

Performance: maximum speed 26·5 kt; range 11,125 km (6,915 miles) at 15 kt

Complement: 31 + 414 plus provision for 182 cadets

Class				Com-
1. France				
Name	**No.**	**Builder**	**Laid down**	**missioned**
Jeanne d'Arc	R97	Brest ND	Jul 1960	Jun 1964

Note: This comparatively simple ship is designed for officer cadet training in time of peace, and for assault commando operations in time of war.

The *Jeanne d'Arc* is a useful dual-role ship used for training in time of peace but with an anti-submarine/commando assault role in time of war.

'John F. Kennedy' class CV

(USA)

Type: multi-role aircraft-carrier

Displacement: 61,000 tons standard and 80,940 tons full load

Dimensions: length 1,052·0 ft (328·7 m); beam 130·0 ft (39·6 m); draught 35·9 ft (10·9 m); flightdeck length 1,052·0 ft (328·7 m) and width 252·0 ft (76·8 m)

Gun armament: three 20-mm Phalanx Mk 15 CIWS mounting

Missile armament: three Mk 29 octuple launchers for RIM-7 NATO Sea Sparrow SAMs

Torpedo armament: none

Anti-submarine armament: aircraft and helicopters (see below)

Aircraft: typically 90 in a multi-role carrier air wing with 20 Grumman F-14 Tomcat, 20 McDonnell Douglas F/A-18 Hornet, 20 Grumman A-6E Intruder, 5 Grumman EA-6B Prowler, 4 Grumman KA-6D Intruder, 5 Grumman E-2C Hawkeye and 10 Lockheed S-3A Viking fixed-wing aircraft, and six Sikorsky SH-3G/H Sea King helicopters

Electronics: one SPS-48C/E 3D radar, one SPS-49 long-range air-search radar, one SPS-65 low-level threat-warning radar, one SPS-10F surface-search radar, one SPN-64 navigation radar, four SPN-series carrier landing radars, or Mk 23 and six Mk 57 radars used in conjunction with three Mk 91 SAM fire-control systems, one Naval Tactical Data System, Link 11 and 14 data-links, one SLQ-17 and one SLQ-26 ESM systems with WLR-3 and WLR-11 warning and jamming elements, four Mk 36 Super RBOC chaff/flare launchers, one OE-82 satellite communications system, one WSC-3 satellite communications transceiver, one SSR-1 satellite communications receiver, and URN-25 TACAN

This view of the *Kennedy* reveals Sea Sparrow and Phalanx defensive systems.

Propulsion: eight Foster-Wheeler boilers supplying steam to four sets of Westinghouse geared turbines delivering 280,000 hp (208,795 kW) to four shafts
Performance: maximum speed 32 kt; range 9,200 miles (14,805 km) at 20 kt
Complement: 155 + 3,045 plus an air group of 320 + 2,160

Note: This is a close relative of the three 'Kitty Hawk' class aircraft-carriers, all four ships being variants of an improved 'Forrestal' class design with the island set farther aft. The ship has an angled flightdeck served by four steam catapults and four deck-edge lifts.

'Kiev' class CVG

(USSR)

Type: multi-role hybrid aircraft-carrier/guided-missile cruiser
Displacement: 30,000 tons standard and 37,100 tons full load
Dimensions: length 273·0 m (895·7 ft); beam 32·7 m (107·3 ft) and width 47·2 m (154·8 ft); draught 10·0 m (32·8 ft); flightdeck length 189·0 m (620·0 ft) and width 20·7 m (68·0 ft) with fore and aft lateral extensions to the maximum width of each ship
Gun armament: four 76-mm (3-in) L/60 DP in two twin mountings, and eight 30-mm ADGM-630 CIWS mountings
Missile armament: four twin container-launchers for 24 SS-N-12 'Sandbox' anti-ship missiles, two twin launchers for 72 SA-N-3 'Goblet' SAMs, two twin launchers for about 40 SA-N-4 'Gecko' SAMs or (*Novorossiysk* only) two groups of six octuple vertical launchers for 96 SA-N-9 SAMs
Torpedo armament: two 533-mm (21-in) quintuple tube mountings for Type 53 dual-role torpedoes
Anti-submarine armament: one twin SUW-N-1 launcher for 20 FRAS-1/SS-N-14 'Silex' missiles, two RBU 6000 12-barrel rocket-launchers, torpedoes (see above), and helicopter-launched weapons (see below)
Aircraft: typically 32, comprising 13 fixed-wing (12 Yakovlev Yak-38 'Forger-As' and one Yak-38 'Forger-B') and 19 rotary-wing (16 Kamov Ka-27

The Novorossiysk of the impressive 'Kiev' carrier/missile cruiser class.

'Helix-As' and three Ka-27 'Helix-Bs')
Electronics: one 'Top Sail' 3D air-surveillance radar, one 'Top Steer/Top Plate' 3D air/surface radar, two 'Strut Pair' air-search radars (*Novorossiysk* only), one 'Trap Door' SSM fire-control radar, two 'Head Light-C' SA-N-3 fire-control radars, two 'Pop Group' SA-N-4 or (*Novorossiysk* only) four 'Cross Sword' SA-N-9 fire-control radars, two 'Owl Screech' 76-mm gun fire-control radars, four 'Bass Tilt' CIWS fire-control radars, one 'Top Knot' aircraft-control radar, four 'Tee Plinth' or (*Novorossiysk* only) 'Tin Man' optronic trackers, one 'Don Kay' and two 'Palm Frond' or (*Novorossiysk* only) three 'Palm Frond' navigation radars, one 'Shot Dome' navigation radar, one low-frequency active search and attack hull sonar, one medium-frequency active search variable-depth sonar, one 'High Pole-A' and one 'High Pole-B' or (*Novorossiysk* only) one 'Salt Pot-A', one 'Salt Pot-B' and one 'Square Head' IFF systems, an extensive electronic warfare suite including eight (not in *Novorossiysk*) 'Bell Globe', four 'Rum Tub', two 'Bell Bash', four 'Bell Nip' and two (not in *Novorossiysk*) 'Cage Pot' antennae/housings, two twin chaff/flare launchers, one towed torpedo-decoy system, and a large variety of conventional and satellite communication and navigation systems including a 'Punch Bowl' antenna for SS-N-12 midcourse guidance update via satellite

Propulsion: eight boilers supplying steam to four sets of geared turbines delivering 150,000 kW (201,180 hp) to four shafts
Performance: maximum speed 32 kt; range 24,100 km (14,975 miles) at 18 kt or 7400 km (4,600 miles) at 30 kt
Complement: 1,200 excluding air group

Class
1. USSR

Name	Builder	Laid down	Commissioned
Kiev	Nikolayev South	Jul 1970	May 1975
Minsk	Nikolayev South	Dec 1972	Feb 1978
Novorossiysk	Nikolayev South	Oct 1975	Aug 1982

Note: These highly impressive ships are the largest combatants yet fielded by the USSR, and mark a new departure from Soviet norms as they indicate a tardy appreciation of the need for organic air capability in Soviet deep-water battle groups. The type possesses a high level of capability in several roles, but is also being used for the development of the various systems required for a fully fledged aircraft-carrier type able to operate conventional rather than STOVL aircraft. The sensor and weapon fits have been considerably improved in the third vessel, which is a hybrid type combining features of the 'Kiev' and 'Kiev (Modified)' classes. The flightdeck is angled at 4·5° and served by two lifts. The Soviets initially classified the type as an anti-submarine cruiser, since modified to tactical aircraft-carrying cruiser.

'Kiev (Modified)' class CVG

(USSR)

Type: multi-role hybrid aircraft-carrier/guided-missile cruiser
Displacement: 30,000 tons standard and 37,100 tons full load
Dimensions: length 273·0 m (895·7 ft); beam 32·7 m (107·3 ft) and width 47·2 m (154·8 ft); draught 10·0 m (32·8 ft); flightdeck length 189·0 m (620·0 ft) and width 20·7 m (68·0 ft) with fore and aft lateral extensions to the maximum width of each ship
Gun armament: two 100-mm (3·93-in) L/70 DP in single mountings, and eight 30-mm ADGM-630 CIWS mountings
Missile armament: six twin container-launchers for 28 SS-N-12 'Sandbox' anti-ship missiles, and four groups of six octuple vertical launchers for 192 SA-N-9 SAMs
Torpedo armament: none
Anti-submarine armament: two new RBU-series 10-barrel rocket-launchers, and helicopter-launched weapons (see below)
Aircraft: typically 32, comprising 13 fixed-wing (12 Yakovlev Yak-38 'Forger-As' and one Yak-38 'Forger-B') and 19 rotary-wing (16 Kamov Ka-27 'Helix-As' and three Ka-27 'Helix-Bs')
Electronics: one 'Sky Watch' 3D surveillance radar with four planar arrays, one 'Cylinder Blanc' air-search radar, one 'Top Steer/Top Plate' 3D air/surface radar, two 'Strut Pair' air-search radars, one 'Trap Door' SSM fire-control radar, four 'Cross Sword' SAM fire-control radars, two 'Hawk Screech' 100-mm gun fire-control radars, four 'Bass Tilt' CIWS fire-control radars, one 'Top Knot' aircraft control radar, three 'Tin Man' optronic trackers, three 'Palm Frond' navigation radars, one 'Shot Dome' navigation radar, one low-frequency active search and attack hull sonar, one medium-frequency active search variable-depth sonar, one 'Salt Pot-A', one 'Salt Pot-B' and one 'Cake Stand' IFF systems, an extensive electronic warfare suite including four 'Wine Flask', 12 'Bell' series and four 'Ball' series antennae/housings, two twin chaff/flare launchers, one towed torpedo-decoy system, and a large variety of conventional and satellite communication and navigation systems including two 'Punch Bowl' antennae for SS-N-12 midcourse guidance update via satellite and two 'Low Ball' satellite navigation systems
Propulsion: eight boilers supplying steam to four sets of geared turbines delivering 150,000 kW (201,180 hp) to four shafts
Performance: maximum speed 32 kt; range 24,100 km (14,975 miles) at 18 kt or 7400 km (4,600 miles) at 30 kt
Complement: 1,200 excluding air group

The *Baku* of the still more impressive 'Kiev (Modified)' class.

Note: This is a considerable improvement on the 'Kiev' class, the most obvious modifications being considerably improved electronics, revised gun and missile armament, alteration of the anti-submarine weapons, and deletion of the torpedo armament.

Class
1. USSR

Name	Builder	Laid down	Commissioned
Baku	Nikolayev South	Dec 1978	Jun 1987

'Kitty Hawk' class CV

(USA)

Type: multi-role aircraft-carrier

Displacement: (CV63) 60,100 tons standard and 81,125 tons full load, (CV64) 60,100 tons standard and 81,775 tons full load, and (CV66) 60,300 tons standard and 79,725 tons full load

Dimensions: length 1,046·0 ft (318·8 m); beam 129·5 ft (39·5 m) or (CV66) 130·0 ft (39·6 m); draught 37·0 ft (11·3 m); flightdeck length 1,046·0 ft (318·8 m) and width 252·0 ft (76·8 m)

Gun armament: three 20-mm Phalanx Mk 15 CIWS mountings

Missile armament: three Mk 29 octuple launchers for RIM-7 NATO Sea Sparrow SAMs

Torpedo armament: none

Anti-submarine armament: aircraft and helicopters (see below)

Aircraft: typically 90 in a multi-role carrier air wing with 20 Grumman F-14 Tomcat, 20 McDonnell Douglas F/A-18 Hornet, 20 Grumman A-6E Intruder, 5 Grumman EA-6B Prowler, 4 Grumman KA-6D Intruder, 5 Grumman E-2C Hawkeye and 10 Lockheed S-3A Viking fixed-wing aircraft, and six Sikorsky SH-3G/H Sea King helicopters

Electronics: one SPS-48C/E 3D radar, one SPS-49 long-range air-search radar, one SPS-65 low-level threat-warning radar, one SPS-67 surface-search radar, one SPN-64 navigation radar, four SPN-series carrier landing radars, one Mk 23 and two or (CV66) three Mk 57 radars used in conjunction with two or (CV66) three Mk 91 SAM fire-control systems, one Naval Tactical Data System, Link 11 and 14 data-links, one SLQ-29(V)3 ESM system with WLR-8 warning and SLQ-17 jamming elements, four Mk 36 Super RBOC chaff/flare launchers, one OE-82 satellite communications system, one WSC-3 satellite communications transceiver, one SSR-1 satellite communications receiver, and URN-25 TACAN

Propulsion: eight Foster-Wheeler boilers supplying steam to four sets of Westinghouse geared turbines delivering 280,000 hp (208,795 kW) to four shafts

Performance: maximum speed 32 kt; range 9,200 miles (14,805 km) at 20 kt

Complement: (CV63) 139+2,634, (CV64) 156+2,861 and (CV66) 152+2,811 plus an air group of 320+2,160

Class

1. USA

Name	No.	Builder	Laid down	Com-missioned
Kitty Hawk	CV63	New York SB	Dec 1956	Apr 1961
Constellation	CV64	New York NY	Sep 1957	Oct 1961
America	CV66	Newport News	Jan 1961	Jan 1965

Note: These are close relatives of the three 'John F. Kennedy' class aircraft-carriers, all four ships being variants of an improved 'Forrestal' class design with the island set farther aft. The ships each have an angled flightdeck served by four steam catapults and four deck-edge lifts, and like the *John F. Kennedy* are being fitted with a system to protect the magazines from ingress by sea-skimming anti-ship missiles.

Above and below left: The *America* of the 'Kitty Hawk' class, the overhead view revealing the angled flightdeck, four catapults and four lifts.

'Kremlin' or 'Tbilisi' class CVGN

(USSR)

Type: nuclear-powered multi-role aircraft-carrier

Displacement: 65,000 tons full load

Dimensions: length 300·0 m (984·2 ft); beam 38·0 m (124·7 ft); draught 11·0 m (36·1 ft); flightdeck length 300·0 m (984·2 ft) and width 73·0 m (239·5 ft)

Gun armament: includes 100-mm (3·93-in) L/70 DP in single mountings or 76-mm (3-in) L/60 DP in twin mountings, and hybrid 30-mm cannon/SA-19 missile CIWS systems

Missile armament: container-launchers for SS-N-19 'Shipwreck' anti-ship missiles, and four groups of six octuple vertical launchers for 192 SA-N-9 SAMs

Torpedo armament: none

Anti-submarine armament: two RBU-series rocket-launchers, and helicopter-launched weapons (see below)

Aircraft: about 50 fixed-wing aircraft and 20 Kamov Ka-27 'Helix' helicopters

Electronics: one 'Sky Watch' 3D surveillance radar with four planar arrays, one 'Plate Steer' air-search radar, one 'Strut Curve' surface-search radar, two or three 'Palm Frond' navigation radars, 'Kite Screech' or 'Owl Screech' gun fire-control radars, four 'Cross Sword' SAM fire-control radars, 'Tin Man' optronic trackers, 'Punch Bowl' SSM-guidance radars, 'Wine Flask' and 'Bell' series ESM antennae/housings, chaff/flare launchers, and other systems as yet unrevealed

Propulsion: probably two pressurized water-cooled reactors supplying steam to four sets of geared turbines delivering 150,000 kW (201,180 hp) to four shafts

Performance: maximum speed 32 kt

Complement: not revealed

Class

1. USSR

Name	Builder	Laid down	Commissioned
Tbilisi	Nikolayev South	Jan 1983	1990
Riga	Nikolayev South	Dec 1985	1992

Note: These useful nuclear-powered aircraft-carriers are due to enter service in the early 1990s and will provide Soviet deep-water battle groups with a true organic air component using conventional rather than STOVL aircraft. The flightdeck has a standard angled section, a forward 12° 'ski-jump', three lifts (two on the starboard edge of the deck and the third inboard of the island) and on the second ship an unknown number of steam catapults (possibly two). At the moment it is not known what aircraft the carriers will embark in their air groups, though it is likely that the *Tbilisi* will carry Yak-38s and the second ship a mixture of this type and its development, the Yak-41 with four-poster vectored-thrust to remove the need for lift jets.

Overleaf; An American impression of the possible appearance of the 'Kremlin' class carrier with a forward 'ski jump' and possible Yakovlev Yak-41 supersonic successor to the Yak-38 transonic carrierborne attack aeroplane.

'Majestic' class CVL

(UK/India)

Type: light aircraft-carrier

Displacement: 16,000 tons standard and 19,500 tons full load

Dimensions: length 700·0 ft (213·4 m); beam 80·0 ft (24·4 m) and width 128·0 ft (39·0 m); draught 24·0 ft (7·3 m); flightdeck length 700·0 ft (213·4 m) and width 112·0 ft (34·1 m)

Gun armament: seven 40-mm Bofors L/70 AA in single mountings

Missile armament: none

Torpedo armament: none

Anti-submarine armament: aircraft and helicopters (see below)

Aircraft: six fixed-wing (BAe Sea Harrier FRS.Mk 51s) and nine rotary-wing (Westland Sea King Mk 42s)

Electronics: one LW-08 air-search radar, one DA-05 air/surface-search radar, one ZW-06 surface-search and navigation radar, one Type 963 aircraft landing radar, one IPN 10 action information system, and various communication and navigation systems

Propulsion: four Admiralty boilers supplying steam to two sets of Parsons geared turbines delivering 40,000 hp (29,830 kW) to two shafts

Performance: maximum speed 24·5 kt; range 13,800 miles (22,210 km) at 14 kt or 7,150 miles (11,505 km) at 23 kt

Complement: 1,075 in time of peace and 1,345 in time of war

Class

1. India

Name	No.	Builder	Laid down	Com-missioned
Vikrant	R11	Vickers-Armstrongs	Oct 1943	Mar 1961

Note: This ship was transferred from the UK in 1957, and has since been modified considerably from the original form. The ship now has an angled flightdeck served by two lifts. The ship has recently been fitted with a 6° 'ski-jump' to facilitate Sea Harrier operations, this requiring the removal of the steam catapult previously used for launch of the ship's flight of four Dassault-Breguet Alizé anti-submarine aircraft.

'Midway' class CV

(USA)

Type: multi-role aircraft-carrier

Displacement: 51,000 tons or (CV43) 52,500 tons standard and 64,000 tons or (CV43) 65,240 tons full load

Dimensions: length 979·0 ft (298·4 m); beam 121·0 ft (36·9 m) or (CV43) 145·9 ft (44·5 m); draught 35·3 ft (10·8 m); flightdeck length 979·0 ft (298·4 m) and width 238·0 ft (72·5 m)

Gun armament: three 20-mm Phalanx Mk 15 CIWS mountings

Missile armament: two Mk 25 octuple launchers for RIM-7 Sea Sparrow SAMs (CV41 only)

Torpedo armament: none

Anti-submarine armament: aircraft and helicopters (see below)

Aircraft: typically 66 in a multi-role carrier air wing with 36 McDonnell Douglas F/A-18 Hornet, 12 Grummam A-6E Intruder or Vought A-7E Corsair II, 4 Grumman KA-6D Intruder, 4 Grumman EA-6B Prowler and 4 Grumman E-2C Hawkeye fixed-wing aircraft, and six Sikorsky SH-3H Sea King helicopters

Electronics: one SPS-48C/E 3D radar, one SPS-49 long-range air-search radar, one SPS-67 surface-search radar, one SPS-64 navigation radar, three SPN-series aircraft landing radars, two Mk 57 radars used in conjunction with two Mk 115 SAM fire-control systems, Naval Tactical Data System, Link 11 and 14 data-links, one SLQ-17(V) or SLQ-29 ESM system with WLR-1, WLR-10 and WLR-11 warning elements and ULQ-6 jamming element, four Mk 36 Super RBOC chaff/flare launchers, one OE-82 satellite communications system, one WSC-3 satellite communications transceiver, one SSR-1 satellite communications receiver, and URN-25 TACAN

Propulsion: 12 Babcock & Wilcox boilers supplying steam to four sets of Westinghouse geared turbines delivering 212,000 hp (158,090 kW) to four shafts

Performance: maximum speed 30 kt; range 17,275 miles (27,800 km) at 15 kt

Complement: 142 + 2,684 plus an air group of 1,854, or (CV43) 145 + 2,357 plus an air group of 2,229

Class

1. USA

Name	No.	Builder	Laid down	Com-missioned
Midway	CV41	Newport News	Oct 1943	Sep 1945
Coral Sea	CV43	Newport News	Jul 1944	Oct 1947

Note: These are the two surviving units of a three-strong class that was the largest type of aircraft-carrier built in World War II. After the war both ships were gradually stripped of most of their considerable gun armaments, and then revised with an angled flightdeck served by three deck-edge lifts and two (CV41) or three (CV43) steam catapults. *Coral Sea's* last refit resulted in the addition of large external blisters to improve buoyancy and thus enhance seaworthiness, but an unfortunate side effect has been a livelier roll rate and therefore an increase in the difficulty of recovering aircraft in poor weather conditions.

'Moskva' class CVHS

(USSR)

Type: anti-submarine helicopter-carrier

Displacement: 14,000 tons standard and 17,500 tons full load

Dimensions: length 189·0 m (620·1 ft); beam 23·0 m (75·4 ft) and width 34·0 m (111·5 ft); draught 10·0 m (32·8 ft); flightdeck length 81·0 m (265·7 ft) and width 34·0 m (111·5 ft)

Gun armament: four 57-mm L/80 AA in two twin mountings

Missile armament: two twin launchers for 48 SA-N-3 'Goblet' SAMs

Torpedo armament: none

Anti-submarine armament: one SUW-N-1 twin launcher for 18 FRAS-1 missiles, two RBU 6000 12-barrel rocket-launchers, and helicopter-launched weapons (see below)

Aircraft: 14 Kamov Ka-25 'Hormone-A' or Ka-27 'Helix-A' helicopters

Electronics: one 'Top Sail' 3D radar, one 'Head Net-C' air-search radar, two 'Don-2' surface-search and navigation radars, two 'Head Light-C' SAM-control radars, two 'Muff Cob' AA gun-control radars, one low-frequency search and attack hull sonar, one medium-frequency active variable-depth sonar, a very extensive ESM system including eight 'Side Globe', two 'Bell Clout', two 'Bell Slam' and four 'Bell Tap' antennae/housings, two twin chaff launchers, and one 'High Pole-A' and one 'High Pole-B' or (*Leningrad*) 'Salt Pot' IFF systems

Propulsion: four boilers supplying steam to two sets of geared turbines delivering 75,000 kW (100,590 hp) to two shafts

Performance: maximum speed 31 kt; range 16,675 km (10,360 miles) at 18 kt or 5200 km (3,230 miles) at 30 kt

Complement: 840 excluding air group

Above: The *Coral Sea* is one of two surviving members of a three-strong class built in World War II and still effective in secondary theatres.

Above: The *Moskva* is an interesting hybrid with a large helicopter deck aft and gun/missile/anti-submarine armament forward of the superstructure.

Note: Of a hybrid design employing features of helicopter-carrier and missile cruiser designs, the two 'Moskva' class ships are used mainly to provide Soviet navy battle groups with command and anti-submarine capabilities during out-of-area deployments, and have also generated much useful data about the operation of substantial helicopter forces on major warships.

Class
1. USSR

Name	Builder	Laid down	Commissioned
Moskva	Nikolayev South	1962	May 1967
Leningrad	Nikolayev South	1964	1968

'Nimitz' class CVN

(USA)

Type: nuclear-powered multi-role aircraft-carrier

Displacement: 81,600 tons standard and 90,945 tons or (CVN71/75) 91,485 tons full load

Dimensions: length 1,092·0 ft (332·9 m); beam 134·0 ft (40·8 m); draught 37·0 ft (11·2 m) or (CVN71/75) 38·7 ft (11·8 m); flightdeck length 1,092·0 ft (332·9 m) and width 252·0 ft (76·8 m) or (CVN71/75) 257·0 ft (78·4 m)

Gun armament: three or four (CVN70/75) 20-mm Phalanx Mk 15 CIWS mountings

Missile armament: three Mk 29 octuple launchers for RIM-7 Sea Sparrow SAMs

Torpedo armament: none

Anti-submarine armament: aircraft and helicopters (see below)

Aircraft: typically 91 in a multi-role carrier air wing with 20 Grumman F-14 Tomcat, 20 McDonnell Douglas F/A-18 Hornet, 6 Grumman EA-6B Prowler, 4 Grumman KA-6D Intruder, 20 Grumman A-6E Intruder or Vought A-7E Corsair II, 5 Grumman E-2C Hawkeye and 10 Lockheed S-3A Viking fixed-wing aircraft, and 6 Sikorsky SH-3G/H Sea King helicopters

Above: The Grumman F-14 Tomcat is the US Navy's prime carrier-borne fighter. Below: Nuclear-powered carriers such as the *Nimitz* are limited not by ship's fuel but rather by 'consumables' such as aircraft warloads and fuel.

Armour: belt 2·5 in (63·5 mm) over certain areas, plus box protection for the magazines and machinery spaces

Electronics: one SPS-48 3D radar (SPS-48B in CVN68/71 and SPS-48E in CVN72/75), one SPS-49 long-range air-search radar, one SPS-67(V) surface-search radar, one SPN-64 or (CVN70/75) LN-66 navigation radar, four SPN-series aircraft landing radars, one Mk 23 and six Mk 57 radars used in conjunction with three Mk 91 SAM fire-control systems, Naval Tactical Data System, Link 11 and 14 data-links, one SLQ-29(V)3 ESM system with WLR-8 warning and SLQ-17AV jamming elements, four Mk 36 Super RBOC chaff/flare launchers, one OE-82 satellite communications system, one WSC-3 satellite communications transceiver, one SSR-1 satellite communications receiver, and URN-25 TACAN

Propulsion: two Westinghouse A4W or General Electric A1G pressurized water-cooled reactors supplying steam to four sets of geared turbines delivering 260,000 hp (193,880 kW) to four shafts

Performance: maximum speed 30 + kt

Complement: 155 + 2,981 plus an air group of 366 + 2,434

Class

1. USA

Name	No.	Builder	Laid down	Com-missioned
Nimitz	CVN68	Newport News	Jun 1968	May 1975
Dwight D. Eisenhower	CVN69	Newport News	Aug 1970	Oct 1977
Carl Vinson	CVN70	Newport News	Oct 1975	Feb 1982
Theodore Roosevelt	CVN71	Newport News	Oct 1981	Oct 1986
Abraham Lincoln	CVN72	Newport News	Nov 1984	Dec 1989
George Washington	CVN73	Newport News	Aug 1986	Dec 1991
John C. Stennis	CVN74	Newport News	1991	1998
	CVN75	Newport News	1992	1998

Note: These are without doubt the world's most powerful surface combatants, and a total of eight is planned to provide the backbone of the US Navy's carrier battle groups until well into the next century. The large angled flightdeck of each ship is served by four deck-edge lifts (three to starboard and one to port) as well as by four steam catapults (two on the forward section of the deck and the other two on the angled section). Each ship carries sufficient aviation consumables (fuel and weapons) for 16 days of sustained operations, volume for the additional four days' worth of consumables (by comparison with the 'Enterprise' class design) resulting from the considerably more compact reactor design. From CVN70 onwards the ships are fitted with an anti-submarine warfare control centre to make these ships into attack and ASW aircraft-carriers, and such facilities are to be retrofitted in CVN68 and CVN69.

Nothing is more indicative of the *Abraham Lincoln's* huge bulk than the diminutive size of the people in the quayside crowd and on the three lifts.

'Principe de Asturias' class CVL

(Spain)

Type: light aircraft-carrier

Displacement: 14,700 tons standard and 16,700 tons full load

Dimensions: length 195·9 m (642·7 ft); beam 24·3 m (79·7 ft) and width 32·0 m (105·0 ft); draught 9·4 m (30·8 ft); flightdeck length 175·0 m (574·0 ft) and width 27·0 (88·6 ft)

Gun armament: four 20-mm Meroka CIWS mountings

Missile armament: none

Torpedo armament: none

Anti-submarine armament: none

Aircraft: typically 24 with between 6 and 12 BAe/McDonnell Douglas AV-8B Harrier II fixed-wing aircraft plus between 2 and 4 Agusta (Bell) AB.212, between 6 and 10 Sikorsky SH-3 Sea King, and two Sikorsky S-70L Seahawk helicopters

Electronics: one SPS-52D 3D air-search radar, one SPS-55 surface-search radar, one SPN-35A aircraft landing radar, one RTN 11L/X missile-warning radar, four VPS-2 Meroka fire-control radars, one Naval Tactical Data System, Link 11 and 14 data-links, one Nettuno ESM system with warning and jamming elements, one SLQ-25 Nixie towed torpedo-decoy system, two Prairie/Masker hull/propeller blade noise suppressors, four Mk 36 Super RBOC chaff/flare launchers, and URN-22 TACAN

Propulsion: COGAG arrangement, with two General Electric LM2500 gas turbines delivering 46,400 hp (34,600 kW) to two shafts

Performance: maximum speed 26 kt; range 12,000 km (7,455 miles) at 20 kt

Complement: 90 + 465 plus 208 air group and flag staff

Class

1. Spain			Laid	Com-
Name	No.	Builder	down	missioned
Principe de Asturias	R11	Bazan	Oct 1979	May 1988

Note: Designed to replace the now-deleted *Dedalo*, this singleton ship is based on the US Navy's abortive Sea Control Ship design, and has a 12° 'ski-jump' and two lifts. The aircraft complement can be increased to 37 in time of war.

'Iowa' class BB

(USA)

Type: battleship

Displacement: 45,000 tons standard and 57,355 tons full load

Dimensions: length 887·2 ft (270·4 m); beam 108·2 ft (33·0 m); draught 38·0 ft (11·6 m)

Gun armament: nine 16-in (406-mm) L/50 in three Mk 7 triple mountings, 12 5-in (127-mm) L/38 DP in six Mk 28 twin mountings, and four 20-mm Phalanx Mk 16 CIWS mountings

Missile armament: eight quadruple Armored Box Launchers Mk 143 for 32 BGM-109 Tomahawk land-attack and anti-ship cruise missiles, and four quadruple Mk 141 container-launchers for 16 RGM-84 Harpoon anti-ship missiles

Torpedo armament: none

Anti-submarine armament: none

Aircraft: provision for three or four Kaman SH-60F/G Seasprite or Sikorsky SH-60B Seahawk helicopters on a platform aft

Armour: belt 13·5/1·62 in (343/41 mm), decks 6 in (152 mm), turrets 17/7·25 in (432/184 mm), barbettes 17·3 in (439 mm), and conning tower 17·5/7·25 in (445/184 mm)

Electronics: one SPS-49(V) long-range air-search radar, one SPS-67(V) medium-range air/surface-search radar, one SPS-10F surface-search radar, one SPN-64 navigation radar, one SPG-53F and two Mk 25 radars used in conjunction with three Mk 37 5-in gun directors, two Mk 13 radars used in conjunction with two Mk 38 5-in gun directors and one Mk 27 radar used in conjunction with one Mk 40 5-in gun director all controlled by the Mk 160 fire-control system with SKY-1 digital computing, one Combat Engagement Center, Link 1 data link, one SLQ-32(V)3 ESM system with warning and jamming elements, eight Mk 36 Super RBOC chaff/flare launchers, one SLQ-25 Nixie towed torpedo-decoy system, one OE-82 satellite communications system, three WSC-3 satellite communications transceivers, and one SSR-1 satellite communications receiver

Propulsion: eight Babcock & Wilcox boilers supplying steam to four sets of geared turbines (General Electric in BB61 and 63, and Westinghouse in BB62 and 64) delivering 212,000 hp (158,090 kW) to four shafts

Performance: maximum speed 35 kt; range 17,275 miles (27,800 km) at 17 kt and 5,750 miles (9250 km) at 30 kt

Complement: 65 + 1,453

Right and below: The ships of the 'Iowa' class are potent projectors of American power, mainly in secondary theatres, but even so it was decided in 1990 that two of the ships would be placed in reserve.

Class

1. USA Name	No.	Builder	Laid down	Commissioned
Iowa	BB61	New York NY	Jun 1940	Feb 1943
New Jersey	BB62	Philadelphia NY	Sep 1940	May 1943
Missouri	BB63	New York NY	Jan 1941	Jun 1944
Wisconsin	BB64	Philadelphia NY	Jan 1941	Apr 1944

Note: Though these four ships were mothballed from shortly after the end of World War II, with brief operational excursions for all four in the Korean War and for *New Jersey* in the Vietnam War, the development of the Soviet navy's long-range surface capability in the 1970s prompted a reappraisal of the battleship's role. This reappraisal led to the conclusion that the battleship still had much to offer in terms of speed, protection and the ability to accommodate modern missiles and electronic features without detriment to the massive conventional firepower that offered such advantages in support of amphibious operations. It was decided, therefore, to recommission all four units as extensively modernized command and support ships for amphibious forces: the ships were recommissioned in April 1984, December 1982, May 1986 and October 1988 respectively, and now serve mainly as the core of surface battle groups in areas where the full capability of modern air and missile powers are unlikely to be found.

'Kirov' class CBGN

(USSR)

Type: nuclear-powered guided-missile battle-cruiser
Displacement: 19,000 tons standard and 23,400 tons full load
Dimensions: length 247·5 m (812·0 ft); beam 28·5 m (93·5 ft); draught 9·1 m (29·9 ft)
Gun armament: (Kirov) two 100-mm (3·93-in) L/70 DP in single mountings or (others) two 130-mm (5·12-in) L/70 DP in one twin mounting, and eight 30-mm ADGM-630 CIWS mountings or (in Kalinin) six combined gun/ missile-launcher mountings
Missile armament: 20 vertical launch tubes for 20 SS-N-19 'Shipwreck' anti-ship missiles, two twin launchers for 40 SA-N-4 'Gecko' SAMs, 12 octuple vertical launchers for 96 SA-N-6 'Grumble' SAMs, and (not in Kirov) three groups (one of eight and two of four) of quadruple vertical launchers for 64 SA-N-9 SAMs
Torpedo armament: two quintuple 533-mm (21-in) mountings for Type 53 dual-role torpedoes
Anti-submarine armament: one twin launcher for 14 SS-N-14 'Silex' missiles (in Kirov), one RBU 6000 12-barrel or (in Kalinin) one new RBU-series 10-barrel rocket-launcher, two RBU 1000 six-barrel rocket-launchers, torpedoes (see above) and helicopter-launched weapons (see below)
Aircraft: three Kamov Ka-25 'Hormone-A/B' (Kirov) or Ka-27 'Helix-A/B' helicopters in a hangar aft''
Electronics: one 'Top Pair' ('Top Sail/Big Net') 3D radar, one 'Top Steer' or (in Kalinin) 'Top Plate' air/sea surveillance radar, three 'Palm Frond' surface-search and navigation radars, two 'Eye Bowl' SS-N-14 control radars (in Kirov only), two 'Pop Group' SA-N-4 control radars, two 'Top Dome' SA-N-6 control radars, four 'Cross Sword' SA-N-9 control radars (not in Kirov), one 'Kite Screech' main armament gun-control radar, four 'Bass Tilt' CIWS control radars (not in Kalinin), four 'Tin Man' optronic trackers, one 'Flyscreen' helicopter-control radar, one low-frequency active search and attack bow sonar, one medium-frequency active search and attack variable-depth sonar, an extremely extensive ESM system including eight 'Side Globe' and four 'Rum Tub' (in Kirov) or eight 'Foot Ball' and 10 'Bell' series housings, two 'Round House' TACAN, two 'Vee Tube-C' (in Kirov) communications antennae or two 'Big Ball' satellite communications systems, two 'Punch Ball' (in Kirov) or 'Big Ball' satellite navigation systems, two chaff/flare launchers, and two 'High Pole-B' (in Kirov) or 'Salt Pot-A/B' IFF systems
Propulsion: two pressurized water-cooled reactors and an unknown number of oil-fired superheating boilers supplying steam to two sets of geared turbines delivering 111,850 kW (150,015 hp) to two shafts
Performance: maximum speed 32 kt; range 26,000 km (16,155 miles) at 33 kt
Complement: 840

Class

1. USSR

Name	Builder	Laid down	Commissioned
Kirov	Baltic Yard 189	Jun 1973	Jul 1980
Frunze	Baltic Yard 189	Dec 1977	Nov 1983
Kalinin	Baltic Yard 189	May 1983	Oct 1988
	Baltic Yard 189	Apr 1986	1991

Note: These are exceptionally powerful missile cruisers of a new concept and size, powered by a hybrid propulsion system of novel type with oil-fired boilers to superheat the steam provided from the nuclear reactors. The four units are fitted out with extensive electronics and the command facilities to serve as escorts for the USSR's new breed of aircraft-carriers or as leaders of detached battle groups. They sport the whole range of weapons needed for the gamut of surface-to-surface, surface-to-underwater and surface-to-air tasks. Their one real limitation is lack of large-calibre gun armament, a fact that precludes their use in the gunfire support of amphibious landings. However, while the Kirov is clearly optimized for the anti-submarine role with a large number of the powerful SS-N-14 missiles, the later units have been modified for a higher level of air-defence capability with the SA-N-9 missile. The third unit, Kalinin, has an improved electronic fit with planar arrays and, in replacement for the eight CIWS mountings of the first two units, six radar-controlled combined gun/missile-launcher mountings, each mounting probably being capable of autonomous operation with two 30-mm 'Gatling' type cannon for last-ditch engagement of targets that have evaded the same mounting's maximum of eight point-defence missiles, which are probably navalized versions of a land system such as the SA-18. It is anticipated that the fourth unit will resemble Kalinin.

The large area forward of the bridge of the two later 'Kirov' class battle-cruisers is devoted to vertical-launch silos for SS-N-19 anti-ship missiles, SA-N-6 SAMs and, on the forecastle, SA-N-9 SAMs.

'Andréa Doria' class CG

(Italy)

Type: anti-submarine and anti-aircraft guided-missile escort cruiser
Displacement: 5,000 tons standard and 7,300 tons full load
Dimensions: length 149·3 m (489·8 ft); beam 17·2 m (56·4 ft); draught 5·0 m (16·4 ft)
Gun armament: eight or (C554) six 76-mm (3-in) L/62 DP in OTO Melara single mountings
Missile armament: one twin launcher for 40 RIM-67A Standard SM-1 ER SAMs
Torpedo armament: none
Anti-submarine armament: two Mk 32 triple 12·75-in (324-mm) mountings for Mk 46 torpedoes, and helicopter-launched weapons (see below)
Aircraft: four or (C554) two Agusta (Bell) AB.212ASW helicopters in a hangar aft
Electronics: one SPS-39 3D radar, one RAN 3L long-range air/surface-search radar, two SPG-55C radars used in conjunction with the Mk 76 SAM fire-control system, four or (C554) three RTN 10X radars used in conjunction with four or (C554) three Argo NA9 gun fire-control systems, one 3RM 20 navigation radar, one SQS-23F or (C554) SQS-39 long-range active/passive search and attack hull sonar, one SADOC 1 action information system, one ESM system with warning and jamming elements, two SCLAR chaff/flare launchers, and (C553 only) URN-20 TACAN
Propulsion: four Foster-Wheeler boilers supplying steam to two sets of geared turbines (CNR in C553 and Ansaldo in C554) delivering 44,750 kW (60,020 hp) to two shafts
Performance: maximum speed 31 kt; range 9250 km (5,750 miles) at 17 kt
Complement: 45 + 425

The *Caio Duilio* differs from her sistership in details that include six rather than eight main guns and two rather than four helicopters.

Class

1. Italy			Laid	Com-
Name	No.	Builder	down	missioned
Andrea Doria	C553	CNR	May 1958	Feb 1964
Caio Duilio	C554	Navalmeccanica	May 1958	Nov 1964

Note: Designed specifically for Mediterranean operations, these interesting ships are in essence small helicopter carriers, though the helicopter facility is somewhat cramped at a length of 30 m (98·5 ft) and width of 16 m (52 ft), with electronics and weapons for the surface-to-underwater and surface-to-air roles.

'Bainbridge' class CGN

(USA)

Type: nuclear-powered anti-aircraft and anti-ship guided-missile escort cruiser
Displacement: 7,700 tons standard and 8,590 tons full load
Dimensions: length 565·0 ft (172·3 m); beam 57·9 ft (17·6 m); draught 29·0 ft (8·8 m)
Gun armament: two 20-mm Phalanx Mk 16 CIWS mountings
Missile armament: two Mk 141 quadruple container-launchers for eight RGM-84 Harpoon anti-ship missiles, and two Mk 10 twin launchers for 80 RIM-67B Standard SM-2 ER SAMs
Torpedo armament: none
Anti-submarine armament: one Mk 16 octuple launcher for eight RUR-5A ASROC anti-submarine missiles, and two Mk 32 triple 12·75-in (324-mm) mountings for Mk 46 torpedoes
Aircraft: provision for one helicopter on a platform aft
Electronics: one SPS-48E 3D radar, one SPS-49 long-range air-search radar, one SPS-67 surface-search radar, one LN-66 navigation radar, four SPG-55C illumination and guidance radars used in conjunction with four Mk 76 SAM

The provision of two Mk 10 twin launchers gives the *Bainbridge* a double-ended SAM capability supported by four dedicated SPG-51 radars.

fire-control systems, one Mk 14 weapon direction system, one SQQ-23A active/passive long-range search and attack bow sonar and one BQR-20A sonar receiver used in conjunction with one Mk 111 underwater weapons fire-control system, Naval Tactical Data System, one SLQ-32(V)3 ESM system with one WLR-1 warning and one jamming element, four Mk 36 Super RBOC chaff/flare launchers, one OE-82 satellite communications system, three WSC-3 satellite communications transceivers, one SRR-1 satellite communications receiver, and URN-25 TACAN
Propulsion: two General Electric D2G pressurized water-cooled reactors supplying steam to two sets of geared turbines delivering 70,000 hp (52,190 kW) to two shafts
Performance: maximum speed 38 kt
Complement: 42 + 516 plus provision for 6 + 12 flag staff

Class

1. USA			Laid	Com-
Name	No.	Builder	down	missioned
Bainbridge	CGN25	Bethlehem Steel	May 1959	Oct 1962

Note: This is a nuclear-powered version of the 'Leahy' class cruisers, the double ended missile layout and four guidance systems allowing for the simultaneous engagement of four target aircraft. The type also possesses good anti-submarine capability marred only by the absence of an embarked helicopter.

'Belknap' class CG

(USA)

Type: anti-aircraft, anti-submarine and anti-ship guided-missile escort cruiser

Displacement: 6,570 tons standard and (CG26/28) 8,200 tons, (CG229/33) 8,065 tons or (CG34) or 8,250 tons full load

Dimensions: length 547·0 ft (166·7 m); beam 54·8 ft (16·7 m); draught 28·8 ft (8·8 m)

Gun armament: one 5-in (127-mm) L/54 DP in a Mk 42 mounting, and two 20-mm Phalanx Mk 16 CIWS mountings

Missile armament: two Mk 141 quadruple container-launchers for eight RGM-84 Harpoon anti-ship missiles, one Mk 10 twin launcher for 40 RIM-67B Standard SM-2 ER SAMs, and (possibly to be retrofitted) BGM-109 Tomahawk cruise missiles

Torpedo armament: none

Anti-submarine armament: two Mk 32 triple 12·75-in (324-mm) mountings for Mk 46 torpedoes, up to 20 RUR-5A ASROC missiles fired from the Mk 10 launcher, and helicopter-launched weapons (see below)

Aircraft: one Kaman SH-2F Seasprite helicopter in a hangar aft

Electronics: one SPS-48C 3D radar, one SPS-49(V)3 or (CG31/34) SPS-40 long-range air-search radar, one SPS-67 surface-search radar, one LN-66 navigation radar, two SPG-55B illumination and guidance radars used in conjunction with two Mk 76 SAM fire-control systems, one Mk 7 or (CG28/34) Mk 11 weapon direction system (being replaced by one Mk 14 weapon direction system), one SPG-53F radar used in conjunction with one Mk 68 gun fire-control system, one SQS-53C (CG26) or SQS-26 active/passive search and attack bow sonar used in conjunction with one Mk 116 (CG26) or Mk 114 underwater weapons fire-control system, Naval Tactical Data System, one SLQ-32(V)3 ESM system with warning and jamming elements, four Mk 36 Super RBOC chaff/flare launchers, one OE-82 satellite communications system, four or (CG30) one WSC-3 satellite communications transceiver, SRR-1 satellite communications receiver, and URN-25 or SRN-6 TACAN

Propulsion: four Babcock & Wilcox or (CG29/31) Combustion Engineering boilers supplying steam to two sets of General Electric or (CG29/31 and 33) De Laval geared turbines delivering 85,000 hp (63,385 kW) to two shafts

Performance: maximum speed 32·5 kt; range 8,175 miles (13,155 km) at 20 kt

Complement: 26 + 454 and (CG26) plus provision for 6 + 12 flag staff

Right: The *Jouett* is the fourth of the important 'Belknap' class cruisers.

Below: The *Josephus Daniels* reveals its forward SAM launcher.

Class 1. USA Name	No.	Builder	Laid down	Com- missioned
Belknap	CG26	Bath Iron Works	Feb 1962	Nov 1964
Josephus Daniels	CG27	Bath Iron Works	Apr 1962	May 1965
Wainwright	CG28	Bath Iron Works	Jul 1962	Jan 1966
Jouett	CG29	Puget Sound NY	Sep 1962	Dec 1966
Horne	CG30	San Francisco NY	Dec 1962	Apr 1967
Sterett	CG31	Puget Sound NY	Sep 1962	Apr 1967
William H. Standley	CG32	Bath Iron Works	Jul 1963	Jul 1966
Fox	CG33	Todd Shipyard	Jan 1963	May 1966
Biddle	CG34	Bath Iron Works	Dec 1963	Jan 1967

Note: These ships were finally built only after a tortuous design phase and have since been used for a host of trials purposes. They were designed principally for the surface-to-underwater and surface-to-air escort of aircraft-carriers, but are limited in the former role by carrying only one LAMPS I helicopter and in the latter role by being single-ended ships able to engage only two targets simultaneously. In recent years the ships have been made more balanced in overall terms by the addition of Harpoon anti-ship missiles for a useful surface-to-surface capability. A limited upgrade is being undertaken with SPS-48E 3D radar, the Mk 14 weapon direction system and the SYS-2 action information system.

'California' class CGN

(USA)
Type: nuclear-powered anti-submarine, anti-ship and anti-aircraft guided-missile escort cruiser
Displacement: 9,560 tons standard and 9,475 or (CGN36) 10,450 tons full load
Dimensions: length 596·0 ft (181·7 m); beam 61·0 ft (18·6 m); draught 31·5 ft (9·6 m)
Gun armament: two 5-in (127-mm) L/54 DP in Mk 45 single mountings, and two 20-mm Phalanx Mk 16 CIWS mountings
Missile armament: two Mk 141 quadruple container-launchers for eight RGM-84 Harpoon anti-ship missiles, and two Mk 13 single launchers for 80 RIM-66B Standard SM-1 MR SAMs
Torpedo armament: none
Anti-submarine armament: one Mk 16 octuple launcher for eight RUR-5A ASROC anti-submarine missiles, and two Mk 32 twin 12·75-in (324-mm) mountings for Mk 46 torpedoes
Aircraft: provision for one helicopter on a platform aft
Electronics: one SPS-48C/E 3D radar, one SPS-40B air-search radar, one SPS-10 or SPS-67 surface-search radar, one LN-66 navigation radar, four SPG-51D illumination and tracking radars used in conjunction with two Mk 74 SAM fire-control systems, one SPG-60 search-and-track radar and one SPQ-9A track-while-scan radar used in conjunction with one Mk 86 forward missile launcher/gun fire-control system, one Mk 11 (being replaced by Mk 13) weapon direction system, one SQS-26CX active/passive search and attack bow sonar used in conjunction with one Mk 114 underwater weapons fire-control system, Naval Tactical Data System, one T Mk 6 Fanfare torpedo decoy system, one SLQ-32(V)3 ESM system with warning and jamming elements, four Mk 36 Super RBOC chaff/flare launchers, one OE-82 satellite communications system, four WSC-3 satellite communications transceivers, one SRR-1 satellite communications receiver, and URN-25 TACAN
Propulsion: two General Electric D2G pressurized water-cooled reactors supplying steam to two sets of geared turbines delivering 70,000 hp (52,190 kW) to two shafts
Performance: maximum speed 30 + kt
Complement: 44 + 559

Class
1. USA
Name	No.	Builder	Laid down	Commissioned
California	CGN36	Newport News	Jan 1970	Feb 1974
South Carolina	CGN37	Newport News	Dec 1970	Jan 1975

Note: This class was originally to have comprised five ships, but was curtailed so that additional financial and yard resources could be allocated to the more capable 'Virginia' class. The 'California' class is notable for its nuclear propulsion, whose cores have three times the life of those used in the preceding 'Bainbridge' class. At the operational level, however, the type suffers from its lack of an embarked helicopter for longer-range anti-submarine operations. Though four missile-control radars are carried, the use of two single-arm SAM launchers means that salvo rate is necessarily poor, which could have unfortunate consequences in the event of saturation air attack. It was planned to fit two quadruple Armored Box Launchers Mk 143 for eight BGM-109 Tomahawk land-attack cruise missiles, but topweight considerations led to the abandonment of this scheme. A limited upgrade programme is to replace the SPS-40B radar with SPS-49 radar, the Mk 11 weapon direction system with the Mk 14 system, and improve the SPG-51D radars and associated Mk 74 fire-control systems.

USS *South Carolina* of the US 6th Fleet.

'Colbert' class CG

(France)
Type: anti-aircraft and anti-ship guided-missile escort cruiser
Displacement: 8,500 tons standard and 11,300 tons full load
Dimensions: length 180·8 m (593·2 ft); beam 20·2 m (66·1 ft); draught 7·7 m (25·2 ft)
Gun armament: two 100-mm (3·9-in) Creusot Loire L/55 DP in Modèle 1968 single mountings, and 12 57-mm Bofors L/60 AA in six Modèle 1951 twin mountings
Missile armament: four container-launchers for four MM.38 Exocet anti-ship missiles, and one twin launcher for 48 Masurca SAMs
Torpedo armament: none
Anti-submarine armament: none
Aircraft: provision for a helicopter on a platform aft
Armour: belt 50/80 mm (2/3·15 in), and deck 50 mm (2 in)
Electronics: one DRBV 23C air-search radar, one DRBV 20C air-warning radar, one DRBI 10D height-finding radar, one DRBV 50 air/surface-search radar, two DRBR 51 SAM illumination and tracking radars, one DRBC 32C 100-mm gun fire-control radar, two DRBC 31 57-mm gun fire-control radars, one RM416 navigation radar, one SENIT 1 action information system, one ESM system with ARBR 10F warning and ARBB 31/32 jamming elements, one Syracuse satellite communications system, two Syllex chaff launchers, and URN-20 TACAN
Propulsion: four Indret boilers supplying steam to two sets of CEM/Parsons geared turbines delivering 64,000 kW (85,385 hp) to two shafts
Performance: maximum speed 31·5 kt; range 7400 km (4,600 miles) at 25 kt
Complement: 24 + 536

Class
1. France
Name	No.	Builder	Laid down	Commissioned
Colbert	C611	Brest ND	Dec 1953	May 1959

Note: This singleton unit was developed from the 'De Grasse' class design of the period just before World War II though of course considerably modernized, and is designed for area defence of major surface groups. The ship is extensively equipped for her primary role as flagship of the French Mediterranean fleet.

'Kara' class CG

(USSR)

Type: anti-submarine and anti-aircraft guided-missile cruiser

Displacement: 8,000 tons standard and 9,700 tons full load

Dimensions: length 173·2 m (568·0 ft); beam 18·6 m (61·0 ft); draught 6·7 m (22·0 ft)

Gun armament: four 76-mm (3-in) L/60 DP in two twin mountings, and four 30-mm ADGM-630 CIWS mountings

Missile armament: two twin launchers for 72 SA-N-3 'Goblet' SAMs and two twin launchers for 40 SA-N-4 'Gecko' SAMs, or (in *Azov*) one twin launcher for 36 SA-N-3 'Goblet' SAMS, two twin launchers for 40 SA-N-4 'Gecko' SAMs, and six twin vertical launchers for 24 SA-N-6 'Grumble' SAMs

Torpedo armament: two quintuple or (in *Azov*) twin 533-mm (21-in) mountings for Type 53 dual-role torpedoes

Anti-submarine armament: two quadruple container-launchers for eight SS-N-14 'Silex' anti-submarine missiles, torpedoes (see above), two RBU 6000 12-barrel rocket-launchers, two RBU 1000 six-barrel rocket-launchers, and helicopter-launched weapons (see below)

Aircraft: one Kamov Ka-25 'Hormone-A' or Ka-27 'Helix-A' helicopter in a hangar aft

Electronics: one 'Top Sail' or (in *Kerch*) one other 3D air-search radar, one 'Head Net-C' 3D air/surface-search radar (not in *Azov*), two 'Don Kay' or (in *Nikolayev*) 'Palm Frond' surface-search and navigation radars, one 'Don-2' navigation radar (not in *Azov*), two or (in *Azov*) one 'Head Light-C' SA-N-3 fire-control radar, two 'Pop Group' SA-N-4 fire-control radars, one 'Top Dome' SA-N-6 fire-control radar (in *Azov*), two 'Owl Screech' 76-mm gun fire-control radars, two 'Bass Tilt' 30-mm gun fire-control radars, two 'Tee Plinth' optronic directors, one low-frequency active/passive search and attack hull sonar, one medium-frequency active/passive variable-depth sonar, one BAT-1 torpedo decoy system, an extremely comprehensive ESM suite including eight 'Side Globe', two 'Bell Slam', one 'Bell Clout' and two 'Bell Tap' (in *Nikolayev* and *Ochakov*) or four 'Rum Tub' (in *Kerch*) antennae/housings, one 'High Pole-A' and one 'High Pole-B' or (in *Nikolayev*) one 'Salt Pot' and one 'Square Head' IFF systems, two twin chaff launchers, and one 'Fly Screen' or (in *Petropavlovsk*) two 'Round House' TACAN

Propulsion: COGOG arrangement, with four gas turbines delivering 89,400 kW (119,905 hp) or two gas turbines delivering 10,500 kW (14,080 hp) to two shafts

Performance: maximum speed 34 kt; range 18,500 km (11,495 miles) at 15 kt or 5500 km (3,420 miles) at 32 kt

Complement: 30 + 510

Class
1. USSR

Name	Builder	Laid down	Commissioned
Nikolayev	Nikolayev North	Jan 1969	Sep 1971
Ochakov	Nikolayev North	Mar 1970	Mar 1973
Kerch	Nikolayev North	Jun 1971	Sep 1974
Azov	Nikolayev North	Aug 1972	Nov 1975
Petropavlovsk	Nikolayev North	Nov 1973	Nov 1976
Tashkent	Nikolayev North	Jan 1975	Nov 1977
Tallinn	Nikolayev North	Dec 1975	Apr 1980

Note: Built at Nikolayev North, this class is essentially a refined and updated version of the 'Kresta II' class with COGOG propulsion, more advanced weapons and optimization for the anti-submarine role though still retaining a very useful air-defence capability, further enhanced in the revision to *Azov* completed during 1986. The ships also have good command facilities, and are thus well suited to lead anti-submarine task groups.

Left: The sole French cruiser *Colbert*.

Above: A frontal aspect of a Soviet Kara class.

'Krasina' or 'Slava' class CG

(USSR)
Type: anti-ship and anti-aircraft guided-missile cruiser
Displacement: 10,500 tons standard and 12,500 tons full load
Dimensions: length 187·0 m (613·5 ft); beam 20·0 m (65·6 ft); draught 7·6 m (25·0 ft)
Gun armament: two 130-mm (5·1-in) L/70 in one twin mounting, and six 30-mm ADGM-630 CIWS mountings
Missile armament: eight twin container-launchers for 16 SS-N-12 'Sandbox' anti-ship missiles, eight vertical octuple launchers for 64 SA-N-6 'Grumble' SAMs, and two twin launchers for 40 SA-N-4 'Gecko' SAMs
Torpedo armament: two quintuple 533-mm (21-in) mountings for Type 53 dual-role torpedoes
Anti-submarine armament: two RBU 6000 12-barrel rocket-launchers, and torpedoes (see above)
Aircraft: one Kamov Ka-25 'Hormone-B' missile-targeting helicopter
Electronics: one 'Top Pair' ('Top Sail/Big Net') 3D air-search radar, one 'Top Steer' 3D air/surface-search radar, three 'Palm Frond' surface-search and navigation radars, one 'Trap Door' ('Front Door/Front Piece') SS-N-12 fire-control radar, one 'Top Dome' SA-N-6 fire-control radar, two 'Pop Group' SA-N-4 fire-control radars, one 'Kite Screech' 130-mm gun fire-control radar, three 'Bass Tilt' CIWS fire-control radars, four 'Tee Plinth' optronic directors, one low-frequency active/passive search and attack hull sonar, one medium-frequency active/passive search variable-depth sonar, an extremely extensive ESM system including eight 'Side Globe', four 'Rum Tub' and several 'Bell' series antennae/housings, one IR surveillance system, two 'Punch Bowl' satellite data-receiving and missile-targeting systems, two twin chaff launchers, and one 'Salt Pot-A' and one 'Salt Pot-B' IFF systems
Propulsion: COGAG arrangement, with four gas turbines delivering about 90,000 kW (120,710 hp) to two shafts
Performance: maximum speed 34 kt; range 16,675 km (10,360 miles) at 15 kt or 4600 km (2,860 miles) at 30 kt
Complement: about 600

Class
1. USSR

Name	Builder	Laid down	Commissioned
Slava	61 Kommuna Yard, Nikolayev	1976	1982
Marshal Ustinov	61 Kommuna Yard, Nikolayev	1978	1986
Chervona Ukraina	61 Kommuna Yard, Nikolayev	1979	1988
	61 Kommuna Yard, Nikolayev	1988	

Note: Built in succession to the 'Kara' class at Nikolayev North, this highly impressive class has the same basic escort role as its predecessor type but features more advanced weapons (though centred on anti-ship missiles) and electronics on a development of the basic hull of the 'Kara' class. It was originally thought that the class would comprise eight units, but recent indications are that it will terminate with the fourth unit.

The *Slava* is lead ship of a notably capable cruiser class optimized for anti-ship and anti-air warfare with effective sensors and potent armament.

'Kresta I' class CG

(USSR)
Type: anti-ship and anti-submarine guided-missile cruiser
Displacement: 6,140 tons standard and 7,600 tons full load
Dimensions: length 155·5 m (510·0 ft); beam 17·0 m (55·7 ft); draught 6·0 m (19·7 ft)
Gun armament: four 57-mm L/80 DP in two twin mountings, and (in *Drozd*) four 30-mm ADGM-630 CIWS mountings
Missile armament: two twin container-launchers for four SS-N-3B 'Shaddock' anti-ship missiles, and two twin launchers for 32 or 44 SA-N-1 'Goa' SAMs
Torpedo armament: two quintuple 533-mm (21-in) mountings for Type 53 dual-role torpedoesG
Anti-submarine armament: torpedoes (see above), two RBU 6000 12-barrel rocket-launchers, and two RBU 1000 six-barrel rocket-launchers
Aircraft: one Kamov Ka-25 'Hormone-B' missile-targeting helicopter in a hangar aft
Electronics: one 'Head Net-C' 3D radar, one 'Big Net' air-search radar, two 'Plinth Net' surface-search radars, one 'Don 2' and one 'Don Kay' or (in *Admiral Zozulya*) two 'Palm Frond' navigation radar, one 'Scoop Pair' SSM fire-control radar, two 'Peel Group' SAM fire-control radars, two 'Muff Cob' 57-mm gun fire-control radars, two 'Bass Tilt' CIWS fire-control radars (in *Drozd*), one medium-frequency active/passive search and attack hull sonar, a comprehensive ESM suite including eight 'Side Globe', two 'Bell Slam', two 'Bell Tap', two 'Bell Strike' and several 'Bell Clout' antennae/housings, two twin chaff launchers, and one 'High Pole-B' IFF system
Propulsion: four boilers supplying steam to two sets of geared turbines delivering 82,000 kW (109,980 hp) to two shafts
Performance: maximum speed 35 kt; range 13,000 km (8,080 miles) at 18 kt, or 19,450 km (12,085 miles) at 14 kt or 3700 km (2,300 miles) at 32 kt
Complement: 360

Class
1. USSR

Name	Builder	Laid down	Commissioned
Admiral Zozulya	Zhdanov Yard	Sep 1964	Mar 1967
Vladivostok	Zhdanov Yard	1965	Jan 1968
Vitse-Admiral Drozd	Zhdanov Yard	1965	Aug 1968
Sevastopol	Zhdanov Yard	1966	Jul 1969

Note: This is essentially an interim type between the 'Kynda' class (optimized for the anti-ship role) and the 'Kresta II' class (optimized for the anti-submarine role). The 'Kresta I' is well provided for both roles, but is perhaps optimized for the anti-ship role with weapons that are now obsolescent. These were the first Soviet ships with full helicopter facilities, in this instance the 'Hormone-B' type required for midcourse guidance update of the long-range SS-N-3 missile without support from shore-based aircraft.

Watched by a US Navy escort, a 'Kresta I' class cruiser passes through Hawaiian waters. Notable is the mass of offensive and defensive electronic antennae on the ship's main, forward and after superstructure arrangements.

'Kresta II' class CG

(USSR)

Type: anti-submarine and anti-aircraft guided-missile cruiser

Displacement: 6,400 tons standard and 7,800 tons full load

Dimensions: length 158·5 m (520·0 ft); beam 16·9 m (55·45 ft); draught 6·0 m (19·7 ft)

Gun armament: four 57-mm L/80 DP in two twin mountings, and four 30-mm ADGM-630 CIWS mountings

Missile armament: two twin launchers for 48 SA-N-3 'Goblet' SAMs

Torpedo armament: two quintuple 533-mm (21-in) mountings for Type 53 dual-role torpedoes

Anti-submarine armament: two quadruple container-launchers for eight SS-N-14 'Silex' anti-submarine missiles, torpedoes (see above), two RBU 6000 12-barrel rocket-launchers, two RBU 1000 six-barrel rocket-launchers, and helicopter-launched weapons (see below)

Aircraft: one Kamov Ka-25 'Hormone-A' helicopter in a hangar aft

Electronics: one 'Top Sail' 3D air-search radar, one 'Head Net-C' 3D air/surface-search radar, two 'Don Kay' or 'Palm Frond' surface-search and navigation radars, two 'Head Light-A/B/C' SAM fire-control radars, two 'Muff Cob' 57-mm gun fire-control radars, two 'Bass Tilt' CIWS fire-control radars (not in first four ships), one medium-frequency active/passive search and attack hull sonar, a comprehensive ESM suite including eight 'Side Globe', two 'Bell Slam', one 'Bell Clout' and two 'Bell Tap' antennae/housings, two twin chaff launchers, and one 'High Pole-A' and one 'High Pole-B' IFF systems

Propulsion: four boilers supplying steam to two sets of geared turbines delivering 82,000 kW (109,980 hp) to two shafts

Performance: maximum speed 35 kt; range 13,000 km (8,080 miles) at 18 kt, or 19,450 km (12,085 miles) at 14 kt or 3250 km (2,020 miles) at 32 kt

Complement: 400

A 'Kresta II' class cruiser at speed reveals elegant hull lines as well as many sensors, two SA-N-3 SAM launchers and, to port of the forward superstructure, one of two SS-N-14 anti-submarine missile launchers.

Class

1. USSR

Name	Builder	Laid down	Commissioned
Kronshtadt	Zhdanov Yard	Jun 1966	Sep 1969
Admiral Isakov	Zhdanov Yard	Jun 1966	Sep 1970
Admiral Nakhimov	Zhdanov Yard	May 1967	Aug 1971
Admiral Makarov	Zhdanov Yard	Mar 1969	Jun 1972
Marshal Voroshilov	Zhdanov Yard	Jan 1970	May 1973
Admiral Oktyabrsky	Zhdanov Yard	May 1969	Sep 1973
Admiral Isachenko	Zhdanov Yard	Feb 1970	Aug 1974
Marshal Timoshenko	Zhdanov Yard	Jun 1971	Aug 1975
Vasily Chapaev	Zhdanov Yard	Feb 1972	Sep 1976
Admiral Yumaschev	Zhdanov Yard	Nov 1973	Oct 1977

Note: This class followed the 'Kresta I' class in Leningrad, and the ships are optimized for the anti-submarine role though the air-defence task is also well served by a more advanced type of SAM than that carried in the 'Kresta I' class ships.

'Kynda' class CG

(USSR)

Type: anti-ship guided-missile cruiser

Displacement: 4,400 tons standard and 5,700 tons full load

Dimensions: length 142·0 m (465·8 ft); beam 15·8 m (51·8 ft); draught 5·3 m (17·4 ft)

Gun armament: four 76-mm (3-in) L/60 DP in two twin mountings, and four 30-mm ADGM-630 CIWS mountings

Missile armament: two quadruple container-launchers for 16 SS-N-3B 'Shaddock' anti-ship missiles, and one twin launcher for 16 or 22 SA-N-1 'Goa' SAMs

Torpedo armament: two triple 533-mm (21-in) mountings for Type 53 dual-role torpedoes

Anti-submarine armament: two 12-barrel RBU 6000 rocket-launchers, torpedoes (see above), and helicopter-launched weapons (see below)

Aircraft: provision for one Kamov Ka-25 'Hormone-A' helicopter on a platform aft

Electronics: two 'Head Net-A' air-search radars or (*Fokin* and *Varyag*) one 'Head Net-A' air-search radar and one 'Head Net-C' 3D radar, two 'Plinth Net' surface-search radars, two 'Don 2' navigation radars, two 'Scoop Pair' SSM fire-control radars, one 'Peel Group' SAM fire-control radar, two 'Owl Screech' 76-mm gun fire-control radars, two 'Bass Tilt' CIWS fire-control radars, one medium-frequency active/passive search and attack hull sonar, one ESM system with four 'Top Hat' and several 'Bell Clout', 'Bell Tap' and 'Bell Slam' antennae/housings, and one 'High Pole-B' IFF system

Propulsion: four boilers supplying steam to two sets of geared turbines delivering 67,000 kW (89,960 hp) to two shafts

Performance: maximum speed 34 kt; range 11,125 km (6,915 miles) at 15 kt or 2775 km (1,725 miles) at 34 kt

Complement: 390

Note: Built as dedicated anti-ship cruisers with long-range missiles, these vessels introduced the now-standard pattern of enclosed pyramid mast for the support of the mass of electronic equipment increasingly characteristic of Soviet surface combatants. The class was to have been larger, but was curtailed at four units as the Soviets began to appreciate the growing importance of anti-submarine warfare over anti-ship operations as the US Navy began to place increasing emphasis on nuclear-powered missile and attack submarines during the 1960s.

Class

1. USSR

Name	Builder	Laid down	Commissioned
Grozny	Zhdanov Yard	Jun 1959	May 1962
Admiral Fokin	Zhdanov Yard	Dec 1960	May 1963
Admiral Golovko	Zhdanov Yard	Dec 1961	Jun 1963
Varyag	Zhdanov Yard	Dec 1962	Jul 1964

The most notable feature of the 'Kynda' class cruiser's foredeck is the quadruple launcher (with eight missiles) of the SS-N-3 anti-ship system.

'Leahy' class CG

(USA)

Type: anti-aircraft, anti-submarine and anti-aircraft guided-missile escort cruiser

Displacement: 5,670 tons standard and 8,205 tons full load

Dimensions: length 533·0 ft (162·5 m); beam 54·9 ft (16·6 m); draught 24·8 ft (7·6 m)

Gun armament: two 20-mm Phalanx Mk 16 CIWS mountings

Missile armament: two Mk 141 quadruple container-launchers for eight RGM-84 Harpoon anti-ship missiles, and two Mk 10 twin launchers for 80 RIM-67B Standard SM-2 ER SAMs

Torpedo armament: none

Anti-submarine armament: one Mk 16 octuple launcher for eight RUR-5A ASROC missiles, two Mk 32 triple 12·75-in (324-mm) mountings for Mk 46 torpedoes, and helicopter-launched weapons (see below)

Aircraft: provision for one Kaman SH-2F Seasprite helicopter on a platform aft

Electronics: one SPS-48A/E 3D air-search radar, one SPS-49(V)3 long-range air-search radar, one SPS-10F or SPS-67 surface-search radar, one LN-66 navigation radar, four SPG-55C illumination and guidance radars used in conjunction with four Mk 76 SAM fire-control systems, one Mk 14 weapon direction system, one SQQ-23B (CG17) hull-mounted or SQS-23 bow-mounted active/passive search and attack sonar used in conjunction with one Mk 114 underwater weapons fire-control system, Naval Tactical Data System, one SLQ-32(V)3 ESM system with warning and jamming elements, four Mk 36 Super RBOC chaff/flare launchers, one OE-82 satellite communications system, three WSC-3 satellite communications transceivers, one SRR-1 satellite communications receiver, and URN-25 TACAN

Propulsion: four Babcock & Wilcox or (CG21/24) Foster-Wheeler boilers supplying steam to two sets of geared turbines (General Electric in CG16/18, De Laval in CG19/22 and Allis-Chalmers in CG23/24) delivering 85,000 hp (63,385 kW) to two shafts

Performance: maximum speed 33 kt; range 9,200 miles (14,805 km) at 20 kt

Complement: 26 + 397 plus provision for 6 + 12 flag staff

Class

1. USA Name	No.	Builder	Laid down	Commissioned
Leahy	CG16	Bath Iron Works	Dec 1959	Aug 1962
Harry E. Yarnell	CG17	Bath Iron Works	May 1960	Feb 1963
Worden	CG18	Bath Iron Works	Sep 1960	Aug 1963
Dale	CG19	New York SB	Sep 1960	Nov 1963
Richmond K. Turner	CG20	New York SB	Jan 1961	Jun 1964
Gridley	CG21	Puget Sound Bridge	Jul 1960	May 1963
England	CG22	Todd SB	Oct 1960	Dec 1963
Halsey	CG23	San Francisco NY	Aug 1960	Jul 1963
Reeves	CG24	Puget Sound NY	Jul 1960	May 1964

Note: This was the first US cruiser class optimized for the escort of aircraft-carriers, and was thus designed with a primary armament of surface-to-air missiles in a double-ended arrangement that allows both the simultaneous engagement of four targets and, because the launchers are of the twin-arm type, rapid response to saturation attack. Anti-submarine warfare is moderately well provided for, though the provision of only a helicopter platform with only limited facilities is a definite disadvantage. The ships have no major gun armament, anti-ship capability being provided by the addition of the standard Harpoon missile installation. Recent developments are considerably improving the ships' electronic capabilities with SPS-48E radar and improvements to the missile launchers, SPG-55 radars and Mk 76 fire-control systems.

Below: The *England* of the 'Leahy' class reveals the design's ASROC, Harpoon, Phalanx and double-ended SAM features. Bottom: The *Long Beach* has two twin SAM launchers forward.

'Long Beach' class CGN

(USA)

Type: nuclear-powered anti-aircraft, anti-submarine and anti-ship guided-missile escort cruiser

Displacement: 14,200 tons standard and 17,525 tons full load

Dimensions: length 721·2 ft (219·9 m); beam 73·2 ft (22·3 m); draught 29·7 ft (9·1 m)

Gun armament: two 5-in (127-mm) L/38 DP in Mk 30 single mountings, and two 20-mm Phalanx Mk 16 CIWS mountings

Missile armament: two quadruple Armored Box Launchers Mk 143 for eight BGM-109 Tomahawk anti-ship and land-attack cruise missiles, two Mk 141 quadruple container-launchers for eight RGM-84 Harpoon anti-ship missiles, and two Mk 10 twin launchers for 120 RIM-67B Standard SM-2 ER SAMs

Torpedo armament: none

Anti-submarine armament: one Mk 16 octuple launcher for 20 RUR-5A ASROC anti-submarine missiles, and two Mk 32 triple 12·75-in (324-mm) mountings for Mk 46 torpedoes

Aircraft: provision for one helicopter on a platform aft

Electronics: one SPS-48C 3D air-search radar, one SPS-49B long-range air-search radar, one SPS-65 low-level threat-warning radar, one SPS-67 surface-search radar, one LN-66 navigation radar, four SPG-55D illumination and guidance radars used in conjunction with four Mk 76 SAM fire-control systems, two Mk 35 radars used in conjunction with two Mk 56 gun fire-control systems, one Mk 14 weapon direction system, Naval Tactical Data System, one SQQ-23B active/passive search and attack hull sonar used in conjunction with one Mk 111 underwater weapons fire-control system, one SLQ-32(V)3 ESM system with warning and jamming elements, four Mk 36 Super RBOC chaff/flare launchers, one OE-82 satellite communications system, four WSC-3 satellite communications transceivers, one SRR-1 satellite communications receiver, and URN-25 TACAN

Propulsion: two Westinghouse C1W pressurized water-cooled reactors supplying steam to two sets of General Electric geared turbines delivering 80,000 hp (59,655 kW) to two shafts

Performance: maximum speed 36 kt

Complement: 65 + 893 plus provision for 10 + 58 flag staff

Class

1. USA Name	No.	Builder	Laid down	Com-missioned
Long Beach	CGN9	Bethlehem	Dec 1957	Sep 1961

Note: This singleton unit was the world's first nuclear-powered surface combatant, and was designed for the air defence of carrier battle groups with two twin Talos and two twin Terrier launchers for long- and medium-range interceptions respectively. The ship has been extensively upgraded in its electronic and weapon systems since that time, and is currently configured as a single-ended ship with two twin launchers on the forecastle. The provision of surface-to-surface and surface-to-underwater missiles adds potent secondary capabilities in the anti-ship, land-attack and anti-submarine roles, the last being hampered slightly by lack of an embarked helicopter. The main radar is to be upgraded to SPS-48E standard, and the missile launchers and illuminating radars are also to be improved.

'Ticonderoga' class CG

(USA)

Type: anti-aircraft, anti-submarine and anti-ship guided-missile escort cruiser

Displacement: 7,015 tons light and 9,590 tons or (CG49 onward) 9,460 tons full load

Dimensions: length 565·8 ft (172·5 m); beam 55·0 ft (16·8 m); draught 31·0 ft (9·5 m)

Gun armament: two 5-in (127-mm) L/54 DP in Mk 45 single mountings, two 20-mm Phalanx Mk 16 CIWS mountings, and four 0·5-in (12·7-mm) machine-guns

Missile armament: two MK 141 quadruple container-launchers for 16 RGM-84 Harpoon anti-ship missiles, and two Mk 26 twin launchers for up to 68 RIM-66C Standard SM-2 MR SAMs; from CG52 onwards the ships each have two 61-cell Mk 41 Vertical Launch Systems for 12 BGM-109 Tomahawk land-attack and anti-ship cruise missiles, plus ASROC(VL) and Standard missiles in a total of 122 missiles

Torpedo armament: none

Anti-submarine armament: two Mk 32 triple 12·75-in (324-mm) mountings for Mk 46 torpedoes, up to 20 RUR-5A ASROC missiles as part of the total missile strength of the Mk 26 launchers (see above), and helicopter-launched weapons (see below)

Aircraft: two Kaman SH-2F Seasprite or (CG49 onwards) Sikorsky SH-60B Seahawk helicopters in a hangar aft

Electronics: two SPY-1A or (CG59 onwards) SPY-1B 3D phased-array pairs of long-range search, target-tracking and missile-control radars used in conjunction with the AEGIS Weapon-Control System Mk 7 and four SPG-62 illumination radars, four Mk 99 SAM fire-control systems and four Mk 80 illuminator directors, one SPS-49(V)6 long-range air-search radar, one SPS-55 surface-search radar, one LN-66 or (CG49 onwards) SPS-64 navigation radar, one SPQ-9A track-while-scan radar used in conjunction with the Mk 86 gun fire-control system, one SQS-53A/B and one SQR-19 passive search towed-array sonar or (CG56 onwards) one SQQ-89 (combined SQQ-53B and SQR-19) sonar system used in conjunction with the Mk 116 underwater weapons fire-control system, one SQQ-28 helicopter data-link sonar, one Link 11 data-link, one SLQ-32(V)3 ESM system with warning and jamming elements, four Mk 36 Super RBOC chaff/flare launchers, one OE-82 satellite communications system, two WSC-3 satellite communications transceivers, and four SRR-1 satellite communications receivers

Propulsion: COGAG arrangement, with four General Electric LM2500 gas turbines delivering 86,000 hp (64,120 kW) to two shafts

Performance: maximum speed 30 + kt; range 6,900 miles (11,105 km) at 20 kt

Complement: 33 + 325

Note: Though originally planned as a class of 18, this has now grown to a projected 27 units as primary escorts of US carrier battle groups against air attacks of all intensities and types. The hull and propulsion arrangement used in the 'Ticonderoga' class are basically those of the 'Spruance' class, the hull lengthened slightly and strengthened as required. The design also includes Kevlar armour for the protection of key spaces. The core of the system is the combination of SPY-1 radar, the AEGIS weapon system and Standard SM-2 ER missiles to provide hemispherical target detection, prioritization and destruction, though anti-ship and anti-submarine capabilities have not been ignored in this nicely balanced design. A constant programme of electronic improvement is being undertaken, and the replacement of conventional twin-arm missile launchers by vertical launchers in later units has provided a most useful increase in salvo rate against saturation attack. There are currently four baseline standards: CG47 is to Baseline I standard with the SH-60B helicopter, CG52 marks the beginning of the Baseline II standard with the vertical launch system, BGM-109 Tomahawk cruise missiles and the SQQ-89 sonar system, CG59 is the start of the Baseline III standard with SPY-1B planar-array radar with UYQ-21 displays, and CG65 is the first ship to Baseline IV standard with considerably upgraded UYK-43/44 computers for faster data handling.

Class

1. USA Name	No.	Builder	Laid down	Com-missioned
Ticonderoga	CG47	Ingalls SB	Jan 1980	Jan 1983
Yorktown	CG48	Ingalls SB	Oct 1981	Jul 1984
Vincennes	CG49	Ingalls SB	Oct 1982	Jul 1985
Valley Forge	CG50	Ingalls SB	Apr 1983	Jan 1986
Thomas S. Gates	CG51	Bath Iron Works	Aug 1984	Aug 1987
Bunker Hill	CG52	Ingalls SB	Jan 1984	Sep 1986
Mobile Bay	CG53	Ingalls SB	Jun 1984	Feb 1987
Antietam	CG54	Ingalls SB	Nov 1984	Jun 1987
Leyte Gulf	CG55	Ingalls SB	Mar 1985	Aug 1987
San Jacinto	CG56	Ingalls SB	Jul 1985	Jan 1988
Lake Champlain	CG57	Ingalls SB	Mar 1986	Aug 1988
Philippine Sea	CG58	Bath Iron Works	May 1986	Mar 1989
Princeton	CG59	Ingalls SB	Oct 1986	Feb 1989
Normandy	CG60	Bath Iron Works	Apr 1987	Dec 1989
Monterey	CG61	Bath Iron Works	Aug 1987	Mar 1990
Chancellorsville	CG62	Ingalls SB	Jun 1987	Nov 1989
Cowpens	CG63	Ingalls SB	Jun 1987	Jul 1990
Gettysburg	CG64	Ingalls SB	Aug 1988	Nov 1990
Chosin	CG65	Ingalls SB	Jul 1988	Nov 1990
Hue City	CG66	Ingalls SB	Feb 1989	Jun 1991
Shiloh	CG67	Bath Iron Works	Jul 1989	Dec 1991
Anzio	CG68	Ingalls SB	Aug 1989	Dec 1991
	CG69	Ingalls SB	May 1990	Sep 1992
	CG70	Bath Iron Works	Nov 1990	Dec 1992
	CG71	Ingalls SB	Nov 1990	Mar 1993
	CG72	Ingalls SB	Feb 1991	Jun 1993
	CG73	Ingalls SB	1991	1993

The *Philippine Sea* is the last unit of the improved Baseline II standard for the 'Ticonderoga' class with a vertical launch missile system.

The *Ticonderoga* reveals her armament and two of the four planar-array antennae for the SPY-1A radar on the forward and after superstructures.

'Truxtun' class CGN

(USA)

Type: nuclear-powered anti-aircraft, anti-submarine and anti-ship guided-missile escort cruiser

Displacement: 8,200 tons standard and 9,125 tons full load

Dimensions: length 564·0 ft (171·9 m); beam 58·0 ft (17·7 m); draught 31·0 ft (9·4 m)

Gun armament: one 5-in (127-mm) L/54 DP in a Mk 42 mounting, and two 20-mm Phalanx Mk 16 CIWS mountings

Missile armament: two Mk 141 quadruple container-launchers for eight RGM-84 Harpoon anti-ship missiles, and one Mk 10 twin launcher for 60 RIM-67B Standard SM-2 ER SAMs

Torpedo armament: none

Anti-submarine armament: two Mk 32 twin 12·75-in (324-mm) mountings for Mk 46 torpedoes, up to 20 RUR-5A ASROC anti-submarine missiles included in the Mk 10 launcher total (see above), and helicopter-launched weapons (see below)

Aircraft: one Kaman SH-2F Seasprite helicopter in a hangar aft

Electronics: one SPS-48E 3D air-search radar, one SPS-49 long-range air-search radar, one SPS-67 surface-search radar, one LN-66 navigation radar, two SPG-55B illumination and guidance radars used in conjunction with two Mk 76 SAM fire-control systems, one SPG-53F radar used in conjunction with the Mk 86 gun fire-control system, one Mk 14 weapon direction system, one SQS-26 active/passive search and attack bow sonar used in conjunction with the Mk 111 underwater weapons fire-control system, Naval Tactical Data System, one SLQ-32(V)3 ESM system with warning and jamming elements, four Mk 36 Super RBOC chaff/flare launchers, one OE-82 satellite communications system, four WSC-3 satellite communications transceivers, one SRR-1 satellite communications receiver, and URN-25 TACAN

Propulsion: two General Electric D2G pressurized water-cooled reactors supplying steam to two sets of geared turbines delivering 70,000 hp (52,190 kW) to two shafts

Performance: maximum speed 38 kt

Complement: 39 + 522 plus provision for 6 + 12 flag staff

Class
1. USA			Laid	Com-
Name	No.	Builder	down	missioned
Truxtun	CGN35	New York SB	Jun 1963	May 1967

Note: This is a singleton nuclear-powered equivalent to the otherwise generally similar 'Belknap' class ships. By modern standards the ship's main limitation is its single twin-arm SAM launcher, located on the quarterdeck rather than on the forecastle as in the 'Belknap' class ships.

Above right: The *Truxtun* is basically a nuclear-powered 'Belknap' unit. Right: The *Virginia* is lead ship of a four-strong derivative of the 'California' class with a nuclear propulsion arrangement.

'Virginia' class CGN

(USA)

Type: nuclear-powered anti-aircraft, anti-ship and anti-submarine guided-missile escort cruiser

Displacement: 8,625 tons standard and 11,300 tons full load

Dimensions: length 585·0 ft (178·4 m); beam 63·0 ft (19·2 m); draught 29·5 ft (9·0 m)

Gun armament: two 5-in (127-mm) L/54 DP in Mk 45 single mountings, and two 20-mm Phalanx Mk 16 CIWS mountings

Missile armament: two quadruple Armored Box Launchers Mk 143 for eight BGM-109 Tomahawk anti-ship and land-attack cruise missiles, two Mk 141 quadruple container-launchers for eight RGM-84 Harpoon anti-ship missiles, and two Mk 26 twin launchers for 68 RIM-66C Standard SM-2 MR SAMs

Torpedo armament: none

Anti-submarine armament: two Mk 32 triple 12·75-in (324-mm) mountings for Mk 46 torpedoes, and up to 20 RUR-5A ASROC anti-submarine missiles in the Mk 26 total (see above)

Aircraft: provision for two helicopters has been deleted to provide space for the Tomahawk ABLs (see above)

Electronics: one SPS-48D/E 3D air-search radar, one SPS-40B long-range air-search radar, one SPS-55 surface-search radar, one LN-66 navigation radar, two SPG-51D illumination and tracking radars used in conjunction with one Mk 74 SAM-control director, one SPG-60D search-and-tracking radar and one SPQ-9A track-while-scan radar used in conjunction with one Mk 86 SAM and gun fire-control system, one Mk 14 weapon direction system, one SQS-53A active/passive search and attack bow sonar used in conjunction with one Mk 116 underwater weapons fire-control system, Naval Tacti-cal Data System, one SLQ-32(V)3 ESM system with warning and jamming elements, four Mk 36 Super RBOC chaff/flare launchers, one T Mk 6 Fanfare torpedo decoy system, one OE-82 satellite communications system, four WSC-3 satellite communications transceivers, one SRR-1 satellite communications receiver, and URN-25 TACAN

Propulsion: two General Electric D2G pressurized water-cooled reactors supplying steam to two sets of geared turbines delivering 100,000 hp (74,570 kW) to two shafts

Performance: maximum speed 40 kt

Complement: 34/45 + 520/579

Class

1. USA Name	No.	Builder	Laid down	Com-missioned
Virginia	CGN38	Newport News	Aug 1972	Sep 1976
Texas	CGN39	Newport News	Aug 1973	Sep 1977
Mississippi	CGN40	Newport News	Feb 1975	Aug 1978
Arkansas	CGN41	Newport News	Feb 1975	Oct 1980

Note: These ships are in essence improved 'California' class cruisers optimized for the area defence of nuclear-powered aircraft-carriers against air and submarine attack. The key feature of the double-ended design is the use of twin SAM launchers with two SPG-51 radars aft and the combined gun/missile Mk 86 system with SPG-60 and SPQ-9 radars forward. The electronics have been considerably upgraded in recent years, and potent anti-ship, land-attack and anti-submarine capabilities are offered by the rest of the missile equipment.

'Vittorio Veneto' class CG

(Italy)

Type: anti-submarine, anti-aircraft and anti-ship guided-missile escort cruiser

Displacement: 7,500 tons standard and 8,850 tons full load

Dimensions: length 179·6 m (589·0 ft); beam 19·4 m (63·6 ft); draught 6·0 m (19·7 ft)

Gun armament: eight 76-mm (3-in) L/62 DP in OTO Melara MMK single mountings, and six 40-mm Breda L/70 AA in three Breda Compact twin mountings

Missile armament: two twin Teseo 2 container-launchers for four Otomat anti-ship missiles, and one Mk 20 Aster twin launcher for 60 RIM-67A Standard SM-1 ER SAMs

Torpedo armament: none

Anti-submarine armament: two Mk 32 triple 12·75-in (324-mm) mountings for Mk 46 torpedoes, up to 20 RUR-5A ASROC anti-ship missiles included in the Mk 20 Aster total (see above), and helicopter-launched weapons (see below)

Aircraft: up to nine Agusta (Bell) AB.212ASW helicopters on a flight deck aft

Electronics: one SPS-52C 3D air-search radar, one RAN 3L medium-range air-search radar, one SPS 702 surface-search and target indication radar, one 3RM 7 navigation radar, two SPG-55C illumination and guidance radars used in conjunction with the Aster SAM fire-control system, four RTN 10X radars used in conjunction with four Argo NA9 76-mm gun fire-control systems, three RTN 20X radars used in conjunction with three Dardo 40-mm fire-control systems, one SQS-23G long-range active/passive search and attack bow sonar, one SADOC 1 action information system, one UAA-1 Abbey Hill ESM system with warning and jamming elements, two SCLAR chaff/flare launchers, and URN-20 TACAN

Propulsion: four Ansaldo/Foster-Wheeler boilers supplying steam to two sets of Tosi geared turbines delivering 54,500 kW (73,095 hp) to two shafts

Performance: maximum speed 32 kt; range 9250 km (5,750 miles) at 17 kt

Complement: 50 + 500

Class

1. Italy Name	No.	Builder	Laid down	Com-missioned
Vittorio Veneto	C550	Italcantieri	Jun 1965	Jul 1969

Note: Based in design on the 'Andrea Doria' class but scaled up in size and displacement, the *Vittorio Veneto* was recast radically when it was realized that the earlier ships' helicopter facilities were far too small. The result is a dual-role ship with impressive anti-aircraft and anti-submarine capabilities, the latter provided by a combination of ASROC missiles and weapons from helicopters operating from the large quarterdeck flight area, which is 40 m (131 ft) long and 18·6 m (61 ft) wide above a substantial hangar.

The *Vittorio Veneto* is an enlarged version of the two 'Andrea Doria' class ships, and combines anti-ship and anti-air missile armament with up to nine helicopters for the primary anti-submarine role.

Two lifts provide helicopter movement between the *Vittorio Veneto's* flightdeck and the hangar, two decks deep, located immediately below it.

The *Vittorio Veneto's* anti-air capability rests on the twin-arm SAM launcher and no fewer than eight 76-mm (3-in) single MMK gun mountings.

'Brooklyn' class CA

(USA/Chile)
Type: gun cruiser
Displacement: 10,000 tons standard and 13,500 tons full load
Dimensions: length 608·3 ft (185·4 m); beam 69·0 ft (21·0 m); draught 24·0 ft (7·3 m)
Gun armament: 15 6-in (152-mm) L/47 in five Mk 16 triple mountings, eight 5-in (127-mm) L/25 DP in four Mk 27 twin mountings, 28 40-mm Bofors L/60 AA in four quadruple and six Mk 1 and Mk 2 twin mountings, and 24 20-mm Oerlikon L/80 AA in single and twin mountings
Missile armament: none
Torpedo armament: none
Anti-submarine armament: none
Aircraft: one Bell Model 206B JetRanger in a hangar aft
Armour: belt 1·5/4 in (38/102 mm); decks 2/3 in (51/66 mm); turrets 3/5 in (76/127 mm); conning tower 8 in (203 mm)
Electronics: one SPS-12 air-search radar, one SPS-10 surface-search radar, and two Mk 34 6-in gun directors
Propulsion: eight Babcock & Wilcox boilers supplying steam to four sets of Parsons geared turbines delivering 100,000 hp (74,560 kW) to four shafts
Performance: maximum speed 32·5 kt; range 8,750 miles (14,080 km) at 15 kt
Complement: 888/975
Class

1. Chile Name	No.	Builder	Laid down	Commissioned
O'Higgins	02	New York NY	Mar 1935	Sep 1937

Note: This was originally the US Navy's *Brooklyn* (CL40). The ship was sold to Chile in 1951, and though completely obsolete by modern standards is still in excellent condition. The hangar is large enough to accommodate six helicopters.

'De Ruyter' class CA

(Netherlands/Peru)
Type: gun cruiser with limited anti-ship and anti-aircraft missile capability
Displacement: 9,530 tons or (CH84) 9,850 tons standard and 12,165 tons or (CH84) 12,250 tons full load
Dimensions: length 190·3 m (624·5 ft) or (CH84) 185·6 m (609·0 ft); beam 17·3 m (56·7 ft); draught 6·7 m (22·0 ft)
Gun armament: eight or (CH84) four 152-mm (6-in) Bofors L/53 DP in four or (CH84) two twin mountings, six 57-mm Bofors L/60 DP in three twin mountings (CH84 only), and six or (CH84) four 40-mm Bofors L/70 AA in three or (CH84) two twin mountings
Missile armament: (CH81 only) four twin Teseo 2 container-launchers for eight Otomat anti-ship missiles, and one Albatros octuple launcher for Aspide SAMs
Torpedo armament: none
Anti-submarine armament: (CH81 only) helicopter-launched weapons (see below)
Aircraft: (CH81 only) three Agusta (Sikorsky) ASH-3D Sea King helicopters in a hangar aft
Electronics: one LW-08 or (CH84) LW-02 air-search radar, one DA-08 or (CH84) DA-02 surface-search and target indication radar, one Decca or (CH84) ZW-01 navigation radar, one STIR SSM fire-control radar (CH81 only), one WM-25 152-mm gun fire-control system, two WM-45 57-mm gun fire-control systems, and one CWC 10N active search hull sonar
Propulsion: four Werkspoor/Yarrow boilers supplying steam to two sets of De Schelde/Parsons geared turbines delivering 63,500 kW (85,165 hp) to two shafts
Performance: maximum speed 32 kt; range 13,000 km (8,080 miles) at 12 kt
Complement: 49 + 904
Class

1. Peru Name	No.	Builder	Laid down	Commissioned
Almirante Grau	CH81	Wilton-Fijenoord	Sep 1939	Nov 1953
Aguirre	CH84	Rotterdamse Droogdok	May 1939	Dec 1953

Note: The building of these two Dutch cruisers was interrupted by World War II, and the ships were sold to Peru in March 1973 and August 1976 respectively. *Aguirre* was then transformed into a helicopter cruiser with a hangar in place of the Terrier SAM system of the Dutch vessel, this hangar measuring 20·4 m (67 ft) in length and 16·5 m (54·1 ft) in width; the Sea Kings carried by the *Aguirre* can carry AM.39 Exocet anti-ship missiles. *Almirante Grau* was converted into a missile cruiser during the mid-1980s, the potent anti-ship missile armament being balanced by a light air-defence missile capability.

Opposite page, top left: Seen with an old pennant number, the *Aguirre* has been modernized with quarterdeck provision for three large helicopters.
Opposite page, top right: The gun-armed cruisers of the 'Sverdlov' class are used primarily for support of amphibious assault operations.
Opposite page, bottom: The *Amatsukaze* in an obsolescent guided-missile destroyer. An ASROC system was retrofitted between the funnels in 1968.

'Sverdlov' class CA

(USSR)

Type: gun cruiser

Displacement: 16,000 tons standard and 17,500 tons full load

Dimensions: length 210·0 m (689·0 ft); beam 22·0 m (72·2 ft); draught 7·5 m (24·5 ft)

Gun armament: 12, nine (in *Zhdanov*) or six (in *Admiral Senyavin*) 152-mm (6-in) L/50 in four, three or two triple mountings, 12 100-mm (3·94-in) L/50 DP in six twin mountings, 32 37-mm L/63 AA in 16 twin mountings, and 16 or eight (in *Zhdanov*) 30-mm L/65 AA in eight or four twin mountings

Missile armament: one twin launcher for 20 SA-N-4 'Gecko' SAMs (in *Admiral Senyavin* and *Zhdanov*)

Torpedo armament: none

Anti-submarine armament: none

Aircraft: none

Mines: up to 150 (not in *Admiral Senyavin* and *Zhdanov*)

Armour: belt 100/125 mm (3·93/4·92 in), ends 40/50 mm (1·6/2 in), decks 25/76 mm (1/3 in) decks, turrets 125 mm (4·92 in), and conning tower 150 mm (5·9 in)

Electronics: one 'Top Trough' air-search radar, one 'High Sieve' or (in *Admiral Senyavin* and *Zhdanov*) 'Low Sieve' surface-search radar, two or (in *Admiral Senyavin* and *Zhdanov*) three 'Don 2' navigation radars, one 'Neptun' navigation radar (in *Admiral Senyavin* and *Zhdanov*), one 'Pop Group' SAM fire-control radar (in *Admiral Senyavin* and *Zhdanov*), two 'Top Bow' 152-mm gun fire-control radars, six 'Egg Cup' 152- and 100-mm gun fire-control radars, two 'Sun Visor-A' 100-mm gun fire-control radars, one 'Half Bow' gun fire-control radar, four (in *Admiral Senyavin*) or two (*Zhda-*

nov) 30-mm fire-control radars, and various ECM systems

Propulsion: six boilers supplying steam to two sets of geared turbines delivering 82,000 kW (109,965 hp) to two shafts

Performance: maximum speed 32 kt; range 16,000 km (9,945 miles) at 18 kt

Complement: about 70 + 930

Class

1. USSR

Name

Sverdlov
Admiral Lazarev
Aleksandr Nevsky
Zhdanov
Admiral Ushakov
Aleksandr Suvorov
Mikhail Kutuzov
Murmansk
Dmitri Pozharsky
Admiral Senyavin

Note: These 10 ships are the survivors of a class that was projected at 24 units. In the event only 20 were laid down at Leningrad, Nikolayev and Severodvinsk from 1949, and 17 were launched from 1951 onwards. Only 14 ships had been completed when the building programme was terminated in 1956. In the early 1970s the *Admiral Senyavin* (1971) and *Zhdanov* (1972) were revised with limited surface-to-air missile armament plus extended staff and communications facilities as command ships, while the others retain their original layout as gunfire support ships for amphibious operations. Most are now in reserve.

'Amatsukaze' or 'Type 163' class DDG

(Japan)

Type: anti-aircraft and anti-submarine guided-missile destroyer

Displacement: 3,050 tons standard and 4,000 tons full load

Dimensions: length 131·0 m (429·8 ft); beam 13·4 m (44·0 ft); draught 4·2 m (13·8 ft)

Gun armament: four 3-in (76-mm) L/50 DP in two Mk 33 twin mountings

Missile armament: one Mk 13 single launcher for 40 RIM-66B Standard SM-1 MR SAMs

Torpedo armament: none

Anti-submarine armament: one Mk 16 octuple launcher for eight RUR-5A ASROC missiles, two Mk 32 triple 12·75-in (324-mm) mountings for Mk 46 torpedoes, and two Hedgehog Mk 15 mortars

Aircraft: none

Electronics: one SPS-52 3D radar, one SPS-29A medium-range air-search radar, one OPS-17 surface-search radar, two SPG-51C illumination and tracking radars used in conjunction with two Mk 73 SAM fire-control systems, one Type 2-21 gun fire-control system, one SQS-23C long-range active search and attack hull sonar used in conjunction with the Mk 114 underwater weapons fire-control system, one ESM system with NOLR-6 warning and OLT-3 jamming elements, and two chaff launchers

Propulsion: two Ishikawajima/Foster-Wheeler boilers supplying steam to two sets of Ishikawajima/General Electric geared turbines delivering 44,750 kW (60,010 hp) to two shafts

Performance: maximum speed 33 kt; range 12,975 km (8,065 miles) at 18 kt

Complement: 290

Class

1. Japan

Name	No.	Builder	Laid down	Commissioned
Amatsukaze	DD163	Mitsubishi	Nov 1962	Feb 1965

Note: This is an unexceptional missile destroyer optimized for the anti-submarine and, to a lesser extent, air-defence roles.

'Animoso' class DDG

(Italy)

Type: anti-ship, anti-submarine and anti-aircraft guided-missile destroyer

Displacement: 4,330 tons standard and 5,045 tons full load

Dimensions: length 147·7 m (484·6 ft); beam 15·0 m (49·5 ft); draught 5·0 m (16·5 ft)

Gun armament: one 127-mm (5-in) OTO Melara L/54 DP in an OTO Melara Compact single mounting, and three 76-mm (3-in) OTO Melara L/62 DP in OTO Melara Super Rapid single mountings

Missile armament: four twin Teseo 2 container-launchers for eight Otomat Mk 2 anti-ship missiles, one Mk 13 single launcher for RIM-67B Standard SM-2 ER SAMs, and one Albatros Mk 2 octuple launcher for 16 Aspide SAMs

Torpedo armament: two B515 single 533-mm (21-in) launcher for A 184 wire-guided dual-role torpedoes

Anti-submarine armament: two ILAS 3 triple 324-mm (12·75-in) mountings for 12 A 244/S torpedoes, plus helicopter-launched weapons (see below)

Aircraft: two Agusta (Bell) AB.212ASW helicopters in a hangar aft

Electronics: one SPS-52C 3D radar, one RAN 3L medium-range air-search radar, one RAN 10S air/surface-search radar, one SPS 702 surface-search radar, one 3RM 20 navigation radar, two SPG-51D illumination and tracking radars used in conjunction with two Mk 74 SAM fire-control systems, one RTN 30X target-indication radar used in conjunction with one Argo 127-mm gun fire-control system, four RTN 30X radars used in conjunction with four Dardo-E 76-mm gun and Albatros SAM fire-control systems, one Raytheon DE 1164 active/passive search and attack bow sonar integrated with one Raytheon DE 1167 variable-depth sonar for use in conjunction with an underwater weapons fire-control system, one IPN 20 (SADOC 2) action information system, one Nettuno ESM system with warning and jamming elements, four SCLAR chaff/flare launchers, and two Sagaie chaff/flare launchers

Propulsion: CODOG arrangement, with two Fiat/General Electric LM2500 gas turbines delivering 55,000 hp (41,015 kW) and two GMT BL 230·20 DVM diesels delivering 12,500 hp (9320 kW) to two shafts

Performance: maximum speed 31·5 kt; range 13,000 km (8,080 miles) at 18 kt

Complement: about 35 + 365

Class

1. Italy Name	No.	Builder	Laid down	Commissioned
Animoso	D560	Fincantieri, Riva Trigoso	Jul 1986	1992
Ardimentoso	D561	Fincantieri, Riva Trigoso	Jul 1986	1992

Note: These are in essence improved versions of the two 'Audace' class units with a longer hull for increased habitability and the volume for the retrofit of more advanced systems. The ships carry a more capable primary SAM, and of particular interest is the use of Super Rapid medium-calibre guns for combined anti-ship and anti-missile CIWS capability. The result is a pair of multi-role ships able to tackle air, surface and underwater threats within the context of an integrated battle group or as leaders of convoy-escort forces.

'Arleigh Burke' class DDG

(USA)

Type: anti-ship, anti-submarine and air defence guided-missile escort destroyer

Displacement: 8,200 tons standard and 8,500 tons full load

Dimensions: length 504·0 ft (153·6 m); beam 66·9 ft (20·4 m); draught 29·6 ft (9·1 m)

Gun armament: one 5-in (127-mm) L/54 DP in a Mk 45 single mounting, and two 20-mm Phalanx Mk 16 CIWS mountings

Missile armament: two Mk 141 quadruple container-launchers for eight RGM-84 Harpoon anti-ship missiles, and two Vertical Launch Systems (one 29-cell and one 61-cell) for 90 RUR-5A ASROC anti-submarine, RIM-66C Standard SM-2 MR surface-to-air and BGM-109 Tomahawk anti-ship and land-attack cruise missiles

Torpedo armament: none

Anti-submarine armament: ASROC missiles in the VLS (see above), two Mk 32 triple 12·75-in (324-mm) mountings for Mk 46 or Mk 50 Barracuda torpedoes, and helicopter-launched weapons (see below)

Aircraft: one Sikorsky SH-60B Seahawk helicopter on a platform aft

Electronics: one SPY-1D 3D phased-array air-search radar used in conjunction with the AEGIS Weapon-Control System Mk 7, one SPS-67(V) surface-search radar, three SPG-62 illumination radars used in conjunction with three Mk 99 SAM fire-control systems, one Mk 160 Seafire laser gun fire-control) system, one SQQ-89 sonar suite (comprising one SQS-53C active/passive search and attack hull sonar and one SQR-19 passive towed-array sonar) used in conjunction with the Mk 116 underwater weapons fire-control system, one SQQ-28 helicopter data-link sonar, one SLQ-25 Nixie towed torpedo-decoy system, Automatic Data Action System, Link 10, 14 and 16 data-links, one SLQ-32(V)2 ESM system with warning and jamming elements, four Mk 36 Super RBOC chaff/flare launchers, satellite navigation and navigation systems including WSC-3 satellite communications transceivers, and URN-25 TACAN

Propulsion: COGAG arrangement, with four General Electric LM2500-30 gas turbines delivering 100,000 hp (74,570 kW) to two shafts

Performance: maximum speed 32 kt; range 5,750 miles (9250 km) at 20 kt

Complement: 23 + 280

Class

1.USA Name	No.	Builder	Laid down	Commissioned
Arleigh Burke	DDG51	Bath Iron Works	Apr 1987	Feb 1991
John Barry	DDG52	Ingalls SB	Sep 1989	Sep 1991
John Paul Jones	DDG53	Ingalls SB	Apr 1990	Jul 1992
Curtis Wilbur	DDG54	Ingalls SB		

Note: This is an impressive design for an advanced guided-missile destroyer (little short of cruiser size and capability) intended as replacement for the 'Leahy' and 'Belknap' class CGs and the 'Coontz' class DDGs as main partner for the 'Ticonderoga' class cruisers. The core of the design is an austere version of the 'Ticonderoga' class's AEGIS radar/SAM system. Current plans call for a total of 29 units.

The *Arleigh Burke* is in essence a 'Ticonderoga' class austere variant.

'Asagiri' or 'Type 134' class DDG

(Japan)
Type: anti-submarine and anti-ship guided-missile destroyer
Displacement: 3,500 tons standard and 4,200 tons full load
Dimensions: length 137·0 m (449·5 ft); beam 14·6 m (47·9 ft); draught 4·45 m (14·6 ft)
Gun armament: one 76-mm (3-in) OTO Melara L/62 DP in an OTO Melara Compact single mounting, and two 20-mm Phalanx Mk 15 CIWS mountings
Missile armament: two Mk 141 quadruple container-launchers for eight RGM-84 Harpoon anti-ship missiles, and one Mk 29 octuple launcher for RIM-7 NATO Sea Sparrow SAMs
Torpedo armament: none
Anti-submarine armament: one Mk 16 octuple launcher for 16 RUR-5A ASROC missiles, two Type 68 triple 12·75-in (324-mm) mountings for Mk 46 torpedoes, and helicopter-launched weapons (see below)
Aircraft: one Mitsubishi (Sikorsky) HSS-2B Sea King or Mitsubishi (Sikorsky) SH-60J Seahawk helicopter in a hangar aft
Electronics: one OPS-14C or (DD156/158 or OPS-24 air-search radar, one OPS-28C surface-search radar, one Type 2-12E radar used in conjunction with the SAM fire-control system, one Type 2-22 radar used in conjunction with the 76-mm gun fire-control system, one OQS-4A(II) active search and attack hull sonar, one passive search variable-depth sonar (to be fitted), one OYQ-6 action information system, one ESM system with OLR-9R warning and NOLR-6C jamming elements, one SLQ-25 Nixe towed torpedo-decoy system, and two Mk 36 Super RBOC chaff/flare launchers
Propulsion: COGAG arrangement, with four Rolls-Royce Spey SM1A gas turbines delivering 54,000 hp (40,260 kW) to two shafts
Performance: maximum speed 30 + kt
Complement: 220

Above: The *Asagiri's* broad stacks contain the exhausts for four Spey gas turbines, which offer high performance as well as great operating economy.

Class

1. Japan

Name	No.	Builder	Laid down	Com-missioned
Asagiri	DD151	Ishikawajima-Harima	Feb 1985	Mar 1988
Yamagiri	DD152	Mitsui	Feb 1986	Jan 1989
Yuugiri	DD153	Sumitomo	Feb 1986	Feb 1989
Amagiri	DD154	Ishikawajima-Harima	Mar 1986	Mar 1989
Hamagiri	DD155	Hitachi	Jan 1987	Jan 1990
Setogiri	DD156	Sumitomo	Mar 1987	Feb 1990
Sawagiri	DD157	Mitsubishi	Jan 1987	Mar 1990
	DD158	Ishikawajima-Harima	Oct 1988	Mar 1991

Note: This is in essence an improved version of the 'Hatsuyuki' class with a quadruple Spey installation.

Right: The *Audace* features an attractive and effective blend of sensors and weapons in the anti-air, anti-ship and anti-submarine escort roles.

'Audace' class DDG

(Italy)
Type: anti-submarine and anti-aircraft guided-missile escort destroyer
Displacement: 3,600 tons standard and 4,400 tons full load
Dimensions: length 136·6 m (448·0 ft); beam 14·2 m (46·6 ft); draught 4·6 m (15·1 ft)
Gun armament: one 127-mm (5-in) OTO Melara L/54 DP in an OTO Melara Compact single mounting, and four 76-mm (3-in) OTO Melara L/62 DP in OTO Melara Compact single mountings
Missile armament: four twin Teseo 2 container-launchers for eight Otomat anti-ship missiles, one Mk 13 single launcher for 40 RIM-66B Standard SM-1 MR SAMs, and one Albatros octuple launcher for Aspide SAMs
Torpedo armament: four 533-mm (21-in) single launchers for 12 A 184 wire-guided dual-role torpedoes
Anti-submarine armament: two Mk 32 triple 12·75-in (324-mm) mountings for 12 Mk 46 or 324-mm (12·75-in) A 244/S torpedoes, and helicopter-launched weapons (see below)
Aircraft: two Agusta (Bell) AB.212ASW or one Agusta (Sikorsky) ASH-3D Sea King helicopter in a hangar aft
Electronics: one SPS-52C 3D radar, one RAN 3L medium-range air-search radar, one RAN 10S air/surface-search radar, one SPQ 2D surface-search radar, one SPN 748 navigation radar, two SPG-51 illumination and tracking radars used in conjunction with two Mk 74 SAM fire-control systems, three RTN 10X radars used in conjunction with one Argo NA10 127-mm gun and two Dardo-E 40-mm gun fire-control systems, one CWE 610 active/passive search and attack hull sonar, one ESM system with warning and jamming elements, and one SCLAR chaff/flare launcher
Propulsion: four boilers (Ansaldo/Foster-Wheeler in D550 and CNR/Foster-Wheeler in D551) supplying steam to two sets of geared turbines delivering 54,500 kW (73,085 hp) to two shafts
Performance: maximum speed 34 kt; range 5560 km (3,455 miles)
Complement: 30 + 350

Class

1. Italy

Name	No.	Builder	Laid down	Com-missioned
Ardito	D550	Italcantieri	Jul 1968	Dec 1973
Audace	D551	CNR, Riva Trigoso	Apr 1968	Nov 1972

Note: Developed from the 'Impavido' class, the two 'Audace' class ships have greater seaworthiness and habitability combined with the electronics and weapons suiting them to the anti-submarine and anti-aircraft roles. In the late 1980s both ships were modernized with an Albatros short-range SAM launcher in place of the second 127-mm (5-in) guns, and Teseo 2 anti-ship missile launchers in the space between the funnels.

'Charles F. Adams' class DDG

(USA)

Type: anti-aircraft, anti-ship and anti-submarine guided-missile escort destroyer

Displacement: 3,370 tons standard and 4,825 tons full load

Dimensions: length 437·0 ft (133·2 m); beam 47·0 ft (14·3 m); draught 20·0 ft (6·1 m)

Gun armament: two 5-in (127-mm) L/54 DP in Mk 42 single mountings

Missile armament: one Mk 11 twin launcher (DDG2/14) or one Mk 13 single launcher (DDG15/24) for 42 or 40 RIM-66B Standard SM-1 MR SAMs respectively; in all but DDG8, 12, 21 and 23 four to six RGM-84 Harpoon anti-ship missiles can be carried instead of the same number of Standard SAMs

Torpedo armament: none

Anti-submarine armament: one Mk 16 octuple launcher for eight or (some ships only) 12 RUR-5A ASROC missiles, and two Mk 32 triple 12·75-in (324-mm) mountings for Mk 46 torpedoes

Aircraft: none

Electronics: one SPS-52B/C 3D radar, one SPS-40B/D long-range air-search radar, one SPS-10 surface-search radar, one LN-66 navigation radar, two SPG-51C illumination and tracking radars used in conjunction with two Mk 70 or (DDG19, 20 and 22) Mk 74 SAM fire-control systems, one SPG-53A radar or (DDG19, 20 and 22) one SPG-60 search-and-track radar and one SPQ-9A track-while-scan radar used in conjunction with one Mk 68 or (DDG19, 20 and 22) gun fire-control system, one Mk 4 or (DDG19, 20 and 22) Mk 13 weapon direction system, one SQQ-23A or SQS-23D long-range active search-and-attack sonar (hull-mounted in DDG2/19 and bow-mounted in DDG20/24) used in conjunction with the Mk 111 or (DDG16/24) Mk 114 underwater weapons fire-control system, one T Mk 6 Fanfare torpedo decoy system, one SLQ-32(V) ESM system with WLR-6 warning and ULQ-6B jamming elements, one T Mk 6 Fanfare torpedo decoy system, four Mk 36 Super RBOC chaff/flare launchers, one OE-82 satellite communications system, two WSC-3 satellite communications transceivers, one SRR-1 satellite communications receiver, and URN-25 or SRN-6 TACAN

Propulsion: four boilers (Babcock & Wilcox in DDG2, 3, 7, 8, 10/13 and 20/22, Foster-Wheeler in DDG4/6, 9, 14 and 23/24, and Combustion Engineering in DDG15/19) supplying steam to two sets of geared turbines (General Electric in DDG2, 3, 7, 8, 10/13 and 15/22, or Westinghouse in DDG4/6, 9, 14 and 22/23) delivering 70,000 hp (52,200 kW) to two shafts

Performance: maximum speed 31·5 kt; range 6,900 miles (11,105 km) at 14 kt or 1,840 miles (2960 km) at 30 kt

Complement: 20 + 340

The *Tattnall* is seen leaving port after being revised with the Hughes SPS-52C (in place of SPS-39A) 3D radar on the front of the after funnel.

Class

1. Australia ('Perth' class)

Name	No.	Builder	Laid down	Com-missioned
Perth	D38	Defoe SB	Sep 1962	Jul 1965
Hobart	D39	Defoe SB	Oct 1962	Dec 1965
Brisbane	D41	Defoe SB	Feb 1965	Dec 1967

(The Australian ships are similar to the American norm with the Mk 13 single launcher for Standard SAMs, but have the Ikara anti-submarine system [two single launchers and 32 missiles per ship] with SQS-23F sonar and Type 975 navigation radar plus a number of other differences in the electronic fit.)

2. USA

Name	No.	Builder	Laid down	Com-missioned
Charles F. Adams	DDG2	Bath Iron Works	Jun 1958	Sep 1960
John King	DDG3	Bath Iron Works	Aug 1958	Feb 1961
Lawrence	DDG4	New York SB	Oct 1958	Jan 1962
Claude V. Ricketts	DDG5	New York SB	May 1959	May 1962
Barney	DDG6	New York SB	May 1959	Aug 1962
Henry B. Wilson	DDG7	Defoe SB	Feb 1958	Dec 1960
Lynde McCormick	DDG8	Defoe SB	Apr 1958	Jun 1961
Towers	DDG9	Todd Pacific	Apr 1958	Jun 1961
Sampson	DDG10	Bath Iron Works	Mar 1959	Jun 1961
Sellers	DDG11	Bath Iron Works	Aug 1959	Oct 1961
Robison	DDG12	Defoe SB	Apr 1959	Dec 1961
Hoel	DDG13	Defoe SB	Jun 1959	Jun 1962
Buchanan	DDG14	Todd Pacific	Apr 1959	Feb 1962
Berkeley	DDG15	New York SB	Jun 1960	Dec 1962
Joseph Strauss	DDG16	New York SB	Dec 1960	Apr 1963
Conyngham	DDG17	New York SB	May 1961	Jul 1963
Semmes	DDG18	Avondale Marine	Aug 1960	Dec 1962
Tattnall	DDG19	Avondale Marine	Nov 1960	Apr 1963
Goldsborough	DDG20	Puget Sound Bridge	Jan 1961	Nov 1963
Cochrane	DDG21	Puget Sound Bridge	Jul 1961	Mar 1964
Benjamin Stoddert	DDG22	Puget Sound Bridge	Jun 1962	Sep 1964
Richard E. Byrd	DDG23	Todd Pacific	Apr 1961	Mar 1964
Waddell	DDG24	Todd Pacific	Feb 1962	Aug 1964

(The basic design is an improvement on the 'Forrest Sherman' class design with an aluminium superstructure to reduce topweight. It was planned to undertake a complete modernization of the class from 1980s, but as funds were not available a measure of updating has been achieved on a piecemeal basis, starting with DDG19, 20 and 22, which approximate to the standard intended in the 'DDG Upgrade' programme.)

The *Conyngham* of the 'Charles F. Adams' class is seen during under-way replenishment. Highly visible between the funnels is the ASROC launcher.

Visible on the *Hoel's* after section are the two SPG-51C SAM radars, the after 5-in (127-mm) gun, and the Mk 11 twin-arm SAM launcher.

'Charles F. Adams (Modified)' or 'Type 103B' class DDG

(USA/West Germany)

Type: anti-aircraft, anti-submarine and anti-ship guided-missile destroyer

Displacement: 3,370 tons standard and 4,500 tons full load

Dimensions: length 437·0 ft (133·2 m); beam 47·0 ft (14·3 m); draught 222·0 ft (6·7 m)

Gun armament: two 5-in (127-mm) L/54 DP in Mk 42 single mountings

Missile armament: one Mk 13 single launcher for 40 RIM-67B Standard SM-1 MR SAMs and, with the SAM numbers reduced, several RGM-84 Harpoon anti-ship missiles, and (to be fitted) two EX-31 container-launchers for 48 RIM-116 RAM SAMs

Torpedo armament: none

Anti-submarine armament: one Mk 16 octuple launcher for eight RUR-5A ASROC missiles, two Mk 32 triple 12·75-in (324-mm) mountings for Mk 46 torpedoes, and one depth-charge mortar

Aircraft: none

Electronics: one SPS-52 3D radar, one SPS-40 long-range air-search radar, one SPS-10 surface-search radar, two SPG-51 illumination and tracking radars used in conjunction with two Mk 74 SAM fire-control systems, one SPG-60 search-and-track radar and one SPQ-9 track-while-scan radar used in conjunction with the Mk 86 gun fire-control system, one Krupp-Atlas DSQS-21 active/passive search and attack hull sonar, one SATIR 1 action information system, Link 11 data-link, one FL-1800S ESM system with warning and jamming elements, one satellite communications system (to be fitted), one Mk 36 Super RBOC chaff/flare launcher, and URN-20 TACAN

Propulsion: four Combustion Engineering boilers supplying steam to two sets of geared turbines delivering 70,000 hp (52,200 kW) to two shafts

Performance: maximum speed 31·5 kt; range 5,200 miles (8370 km) at 20 kt

Complement: 19 + 318

Class

1. West Germany ('Lütjens' class)

Name	No.	Builder	Laid down	Commissioned
Lütjens	D185	Bath Iron Works	Mar 1966	Mar 1969
Mölders	D186	Bath Iron Works	Apr 1966	Sep 1969
Rommel	D187	Bath Iron Works	Aug 1967	May 1970

Note: These are very seaworthy multi-role ships modelled closely on the American norm but fitted with a 'mack' (combined mast and stack) layout and a number of German electronic items. The ships were modernized in the early 1980s to a standard approximating to that of the US Navy's proposed 'DDG Upgrade' programme.

The *Lutjens* of the 'Charles F. Adams (Modified)' class makes an interesting comparison with the American 'Charles F. Adams' class.

'China' class DDG

(China)

Type: anti-ship, anti-aircraft and anti-submarine guided-missile destroyer
Displacement: 4,200 tons full load
Dimensions: length 132·0 m (249·3 ft); beam 12·8 m (42·0 ft); draught 4·0 m (13·1 ft)
Gun armament: one 100-mm (3·94-in) Creusot Loire L/55 DP in a Creusot Loire Compact single mounting, eight 37-mm L/63 AA in four twin mountings, and one 20-mm Phalanx Mk 15 CIWS mounting
Missile armament: eight container-launchers for eight C-801 anti-ship missiles, and two twin launchers for HQ-61 SAMs
Torpedo armament: none
Anti-submarine armament: two ILAS 3 triple 324-mm (12·75-in) mountings for lightweight torpedoes, and helicopter-launched weapons (see below)
Aircraft: one Harbin Zhi-9A helicopter in a hangar aft

'County' class DDG

(UK/Chile)

Type: anti-aircraft and anti-ship guided-missile destroyer
Displacement: 5,440 tons standard and 6,200 tons full load
Dimensions: length 520·5 ft (158·7 m); beam 54·0 ft (16·5 m); draught 20·5 ft (6·3 m)
Gun armament: two 4·5-in (114-mm) Vickers L/45 DP in one Mk 6 twin mounting, and two 20-mm Oerlikon AA in Mk 9 single mountings
Missile armament: two twin container-launchers for four MM.38 Exocet anti-ship missiles, one twin launcher for 36 Sea Slug Mk 2 SAMs (12 and 14 only), and two quadruple launchers for 32 Sea Cat SAMs (not in 14); from 1990 the Sea Slug and Sea Cat systems are to be replaced by one Barak 1 SAM system
Torpedo armament: none
Anti-submarine armament: two STWS-2 triple 12·75-in (324-mm) mountings for Mk 46 or Stingray torpedoes, and helicopter-launched weapons (see below)
Aircraft: one Aérospatiale SA 319B Alouette III Astazou helicopter (12 and 14) or two Aérospatiale/Nurtanio NAS 332F Super Puma helicopters (11 and 15) in a hangar aft
Electronics: one Type 965M or (14 and 15) Type 966 air-search radar, one Type 992R surface-search radar, one Type 977M air control radar, one Type 901 radar used in conjunction with the Sea Slug fire-control system (not in 15), two Type 904 radars used in conjunction with two GWS 22 Sea Cat fire-control systems (not in 14), one Type 903 radar used in conjunction with the MRS3 gun fire-control system, one Type 978 or Type 1006 navigation radar, one Type 162M side-looking classification hull sonar, one Type 184M or (15) Type 184S active search and attack hull sonar, one ADAWS 1 action information system, one Type 182 towed torpedo-decoy system, one UA-8/9 ESM system with warning element, two Corvus chaff launchers, and two Barricade chaff launchers
Propulsion: COSAG arrangement, with two Babcock & Wilcox boilers supplying steam to two sets of AEI geared turbines delivering 30,000 hp (22,370 kW) and four English Electric G.6 gas turbines delivering 30,000 hp (22,370 kW) to two shafts
Performance: maximum speed 30 kt; range 4,000 miles (6440 km) at 28 kt
Complement: 36 + 444

Class
1. Chile

Name	No.	Builder	Laid down	Commissioned
Capitan Prat	11	Swan Hunter	Mar 1966	Mar 1970
Almirante Cochrane	12	Fairfield SB	Jan 1966	Jul 1970
Almirante Latorre	14	Vickers	Sep 1962	Oct 1966
Blanco Encalada	15	Fairfield SB	Jun 1962	Jun 1966

(These Chilean ships were transferred in April 1982, June 1984, October 1986 and August 1987 respectively. They are currently seen in two standard forms after conversion in local yards on delivery from the UK between 1982 and 1987. The *Capitan Prat* and *Blanco Encalada* have been stripped of their Sea Slug launchers, the quarterdeck space thus made available being used for a larger helicopter platform and hangar: this can accommodate up to four Alouette IIIs or, for enhanced anti-submarine capability in conjunction with a possible towed-array sonar, up to two NAS 332F Super Pumas. The Chilean navy has recently revealed that from 1990 the ships are to be fitted with a point-defence SAM system of the vertical-launch type, the choice between the GWS 26 Vertical-Launch Seawolf from the UK and the IAI Barak from Israel having been decided in favour of the Israeli system.)

Electronics: not revealed
Propulsion: CODOG arrangement, with two General Electric LM2500 gas turbines delivering 50,000 hp (37,280 kW) or two SEMT-Pielstick diesels delivering unrevealed power to two shafts
Performance: maximum speed 32 kt; range 9250 km (5,750 miles) at 16 kt
Complement: 220

Class
1. China

Name	No.	Builder	Laid down	Commissioned
		Jiangnan, Shanghai		1990
		Jiangnan, Shanghai		

Note: This new destroyer class appears to have a hull based on that of the 'Luda' class but in this instance mounting a Franco-American propulsion arrangement and a mix of Chinese and Western weapons.

2. Pakistan

Name	No.	Builder	Laid down	Commissioned
Babur	C84	Swan Hunter	Feb 1960	Nov 1963

(This ship was transferred in May 1982, and is classified by the Pakistani navy as a cruiser. The Sea Slug SAM system and its associated electronics have been removed to create additional volume for accommodation and classrooms for trainees. The ship currently operates an Aérospatiale SA 319B Alouette III Astazou light helicopter, but the flight deck and hangar are being extended to make possible the embarkation of three or four Westland Sea King Mk 45 medium helicopters with anti-ship missiles in addition to their conventional anti-submarine weapons and sensors. The sonar suite comprises four British equipments, namely Type 176 passive search and torpedo warning, Type 177 active search and attack, and Type 162 active classification and attack types.)

The Royal Navy's 'County' class *Norfolk* is now the Chilean navy's *Almirante Cochrane*, one of four such units in Chilean service.

'F65' class DDG

(France)

Type: anti-submarine and anti-ship guided-missile escort destroyer
Displacement: 3,500 tons standard and 3,900 tons full load
Dimensions: length 127·0 m (416·7 ft); beam 13·4 m (44·0 ft); draught 5·8 m (18·9 ft)
Gun armament: two 100-mm (3·9-in) Creusot Loire L/55 DP in Modèle 1968 single mountings
Missile armament: two quadruple container-launchers for eight MM.40 Exocet anti-ship missiles
Torpedo armament: none
Anti-submarine armament: one single launcher for 13 Malafon anti-submarine missiles, and two single 533-mm (21-in) launchers for 10 L5 torpedoes
Aircraft: none
Electronics: one DRBV 22A air-search radar, one DRBV 15 air/surface-search radar, one DRBN 32 navigation radar, one DRBC 32B radar used in conjunction with the gun fire-control system, one DUBV 23 active/passive search and attack hull sonar, one DUBV 43 passive variable-depth sonar, one SENIT 3 action information system, one ESM system with ARBR 16 warning and ARBB 32 jamming elements, one SLQ-25 Nixie towed torpedo-decoy system, and two Syllex chaff launchers
Propulsion: two boilers supplying steam to one Rateau geared turbine delivering 21,350 kW (28,635 hp) to one shaft
Performance: maximum speed 27 kt; range 9250 km (5,750 miles) at 18 kt
Complement: 15 + 213

Seen with an earlier pennant number, the *Aconit* has the antenna for its DRBV-13 search radar in the large radome above the forward superstructure.

Class

1. France			Laid	Com-
Name	No.	Builder	down	missioned
Aconit	D609	Lorient ND	Jan 1966	Mar 1973

Note: This ship was the only example of the 'C65' (now 'F65') class, and was produced as the forerunner of the 'C67' (now 'F67') class. It has recently been fitted with a second quadruple container-launcher for Exocet anti-ship missiles, now of the longer-range MM.40 rather than the original MM.38 variety. DSBV 61/62 passive towed-array sonar is to be fitted.

'F67' class DDG

(France)

Type: anti-submarine and anti-ship guided-missile destroyer
Displacement: 4,580 tons standard and 5,745 tons full load
Dimensions: length 152·75 m (501·1 ft); beam 15·3 m (50·2 ft); draught 5·7 m (18·7 ft)
Gun armament: two 100-mm (3·9-in) Creusot Loire L/55 DP in Modèle 1968 single mountings, and two 20-mm AA in single mountings
Missile armament: two triple container-launchers for six MM.38 Exocet anti-ship missiles, and one Naval Crotale octuple launcher for 26 R.440 SAMs
Torpedo armament: none
Anti-submarine armament: one launcher for 13 Malafon missiles, and two single 533-mm (21-in) launchers for 10 L5 torpedoes
Aircraft: two Westland Lynx HAS.Mk 2/4 helicopters in a hangar aft
Electronics: one DRBV 26 air-search radar, one DRBV 51 air/surface-search radar, two RM1226 navigation radars, one DRBC 32D radar used in conjunction with the 100-mm gun fire-control system, one Vega weapon direction system, one DUBV 23B active/passive search and attack hull sonar, one DUBV 43B/C variable-depth sonar, one DUBV 61 passive search towed-array sonar, one SENIT 3 action information system, one ESM system with ARBR 16 warning and ARBB 32 jamming elements, one Syracuse satellite communications system, and two Syllex (being replaced by Dagaie) chaff launchers
Propulsion: four boilers supplying steam to two sets of Rateau geared turbines delivering 40,500 kW (54,320 hp) to two shafts
Performance: speed 32 kt; range 9250 km (5,750 miles) at 18 kt or 3500 km (2,175 miles) at 30 kt
Complement: 21 + 280

Class

1. France			Laid	Com-
Name	No.	Builder	down	missioned
Tourville	D610	Lorient ND	Mar 1970	Jun 1974
Duguay-Trouin	D611	Lorient ND	Feb 1971	Sep 1975
De Grasse	D612	Lorient ND	Jun 1972	Oct 1977

Note: Developed from the 'Aconit' class units, these capable ships are to be upgraded in the early 1990s to incorporate improved anti-submarine capability through the retrofit of the SLASM active/passive towed-array sonar, Murène torpedoes, and the OTO-Melara/Matra Milas rather than Malafon vehicle for the stand-off delivery of anti-submarine torpedoes.

The *Tourville* is leader of a three-strong development of the 'F65' class.

'F70/AA' class DDG

(France)

Type: anti-aircraft and anti-ship guided-missile escort destroyer
Displacement: 4,000 tons standard and 4,340 tons full load
Dimensions: length 139·0 m (456·0 ft); beam 14·0 m (45·9 ft); draught 5·7 m (18·7 ft)
Gun armament: one 100-mm (3·9-in) Creusot Loire L/55 DP in a Modèle 1968-II single mounting, and two 20-mm AA in single mountings
Missile armament: four twin container-launchers for eight MM.40 Exocet anti-ship missiles, one Mk 13 single launcher for 40 RIM-66C Standard SM-1 MR SAMs, and two SADRAL sextuple launchers for Mistral SAMs
Torpedo armament: none
Anti-submarine armament: two single 533-mm (21-in) launchers for 10 L5 torpedoes, and helicopter-launched weapons (see below)
Aircraft: one Westland Lynx Mk 2/4 helicopter on a platform aft
Electronics: one DRBJ 11B 3D air-search radar, one DRBV 26 air/surface-search radar, two RM1229 navigation radars, one DRBC 33 radar used in conjunction with the 100-mm gun fire-control system, two DRBR 51 (SPG-51C) radars used with the SAM fire-control system, one Vega weapon direction system, one Naja optronic, one Piranha II and one Piranha IV directors, one SENIT 6 action information system, Link 11 and 14 data-links, one DUBA 25A active search and attack hull sonar, one DSBV 61A passive search towed-array sonar (possibly to be fitted), one ESM system with ARBR 17 warning and ARBB 33 jamming elements, one DIBV 10 Vampir IR surveillance system, one SLQ-25 Nixie towed torpedo-decoy system, two Dagaie chaff/flare launchers, two Sagaie chaff/flare launchers, one Syracuse satellite communications system, and URN-20 TACAN
Propulsion: four SEMT-Pielstick 18 PA6 V280 BTC diesels delivering 31,600 kW (42,380 hp) to two shafts
Performance: maximum speed 29·5 kt; range 15,200 km (9,445 miles) at 17 kt or 9250 km (5,750 miles) at 24 kt
Complement: 22 + 218 with a maximum of 251 possible

Class

1. France Name	No.	Builder	Laid down	Commissioned
Cassard	D614	Lorient ND	Sep 1982	Jul 1988
Jean Bart	D615	Lorient ND	Mar 1986	1991

Note: Though this used the same hull as the 'F70/ASW' class, the armament and propulsion of this variant (originally designated the 'C70/AA' class) have been completely revised for the ships' primary air-defence role, though useful anti-ship and anti-submarine capabilities are still featured. The third and fourth units of the class *Courbet* [D616] and *Chevalier Paul* [D617] have been postponed pending availability of the new SAMP system with Arabel 3D radar and the SAN 90/Aster SAM. As this missile is designed for a vertical launch system, the last two units will inevitably have an appearance considerably different from that of their half-sisters.

A model reveals the salient features of the 'F70/AA' class destroyer in its present form of just two ships. Later units may be considerably different.

'F70/ASW' class DDG

(France)

Type: anti-submarine and anti-ship guided-missile destroyer
Displacement: 3,830 tons standard and 4,170 tons full load
Dimensions: length 139·0 m (456·0 ft); beam 14·0 m (45·9 ft); draught 5·7 m (18·7 ft)
Gun armament: one 100-mm (3·9-in) Creusot Loire L/55 DP in a Modèle 1968-II single mounting, and two 20-mm AA in single mountings
Missile armament: four container-launchers for four MM.38 Exocet (MM.40 Exocet in D642 onwards) anti-ship missiles, and one Naval Crotale octuple launcher for 26 R.440 SAMs
Torpedo armament: none
Anti-submarine armament: two single 533-mm (21-in) launchers for 10 L5 torpedoes, and helicopter-launched weapons (see below)
Aircraft: two Westland Lynx Mk 2/4 helicopters in a hangar aft
Electronics: one DRBV 26 air-search radar (not in D644/646), one DRBV 51C or (D644/646) DRBV 15 air/surface-search radar, two RM1226 navigation radars, one DRBC 32D or (D644/646) DRBC 32E radar used in conjunction with the 100-mm gun fire-control system, one SENIT 4 action information system, one Vega weapon direction system, one Panda optical director, one DUBV 23D or (D644/646) DUBV 24C active search and attack hull sonar, one DUBV 43B or (D643/646) DUBV 43C passive search variable-depth sonar and (D644 onwards with retrofit in earlier ships from 1991) one DSBV 61A passive search towed-array sonar used in conjunction with the SLASM underwater weapons fire-control system, one ESM system with ARBR 16 or (D643

onwards with retrofit in earlier ships) ARBR 17 warning and ARBB 32B jamming elements, one DIBV 10 IR detector, and two Dagaie chaff/decoy launchers
Propulsion: CODOG arrangement, with two Rolls-Royce Olympus TM3B gas turbines delivering 46,200 hp (34,445 kW) or two SEMT-Pielstick 16 PA6 CV280 diesels delivering 7750 kW (10,395 hp) to two shafts
Performance: maximum speed 30 kt on gas turbines or 18 kt on diesels; range 15,750 km (9,785 miles) at 17 kt on diesels
Complement: 15 + 201 with a maximum of 250 possible

Class

1. France Name	No.	Builder	Laid down	Commissioned
Georges Leygues	D640	Brest ND	Sep 1974	Dec 1979
Dupleix	D641	Brest ND	Oct 1975	Jun 1981
Montcalm	D642	Brest ND	Dec 1975	May 1982
Jean de Vienne	D643	Brest ND	Oct 1979	May 1984
Primauguet	D644	Brest ND	Nov 1981	Nov 1986
La Motte-Piquet	D645	Brest ND	Feb 1982	Feb 1988
Latouche-Tréville	D646	Brest ND	May 1985	1990

Note: These are basically anti-submarine ships relying on helicopters as their main weapon platforms in this role. The anti-ship secondary weapon fit is also good, but the air-defence armament is intended only for self-defence.

***Georges Leygues* is lead ship of the 'F70/ASW' class, whose main anti-submarine weapons are its embarked helicopters and ship-launched torpedoes.**

'Farragut' or 'Coontz' class DDG

(USA)
Type: anti-aircraft, anti-submarine and anti-ship guided-missile destroyer
Displacement: 4,580 tons standard and 6,150 tons full load
Dimensions: length 512·5 ft (156·3 m); beam 52·5 ft (16·0 m); draught 23·4 ft (7·1 m)
Gun armament: one 5-in (127-mm) L/54 DP in a Mk 42 single mounting
Missile armament: two Mk 141 quadruple container-launchers for eight RGM-84 Harpoon anti-ship missiles, and one Mk 10 twin launcher for 40 RIM-67B Standard SM-2 ER SAMs
Torpedo armament: none
Anti-submarine armament: one Mk 16 octuple launcher for eight RUR-5A ASROC missiles, two Mk 32 triple 12·75-in (324-mm) mountings for Mk 46 torpedoes, and (sometimes) helicopter-launched weapons (see below)
Aircraft: provision for one Kaman SH-2F Seasprite helicopter on a platform aft
Electronics: one SPS-48C or (DDG42) SPS-48E 3D radar, one SPS-49(V)5 long-range air-search radar, one SPS-10B surface-search radar, one LN-66 navigation radar (only in DDG37, 39, 40, 42 and 44), two SPG-55B illumination and guidance radars used in conjunction with two Mk 76 SAM fire-control systems, one SPG-53 radar used in conjunction with one Mk 68 gun fire-control system, one Mk 14 weapon direction system, one SQQ-23A active search and attack hull sonar used in conjunction with the Mk 111 underwater weapons fire-control system, Naval Tactical Data System, Link 11 and 14 data-links, one T Mk 6 Fanfare torpedo decoy system, one SLQ-32(V) ESM system with warning and jamming elements, four Mk 36 Super RBOC chaff/flare launchers, one OE-82 satellite communications system, two WSC-3 satellite communications transceivers, one SRR-1 satellite communications receiver, and URN-25 TACAN
Propulsion: four boilers (Foster-Wheeler in DDG37/39 and Babcock & Wilcox in DDG40/46) supplying steam to two sets of geared turbines (De Laval in DDG37/39 and Allis-Chalmers in DDG40/45) delivering 85,000 hp (63,385 kW) to two shafts
Performance: speed 33 kt; range 5,750 miles (9255 km) at 20 kt
Complement: 25 + 377 plus provision for 7 + 12 flag staff

Note: Also known as the **'Coontz' class** because this was the first ship of the class ordered as a guided-missile frigate rather than as a frigate, these ships are highly capable anti-submarine and long-range anti-aircraft destroyers, though the high quality of the electronic suite and the provision of Harpoon missiles provides a powerful anti-ship capability. The ships are being upgraded in the 'New Threat Upgrade' programme with RIM-67B rather than RIM-67A SAMs, improved search and fire-control radars, and (when available) the SYS-2 computerized action information system.

Class
1. USA

Name	No.	Builder	Laid down	Commissioned
Farragut	DDG37	Bethlehem Steel	Jun 1957	Dec 1960
Luce	DDG38	Bethlehem Steel	Oct 1957	May 1961
MacDonough	DDG39	Bethlehem Steel	Apr 1958	Nov 1961
Coontz	DDG40	Puget Sound NY	Mar 1957	Jul 1960
King	DDG41	Puget Sound NY	Mar 1957	Nov 1960
Mahan	DDG42	San Francisco NY	Jul 1957	Aug 1960
Dahlgren	DDG43	Philadelphia NY	Mar 1958	Apr 1961
William V. Pratt	DDG44	Philadelphia NY	Mar 1958	Nov 1961
Dewey	DDG45	Bath Iron Works	Aug 1957	Dec 1959
Preble	DDG46	Bath Iron Works	Dec 1957	May 1960

The *Luce* is a typical unit of the 'Farragut' class, which is somewhat elderly but retains a high level of operational capability because of its updated electronic and weapon suites.

'Halifax' class DDG

(Canada)
Type: anti-submarine and anti-ship guided-missile destroyer
Displacement: 4,750 tons full load
Dimensions: length 440·0 ft (134·1 m); beam 53·8 ft (16·4 m); draught 15·1 ft (4·6 m)
Gun armament: one 57-mm L/70 DP in a Bofors Mk 2 single mounting, one 20-mm Phalanx Mk 16 CIWS mounting, and eight 7·62-mm (0·3-in) machine-guns
Missile armament: two Mk 141 quadruple container-launchers for eight RGM-84 Harpoon anti-ship missiles, and two octuple vertical-launch systems for 28 RIM-7 Sea Sparrow SAMs
Torpedo armament: none
Anti-submarine armament: two Mk 32 twin 12·75-in (324-mm) mountings for Mk 46 torpedoes, and helicopter-launched weapons (see below)
Aircraft: one Sikorsky CH-124A Sea King or European Helicopter Industries EH.101 helicopter in a hangar aft
Electronics: one SPS-49(V)5 long-range air-search radar, one Sea Giraffe HC 150 medium-range air/surface-search radar, one Raytheon Mk 340 navigation radar, two WM-25 STIR illuminating and tracking radars used in conjunction with two SAM fire-control systems, one SQS-505 active search and attack hull sonar and one SQR-501 CANTASS passive search towed-array sonar used in conjunction with the UCS 257 underwater weapons fire-control system, one IR search and target designation system, one SLQ-25 Nixie towed torpedo-decoy system, one ESM system with SLQ-501 CANEWS warning and SLQ-503 RAMSES jamming elements, two Shield chaff/flare launchers, and one WSC-3 satellite communications transceiver

Propulsion: CODOG arrangement, with two General Electric LM2500 gas turbines delivering 50,000 hp (37,285 kW) or one SEMT-Pielstick 20 PA6 V20 diesel delivering 6000 kW (8,045 hp) to two shafts
Performance: speed 29 + kt; range 5,200 miles (8370 km) at 15 kt
Complement: 185 in time of peace, or 225 in time of war

Class
1. Canada

Name	No.	Builder	Laid down	Commissioned
Halifax	DD330	St John SB	Mar 1987	1990
Vancouver	DD331	Marine Industries	Feb 1988	1990
Ville de Quebec	DD332	St John SB	Dec 1988	1990
Toronto	DD333	Marine Industries	Feb 1988	1991
Regina	DD334	St John SB		1991
Calgary	DD335	Marine Industries		1992
Montreal	DD336	St John SB		1992
Fredericton	DD337	St John SB		1993
Winnipeg	DD338	St John SB		1994
Charlottetown	DD339	St John SB		1995
St John's	DD340	St John SB		1995
Ottawa	DD341	St John SB		1996

Note: This is a nicely balanced design offering a judicious blend of anti-ship and anti-submarine capability (the latter through use of medium helicopters) together with a capable short-range anti-aircraft defence. Canada had planned to produce the last six ships as the generally similar **'Montreal' class** subvariant with the length stretched by 33 ft (10·0 m) to provide better habitability and to allow an increase in Sea Sparrow numbers to 56, but this idea seems to have been abandoned.

'Hamburg' or 'Type 101A' class DDG

(West Germany)

Type: anti-ship and anti-submarine guided-missile destroyer

Displacement: 3,340 tons standard and 4,680 tons full load

Dimensions: length 133·7 m (438·6 ft); beam 13·4 m (44·0 ft); draught 6·2 m (20·3 ft)

Gun armament: three 100-mm (3·9-in) Creusot Loire L/55 DP in Modèle 1954 single mountings, and eight 40-mm Bofors L/70 AA in four Breda twin mountings

Missile armament: two twin container-launchers for four MM.38 Exocet anti-ship missiles

Torpedo armament: none

Anti-submarine armament: two 375-mm (14·76-in) Bofors four-barrel rocket-launchers, one quadruple 533-mm (21-in) mounting for torpedoes, two depth-charge throwers, and depth-charge rails

Aircraft: none

Mines: 60/80 depending on type

Electronics: one LW-04 air-search radar, one DA-08 air/surface-search radar, one ZW-01 surface-search radar, one Kelvin Hughes 14/9 navigation radar, three radars used in conjunction with three WM-45 gun fire-control systems, one ELAC 1BV active search and attack hull sonar used in conjunction with a Hollandse Signaalapparaten underwater weapons fire-control system, one ESM system with WLR-6 warning element, and two SCLAR chaff launchers

Propulsion: four Wahodag boilers supplying steam to two sets of Wahodag geared turbines delivering 50,700 kW (67,990 hp) to two shafts

Performance: maximum speed 34 kt; range 11,125 km (6,915 miles) at 13 kt or 1700 km (1,055 miles) at 34 kt

Complement: 19 + 249

The obsolescent 'Hamburg' class destroyer *Schleswig-Holstein* reveals key elements of the type's largely imported sensor and weapon suites.

Class

1. West Germany			Laid	Com-
Name	No.	Builder	down	missioned
Hamburg	D181	H.C.Stulcken	Jan 1959	Mar 1964
Schleswig-Holstein	D182	H.C.Stulcken	Aug 1959	Oct 1964
Bayern	D183	H.C.Stulcken	Sep 1960	Jul 1965
Hessen	D184	H.C.Stulcken	Feb 1961	Oct 1968

Note: Though modernized in the mid-1970s with more modern radars and anti-ship missiles, these vessels are at best obsolescent by Western European standards because of their indifferent anti-aircraft defences.

'Haruna' or 'Type 141' class DDG

(Japan)

Type: anti-submarine and anti-ship guided-missile destroyer

Displacement: 4,700 tons (DD142) or 4,950 tons standard and 6,300 tons full load

Dimensions: length 153·0 m (502·0 ft); beam 17·5 m (57·4 ft); draught 5·1 m (16·7 ft)

Gun armament: two 5-in (127-mm) L/54 DP in Mk 42 single mountings, and two 20-mm Phalanx Mk 15 CIWS mountings

Missile armament: two Mk 141 quadruple container-launchers for eight RGM-84 Harpoon anti-ship missiles, and one octuple launcher for 24 RIM-7 Sea Sparrow SAMs

Torpedo armament: none

Anti-submarine armament: one Mk 16 octuple launcher for 16 RUR-5A ASROC missiles, two Type 68 triple 12·75-in (324-mm) mountings for Mk 46 torpedoes, and helicopter-launched weapons (see below)

Aircraft: three Mitsubishi (Sikorsky) HSS-3B Sea King helicopters in a hangar aft

Electronics: one OPS-11C air-search radar, one OPS-28 surface-search radar, two radars used in conjunction with two Type 1A gun fire-control systems, one radar used in conjunction with one Type 2-12 SAM fire-control system, one OQS-3 active search and attack hull sonar, one OYQ-6 action information system, one ESM system with OLR-9 warning and NOLQ-1 jamming elements, four Mk 36 Super RBOC chaff launchers, and URN-6 TACAN

Propulsion: two boilers supplying steam to two sets of Ishikawajima/General Electric geared turbines delivering 52,200 kW (70,000 hp) to two shafts

Performance: speed 32 kt

Complement: 36 + 334

Class

1. Japan			Laid	Com-
Name	No.	Builder	down	missioned
Haruna	DD141	Mitsubishi	Mar 1970	Feb 1973
Hiei	DD142	Ishikawajima	Mar 1972	Nov 1974

Note: Predecessors of the 'Shirane' class ships, the two 'Haruna' class units are in essence small helicopter cruisers whose primary task is anti-submarine warfare with their three helicopters and ASROC missiles. Anti-ship and anti-aircraft capabilities are well provided.

The 'Haruna' class *Hiei* has a particularly striking appearance, and includes a substantial platform for its three large helicopters.

'Hatakaze' or 'Type 171' class DDG

(Japan)

Type: anti-aircraft, anti-submarine and anti-ship guided-missile destroyer

Displacement: 4,600 tons or (DD172) 4,650 tons standard and 5,500 tons full load

Dimensions: length 150·0 m (492·1 ft); beam 16·4 m (53·8 ft); draught 4·7 m (15·4 ft)

Gun armament: two 5-in (127-mm) L/54 DP in Mk 42 single mountings, and two 20-mm Phalanx Mk 15 CIWS mountings

Missile armament: two Mk 141 quadruple container-launchers for eight RGM-84 Harpoon anti-ship missiles, and one Mk 13 single launcher for 40 RIM-66B Standard SM-1 MR SAMs

Torpedo armament: none

Anti-submarine armament: one Mk 16 octuple launcher for 16 RUR-5A ASROC missiles, and two Type 68 triple 12·75-in (324-mm) mountings for Mk 46 torpedoes

Aircraft: provision for one Mitsubishi (Sikorsky) HSS-3B Sea King helicopter on a platform aft

Electronics: one SPS-52C 3D radar, one OPS-11 air-search radar, one OPS-28B surface-search radar, two SPG-51 illumination and tracking radars used in conjunction with two Mk 74 SAM fire-control systems, one Type 127 radar used in conjunction with one Type 2-21C 127-mm gun fire-control system, one OQS-4 active/passive search and attack hull sonar used in conjunction with the Mk 114 underwater weapons fire-control system, one OYQ-4 action information system, one ESM system with NOLQ-1 warning and OLT-3 jamming elements, two Mk 36 Super RBOC chaff/flare launchers, and URN-25 TACAN

Propulsion: COGAG arrangement, with two Rolls-Royce Olympus SM3B gas turbines and two Rolls-Royce Spey SM1A gas turbines delivering a total of 90,200 hp (67,260 kW) to two shafts

Performance: speed 32 kt

Complement: 260

The 'Hatakaze' class *Shimakaze's* foredeck sports three weapon systems.

Class 1. Japan Name	No.	Builder	Laid down	Commissioned
Hatakaze	DD171	Mitsubishi	May 1983	Mar 1986
Shimakaze	DD172	Mitsubishi	Jan 1985	Mar 1988

Note: This is a nicely balanced design optimized for anti-submarine warfare but possessing good anti-ship and anti-aircraft capabilities.

'Hatsuyuki' or 'Type 122' class DDG

(Japan)

Type: anti-submarine and anti-ship guided-missile destroyer

Displacement: 2,950 tons or (DD129 onwards) 3,050 tons standard and 3,700 tons full load

Dimensions: length 130·0 m (426·5 ft); beam 13·6 m (44·6 ft); draught 4·2 m (13·8 ft) or (DD129 onward) 4·4 m (14·4 ft)

Gun armament: one 76-mm (3-in) OTO Melara L/62 DP in an OTO Melara Compact single mounting, and (DD124 onwards) two 20-mm Phalanx Mk 15 CIWS mountings

Missile armament: two Mk 141 quadruple container-launchers for eight RGM-84 Harpoon anti-ship missiles, and one Type 3 (Mk 29) octuple launcher for 12 RIM-7 NATO Sea Sparrow SAMs

Torpedo armament: none

Anti-submarine armament: one Mk 16 octuple launcher for 16 RUR-5A ASROC missiles, two Type 68 triple 12·75-in (324-mm) mountings for Mk 46 torpedoes, and helicopter-launched weapons (see below)

Aircraft: one Mitsubishi (Sikorsky) HSS-3B Sea King helicopter in a hangar aft

Electronics: one OPS-14B air-search radar, one OPS-18 surface-search radar, one radar used in conjunction with the Type 2-12A SAM fire-control system, two radars used in conjunction with two Type 2-21A gun fire-control systems, one OQS-4A(II) active search and attack hull sonar and (to be fitted) one SQR-19 passive search towed-array sonar, one OYQ-5 action information system, Link 14 data-link, one ESM system with NOLR-6C warning and OLT-3 jamming elements, two Mk 36 Super RBOC chaff/flare launchers, and one URN-25 TACAN

Propulsion: COGOG arrangement, with two Kawasaki/Rolls-Royce Olympus TM3B gas turbines delivering 33,550 kW (45,000 hp) or two Rolls-Royce Tyne RM1C gas turbines delivering 9,240 hp (6890 kW) to two shafts

Performance: speed 30 kt

Complement: 195 or (DD129 onwards) 200

Note: Though they are comparatively small for destroyers, these Japanese ships offer a judicious blend of capabilities against submarines, ships and aircraft in full keeping with Japan's constitutionally mandated defensive military posture.

The *Shimayuki* is the last unit of the 12-strong 'Hatsuyuki' class.

Class 1. Japan Name	No.	Builder	Laid down	Commissioned
Hatsuyuki	DD122	Sumitomo	Mar 1979	Mar 1982
Shirayuki	DD123	Hitachi	Dec 1979	Feb 1983
Mineyuki	DD124	Mitsubishi	May 1981	Mar 1984
Sawayuki	DD125	Ishikawajima	Apr 1981	Feb 1984
Hamayuki	DD126	Mitsui	Apr 1981	Jan 1984
Isoyuki	DD127	Ishikawajima	Apr 1982	Jan 1985
Harayuki	DD128	Sumitomo	Apr 1982	Mar 1985
Yamayuki	DD129	Hitachi	Oct 1983	Dec 1985
Matsuyuki	DD130	Ishikawajima	Oct 1983	Mar 1986
Setoyuki	DD131	Mitsui	Jan 1984	Dec 1986
Asayuki	DD132	Sumitomo	Dec 1983	Feb 1987
Shimayuki	DD133	Mitsubishi	May 1984	Feb 1987

'Impavido' class DDG

(Italy)
Type: anti-aircraft guided-missile escort destroyer
Displacement: 3,200 tons standard and 3,850 tons full load
Dimensions: length 131·3 m (429·5 ft); beam 13·6 m (44·7 ft); 4·5 m (14·8 ft)
Gun armament: two 5-in (127-mm) L/38 DP in one Mk 38 twin mounting, and four 76-mm (3-in) OTO Melara L/62 DP in OTO Melara single mountings
Missile armament: one Mk 13 single launcher for 40 RIM-66B Standard SM-1 MR SAMs
Torpedo armament: none
Anti-submarine armament: two Mk 32 triple 12·75-in (324-mm) mountings for Mk 46 torpedoes
Aircraft: provision for one light helicopter on a platform aft
Electronics: one SPS-39A 3D air-search radar, one SPS-12 air-search radar, one SPQ 2A2 surface-search radar, one SPN 748 navigation radar, two SPG-51B illumination and tracking radars used in conjunction with two Mk 73 SAM fire-control systems, three RTN 10X radars used in conjunction with three Argo NA10 gun fire-control systems, one SQS-39 active search and attack hull sonar, one ESM system with warning element, and two SCLAR chaff launchers
Propulsion: four Foster-Wheeler boilers supplying steam to two sets of Tosi geared turbines delivering 52,200 kW (70,000 hp) to two shafts
Performance: maximum speed 33 kt; range 6100 km (3,790 miles) at 20 kt or 2775 km (1,725 miles) at 30 kt
Complement: 23 + 317

Class

1. Italy Name	No.	Builder	Laid down	Com- missioned
Impavido	D570	CNR, Riva Trigoso	Jun 1957	Nov 1963
Intrepido	D571	Italcantieri	May 1959	Jul 1964

Note: Though capable ships in terms of their armament and electronics, these ships are hampered by their small size, which reduces seaworthiness and habitability.

The *Impavido*, lead unit of a two-ship class, has effective sensors and weapons, but is hampered operationally by being too cramped. This resulted from an effort to get too much capability into too small a hull.

'Iroquois' or 'Tribal' class DDG

(Canada)
Type: anti-aircraft guided-missile destroyer
Displacement: 3,550 tons standard and 4,700 tons full load
Dimensions: length 426·0 ft (129·8 m); beam 50·0 ft (15·2 m); draught 21·5 ft (6·6 m)
Gun armament: one 76-mm (3-in) OTO Melara L/62 DP in an OTO Melara Super Rapid single mounting, and one 20-mm Phalanx Mk 15 CIWS mountings
Missile armament: one Mk 41 Vertical-Launch System for 32 RIM-66C Standard SM-2 MR SAMs
Torpedo armament: none
Anti-submarine armament: two Mk 32 triple 12·75-in (324-mm) mountings for Mk 46 torpedoes, and helicopter-launched weapons (see below)
Aircraft: two Sikorsky CH-124A Sea King helicopters in a hangar amidships
Electronics: one LW-8 air-search radar, one DA-08 surface-search and navigation radar, two STIR 1·8 radars used in conjunction with the WM-25 fire-control system, one Mk 69 (to be rebuilt as solid-state Mk 60) gun fire-control system, one SQS-505 active/passive search and attack combined hull and variable-depth sonar, one SQS-501 classification hull sonar, one SQR-19 passive search towed-array sonar, one SLQ-26 Nixie towed torpedo-decoy system, one SHINPADS action information system, Link 11 and Link 14 data links, one ESM system with CANEWS warning and RAMSES jamming elements, two Shield chaff/flare launchers, one WSC-3 satellite communications transceiver, and URN-25 TACAN
Propulsion: COGOG arrangement, with two Pratt & Whitney FT4A2 gas turbines delivering 50,000 hp (37,285 kW) or two Allison 570KF gas turbines delivering 12,800 hp (9545 kW) to two shafts
Performance: maximum speed 29 + kt on main engines or 18 kt on cruising engines; range 5,200 miles (8370 km) at 20 kt
Complement: 20 + 225 plus an air unit of 7 + 33

Opposite page, top: In its original form, the *Iroquois* of the 'Tribal' class lacked all but close-range SAMs as it was optimized for deep-ocean anti-submarine operations with the Limbo mortar, Mk 44 torpedoes and, most importantly, two large helicopters. A notable

Class

1. Canada Name	No.	Builder	Laid down	Com- missioned
Iroquois	280	Marine Industries	Jan 1969	Jul 1972
Huron	281	Marine industries	Jan 1969	Dec 1972
Athabaskan	282	Davies SB	Jun 1969	Nov 1972
Algonquin	283	Davies SB	Sep 1969	Sep 1973

Note: Though not fitted originally with any major offensive/defensive missile armament, these four units are still capable anti-submarine vessels as a result of their size, sensors and advanced anti-submarine helicopters. Between 1986 and 1991 the ships are being taken in hand under the TRUMP (TRibal Update and Modernization Project) for development into dual-role area-defence and anti-submarine DDGs. This is an extensive programme involving the strengthening of the hull to permit operations under all Atlantic conditions, a host of engineering improvements (including the replacement of the two 3,700-hp (2760-kW FT12AH3 gas turbines by two Allison 570KF gas turbine cruising engines), the replacement of the two quadruple launchers for 32 RIM-7 Sea Sparrow SAMs by a 32-cell Mk 41 Vertical-Launch System for Standard SM-2 MR SAMs, the replacement of the current 5-in (127-mm) OTO Melara Compact L/54 main gun by a 76-mm (3-in) OTO Melara Super Rapid gun and the addition of one Phalanx Mk 15 CIWS mounting, the modernization of the electronic suite (from the original fit of one SPS-501 air-search radar, one SPQ 2D surface-search radar, two WM-22 radar fire-control systems, Mk 69 gun fire-control system, CCS 280 action information system, ESM system with WLR-series warning and ULQ-6 jamming elements, and two Corvus chaff launchers) and a new torpedo-handling system for the retained anti-submarine capability (based on the same sensors and helicopters) despite the elimination of the obsolete Limbo Mk 10 three-barrel mortar. The first conversion was due to get the *Algonquin* back into service by the end of 1989, with the other three ships following by 1992.

feature is the outward angling of the stacks to keep corrosive exhaust gases away from the mast-mounted antennae. The ship also boasts advanced sonar, a central citadel, and a pre-wetting system to mitigate the effect of radio-active fallout.

'Japanese AEGIS' class DDG

(Japan)

Type: anti-aircraft, anti-ship and anti-submarine guided-missile destroyer

Displacement: 7,200 tons standard and 8,900 tons full load

Dimensions: length 161·0 m (528·2 ft); beam 21·0 m (68·9 ft); draught 6·1 m (20·0 ft)

Gun armament: one 127-mm (5-in) OTO Melara L/54 DP in an OTO Melara Compact single mounting, and two 20-mm Phalanx Mk 15 CIWS mountings

Missile armament: two Mk 141 quadruple container-launchers for eight RGM-84 Harpoon anti-ship missiles, and two Vertical-Launch Systems Mk 41 (32 cells forward and 64 cells aft) for 90 RIM-66C Standard SM-2 MR SAMs and VL ASROC anti-submarine missiles

Torpedo armament: none

Anti-submarine armament: VL ASROC missiles (see above), two Type 68 triple 12·75-in (324-mm) mountings for Mk 46 or Mk 50 Barracuda torpedoes, and helicopter-launched weapons (see below)

Aircraft: provision for one Mitsubishi (Sikorsky) SH-60J Seahawk helicopter on a platform aft

Electronics: one SPY-1D 3D radar with four planar arrays, one OPS-28D surface-search radar, one OPS-19C navigation radar, three SPG-62 illuminating radars used in conjunction with three Mk 99 SAM fire-control systems, one radar used in conjunction with one Type 2-21 gun fire-control system, one OQS-101 active search and attack hull sonar and one SQR-19A(V) passive search towed-array sonar used in conjunction with the Mk 116 underwater weapons fire-control system, one action information system, one ESM system with warning and NOLQ-2 jamming elements, and four Mk 36 Super RBOC chaff/flare launchers

Propulsion: COGAG arrangement, with four General Electric LM2500 gas turbines delivering 80,000 hp (59,650 kW) to two shafts

Performance: speed 31 kt

Complement: 310

Class

1. Japan

Name	No.	Builder	Laid down	Commissioned
	DD173	Mitsubishi	Sep 1990	Mar 1993

Note: The Japanese plan to build four (and possibly eight) of this class, which is in essence an enlarged version of the American 'Arleigh Burke' design with a lightweight SPY-1/AEGIS system.

'Kanin' class DDG

(USSR)

Type: anti-aircraft guided-missile escort destroyer

Displacement: 3,700 tons standard and 4,750 tons full load

Dimensions: length 139·0 m (455·9 ft); beam 14·7 m (48·2 ft); draught 5·0 m (16·4 ft)

Gun armament: eight 57-mm L/70 AA in two quadruple mountings, and eight 30-mm L/65 AA in four twin mountings

Missile armament: one twin launcher for 16 SA-N-1 'Goa' SAMs

Torpedo armament: two quintuple 533-mm (21-in) mountings for Type 53 dual-role torpedoes

Anti-submarine armament: three RBU 6000 12-barrel rocket-launchers, and torpedoes (see above)

Aircraft: provision for one Kamov Ka-25 'Hormone' helicopter on a platform aft

Electronics: one 'Head Net-C' 3D radar, two 'Don Kay' surface-search and navigation radars, one 'Peel Group' SAM fire-control radar, one 'Hawk Screech' 57-mm gun fire-control radar, two 'Drum Tilt' 30-mm gun fire-control radars, one high/medium-frequency active search and attack hull sonar, one ESM system including four 'Top Hat' and four 'Bell Squat' antennae/housings, and one 'High Pole-B' IFF system

Propulsion: four boilers supplying steam to two sets of geared turbines delivering 63,500 kW (85,165 hp) to two shafts

Performance: maximum speed 35 kt; range 8350 km (5,190 miles) at 16 kt or 2050 km (1,275 miles) at 33 kt

Complement: 350

Class

1. USSR

Name
Derzky
Gnevny
Uporny
Zorky

Note: These obsolete ships are disappearing from service. They were built between 1957 and 1962 as 'Krupny' class anti-submarine destroyers with an anti-ship missile capability. These are the survivors (two active and two in reserve) of eight units were converted to anti-aircraft destroyers at the Zhdanov Yard, Leningrad (five ships between 1974 and 1978) and at Komsomolsk (three ships between 1974 and 1978).

'Kashin' class DDG

(USSR)

Type: anti-aircraft and anti-submarine guided-missile escort destroyer
Displacement: 3,500 tons standard and 4,500 tons full load
Dimensions: length 144·0 m (472·4 ft); beam 15·8 m (51·8 ft); draught 4·7 m (15·4 ft)
Gun armament: four 76-mm (3-in) L/60 DP in two twin mountings
Missile armament: two twin launchers for 32 SA-N-1 'Goa' SAMs
Torpedo armament: one quintuple 533-mm (21-in) mounting for Type 53 dual-role torpedoes
Anti-submarine armament: two RBU 6000 12-barrel rocket-launchers, two RBU 1000 six-barrel rocket-launchers, torpedoes (see above), and helicopter-launched weapons (see below)
Mines: provision for minelaying
Aircraft: one Kamov Ka-25 'Hormone-A' helicopter on a platform aft
Electronics: one 'Head Net-C' 3D radar and one 'Big Net' air-search radar (eight ships) or two 'Head Net-A/C' air-search radars (others), two 'Don 2', 'Don Kay' or 'Palm Frond' navigation radars, two 'Peel Group' SAM fire-control radars, two 'Owl Screech' gun fire-control radars, one high-frequency active search and attack hull sonar, one ESM system with two 'Watch Dog' antennae/housings, two towed torpedo decoys, and one 'High Pole-B' IFF system
Propulsion: four gas turbines delivering 70,100 kW (94,020 hp) to two shafts
Performance: maximum speed 38 kt; range 8350 km (5,190 miles) at 18 kt or 2600 km (1,615 miles) at 36 kt
Complement: 20 + 260

The 'Kashin' class destroyers were the world's first major warships with gas turbine propulsion, the gases being vented through four large funnels.

'Kashin (Modified)' class DDG

(USSR)

Type: anti-aircraft, anti-ship and anti-submarine guided-missile escort destroyer
Displacement: 3,950 tons standard and 4,900 tons full load
Dimensions: length 147·0 m (482·3 ft); beam 15·8 m (51·8 ft); draught 4·7 m (15·4 ft)
Gun armament: four 76-mm (3-in) L/60 DP in two twin mountings, and four 30-mm ADGM-630 CIWS mountings
Missile armament: four container-launchers for four SS-N-2C 'Styx' anti-ship missiles, and two twin launchers for 32 SA-N-1 'Goa' SAMs
Torpedo armament: one quintuple 533-mm (21-in) mounting for Type 53 dual-role torpedoes
Anti-submarine armament: two RBU 6000 12-barrel rocket-launchers, torpedoes (see above), and helicopter-launched weapons (see below)
Aircraft: provision for one Kamov Ka-25 'Hormone-A' helicopter on a platform aft
Electronics: one 'Head Net-C' 3D radar, one 'Big Net' air-search radar, two 'Don 2', 'Don Kay' or 'Palm Frond' surface-search and navigation radars, two 'Peel Group' SAM fire-control radars, two 'Owl Screech' 76-mm gun fire-control radars, two 'Bass Tilt' CIWS fire-control radars, one medium-frequency active search and attack sonar, one medium-frequency variable-depth sonar, two towed torpedo decoys, one ESM system with two 'Bell Shroud' and two 'Bell Squat' housings, four chaff launchers, and one 'High Pole-B' IFF system

Class
1. USSR

Name	Builder
Komsomolets Ukrainy	Nikolayev North
Krazny-Kavaz	Nikolayev North
Krazny-Krim	Nikolayev North
Obraztsovy	Zhdanov Yard
Odarenny	Zhdanov Yard
Provorny	Nikolayev North
Reshitelny	Nikolayev North
Skory	Nikolayev North
Smetlivy	Nikolayev North
Soobrazitelny	Nikolayev North
Sposobny	Nikolayev North
Steregushchy	Zhdanov Yard
Strogy	Nikolayev North

Note: Built between 1961 and 1972 as anti-submarine destroyers, these were the world's first major warship class relying exclusively on gas turbine propulsion. The ships were delivered from Nikolayev North between 1962 and 1972, and from the Zhdanov Yard between 1965 and 1967. Though classified by the Soviets as anti-submarine ships, they are tasked with the screening of anti-submarine task groups, which explains their anti-aircraft armament. *Provorny* is somewhat different from her sisters, having been used as trials ship for the SA-N-7 SAM system: in addition to its twin SAM launcher with 20 missiles, the ship has one 'Top Steer' air-search radar and eight 'Front Dome' SAM-control radars, but no RBU 1000 anti-submarine rocket-launchers.

The 'Kashin (Modified)' class is a comparatively simple adaptation of the basic 'Kashin' class for considerably enhanced operational effectiveness.

Propulsion: four gas turbines delivering 70,100 kW (94,020 hp) to two shafts
Performance: maximum speed 37 kt; range 8350 km (5,190 miles) at 18 kt
Complement: 25 + 255

Class
1. Poland

Name	Builder
Warszawa	Nikolayev North

(This is identical with the Soviet ships, and was originally the Soviet *Smely* transferred in 1988.)

2. USSR

Name	Builder
Ognevoy	Zhdanov Yard
Sderzhanny	Nikolayev North
Slavny	Zhdanov Yard
Smyshlenny	Nikolayev North
Stroyny	Nikolayev North

(These were built as standard 'Kashin' class destroyers, but were modified between 1972 and 1980 with additional anti-ship and anti-submarine capabilities: the hull was lengthened slightly, four anti-ship missiles were added, variable-depth sonar was added and, for self-defence, four CIWS mountings were shipped. In common with the 'Kashin' class ships, however, these vessels suffer in anti-submarine capability from their lack of long-range weapons and full helicopter facilities.)

'Kashin II' class DDG

(USSR/India)
Type: anti-aircraft and anti-ship guided-missile destroyer
Displacement: 3,950 tons standard and 4,950 tons full load
Dimensions: length 146·5 m (480·5 ft); beam 15·8 m (51·8 ft); draught 4·8 m (15·7 ft)
Gun armament: two 76-mm (3-in) L/60 DP in a twin mounting, eight 30-mm L/65 AA in four twin mountings or ('Kashin II [Mod]' class) four 30-mm ADGM-630 CIWS mountings
Missile armament: four container-launchers for four SS-N-2C 'Styx' anti-ship missiles, and two twin launchers for 44 SA-N-1 'Goa' SAMs
Torpedo armament: one quintuple 533-mm (21-in) mounting for five Type 53 dual-role torpedoes
Anti-submarine armament: two RBU 6000 12-barrel rocket-launchers, torpedoes (see above), and helicopter-launched weapons (see below)
Aircraft: one Kamov Ka-25 'Hormone-A' or ('Kashin II [Mod]' class and to be retrofitted in 'Kashin II' class) Ka-27 'Helix-A' helicopter in a hangar aft
Electronics: one 'Big Net-A' medium-range air-search radar, one 'Head Net-C' air/surface-search radar, two 'Don Kay' navigation radars, two 'Peel Group' SAM fire-control radars, one 'Owl Screech' 76-mm gun fire-control radar, two 'Drum Tilt' AA gun fire-control radars or ('Kashin II [Mod]' class) two 'Bass Tilt' CIWS fire-control radars, one medium-frequency active search and attack sonar, one medium-frequency variable-depth sonar, one

ESM system with two 'Watch Dog', two 'Top Hat-A' and two 'Top Hat-B' antennae/housings, four chaff launchers, and two 'High Pole-B' IFF systems
Propulsion: four gas turbines delivering 71,575 kW (95,995 hp) to two shafts
Performance: maximum speed 35 kt; range 8350 km (5,190 miles) at 18 kt or 1675 km (1,040 miles) at 35 kt
Complement: 35 + 285

Class

1. India Name	No.	Builder	Laid down	Com-missioned
Rajput	D51	Nikolayev		Sep 1980
Rana	D52	Nikolayev		Jun 1982
Ranjit	D53	Nikolayev		Nov 1983
Ranvir	D54*	Nikolayev		Aug 1986
Ranvijay	D55*	Nikolayev		Jan 1988
	D56*	Nikolayev		

* 'Kashin II [Mod]' class
Note: These are 'Kashin (Modified)' class variants with fairly radical modifications to suit them to the Indian role and operational area: the after 76-mm (3-in) gun mounting of the Soviet ships is replaced by a hangar, and in the 'Kashin II (Modified)' subclass four CIWS mountings replace the eight 30-mm AA mountings, and it is possible that an IR guidance package is added to the SS-N-2C anti-ship missiles. It is possible that the planned third unit of the 'Kashin II (Mod)' class has been cancelled.

'Kidd' class DDG

(USA)
Type: anti-aircraft, anti-submarine and anti-ship guided-missile destroyer
Displacement: 6,950 tons light and 9,750 tons full load
Dimensions: length 563·3 ft (171·8 m); beam 55·0 ft (16·8 m); draught 30·0 ft (9·1 m)
Gun armament: two 5-in (127-mm) L/54 DP in Mk 45 single mountings, and two 20-mm Phalanx Mk 16 CIWS mountings
Missile armament: two Mk 141 quadruple container-launchers for eight RGM-84A Harpoon anti-ship missiles, and two Mk 26 twin launchers for 52 RIM-66C Standard SM-2 MR SAMs
Torpedo armament: none
Anti-submarine armament: two Mk 32 triple 12·75-in (324-mm) launchers for Mk 46 torpedoes, 16 RUR-5A ASROC missiles fired from the Mk 26 launcher, and helicopter-launched weapons (see below)
Aircraft: two Kaman SH-2F Seasprite helicopters or one Sikorsky SH-60B Seahawk helicopter in a hangar amidships
Electronics: one SPS-48C/E 3D radar, one SPS-55 surface-search radar, one SPS-53 navigation radar, two SPG-55D illumination and tracking radars used in conjunction with two Mk 74 SAM fire-control systems, one SPG-60 search-and-track radar and one SPQ-9A track-while-scan radar used in conjunction with one Mk 86 gun fire-control system, one SQS-53A (to be replaced by SQS-53C) active search and attack bow sonar and one SQR-19 passive search towed-array sonar used in conjunction with one Mk 116 underwater weapons fire-control system, one Mk 13 (to be replaced by Mk 14) weapon direction system, Naval Tactical Data System, one SLQ-32(V)2 ESM system with warning and jamming elements, one SLQ-25 Nixie torpedo-decoy system, four Mk 36 Super RBOC chaff/flare launchers, one OE-82 satellite communications system, three WSC-3 satellite communications transceivers, one SSR-1 satellite communications receiver, and URN-25 TACAN
Propulsion: four General Electric LM2500 gas turbines delivering 80,000 hp (59,655 kW) to two shafts
Performance: maximum speed 33 kt; range 9,200 miles (14,805 km) at 17 kt or 3,800 miles (6115 km) at 30 kt
Complement: 20 + 319

Note: These are the world's most powerful destroyers, cruisers in all but name. They were built to an Iranian order cancelled in 1979, and are notable for their excellent blend of anti-aircraft, anti-ship and anti-submarine capability. The one drawback to the armament/sensor fit is the provision of only two SPG-55 SAM-control radars, limiting the ship to the simultaneous engagement of only two targets despite the availability of four launcher arms. The standard is that to which the whole 'Spruance' class was to have been built, though these ships were later downgraded in capability for financial reasons.

The *Callaghan* is the second of four 'Kidd' class destroyers derived from the 'Spruance' class but so improved that the ships must be regarded as not significantly inferior to cruisers in operational terms.

Class

1. USA Name	No.	Builder	Laid down	Com-missioned
Kidd	DDG993	Ingalls SB	Jun 1978	May 1981
Callaghan	DDG994	Ingalls SB	Oct 1978	Aug 1981
Scott	DDG995	Ingalls SB	Feb 1979	Oct 1981
Chandler	DDG996	Ingalls SB	May 1979	Mar 1982

'Kildin (Modified)' class DDG

(USSR)
Type: anti-ship guided-missile destroyer
Displacement: 3,000 tons standard and 3,500 tons full load
Dimensions: length 126·6 m (414·9 ft); beam 13·0 m (42·6 ft); draught 4·6 m (15·1 ft)
Gun armament: four 76-mm (3-in) L/60 DP in two twin mountings, and 16 57-mm L/70 AA in four quadruple mountings or (in *Bedovy*) 16 45-mm L/85 AA in four quadruple mountings
Missile armament: four container-launchers for four SS-N-2C 'Styx' anti-ship missiles
Torpedo armament: two twin 533-mm (21-in) mountings for Type 53 dual-role torpedoes
Anti-submarine armament: two RBU 2500 16-barrel rocket-launchers, and torpedoes (see above)
Aircraft: none
Electronics: one 'Head Net-C' or (in *Bedovy*) one 'Strut Pair' air-search radar, two 'Don 2' surface-search and navigation radars, one 'Owl Screech' 76-mm gun fire-control radar, two 'Hawk Screech' 57-mm gun fire-control radars, one high/medium-frequency active search and attack hull sonar, one ESM system with two 'Watch Dog' antennae/housings, and one 'Square Head' and one 'High Pole-A' IFF systems
Propulsion: four boilers supplying steam to two sets of geared turbines delivering 53,700 kW (72,025 hp) to two shafts
Performance: maximum speed 36 kt; range 8350 km (5,190 miles) at 16 kt or 1850 km (1,150 miles) at 34 kt
Complement: 300

Class
1. USSR

Name	Builder
Bedovy	Nikolayev
Neulovimy	Leningrad
Prozorlivy	Nikolayev

Note: These obsolescent anti-ship destroyers (of which the *Neulovimy* is in reserve) were completed in 1957 and 1958 as 'Kildin' class destroyers with a primary armament of SS-N-1 anti-ship missiles on the quarterdeck. The design is basically a development of the 'Kotlin' class design, and it is thought that *Bedovy* was in fact laid down as a 'Kotlin' class destroyer. The ships were modernized to their present standard between 1973 and 1976.

'Luda' or 'Type 051' class DDG

(China)
Type: anti-ship guided-missile destroyer
Displacement: 3,250 tons standard and 3,800 tons full load
Dimensions: length 132·0 m (433·1 ft); beam 12·8 m (42·0 ft); draught 4·6 m (15·0 ft)
Gun armament: four 130-mm (5·1-in) L/58 DP in two twin mountings or (105 only) two 130-mm (5·1-in) L/58 DP in a twin mounting and two 100-mm (3·94-in) L/56 DP in a twin mounting, six or eight 37-mm L/63 AA in three or four twin mountings, and eight 25-mm L/60 AA in four twin mountings
Missile armament: two triple container-launchers for six HY-2 (CSS-N-2) anti-ship missiles
Torpedo armament: none
Anti-submarine armament: two FQF-2500 12-barrel rocket-launchers, two or four BMB-series depth-charge throwers, and two or four depth-charge racks
Mines: up to 38
Aircraft: none
Electronics: one 'Rice Screen' 3D radar (in some ships only), one 'Knife Rest', 'Cross Slot', 'Bean Sticks' or 'Pea Sticks' air-search radar, one 'Eye Shield' surface-search radar, one 'Square Tie' surface-search radar (in some ships only), one 'Fin Curve' navigation radar, 'Wasp Head' ('Wok Won') and 'Post Lamp' (105/108) or 'Sun Visor-B' and 'Rice Lamp' (others) gun fire-control radars, one Pegas-2M high-frequency active search and attack hull sonar, one Tamir high-frequency active search and attack hull sonar, one ESM system with 'Jug Pair' antennae/housings, chaff launchers (in some ships only), and one 'High Pole' IFF system
Propulsion: four boilers supplying steam to two sets of geared turbines delivering 44,750 kW (60,020 hp) to two shafts
Performance: maximum speed 32 kt; range 5925 km (3,680 miles) at 18 kt or 2000 km (1,245 miles) at 32 kt
Complement: 27 + 258

Class
1. China

Name	No.	Builder	Laid down	Commissioned
Jinan	105	Luda	1969	1971
Xian	106	Luda	1969	1972
Yinchuan	107	Guangzhou	1970	1974
Xining	108	Luda	1970	1974
Kaifeng	109	Luda	1977	1980
Dalian	110	Chunghua	1977	1980
Nanjing	131	Chunghua	1969	1973
Hefei	132	Chunghua	1970	1973
Chongqing	133	Chunghua	1979	1982
Zunyi	134	Chunghua	1981	1984
Changsha	161	Guangzhou	1972	1975
Nanning	163	Guangzhou	1979	1983
Nanchang	164	Guangzhou	1980	1984
Guilin	165	Guangzhou	1981	1985

Note: These were China's first indigenously designed destroyers, though they have several features clearly derived from the Soviet 'Kotlin' class. The considerable gap in the middle of the complete programme is attributable to the death in 1971 of Lin Piao and a consequent cutback in funding for military and naval programmes. Starting with 105, some of these ships are being modified to a considerably more powerful standard with a quadruple container-launcher for C-801 anti-ship missiles instead of the previous HY-2 launchers, the forward 130-mm gun mounting replaced by either two 100-mm (3·94-in) DP guns in a twin mounting or a Naval Crotale octuple launcher for R.440 SAMs, and an Aérospatiale SA 365N Dauphin 2 (or Chinese copy) on a platform that replaces the after 13-mm gun mounting; the variant also has a Thomson-CSF Castor tracker radar on the mast, probably for use in conjunction with the light AA armament. China has recently bought from Italy a number of ILAS 3 triple mountings for 324-mm (12·75-in) anti-submarine torpedoes, and it is conceivable that these will be shipped on the modernized 'Luda' class destroyers.

Almirante Brown is the lead ship of the Argentine navy's four-strong 'Meko 360' class of destroyers, which are very cost effective surface combatants.

'Meko 360' class DDG

(West Germany/Argentina)
Type: anti-ship and anti-submarine guided-missile destroyer
Displacement: 2,900 tons standard and 3,360 tons full load
Dimensions: length 125·9 m (413·1 ft); beam 14·0 m (46·0 ft); draught 5·8 m (19·0 ft)
Gun armament: one 127-mm (5-in) OTO Melara L/54 DP in an OTO Melara Compact single mounting, and eight 40-mm Bofors L/70 AA in four Breda twin mountings
Missile armament: two quadruple container-launchers for eight MM.40 Exocet anti-ship missiles, and one Albatros octuple launcher for 24 Aspide SAMs
Torpedo armament: none
Anti-submarine armament: two ILAS 3 triple 324-mm (12·75-in) mountings for 24 A 244/S torpedoes, and helicopter-launched weapons (see below)
Aircraft: two Aérospatiale SA 319B Alouette III Astazou helicopters in a hangar aft
Electronics: one DA-08A air/surface-search radar, one RM1226 navigation radar, one ZW-06 navigation radar, one STIR 127-mm gun fire-control radar, one WM-25 gun fire-control radar, two LIROD 40-mm gun radar/optronic directors, one Krupp-Atlas 80 active search and attack hull sonar, one SEWACO action information system, one AEG-Telefunken ESM system with

Almirante Brown and *La Argentina* reveal the salient features of this useful and very flexible guided-missile destroyer's concept and design.

warning and jamming elements, one G1738 towed torpedo-decoy system, two SCLAR chaff/flare launchers, and two Dagaie decoy launchers
Propulsion: COGOG arrangement, with two Rolls-Royce Olympus TM3B gas turbines delivering 51,600 hp (38,475 kW) or two Rolls-Royce Tyne RM1C gas turbines delivering 10,680 hp (7965 kW) to two shafts
Performance: maximum speed 30·5 kt on Spey gas turbines, or 20·5 kt on Tyne gas turbines; range 8350 km (5,190 miles) at 18 kt
Complement: 26 + 174

Class
1. Argentina

Name	No.	Builder	Laid down	Com- missioned
Almirante Brown	D10	Blohm und Voss	Sep 1980	Feb 1983
La Argentina	D11	Blohm und Voss	Mar 1981	May 1983
Heroina	D12	Blohm und Voss	Aug 1981	Nov 1983
Sarandi	D13	Blohm und Voss	Mar 1982	Apr 1984

Note: These Argentine ships differ from the Nigerian 'Meko 360H2' unit in several respects. Six ships had been planned, but the order was reduced to four when Argentina selected the 'Mako 140' class frigate.

'Muntenia' class DDG

(Romania)
Type: anti-aircraft and anti-ship guided-missile destroyer
Displacement: 4,500 tons standard
Dimensions: length 148·0 m (485·6 ft); beam 14·8 m (48·6 ft); draught 7·0 m (23·0 ft)
Gun armament: four 76-mm (3-in) L/60 DP in two twin mountings, and eight 30-mm L/65 AA in four twin mountings
Missile armament: four twin container-launchers for eight SS-N-2C 'Styx' anti-ship missiles, and seven multiple launchers for SA-N-7 SAMs
Torpedo armament: two triple 533-mm (21-in) mountings for Type 53 dual-role torpedoes
Anti-submarine armament: torpedoes (see above), and helicopter-launched weapons (see below)
Aircraft: three IAR-316B Alouette III helicopters in a hangar aft

Electronics: one 'Strut Curve' air/surface-search radar, one 'Hawk Screech' 76-mm gun fire-control radar, two 'Drum Tilt' 30-mm gun fire-control radars, one medium-frequency active search and attack hull sonar, and other systems
Propulsion: CODAG arrangement, with two gas turbines and two diesels delivering a total of 71,600 kW (96,030 hp) to two shafts
Performance: maximum speed 32 kt
Complement: not revealed

Class
1. Romania

Name	Builder	Laid down	Commissioned
Muntenia	Mangalia		Aug 1985

Note: Little is known of this indigenously designed Romanian destroyer. The ship was placed in reserve during 1988 for lack of manpower, but it is known that Romania would like to procure another unit of the same class.

'SAM Kotlin' class DDG

(USSR)

Type: anti-aircraft guided-missile escort destroyer

Displacement: 2,850 tons standard and 3,500 tons full load

Dimensions: length 126·5 m (415·0 ft); beam 12·9 m (42·3 ft); draught 4·6 m (15·1 ft)

Gun armament: two 130 mm (5·1-in) L/58 DP in a twin mounting, four 45-mm L/85 AA in a quadruple mounting, and (in *Nesokrushimy, Skrytny, Soznatelny* and *Vozbuzhdenny*) eight 30-mm AA in four twin mountings

Missile armament: one twin launcher for 16 SA-N-1 'Goa' SAMs

Torpedo armament: one quintuple 533-mm (21-in) mounting for Type 53 dual-role torpedoes

Anti-submarine armament: two RBU 6000 12-barrel rocket-launchers and (in *Skromny*) two RBU 2500 16-barrel rocket-launchers, and torpedoes (see above)

Aircraft: none

Mines: up to 60

Electronics: one 'Head Net-C' 3D radar, one 'Don 2' or (in *Nastoychivy*) one 'Low Trough' surface-search and navigation radar, one 'Peel Group' SAM fire-control radar, one 'Sun Visor-B' 130-mm gun fire-control radar, one 'Hawk Screech' 45-mm gun fire-control radar, two 'Drum Tilt' 30-mm gun fire-control radars (in *Nesokrushimy, Skrytny, Soznatelny* and *Vozbuzhdenny*), one high-frequency active search and attack hull sonar, one ESM system with two 'Watch Dog' antennae/housings, and one 'High Pole-B' IFF system

Propulsion: four boilers supplying steam to two sets of geared turbines delivering 53,700 kW (72,025 hp) to two shafts

Performance: maximum speed 36 kt; range 8350 km (5,190 miles) at 15 kt or 2000 km (1,245 miles) at 35 kt

Complement: 300

Class

1. USSR

Name
Näkhodchivy
Nastoychivy
Nesokrushimy
Skromny
Skrytny
Soznatelny
Vozbuzhdenny

Note: These seven units were built in the late 1950s as conventional gun destroyers of the 'Kotlin' class. In 1961 the *Bravy* was converted as the prototype for the class, and another eight were similarly converted between 1967 and 1972 for the screening of less important surface task groups. The ships are now obsolete, and the two that have already disappeared are the *Bravy* and the sole Polish ship.

'Sheffield' or 'Type 42' class DDG

(UK)

Type: anti-aircraft and anti-submarine guided-missile escort destroyer

Displacement: 3,850 tons standard and 4,350 tons full load, or (Batch 3 ships) 4,775 tons standard and 5,350 tons full load

Dimensions: length 412·0 ft (125·6 m) or (Batch 3 ships) 462·8 ft (141·1 m); beam 47·0 ft (14·3 m) or (Batch 3 ships) 49·0 ft (14·9 m); draught 19·0 ft (5·8 m)

Gun armament: one 4·5-in (114-mm) Vickers L/55 DP in a Mk 8 single mounting, two 20-mm Oerlikon 20-mm L/120 AA in two GAM-B01 single mountings, two 20-mm Oerlikon AA in Mk 9 single mountings, and two 20-mm Phalanx Mk 15 CIWS mountings

Missile armament: one twin launcher for 24 or (Batch 3) or 40 Sea Dart SAMs

Torpedo armament: none

Anti-submarine armament: two STWS-2 triple 12·75-in (324-mm) mountings for Stingray or Mk 46 torpedoes, and helicopter-launched weapons (see below)

Aircraft: one Westland Lynx HAS.Mk 2/3 helicopter in a hangar aft

Electronics: one Type 1022 air-search radar, one Type 992Q or Type 992R surface-search radar (being replaced by Type 996 3D radar), one Type 1006 navigation radar, two Type 909 or Type 909I radars used in conjunction with the GWS 30 SAM fire-control system, one Type 2016 active/passive search and attack hull sonar, one Type 162M classification hull sonar, one Type 208 hull sonar (Batch 3 ships only), one ADAWS 4 or (Batch 3 ships) ADAWS 8 action information system, one Type 182 towed torpedo-decoy system, one UAA-1 Abbey Hill ESM system with Type 670 (or Type 675) jammer, two Corvus or Shield chaff launchers, two Mk 36 Super RBOC chaff/flare launchers, and two SCOT satellite communications antennae

Propulsion: COGOG arrangement, with two Rolls-Royce Olympus TM3B gas turbines delivering 50,000 hp (37,280 kW) or two Rolls-Royce Tyne RM1C gas turbines delivering 9,700 hp (7230 kW) to two shafts

Performance: maximum speed 29 kt or (Batch 3 ships) 30 + kt on Olympus turbines, or 18 kt on Tyne turbines; range 4,600 miles (7400 km) at 18 kt or 750 miles (1205 km) at 29 kt

Complement: 24 + 229, with a maximum of 312 possible, or (Batch 3 ships) 26 + 275

Class

1. Argentina

Name	No.	Builder	Laid down	Commissioned
Hercules	D1	Vickers	Jun 1971	Jul 1976
Santisima Trinidad	D2	AFNE Rio Santiago	Oct 1971	Jul 1981

(These Argentine units have suffered severe maintenance problems since the Falklands campaign of 1982 as no British spares have been obtainable. The ships are basically 'Type 42 Batch 1' class vessels, but have standard and full-load displacements of 3,150 tons and 4,100 tons respectively, a gun armament of one 4·5-in/114-mm gun and two 20-mm Oerlikon AA in single mountings, an anti-ship missile armament of four single MM.38 Exocet anti-

The *Nottingham* is the third of four 'Type 42 Batch 2' class destroyers, which differ only insignificantly from the four 'Type 42 Batch 1' ships.

ship missile container/launchers, two ILAS 3 triple mountings for A 244/S anti-submarine torpedoes, Type 965M air-search radar with twin AKE-2 arrays, Type 184M active search and attack hull sonar, two Rolls-Royce Tyne RM1A cruising engines delivering 6,000 hp/4475 kW, and one Aérospatiale SA 319B Alouette III helicopter.)

2. UK ('Type 42 Batch 1' or 'Sheffield' class)

Name	No.	Builder	Laid down	Commissioned
Birmingham	D86	Cammell Laird	Mar 1972	Dec 1976
Newcastle	D87	Swan Hunter	Feb 1973	Mar 1978
Glasgow	D88	Swan Hunter	Apr 1974	May 1979
Cardiff	D108	Vickers	Nov 1972	Sep 1979

3. UK ('Type 42 Batch 2' or 'Exeter' class)

Name	No.	Builder	Laid down	Commissioned
Exeter	D89	Swan Hunter	Jul 1976	Sep 1980
Southampton	D90	Vosper Thornycroft	Oct 1976	Oct 1981
Nottingham	D91	Vosper Thornycroft	Feb 1978	Apr 1982
Liverpool	D92	Cammell Laird	Jul 1978	Jul 1982

4. UK ('Type 42 Batch 3' or 'Manchester' class)

Name	No.	Builder	Laid down	Com-missioned
Manchester	D95	Vickers	May 1978	Dec 1982
Gloucester	D96	Vosper Thornycroft	Oct 1979	Sep 1985
Edinburgh	D97	Cammell Laird	Sep 1980	Dec 1985
York	D98	Swan Hunter	Jan 1980	Aug 1985

This view of the *Gloucester* emphasizes the longer bow of the 'Type 42 Batch 3' destroyer variant, which has much improved seakeeping qualities.

(These are capable ships, but the seaworthiness and missile capacity were improved in the 'Batch 3' ships by increasing length and beam. All the ships have a considerably heavier AA and CIWS defence as a result of the British experience in the Falklands War of 1982. The long-term plan is to retrofit the Lightweight Sea Wolf SAM system [two Type 911(3) radars and the GWS 26 Mod 2 fire-control system] on all ships, but cost considerations will probably limit the plan to just the 'Batch 3' ships. Some of the other modifications planned for the class in the future include Type 996 3D radar in place of the current Type 992, and, in addition, the standard Type 670 jammer is replaced by the Type 675 [Thorn EMI Guardian] in ships destined for higher-threat areas.)

'Shirane' or 'Type 143' class DDG

(Japan)

Type: anti-submarine and anti-ship guided-missile destroyer

Displacement: 5,200 tons standard and 6,800 tons full load

Dimensions: length 159·0 m (521·5 ft); beam 17·5 m (57·5 ft); draught 5·3 m (17·5 ft)

Gun armament: two 5-in (127-mm) L/54 DP in Mk 42 single mountings, and (DD144 only) two 20-mm Phalanx Mk 16 CIWS mountings

Missile armament: one Mk 29 octuple launcher for 24 RIM-7 Sea Sparrow SAMs

Torpedo armament: none

Anti-submarine armament: one Mk 16 octuple launcher for 16 RUR-5A ASROC missiles, two Type 68 triple 12·75-in (324-mm) mountings for Type 46 torpedoes, and helicopter-launched weapons (see below)

Aircraft: three Mitsubishi (Sikorsky) HSS-2B Sea King helicopters in a hangar amidships

Electronics: one OPS-12 air-search radar, one OPS-28 surface-search radar, one NOPN-1 navigation radar, two radars used in conjunction with two Type 72-1A gun fire-control systems, one WM-25 missile fire-control radar, one OQS-101 active/passive search and attack hull sonar, one SQS-35(J) active/passive search and attack variable-depth sonar and (DD144 only) one SQR-18A passive search towed-array sonar used in conjunction with the Mk 114 underwater weapons fire-control system, one action information system, Link 11 and 14 data-links, one ESM system with OLR-9B warning and NOLQ-1 jamming elements, one Prairie Masker hull/propeller blade noise-suppression system, and URN-25 TACAN

Propulsion: four boilers supplying steam to two sets of geared turbines delivering 52,200 kW (70,010 hp) to two shafts

Performance: maximum speed 32 kt

Complement: 350 or (DD144) 360

Class

1. Japan

Name	No.	Builder	Laid down	Com-missioned
Shirane	DD143	Ishikawajima	Feb 1977	Mar 1980
Kurama	DD144	Ishikawajima	Feb 1978	Mar 1981

Note: These are of an improved 'Haruna' class design with reduced noise and improved electronics. The ships are in essence small helicopter carriers, and in conjunction with their ASROC missiles this gives a good anti-submarine capability. Anti-aircraft weaponry is limited to self-defence Sea Sparrows, and anti-ship capability is notably absent.

'Sovremenny' class DDG

(USSR)
Type: anti-ship guided-missile destroyer
Displacement: 6,000 tons standard and 7,300 tons full load
Dimensions: length 156·0 m (511·8 ft); beam 17·3 m (56·8 ft); draught 6·2 m (20·3 ft)
Gun armament: four 130-mm (5·1-in) L/70 DP in two twin mountings, and four 30-mm ADGM-630 CIWS mountings
Missile armament: two quadruple container-launchers for eight SS-N-22 'Sunburn' anti-ship missiles, and two single launchers for 44 SA-N-7 'Gadfly' SAMs
Torpedo armament: two twin 533-mm (21-in) mountings for Type 53 dual-role torpedoes
Anti-submarine armament: two RBU 1000 six-barrel rocket-launchers, and torpedoes (see above)
Aircraft: one Kamov Ka-25 'Hormone-B' or Ka-27 'Helix' helicopter in a hangar amidships
Mines: fitted with rails for 40 mines
Electronics: one 'Top Steer' (first three ships), one 'Plate Steer' (fourth and fifth ships) or one 'Top Plate' (others) 3D radar, three 'Palm Frond' surface-search and navigation radars, one 'Band Stand' SSM fire-control radar, six 'Front Dome' SAM fire-control radars, one 'Kite Screech' 130-mm gun fire-control radar, two 'Bass Tilt' CIWS fire-control radars, two medium-frequency active/passive search and attack hull sonars, one ESM system with four 'Foot Ball' antennae/housings, two twin chaff launchers, one 'Salt Pot-A', one 'Salt Pot-B' and one 'High Pole-B' IFF systems, and two 'Shot Rock' satellite navigation systems
Propulsion: four boilers supplying steam to two sets of turbo-pressurized turbines delivering 82,000 kW (109,965 hp) to two shafts
Performance: maximum speed 34 kt; range 26,000 km (16,155 miles) at 14 kt or 4450 km (2,765 miles) at 32 kt
Complement: 320

Class
1. USSR

Name	Builder	Laid down	Commissioned
Sovremenny	Zhdanov Yard	1976	Aug 1980
Otchyanny	Zhdanov Yard	1977	May 1982
Otlichny	Zhdanov Yard	1978	May 1983
Osmotritelny	Zhdanov Yard	1979	Jun 1984
Bezuprechny	Zhdanov Yard	1980	Jun 1985
Boyevoy	Zhdanov Yard	1981	Jun 1986
Stoyky	Zhdanov Yard	1982	Sep 1986
Okrylenny	Zhdanov Yard	1983	Sep 1987
Burnyy	Zhdanov Yard	1984	Apr 1988
Gremyashchy	Zhdanov Yard	1984	Nov 1988
	Zhdanov Yard	1985	1989
	Zhdanov Yard	1986	1990
	Zhdanov Yard	1986	1990
	Zhdanov Yard	1987	1991

Note: This is an extremely capable multi-role type with little short of cruiser capacity in its primary surface-strike role. The class is being built at the same yard as the 'Kresta II' class cruisers, and can be regarded as successor to those ships. The ships generally work with 'Udaloy' class destroyers, the anti-ship capabilities of the 'Sovremenny' class ships complementing the anti-submarine capabilities of the 'Udaloy' class ships.

'Spruance' class DDG

(USA)
Type: anti-submarine and anti-ship guided-missile escort destroyer
Displacement: 5,770 tons light and 8,040 tons full load
Dimensions: length 563·2 ft (171·7 m); beam 55·1 ft (16·8 m); draught 29·0 ft (8·8 m)
Gun armament: two 5-in (127-mm) L/54 DP in Mk 45 single mountings, two 20-mm Phalanx Mk 16 CIWS mountings, and four 0·5-in (12·7-mm) machine-guns
Missile armament: two Mk 141 quadruple container-launchers for eight RGM-84 Harpoon anti-ship missiles, two Mk 143 Armored Box Launchers for eight BGM-109 Tomahawk anti-ship and land-attack cruise missiles (DD974, 976, 979, 983, 984, 989 and 990) or (others in place of the Mk 16 ASROC launcher currently fitted) one Mk 41 Vertical-Launch System for up to 61 BGM-109 Tomahawk anti-ship and land attack cruise missiles, RIM-66B Standard SM-1 MR SAMs (possibly) and RUR-5A ASROC anti-submarine missiles, and one Mk 29 octuple launcher for 24 RIM-7 Sea Sparrow SAMs
Torpedo armament: none
Anti-submarine armament: one Mk 16 octuple launcher for 24 RUR-5A ASROC missiles (to be replaced, see above), two Mk 32 12·75-in (324-mm) triple mountings for 14 Mk 46 torpedoes, and helicopter-launched weapons (see below)
Aircraft: one Sikorsky SH-3 Sea King or two Kaman SH-2F Seasprite helicopters (being replaced by one Sikorsky SH-60B Seahawk helicopter) in a hangar aft
Electronics: one SPS-40B or (DD997) SPS-49(V) air-search radar, one SPS-55 surface-search radar, two Mk 23 radars used in conjunction with the Mk 91 SAM fire-control system, one SPG-60 search-and-track radar and one SPQ-9A track-while-scan radar used in conjunction with the Mk 86 gun fire-control system, one SQS-53 (to be modernized to SQS-53C) active/passive search and attack bow sonar and one SQR-19 passive search towed-array sonar used in conjunction with the Mk 116 underwater weapons fire-control system, Naval Tactical Data System, one SLQ-25 Nixie towed torpedo-decoy system, one Prairie Masker hull/propeller blade noise-suppression system, one SLQ-32(V)2 or (some ships) SLQ-34 ESM system with warning and jamming elements, four Mk 36 Super RBOC chaff/flare launchers, one OE-82 satellite communications system, three WSC-3 satellite communications transceivers, one SRR-1 satellite communications receiver, and URN-20 or URN-25 TACAN
Propulsion: four General Electric LM2500 gas turbines delivering 80,000 hp (59,655 kW) to two shafts
Performance: maximum speed 33 kt; range 6,900 miles (11,105 km) at 20 kt
Complement: 20 + 299/319
Note: This is in numerical terms the US Navy's most important multi-role destroyer class, and its ships have the electronic and weapon capabilities for the whole gamut of escort and independent tasks. The high level of automation inbuilt into the class has permitted an average 20% reduction in crew numbers by comparison with ships of similar capability, and the importance of the class is attested by the US Navy's plans to modernize through to 1996 so that the class can remain in effective service until well into the next century. The *David R. Ray* is the trials ship for the RIM-116 RAM surface-to-air missile system, and others of the class may be fitted with this system in the early 1990s.

Above: The *Paul F. Foster* is the second unit of the 'Spruance' class, in numerical and operational terms the US Navy's most vital destroyer asset.
Left: The 'Sovremenny' class provides the Soviet navy with a superb multi-role destroyer type optimized for the anti-ship role with potent weapons.

Class

1. USA

Name	No.	Builder	Laid down	Com-missioned
Spruance	DDG963	Ingalls SB	Nov 1972	Sep 1975
Paul F. Foster	DDG964	Ingalls SB	Feb 1973	Feb 1976
Kinkaid	DDG965	Ingalls SB	Apr 1973	Jul 1976
Hewitt	DDG966	Ingalls SB	Jul 1973	Sep 1976
Elliott	DDG967	Ingalls SB	Oct 1973	Jan 1976
Arthur W. Radford	DDG968	Ingalls SB	Jan 1974	Apr 1977
Peterson	DDG969	Ingalls SB	Apr 1974	Jul 1977
Caron	DDG970	Ingalls SB	Jul 1974	Oct 1977
David R. Ray	DDG971	Ingalls SB	Sep 1974	Nov 1977
Oldendorf	DDG972	Ingalls SB	Dec 1974	Mar 1978
John Young	DDG973	Ingalls SB	Feb 1975	May 1978
Comte de Grasse	DDG974	Ingalls SB	Apr 1975	Aug 1978
O'Brien	DDG975	Ingalls SB	May 1975	Dec 1977
Merrill	DDG976	Ingalls SB	Jun 1975	Mar 1978
Briscoe	DDG977	Ingalls SB	Jul 1975	Jun 1978
Stump	DDG978	Ingalls SB	Aug 1975	Aug 1978
Conolly	DDG979	Ingalls SB	Sep 1975	Oct 1978
Moosbrugger	DDG980	Ingalls SB	Nov 1975	Dec 1978
John Hancock	DDG981	Ingalls SB	Jan 1976	Mar 1979
Nicholson	DDG982	Ingalls SB	Feb 1976	May 1979
John Rodgers	DDG983	Ingalls SB	Aug 1976	Jul 1979
Leftwich	DDG984	Ingalls SB	Nov 1976	Aug 1979
Cushing	DDG985	Ingalls SB	Dec 1976	Sep 1979
Harry W. Hill	DDG986	Ingalls SB	Jan 1977	Nov 1979
O'Bannon	DDG987	Ingalls SB	Feb 1977	Dec 1979
Thorn	DDG988	Ingalls SB	Aug 1977	Feb 1980
Deyo	DDG989	Ingalls SB	Oct 1977	Mar 1980
Ingersoll	DDG990	Ingalls SB	Dec 1977	Apr 1980
Fife	DDG991	Ingalls SB	Mar 1978	May 1980
Fletcher	DDG992	Ingalls SB	Apr 1978	Jul 1980
Hayler	DDG997	Ingalls SB	Oct 1980	Mar 1983

By far the most striking feature of the 'Suffren' class *Duquesne* is the huge dome covering the antenna for the DRBI 23 air-search radar. Farther aft are the two DRBR 51 radars for use with the Masurca SAM system.

'Suffren' class DDG

(France)

Type: anti-aircraft, anti-submarine and anti-ship guided-missile escort destroyer

Displacement: 5,090 tons standard and 6,090 tons full load

Dimensions: length 157·6 m (517·1 ft); beam 15·5 m (51·0 ft); draught 6·1 m (20·0 ft)

Gun armament: two 100-mm (3·9-in) Creusot Loire L/55 DP in Modèle 1953 single mountings, and four 20-mm AA in single mountings

Missile armament: two twin container-launchers for four MM.38 Exocet anti-ship missiles, and one twin launcher for 48 Masurca SAMs

Torpedo armament: none

Anti-submarine armament: one single launcher for 13 Malafon missiles, and four single 533-mm (21-in) launchers for L5 torpedoes

Aircraft: none

Electronics: one DRBI 23 air-search radar, one DRBV 15 air/surface-search radar, one DRBN 32 navigation radar, two DRBR 51 radars used in conjunction with the SAM fire-control system, one DRBC 32A gun fire-control radar, one DUBV 23D active search and attack hull sonar, one DUBV 43B/C active search variable-depth sonar, SENIT 1 action information system, one ESM system with warning and ARBB 32 jamming elements, two Dagaie chaff/flare launchers, two Syllex chaff launchers, one Syracuse satellite communications system, and URN-20 TACAN

Propulsion: four boilers supplying steam to two sets of Rateau geared turbines delivering 54,000 kW (72,425 hp) to two shafts

Performance: maximum speed 34 kt; range 9500 km (5,905 miles) at 18 kt or 4450 km (2,765 miles) at 29 kt

Complement: 23 + 332

Class

1. France

Name	No.	Builder	Laid down	Com-missioned
Suffren	D602	Lorient ND	Dec 1962	Jul 1967
Duquesne	D603	Brest ND	Nov 1964	Apr 1970

Note: These highly seaworthy ships were designed as the primary escorts for French aircraft-carriers, and are capable ships providing an excellent platform for a nicely balanced anti-aircraft, anti-ship and anti-submarine armament.

'T47' class DDG

(France)
Type: anti-aircraft guided-missile escort destroyer
Displacement: 2,750 tons standard and 3,740 tons full load
Dimensions: length 128·6 m (421·9 ft); beam 12·7 m (41·7 ft); draught 6·3 m (20·7 ft)
Gun armament: six 57-mm Bofors L/60 DP in three Modèle 1951 twin mountings
Missile armament: one Mk 13 single launcher for 40 RIM-24B Tartar and RIM-66B Standard SM-1 MR SAMs
Torpedo armament: none
Anti-submarine armament: one 375-mm (14·76-in) Modèle 1954 six-barrel rocket-launcher, and two triple 550-mm (21·7-in) mountings for L3 torpedoes
Aircraft: none
Electronics: one SPS-39A/B 3D radar, one DRBV 22 air-search radar, one DRBV 31 surface-search and navigation radar, two SPG-51B radars used in conjunction with the Mk 73 SAM fire-control system, one DRBC 31 gun fire-control radar, one DUBA 1 active search and attack hull sonar, one DUBV 24 active search and attack hull sonar, SENIT 2 action information system, one ESM system with ARBR 10 warning element, and URN-20 TACAN
Propulsion: four Indret boilers supplying steam to two sets of geared turbines delivering 47,000 kW (63,035 hp) to two shafts
Performance: maximum speed 32 kt; range 9250 km (5,750 miles) at 18 kt or 2225 km (1,385 miles) at 32 kt
Complement: 17 + 260 in peace and 320 in war

Class
1. France			Laid	Com-
Name	No.	Builder	down	missioned
Du Chayla	D630	Brest ND	Jul 1953	Jun 1957

Note: This is the sole survivor of the four-strong anti-aircraft half-sister class to the 'T47' anti-submarine destroyers. The first two ships were paid off to provide missile systems for the newer 'C70 AA' class ships, the *Dupetit Thouars* was placed in reserve in 1988, and the *Du Chayla* is scheduled to pay off in 1990.

Sistership *Maille Brézé* (D627) commissioned in May 1957 and now stood down.

'Type 82' class CG

(UK)
Type: guided-missile cruiser
Displacement: 6,300 tons standard and 7,100 tons full load
Dimensions: length 507·0 ft (154·5 m); beam 55·0 ft (16·8 m); draught 23·0 ft (7·0 m)
Gun armament: one 4·5-in (114-mm) Vickers L/55 DP in a Mk 8 single mounting, four 30-mm Oerlikon AA in two GCM-A03 twin mountings, two 20-mm Oerlikon AA in GAM-B01 single mountings, and two 20-mm Oerlikon AA in Mk 7 single mountings
Missile armament: one twin launcher for 40 Sea Dart SAMs
Torpedo armament: none
Anti-submarine armament: helicopter-launched weapons (see below)
Aircraft: one Westland Wasp HAS.Mk 1 helicopter on a platform aft
Electronics: one Type 1022 long-range air-search radar, one Type 992R surface-search and target indication radar, one Type 1006 navigation radar, two Type 909 radars used in conjunction with two GWS 30 SAM fire-control systems, one Type 184P medium-range active/passive search and attack hull sonar, one Type 162M side-looking classification hull sonar, one Type 182 towed torpedo-decoy system, one ADAWS 2 action-information system, Link 10, 11 and 14 data-links, one UAA-1 Abbey Hill ESM system with two Type 675 jamming elements, two Corvus chaff launchers, and one SCOT satellite communications system
Propulsion: COSAG arrangement, with two boilers supplying steam to two sets of Admiralty Standard Range geared turbines delivering 30,000 hp (22,370 kW), and two Rolls-Royce Olympus TM1A gas turbines delivering 30,000 hp (22,370 kW) to two shafts
Performance: maximum speed 28 kt; range 5,750 miles (9255 km) at 18 kt
Complement: 30 + 367

Note: Classified by the British as a destroyer, in size and capability the single 'Type 82' class ship is similar to many of the guided-missile cruisers operated by other navies. The *Bristol* was to have been the lead vessel of a four-ship class designed for the protection of aircraft-carriers against air and submarine attack, but the phasing out of the Royal Navy's large carriers combined with rising costs to curtail this plan at just the one ship. The type has the size and facilities to operate as a flagship.

The *Bristol* was produced as lead ship for a class of escorts for aircraft-carriers that did not appear, and thus remains a singleton unit.

Class
1. UK			Laid	Com-
Name	No.	Builder	down	missioned
Bristol	D23	Swan Hunter	Nov 1967	Mar 1973

'Tachikaze' or 'Type 168' class DDG

(Japan)
Type: guided-missile destroyer
Displacement: 3,850 tons or (DD170) 3,900 tons standard and 4,800 tons full load
Dimensions: length 143·0 m (469·2 ft); beam 14·3 m (46·9 ft); draught 4·6 m (15·0 ft)
Gun armament: two 5-in (127-mm) L/54 DP in Mk 42 single mountings, and two 20-mm Phalanx Mk 15 CIWS mountings
Missile armament: two Mk 141 quadruple container-launchers for eight RGM-84 Harpoon anti-ship missiles, and one Mk 13 single launcher for 40 RIM-66B Standard SM-1 MR SAMs
Torpedo armament: none
Anti-submarine armament: one Mk 16 octuple launcher for 16 RUR-5A ASROC missiles, and two Mk 32 triple 12·75-in (324-mm) mountings for Mk 46 torpedoes
Aircraft: none
Electronics: one SPS-52B 3D radar, one OPS-11B air-search radar, one OPS-16 or (DD170) OPS-28 surface-search radar, two SPG-51C radars used in conjunction with two Mk 74 SAM fire-control systems, one Type 2 radar used in conjunction with the Type 1A or (DD170) Type 2 gun fire-control system, Link 14 data-link, one OQS-4 active search and attack hull sonar used in conjunction with the Mk 114 underwater weapons fire-control system, one ESM system with NOLQ-1 or (DD168) NOLR-6 warning and OLT-3 jamming elements, and four Mk 36 Super RBOC chaff/flare launchers
Propulsion: two boilers supplying steam to two sets of Mitsubishi geared turbines delivering 52,200 kW (70,010 hp) to two shafts
Performance: maximum speed 32 kt
Complement: 250 or (DD170) 255
Note: Though comparatively small, these destroyers are well suited to Japan's defence stance with a balanced anti-aircraft, anti-ship and anti-submarine capability.

Class 1. Japan Name	No.	Builder	Laid down	Com- missioned
Tachikaze	DD168	Mitsubishi	Jun 1973	Mar 1976
Asakaze	DD169	Mitsubishi	May 1976	Mar 1979
Sawakaze	DD170	Mitsubishi	Sep 1979	Mar 1983

The *Sawakaze* is the third and last unit of the 'Tachikaze' class, whose ships are small but nicely balanced in their capabilities.

'Takatsuki' or 'Type 164' class DDG

(Japan)
Type: anti-submarine and anti-ship guided-missile destroyer
Displacement: 3,250 tons or (DD166/167) 3,100 tons standard and 4,500 tons full load
Dimensions: length 136·0 m (446·2 ft); beam 13·4 m (44·0 ft); draught 4·4 m (14·5 ft)
Gun armament: one or (DD166/167) two 5-in (127-mm) L/54 DP in Mk 42 single mountings, and (DD164/165 only) one 20-mm Phalanx Mk 15 CIWS mountings
Missile armament: (DD164/165 only) two Mk 141 quadruple container-launchers for eight RGM-84 Harpoon anti-ship missiles, and one Mk 29 octuple launcher for 16 RIM-7 Sea Sparrow SAMs
Torpedo armament: none
Anti-submarine armament: one Mk 16 octuple launcher for 16 RUR-5A ASROC missiles, one 375-mm (14·76-in) Bofors Type 71 four-barrel rocket-launcher, two Type 68 triple 12·75-in (324-mm) mountings for Mk 46 torpedoes, and (DD166/167 only) helicopter-launched weapons (see below)
Aircraft: (DD166/167 only) provision for one helicopter on a platform aft
Electronics: one OPS-11B air-search radar, one OPS-17 surface-search radar, one Type 2 radar used in conjunction with the Type 2-12B SAM fire-control system (DD164/165 only), one Mk 35 radar used in conjunction with the Mk 56 or Type 1 5-in gun fire-control system, one OQS-3 active search and attack hull sonar, one SQS-35J active search variable-depth sonar or (DD164/165 only) one SQR-18 passive search towed-array sonar, one ESM system with NOLQ-6C warning element, and (DD164/165 only) two Mk 36 Super RBOC chaff/flare launchers
Propulsion: two Foster-Wheeler or (DD166/167) Mitsubishi boilers supplying steam to two sets of Kawasaki/General Electric or (DD166/167) Mitsubishi/Westinghouse geared turbines delivering 44,750 kW (60,020 hp) to two shafts
Performance: maximum speed 31 kt or (DD166/167) 32 kt; range 12,975 km (8,065 miles) at 20 kt
Complement: 260 or (DD166/167) 270

The *Takatsuki* is the lead ship of a class of small but well balanced destroyers built for the anti-submarine role and then improved with anti-ship missiles. The ships use the hull and propulsion arrangement of the 'Amatsukaze' class, but have a 'mack' (combined mast and stack).

Class 1. Japan Name	No.	Builder	Laid down	Com- missioned
Takatsuki	DD164	Ishikawajima	Oct 1964	Mar 1967
Kikuzuki	DD165	Mitsubishi	Mar 1966	Mar 1968
Mochizuki	DD166	Ishikawajima	Nov 1966	Mar 1969
Nagatsuki	DD167	Mitsubishi	Mar 1968	Feb 1970

Note: These small destroyers are well balanced with the hull and propulsion of the 'Amatsukaze' class and a weapon/sensor fit based on licence-made US equipment. The ships of the first pair were extensively updated in the first half of the 1980s with the after 5-in (127-mm) gun and helicopter hangar removed in favour of anti-ship and anti-aircraft missile armament, the variable-depth sonar replaced by towed-array sonar, and a CIWS mounting added. The ships of the second pair are not to receive the modernization, the Japanese preferring to allocate the funding to new construction.

'Tromp' class DDG

(Netherlands)
Type: anti-submarine, anti-aircraft and anti-ship guided-missile destroyer
Displacement: 3,665 tons standard and 4,310 tons full load
Dimensions: length 138·4 m (454·0 ft); beam 14·8 m (48·6 ft); draught 4·6 m (15·1 ft)
Gun armament: two 120-mm (4·7-in) Bofors L/50 DP in a Bofors twin mounting
Missile armament: two Mk 141 quadruple container-launchers for eight RGM-84 Harpoon anti-ship missiles, one Mk 13 single launcher for 40 RIM-66B Standard SM-1 MR SAMs, and one Mk 29 octuple launcher for 16 RIM-7 NATO Sea Sparrow SAMs
Torpedo armament: none
Anti-submarine armament: two Mk 32 triple 12·75-in (324-mm) mountings for Mk 46 torpedoes, and helicopter-launched weapons (see below)
Aircraft: one Westland SH-14B Lynx helicopter in a hangar aft
Electronics: one MTTR/SPS 01 3D radar, two Decca 1226 navigation radars, two SPG-51C radars used in conjunction with the RIM-66 fire-control system, one radar used in conjunction with the WM-25 gun and Sea Sparrow fire-control system, one CWE-610 active search and attack hull sonar and one Type 162M side-looking classification hull sonar used in conjunction with a Hollandse Signaalapparaten underwater weapons fire-control system, one SEWACO I action information system, one Daisy data-handling system, Link 10 and 11 data-links, one Sphinx ESM system with warning and jamming elements, and two Corvus chaff launchers
Propulsion: COGOG arrangement, with two Rolls-Royce Olympus TM3B gas turbines delivering 50,000 hp (37,285 kW) or two Rolls-Royce Tyne RM1C gas turbines delivering 8,000 hp (5965 kW) to two shafts

Like other destroyers optimized for the anti-air role, the *Tromp* has a large randome over its 3D radar, in this instance the MTTR/SPS 01 equipment.

Performance: maximum speed 30 kt; range 9250 km (5,750 miles) at 18 kt
Complement: 34 + 272

Class

1. Netherlands			Laid	Com-
Name	No.	Builder	down	missioned
Tromp	F801	Koninklijke Maatschappij	Sep 1971	Oct 1975
De Ruyter	F802	Koninklijke Maatschappij	Dec 1971	Jun 1976

Note: These are anti-aircraft ships with useful medium- and short-range missile fits together with an anti-ship capability. Both ships serve as flagships, and the planned update with a 30-mm Goalkeeper CIWS mounting was cancelled in 1988 for financial reasons.

'Udaloy' class DDG

(USSR)
Type: anti-submarine and anti-aircraft guided-missile escort destroyer
Displacement: 6,400 tons standard and 8,300 tons full load
Dimensions: length 163·5 m (536·4 ft); beam 19·3 m (63·3 ft); draught 6·2 m (20·3 ft)
Gun armament: two 100-mm (3·9-in) L/70 DP in single mountings, and four 30-mm ADGM-630 CIWS mountings
Missile armament: eight silo groups (four forward, two amidships and two aft) each containing an octuple vertical launcher for 64 SA-N-9 SAMs
Torpedo armament: two quadruple 533-mm (21-in) mountings for Type 53 dual-role torpedoes
Anti-submarine armament: two quadruple container-launchers for eight SS-N-14 'Silex' missiles, two RBU 6000 12-barrel rocket-launchers, torpedoes (see above), and helicopter-launched weapons (see below)
Aircraft: two Kamov Ka-27 'Helix-A' helicopters in twin hangars aft
Mines: fitted with rails for 30 mines
Electronics: two 'Strut Pair' air/surface-search radars or (in *Marshal Vasilevsky* onwards) one 'Top Plate' 3D and one 'Strut Pair' air/surface-search radars, three 'Palm Frond' surface-search and navigation radars, two 'Eye Bowl' SS-N-14 fire-control radars, two 'Cross Sword' SA-N-9 fire-control radars (third ship onwards), one 'Kite Screech' 100-mm gun fire-control radar, two 'Bass Tilt' CIWS fire-control radars, one 'Fly Screen-B' aircraft control radar, one low/medium-frequency active search and attack bow sonar, one medium-frequency active search variable-depth sonar, one ESM system including two 'Bell Shroud' and two 'Bell Squat' antennae/housings, two chaff launchers, one noise-reduction system, one 'Salt Pot-A' and one 'Salt Pot-B' IFF systems, and two 'Round House' TACAN
Propulsion: COGOG arrangement, with four gas turbines delivering about 82,000 kW (109,965 hp) to two shafts
Performance: maximum speed 32 kt; range 11,125 km (6,915 miles) at 20 kt or 3700 km (2,300 miles) at 32 kt
Complement: 35 + 275

Note: These extremely impressive ships are successors to the 'Kresta II' class cruisers but based on the 'Krivak' class destroyer design, and have good sea-keeping and endurance records. The type is optimized for general-purpose duties with a leaning towards anti-submarine capability, and are generally paired with 'Sovremenny' class destroyers for the escort of major surface combatants.

Class

1. USSR			Com-
Name	Builder	Laid down	missioned
Udaloy	Yantar, Kaliningrad	1978	Nov 1980
Vitse-Admiral Kulakov	Zhdanov Yard, Leningrad	1978	Sep 1981
Marshal Vasilevsky	Zhdanov Yard, Leningrad	1979	Jun 1983
Admiral Zakharov	Yantar, Kaliningrad	1979	Oct 1983
Admiral Spiridonov	Yantar, Kaliningrad	1981	Sep 1984
Admiral Tributs	Zhdanov Yard, Leningrad	1980	Aug 1985
Marshal Shaposhnikov	Yantar, Kaliningrad	1983	Oct 1985
Simferopol	Zhdanov Yard, Leningrad	1981	Dec 1986
Admiral Levchenko	Yantar, Kaliningrad	1984	Nov 1987
Admiral Vinogradov	Yantar, Kaliningrad	1985	Sep 1988
Admiral Charlamov	Yantar, Kaliningrad	1987	Dec 1989
	Yantar, Kaliningrad	1988	1991
	Yantar, Kaliningrad	1988	

Designed to partner the 'Sovremenny' class, the 'Udaloy' class destroyer is further proof of the Soviets' ability to produce powerful warships.

'Allen M. Sumner' class DD

(USA/Taiwan)

Type: gun destroyer with anti-ship missile capability

Displacement: 2,200 tons standard and 3,320 tons full load

Dimensions: length 376·5 ft (114·8 m); beam 40·9 ft (12·5 m); draught 19·0 ft (5·8 m)

Gun armament: four 5-in (127-mm) L/38 DP in two Mk 38 twin mountings, and four 40-mm Bofors L/70 AA in two twin mountings or (906 and 910 only) one 76-mm (3-in) OTO Melara L/62 DP in an OTO Melara Compact single mounting

Missile armament: two triple or one triple and two single container-launchers for six or five Hsiung Feng I anti-ship missiles, and one quadruple Sea Chaparral launcher for 20 MIM-72 SAMs

Torpedo armament: none

Anti-submarine armament: two Mk 32 triple 12·75-in (324-mm) mountings for Mk 46 torpedoes, and two Hedgehog Mk 10 rocket-launchers

Aircraft: none

Electronics: one SPS-6C or SPS-40 air-search radar, one SPS-10 surface-search radar, one Mk 25 radar used in conjunction with the Mk 37 gun fire-control system, one RTN 10X radar used in conjunction with the H 930 anti-ship missile fire-control system or (906 and 910) two HR 76 optronic directors used in conjunction with an RCA 76-mm gun/anti-ship missile fire-control system, one Mk 51 40-mm gun fire-control system, one Kollmorgen optronic director, one SQS-29 active search and attack hull sonar, one SLQ-25 Nixie towed torpedo-decoy system, one ESM system with Argo 680/681 warning and jamming elements, and four Kung Fen 6 chaff launchers

Propulsion: four Babcock & Wilcox boilers supplying steam to two sets of geared turbines delivering 60,000 hp (44,740 kW) to two shafts

Performance: maximum speed 34 kt; range 5,300 miles (8530 km) at 15 kt or 1,140 miles (1835 km) at 31 kt

Complement: 275

Class

1. Brazil

Name	No.	Builder	Laid down	Commissioned
Mato Grosso	D34	Federal SB	Mar 1944	Nov 1944

(This ship was transferred in September 1972, and still resembles the baseline World War II destroyer in most vital respects. Despite its quadruple launcher for Sea Cat SAMs, used with a WM-20 optical fire-control system, this is an obsolete ship. The rest of the armament comprises six 5-in/127-mm L/38 DP guns in three Mk 38 twin mountings, and the electronic fit includes SPS-6 air-search radar, SPS-10 surface-search radar, Mk 25 radar used in conjunction with the Mk 37 gun fire-control system, and an ESM system with WLR-3 warning element. The anti-submarine weapons include two Mk 32 triple mountings, two Hedgehog rocket-launchers and one rack of depth charges used with the SQS-31 active search and attack hull sonar. The complement is 15 + 261.)

2. Taiwan

Name	No.	Builder	Laid down	Commissioned
Hsiang Yang	901	Bethlehem Steel	Jul 1943	Apr 1944
Heng Yang	902	Bethlehem Steel	Sep 1943	Jun 1944
Hua Yang	903	Bethlehem Steel	May 1944	Mar 1945
Yuen Yang	905	Federal SB	Dec 1943	Jun 1944
Huei Yang	906	Federal SB	Oct 1943	May 1944
Po Yang	910	Bath Iron Works	Oct 1943	Jun 1944

(The Taiwanese ships were transferred between 1969 and 1972 and, though originally similar to the Brazilian vessel in baseline weapon and electronic fit, have been converted into anti-ship missile destroyers.)

A former Iranian Navy vessel of the 'Allen M. Sumner' class destroyer.

'Allen M. Sumner (FRAM II)' class DD

(USA/Brazil)

Type: gun destroyer
Displacement: 2,200 tons standard and 3,320 tons full load
Dimensions: length 376·5 ft (114·8 m); beam 40·9 ft (12·5 m); draught 19·0 ft (5·8 m)
Gun armament: six 5-in (127 mm) L/38 DP in three Mk 38 twin mountings
Missile armament: none
Torpedo armament: none
Anti-submarine armament: two Mk 32 triple 12·75-in (324-mm) mountings for Mk 46 torpedoes, two Hedgehog rocket-launchers, and helicopter-launched weapons (see below)
Aircraft: provision for one Westland Wasp HAS.Mk 1 light helicopter in a hangar aft
Electronics: one SPS-29 (D38 only) or SPS-40 air-search radar, one SPS-10 surface-search radar, one Mk 25 radar used in conjunction with the Mk 37 gun fire-control system, one SQS-40 active search and attack sonar and one SQA-10 variable-depth sonar used in conjunction with the Mk 105 underwater weapons fire-control system, and one ESM system with WLR-3 warning and (D38 only) ULQ-6 jamming elements
Propulsion: four Babcock & Wilcox boilers supplying steam to two sets of geared turbines delivering 60,000 hp (44,740 kW) to two shafts
Performance: maximum speed 34 kt; range 5,300 miles (8530 km) at 15 kt or 1,140 miles (1835 km) at 31 kt
Complement: 15 + 259

Class

1. Brazil

Name	No.	Builder	Laid down	Commissioned
Sergipe	D35	Bethlehem Steel	Apr 1944	Feb 1945
Alagoas	D36	Bethlehem Steel	Feb 1944	Jun 1946
Rio Grande do Norte	D37	Bethlehem Steel	Jul 1943	Mar 1945
Espirito Santo	D38	Bethlehem Steel	Aug 1943	Jul 1944

(These are standard gun destroyers of the World War II type with a slight enhancement in their anti-submarine capabilities through the addition of more modern sonar and a helicopter.)

2. Chile

Name	No.	Builder	Laid down	Commissioned
Ministro Zenteno	16	Todd Pacific	1944	Dec 1944
Ministro Portales	17	Federal SB	1943	May 1944

(The Chilean ships are similar to the Brazilian units, but have fittings for two MM.38 Exocet anti-ship missiles, two 40-mm AA in single mountings, Mk 44 rather than Mk 46 anti-submarine torpedoes, SPS-37 or SPS-40 air-search radar, SQS-40 hull sonar, and an Aérospatiale SA 319B Alouette III Astazou helicopter.)

The Miaoulis is Greece's sole 'Allen M. Sumner (FRAM II)' class destroyer.

3. Greece

Name	No.	Builder	Laid down	Commissioned
Miaoulis	D211	Federal SB	Aug 1943	Mar 1944

(This ship has an Agusta [Bell] AB.212ASW helicopter in a larger hangar, and its armament has been upgraded by the addition of two 20-mm cannon and shoulder-launched FIM-43 Redeye SAMs.)

4. Iran

Name	No.	Builder	Laid down	Commissioned
Babr	61	Todd Pacific	Dec 1943	Oct 1944
Palang	62	Todd Pacific	Apr 1944	Jan 1945

(The Iranian vessels were laid up for lack of spares in the mid-1980s, but are now both back in commission. The ships are each fitted with four launchers for eight RIM-66B Standard SM-1 MR missiles, have a gun armament of four 5-in/127-mm guns in two twin mountings and four 14·5-mm/0·57-in machine-guns in a quadruple mounting, carry SPS-29C air-search radar, have SQS-43 or SQS-44 hull sonar, and have accommodation for a single Agusta [Bell] AB.204AS helicopter in a hangar aft.)

5. South Korea

Name	No.	Builder	Laid down	Commissioned
Dae Gu	DD917	Bath Iron Works	Apr 1944	Sep 1944
Inchon	DD918	Federal SB	Oct 1943	Mar 1944

(The South Korean ships each have a gun armament of six 5-in/127-mm L/38 DP in three twin mountings, four 40-mm Bofors L/56 AA in two twin mount-ings and [DD918 only] one 20-mm Phalanx Mk 15 CIWS mounting. The embarked helicopter is an Aérospatiale SA 316B Alouette III or McDonnell Douglas MD-500D Defender in a hangar aft.)

6. Taiwan

Name	No.	Builder	Laid down	Commissioned
Lo Yang	914	Bethlehem Steel	Aug 1943	May 1944
Nan Yang	917	Bethlehem Steel	Nov 1944	Oct 1945

(These Taiwanese units are generally similar to the same country's 'Allen M. Sumner' class destroyers in updated form with one triple and two single container-launchers for five Hsiung Feng I anti-ship missiles, but possess only two 5-in/127-mm guns while also having one quadruple launcher for 20 Sea Chaparral SAMs, an Argo AR 680/681 ESM system with warning and jamming elements, and a McDonnell Douglas MD-500MD helicopter on an Israeli-supplied flightdeck carried in place of Y turret.)

7. Turkey

Name	No.	Builder	Laid down	Commissioned
Zafer	D356	Federal SB	1944	Mar 1945

(The Turkish ship is similar to the Greek unit, but its helicopter capability has been removed in favour of an enhanced AA defence in the form of four Bofors 40-mm L/56 AA in two twin mountings and two Oerlikon 35-mm L/90 AA in a GDM-A twin mounting.)

'Almirante' class DD

(Chile)

Type: gun destroyer with secondary anti-ship missile capability

Displacement: 2,730 tons standard and 3,300 tons full load

Dimensions: length 402·0 ft (122·5 m); beam 43·0 ft (13·1 m); draught 13·3 ft (4·0 m)

Gun armament: four 4-in (102-mm) Vickers L/60 DP in Mk(N)R single mountings, and four 40-mm Bofors L/70 AA in single mountings

Missile armament: four container-launchers for four MM.38 Exocet anti-ship missiles, and two quadruple launchers for 24 Sea Cat SAMs; from 1990 the Sea Cat system is to be replaced by one Barak 1 vertical-launch SAM system

Torpedo armament: none

Anti-submarine armament: two Mk 32 triple 12·75-in (324-mm) mountings for Mk 44 torpedoes, and two Squid three-barrel depth-charge mortars

Aircraft: none

Electronics: one AWS 1 air-search radar, one SNW 10 air/surface-search radar, one Decca 1629 navigation radar, two SGR 102 radars used in conjunction with the 4-in gun fire-control system, two WM-4 SAM optical directors, one Type 184B active search and attack hull sonar, one Ferranti action information system, and one ESM system with WLR-1 warning element

Propulsion: two Babcock & Wilcox boilers supplying steam to two sets of Parsons/Pametrada geared turbines delivering 54,000 hp (40,270 kW) to two shafts

Performance: maximum speed 34·5 kt; range 6,900 miles (11,100 km)

Complement: 17 + 249

Despite their defensive SAM armament, which oddly enough is apparently to be updated, the Chilean navy's two 'Almirante' class destroyers are obsolete. This is the *Almirante Riveros* in original configuration.

Class 1. Chile			Laid	Com-
Name	No.	Builder	down	missioned
Almirante Riveros	18	Vickers-Armstrongs	Apr 1957	Dec 1960
Almirante Williams	19	Vickers-Armstrongs	June 1956	Mar 1960

Note: These were ordered as conventional gun destroyers in 1955, and converted during the early 1970s, with upgraded electronics following later in the decade. Despite their missile armament, these are little more than gun destroyers because of the limitations of their other armament and sensors.

'Anshan' or 'Type 07' class DD

(China)

Type: gun destroyer with secondary anti-ship missile capability

Displacement: 1,660 tons standard and 2,040 tons full load

Dimensions: length 112·8 m (370·0 ft); beam 10·2 m (33·5 ft); draught 3·8 m (12·5 ft)

Gun armament: four 130-mm (5·1-in) L/50 DP in single mountings, and eight 37-mm L/63 AA in four twin mountings

Missile armament: two twin container-launchers for four HY-2 (CSS-N-1) anti-ship missiles

Torpedo armament: none

Anti-submarine armament: two BMB-1 mortars with 24 depth charges, and two depth charge racks

Mines: up to 60

Aircraft: none

Electronics: one 'Cross Bird' air-search radar, one 'High Sieve' air/surface-search radar, one 'Ball End' surface-search radar, one 'Square Tie' surface-search and missile fire-control radar, one 'Fin Curve' or 'Neptun' navigation radar, one 'Post Lamp' radar used in conjunction with the 'Mina' gun fire-control system, one 'Four Eyes' optronic director, one Pegas-2M active search and attack hull sonar, and one 'Yard Rake' IFF system

Propulsion: three boilers supplying steam to two sets of Tosi geared turbines delivering 35,800 kW (48,010 hp) to two shafts

Performance: maximum speed 32 kt; range 4800 km (2,980 miles) at 19 kt

Complement: 15 + 190

Class 1. China			Laid	Com-
Name	No.	Builder	down	missioned
Anshan	101	Nikolayev-Dalzavod	1935	1940
Fushun	102	Nikolayev-Komsomolsk	1935	1942
Changchun	103	Nikolayev-Dalzavod	1935	1941
Qingdao	104	Nikolayev-Komsomolsk	1936	1942

Note: These ships were supplied from the USSR in December 1954 (two ships) and July 1955 (two ships). They were converted to semi-missile destroyers between 1971 and 1974, and are now nearing the end of their lives.

Closest to the camera in this three-ship line-up is the 'Anshan' class destroyer *Changchun* complete with midships anti-ship missile launchers.

'Carpenter (FRAM I)' class DD

(USA/Turkey)

Type: gun destroyer
Displacement: 2,425 tons standard and 3,540 tons full load
Dimensions: length 390·5 ft (119·0 m); beam 41·0 ft (12·5 m); draught 20·9 ft (6·4 m)
Gun armament: two 5-in (127-mm) L/38 DP in a Mk 38 twin mounting, two 3-in (76-mm) L/50 DP in a twin mounting, and two 35-mm Oerlikon L/90 AA in a GDM-A twin mounting
Missile armament: none
Torpedo armament: none
Anti-submarine armament: one Mk 16 octuple launcher for eight RUR-5A ASROC missiles, two Mk 32 triple 12·75-in (324-mm) mountings for Mk 46 torpedoes, helicopter-launched weapons (see below), and one rack for nine depth charges
Aircraft: provision for one Agusta (Bell) AB.212ASW on a platform aft
Electronics: one SPS-40 air-search radar, one SPS-10 surface-search radar, one Mk 35 radar used in conjunction with the Mk 56 gun fire-control system, one Mk 1 target designation system, one SQS-23 active search and attack hull sonar used in conjunction with the Mk 114 underwater weapons fire-control system, and one ESM system with WLR-1 warning and ULQ-6 jamming elements
Propulsion: four Babcock & Wilcox boilers supplying steam to two sets of General Electric geared turbines delivering 60,000 hp (44,740 kW) to two shafts
Performance: maximum speed 33 kt; range 6,900 miles (7945 km) at 12 kt
Complement: 15 + 260

Class

1. Turkey			Laid	Com-
Name	No.	Builder	down	missioned
Alcitepe	D346	Bath Iron Works	Oct 1945	Nov 1949
Anittepe	D348	Consolidated Steel	Jul 1945	Dec 1949

Note: These two ships were transferred in 1981 and 1982 respectively, and retain a limited utility through their comparatively modern anti-submarine sensors and weapons. It is reported that the two ships are to be further upgraded with STIR radar and the VLS Sea Sparrow SAM system.

'Daring' class DD

(UK/Peru)

Type: gun destroyer with anti-ship missile capability
Displacement: 2,800 tons standard and 3,600 tons full load
Dimensions: length 390·0 ft (118·9 m); beam 43·0 ft (13·1 m); draught 18·0 ft (5·5 m)
Gun armament: six or (DM73) four 4·5-in (114-mm) L/45 DP in three or (DM73) two Mk 6 twin mountings, and four 40-mm Bofors L/70 AA in two Mk 5 twin mountings
Missile armament: eight container-launchers for eight MM.38 Exocet anti-ship missiles
Torpedo armament: none
Anti-submarine armament: one Squid rocket-launcher
Aircraft: provision for one light helicopter on a platform aft
Electronics: one AWS 1 air/surface-search radar, one Decca navigation radar, one TSF radar used in conjunction with the gun fire-control system, and one active search and attack hull sonar
Propulsion: two Foster-Wheeler boilers supplying steam to two sets of English Electric geared turbines delivering 54,000 hp (40,270 kW) to two shafts
Performance: speed 32 kt; range 3,450 miles (5550 km) at 20 kt
Complement: 297

Class

1. Chile			Laid	Com-
Name	No.	Builder	down	missioned
Palacios	DM73	Yarrow	Apr 1947	Mar 1954
Ferre	DM74	Yarrow	Sep 1946	Apr 1953

Note: These ships were bought from the UK in 1969, and are now obsolete in all respects but their potent anti-ship missile armament. *Palacios* has only four main guns as the after twin turret was removed in 1970s to make way for a helicopter hangar that has since been removed.

Below: The pennant number 85 identifies this 'Fletcher' class destroyer as the *Sfendoni*, one of the Greek navy's four such ships now in reserve.

Above: A previous operator of the 'Daring' class destroyer was Australia, and seen here is the *Vampire*, one of that country's three such ships.

'Fletcher' class DD

(USA/Greece)
Type: gun destroyer
Displacement: 2,050 tons standard and 3,050 tons full load
Dimensions: length 376·5 ft (114·7 m); beam 39·5 ft (12·0 m); draught 18·0 ft (5·5 m)
Gun armament: four 5-in (127-mm) L/38 DP in Mk 30 single mountings, six 3-in (76-mm) L/55 DP in three Mk 33 twin mountings, and two 0·5-in (12·7-mm) machine-gunsl
Missile armament: shoulder-launched FIM-43 Redeye SAMs
Torpedo armament: one quintuple 21-in (533-mm) mounting for NT 37E wire-guided dual-role torpedoes
Anti-submarine armament: two Mk 32 triple 12·75-in (324-mm) mountings for Mk 46 torpedoes, two Hedgehog Mk 10 rocket-launchers, and one depth-charge rack
Aircraft: none
Electronics: one SPS-6 air-search radar, one SPS-10 surface-search radar, one Decca navigation radar, one Mk 35 radar used in conjunction with the Mk 37 5-in gun fire-control system, one Mk 25 radar used in conjunction with the one Mk 56 and two Mk 63 3-in gun fire-control systems, one SQS-39 or SQS-43 active search and attack hull sonar, and one ESM system with WLR-3 warning element
Propulsion: four Babcock & Wilcox boilers supplying steam to two sets of General Electric geared turbines delivering 60,000 hp (44,740 kW) to two shafts
Performance: maximum speed 32 kt; range 6,900 miles (11,105 km) at 15 kt or 1,450 miles (2335 km) at 32 kt
Complement: 250

Class
1. Brazil

Name	No.	Builder	Laid down	Com-missioned
Piaui	D31	Federal SB	Mar 1943	Sep 1943
Maranhao	D33	Puget Sound NY	Aug 1943	Feb 1945

(These Brazilian ships are similar to the Greek vessels, and were purchased by Brazil in the early 1970s. The ships have no 3-in guns, but retain the original AA armament of 10 40-mm Bofors L/60 in one twin and two quadruple mountings. The sonar equipment comprises one SQS-4 hull set.)

2. Greece

Name	No.	Builder	Laid down	Com-missioned
Aspis	D06	Boston NY	Apr 1942	June 1943
Velos	D16	Boston NY	Feb 1941	May 1943
Lonchi	D56	Boston NY	Apr 1942	Jul 1943
Sfendoni	D85	Consolidated Steel	May 1941	Oct 1942

(These Greek ships are now in reserve, and were bought in April 1977 after transfer in 1959. Some ex-West German ships were also bought for cannibalization as a source of spares.)

3. Mexico

Name	No.	Builder	Laid down	Com-missioned
Cuitlahuac	E02	Consolidated Steel	Jul 1941	Feb 1943

(This ship lacks 3-in/76-mm secondary armament but carries 10 40-mm Bofors L/60 AA in five Mk 2 twin mountings, and has no anti-submarine capability. The radar comprises Kelvin Hughes 17/9 surface-search and Kelvin Hughes 14/9 navigation sets.)

4. Taiwan

Name	No.	Builder	Laid down	Com-missioned
Kwei Yang	908	Bethlehem Steel	Nov 1942	Dec 1943
Chiang Yang	909	Bethlehem Steel	Jan 1942	Apr 1943
An Yang	918	Bethlehem Steel	Jul 1942	May 1943
Kun Yang	919	Bethlehem Steel	Dec 1942	Dec 1943

(The Taiwanese ships differ considerably from the Greek vessels, having been converted to a standard approximating that of the Taiwanese 'Allen M. Sumner' class ships with one triple container-launcher for three Hsiung Feng I anti-ship missiles supported by two HR 76 radars used in conjunction with an H 930 fire-control system, one quadruple launcher for 20 Sea Chaparral SAMs, two 5-in/127-mm guns in a twin mounting controlled by the Mk 37 fire-control system upgraded with a Kollmorgen optronic director, one 3-in/76-mm OTO Melara L/62 DP in an OTO Melara Compact single mounting, two triple mountings for Mk 46 torpedoes, two Hedgehog Mk 10 rocket-launchers, and one or [919 only] two minelaying rails. 918 and 919 have SQS-50, 909 has SQS-40 and 908 has SQS-41 hull-mounted sonar, and all ships have an ESM system with Argo 680/681 warning and jamming elements. The complements are 261 [908], 279 [909] and 270 [918 and 919].)

'Friesland' class DD

(Netherlands/Peru)
Type: gun destroyer
Displacement: 2,495 tons standard and 3,070 tons full load
Dimensions: length 116·0 m (380·5 ft); beam 11·7 m (38·5 ft); draught 5·2 m (17·0 ft)
Gun armament: four 120-mm (4·7-in) Bofors L/50 DP in two Bofors twin mountings, and four 40-mm Bofors L/70 AA in single mountings
Missile armament: none
Torpedo armament: none
Anti-submarine armament: two 375-mm (14·76-in) Bofors four-barrel rocket-launchers, and two depth-charge racks
Aircraft: none
Electronics: one LW-03 air-search radar, one DA-05 air/surface-search radar, one ZW-06 surface-search radar, one TM1229 navigation radar, one radar used in conjunction with the WM-45 gun fire-control system, one CWE 10-N active search and attack hull sonar, and one PAE 1-N active search and attack hull sonar
Propulsion: four Babcock & Wilcox boilers supplying steam to two sets of Werkspoor geared turbines delivering 44,750 kW (60,020 hp) to two shafts
Performance: maximum speed 36 + kt; range 7400 km (4,600 miles) at 18 kt
Complement: 284

Class
1. Peru

Name	No.	Builder	Laid down	Com-missioned
Bolognesi	DD70	Dok en Werfmaatschappij	Oct 1953	Oct 1957
Castilla	DD71	Koninklijke Maatschappij	Feb 1954	Oct 1957
Capitan Quinones	DD76	Koninklijke Maatschappij	Nov 1953	Oct 1956
Villar	DD77	Nederlandse Dok	Mar 1956	Aug 1958
Galvez	DD78	Nederlandse Dok	Feb 1952	Sep 1956
Diez Canseco	DD79	Rotterdamse Droogdok	Jan 1954	Feb 1957

Note: These are obsolete gun destroyers bought from the Netherlands between 1980 and 1982. Two are currently in reserve, and it is thought that the deletion of the class is to begin shortly.

'Gearing (FRAM I)' class DD

(USA/Greece)
Type: gun destroyer with anti-ship missile capability
Displacement: 2,425 tons standard and 3,500 tons full load
Dimensions: length 390·5 ft (119·0 m); beam 41·2 ft (12·6 m); draught 19·0 ft (5·8 m)
Gun armament: four 5-in (127-mm) L/38 DP in two Mk 38 twin mountings, one 76-mm (3-in) OTO Melara L/62 DP in an OTO Melara Compact single mounting, one 40-mm Bofors L/70 AA in a single mounting (D216/217 only), and two 0·5-in (12·7-mm) machine-guns
Missile armament: two Mk 141 quadruple container-launchers for eight RGM-84 Harpoon anti-ship missiles (D212/215 only), and shoulder-launched FIM-43 Redeye SAMs
Torpedo armament: none
Anti-submarine armament: one Mk 16 octuple launcher for eight RUR-5A ASROC missiles, two Mk 32 triple 12·75-in (324-mm) mountings for Mk 46 torpedoes, and two depth-charge racks
Aircraft: none
Electronics: one SPS-37 or (D213, 214 and 217) SPS-40 air-search radar, one SPS-10 surface-search radar, one Decca navigation radar, one Mk 25 radar used in conjunction with the Mk 37 5-in fire-control system, one RTN 10X radar used in conjunction with the Argo NA21/30 76-mm gun fire-control system, one Mk 51 40-mm gun fire-control system, one SQS-23 active search

and attack hull sonar used in conjunction with the Mk 114 underwater weapons fire-control system, one ESM system with WLR-1 warning and ULQ-6 jamming elements, and two Mk 36 Super RBOC chaff/flare launchers
Propulsion: four Babcock & Wilcox boilers supplying steam to two sets of Westinghouse geared turbines delivering 60,000 hp (44,740 kW) to two shafts
Performance: maximum speed 32·5 kt; range 5,525 miles (8890 km) at 15 kt
Complement: 16 + 253

Class
1. Brazil

Name	No.	Builder	Laid down	Com-missioned
Marcilio Dias	D25	Consolidated Steel	May 1944	Mar 1945
Mariz E. Barros	D26	Consolidated Steel	Dec 1944	Oct 1945

(The Brazilian ships are similar to the Greek units, but lack the 76-mm/3-in gun and its associated fire-control system, having instead provision for a Westland Wasp HAS.Mk 1 light helicopter in a hangar amidships.)

2. Ecuador

Name	No.	Builder	Laid down	Com-missioned
Presidente E. Alfaro	DD01	Consolidated Steel	Apr 1945	May 1946

(This unit is comparable to the Brazilian ships, but lacks the Mk 16 ASROC launcher and has provision for a Bell Model 206B JetRanger light helicopter on a platform aft.)

3. Greece

Name	No.	Builder	Laid down	Com-missioned
Kanaris	D212	Consolidated Steel	Jan 1945	Sep 1945
Kountouriotis	D213	Bethlehem Steel	May 1945	Mar 1946
Sachtouris	D214	Bethlehem Steel	Mar 1945	Jan 1946
Tompazis	D215	Todd Pacific	Oct 1944	May 1945
Apostolis	D216	Bath Iron Works	Dec 1944	Jun 1945
Kriezis	D217	Consolidated Steel	Apr 1945	Feb 1946

(These Greek ships were transferred between 1973 and 1980, and have been upgraded to limited utility in Mediterranean anti-submarine requirements.)

4. Mexico

Name	No.	Builder	Laid down	Com-missioned
Quetzalcoatl	E03	Bethlehem Steel	Aug 1944	Apr 1945
Netzahualcoyotl	E04	Bethlehem Steel	Sep 1944	May 1945

(The ships are generally similar to the Brazilian ships but embark an MBB BO105C light helicopter.)

5. Pakistan

Name	No.	Builder	Laid down	Com-missioned
Alamgir	D160	Bethlehem Steel	Nov 1944	Dec 1946
Shah Jahan	D164	Bethlehem Steel	Oct 1944	Jun 1945
Tariq	D165	Federal SB	Mar 1945	Jan 1946
Taimur	D166	Todd Pacific	Jun 1945	Mar 1949
Tughril	D167	Todd Pacific	Oct 1944	Aug 1945
Tippu Sultan	D168	Bethlehem Steel	May 1945	Apr 1946

(These ships are comparable with the Greek navy's units, but have two triple container-launchers for six RGM-84 Harpoon anti-ship missiles and lack the 76-mm/3-in gun and and its associated fire-control system, instead possessing provision for an Aérospatiale SA 319B Alouette III light helicopter. Other differences are a 20-mm Phalanx Mk 15 CIWS mounting, improved SQS-23D hull sonar, replacement in some ships of the ESM system with WLR-1 warning element by an Argo Phoenix II suite, and two Shield chaff/flare launchers. Two ships are in reserve as a source of spares for the four operational ships.)

6. South Korea

Name	No.	Builder	Laid down	Com-missioned
Taejon	DD919	Consolidated Steel	Apr 1945	Apr 1946
Kwang Ju	DD921	Bath Iron Works	Jul 1945	May 1946
Kang Won	DD922	Federal SB	Oct 1944	Sep 1945
Kyong Ki	DD923	Consolidated Steel	Oct 1944	Jul 1945
Jeon Ju	DD925	Consolidated Steel	Jun 1944	Mar 1945

(The South Korean ships were closer to the original American pattern of this class, but now feature two Mk 141 quadruple container-launchers for eight RGM-84 Harpoon anti-ship missiles [not in DD923 and 925 which have a Mk 16 octuple launcher for RUR-5A ASROC anti-submarine missiles], six 5-in/127-mm guns in three twin mountings, two 40-mm Bofors L/56 AA in a twin

mounting, two 20-mm Phalanx Mk 15 CIWS mountings [not in DD923 and 925], four 30-mm AA in two EMERLEC-30 twin mountings [DD925 only], and provision for an Aérospatiale SA 316B Alouette III or McDonnell Douglas Helicopters MD-500D Defender light helicopter for longer-range anti-submarine work.)

7. Spain ('D60' class)

Name	No.	Builder	Laid down	Com-missioned
Churruca	D61	Federal SB	1944	Jun 1945
Gravina	D62	Consolidated Steel	1944	Jul 1945
Mendez Nunez	D63	Consolidated Steel	1945	Nov 1945
Langara	D64	Consolidated Steel	1944	May 1945
Blas de Lezo	D65	Bath Iron Works	1945	Nov 1945

(These ships are close to the Greek standard, but have a McDonnell Douglas Helicopters MD-500M helicopter instead of the 76-mm/3-in gun. D65 has six 5-in/127-mm guns in three twin mountings, and as it lacks an ASROC launcher is used for economic zone protection duties.)

8. Taiwan

Name	No.	Builder	Laid down	Com-missioned
Chien Yang	912	Todd Pacific	Dec 1944	Feb 1946
Han Yang	915	Bath Iron Works	Oct 1944	May 1945
Lao Yang	920	Bethlehem Steel	May 1945	Jun 1946
Liao Yang	921	Bath Iron Works	Oct 1944	May 1945
Kai Yang	923	Todd Pacific	Dec 1944	Oct 1945
Shen Yang	924	Bath Iron Works	Feb 1945	Sep 1945
Te Yang	925	Bath Iron Works	Jan 1945	Jul 1945
Lai Yang	926	Todd Pacific	Jun 1945	Jun 1946
Chao Yang	927	Federal SB	Apr 1945	Jul 1946
Yung Yang	928	Consolidated Steel	May 1945	Oct 1946
Chen Yang	929	Todd Pacific	Jan 1945	Mar 1946
Shao Yang	930	Federal SB	May 1944	Jul 1946

(By comparison with the Greek ships, these Taiwanese units were revised in the early 1980s to a somewhat modified standard in a number of different forms approximating to Taiwan's local development of its 'Allen M. Sumner' and 'Fletcher' class destroyers. The gun armament comprises two or four 5-in/127-mm L/38 DP in one or two twin Mk 38 mountings, one 76-mm/3-in OTO Melara L/62 DP in an OTO Melara Compact single mounting [not in all ships], and two or four 40-mm Bofors L/70 AA in one or two twin mountings. The missile armament comprises one triple and two single container-launchers for five Hsiung Feng I or II anti-ship missiles, and [not in all ships] two Sea Chaparral quadruple launchers for 40 MIM-72 SAMs. The anti-submarine armament comprises one Mk 16 octuple laucher for eight ASROC missiles [not in all ships], and two Mk 32 triple mountings for Mk 46 torpedoes. These weapons are operated in co-operation with an electronic fit that includes SPS-29 or SPS-37 [to be replaced in some ships by DA-08] air-search radar, SPS-10 or Elta 1040 surface-search radar, Mk 25 radar used in conjunction with the Mk 37 5-in gun fire-control system upgraded with a Kollmorgen optronic director, RTN 10X radar used in conjunction with the Argo NA21/30 fire-control system in ships fitted with the 76-mm gun, one Galileo optronic director [in some ships only], two HR 76 optronic directors used in conjunction with the H 930 anti-ship missile fire-control system, one ESM system with WLR-1/3 warning and ULQ-6 jamming elements or [in upgraded ships] Argo 670/671 warning and jamming elements, one SLQ-25 Nixie towed torpedo-decoy system, and four Kung Fen 6 chaff launchers. The ships each have one McDonnell Douglas Helicopters MD-500D Defender light helicopter in a hangar aft, and possess a complement of about 275.)

9. Turkey

Name	No.	Builder	Laid down	Com-missioned
Yucatepe	D345	Todd Pacific	Sep 1944	Jun 1945
Savastepe	D348	Consolidated Steel	Jan 1945	Dec 1945
Kilic Ali Pasha	D349	Consolidated Steel	Jun 1945	Oct 1946
Piyale Pasha	D350	Bath Iron Works	Apr 1945	Nov 1945
M. Fevzi Cakmak	D351	Bethlehem Steel	1944	Sep 1946
Gayret	D352	Todd Pacific	1945	Jul 1946
Adatepe	D353	Bethlehem Steel	1945	Jun 1946

(The Turkish ships are very similar to the Greek units, but have one or [D351 and 352] two GDM-A twin mounting aft for two or four 35-mm Oerlikon L/90 AA guns, and other modifications planned for some of the class include STIR radar and a vertical-launch Sea Sparrow SAM system.)

'Gearing (FRAM II)' class DD

(USA/South Korea)

Type: gun destroyer with anti-ship missile capability

Displacement: 2,425 tons standard and 3,500 tons full load

Dimensions: length 390·5 ft (119·0 m); beam 41·2 ft (12·6 m); draught 19·0 ft (5·8 m)

Gun armament: six 5-in (127-mm) L/38 DP in three Mk 38 twin mountings, and two 20-mm Phalanx Mk 15 CIWS mountings

Missile armament: two Mk 141 quadruple container-launchers for eight RGM-84 Harpoon anti-ship missiles

Torpedo armament: none

Anti-submarine armament: two Mk 32 triple 12·75-in (324-mm) mountings for Mk 46 torpedoes, two Hedgehog Mk 11 rocket-launchers, one Mk IX depth-charge rack, and helicopter-launched weapons (see below)

Aircraft: one Aérospatiale SA 316B Alouette III or McDonnell Douglas Helicopters MD-500D Defender helicopter in a hangar aft

Electronics: one SPS-40 air-search radar, one SPS-10 surface-search radar, one Mk 25 radar used in conjunction with the Mk 37 gun fire-control system, one SQS-29 active search and attack hull sonar, and one ESM system with WLR-1 or (DD916) WJ1140 warning element

Propulsion: four Babcock & Wilcox boilers supplying steam to two sets of General Electric geared turbines delivering 60,000 hp (44,740 kW) to two shafts

Performance: maximum speed 32·5 kt; range 6,675 miles (10,740 km) at 15 kt

Complement: 280

Class

1. Greece

Name	No.	Builder	Laid down	Commissioned
Themistocles	D210	Bath Iron Works	May 1944	Dec 1944

Top: A 'Gearing' class destroyer in original FRAM I form.
Above: A 'Gearing' class destroyer in original FRAM II form.

(This ship is similar to the South Korean units, and has provision for an Agusta [Bell] AB.212ASW helicopter plus SQA-10 active variable-depth sonar. The ship lacks Harpoon missile armament, but in common with other Greek units has shoulder-launcher FIM-43 Redeye SAMS for point defence.)

2. South Korea

Name	No.	Builder	Laid down	Commissioned
Chung Buk	DD915	Bath Iron Works	Jun 1944	Jan 1945
Jeong Buk	DD916	Bath Iron Works	Sep 1944	Apr 1945

(Having started in a configuration very similar to that of the baseline US ships, these two South Korean units have become considerably more potent thanks to the addition of anti-ship missile armament.)

3. Taiwan

Name	No.	Builder	Laid down	Commissioned
Fu Yang	907	Bath Iron Works	Jan 1945	Aug 1945
Dang Yang	911	Bethlehem Steel	Mar 1944	Mar 1947

(These units were similar to the South Korean ships, but have since been fitted to a standard very similar to the Taiwanese 'Gearing [FRAM I]' class destroyers.)

4. Turkey

Name	No.	Builder	Laid down	Commissioned
Kocatepe	D354	Bethlehem Steel	Jan 1944	Jun 1945

(This ship lacks missile armament, and the gun armament comprises four 5-in/127-mm DP in two twin mountings, four 40-mm AA in two twin mountings, and two 35-mm Oerlikon L/90 AA in a GDM-A twin mounting. Further development is thought to be in hand with the adoption of STIR radar and a vertical-launch Sea Sparrow SAM system.)

'Kotlin' and 'Kotlin (Modified)' class DDs

(USSR)

Type: gun destroyer

Displacement: 2,850 tons standard and 3,600 tons full load

Dimensions: length 126·5 m (414·9 ft); beam 12·9 m (42·3 ft); draught 4·6 m (15·1 ft)

Gun armament: four 130-mm (5·1-in) L/58 DP in two twin mountings, 16 45-mm L/85 AA in four quadruple mountings, and ('Kotlin [Modified]' class ships) four or eight 25-mm L/80 AA guns in two or four twin mountings

Missile armament: none

Torpedo armament: two or ('Kotlin [Modified]' class ships) one quintuple 533-mm (21-in) mountings for Type 53 dual-role torpedoes

Anti-submarine armament: two RBU 2500 16-barrel rocket-launchers, two RBU 600 six-barrel rocket-launchers, torpedoes (see above), two depth-charge racks, and (not in *Svetly*, *Vesky* and 'Kotlin [Modified]' class ships) six depth-charge throwers

Mines: 56

Aircraft: one Kamov Ka-25 'Hormone' helicopter on a platform aft (in *Svetly* only)

Electronics: one 'Slim Net' surface-search radar, one or two 'Don 2' or one 'Neptun' navigation radar, one 'Sun Visor' 130-mm gun fire-control radar, two 'Egg Cup' 130-mm gun fire-control radars, two 'Hawk Screech' 45-mm gun-control radars, one 'Post Lamp' torpedo fire-control radar, one medium-frequency active search and attack hull sonar, one ESM system with two 'Watch Dog' antennae/housings, and one 'Square Head' and one 'High Pole-A' IFF systems

Propulsion: four boilers supplying steam to two sets of geared turbines delivering 53,700 kW (72,020 shp) to two shafts

Performance: maximum speed 36 kt; range 8350 km (5,190 miles) at 15 kt or 2050 km (1,275 miles) at 35 kt

Complement: 285

Class

1. USSR ('Kotlin' class)

Name

Spleshny
Spokoyny
Svetly
Vesky

2. USSR ('Kotlin [Modified]' class)

Name

Blagorodny
Burlivy
Byvaly
Plamenny
Svedushchy
Vyderzhanny
Vyzyvayushchy

Note: These ships were completed between 1954 and 1956, and are now completely obsolete. The Soviets maintain only three ships (one 'Kotlin' and two 'Kotlin [Modified]' class units) in the active fleet, the other eight (three 'Kotlin' and five 'Kotlin [Modified]' class units) being maintained in reserve.

Typical of the gun destroyers built in the mid-1950s, the 'Kotlin' class is now obsolete for all but the patrol and perhaps training roles.

'Minegumo' or 'Type 116' class DD

(Japan)
Type: gun destroyer
Displacement: 2,100 tons or (DD118) 2,150 tons standard and 2,550 tons full load
Dimensions: length 114·0 m (374·0 ft or (DD118) 115·0 m (377·2 ft); beam 11·8 m (38·7 ft); draught 4·0 m (13·1 ft)!
Gun armament: four or (DD118) two 3-in (76-mm) L/50 DP in two or one Mk 33 twin mountings, and (DD118 only) one 76-mm (3-in) OTO Melara Compact L/62 DP in a Mk 75 single mounting
Missile armament: none
Torpedo armament: none
Anti-submarine armament: one Mk 16 octuple launcher for eight RUR-5A ASROC missiles, one 375-mm (14·76-in) Bofors Type 71 four-barrel rocket-launcher, and two Type 68 triple 12·75-in (324-mm) mountings for Mk 46 torpedoes
Aircraft: none
Electronics: one OPS-11 air-search radar, one OPS-17 surface-search radar, one Type 2 or (DD118) SPG-34 radar used in conjunction with the Type 2-12B gun fire-control system, one Type 1A fire-control system, one

OQS-3 active/passive search and attack hull sonar and (DD118 only) one SQS-35(J) active/passive search variable-depth sonar used in conjunction with the Mk 114 underwater weapons fire-control system, and one ESM system with NOLR-5 warning element
Propulsion: six Mitsubishi 12UEV 30/40N diesels delivering 19,800 kW (26,555 hp) to two shafts
Performance: maximum speed 27 kt; range 12,975 km (8,065 miles) at 20 kt
Complement: 19 + 291 or (DD118) 19 + 201

Class
1. Japan

Name	No.	Builder	Laid down	Com- missioned
Minegumo	DD116	Mitsui	Mar 1967	Aug 1968
Natsugumo	DD117	Uraga	Jun 1967	Apr 1969
Murakumo	DD118	Maizuru	Oct 1968	Aug 1970

Note: These are obsolescent ships retaining a limited anti-submarine capability through their sonar and associated ASROC system.

Despite the ASROC launcher on her quarterdeck, the *Minegumo* and her two sisterships are obsolescent in their primary anti-submarine role.

'Skory' and 'Skory (Modified)' class DDs

(USSR)
Type: gun destroyer
Displacement: 2,240 tons standard and 3,150 tons full load
Dimensions: length 120·5 m (395·2 ft); beam 11·9 m (38·9 ft); draught 4·6 m (15·1 ft)
Gun armament: four 130-mm (5·1-in) L/50 DP in two twin mountings, two 85-mm (3·5-in) L/55 DP in a twin mounting ('Skory' class ships only), two 57-mm L/77 AA in a twin mounting or ('Skory [Modified]' class ships) five 57-mm L/77 AA in single mountings, eight 37-mm L/70 AA in four twin mountings or seven 37-mm L/70 AA in seven single mountings ('Skory' class ships only), and four or six 25-mm L/80 AA in two or three twin mountings ('Skory' class ships only)
Missile armament: none
Torpedo armament: two or ('Skory [Modified]' class ships) one quintuple 533-mm (21-in) mounting for Type 53 torpedoes
Anti-submarine armament: two depth-charge racks or ('Skory [Modified]' class ships) two RBU 2500 16-barrel rocket-launchers
Mines: 50
Aircraft: none
Electronics: ('Skory' class ships) one 'Cross Bird' or 'Knife Rest' air-search radar, one 'High Sieve' surface-search radar, one 'Don' navigation radar, one 'Top Bow' 130-mm gun fire-control radar, one 'Post Lamp' torpedo fire-control radar, one high-frequency active search and attack hull sonar, one

ESM system with two 'Watch Dog' antennae/housings, one 'Square Head' IFF system, and one 'High Pole-A' IFF system
Electronics: ('Skory [Modified]' class ships) one 'Slim Net' surface-search radar, one 'Top Bow' 130-mm gun fire-control radar, two 'Hawk Screech' 57-mm gun fire-control radars, one 'Don' navigation radar, one 'Post Lamp' torpedo fire-control radar, one high-frequency active search and attack hull sonar, one ESM system with two 'Watch Dog' antennae/housings, one 'Square Head' IFF system, and one 'High Pole-A' IFF system
Propulsion: four boilers supplying steam to two sets of geared turbines delivering 44,750 kW (60,020 hp) to two shafts
Performance: maximum speed 33 kt; range 7225 km (4,490 miles) at 13 kt or 1700 km (1,055 miles) at 32 kt
Complement: 280

Class
1. USSR
9 'Skory' and 'Skory (Modified)' class ships

Note: These are the survivors (including five ships in reserve) of a class completed between 1949 and 1954 to a total of 72 ships. Of the four active ships, two are standard 'Skory' class units while the other two belong to the 'Skory (Modified)' class. All are to be deleted in the near future. Some 16 ships were exported (four to Egypt between 1956 and 1961 with two replacements following in 1968, eight to Indonesia between 1959 and 1965, and two to Poland in 1958), but these have already been deleted.

'T53 (Modified)' class DD

(France)
Type: gun destroyer with anti-ship missile capability
Displacement: 2,800 tons standard and 3,900 tons full load
Dimensions: length 132·8 m (435·7 ft); beam 12·5 m (41·7 ft); draught 6·1 m (20·0 ft)
Gun armament: one 100-mm (3·94-in) Creusot Loire L/55 DP in a Modèle 68 single mounting
Missile armament: two twin container-launchers for four MM.38 Exocet anti-ship missiles
Torpedo armament: none
Anti-submarine armament: two single 533-mm (21-in) launchers for eight L5 dual-role torpedoes
Aircraft: one Westland Lynx HAS.Mk 2/4 helicopter in a hangar amidships
Electronics: one DRBV 22A air-search radar, one DRBV 51 air/surface-search radar, one Decca navigation radar, one DRBC 32E gun fire-control radar used in conjunction with the Vega weapon direction system, one DUBV 23 active search and attack hull sonar, one DUBV 43 active/passive search and attack variable-depth sonar, SENIT 2 action information system, one ESM system with ARBR 16 warning element, and two Corvus chaff launchers
Propulsion: four Indret boilers supplying steam to two sets of geared turbines delivering 47,000 kW (63,035 hp) to two shafts
Performance: maximum speed 32 kt; range 9250 km (5,750 miles) at 18 kt or 2225 km (1,385 miles) at 32 kt
Complement: 15 + 257

Class

1. France			Laid	Com-
Name	No.	Builder	down	missioned
Duperré	D633	Lorient ND	Nov 1954	Oct 1957

Note: This ship was built as a radar picket, and though due for deletion in the near future still serves usefully as an anti-submarine type with flagship capability.

Right: The *Duperré* has a helicopter and stern-mounted variable-depth sonar.

'T56' class DD

(France)
Type: gun destroyer
Displacement: 2,750 tons standard and 3,910 tons full load
Dimensions: length 132·8 m (435·7 ft); beam 12·7 m (41·7 ft); draught 6·3 m (20·7 ft)
Gun armament: two 100-mm (3·94-in) Creusot Loire L/55 DP in Modèle 1953 single mountings, and one 20-mm AA in a single mounting
Missile armament: none
Torpedo armament: none
Anti-submarine armament: one launcher for 13 Malafon missiles, and two triple 550-mm (21·7-in) mountings for L3 torpedoes
Aircraft: one Aérospatiale SA 319B Alouette III Astazou helicopter in a hangar aft
Electronics: one DRBV 22 air-search radar, one DRBV 50 air/surface-search radar, one DRBN 32 navigation radar, one DRBC 32A gun fire-control radar, one DUBV 23 active search and attack hull sonar, one DUBV 43 active/passive search variable-depth sonar, action information system, one ESM system with ARBR 10 warning element, and URN-20 TACAN
Propulsion: four Indret boilers supplying steam to two sets of geared turbines delivering 47,000 kW (63,035 hp) to two shafts
Performance: maximum speed 34 kt; range 9250 km (5,750 miles) at 18 kt or 2225 km (1,385 miles) at 32 kt
Complement: 15 + 255

Class

1. France			Laid	Com-
Name	No.	Builder	down	missioned
La Galissonnière	D638	Lorient ND	Nov 1958	July 1962

Note: This singleton unit has the same hull and propulsion machinery as the 'T47' and 'T53' class destroyers, but a different armament and sensor arrangement optimized for the anti-submarine role. The hangar hinges outward when opening to create a helicopter platform. The ship is due for deletion in the near future.

Above: The singleton *La Galissonnière* has stern-mounted variable-depth sonar and a helicopter hangar that opens out into the flight patform.

'Yamagumo' or 'Type 113' class DD

(Japan)

Type: gun destroyer

Displacement: 2,050 tons or (DD119/121) 2,150 tons standard and 2,150 tons or (DD119/121) 2,250 tons full load

Dimensions: length 114·0 m (373·9 ft) or (DD115 and 119/21) 114·9 m (377·2 ft); beam 11·8 m (38·7 ft); draught 4·0 m (13·1 ft)

Gun armament: four 3-in (76-mm) L/50 DP in two Mk 33 twin mountings

Missile armament: none

Torpedo armament: none

Anti-submarine armament: one Mk 16 octuple launcher for eight RUR-5A ASROC missiles, one 375-mm (14·76-in) Bofors Type 71 four-barrel rocket-launcher, and two Type 68 triple 12·75-in (324-mm) mountings for Mk 46 torpedoes

Aircraft: none

Electronics: one OPS-11 air-search radar, one OPS-17 surface-search radar, two Mk 35 radars used in conjunction with one Mk 56 or Mk 63 (DD113/116 and 119) or Type 1 (DD120/121) gun fire-control system, one SQS-23 (DD113/115) or OQS-3 (DD119/121) active search and attack hull sonar, one SQS-35(J) active search variable-depth sonar (DD113/114 and DD120/121), and one ESM system with SLR-1 or (DD119/121) SLR-2 warning and NOLR-1B or (DD119/121) NOLR-5 jamming elements

Propulsion: six Mitsubishi 12UEV 30/40N diesels delivering 19,800 kW (26,555 hp) to two shafts

Performance: maximum speed 27 kt; range 12,975 km (8,065 miles) at 20 kt

Complement: 19 + 191

Like other Japanese gun destroyers, the *Yamagumo* and her sisterships are obsolete despite the ASROC launchers located between the funnels.

Class				
1. Japan			**Laid**	**Com-**
Name	**No.**	**Builder**	**down**	**missioned**
Yamagumo	DD113	Mitsui	Mar 1964	Jan 1966
Makigumo	DD114	Uraga	Jun 1964	Mar 1966
Asagumo	DD115	Maizuru	Jun 1965	Aug 1967
Aokumo	DD119	Sumitomo	Oct 1970	Nov 1972
Akigumo	DD120	Sumitomo	Jul 1972	Jul 1974
Yugumo	DD121	Sumitomo	Feb 1976	Mar 1978

Note: This is an obsolescent class retaining a limited anti-submarine capability thanks to its sensors and ASROC system.

'A69' or 'd'Estienne d'Orves' class FFG

(France)

Type: coastal anti-submarine and anti-ship guided-missile frigate

Displacement: 950 tons standard and 1,170 tons or (later ships) 1,250 tons full load

Dimensions: length 80·0 m (262·5 ft); beam 10·3 m (33·8 ft); draught 5·5 m (18·0 ft)

Gun armament: one 100-mm (3·9-in) Creusot Loire L/55 DP in a Modèle 1968 single mounting, and two 20-mm AA in single mountings

Missile armament: two or (F792 onwards) four container-launchers for two MM.38 Exocet or (F792 onwards) four MM.40 Exocet anti-ship missiles, with the MM.40 to be retrofitted in all ships

Torpedo armament: four single 550-mm (21·7-in) tubes for L3 anti-submarine or 533-mm (21-in) L5 dual-role torpedoes

Anti-submarine armament: one 375-mm (14·76-in) Modèle 1954 six-barrel rocket-launcher, and torpedoes (see above)

Aircraft: none

Electronics: one DRBV 51A air/surface-search radar, one Decca 1226 navigation radar, one DRBC 32E radar used in conjunction with the Vega weapon direction system, one DUBA 25 active search and attack hull sonar, one ESM system with ARBR 16 warning element, one SLQ-25 Nixie towed torpedo-decoy system, and two Dagaie chaff/flare launchers

Propulsion: two SEMT-Pielstick 12 PC2-V400 diesels delivering 9000 kW (12,070 hp) to two shafts

Performance: maximum speed 24 kt; range 8340 km (5,185 miles) at 15 kt; endurance 15 days

Complement: 7 + 85

Class				
1. Argentina			**Laid**	**Com-**
Name	**No.**	**Builder**	**down**	**missioned**
Drummond	F31	Lorient ND	Mar 1976	Nov 1978
Guerrico	F32	Lorient ND	Oct 1976	Nov 1978
Granville	F33	Lorient ND	Dec 1978	Jun 1981

(These ships differ from the French standard by having two twin launchers for four MM.38 Exocet anti-ship missiles, additional AA armament [two 40-mm Bofors supported by a Naja optronic director in F31 and F32, and by a Panda Mk 2 optical director in F33], different anti-submarine armament [two Mk 32 12·75-in/324-mm triple mountings for A 244/S torpedoes] and a revised electronic suite with Diodon sonar and improved ESM capability. The ships are used mainly for patrol.)

2. France			**Laid**	**Com-**
Name	**No.**	**Builder**	**down**	**missioned**
D'Estienne d'Orves	F781	Lorient ND	Sep 1972	Sep 1976
Amyot d'Indville	F782	Lorient ND	Sep 1973	Oct 1976
Drogou	F783	Lorient ND	Oct 1973	Sep 1976
Détroyat	F784	Lorient ND	Dec 1974	May 1977
Jean Moulin	F785	Lorient ND	Jan 1875	May 1977
Quartier Maître Anquetil	F786	Lorient ND	Aug 1975	Feb 1978
Commandant de Pimodan	F787	Lorient ND	Sep 1975	May 1978
2er Maître Le Bihan	F788	Lorient ND	Nov 1976	Jul 1979
Lieutenant Le Henaff	F789	Lorient ND	Mar 1977	Feb 1980
Lieutenant Lavallee	F790	Lorient ND	Nov 1977	Aug 1980
Commandant l'Herminier	F791	Lorient ND	May 1979	Dec 1981
1er Maître l'Her	F792	Lorient ND	Jul 1979	Dec 1981
Commandant Blaison	F793	Lorient ND	Nov 1979	Apr 1982
Enseigne Jacoubet	F794	Lorient ND	Jun 1980	Oct 1982
Commandant Ducuing	F795	Lorient ND	Oct 1980	Mar 1983
Commandant Birot	F796	Lorient ND	Mar 1981	Mar 1984
Commandant Bouan	F797	Lorient ND	Oct 1981	Nov 1984

(These useful ships are designed for coastal anti-submarine operations, but have been retrofitted with a significant anti-ship capability.)

The *Drogou* is one of the French navy's limited but nonetheless useful 'd'Estienne d'Orves' class of coastal anti-submarine frigates.

'Abukuma' class FFG

(Japan)

Type: anti-ship and anti-submarine guided-missile frigate
Displacement: 1,950 tons standard and 2,500 tons full load
Dimensions: length 109·0 m (357·6 ft); beam 13·4 m (44·0 ft); draught 3·8 m (12·5 ft)
Gun armament: one 76-mm (3-in) OTO Melara L/62 DP in an OTO Melara Compact single mounting, and one 20-mm Phalanx Mk 15 CIWS mounting
Missile armament: two Mk 141 quadruple container-launchers for eight RGM-84 Harpoon anti-ship missiles
Torpedo armament: none
Anti-submarine armament: one Type 112 octuple launchers for eight RUR-5A ASROC missiles, and two Type 68 triple 12·75-in (324-mm) mountings for Mk 46 torpedoes
Aircraft: none
Electronics: one OPS-14C air-search radar, one OPS-28 surface-search radar, one OPS-19 navigation radar, one Type 2 radar used in conjunction with the Type 2-21 gun fire-control system, one Raytheon DE 1167 active search and attack hull sonar, one ESM system with NOLQ-6Q warning and OLT-3 jamming elements, and two Mk 36 Super RBOC chaff/flare launchers
Propulsion: CODOG arrangement, with one Kawasaki/Rolls-Royce Spey SM1A gas turbine delivering 27,000 hp (20,130 kW) or two Mitsubishi diesels delivering 4500 kW (6,035 hp) to two shafts
Performance: maximum speed 27 kt
Complement: 115

Class

1. Japan			Laid	Com-
Name	No.	Builder	down	missioned
Abukuma	DE229	Mitsui	Mar 1988	Dec 1989
Jintsu	DE230	Hitachi	Apr 1988	Mar 1990
	DE231	Mitsui	Mar 1989	Jan 1991
	DE232	Ishikawajima	Apr 1989	Mar 1991

Note: These are being produced to what is in effect a 'Yubari (Improved)' class design. The ships have useful anti-submarine and anti-ship weapons, but seem deficient in protection against air attack even though the Phalanx mounting provides a measure of defence against anti-ship missiles.

'Amazon' or 'Type 21' class FFG

(UK)

Type: anti-submarine and anti-ship guided-missile frigate
Displacement: 3,100 tons standard and 3,600 tons full load
Dimensions: length 384·0 ft (117·0 m); beam 41·7 ft (12·7 m); draught 19·5 ft (5·9 m)
Gun armament: one 4·5-in (114-mm) Vickers L/55 DP in a Mk 8 single mounting, and two or four 20-mm L/85 AA in GAM-B01 single mountings
Missile armament: four container-launchers for four MM.38 Exocet anti-ship missiles, and one quadruple launcher for 24 Sea Cat SAMs (to be replaced by GWS 25 Sea Wolf)
Torpedo armament: none
Anti-submarine armament: two STWS-1 triple 12·75-in (324-mm) mountings for Stingray and Mk 46 torpedoes, and helicopter-launched weapons (see below)
Aircraft: one Westland Lynx HAS.Mk 2/3 helicopter in a hangar aft
Electronics: one Type 992R air/surface-search radar, one Type 1006 navigation radar, one two Type 912 (RTN 10X) radars used in conjunction with one GWS 24/WSA-4 SAM/gun fire-control system, one GWS 50 SSM fire-control system, one Type 184P hull-mounted medium-range search and attack sonar, one Type 162M bottom classification hull sonar, one CAAIS action information system, one Type 182 towed torpedo-decoy system, one UAA-1 Abbey Hill ESM system with warning and jamming elements, two Corvus chaff launchers, and two SCOT satellite communications antennae
Propulsion: COGOG arrangement, with two Rolls-Royce Olympus TM3B gas turbines delivering 50,000 hp (37,280 kW) or two Rolls-Royce Tyne RM1C gas turbines delivering 9,700 hp (7235 kW) to two shafts
Performance: maximum speed 30 kt on Olympus gas turbines or 18 kt on Tyne gas turbines; range 4,600 miles (7400 km) at 17 kt or 1,380 miles (2220 km) at 30 kt
Complement: 13 + 162 with a maximum of 192 possible

Class

1. UK			Laid	Com-
Name	No.	Builder	down	missioned
Amazon	F169	Vosper Thornycroft	Nov 1969	May 1974
Active	F171	Vosper Thornycroft	Jul 1971	Jun 1977
Ambuscade	F172	Yarrow	Sep 1971	Sep 1975
Arrow	F173	Yarrow	Sep 1972	Jul 1976
Alacrity	F174	Yarrow	Mar 1973	Jul 1977
Avenger	F175	Yarrow	Oct 1974	Jul 1978

Note: These ships are to a combined Vosper Thornycroft and Yarrow design for a patrol frigate, and in addition to being the first Royal Navy warships designed as such for COGOG propulsion were the first commercially designed combatants accepted for Royal Navy service in many years.

The *Amazon* is lead ship of a class that originally numbered eight units, of which two were sunk in the Falklands war of 1982.

'Bremen' or 'Type 122' class FFG

(West Germany)

Type: anti-submarine and anti-ship guided-missile frigate

Displacement: 2,900 tons standard and 3,600 tons full load

Dimensions: length 130·0 m (426·4 ft); beam 14·5 m (47·6 ft); draught 6·5 m (21·3 ft)

Gun armament: one 76-mm (3-in) OTO Melara L/62 DP in an OTO Melara Compact single mounting

Missile armament: two Mk 141 quadruple container-launchers for eight RGM-84 Harpoon anti-ship missiles, one Mk 29 octuple launcher for 24 RIM-7 NATO Sea Sparrow SAMs, two multi-cell container-launchers for FIM-92 Stinger SAMs, and (to be retrofitted) two EX-31 21-round container-launchers for 42 RIM-116 RAM SAMs

Torpedo armament: none

Anti-submarine armament: two Mk 32 twin 12·75-in (324-mm) mountings for Mk 46 torpedoes, and helicopter-launched weapons (see below)

Aircraft: two Westland Lynx HAS.Mk 88 helicopters in a hangar aft

Electronics: one DA-08 air/surface-search radar, one 3RM 20 navigation radar, one STIR surveillance and target-indication radar used in conjunction with the WM-25 gun and SAM fire-control system (with data provision for SSMs), one SATIR action information system, one DSQS-21BZ(BO) active search and attack hull sonar, one SLQ-51 Nixie towed torpedo-decoy system, one Prairie/Masker hull and propeller blade noise-suppression system, one FL1800S ESM system with warning and jamming elements, one SCLAR chaff/flare launcher, and (some ships only) one SCOT 1A satellite communications system

Propulsion: CODOG arrangement, with two MTU/General Electric LM2500 gas turbines delivering 51,600 hp (38,480 kW) or two MTU 20V 956 TB92 diesels delivering 7750 kW (10,395 hp) to two shafts

Performance: maximum speed 32 kt on gas turbines or 20 kt on diesels; range 7400 km (4,600 miles) at 18 kt

Complement: 204 plus 18 aircrew

Note: The ships are close derivatives of the Dutch 'Kortenaer' class design, and as such highly capable multi-role frigates admirably suited to North Sea operations. The single most notable feature is the three-layer SAM system to provide protection against all levels of air attack, though other features worthy of remark are the full NBC protection and the use of a Prairie/Masker bubbler system to shield the radiated noise emission of the hull and propellers respectively.

Class 1. West Germany Name	No.	Builder	Laid down	Commissioned
Bremen	F207	Bremer Vulkan	Jul 1979	May 1982
Niedersachsen	F208	AG Weser	Nov 1979	Oct 1982
Rheinland-Pfalz	F209	Blohm und Voss	Sep 1979	May 1983
Emden	F210	Thyssen	Jun 1980	Oct 1983
Köln	F211	Blohm und Voss	Jun 1980	Oct 1984
Karlsruhe	F212	Howaldtswerke	Mar 1981	Apr 1984
Augsburg	F213	Bremer Vulkan	Apr 1987	Sep 1989
Lubeck	F214	Thyssen	Jun 1987	Mar 1990

The *Karlsruhe* is a ship of the 'Bremen' class, a development of the Dutch 'Kortenaer' class fully optimized for operation in high-threat areas.

'Broadsword Batch 1/2' or 'Type 22 Batch 1/2' class FFG

(UK)

Type: anti-aircraft, anti-ship and anti-submarine guided-missile escort frigate

Displacement: (F88/91) 3,500 tons standard and 4,400 tons full load, or (F92/96 and F98) 4,100 tons standard and 4,600 tons full load

Dimensions: length (F88/F91) 430·0 ft (131·2 m), or (F92/F93) 485·8 ft (145·0 m), or (F94/96 and F98) 480·5 ft (146·5 m); beam 48·5 ft (14·8 m); draught (F88/91) 19·9 ft (6·0 m) or (others) 21·0 ft (6·4 m)

Gun armament: four 30-mm Oerlikon L/75 AA in two GCM-A03 twin mountings, and two 20-mm Oerlikon L/120 AA in GAM-B01 single mountings

Missile armament: two twin container-launchers for four MM.38 Exocet anti-ship missiles, and two sextuple launchers for 60 Sea Wolf SAMs

Torpedo armament: none

Anti-submarine armament: (F88/89) two STWS-1 triple 12·75-in (324-mm) mountings for Mk 46 torpedoes, or (others) two STWS-2 triple 12·75-in (324-mm) mountings for Stingray torpedoes, and helicopter-launched weapons (see below)

Aircraft: two Westland Lynx HAS.Mk 2 or (F94 onwards) two European Helicopter Industries EH.101 or Westland Sea King HAS.Mk 5/6 helicopters in a hangar aft

Electronics: one Type 967 air-search radar and one Type 968 surface-search radar in a combined mounting, one Type 1006 navigation radar, two Type 911 radars used in conjunction with two GWS 25 Mod 0 or (F94/96 and 98) GWS 25 Mod 3 SAM fire-control systems, one GWS 50 Exocet fire-control system, one Type 2016 (being replaced by Type 2050) active/passive search and attack hull sonar, one Type 2031Z passive search towed-array sonar (F92 onwards), one CAAIS or (F92 onwards) CACS 1 action information

The *Beaver* is of the four-strong 'Broadsword Batch 2' class, enlarged from the 'Batch 1' class for improved seakeeping.

system, Link 11 and 14 data-links, one Type 182 towed torpedo-decoy system, one UAA-1 Abbey Hill ESM system with warning and two Type 690 jammer elements, two Shield decoy launchers, two Mk 36 Super RBOC chaff/flare launchers, and one SCOT satellite communications system

Propulsion: (F88/93) COGOG arrangement, with two Rolls-Royce Olympus TM3B gas turbines delivering 54,600 hp (40,710 kW) or two Rolls-Royce Tyne RM1C gas turbines delivering 9,700 hp (7230 kW) to two shafts

Propulsion: (F94) COGOG arrangement, with two Rolls-Royce Spey SM1C gas turbines delivering 48,000 hp (35,790 kW) or two Rolls-Royce Tyne RM1C gas turbines delivering 9,700 hp (7230 kW) to two shafts

Propulsion: (F95/96 and 98) COGAG arrangement, with two Rolls-Royce Spey SM1A gas turbines delivering 37,540 hp (29,990 kW) and two Rolls-Royce Tyne RM1C gas turbines delivering 9,700 hp (7230 kW) to two shafts

Performance: maximum speed 30 kt on Olympus engines or 28 kt on Spey engines, and 18 kt on Tyne engines; range 5,200 miles (8370 km) at 18 kt on Tyne engines

Complement: (F88/91) 17 + 205 with a maximum of 249 possible, or (F92/96 and F98) 30 + 243 with a maximum of 296 possible

Note: Though rated as frigates, and as such designed as replacements for the 'Leander' class frigates, these are in fact destroyers optimized for anti-submarine operations in North Atlantic waters. The 'Broadsword Batch 1' ships proved too short to carry their planned Type 2031(Z) towed-array sonar and larger helicopters, so the 'Broadsword Batch 2' ships were lengthened and fitted with a revised propulsion arrangement. The lengthening was mainly in the bows, providing these ships with a finer entry and improved sea-keeping qualities.

The *Beaver* of the 'Broadsword Batch 2' class shows off the design's forward armament of four Exocet missiles and the sextuple Sea Wolf SAM launcher.

Class

1. UK ('Broadsword Batch 1' class)

Name	No.	Builder	Laid down	Commissioned
Broadsword	F88	Yarrow	Feb 1975	May 1979
Battleaxe	F89	Yarrow	Feb 1976	Mar 1980
Brilliant	F90	Yarrow	Mar 1977	May 1981
Brazen	F91	Yarrow	Aug 1978	Jul 1982

2. UK ('Broadsword Batch 2' or 'Boxer' class)

Name	No.	Builder	Laid down	Commissioned
Boxer	F92	Yarrow	Nov 1979	Jan 1984
Beaver	F93	Yarrow	Jun 1980	Dec 1984
Brave	F94	Yarrow	May 1982	Jul 1986
London	F95	Yarrow	Feb 1983	Jun 1987
Sheffield	F96	Swan Hunter	Mar 1984	Jul 1988
Coventry	F98	Swan Hunter	Mar 1984	Oct 1988

'Broadsword Batch 3' or 'Cornwall' class FFG

(UK)

Type: anti-aircraft, anti-ship and anti-submarine guided-missile escort frigate

Displacement: 4,200 tons standard and 4,900 tons full load

Dimensions: length 485·9 ft (148·1 m); beam 48·5 ft (14·8 m); draught 21·0 ft (6·4 m)

Gun armament: one 4·5-in (114-mm) L/55 DP in a Mk 8 single mounting, two 30-mm Oerlikon L/75 DP in two DS30 single mountings, and one 30-mm Goalkeeper CIWS mounting

Missile armament: two quadruple Mk 141 container-launchers for eight RGM-84 Harpoon anti-ship missiles, and two sextuple launchers for 60 Sea Wolf SAMs

Torpedo armament: none

Anti-submarine armament: two STWS-2 triple 12·75-in (324-mm) mountings for Stingray or Mk 46 torpedoes

Aircraft: two Westland Lynx HAS.Mk 2 helicopters in a hangar aft, with provision for embarking two European Helicopter Industries EH.101 or Westland Sea King HAS.Mk 5/6 helicopters

Electronics: one Type 967 air-search radar and one Type 968 surface-search radar in a combined mounting, one Type 1006 navigation radar, two Type 911 radars used in conjunction with two GWS 25 Mod 3 SAM fire-control systems, one Sea Archer gun fire-control system, one Type 2016 (being replaced by Type 2050) active/passive search and attack hull sonar, one Type 2031Z passive search towed-array sonar, one CACS 5 action information system, Link 11 and 14 data-links, one Type 182 towed torpedo-decoy system, one Guardian ESM system with warning and jamming elements, four Sea Gnat decoy launchers, and two SCOT satellite communications systems

Propulsion: COGAG arrangement, with two Rolls-Royce Spey SM1A gas turbines delivering 37,540 hp (27,995 kW) and two Rolls-Royce Tyne RM3C gas turbines delivering 9,700 hp (7230 kW) to two shafts

Performance: maximum speed 30 kt on Spey engines, and 18 kt on Tyne engines; range 5,200 miles (8370 km) at 18 kt on Tyne engines

Complement: 31 + 219, with a maximum of 301 possible

Class

1. UK

Name	No.	Builder	Laid down	Commissioned
Cornwall	F99	Yarrow	Dec 1983	Apr 1988
Cumberland	F85	Yarrow	Oct 1984	Jun 1989
Campbeltown	F86	Cammell Laird	Dec 1985	May 1989
Chatham	F87	Swan Hunter	May 1986	Feb 1990

Note: The third batch of 'Type 22' destroyers was considerably revised in the planning stage in light of the lessons of the 1982 Falklands war with all the improvements of the 'Type 22 Batch 2' class ships plus a revised air-defence armament centred on a 4·5-in (114-mm) DP gun, improved short-range AA armament and a new CIWS mounting, as well as improved anti-ship armament in the form of eight Harpoon anti-ship missiles in place of the other variants' four Exocet missiles.

Comparison of the *Campbeltown* with the *Beaver* reveals the modifications introduced on the 'Broadsword Batch 3' class, including the forward-mounted 4·5-in (114-mm) gun in place of four Exocet missiles, which are replaced by eight Harpoon missiles located between the bridge and the foremast.

'Brooke' class FFG

(USA)

Type: anti-submarine and anti-aircraft guided-missile escort frigate
Displacement: 2,645 tons standard and 3,425 tons full load
Dimensions: length 414·5 ft (126·3 m); beam 44·2 ft (13·5 m); draught 15·0 ft (4·6 m)
Gun armament: one 5-in (127-mm) L/38 DP in a Mk 30 single mounting
Missile armament: one Mk 22 single launcher for 16 RIM-66B Standard SM-1 MR SAMs
Torpedo armament: none
Anti-submarine armament: one Mk 16 octuple launcher for eight or (last three ships) 16 RUR-5A ASROC missiles, two Mk 32 triple 12·75-in (324-mm) mountings for Mk 46 torpedoes, and helicopter-launched weapons (see below)
Aircraft: one Kaman SH-2F Seasprite helicopter in a hangar aft
Electronics: one SPS-52B 3D radar, one SPS-10F surface-search radar, one Pathfinder (in *Khyber*) or LN-66 navigation radar, one SPG-51C radar used in conjunction with the Mk 74 SAM fire-control system, one Mk 35 radar used in conjunction with the Mk 56 gun fire-control system, one active search and attack bow sonar (SQS-26AXR in the first four ships and SQS-26BX in the last two ships) used in conjunction with the Mk 114 underwater weapons fire-control system, one Mk 4 weapon direction system, one SLQ-32(V)2 ESM system with WLR-6 warning and ULQ-6 jamming elements, four Mk 36 Super RBOC chaff/flare launchers, and SRN-15 TACAN
Propulsion: two Foster-Wheeler boilers supplying steam to one set of West-inghouse or (last three ships) General Electric geared turbines delivering 35,000 hp (26,100 kW) to one shaft
Performance: maximum speed 27·2 kt; range 4,600 miles (7400 km) at 20 kt
Complement: 17 + 260

Class

1. Pakistan			Laid	Com-
Name	No.	Builder	down	missioned
Saif		Bath Iron Works	Jul 1965	Nov 1967
Khaiber		Lockheed SB	Dec 1962	Mar 1966
Tabuk		Bath Iron Works	Jan 1965	Aug 1967
Hunain		Bath Iron Works	May 1964	Apr 1967

(These were the *Julius A. Furer*, *Brooke*, *Richard L. Page* and *Talbot* [FFG6, 1, 5 and 3], which were decommissioned by the US Navy and transferred to Pakistan in January, February, March and April 1989 respectively.)

Note: This class is based on the same hull and machinery combination as the 'Garcia' class, but is optimized for air defence whereas the 'Garcia' is optimized for anti-submarine warfare. The design was created for the support of smaller task forces, for which the single-ended launcher arrangement and small missile complement were deemed sufficient. The provision of an ASROC launcher and a helicopter means that little anti-submarine capability is lost. In July 1989 Turkey decided not to proceed with its proposed lease of the ex-*Ramsey* (FFG2) and ex-*Schofield* (FFG3), both built by Lockheed Ship Building for commissioning in June 1967 and May 1968 respectively.

The *Talbot* is seen before her transfer to Pakistan as the *Hunain*.

'Chengdu' or 'Type 01' class FFG

(China)

Type: anti-ship guided-missile frigate
Displacement: 1,240 tons standard and 1,460 tons full load
Dimensions: length 91·5 m (300·1 ft); beam 10·1 m (33·1 ft); draught 3·2 m (10·5 ft)
Gun armament: three 100-mm (3·94-in) L/56 DP in single mountings, four 37-mm L/63 AA in two twin mountings, and four 14·5-mm (0.57-in) L/93 AA in two twin mountings
Missile armament: one twin container-launcher for two HY-2 (CSS-N-1) anti-ship missiles
Torpedo armament: none
Anti-submarine armament: four BMB-2 depth-charge throwers
Mines: 50
Aircraft: none
Electronics: one 'Slim Net' air/surface-search radar, one 'Neptun' naviga-tion radar, one 'Sun Visor-B' 100-mm gun fire-control radar, one 'Square Tie' missile fire-control radar, one high/medium-frequency active search and attack hull sonar, one ESM system with one 'Watch Dog' antennae/housing, and one 'High Pole-A' IFF system
Propulsion: two boilers supplying steam to two sets of geared turbines delivering 14,900 kW (19,985 hp) to two shafts
Performance: maximum speed 28 kt; range 3700 km (2,300 miles) at 10 kt
Complement: 16 + 154

Class

1. China			Laid	Com-
Name	No.	Builder	down	missioned
Kunming	505	Hutong,Shanghai	1955	1958
Chengdu	506	Guangzhou	1955	1959
Pingxiang	507	Hutong, Shanghai	1955	1958
Xichang	508	Guangzhou	1955	1959

Note: These obsolescent ships are essentially similar to the Soviet 'Riga' class frigates, and were assembled from Soviet-supplied components as standard gun-armed patrol frigates. In the 1970s all were modified with anti-ship missiles and additional AA defences.

'Commandant Rivière' class FFG

(France)

Type: anti-ship and anti-submarine guided-missile escort frigate
Displacement: 1,750 tons standard and 2,250 tons full load
Dimensions: length 102·7 m (336·9 ft); beam 11·7 m (38·4 ft); draught 4·3 m (14·1 ft)
Gun armament: two or (F729) three 100-mm (3·9-in) Creusot Loire L/55 DP in Modèle 1953 single mountings, and two 30-mm L/70 AA in single mountings
Missile armament: two (not in F729) twin container-launchers for four MM.38 Exocet anti-ship missiles
Torpedo armament: none

The *Balny* is identical to the other 'Commandant Rivière' class frigates in all but her CODAG propulsion arrangement.

Anti-submarine armament: two triple 533-mm (21-in) mountings for L3 torpedoes, and one 305-mm (12-in) quadruple rocket-launcher
Aircraft: none
Electronics: one DRBV 22A air/surface-search radar, one Decca 1226 navigation radar, one DRBC-32C or (F729 only) one DRBC-32A gun fire-control radar, one SQS-17 active search hull sonar, one DUBA 3 active attack hull sonar, one ESM system with ARBR 16 warning element, and two Dagaie chaff/flare launchers
Propulsion: four SEMT-Pielstick 12PC diesels delivering 11,920 kW (15,990 hp) to two shafts, except F729 which has a CODAG arrangement with two diesels and one Turboméca M38 gas turbine
Performance: maximum speed 25 kt; range 13,900 km (8,635 miles) at 15 kt
Complement: 10 + 157

Class
1. France

Name	No.	Builder	Laid down	Com-missioned
Commandant Bory	F726	Lorient ND	Mar 1958	Mar 1964
Amiral Charner	F727	Lorient ND	Nov 1958	Dec 1962
Doudart de Lagrée	F728	Lorient ND	Mar 1960	May 1963
Balny	F729	Lorient ND	Mar 1960	Mar 1962
Commandant Bourdais	F740	Lorient ND	Apr 1959	Mar 1963
Protet	F748	Lorient ND	Sep 1961	May 1964
Enseigne Henry	F749	Lorient ND	Sep 1962	Jan 1965

(These are nicely balanced escort frigates with provision for operation in all climatic regions. The ships have flag accommodation capability, and can also carry 80 soldiers as well as two LCPs.)

2. Uruguay

Name	No.	Builder	Laid down	Com-missioned
General Artigas	2	Lorient ND	Oct 1957	Oct 1962

(This was the *Victor Schoelcher*, lead ship of the French class, and was transferred to Uruguay in May 1989 fitted for, but not with, Exocet anti-ship missiles. It is anticipated that another two ships of the same class will be bought from France.)

'Descubierta' or 'F30' class FFG

(Spain)

Type: anti-ship and anti-submarine guided-missile escort frigate
Displacement: 1,235 tons standard and 1,480 tons full load
Dimensions: length 88·8 m (291·3 ft); beam 10·4 m (34·0 ft); draught 3·8 m (12·5 ft)
Gun armament: one 76-mm (3-in) OTO Melara L/62 DP in an OTO Melara Compact single mounting, one 40-mm Bofors L/70 AA in a single Breda mounting, and one 20-mm Meroka CIWS mounting
Missile armament: two Mk 141 quadruple container-launchers for eight RGM-84 Harpoon anti-ship missiles, and one Albatros octuple launcher for 24 RIM-7 Sea Sparrow SAMs
Torpedo armament: none
Anti-submarine armament: two Mk 32 triple 12·75-in (324-mm) mountings for Mk 46 torpedoes, and one 375-mm (14·76-in) Bofors twin-barrel rocket-launcher
Aircraft: none
Electronics: one DA-05/2 air/surface-search radar, one ZW-06 surface-search and navigation radar, one radar used in conjunction with the WM-22/41 or WM-25 gun and SAM fire-control system (with data provision for SSMs), one RAN 12L and one VPS-2 radars used in conjunction with the Meroka fire-control system, one optronic director, one Raytheon DE 1160B active search and attack hull sonar, one SEWACO action information system, one Prairie/Masker hull and propeller blade noise-suppression system, one Beta ESM system with warning and jamming elements, and two chaff launchers
Propulsion: four MTU/Bazan 16V 956 TB91 diesels delivering 13,400 kW (17,970 hp) to two shafts
Performance: maximum speed 25·5 kt; range 7400 km (4,600 miles) at 18 kt
Complement: 10 + 108 plus provision for 30 marines

Class
1. Egypt

Name	No.	Builder	Laid down	Com-missioned
El Suez	941	Bazan	Oct 1978	May 1984
Abu Qir	946	Bazan	Feb 1979	Oct 1984

(These Egyptian ships are similar to the Spanish units, but have two 40-mm Bofors L/70 AA in Breda single mountings rather than the Spanish ships' single 40-mm gun and a Meroka CIWS mounting, carry the Aspide SAM in place of the Spanish ships' RIM-7 Sea Sparrows, have the WM-25 fire-control radar system, fire the Stingray anti-submarine torpedo from their Mk 32 tube mountings, and are fitted with the Raytheon DE 1167 active search variable-depth sonar.)

2. Morocco

Name	No.	Builder	Laid down	Com-missioned
Colonel Errhamani	501	Bazan	Mar 1979	Feb 1982

(This Moroccan unit differs from the Spanish norm in having two 40-mm Bofors L/70 AA in two Breda single mountings, no Meroka CIWS mounting, two twin mountings for four MM.40 Exocet rather than RGM-84 Harpoon anti-ship missiles, Aspide rather than RIM-7 Sea Sparrow SAMs, a revised electronic fit including an Elettronica ELT 715 ESM system and twin Dagaie chaff/flare launchers, and less powerful MTU/Bazan 16MA 996 TB91 diesels delivering 12,000 kW [16,095 hp] for a speed of 26 kt. The complement is 100.)

3. Spain

Name	No.	Builder	Laid down	Com-missioned
Descubierta	F31	Bazan	Nov 1974	Nov 1978
Diana	F32	Bazan	Jul 1975	Jun 1979
Infanta Elena	F33	Bazan	Jan 1976	Apr 1980
Infanta Cristina	F34	Bazan	Sep 1976	Nov 1980
Cazadora	F35	Bazan	Dec 1977	Jul 1981
Vencedora	F36	Bazan	May 1978	Mar 1982

(This is basically a Spanish development of the Portuguese 'Joao Coutinho' class design with a number of significant improvements, and is fitted with the Prairie/Masker bubbler system to reduce noise radiated by the hull and propellers. The sensor and armament fits provide nice balance of anti-ship, anti-submarine and anti-aircraft capabilities on a comparatively small hull. Raytheon DE 1167 active search variable-depth sonar may be retrofitted to improve anti-submarine capability.)

Above right: The *Descubierta* and her five sisterships were based on the 'Joao Coutinho' class design but introduced features important in making the type suitable for a higher-intensity level of warfare.

'Duke' or 'Type 23' class FFG

(UK)

Type: anti-submarine, anti-ship and anti-aircraft guided-missile frigate

Displacement: 3,500 tons standard and 4,200 tons full load

Dimensions: length 436·2 ft (133·0 m); beam 52·8 ft (16·1 m); draught 18·0 ft (5·5 m)

Gun armament: one 4·5-in (114-mm) Vickers L/55 DP in a Mk 8 single mounting, and four 30-mm Oerlikon L/75 AA in two GCM-A03 twin mountings

Missile armament: two Mk 141 quadruple container-launchers for eight RGM-84 Harpoon anti-ship missiles, and one GWS 26 vertical launch system (24-round silo forward and 8-round silo aft) for 32 Sea Wolf SAMs

Torpedo armament: none

Anti-submarine armament: two STWS-2 twin 12·75-in (324-mm) mountings for Stingray torpedoes, and helicopter-launched weapons (see below)

Aircraft: one or two Westland Lynx HAS.Mk 2/3 or one EHI EH.101 helicopter in a hangar aft

Electronics: one Type 996 3D radar, one Type 1007 navigation radar, two Type 911 radars used in conjunction with the GWS 26 Mod 1 SAM fire-control system, one GSA 8B/GPEOD optronic director, one Type 2050 active search and attack bow sonar, one Type 2031Z (to be replaced by Type 2057) passive search towed-array sonar, one Surface Ship Command System action information system, one Type 182 towed torpedo-decoy system, one Racal ESM system (with UAF-1 Cutlass warning and Cygnus jamming elements in earlier ships or UAF-X warning and Type 965 jamming elements in later ships), one Type 182 towed torpedo-decoy system, four Sea Gnat chaff/decoy launchers, and two SCOT 1D satellite communications systems

Propulsion: CODAG arrangement, with two Rolls-Royce Spey SM1A gas turbines delivering 34,000 hp (25,355 kW) and four Paxman Valenta 12 RPA 200 CZ diesels delivering 7,000 hp (5220 kW) to two shafts

Performance: maximum speed 28 kt; range 9,000 miles (14,485 km) at 15 kt

Complement: 12 + 134 with a maximum of 17 + 168 possible

Class 1. UK Name	No.	Builder	Laid down	Com-missioned
Norfolk	F230	Yarrow	Dec 1985	Nov 1989
Argyll	F231	Yarrow	Mar 1987	1991
Lancaster	F232	Yarrow	Dec 1987	1991
Marlborough	F233	Swan Hunter	Oct 1987	1990
Iron Duke	F234	Yarrow	Dec 1988	1992
Monmouth	F235	Yarrow	Aug 1989	1992
Montrose	F236	Yarrow	Mar 1990	1993

Note: This promises to be a highly capable multi-role frigate design with powerful capabilities in all of its design roles if an effective computerized action information and command system can be produced to replace the proposed but now cancelled CACS 4 system. The type should total 16 units, and was designed with 'stealth' in mind, obtuse angles and curved edges being employed to keep radar signature to a minimum and a hull 'bubbler' system being used to reduced underwater radiated noise. There was the strong possibility that the third batch of four ships would be lengthened by 23 ft (7·0 m) to allow one or two 30-mm Goalkeeper CIWS mountings to be carried on each ship, but in 1989 it was revealed that such would not be the case. Later in 1989 it was revealed that the Royal Navy is considering an enhanced version of the 'Duke' class design for later procurement with several of the previously discarded features such as a hull lengthened by 32·8 ft (10 m), missile capacity of the Vertical-Launch Sea Wolf SAM system increased to 48 (40 missiles forward and 8 aft), and two 30-mm Goalkeeper CIWS mountings. Still further into the future may be a development of the 'Duke' class design optimized for the anti-aircraft role.

The *Norfolk* (seen here on trials) is lead ship of a very important class of British frigates that should offer very good capabilities when the much-troubled command and control system is finally developed and installed.

'F2000S' or 'Al Madinah' class FFG

(France/Saudi Arabia)

Type: anti-ship and anti-submarine guided-missile frigate

Displacement: 2,000 tons standard and 2,870 tons full load

Dimensions: length 115·0 m (377·3 ft); beam 12·5 m (41·0 ft); draught 4·7 m (15·3 ft)

Gun armament: one 100-mm (3·9-in) Creusot Loire L/55 DP in a Creusot Loire Compact single mounting, and four 40-mm Breda L/70 AA in two twin Dardo mountings

Missile armament: two Teseo 2 quadruple container-launchers for eight Otomat Mk 2 anti-ship missiles, and one Naval Crotale EDIR octuple launcher for 26 Matra R.440 SAMs

Torpedo armament: none

Anti-submarine armament: four single 533-mm (21-in) single K 66A mountings for F17P wire-guided torpedoes, and two Mk 32 single mountings for 12·75-in (324-mm) Mk 46 torpedoes

Aircraft: one Aérospatiale SA 365F Dauphin 2 helicopter in a hangar aft

Electronics: one DRBV 15 Sea Tiger air/surface-search radar, two TM1226 navigation radars, one DRBC 32E SAM-control radar, one radar used in conjunction with the Castor IIC 100-mm gun fire-control system, one DRBC 32 SAM fire-control radar, one Vega weapon direction system, three Naja optronic directors (two for the Dardo installations and the third as back-up for the Castor IIC), one Diodon TSM 2630 active search and attack hull sonar and one Sorel active variable-depth sonar used in conjunction with the Alcatel DLA underwater weapons fire-control system, one TAVITAC (SENIT VI) action information system with Erato for Otomat control, one ESM system with DR 4000S warning and Jamet jamming elements, one Telegon VI direction-finding system, two Dagaie chaff/flare launchers, and one Sylosat satellite navigation system

Propulsion: CODAD arrangement, with four SEMT-Pielstick 16 PA6-V280 BTC diesels delivering 24,240 kW (32,510 hp) to two shafts

Performance: maximum speed 30 kt; range 12,000 km (7,455 miles) at 18 kt

Complement: 15 + 164

Class

1. Saudi Arabia

Name	No.	Builder	Laid down	Com-missioned
Al Madinah	702	Lorient ND	Oct 1981	Jan 1985
Hofouf	704	CNIM	Jun 1982	Oct 1985
Abha	706	CNIM	Dec 1982	Apr 1986
Taif	708	CNIM	Jun 1983	Aug 1986

Right and below: *Al Madinah* is lead ship of Saudi Arabia's 'F2000S' frigate class, which offers a high level of capabilities in a fairly small hull.

Note: This is a very ambitious design produced for a technologically immature navy, and combines state-of-the-art sensors and weapons in a nicely arranged multi-role package. The predominant feature of this balanced design is the choice of ship-launched Otomat Mk 2 long-range anti-ship missiles and helicopter-launched AS.15TT short-range anti-ship missiles. The helicopter can also provide mid-course guidance update for the Otomat missiles.

'Fatahillah' class FFG

(Netherlands/Indonesia)
Type: anti-submarine and anti-ship guided-missile frigate
Displacement: 1,200 tons standard and 1,450 tons full load
Dimensions: length 84·0 m (275·6 ft); beam 11·1 m (36·4 ft); draught 3·3 m (10·7 ft)
Gun armament: one 120-mm (4·7-in) Bofors L/46 DP in a Bofors single mounting, one or (363) two 40-mm Bofors L/70 AA in single mountings, and two 20-mm AA in single mountings
Missile armament: four container-launchers for four MM.38 Exocet anti-ship missiles
Torpedo armament: none
Anti-submarine armament: one 375-mm (14·76-in) Bofors two-barrel rocket-launcher, and two Mk 32 triple 12·75-in (324-mm) mountings for 12 Mk 44 torpedoes or (362) two ILAS 3 triple 324-mm (12·75-in) mountings for 12 A 244/S torpedoes or (363 only) helicopter-launched weapons (see below)
Aircraft: (363 only) one Nurtanio-MBB BO105 helicopter in a hangar aft
Electronics: one DA-05 air/surface-search radar, one AC1229 surface-search and navigation radar, one radar used in conjunction with the WM-28 gun and SSM fire-control system, two LIROD optronic directors, one PHS-32 active search and attack hull sonar, one Daisy action information system, one T Mk 6 Fanfare torpedo decoy system, one ESM system with Susie I warning element, and two Corvus chaff launchers
Propulsion: CODOG arrangement, with one Rolls-Royce Olympus TM3B gas turbine delivering 28,000 hp (20,875 kW) or two MTU 16V 956 TP61 diesels delivering 4480 kW (6,010 hp) to two shafts
Performance: maximum speed 30 kt; range 7875 km (4,895 miles) at 18 kt
Complement: 11 + 78

Class 1. Indonesia			Laid	Com-
Name	No.	Builder	down	missioned
Fatahillah	361	Wilton-Fijenoord	Jan 1977	Jul 1979
Malahayati	362	Wilton-Fijenoord	Jul 1977	Mar 1980
Nala	363	Wilton-Fijenoord	Jan 1978	Aug 1980

Note: This class has dual-role capability thanks to the installation of adequate weapons and advanced sensors (electronic and optronic), and is notable for its small complement and provision with full NBC defence.

Though small, the *Fatahillah* and her two sisters are capable ships by the standards prevailing in South-East Asia.

'FL 3000' class FFG

(France)
Type: anti-aircraft and anti-ship guided-missile frigate
Displacement: 3,200 tons full load
Dimensions: length 119·0 m (390·4 ft); beam 13·8 m (45·3 ft); draught 4·0 m (13·1 ft)
Gun armament: one 100-mm (3·9-in) Creusot Loire L/55 DP in a Creusot Loire Compact single mounting, and two 20-mm AA in single mountings
Missile armament: two quadruple container-launchers for eight MM.40 Exocet anti-ship missiles, one Naval Crotale octuple launcher for R.440 SAMs or SAAM vertical launch system for SAN 90 Aster SAMs, and two SADRAL launchers for Mistral SAMs
Torpedo armament: none
Anti-submarine armament: four single 324-mm (12·75-in) tubes for Murène torpedoes
Aircraft: one Aérospatiale SA 365F Dauphin 2 helicopter in a hangar aft
Electronics: one DRBV 27 (Jupiter III) air-search radar, one DRBV 15 (Sea Tiger) air/surface-search radar, two Decca 1226 navigation radars, one DRBC 33 100-mm gun fire-control radar, one Vega weapon direction system, one active search and attack hull sonar, one DSBV 61 passive towed-array sonar, one ESM system with ARBR 17 warning and ARBB 33 jamming elements, one DIBV 10 Vampir IR detector, two Dagaie chaff/flare launchers, and one Syracuse II satellite communications system
Propulsion: CODAD arrangement, with four SEMT-Pielstick 16 PA6-V280 BTC diesels delivering 26,000 kW (34,870 hp) to two shafts
Performance: maximum speed 29 kt; range 13,000 km (8,080 miles) at 15 kt; endurance 50 days
Complement: 156

Class 1. France			Laid	Com-
Name	No.	Builder	down	missioned
La Fayette		Lorient ND		1994
Surcouf		Lorient ND		1995
Courbet		Lorient ND		1996

Note: Though designed as general-purpose frigates with optimization for the anti-aircraft and anti-ship roles, this class of six patrol FFGs could eventually be built in two subvariants, one in the general-purpose form described above and the other with modifications to alter the optimization to the anti-submarine role.

'Floreal' class FFG

(France)
Type: anti-submarine and anti-ship guided-missile frigate
Displacement: 2,600 tons standard and 1,850 tons full load
Dimensions: length 93·5 m (306·8 ft); beam 14·0 m (45·9 ft); draught 4·3 m (13·1 ft)
Gun armament: one 100-mm (3·9-in) Creusot Loire L/55 DP in a Creusot Loire Compact single mounting, and two 20-mm AA in single mountings
Missile armament: two twin container-launchers for four MM.40 Exocet anti-ship missiles, and two SADRAL sextuple launchers for Mistral SAMs
Torpedo armament: none
Anti-submarine armament: none
Aircraft: one Aérospatiale AS 332F Super Puma helicopter in a hangar aft
Electronics: one DRBV 15 (Sea Tiger) air/surface-search radar, one Decca 1226 navigation radar, one DRBC 33 100-mm gun fire-control radar, one Naja optronic director, one active search hull sonar, one ESM system with ARBR 17 warning element, two Dagaie chaff/flare launchers, and one Syracuse satellite communications system
Propulsion: CODAD arrangement, with four SEMT-Pielstick diesels delivering 6000 kW (8,050 hp) to two shafts
Performance: maximum speed 20 kt; range 16,675 km (10,360 miles) at 15 kt; endurance 50 days
Complement: 100 plus provision for 24 commandos

Class 1. France			Laid	Com-
Name	No.	Builder	down	missioned
Floreal	F800	Chantiers de l'Atlantique		1990
Prairial	F801	Chantiers de l'Atlantique		1991

Note: This light frigate class is projected to a total of 10 ships to be built to mercantile standards for the offshore patrol role, with capability for wartime operations in low-intensity theatres.

'Godavari' class FFG

(India)
Type: anti-ship and anti-submarine guided-missile escort frigate
Displacement: 3,600 tons standard and 4,000 tons full load
Dimensions: length 414·9 ft (126·5 m); beam 47·6 ft (14·5 m); draught 29·5 ft (9·0 m)
Gun armament: two 57-mm L/70 DP in a single mounting, and eight 30-mm L/65 AA in four twin mountings
Missile armament: two twin container-launchers for four SS-N-2C 'Styx' anti-ship missiles, and one twin launcher for 20 SA-N-4 'Gecko' SAMs
Torpedo armament: none
Anti-submarine armament: two ILAS 3 triple 324-mm (12·75-in) mountings for A 244/S torpedoes, and helicopter-launched weapons (see below)
Aircraft: two Westland Sea King Mk 42, or one Sea King Mk 42 and one HAL Chetak helicopter in a hangar aft
Electronics: one LW-08 air-search radar, one 'Head Net-C' air/surface-search radar, one ZW-06 surface-search and navigation radar, one MR301 SSM-control system, one 'Pop Group' SAM fire-control radar, one 'Muff Cob' 57-mm gun fire-control radar used in conjunction with the MR103 gun fire-control system, two 'Drum Tilt' 30-mm gun fire-control radars, one Graseby 750 (F20) or APSOH active search and attack hull sonar, one Type 162M bottom classification hull sonar, one Fathoms Oceanic active/passive search

variable-depth sonar, one IPN 10 action information system, one G738 towed torpedo-decoy system, one INS-3 ESM system with warning and jamming elements, two chaff launchers, and one satellite communications system
Propulsion: two boilers supplying steam to two sets of geared steam turbines delivering 30,000 hp (22,370 kW) to two shafts
Performance: maximum speed 27 kt; range 5,200 miles (8370 km) at 12 kt
Complement: 40 + 273

Class

1. India			Laid	Com-
Name	No.	Builder	down	missioned
Godavari	F21	Mazagon Docks	Jun 1978	Dec 1983
Ganga	F22	Mazagon Docks	1980	Dec 1985
Gomati	F23	Mazagon Docks	1981	Apr 1988

Note: This interesting class is an Indian development of the British 'Leander' class design with two large anti-submarine helicopters, British, Dutch and Soviet electronics, Italian anti-submarine armament, and Soviet guns. It was thought that the Indians might build another three of the class, possibly in Calcutta, but in the late 1980s it was disclosed that the scheme had been shelved.

'Hajar Dewantara' class FFG

(Yugoslavia/Indonesia)
Type: anti-ship guided-missile frigate
Displacement: 1,850 tons full load
Dimensions: length 96·7 m (317·3 ft); beam 11·2 m (36·7 ft); draught 4·5 m (14·8 ft)
Gun armament: one 57-mm SAK 57 Mk 1 L/70 DP in a Bofors single mounting, and four 20-mm AA in two twin mountings
Missile armament: two twin container-launchers for four MM.38 Exocet anti-ship missiles
Torpedo armament: two single 533-mm (21-in) mountings for SUT wire-guided dual-role torpedoes
Anti-submarine armament: torpedoes (see above), and one depth-charge thrower
Aircraft: one Nurtanio-MBB BO105C helicopter on a platform aft
Electronics: one Decca 1229 surface-search and navigation radar, one radar used in conjunction with the WM-28 fire-control system, one PHS 32 active search and attack hull sonar, one SEWACO action information system, one ESM system with Susie warning element, and two chaff/decoy launchers
Propulsion: CODOG arrangement, with one Rolls-Royce Olympus gas turbine delivering 27,250 hp (20,320 kW) and two MTU 16V 956 TB91 diesels delivering 5600 kW (7,510 hp) to two shafts
Performance: maximum speed 26 kt on gas turbine or 20 kt on diesels; range 7400 km (4,600 miles) at 18 kt
Complement: 11 + 180 including 14 instructors and 100 cadets

Class

1. Indonesia			Laid	Com-
Name	No.	Builder	down	missioned
Hajar Dewantara	364	Split SY	May 1979	Oct 1981

(This is a simple frigate type of Yugoslav design and manufacture used mainly for cadet training in peace, but its war roles would include escort, anti-submarine operations and, as a secondary task, troop transport for which two LCVPs are shipped. The success of the first unit prompted the ordering of a second unit in 1983, but lack of further information suggests that this may have been cancelled.)

2. Iraq			Laid	Com-
Name	No.	Builder	down	missioned
Ibn Khaldoum	507	Split SY	1977	Mar 1980

(This is near-sister to the Indonesian type, possessing a standard armament of one 57-mm Bofors SAK 57 Mk 1 L/70 DP gun, one 40-mm Bofors L/70 AA gun, and eight 20-mm AA in four twin mountings; the type is also fitted for but not with two twin container-launchers for four MM.38 Exocet anti-ship missiles, and the torpedo and anti-submarine armaments are identical to those of the Indonesian ships. The electronics include two Decca 1229 surface-search and navigation radars, and one 9LV 200 Mk 2 fire-control radar. The type lacks any helicopter capability, but the propulsion is identical to that of the Indonesian ships. The complement is 93, with provision for 100 trainees or, in time of war, troops.)

'Inhauma' class FFG

(Brazil)
Type: anti-submarine and anti-ship guided-missile frigate
Displacement: 1,600 tons standard and 1,970 tons full load
Dimensions: length 95·8 m (314·2 ft); beam 11·4 m (37·4 ft); draught 3·7 m (12·1 ft)
Gun armament: one 4·5-in (114-mm) Vickers L/55 DP in a Mk 8 single mounting, two 40-mm Bofors L/70 AA in single mountings, and one 20-mm Phalanx Mk 15 CIWS mounting
Missile armament: two twin container-launchers for four MM.40 Exocet anti-ship missiles
Torpedo armament: none
Anti-submarine armament: two Mk 32 triple 12·75-in (324-mm) mountings for Mk 46 torpedoes, and helicopter-launched weapons (see below)
Aircraft: one Westland Lynx Mk 21 or Aérospatiale SA 365F Dauphin 2 helicopter in a hangar aft
Electronics: one ASW 4 surface-search radar, one navigation radar, one RTN 10X radar used in conjunction with the WSA 420 SSM and gun fire-control system, one ASO 4 Mod 2 active search and attack hull sonar, one CAAIS 450 action information system, one data-link, one ESM system with warning element, and two Shield chaff/decoy launchers
Propulsion: CODOG arrangement, with one General Electric LM2500 gas turbine delivering 27,500 hp (20,505 kW) and two MTU 16V 956 TB91 diesels delivering 5800 kW (7,780 hp) to two shafts
Performance: maximum speed 29 kt on gas turbine or 15 kt on diesels; range 7400 km (4,600 miles) at 15 kt
Complement: 15 + 100

Class

1. Brazil			Laid	Com-
Name	No.	Builder	down	missioned
Inhauma	V30	Arsenal de Marinha	Sep 1983	Mar 1989
Jaceguary	V31	Arsenal de Marinha	Oct 1984	1990
Julio de Noronha	V32	Verolme	May 1987	1989
Frontin	V33	Verolme	Aug 1987	1989

Note: Though small for a frigate design, this type offers great capabilities in the multi-role escort task through the use of high-quality imported sensors and weapons on a locally designed hull. Current plans call for a total of 16 units, and the navy is taking full advantage of funding delays to reassess the weapon fit of these vessels, whose later units may have Brazilian weapons in the form of Barracuda SSMs, eight Avibras SSAI-N anti-submarine rocket-launchers and Avibras FILA 20-mm AA cannon mountings.

'Ishikari' or 'Type 226' class FFG

(Japan)

Type: anti-ship and anti-submarine guided-missile frigate
Displacement: 1,290 tons standard and 1,450 tons full load
Dimensions: length 85·0 m (278·8 ft); beam 10·6 m (34·7 ft); draught 5·9 m (19·2 ft)
Gun armament: one 76-mm (3-in) OTO Melara L/62 DP in an OTO Melara Compact single mounting
Missile armament: two Mk 141 quadruple container-launchers for eight RGM-84 Harpoon anti-ship missiles
Torpedo armament: none
Anti-submarine armament: one 375-mm (14·76-in) Bofors Type 71 four-barrel rocket-launcher, and two Type 68 triple 12·75-in (324-mm) mountings for Mk 46 torpedoes
Aircraft: none
Electronics: one OPS-28 surface-search radar, one OPS-19 navigation radar, one Type 2 radar used in conjunction with the Type 2-21 gun fire-control system, one OQS-4 active search and attack hull sonar, one ESM system with NOLQ-6Q warning and OLT-2 jamming elements, and one Mk 36 Super RBOC chaff/flare launcher
Propulsion: CODOG arrangement, with one Kawasaki/Rolls-Royce Olympus TM3B gas turbine delivering 28,930 hp (21,570 kW) or one Mitsubishi 6 DRV 35/44 diesel delivering 3500 kW (4,695 hp) to two shafts
Performance: maximum speed 25 kt
Complement: 90

Class

1. Japan

Name	No.	Builder	Laid down	Com-missioned
Ishikari	DE226	Mitsui	May 1979	Mar 1981

Note: Though fully operational, this singleton frigate may be regarded more realistically as a prototype for new Japanese frigate construction, being the first new design of this category since the mid-1960s and the obsolescent non-missile 'Chikugo' class.

The *Ishikari* was built as an operational type in which features for later frigates could be evaluated under realistic conditions.

'Jacob van Heemskerck' class FFG

(Netherlands)

Type: anti-aircraft and anti-ship guided-missile frigate
Displacement: 3,000 tons standard and 3,750 tons full load
Dimensions: length 130·5 m (428·1 ft); beam 14·6 m (47·9 ft); draught 6·2 m (20·3 ft)
Gun armament: one 30-mm Goalkeeper CIWS mounting
Missile armament: two Mk 141 quadruple container-launchers for eight RGM-84 Harpoon anti-ship missiles, one Mk 13 single launcher for 40 RIM-66B Standard SM-1 MR SAMs, and one Mk 29 octuple launcher for 24 RIM-7 NATO Sea Sparrow SAMs
Torpedo armament: none
Anti-submarine armament: two Mk 32 twin 12·75-in (324-mm) mountings for Mk 46 torpedoes
Aircraft: none
Electronics: one LW-08 air-search radar, one DA-05 air/surface-search radar (being replaced by SMART [Signaal Multi-beam Acquisition Radar for Targeting] 3D radar), one ZW-06 surface-search and navigation radar, three Signaal Track and Illumination Radars (two STIR 240 and one STIR 180) radars used with the SAM and CIWS fire-control systems, one PHS-36 active search and attack hull sonar, one SQR-18A passive search towed-array sonar (possibly to be retrofitted), one SEWACO II action information system, one Daisy data-handling system, Link 10 and 11 data-links, one ESM system with warning and RAMSES jamming elements, and two Mk 36 Super RBOC chaff/flare launchers
Propulsion: COGOG arrangement, with two Rolls-Royce Olympus TM3B gas turbines delivering 50,000 hp (37,285 kW) or two Rolls-Royce Tyne RM1C gas turbines delivering 8,000 hp (5965 kW) to two shafts
Performance: maximum speed 30 kt; range 8700 km (5,405 miles) at 16 kt
Complement: 23 + 174 plus accommodation for 20 flag staff

Class

1. Netherlands

Name	No.	Builder	Laid down	Com-missioned
Jacob van Heemskerck	F812	Koninklijke Maatschappij	Jan 1981	Jan 1986
Witte de Witt	F813	Koninklijke Maatschappij	Dec 1981	Sep 1986

Note: This is the air-defence counterpart of the anti-submarine 'Kortenaer' class frigate, the helicopter facilities of the 'Kortenaer' class being replaced by a single-ended missile installation. The ships are fitted to serve as flag-ships.

'Jiangdong' or 'Type 053K' class FFG

(China)

Type: anti-aircraft guided-missile escort frigate
Displacement: 1,700 tons standard and 2,000 tons full load
Dimensions: length 103·2 m (338·5 ft); beam 10·2 m (38·5 ft); draught 3·1 m (10·2 ft)
Gun armament: four 100-mm (3·94-in) L/56 DP in two twin mountings, and eight 37-mm L/63 AA in four twin mountings
Missile armament: two twin launchers for HQ-61 (CSA-N-2) SAMs
Torpedo armament: none
Anti-submarine armament: two RBU 1200 five-barrel rocket-launchers, two BMB-2 depth-charge throwers, and two depth-charge racks
Aircraft: none
Electronics: one 'Rice Screen' 3D radar, one 'Square Tie' surface-search radar, one 'Fin Curve' navigation radar, two radars used in conjunction with two 'Fog Lamp' SAM fire-control systems, one 'Sun Visor-B' 100-mm gun fire-control radar, one 'Rice Lamp' 37-mm gun fire-control radar, one 'Pegas-2M' active search and attack hull sonar, one 'Tamir-2' active search

and attack hull sonar, one ESM system with two 'Jug Pair' housings, one 'Ski Pole' and one 'Yard Rake' IFF systems
Propulsion: two SEMT-Pielstick 12 PA6 diesels delivering 12,000 kW (16,095 hp) to two shafts
Performance: maximum speed 26 kt; range 7400 km (4,600 miles) at 15 kt
Complement: 185

Class

1. China

Name	No.	Builder	Laid down	Com-missioned
Yingtan	531	Hutong, Shanghai	1970	1977
	532	Chiuhsin, Shanghai	1972	1978

Note: This was China's first SAM-equipped warship design, and underwent an extremely lengthy development. It was possibly planned to build five units, but it seems more likely now that only these two units will be built, the experience gained in their design, construction and operation being used in the preparation of a more advanced anti-aircraft frigate type.

'Jianghu I' and 'Jianghu II' or 'Type 053H' class FFGs

(China)

Type: anti-ship guided-missile frigate
Displacement: 1,570 tons standard and 2,000 tons full load
Dimensions: length 103·2 m (338·5 ft); beam 10·2 m (38·5 ft); draught 3·1 m (10·2 ft)
Gun armament: two 100-mm (3·94-in) L/56 DP in two single mountings or ('Jianghu II' class ships) four 100-mm (3·94-in) L/56 DP in two twin mountings, and 12 37-mm L/63 AA in six twin mountings
Missile armament: two twin container-launchers for four HY-2 (CSS-N-1) anti-ship missiles
Torpedo armament: none
Anti-submarine armament: four or ('Jianghu II' class ships) two RBU 1200 five-barrel rocket-launchers, two BMB-2 depth-charge throwers, and two depth-charge racks
Mines: 60
Aircraft: none
Electronics: one 'Eye Shield' air/surface-search radar, one 'Square Tie' surface-search radar, one 'Wok Won' 100-mm gun fire-control radar ('Jianghu II' class ships only), one 'Don 2' or 'Fin Curve' navigation radar, one optronic director ('Jianghu II' class ships only), one medium-frequency active search and attack hull sonar, one ESM system with one 'Jug Pair' or 'Watch Dog' antenna/housing, one 'High Pole-A' and one 'Yard Rake' or 'Square Head' IFF systems, and (some ships only) two Mk 36 Super RBOC chaff launchers
Propulsion: two SEMT-Pielstick 12 PA6 diesels delivering 12,000 kW (16,095 hp) to two shafts
Performance: maximum speed 26 kt; range 7400 km (4,600 miles) at 15 kt or 5000 km (3,105 miles) at 18 kt
Complement: 195

Class

1. China

Name	No.	Builder	Laid down	Com-missioned
Changde	509	Hutong, Shanghai	1974	1976
Shaixing	510*	Jiangnan, Shanghai	1975	1977
Nantong	511	Jiangnan, Shanghai	1975	1977
Wuxi	512*	Jiangnan, Shanghai	1975	1977
Huayin	513	Jiangnan, Shanghai	1976	1978
Zhenjiang	514	Jiangnan, Shanghai	1976	1978
Xiamen	515	Hutong, Shanghai	1976	1978
Jiujiang	516	Hutong, Shanghai	1977	1979
Nanping	517	Hutong, Shanghai	1978	1980
Jian	518	Jiangnan, Shanghai	1979	1981
Changzhi	519	Hutong, Shanghai	1980	1982
Chanshao	525	Hutong, Shanghai	1980	1983
Xian	527	Hutong, Shanghai	1981	1983
Ningbo	533	Hutong, Shanghai	1982	1984
Jinhua	534	Hutong, Shanghai	1982	1984
Huangshi	535*	Hutong, Shanghai	1983	1984
	536*	Hutong, Shanghai	1983	1985
	538	Hutong, Shanghai	1984	1986

Name	No.	Builder	Laid down	Com-missioned
Dandong	543	Hutong, Shanghai	1984	1986
Siping	544**	Hutong, Shanghai	1984	1987
	545	Hutong, Shanghai	1984	1987
Maoming	551	Jiangnan, Shanghai	1985	1987
Yibin	552	Hutong, Shanghai	1985	1987
Shaoguan	553	Jiangnan, Shanghai	1985	1987
Anshun	554	Jiangnan, Shanghai	1985	1987

* 'Jianghu IV' class
** 'Jianghu V' class

(The basic 'Jianghu' design developed from the 'Jiangdong' class emphasizing anti-ship warfare, by the missile installation of four HY-2 [Chinese version of the Soviet SS-N-2 'Styx' in early units] and eight smaller C-801 missiles in 'Jianghu IV' class ships. It is believed that the type is to number some 27–30 units in all, built at the Jiangnan and Hutong yards in Shanghai in various subclasses. The 'Jianghu I' class has a square stack and optical fire-control for the main armament of two 100-mm/3·94-in guns. The 'Jianghu II' class has a rounded stack, and two twin rather than two single 100-mm mountings used with radar fire-control. The **'Jianghu IV' class** has 100 tons more full-load displacement for a primary missile armament of eight C-810 anti-ship missiles backed by two twin 100-mm gun mountings and four twin 37-mm mountings with 'Rice Lamp' fire-control radar; the type also possesses three ILAS triple 324-mm/12·75-in mountings for A 224/S anti-submarine torpedoes and two RBU 1200 launchers. Finally, the **'Jianghu V' class** is a development of the 'Jianghu II' class providing improved anti-submarine capability on a lengthened 110-m/360·8-ft hull with a flightdeck and hangar aft for one Harbin Zhi-9 helicopter; the other armament is a twin container-launcher for two HY-2 anti-ship missiles, two 100-m/3·94-in L/56 DP guns in a twin mounting, and eight 37-mm AA in twin mountings; the fire-control system includes 'Wok Won' radar and a Naja optronic director. Older units may be converted to 'Jianghu IV' and 'Jianghu V' standard, possibly with an upgraded electronic fit including the 'Rice Lamp' fire-control radar.)

2. Egypt ('Jianghu III' class)

Name	No.	Builder	Laid down	Com-missioned
Najim al Zaffer	951	Hutong, Shanghai		Oct 1984
El Nasser	956	Hutong, Shanghai		Apr 1985

(These are similar to the Chinese 'Jianghu II' class ships in all respects but for the main armament, of four 57-mm L/70 DP in two twin mountings. The Egyptians plan an upgrade with Western sensors and weapons.)

3. Thailand

Name	No.	Builder	Laid down	Com-missioned
		Hutong, Shanghai		
		Hutong, Shanghai		
		Hutong, Shanghai		
		Hutong, Shanghai		

(These four frigates are two 'Jianghu I' and two 'Jianghu V' class ships fitted with Creusot Loire main guns, fitted with two triple 12·75-in/324-mm mountings for Stingray anti-submarine torpedoes, and re-engined before delivery with MTU diesels and, in the case of the latter pair, with the after 100-mm/3·94-in gun replaced by a platform for a single helicopter. The first two are due in February 1991 and the second two by February 1992.)

The *Zhenjiang* is a typical unit of the Chinese navy's 'Jianghu I'
guided-missile frigate class, which is scoring export successes in
various forms.

'Karel Doorman' class FFG

(Netherlands)

Type: anti-ship and anti-submarine guided-missile frigate
Displacement: 2,650 tons standard and 3,320 tons full load
Dimensions: length 122·3 m (401·1 ft); beam 14·4 m (47·25 ft); draught 6·0 m
(19·7 ft)
Gun armament: one 76-mm (3-in) OTO Melara L/62 DP in an OTO Melara
Super Rapid single mounting, one 30-mm Goalkeeper CIWS mounting, and
two 20-mm AA in single mountings
Missile armament: two Mk 141 quadruple container-launchers for eight
RGM-84 Harpoon anti-ship missiles, and one vertical launch system for 16
RIM-7 Sea Sparrow SAMs
Torpedo armament: none
Anti-submarine armament: two Mk 32 twin 12·75-in (324-mm) mountings
for Mk 46 torpedoes, and helicopter-launched weapons (see below)
Aircraft: one Westland SH-14C Lynx helicopter in a hangar aft
Electronics: one SMART (Signaal Multi-beam Acquisition Radar for Tar-
geting) 3D radar, one LW-08 air/surface-search radar, one ZW-06 surface-
search radar, one Decca 1226 navigation radar, two STIR (Signaal Track and
Illumination Radar) gun and SAM fire-control radars, one PHS-36 active
search and attack hull sonar, one SQR-18A passive towed-array sonar, one
SEWACO VII action information system, Link 10, 11 and 14 data-links, one
towed torpedo-decoy system, one ESM system with warning and RAMSES
jamming elements, two Mk 36 Super RBOC chaff/flare launchers, and one
satellite communications system
Propulsion: CODOG arrangement, with two Rolls-Royce Spey SM1C gas
turbines delivering 48,000 hp (35,790 kW) or two Werkspoor 12 SW280 diesels delivering 6000 kW (8,050 hp) to two shafts

Performance: maximum speed 29 kt on gas turbines and 21 kt on diesels;
range 9250 km (5,750 miles) at 18 kt
Complement: 16 + 125 with a maximum of 158 possible

Class

1. Netherlands Name	No.	Builder	Laid down	Com-missioned
Karel Doorman	F827	Koninklijke Maatschappij	Feb 1985	Jun 1990
Van Amstel	F829	Koninklijke Maatschappij	Nov 1985	Nov 1990
Willem van der Zaan	F830	Koninklijke Maatschappij	Oct 1986	1991
Tjerk Hiddes	F831	Koninklijke Maatschappij	May 1988	1992
Abraham van der Hulst	F832	Koninklijke Maatschappij	Feb 1989	1992
Van Nes	F833	Koninklijke Maatschappij	Feb 1990	1994
Van Galen	F834	Koninklijke Maatschappij	May 1990	1994
Van Speijk	F828	Koninklijke Maatschappij	Aug 1991	1995

Note: This is a capable multi-role type designed to replace the 'Van Speijk'
class. The main part of the radar fit is identical with that planned for West
Germany's 'F123' class guided-missile frigates, and is closely akin to the
suites of the Dutch 'Kortenaer' and related West German 'Type 122' class
guided-missile frigates.

'Knox' class FFG

(USA)

Type: anti-submarine and anti-ship guided-missile escort frigate

Displacement: 3,010 tons standard and 3,875 tons or (FF1078/1097) 4,260 tons full load

Dimensions: length 438·0 ft (133·5 m); beam 46·8 ft (14·3 m); draught 24·8 ft (7·8 m)

Gun armament: one 5-in (127-mm) L/54 DP in a Mk 42 single mounting, and one 20-mm Phalanx Mk 15 CIWS mounting

Missile armament: up to eight RGM-84 Harpoon anti-ship missiles instead of RUR-5A ASROC missiles (see below)

Torpedo armament: none

Anti-submarine armament: one Mk 16 octuple launcher for up to 16 RUR-5A ASROC missiles, two Mk 32 twin 12·75-in (324-mm) mountings for 24 Mk 46 torpedoes, and helicopter-launched weapons (see below)

Aircraft: one Kaman SH-2F Seasprite helicopter in a hangar aft

Electronics: one SPS-40 or (FF1070) Mk 23 air-search radar, one SPS-10 or SPS-67 surface-search radar, one LN-66 navigation radar, one SPG-53A radar used in conjunction with the Mk 68 gun fire-control system, one Mk 1 weapon direction system, one SQS-26CX active search and attack bow sonar, one SQS-35A active variable-depth sonar (most ships) and one passive towed-array sonar (SQR-18[V]1 in VDS ships and SQR-18[V]2 in non-VDS ships) used in conjunction with the Mk 114 underwater weapons fire-control system, one Mk 1 target designation system, one SLQ-32(V)2 ESM system with warning and jamming elements, one Prairie/Masker hull and propeller blade noise-suppression system, four Mk 36 Super RBOC chaff/flare launchers, one OE-82 satellite communications system, one WSC-3 satellite communications transceiver, one SRR-1 satellite communications receiver, and SRN-15 TACAN

Propulsion: two Combustion Engineering or (FF1056/1057, 1061, 1063, 1065, 1072/1074 and 1077) Babcock & Wilcox boilers supplying steam to one set of Westinghouse geared turbines delivering 35,000 hp (26,100 kW) to one shaft

Performance: maximum speed 27 kt; range 5,200 miles (8370 km) at 20 kt

Complement: 17 + 271

Class Name	No.	Builder	Laid down	Commissioned
Baleares	F71	Bazan	Oct 1968	Sep 1973
Andalucia	F72	Bazan	Jul 1969	May 1974
Cataluna	F73	Bazan	Aug 1970	Jan 1975
Asturias	F74	Bazan	Mar 1971	Dec 1975
Extremadura	F75	Bazan	Nov 1971	Nov 1976

1. Spain ('Baleares' or 'F70' class)

(This is the Spanish version of the 'Knox' class design with standard and full-load displacements of 3,015 and 4,175 tons respectively. The ships each have a Mk 22 single launcher for up to 16 RIM-66B Standard SM-1 MR SAMs, two quadruple or two twin container-launchers for eight or four RGM-84 Harpoon anti-ship missiles, two 20-mm Meroka CIWS mountings, and the anti-submarine armament is augmented by two Mk 25 single 19-in/485-mm launchers for 19 Mk 37 wire-guided anti-submarine torpedoes in addition to the 22 Mk 46 torpedoes carried for the Mk 32 tube mountings. The type has no helicopter facilities, and also carries a revised electronic fit with SPS-52A 3D radar, Pathfinder navigation radar, one RAN 12L and two VPS-2 radars used in conjunction with the Meroka fire-control system, Raytheon DE 1160LF active search and attack hull sonar, SQS-35(V) active search and attack variable-depth sonar, a Tritan 1 action information system, an ESM system with Elsag Mk 1000 warning and Deneb jamming elements, and four Mk 36 Super RBOC chaff/flare launchers.)

2. USA

Name	No.	Builder	Laid down	Commissioned
Knox	FF1052	Todd Pacific	Oct 1965	Apr 1969
Roark	FF1053	Todd Pacific	Feb 1966	Nov 1969
Gray	FF1054	Todd Pacific	Nov 1966	Apr 1970
Hepburn	FF1055	Todd Pacific	Jun 1966	Jul 1969
Connole	FF1056	Avondale	Mar 1967	Aug 1969
Rathburne	FF1057	Lockheed SB	Jan 1968	May 1970
Meyerkord	FF1058	Todd Pacific	Sep 1966	Nov 1969
W. S. Sims	FF1059	Avondale	Apr 1967	Jan 1970
Lang	FF1060	Todd Pacific	Mar 1967	Mar 1970
Patterson	FF1061	Avondale	Oct 1967	Mar 1970
Whipple	FF1062	Todd Pacific	Apr 1967	Aug 1970

Name	No.	Builder	Laid down	Commissioned
Reasoner	FF1063	Lockheed SB	Jan 1969	Jul 1971
Lockwood	FF1064	Todd Pacific	Nov 1967	Dec 1970
Stein	FF1065	Lockheed SB	Jun 1970	Jan 1972
Marvin Shields	FF1066	Todd Pacific	Apr 1968	Apr 1971
Francis Hammond	FF1067	Todd Pacific	Jul 1967	Jul 1970
Vreeland	FF1068	Avondale	Mar 1968	Jun 1970
Bagley	FF1069	Lockheed SB	Sep 1970	May 1972
Downes	FF1070	Todd Pacific	Sep 1968	Aug 1971
Badger	FF1071	Todd Pacific	Feb 1968	Dec 1970
Blakely	FF1072	Avondale	Jun 1968	Jul 1970
Robert E. Peary	FF1073	Lockheed SB	Dec 1970	Sep 1972
Harold E. Holt	FF1074	Todd Pacific	May 1968	Mar 1971
Trippe	FF1075	Avondale	Jul 1968	Sep 1970
Fanning	FF1076	Todd Pacific	Dec 1968	Jul 1971
Ouellet	FF1077	Avondale	Jan 1969	Dec 1970
Joseph Hewes	FF1078	Avondale	May 1969	Apr 1971
Bowen	FF1079	Avondale	Jul 1969	May 1971
Paul	FF1080	Avondale	Sep 1969	Aug 1971
Aylwin	FF1081	Avondale	Nov 1969	Sep 1971
Elmer Montgomery	FF1082	Avondale	Jan 1970	Oct 1971
Cook	FF1083	Avondale	Mar 1970	Dec 1971
McCandless	FF1084	Avondale	Jun 1970	Mar 1972
Donald B. Beary	FF1085	Avondale	Jul 1970	Jul 1972
Brewton	FF1086	Avondale	Oct 1970	Jul 1972
Kirk	FF1087	Avondale	Dec 1970	Sep 1972
Barbey	FF1088	Avondale	Feb 1971	Nov 1972
Jesse L. Brown	FF1089	Avondale	Apr 1971	Feb 1973
Ainsworth	FF1090	Avondale	Jun 1971	Mar 1973
Miller	FF1091	Avondale	Aug 1971	Jun 1973
Thomas C. Hart	FF1092	Avondale	Oct 1971	Jul 1973
Capodanno	FF1093	Avondale	Oct 1971	Nov 1973
Pharris	FF1094	Avondale	Feb 1972	Jan 1974
Truett	FF1095	Avondale	Apr 1972	Jun 1974
Valdez	FF1096	Avondale	Jun 1972	Jul 1974
Moinester	FF1097	Avondale	Aug 1972	Nov 1974

(This was the largest single warship class produced in the West between the end of World War II and the advent of the 'Oliver Hazard Perry' class. It was designed to provide the US Navy with a second-line anti-submarine force of ocean-going capability for the escort of convoys and amphibious forces, and was therefore modelled on the preceding 'Garcia' and 'Brooke' classes with the hull enlarged to accommodate non-pressure-fired boilers. The type has proved generally successful, though there has been some criticism of the ships' lack of manoeuvrability, resulting largely from the single-propeller propulsion arrangement, and its lack of anti-ship capability. This latter has been remedied by the use of the left-hand pair of ASROC launchers for Harpoon anti-ship missiles. The class is fitted with the Prairie/Masker bubbler system to reduce the levels of radiated noise from the hull and propeller. Seaworthiness has also been improved by the addition of higher bulwarks and strakes forward, and anti-submarine electronics have been enhanced.)

Above: The *Marvin Shields* with its ASROC launcher forward of the bridge.

Above right: The *Paul* with Sh-2 and Phalanx CIWS toward the stern.

'Koni' class FFG

(USSR)
Type: guided-missile patrol frigate
Displacement: 1,700 tons standard and 1,900 tons full load
Dimensions: length 96·7 m (317·25 ft); beam 12·8 m (42·0 ft); draught 4·2 m (13·7 ft)
Gun armament: four 76-mm (3-in) L/60 DP in two twin mountings, and four 30-mm L/65 AA in two twin mountings
Missile armament: one twin launcher for 20 SA-N-4 'Gecko' SAMs, and (Libyan and Yugoslav vessels only) four container-launchers for four SS-N-2 'Styx' anti-ship missiles (SS-N-2B on Yugoslav vessels and SS-N-2C on Libyan vessels)
Torpedo armament: none
Anti-submarine armament: two (one in Libyan variant) RBU 6000 12-barrel rocket-launchers, two racks for 24 depth charges, and (Libyan variant) four single 400-mm (15·75-in) tubes for Type 40 torpedoes
Mines: 20/30 depending on type
Aircraft: none
Electronics: one 'Strut Curve' air-search radar, one 'Don 2' or 'Palm Frond' surface-search and navigation radar, one 'Plank Shave' SS-N-2 targeting radar (Libyan ships only), one 'Pop Group' SAM fire-control radar, one 'Owl Screech' 76-mm gun fire-control radar, one 'Drum Tilt' 30-mm gun fire-control radar, one 'Herkules' medium-frequency active search and attack hull sonar, one ESM system with two 'Watch Dog' antennae/housings, two chaff launchers, one 'High Pole-B' and two 'Square Head' IFF systems
Propulsion: CODAG arrangement, with one gas turbine delivering 13,400 kW (17,970 hp) and two diesels delivering 9000 kW (12,070 hp) to three shafts
Performance: maximum speed 28 kt on gas turbine or 22 kt on diesels; range 3700 km (2,300 miles) at 14 kt
Complement: 110

Class
1. Algeria

Name	No.	Commissioned
Murat Rais	901	Dec 1980
Rais Kellich	902	Apr 1982
Rais Korfo	903	Jan 1985

(These vessels are of the 'Koni Type II' subclass with the space between the funnel and the after superstructure occupied by a large deckhouse thought to contain air-conditioning equipment.)

2. Cuba

Name	No.	Commissioned
	350	Sep 1981
	353	Feb 1984
	356	Apr 1988

(These Cuban ships are of the 'Koni Type II' subclass.)

3. East Germany

Name	No.	Commissioned
Rostock	141	Jul 1978
Berlin	142	May 1979
Halle	143	Jan 1986

(These East German ships are of the 'Koni Type I' subclass with two RBU 6000 rocket-launchers and TSR 333 navigation radar. It is thought that a fourth unit may be transferred in the near future.)

4. Libya

Name	No.	Commissioned
Al Hani	F212	Jun 1986
Al Qirdabiyah	F213	Oct 1987
	F214	1989

(These Libyan ships are of the 'Koni Type III' subclass based on the 'Koni Type II' subclass with revised anti-submarine armament and anti-ship missiles.)

5. USSR

Name	Commissioned
Delfin	1976

(This single 'Koni Type I' class light general-purpose frigate is retained by the USSR only for training of crews from those countries to which the class has been exported. All the ships have been built at the Zelenodolsk yard on the Black Sea.)

6. Yugoslavia ('Split' class)

Name	No.	Builder	Commissioned
Split	VPB31	Zelenodolsk	Feb 1980
Koper	VPB32	Zelenodolsk	Dec 1982
Kotor	VPB33	S & DE Yard	1988
Pula	VPB34	S & DE Yard	1988

(The first two units are 'Koni Type I' ships. The third and fourth units were built under licence at Kraljevica, and are in essence 'Koni Type III' ships differing from the Soviet-supplied ships in having an improved hull form of slightly greater length, two 4475-kW/6,000-hp SEMT-Pielstick 12 PA6-V80 diesels, the SS-N-2 missiles in a different location facing forward rather than aft, and the after 76-mm/3-in gun mounting replaced by two triple Mk 32 12·75-in/324-mm or ILAS 3 324-mm/12·75-in mountings for Mk 44 or A 244/S anti-submarine torpedoes.)

'Kortenaer' class FFG

(Netherlands)

Type: anti-submarine and anti-ship guided-missile frigate

Displacement: 3,050 tons standard and 3,630 tons full load

Dimensions: length 130·5 m (428·1 ft); beam 14·6 m (47·9 ft); draught 6·2 m (20·3 ft)

Gun armament: one 76-mm (3-in) OTO Melara L/62 DP in an OTO Melara Compact single mounting (to be replaced by a Super Rapid weapon of the same calibre), and one 40-mm Bofors L/70 AA in a single mounting (being replaced by one 30-mm Goalkeeper CIWS mounting)

Missile armament: two Mk 141 quadruple container-launchers for eight RGM-84 Harpoon anti-ship missiles, and one Mk 29 octuple launcher for 24 RIM-7 NATO Sea Sparrow SAMs

Torpedo armament: none

Anti-submarine armament: two Mk 32 twin 12·75-in (324-mm) mountings for Mk 46 torpedoes, and helicopter-launched weapons (see below)

Aircraft: two Westland SH-14B Lynx helicopters in a hangar aft

Electronics: one LW-08 air-search radar, one ZW-06 surface-search and navigation radar, one STIR (Signaal Track and Illumination Radar) surveillance and target-indicator radar, one radar used in conjunction with the WM-25 gun and SAM fire-control system (with data provision for SSMs), one SQS-505 active search and attack bow sonar, one SEWACO II action information system, one Daisy data-handling system, Link 10 and 11 data-links, one ESM system with warning and RAMSES jamming elements, and two Corvus chaff or Mk 36 Super RBOC chaff/flare launchers

Propulsion: COGOG arrangement, with two Rolls-Royce Olympus TM3B gas turbines delivering 51,600 hp (38,480 kW) or two Rolls-Royce Tyne RM1C gas turbines delivering 8,000 hp (5965 kW) to two shafts

Performance: maximum speed 30 kt; range 8700 km (5,405 miles) at 16 ktg

Complement: 18 + 158 with a maximum of 200 possible

Class

1. Greece

Name	No.	Builder	Laid down	Com-missioned
Elli	F450	Koninklijke Maatschappij	Jul 1977	Oct 1981
Limnos	F451	Koninklijke Maatschappij	Jun 1978	Sep 1982

(The Greek ships are very similar to the Dutch units, but have two Agusta [Bell] AB.212ASW helicopters in a lengthened hangar, Aspide rather than Sea Sparrow SAMs, shoulder-launched FIM-43 Redeye SAMs for close-range air defence, a 20-mm Phalanx Mk 15 CIWS mounting, and an ESM system with Sphinx warning element.)

Located forward of the *Kortenaer*'s bridge is the ship's 76-mm (3-in) gun and the Mk 29 octuple launcher for Sea Sparrow SAMs.

2. Netherlands

Name	No.	Builder	Laid down	Com-missioned
Kortenaer	F807	Koninklijke Maatschappij	Apr 1975	Oct 1978
Callenburgh	F808	Koninklijke Maatschappij	Jun 1975	Jul 1979
Van Kinsbergen	F809	Koninklijke Maatschappij	Sep 1975	Apr 1980
Banckert	F810	Koninklijke Maatschappij	Feb 1978	Oct 1980
Piet Heyn	F811	Koninklijke Maatschappij	Apr 1977	Apr 1981
Abraham Crijnssen	F816	Koninklijke Maatschappij	Oct 1978	Jan 1983
Philips Van Almonde	F823	Dok en Werfmaatschappij	Oct 1977	Dec 1981
Bloys Van Treslong	F824	Dok en Werfmaatschappij	April 1978	Nov 1982
Jan Van Brakel	F825	Koninklijke Maatschappij	Nov 1979	Apr 1983
Pieter Florisz	F826	Koninklijke Maatschappij	Jan 1981	Oct 1983

(Designed specifically for anti-submarine operations in the Atlantic, the 'Kortenaer' class has matured as an excellent general-purpose frigate type optimized for the anti-ship and anti-submarine roles. In the first half of the 1990s six of the class are to be extensively modernized while the other four are to be placed in reserve.)

'Krivak I', 'Krivak II' and 'Krivak III' class FFGs

(USSR)

Type: anti-aircraft, anti-ship and anti-submarine guided-missile escort frigate

Displacement: 3,000 tons standard and 3,700 tons or ('Krivak II' and 'Krivak III' class ships) 3,900 tons full load

Dimensions: length 123·5 m (405·2 ft); beam 14·0 m (45·9 ft); draught 5·0 m (16·4 ft)

Gun armament: four 76-mm (3-in) L/60 DP in two twin mountings, or ('Krivak II' class ships) two 100-mm (3·94-in) L/70 DP in single mountings or ('Krivak III' class ships) one 100-mm (3·94-in) L/70 DP in a single mounting and two 30-mm ADGM-630 CIWS mountings

Missile armament: two or ('Krivak III' class ships) one twin launchers for 40 or 20 SA-N-4 'Gecko' SAMs

Torpedo armament: two quadruple 533-mm (21-in) mountings for eight Type 53 dual-purpose torpedoes

Anti-submarine armament: one quadruple container-launcher for four SS-N-14 'Silex' missiles (not in 'Krivak III' class), and two RBU 6000 12-barrel rocket-launchers

Mines: 30/40 depending on type

Aircraft: one Kamov Ka-27 'Helix-A' helicopter in a hangar aft ('Krivak III' class only)

Electronics: one 'Head Net-C' 3D radar, one 'Don Kay', 'Palm Frond-A/B' or

'Don 2' surface-search and navigation radar, two 'Eye Bowl' SS-N-14-control radars (not in 'Krivak III' class ships), two or ('Krivak III' class ships) one 'Pop Group' SAM-control radars, one 'Owl Screech' or ('Krivak II' and 'Krivak III' class ships) 'Kite Screech' gun fire-control radar, one 'Bass Tilt' CIWS-control radar ('Krivak III' class only), one medium-frequency active search and attack hull sonar, one medium-frequency active search variable-depth sonar, one towed torpedo-decoy system, one ESM system with two 'Bell Shroud' and two 'Bell Squat' antennae/housings, four chaff launchers, and one 'High Pole-B' or ('Krivak III' class ships) 'Salt Pot' IFF system

Propulsion: COGAG arrangement, with two gas turbines delivering 41,000 kW (54,980 hp) and two gas turbines delivering 10,500 kW (14,085 hp) to two shafts

Performance: maximum speed 32 kt; range 7400 km (4,600 miles) at 15 kt or 2975 km (1,850 miles) at 30 kt

Complement: 180

Class

1. USSR ('Krivak I' class)

Name	Builder
Bditelny	Zhdanov
Bezukoroznenny	Kamysch-Burun
Bezzavetny	Kamysch-Burun
Bodry	Zhdanov
Deyatelny	Kamysch-Burun
Doblestny	Kamysch-Burun
Dostoyny	Kamysch-Burun
Druzhny	Zhdanov
Ladny	Kamysch-Burun
Leningradsky Komsomolets	Kaliningrad
Letuchy	Kaliningrad
Poryvisty	Kamysch-Burun
Pylky	Kaliningrad
Razumny	Zhdanov
Razyashchy	Zhdanov
Retivy	Kaliningrad
Silny	Zhdanov
Storozhevoy	Zhdanov
Svirepy	Zhdanov
Zadorny	Kaliningrad
Zharky	Kaliningrad

Below left: Lying at anchor off Libya, the *Razytelny* reveals the 'Krivak II' class layout with two 100-mm (3·94-in) guns aft, an SS-N-14 launcher forward and, just forward and aft of these systems, the spray-shielded locations of the pop-up launchers of the SA-N-4 SAM system.

2. USSR ('Krivak II' class)

Name	Builder
Bessmenny	Kaliningrad
Gorelivy	Kaliningrad
Gromky	Kaliningrad
Grozyashchy	Kaliningrad
Neukrotimy	Kaliningrad
Pytlivy	Kaliningrad
Razytelny	Kaliningrad
Revnostny	Kaliningrad
Rezky	Kaliningrad
Rezvy	Kaliningrad
Ryanny	Kaliningrad

3. USSR ('Krivak III' class)

Name	Builder
Dzerzhinsky	Kamysch-Burun
Imeni XXVII Sezda KPSS	Kamysch-Burun
Imeni LXX Letiya Vuk	Kamysch-Burun
Menzhinsky	Kamysch-Burun
	Kamysch-Burun
	Kamysch-Burun

Note: The 'Krivak I' class ships were built at three yards between 1970 and 1982 as anti-submarine frigates, the revised 'Krivak II' class units following from one of the three original yards between 1976 and 1981. In the late 1970s both classes were redesignated as patrol frigates in recognition of the ships' size and endurance limitations in blue-water operations. The 'Krivak III' class appeared in 1984 from another of the original three yards, and remedies some of the earlier classes' limitations, the elimination of the heavyweight anti-submarine and anti-aircraft weapons allowing the installation of a hangar and flightdeck to create a pure patrol frigate type.

'Leander Batch 2 TA' class FFG

(UK)

Type: anti-submarine and anti-ship guided-missile frigate
Displacement: 2,450 tons standard and 3,200 tons full load
Dimensions: length 372·0 ft (113·4 m); beam 41·0 ft (12·5 m); draught 19·0 ft (5·8 m)
Gun armament: two 20-mm Oerlikon AA in single mountings
Missile armament: two twin container-launchers for four MM.38 Exocet anti-ship missiles, and two quadruple launchers for Sea Cat SAMs
Torpedo armament: none
Anti-submarine armament: two Mk 32/STWS-2 triple 12·75-in (324-mm) mountings for Mk 46 or Stingray torpedoes (being removed), and helicopter-launched weapons (see below)
Aircraft: one Westland Lynx HAS.Mk 2/3 helicopter in a hangar aft
Electronics: one Type 994 air/surface-search radar, one Type 1006 navigation radar, two Type 903/904 radars used in conjunction with the MRS 3/GWS 22 gun/SAM fire-control system, one Type 184P active search and attack hull sonar, one Type 162M bottom classification hull sonar, one Type 2031Z passive search towed-array sonar, one CAAIS action information system, one ESM system with UAA-8/9 warning and Type 668/669 jamming elements, one Type 182 towed torpedo-decoy system, two Corvus chaff launchers, one Mk 36 Super RBOC chaff/flare launchers, and one SCOT satellite communications system (some ships only)
Propulsion: two Babcock & Wilcox boilers supplying steam to two sets of White/English Electric geared turbines delivering 30,000 hp (22,370 kW) to two shafts
Performance: maximum speed 28 kt; range 4,600 miles (7400 km) at 15 kt
Complement: 18 + 248

Class

1. New Zealand

Name	No.	Builder	Laid down	Commissioned
Waikato	F55	Harland & Wolff	Jan 1964	Sep 1966
Southland	F104	Yarrow	Dec 1959	Sep 1963

Right: A notable feature of the *Southland* is the Ikara anti-submarine system forward of the bridge in a large circular well. Note also the 40-mm guns flanking the bridge and, in a platform aft, the Sea Cat SAM launcher.

(F55 has two 4·5-in/114-mm guns in a Mk 6 twin mounting, no other gun armament, 12 Sea Cat SAMs for one quadruple launcher, Type 965 air-search radar and a hangar large enough to take a Lynx helicopter but normally carrying a Westland Lynx HAS.Mk 1 helicopter, whereas F104 has two quadruple SAM launchers, no 4·5-in/114-mm guns, two 40-mm Bofors guns, Type Type 993 air/surface-search radar, and one launcher for Ikara anti-submarine missiles.)

2. UK

Name	No.	Builder	Laid down	Commissioned or converted
*Cleopatra**	F28	Devonport Dockyard	Jun 1963	Nov 1975
*Sirius**	F40	Portsmouth Dockyard	Aug 1963	Oct 1977
*Phoebe**	F42	Alexander Stephen	Jun 1963	Apr 1977
Minerva	F45	Vickers	Jul 1973	Mar 1979
Danae	F47	Devonport Dockyard	Dec 1964	Dec 1980
*Juno***	F52	Thornycroft	Jul 1964	Jul 1967
*Argonaut**	F56	Hawthorn Leslie	Nov 1964	Mar 1980
Penelope	F127	Vickers	Mar 1961	Mar 1981

* 'Leander Batch 2 TA' class
** training ship

(Developed in the late 1950s and early 1960s as the Royal Navy's standard general-purpose frigate, the 'Leander' class has since been extensively developed into specialized classes. Of the narrow-beam ships a number were converted with Exocet anti-ship missiles, and these **'Leander Batch 2' class** ships in turn fall into two major subclasses, namely the basic 'Leander Batch 2' class, and 'Leander Batch 2 TA' class when fitted with only two Sea Cat launchers and the Type 2031Z towed-array sonar in addition to the Type

184 equipment. The 'Leander Batch 2' class ships have three quadruple launchers for Sea Cat SAMs, two 40-mm Bofors L/60 AA in single mountings, two 20-mm Oerlikon in GAM-B01 single mountings or (F52) two 20-mm Oerlikon AA in single mountings, Type 996 air-search and Type 994 surface-search radars, and a complement of 20 + 228. F52 has a reduced standard of weapons and electronics in her role as a training ship.)

The *Penelope* was converted as an Exocet-armed type, and was also operated experimentally with the sextuple Sea Wolf SAM system.

'Leander Batch 3' or 'Broad-Beam Leander' class FFG

(UK)

Type: anti-aircraft and anti-ship guided-missile frigate
Displacement: 2,500 tons standard and 2,960 tons full load
Dimensions: length 372·0 ft (113·4 ft); beam 43·0 ft (13·1 m); draught 18·0 ft (5·5 m)
Gun armament: (Batch 3A ships) two or (F58 and 75) three 20-mm Oerlikon AA in GAM-B01 single mountings, or (Batch 3B ships) two 4·5-in (114-mm) Vickers L/45 DP in one Mk 6 twin mounting, two 20-mm Oerlikon L/70 AA in single mountings and one 20-mm Oerlikon AA in a GAM-B01 single mounting
Missile armament: (Batch 3A ships) two twin container-launchers for four MM.38 Exocet anti-ship missiles, and one sextuple launcher for 32 Sea Wolf SAMs, or (Batch 3B ships) one quadruple launcher for Sea Cat SAMs
Torpedo armament: none
Anti-submarine armament: (Batch 3A ships) two Mk 32/STWS-1 triple 12·75-in (324-mm) mountings for Mk 46 torpedoes, and helicopter-launched weapons (see below), or (Batch 3B) one Limbo Mk 10 three-barrel mortar, and helicopter-launched weapons (see below)
Aircraft: one Westland Lynx HAS.Mk 2/3 helicopter in a hangar aft
Electronics: (Batch 3A ships) one Type 967/968 air/surface-search radar, one Type 1006 navigation radar, one Type 910 radar used in conjunction with the GWS 25 Mod 0 SAM fire-control system, one Type 162M bottom classification hull sonar, one Type 2016 active search and attack hull sonar, one CAAIS action information system, one Type 182 towed torpedo-decoy system, one ESM system with UAA-1 Abbey Hill warning and Type 690 jamming elements, two Corvus chaff launchers, and one SCOT satellite communications system (some ships only)
Electronics: (Batch 3B ships) one Type 966 air-search radar, one Type 994 surface-search radar, one Type 1006 navigation radar, one Type 903/904

radar used in conjunction with the GWS 22/MRS 3 SAM/gun fire-control system, one Type 162M bottom classification hull sonar, one Type 170B active search and attack hull sonar, one Type 184P active search and attack hull sonar, one Type 199 active search variable-depth sonar (fitted for but generally not with), one Type 182 towed torpedo-decoy system, one ESM system with UAA-8/9 or UAA-13 warning element, two Corvus chaff launchers, and one SCOT satellite communications system
Propulsion: two Babcock & Wilcox boilers supplying steam to two sets of White/English Electric geared turbines delivering 30,000 hp (22,370 kW) to two shafts
Performance: maximum speed 28 kt; range 4,600 miles (7400 km) at 15 kt
Complement: 19 + 241 in Batch 3A ships, and 15 + 220 in Batch 3B ships

Class
1. Chile

Name	No.	Builder	Laid down	Commissioned
Condell	06	Yarrow	Jun 1971	Dec 1973
Almirante Lynch	07	Yarrow	Dec 1971	May 1974
ex-*Achilles*	08	Yarrow	Dec 1967	Jul 1970

(These Chilean ships are generally similar to the British 'Leander Batch 3B' ships, and have standard and full-load displacements of 2,500 and 2,960 tons. Their weapons fit includes two 4·5-in/114-mm guns in a twin mounting, one quadruple launcher with 20 Sea Cat SAMs [to be replaced by the Israeli Barak 1 vertical-launch missile system], and two Mk 32 triple mountings for Mk 46 torpedoes. The sensors are again similar to those of the British ships, but there is no provision for variable-depth sonar as the ships carry no Limbo Mk 10 mortar, instead relying on an Aérospatiale SA 319B Alouette III Astazou for anti-submarine operations in conjunction with Type 162M, Type 170B and Type 184M hull-mounted sonars. The first two ships were built to Chilean order, and the Chilean navy hopes to buy a further four ex-British ships as these become available.)

2. New Zealand

Name	No.	Builder	Laid down	Commissioned
Canterbury	F421	Yarrow	Apr 1969	Oct 1971
Wellington	F69	Vickers	Oct 1966	Oct 1969

(These two New Zealand ships are fairly similar to the British ships, the standard armament fit being two 4·5-in/114-mm guns, one quadruple SAM launcher and two Mk 32 triple mountings for Mk 46 torpedoes. The ships have no provision for SSMs, and the embarked helicopter is a Westland Wasp HAS.Mk 1 used in conjunction with the Type 162M and Type 170B hull sonars. The radar fit is similar to that of the British 'Leander Batch 3B' ships, but an RCA R76C5 fire-control system is used for the guns and a Plessey NAUTIS command and control system is to be retrofitted.)

3. Pakistan

Name	No.	Builder	Laid down	Commissioned or converted
Shamsher	263	Yarrow	Jan 1968	Apr 1971
Zulfiqar	262	Yarrow	May 1969	May 1972

(These two are the ex-British *Diomede* and *Apollo*, and were sold to Pakistan in 1988 with all their British armament and equipment less the embarked helicopters, which are being replaced by Aérospatiale SA 319B Alouette III Astazous.)

4. UK

Name	No.	Builder	Laid down	Commissioned or converted
*Andromeda**	F57	Portsmouth Dockyard	May 1966	Dec 1980
*Hermione**	F58	Alexander Stephen	Dec 1965	Jan 1983
*Jupiter**	F60	Yarrow	Oct 1966	Jul 1983
*Scylla**	F71	Devonport Dockyard	May 1967	Apr 1983
Ariadne	F72	Yarrow	Nov 1969	Feb 1973
*Charybdis**	F75	Harland & Wolff	Jan 1967	Jun 1982

* 'Leander Batch 3A' ships

(The 'Leander' class was built over a 10-year period as an improved 'Type 12' general-purpose frigate class, the 'Broad-Beam Leander' variant adding 2 ft/0·6 m to the beam for improved seakeeping qualities. The 'Broad-Beam Leander Batch 3B' ships remained essentially unaltered except for electronic updating, but the 'Broad-Beam Leander Batch 3A' ships have been extensively updated with anti-ship missiles, an improved SAM system, STWS triple tubes for anti-submarine torpedoes, better sonar and initially a more advanced helicopter, and more modern electronic warfare equipment. The ships are now reaching the end of their lives in British service, with Chile and Pakistan keen buyers of ex-British vessels as they become available in the late 1980s and early 1990s.)

Below: The *Canterbury* is one of two New Zealand 'Leander Batch 3' class ships, and similar in all essential respects to British units.

'Lupo' class FFG

(Italy)

Type: anti-submarine and anti-ship guided-missile escort frigate

Displacement: 2,210 tons standard and 2,525 tons full load

Dimensions: length 113·2 m (371·3 ft); beam 11·3 m (37·1 ft); draught 3·7 m (12·1 ft)

Gun armament: one 127 mm (5 in) OTO Melara L/54 DP in an OTO Melara Compact single mounting, and four 40-mm Breda L/70 AA in two Dardo twin mountings

Missile armament: eight Teseo 2 container-launchers for eight Otomat Mk 2 anti-ship missiles, and one Mk 29 octuple launcher for 24 Aspide and RIM-7 Sea Sparrow SAMs

Torpedo armament: none

Anti-submarine armament: two Mk 32 triple 12·75-in (324-mm) mountings for Mk 46 torpedoes, and helicopter-launched weapons (see below)

Aircraft: one Agusta (Bell) AB.212ASW helicopter in a hangar aft

Electronics: one RAN 10S air-search radar, one SPQ 2F surface-search radar, one 3RM 20 navigation radar, one RTN 10X radar used in conjunction with two Argo NA10 SAM and 127-mm gun fire-control systems, two RTN 20X radars used in conjunction with two Dardo 40-mm gun fire-control systems, one Raytheon DE 1160B active search and attack hull sonar, one IPN 20 (SADOC 2) action information system, one ESM system with warning and jamming elements, and two SCLAR chaff/flare launchers

Propulsion: CODOG arrangement, with two Fiat/General Electric LM2500 gas turbines delivering 50,000 hp (37,285 kW) or two GMT A 230·20 M diesels delivering 5800 kW (7,780 hp) to two shafts

Performance: maximum speed 35 kt on gas turbines or 21 kt on diesels; range 8000 km (4,970 miles) at 16 kt on diesels

Complement: 16 + 169

Class

1. Iraq

Name	No.	Builder	Laid down	Com-missioned
Hittin	F14	CNR, Ancona	Mar 1982	Mar 1985
Thi Qar	F15	CNR, Ancona	Sep 1982	1986
Al Qadisiya	F16	CNR, Ancona	Dec 1983	1987
Al Yarmouk	F17	CNR, Ancona	Mar 1984	1987

(The Iraqi ships are very similar to the Venezuelan ships and differ from the Italian ships mainly in having a fixed rather than telescopic hangar for two rather than one AB.212ASW helicopters, a change that restricts the SAM armament to 16 Aspide missiles for the Albatros launcher. Other modifications are the variable-depth sonar carried by at least two of the ships, the RAN 11L/X surface-search radar, the Lambda ESM system, and the ILAS 3 triple 324-mm/12·75-in mountings for A 244/S anti-submarine torpedoes.)

2. Italy

Name	No.	Builder	Laid down	Com-missioned
Lupo	F564	CNR, Ancona	Oct 1974	Sep 1977
Sagittario	F565	CNR, Ancona	Feb 1976	Nov 1978
Perseo	F566	CNR, Ancona	Feb 1977	Mar 1980
Orsa	F567	CNR, Ancona	Aug 1977	Mar 1980

(This class was curtailed at just four units when it was realized how much superior the 'Maestrale' class promised to be.)

3. Peru

Name	No.	Builder	Laid down	Com-missioned
Meliton Carvajal	FM51	CNR, Ancona	Aug 1974	Feb 1979
Manuel Villavicencio	FM52	CNR, Ancona	Oct 1976	Jun 1979
Montero	FM53	SIMAC, Peru	Oct 1978	Jul 1984
Mariatequi	FM54	SIMAC, Peru	1979	Oct 1987

(The Peruvian ships are similar to the Italian units, having a telescopic hangar and 24 Aspide SAMs for the Albatros octuple launcher, though the missiles are manually rather than automatically reloaded, and the 40-mm mountings carried higher than in the Italian ships. The anti-submarine armament is two triple ILAS 3 mountings for 324-mm/12·75-in A 244/S torpedoes, and one AB.212SW helicopter.)

4. Venezuela

Name	No.	Builder	Laid down	Com-missioned
Mariscal Sucre	F21	CNR, Ancona	Nov 1976	May 1980
Almirante Brion	F22	CNR, Ancona	Jun 1977	Mar 1981
General Urdaneta	F23	CNR, Ancona	Jan 1978	Aug 1981
General Soublette	F24	CNR, Ancona	Aug 1978	Dec 1981
General Salom	F25	CNR, Ancona	Nov 1978	Apr 1982
Jose Felix Ribas	F26	CNR, Ancona	Aug 1979	Jul 1982

(The Venezuelan ships are similar to the Italian units, but have a fixed hangar, making it impossible to carry reload Aspide rounds for the Albatros SAM launcher, and carry SQS-29 hull-mounted sonar matched to the A 244/S torpedoes fired from the two ILAS 3 triple 324-mm/12·75-in mountings.)

Previous page, bottom: The Italian navy's 'Lupo' class frigate Perseo. Above: The 127-mm (5-in) OTO Melara gun of the 'Lupo' class frigate. Below: Seen before the installation of its Teseo 2 launchers, the Maestrale has one 127-mm (5-in) and four 40-mm guns as well as an Albatros launcher.

'Maestrale' class FFG

(Italy)
Type: anti-submarine and anti-ship guided-missile frigate
Displacement: 2,500 tons standard and 3,200 tons full load
Dimensions: length 122·7 m (405·0 ft); beam 12·9 m (42·5 ft); draught 8·4 m (27·4 ft)
Gun armament: one 127-mm (5-in) OTO Melara L/54 DP in an OTO Melara Compact single mounting, and four 40-mm Breda L/70 AA in two Dardo twin mountings
Missile armament: four Teseo 2 container-launchers for four Otomat Mk 2 anti-ship missiles, and one Albatros octuple launcher for 24 Aspide SAMs
Torpedo armament: two B516 single 533-mm (21-in) mountings for A 184 wire-guided dual-role torpedoes
Anti-submarine armament: two ILAS 3 triple 324-mm (12·75-in) mountings for A 244/S torpedoes, and helicopter-launched weapons (see below)
Aircraft: two Agusta (Bell) AB.212ASW helicopters in a hangar aft
Electronics: one RAN 10S air/surface-search radar, one SPS 702 surface-search radar, one SPN 703 navigation radar, one RTN 30X radar used in conjunction with the Argo NA30 SAM and 127-mm gun fire-control system, two RTN 20X radars used in conjunction with two Dardo fire-control systems, one Raytheon DE 1160B active search and attack hull sonar, one Raytheon DE 1164 active search variable-depth sonar, one IPN 20 (SADOC 2) action information system, one SLQ-25 Nixie towed torpedo-decoy system, one Prairie/Masker hull and propeller blade noise-suppression system, one Newton ESM system with warning and jamming elements, and two SCLAR chaff/flare launchers

Propulsion: CODOG arrangement, with two Fiat/General Electric LM2500 gas turbines delivering 50,000 hp (37,285 kW) or two GMT B 230·50 DVM diesels delivering 8200 kW (11,000 hp) to two shafts
Performance: maximum speed 33 kt on gas turbines or 21 kt on diesels; range 11,125 km (6,915 miles) at 16 kt
Complement: 24 + 208

Class

1. Italy Name	No.	Builder	Laid down	Com-missioned
Maestrale	F570	CNR, Riva Trigoso	Mar 1978	Mar 1982
Grecale	F571	CNR, Muggiano	Mar 1979	Feb 1983
Libeccio	F572	CNR, Riva Trigoso	Aug 1979	Feb 1983
Scirocco	F573	CNR, Riva Trigoso	Feb 1980	Sep 1983
Aliseo	F574	CNR, Riva Trigoso	Aug 1980	Sep 1983
Euro	F575	CNR, Riva Trigoso	Apr 1981	Jan 1984
Espero	F576	CNR, Riva Trigoso	Jul 1982	May 1984
Zeffiro	F577	CNR, Riva Trigoso	Mar 1983	May 1985

Note: The 'Maestrale' class is a development of the 'Lupo' class to meet specifically Italian requirements, sacrificing a small measure of speed to secure the better seakeeping and anti-submarine characteristics provided by a larger hull with its fixed hangar and variable-depth sonar, of which the latter can be fitted with a low-frequency passive towed array. The aft-located flightdeck measures 12·0 m (39·4 ft) by 27·0 m (88·6 ft), giving the type the ability to operate a single helicopter as large as the Agusta (Sikorsky) ASH-3D Sea King.

'Meko 140A16' class FFG

(West Germany/Argentina)
Type: anti-submarine and anti-ship guided-missile frigate
Displacement: 1,470 tons standard and 1,790 tons full load
Dimensions: length 91·2 m (299·1 ft); beam 11·1 m (36·4 ft); draught 3·4 m (11·2 ft)
Gun armament: one 76-mm (3-in) OTO Melara L/62 DP in an OTO Melara Compact single mounting, four 40-mm Breda L/70 AA in two Dardo twin mountings, and two 0·5-in (12·7-mm) machine-guns
Missile armament: two quadruple container-launchers for eight MM.40 Exocet anti-ship missiles
Torpedo armament: none
Anti-submarine armament: two ILAS 3 triple 324-mm (12·75-in) mountings for 12 A 244/S torpedoes, and helicopter-launched weapons (see below)
Aircraft: one Aérospatiale SA 319B Alouette III Astazou helicopter on a platform amidships (first three ships) or in a telescopic hangar (last three ships and due for retrofit on earlier ships)
Electronics: one DA-05/2 air/surface-search radar, one TM1226 navigation radar, one radar used in conjunction with the WM-28 gun and SSM fire-control system, two LIROD optronic directors, one Krupp-Atlas ADS-4 active search and attack hull sonar, one SEWACO action information system one Daisy data-handling system, one G1738 towed torpedo-decoy system, one ESM system with RDC-2ABC warning and RCM-2 jamming elements, and

one twin Dagaie chaff/flare launcher
Propulsion: two SEMT-Pielstick 16 PC2-5V400 diesels delivering 15,200 kW (20,385 hp) to two shafts
Performance: maximum speed 27 kt; range 7400 km (4,600 miles) at 18 kt
Complement: 11 + 82

Class

1. Argentina Name	No.	Builder	Laid down	Com-missioned
Espora	F41	AFNE Rio Santiago	Oct 1980	Jul 1985
Rosales	F42	AFNE Rio Santiago	Jul 1981	Nov 1986
Spiro	F43	AFNE Rio Santiago	Jan 1982	Nov 1987
Parker	F44	AFNE Rio Santiago	Aug 1982	1989
Robinson	F45	AFNE Rio Santiago	Jun 1983	1990
Gomez Roca	F46	AFNE Rio Santiago	Dec 1983	1991

Note: This design is essentially a scaled-down version of the 'Meko 360' frigate from the West German company Blohm und Voss. The last three ships are fitted with a telescopic hangar which is being retrofitted to the earlier ships, and the missile armament is being successively upgraded from the original two twin container-launchers for four MM.38 Exocet anti-ship missiles to eight MM.40 Exocet anti-ship missiles.

Argentina's 'Meko 140A16' class frigates have a modular update capability.

'Meko 200' class FFG

(West Germany/Turkey)

Type: anti-ship and anti-submarine guided-missile frigate

Displacement: 2,000 tons standard and 2,785 tons full load

Dimensions: length 110·5 m (362·5 ft); beam 14·2 m (46·6 ft); draught 4·0 m (13·1 ft)

Gun armament: one 5-in (127-mm) L/54 DP in a Mk 45 single mounting, and three 25-mm Seaguard CIWS mountings

Missile armament: two Mk 141 quadruple container-launchers for eight RGM-84 Harpoon anti-ship missiles, and one Albatros octuple launcher for 24 Aspide SAMs

Torpedo armament: none

Anti-submarine armament: two Mk 32 triple 324-mm (12·75-in) mountings for Mk 46 torpedoes, and helicopter-launched weapons (see below)

Aircraft: one Agusta (Bell) AB.212ASW helicopter in a hangar aft

Electronics: one DA-08 air-search radar, one AW 6 Dolphin air/surface-search radar, one STIR target-designation and tracking radar used in conjunction with the SAM fire-control system, two Contraves Seaguard radars used in conjunction with the Seaguard fire-control system, one radar used in conjunction with the WM-28 gun and SSM fire-control system, two Siemens Albis optronic directors, one Raytheon DE 1160 active search and attack hull sonar, one SEWACO action information system, Link 10 data-link, one SLQ-29 Nixie towed torpedo-decoy system, one ESM system with RAPIDS warning element, and two Mk 36 Super RBOC chaff/flare launchers

Propulsion: CODAD arrangement, with four MTU 20V 1163 TB93 diesels delivering 29,800 kW (39,970 hp) to two shafts

Performance: maximum speed 27 kt; range 7400 km (4,600 miles) at 20 kt

Complement: 24 + 156

Class

1. Australia ('Meko 200ANZ' class)

Name	No.	Builder	Laid down	Com-missioned
		Ameco		
		Ameco		
		Ameco		
		Ameco		
		Ameco		
		Ameco		
		Ameco		
		Ameco		

(The choice of this class as the Royal Australian Navy's standard frigate was announced in August 1989, the losing contender being a derivative of the Dutch 'M' class offered by AWS. The type is to carry a 5-in/127-mm main gun, Standard Missile SAMs and a Sea Sparrow Point-Defence Missile System, and provision is made for the retrofit of Harpoon anti-ship missiles and a CIWS mounting; anti-submarine capability will be considerably enhanced by the shipping of a single Sikorsky S-70B-2 Seahawk helicopter in a hangar aft. The sensor fit will include LW-08 or Sea Giraffe surveillance radar, a 9LV 200 target-acquisition and tracking radar used in conjunction with the 9LV 453 Mk 3 command and weapon-control system, Mulloka or Spherion-B active search hull sonar, and Kariwara passive towed-array sonar. The CODOG propulsion arrangement comprises one General Electric LM2500 gas turbine or two MTU 12V 1163 TB83 diesels delivering power to two shafts for a maximum speed of 27 kt and a range of 8,175 miles/13,155 km at 17 kt.)

2. Greece

Name	No.	Builder	Laid down	Com-missioned
		Blohm und Voss	1988	1992
		Hellenic Shipyards	1990	1996
		Hellenic Shipyards	1990	1996
		Hellenic Shipyards	1990	1997

(These Greek units will be similar in most essential respects to the Turkish ships apart from a CODOG propulsion arrangement with two General Electric LM2500 gas turbines or two MTU 20V 956 diesels for speed of 30 kt and 20 kt respectively, and an electronic suite that includes SPS-49 air-search radar and a combination of SQS-56 and DE 1160 sonars.)

3. New Zealand ('Meko 200ANZ' class)

Name	No.	Builder	Laid down	Com-missioned
		Ameco		
		Ameco		

(These New Zealand units, the first of a possible four ships, will be similar in most essential respects to the Australian ships, but with considerably different electronics including the Krupp 8600 ARPA navigation radar, 9LV 200 fire-control radar, Sea Giraffe target-indication radar, 9LV 453 Mk 3 action information system, Spherion B sonar, Nixie towed torpedo-decoy system, Vesta helicopter data-link system, and Mk 36 Super RBOC chaff launcher.)

4. Portugal ('Vasco da Gama' class)

Name	No.	Builder	Laid down	Com-missioned
Vasco da Gama		Blohm und Voss	Aug 1988	Nov 1990
Alvares Cabral		Howaldtswerke	Feb 1989	May 1991
Corte Real		Howaldtswerke	Aug 1989	Nov 1991

(These Portuguese ships differ somewhat from the Turkish vessels, principally in armament and propulsion. At standard and full-load displacements of 2,900 and 3,180 tons respectively they have an armament comprising eight RGM-84 Harpoon anti-ship missiles, one Mk 29 octuple launcher for RIM-7 Sea Sparrow SAMs, one 100-mm/3·94-in Creusot Loire L/55 DP gun in a Creusot Loire Compact single mounting, one Phalanx Mk 15 CIWS mounting, provision for one 25-mm Seaguard CIWS mounting, two Mk 32 triple 12·75-in/324-mm mountings for Mk 46 torpedoes, and two Westland Super Lynx helicopters. The electronics include DA-08 air-search radar, MW-08 air/surface-search radar, Type 1007 navigation radar, two STIR fire-control radars, SQS-510 active search and attack hull sonar, a SEWACO action information system with STACOS tactical command subsystem, Link 11 and 14 data-links, an ESM system with APECA Rogan II warning and AR 700 jamming elements, one SLQ-25 Nixie towed torpedo-decoy system, and two Mk 36 Super RBOC chaff/flare launchers. The propulsion is of the CODOG type using two General Electric LM2500 gas turbines delivering 53,600 hp/39,965 kW or two MTU 12V 1163 TB83 diesels delivering 6600 kW/8,850 hp to two shafts for a speed of 31 kt on gas turbines and 20 kt on diesels, and for ranges of 17,800 km/11,060 miles at 12 kt or 9100 km/5,655 miles at 18 kt. The complement is 26 + 158.)

5. Turkey ('Yavuz' class)

Name	No.	Builder	Laid down	Com-missioned
Yavuz	F240	Blohm und Voss	May 1985	Jul 1987
Turgutreis	F241	Howaldtswerke	May 1985	Feb 1988
Fatih	F242	Golcuk NY	Jan 1986	Jul 1988
Yildirim	F243	Golcuk NY	Jan 1987	Aug 1989
	F244	Golcuk NY		
	F245	Golcuk NY		

(These useful dual-role frigates are built using the Blohm und Voss modular system that greatly eases the problem of updating the sensors and weapons. Particularly notable is the potent CIWS armament and the use of a helicopter carrying Sea Skua anti-ship missiles. Early in 1989 the Turkish government added the last pair to the originally planned four units. The most important difference between these last two ships and their four predecessors will be the installation on the later ships of the Contraves/Krupp-Atlas COSYS 200 combat system to integrate the air-defence capability provided by the Aspide SAMs of the Albatros system and the three Sea Zenith cannon mountings of the Sea Guard CIWS system. Turkey's mid-1989 decision not to lease frigates of the 'Brooke' and 'Garcia' classes from the USA means it is likely that additional 'Meko 200' class units will be ordered.)

Turkey's 'Yavuz' variant of the 'Meko 200' class design is notable particularly for its potent capability against close-in air and missile attack with the Aspide SAMs of the Albatros missile system and the three large Sea Zenith mountings of the Sea Guard cannon system.

'Meko 360H2' class FFG

(West Germany/Nigeria)

Type: anti-ship and anti-submarine guided-missile frigate
Displacement: 3,630 tons full load
Dimensions: length 125·6 m (412·0 ft); beam 15·0 m (49·2 ft); draught 4·3 m (14·1 ft)
Gun armament: one 127-mm (5-in) OTO Melara L/54 DP in an OTO Melara Compact single mounting, and eight 40-mm Bofors L/70 AA in four Breda twin mountings
Missile armament: two twin and four single container-launchers for eight Otomat anti-ship missiles, and one Albatros octuple launcher for 24 Aspide SAMs
Torpedo armament: none
Anti-submarine armament: two STWS-1B triple 12·75-in (324-mm) mountings for A 244/S torpedoes, one depth-charge rack, and helicopter-launched weapons (see below)
Aircraft: one Westland Lynx Mk 89 helicopter in a hangar aft
Electronics: one AWS 5 air/surface-search radar, one RM1226 navigation radar, one STIR 127-mm gun fire-control radar, one WM-25 40-mm gun fire-control radar, one Krupp-Atlas 80 active search and attack hull sonar, one SEWACO action information system, one ESM system with RDL-2 warning and RCM-2 jamming elements, and two SCLAR chaff/flare launchers
Propulsion: CODOG arrangement, with two Rolls-Royce Olympus TM3B gas turbines delivering 56,000 hp (41,760 kW) or two MTU 20V 956 TB92 diesels delivering 7500 kW (10,060 hp) to two shafts
Performance: maximum speed 30·5 kt on gas turbines; range 12,000 km (7,455 miles) at 15 kt on diesels
Complement: 26 + 174 with a maximum of 235 possible when 35 midshipmen are carried

Above right: Even without the container-launchers for her Otomat anti-ship missiles, the *Aradu* is still impressively armed with the Albatros sytem, 127-mm (5-in) and 40-mm guns, and two triple mountings for A/S torpedoes.

Class
1. Nigeria

Name	No.	Builder	Laid down	Com-missioned
Aradu	F89	Blohm und Voss	Dec 1978	Sep 1981

Note: The modular nature of the Meko system greatly eases building, and has the additional advantage that new weapons and/or sensors can be installed simply by removing an existing module and replacing it with a new module.

'Niels Juel' class FFG

(Denmark)

Type: anti-ship guided-missile patrol frigate
Displacement: 1,320 tons full load
Dimensions: length 84·0 m (275·5 ft); beam 10·3 m (33·8 ft); draught 3·1 m (10·2 ft)
Gun armament: one 76-mm (3-in) OTO Melara L/62 DP in an OTO Melara Compact single mounting, and four 20-mm Oerlikon AA in single mountings
Missile armament: two Mk 141 quadruple container-launchers for eight RGM-84 Harpoon anti-ship missiles, one Mk 29 octuple launcher for eight RIM-7 NATO Sea Sparrow SAMs, and (to be fitted) two EX-31 launchers for 48 RIM-116 RAM SAMs
Torpedo armament: none
Anti-submarine armament: four Mk 32 single 12·75-in (324-mm) mountings for Mk 46 torpedoes, and one depth-charge rack
Mines: have minelaying capability
Aircraft: none
Electronics: one AWS 5 3D radar, one 9GR 600 surface-search radar, one Skanter Mk 009 navigation radar, two RTN 10X radars used in conjunction with the 9LV 200 Mk 2 gun fire-control system, one radar and two optical directors used with the Mk 91 SAM fire-control system, EPLO action informa- tion system, one PMS 26 active search and attack hull sonar, one ESM system with Cutlass warning element, and one SCLAR chaff/flare launcher
Propulsion: CODOG arrangement, with one General Electric LM2500 gas turbine delivering 18,400 hp (13,720 kW) or one MTU 20V 956 TB82 diesel delivering 3350 kW (4,495 hp) to two shafts
Performance: maximum speed 30 kt on gas turbine or 20 kt on diesel; range 4625 km (2,875 miles) at 18 kt
Complement: 18 + 80

Class
1. Denmark

Name	No.	Builder	Laid down	Com-missioned
Niels Juel	F354	Aalborg Vaerft	Oct 1976	Aug 1980
Olfert Fischer	F355	Aalborg Vaerft	Dec 1978	Oct 1981
Peter Tordenskiold	F356	Aalborg Vaerft	Dec 1979	Apr 1982

Note: These ships were designed by a British consortium to fit specifically into the Danish concept of seaward defence, and possess good anti-ship capability with missiles and mines, adequate air-defence capability but only poor anti-submarine potency.

The *Niels Juel* is lead ship of a small but capable Danish frigate class.

'Nilgiri' class FFG

(India)

Type: anti-ship and anti-submarine guided-missile frigate
Displacement: 2,680 tons standard and 2,960 tons full load
Dimensions: length 372·0 ft (113·4 m); beam 43·0 ft (13·1 m); draught 18·0 ft (5·5 m)
Gun armament: two 4·5-in (114-mm) Vickers L/45 DP in a Mk 6 twin mounting, and two 20-mm Oerlikon L/70 AA in single mountings
Missile armament: two container-launchers for two SS-N-2B 'Styx' anti-ship missiles (F41 and 42 only), and one (F33 and 34) or two quadruple launchers for 16 or 32 Sea Cat SAMs
Torpedo armament: none
Anti-submarine armament: one Limbo Mk 10 three-barrel mortar or (F41 and 42) one Bofors 375-mm (14·76-in) twin-barrel rocket-launcher, two ILAS 3 triple 324-mm (12·75-in) mountings for A 244/S or NST 58 torpedoes (F41 and 42), and helicopter-launched weapons (see below)
Aircraft: one HAL Chetak or (F41 and 42) Westland Sea King Mk 42 helicopter in a hangar aft
Electronics: one Type 965M (F33 only) or LW-08 air-search radar, one Type 993 (F33 only) or ZW-06 surface-search radar, one Decca 978 navigation radar, one Type 904 (F33) or HSA radar used in conjunction with one GWS 22 or two WM-44 SAM fire-control systems, one MRS3 (F33 and 34) or WM-44 gun fire-control system, one Graseby 750 active search and attack hull sonar, one Type 199 (first four ships) or Thomson-CSF (other ships) active search variable-depth sonar, one Type 16M bottom classification hull sonar, one G738 towed torpedo-decoy system, and one ESM system with UA-8 warning and Type 667 jamming elements
Propulsion: two Babcock & Wilcox boilers supplying steam to two sets of geared turbines delivering 30,000 hp (22,370 kW) to two shafts; it is believed that F38 and F41 have more power
Performance: maximum speed 27 kt or (F38 and 41) 28 kt; range 5,180 miles (8335 km) at 12 kt
Complement: 17 + 250

Class

1. India

Name	No.	Builder	Laid down	Commissioned
Nilgiri	F33	Mazagon Docks	Oct 1966	Nov 1972
Himgiri	F34	Mazagon Docks	1967	Nov 1974
Udaygiri	F35	Mazagon Docks	Jan 1973	Feb 1977
Dunagiri	F36	Mazagon Docks	Sep 1970	Feb 1976
Taragiri	F41	Mazagon Docks	1974	May 1980
Vindhyagiri	F42	Mazagon Docks	1975	Jul 1981

Note: This is an Indian licence-built version of the 'Broad-Beam Leander' class design with a number of local modifications. It is thought that retrofits are being planned to bring the sensors and armament of the first four FFs into line with the standard of the last two FFGs. Particularly notable, in addition to the anti-ship missiles, are the revisions to the after portion of each ship to enhance anti-submarine capability with a large helicopter that can double in the anti-ship role with Sea Eagle missiles.)

'Niteroi' or 'Vosper Thornycroft Mk 10' class DDG

(UK/Brazil)

Type: anti-ship and anti-submarine guided-missile escort destroyer
Displacement: 3,200 tons standard and 3,800 tons full load
Dimensions: length 424·0 ft (129·2 m); beam 44·2 ft (13·5 m); draught 18·2 ft (5·5 m)
Gun armament: one or (F42/43) two (114-mm) L/55 DP in Mk 8 single mountings, two 40-mm Bofors L/70 AA in single mountings, and (to be fitted in F40/41 and F44/55) one 2-mm Phalanx Mk 15 CIWS mounting
Missile armament: two twin container-launchers for four MM.38 Exocet anti-ship missiles or (F440/41 and F44/45) two single launchers for two MM.38 Exocet anti-ships missiles, and two triple launchers for 60 Sea Cat SAMs
Torpedo armament: none
Anti-submarine armament: one 375-mm (14·76-in) Bofors two-barrel rocket-launcher, two STWS-1 triple 12·75-in (324-mm) mountings for six Mk 46 torpedoes, one depth-charge rail with five depth charges or (F440/41 and F44/45) one Branik launcher for 10 Ikara missiles, and helicopter-launched weapons (see below)
Aircraft: one Westland Lynx Mk 21 helicopter in a hangar aft
Electronics: one AWS 2 air/surface-search radar, one ZW-06 surface-search and navigation radar, two RTN 10X radars used in conjunction with two gun fire-control systems, one CAAIS action information system, one EDO 610E active search and attack hull sonar and (F40/41 and F44/45) one EDO 700E active search variable-depth sonar, and one ESM system with RDL-2/3 warning element
Propulsion: CODOG arrangement, with two Rolls-Royce Olympus TM3B gas turbines delivering 56,000 hp (41,760 kW) or four MTU 16V 956 TB92 diesels delivering 14,600 kW (19,580 hp) to two shafts
Performance: maximum speed 30 kt on gas turbines or 22 kt on diesels; range 9825 km (6,105 miles) at 16 kt on two diesels, or 7775 km (4,830 miles) at 19 kt on four diesels or 2400 km (1,490 miles) at 28 kt on gas turbines
Complement: 22 + 187

Class

1. Brazil

Name	No.	Builder	Laid down	Commissioned
Niteroi	F40	Vosper Thornycroft	Jun 1972	Nov 1976
Defensora	F41	Vosper Thornycroft	Dec 1972	Mar 1977
Constituicao	F42	Vosper Thornycroft	Mar 1974	Mar 1978
Liberal	F43	Vosper Thornycroft	May 1975	Nov 1978
Independencia	F44	Arsenal de Marinha	Jun 1972	Sep 1979
Uniao	F45	Arsenal de Marinha	Jun 1972	Sep 1980

The Liberal is one of four ships in the 'Niteroi' class optimized for the anti-submarine role with the Branik version of the Okara system.

Note: These British-designed destroyers are notable for their high levels of automation resulting in a 50% reduction in crew numbers by comparison with destroyers of similar capabilities. F42 and 43 are in the general-purpose configuration with more powerful SSM and gun armament, while the other four (including the two Brazilian-built ships) are in anti-submarine configuration with the Branik system for Ikara anti-submarine missiles and reduced SSM and gun armament. It is believed that the whole class is to be modernized with better weapons: the two general-purpose ships are to have their four MM.39s replaced, and all the ships are to have their Sea Cat launchers replaced by 20-mm Avibras FILA systems, and to be retrofitted with the Shield decoy system. Brazil has also built a training ship, the Brasil, to the **'Niteroi (Modified)' class** design with a full-load displacement of 3,400 tons, an armament of two 40-mm Bofors AA guns, two 2600-kW (3,485-hp) Pielstick 6 PCZ-5 L-400 diesels for a speed of 18 kt, and a complement of 415 plus 200 midshipmen.

'Oliver Hazard Perry' class FFG

(USA)

Type: anti-aircraft, anti-submarine and anti-ship guided-missile escort frigate

Displacement: 2,750 tons light and 3,585 tons or (FFG8 and 36/61) 4,100 tons full load

Dimensions: length 445·0 ft (135·6 m) or (FFG8 and 36/61) 453·0 ft (138·1 m); beam 45·0 ft (13·7 m); draught 24·5 ft (5·7 m)

Gun armament: one 76-mm (3-in) OTO Melara Compact L/62 DP in a Mk 75 single mounting, and one 20-mm Phalanx Mk 15 CIWS mounting

Missile armament: one Mk 13 single launcher for four RGM-84 Harpoon anti-ship missiles and 36 RIM-66B Standard SM-1 MR SAMs

Torpedo armament: none

Anti-submarine armament: two Mk 32 triple 12·75-in (324-mm) mountings for 14 Mk 46 torpedoes, and helicopter-launched weapons

Aircraft: two Kaman SH-2F Seasprite helicopters in a hangar aft (being replaced in FFG8 and FFG36 onwards by Sikorsky SH-60B Seahawk helicopters in a modification requiring the lengthening of the ships to 453·0 ft/138·1 m by an 8-ft/2·4-m increase of the rearward slope of the transom)

Electronics: one SPS-49(V)2 or SPS-49(V)5 air-search radar, one SPS-55 surface-search and navigation radar, one STIR (modified SPG-60) and one Mk 92/94 radar used in conjunction with the Mk 92/94 (WM-25/28) gun, SAM and SSM fire-control system, one Mk 13 weapon direction system, two Mk 24 optical directors, one SQS-56 active search and attack hull sonar, one SQR-19 passive search towed-array sonar, one T Mk 6 Fanfare torpedo decoy system, one SLQ-32(V)2 ESM system with warning and jamming elements, four Mk 36 Super RBOC chaff launchers, two OE-82 satellite communications systems, one WSC-3 satellite communications transceiver, one SRR-1 satellite communications receiver, and URN-25 TACAN

Propulsion: two General Electric LM2500 gas turbines delivering 41,000 hp (30,575 kW) to one shaft

Performance: maximum speed 29 kt; range 5,200 miles (8370 km) at 20 kt

Complement: 13 + 193 including 19 aircrew

Class

1. Australia

Name	No.	Builder	Laid down	Com-missioned
Adelaide	01	Todd Pacific	Jul 1977	Nov 1980
Canberra	02	Todd Pacific	Mar 1978	Mar 1981
Sydney	03	Todd Pacific	Jan 1980	Jan 1983
Darwin	04	Todd Pacific	Jul 1981	Jul 1984
Melbourne	05	Australian Marine	Jul 1985	1991
Newcastle	06	Australian Marine	Nov 1988	1994

(The Australian ships, which were eventually to have numbered 10 but were then curtailed at six in favour of the forthcoming 'ANZAC' class, are in all vital respects similar to the US units but will be fitted or retrofitted with locally developed Mulloka hull and Kariwara towed-array sonars.)

2. Spain ('Santa Maria' or 'F80' class)

Name	No.	Builder	Laid down	Com-missioned
Santa Maria	F81	Bazan	May 1982	Oct 1986
Victoria	F82	Bazan	Aug 1983	Nov 1987
Numancia	F83	Bazan	Jan 1986	Nov 1988
Reina Sofia	F84	Bazan	Oct 1987	1990

(The Spanish ships have been much delayed as a result of the programme for the light carrier Principe de Asturias, but the ships will be similar to the US units other than having RAN 12L/X missile-detecting radar for use with the 20-mm Meroka CIWS mounting carried in place of the Phalanx, Raytheon navigation radar, and an Elettronica ESM system.)

3. Taiwan

(Early in 1989 Taiwan ordered eight 'Oliver Hazard Perry' clas FFGs, but as yet it is not known how these will differ from the American baseline standard.)

4. USA

Name	No.	Builder	Laid down	Com-missioned
Oliver Hazard Perry	FFG7	Bath Iron Works	Jun 1975	Dec 1977
McInerney	FFG8	Bath Iron Works	Nov 1977	Nov 1979
Wadsworth	FFG9	Todd Pacific	Jul 1977	Feb 1980
Duncan	FFG10	Todd Pacific	Apr 1977	May 1980
Clark	FFG11	Bath Iron Works	Jul 1978	May 1980
George Philip	FFG12	Todd Pacific	Dec 1977	Oct 1980
Samuel Eliot Morison	FFG13	Bath Iron Works	Dec 1978	Oct 1980
Sides	FFG14	Todd Pacific	Aug 1978	May 1981
Estocin	FFG15	Bath Iron Works	Apr 1978	Jan 1981
Clifton Sprague	FFG16	Bath Iron Works	Sep 1979	Mar 1981

Name	No.	Builder	Laid down	Com-missioned
John A. Moore	FFG19	Todd Pacific	Dec 1978	Nov 1981
Antrim	FFG20	Todd Pacific	Jun 1978	Sep 1981
Flatley	FFG21	Bath Iron Works	Nov 1979	Jun 1981
Fahrion	FFG22	Todd Pacific	Dec 1978	Jan 1982
Lewis B. Puller	FFG23	Todd Pacific	May 1979	Apr 1982
Jack Williams	FFG24	Bath Iron Works	Feb 1980	Sep 1981
Copeland	FFG25	Todd Pacific	Oct 1979	Aug 1982
Gallery	FFG26	Todd Pacific	May 1980	Dec 1981
Mahlon S. Tisdale	FFG27	Todd Pacific	Mar 1980	Nov 1982
Boone	FFG28	Todd Pacific	Mar 1970	May 1982
Stephen W. Groves	FFG29	Bath Iron Works	Sep 1980	Apr 1982
Reid	FFG30	Todd Pacific	Oct 1980	Feb 1983
Stark	FFG31	Todd Pacific	Aug 1979	Oct 1982
John L. Hall	FFG32	Bath Iron Works	Jan 1981	Jun 1982
Jarrett	FFG33	Todd Pacific	Feb 1981	Jul 1983
Aubrey Fitch	FFG34	Bath Iron Works	Apr 1981	Oct 1982
Underwood	FFG36	Bath Iron Works	Jul 1981	Jan 1983
Crommelin	FFG37	Todd Pacific	May 1980	Jun 1983
Curts	FFG38	Todd Pacific	Jul 1981	Oct 1983
Doyle	FFG39	Bath Iron Works	Oct 1981	May 1983
Halyburton	FFG40	Todd Pacific	Sep 1980	Jan 1984
McClusky	FFG41	Todd Pacific	Oct 1981	Dec 1983
Klakring	FFG42	Bath Iron Works	Mar 1982	Aug 1983
Thach	FFG43	Todd Pacific	Mar 1982	Mar 1984
Dewert	FFG45	Bath Iron Works	Jun 1982	Nov 1983
Rentz	FFG46	Todd Pacific	Sep 1982	Jun 1984
Nicholas	FFG47	Bath Iron Works	Sep 1982	Mar 1984
Vandergrift	FFG48	Todd Pacific	Oct 1981	Nov 1984
Robert G. Bradley	FFG49	Bath Iron Works	Dec 1982	Aug 1984
Jesse L. Taylor	FFG50	Bath Iron Works	May 1983	Dec 1984
Gary	FFG51	Todd Pacific	Dec 1982	Nov 1984
Carr	FFG52	Todd Pacific	Mar 1982	Jul 1985
Hawes	FFG53	Bath Iron Works	Aug 1983	Feb 1985
Ford	FFG54	Todd Pacific	Jul 1983	Jun 1985
Elrod	FFG55	Bath Iron Works	Nov 1983	May 1985
Simpson	FFG56	Bath Iron Works	Feb 1984	Aug 1985
Reuben James	FFG57	Todd Pacific	Nov 1983	Mar 1986
Samuel B. Roberts	FFG58	Todd Pacific	May 1984	Apr 1986
Kauffman	FFG59	Todd Pacific	Apr 1985	Feb 1987
Rodney M. Davies	FFG60	Todd Pacific	Feb 1985	May 1987
Ingraham	FFG61	Todd Pacific	Dec 1986	Aug 1989

(This is the US Navy's largest class of small combatants, and is a nicely balanced type with a judicious blend of anti-aircraft, anti-ship and anti-submarine weapons supported by advanced sensors.)

Below: The *Nicholas* is a typical unit of the 'Oliver Hazard Perry' class.

Overleaf, top: The 'Oliver Hazard Perry' class packs much into a small hull, including a 76-mm (3-in) gun just forward of the low funnel.

'Oslo' class FFG

(Norway)
Type: anti-ship and anti-submarine guided-missile coastal frigate
Displacement: 1,450 tons standard and 1,745 tons full load
Dimensions: length 96·6 m (317·0 ft); beam 11·2 m (36·7 ft); draught 5·3 m
(17·4 ft)
Gun armament: two 3-in (76-mm) L/50 DP in a Mk 33 twin mounting, one
40-mm Bofors L/70 AA in a single mounting, and two 20-mm Rheinmetall AA
in single mountings
Missile armament: six container-launchers for six Penguin Mk II anti-ship
missiles, and one Mk 29 octuple launcher for 24 RIM-7 NATO Sea Sparrow
SAMs
Torpedo armament: none
Anti-submarine armament: two Mk 32 triple 12·75-in (324-mm) mountings
for Mk 46 torpedoes, and one Terne III six-barrel rocket-launcher
Aircraft: none
Mines: provision for minelaying
Electronics: one DRBV 22 air-search radar, one TM1226 surface-search and
navigation radar, one radar used in conjunction with the Mk 91 SAM fire-
control system, one radar used in conjunction with the 9LV 200 Mk 2 gun
fire-control system, one Spherion TSM 2633 active/passive search and attack
sonar with hull and variable-depth elements, one Terne III Mk 3 active attack
hull sonar, one MSI 3100 action information system, and two chaff launchers
Propulsion: two Babcock & Wilcox boilers supplying steam to one set of
Ljungstrom/De Laval geared turbines delivering 20,000 hp (14,915 kW) to
one shaft
Performance: maximum speed 25 + kt; range 8350 km (5,190 miles) at 15 kt
Complement: 11 + 139

Note: The design of this Norwegian class is based on the US 'Dealey' class
with a higher bow and a sensor/weapon fit suited to operations along
Norway's long coast.

**The 'Oslo' class frigate *Bergen* fires one of her complement of six
Penguin anti-ship missiles, all located on the quarterdeck in
individual containers.**

Class
1. Norway

Name	No.	Builder	Laid down	Com-missioned
Oslo	F300	Marinens Hovedwerft	1963	Jan 1966
Bergen	F301	Marinens Hovedwerft	1964	Jun 1967
Trondheim	F302	Marinens Hovedwerft	1963	Jun 1966
Stavanger	F304	Marinens Hovedwerft	1965	Dec 1967
Narvik	F305	Marinens Hovedwerft	1964	Nov 1966

'Peder Skram' class FFG

(Denmark)

Type: anti-ship and anti-submarine guided-missile frigate

Displacement: 2,030 tons standard and 2,720 tons full load

Dimensions: length 112·6 m (369·4 ft); beam 12·0 m (39·5 ft); draught 3·6 m (11·8 ft)

Gun armament: two 5-in (127-mm) L/38 DP in a Mk 38 twin mounting, four 40-mm Bofors L/60 AA in single mountings, and four 20-mm Oerlikon AA in single mountings

Missile armament: two Mk 141 quadruple container-launchers for eight RGM-84 Harpoon anti-ship missiles, and one Mk 29 octuple 29 launcher for 16 RIM-7 NATO Sea Sparrow SAMs

Torpedo armament: two twin 533-mm (21-in) mountings for Tp 61 wire-guided dual-role torpedoes

Anti-submarine armament: torpedoes (see above), and one depth-charge rack

Aircraft: none

Electronics: two CWS-3 air/surface-search radars, one NWS-1 tactical radar, one Skanter Mk 009 navigation radar, one radar used in conjunction with the Mk 91 SAM fire-control system, three CGS-1 fire-control radars, one PMS 26 active search and attack hull sonar, one EPLO action information system, and one ESM system with Cutlass warning element

Propulsion: CODOG arrangement, with two Pratt & Whitney GG4A-3 gas turbines delivering 44,000 hp (32,810 kW) or two General Motors 16-567D diesels delivering 4,800 hp (3580 kW) to two shafts

Performance: maximum speed 32·5 kt on gas turbines or 13 kts on diesel

Complement: 191

Class

1. Denmark			Laid	Com-
Name	No.	Builder	down	missioned
Peder Skram	F352	Helsingors J&M	Sep 1964	May 1966
Herluf Trolle	F353	Helsingors J&M	Dec 1964	Apr 1967

Note: Featuring good anti-ship and anti-submarine capabilities, these Danish ships have a high level of automation to reduce manning requirements.

The *Peder Skram* carries powerful armament including, in place of the 'B' turret seen here, two Mk 141 quadruple launchers for Harpoon missiles.

'Type 123' class FFG

(West Germany)

Type: anti-ship, anti-submarine and anti-aircraft guided-missile frigate

Displacement: about 4,300 tons standard

Dimensions: not revealed

Gun armament: one 76-mm (3-in) OTO Melara L/62 DP in an OTO Melara Super Rapid single mounting

Missile armament: two twin container-launchers for four MM.38 Exocet anti-ship missiles, one Vertical-Launch System Mk 41 for 48 RIM-66B Standard SM-1 MR SAMs and RGM-84 Harpoon anti-ship missiles, and two EX-31 launchers for 48 RIM-116 RAM SAMs

Torpedo armament: none

Anti-submarine armament: two Mk 32 triple 12·75-in (324-mm) mountings for Mk 46 or Mk 50 Barracuda torpedoes, and helicopter-launched weapons (see below)

Aircraft: two Westland Lynx Mk 88 helicopters in a hangar aft

Electronics: one Triton G or SMART air/surface-search radar, one surface-search radar, one navigation radar, two STIR radars used in conjunction with two fire-control systems, one Krupp-Atlas DSQS-21BZ active/passive search and attack hull sonar, one passive search towed-array sonar, one action information system, one FL1800S ESM system with warning and jamming elements, two SCLAR chaff/flare launchers, and other systems

Propulsion: probably a CODOG arrangement or possibly a CODAD arrangement

Performance: not revealed

Complement: 190 excluding air group

Class

1. West Germany

Note: This promises to be a highly capable multi-role class using the modular design and construction principles developed by Blohm und Voss. The first of a planned four units was scheduled to be laid down in 1989.

'Type FS1500' class FFG

(West Germany/Colombia)
Type: anti-ship and anti-submarine guided-missile frigate
Displacement: 1,500 tons standard and 2,100 tons full load
Dimensions: length 99·1 m (325·1 ft); beam 11·3 m (37·1 ft); draught 3·7 m (12·1 ft)
Gun armament: one 76-mm (3-in) OTO Melara L/62 DP in an OTO Melara Compact single mounting, two 40-mm Bofors L/70 AA in a Breda twin mounting, and four 30-mm Oerlikon L/75 AA in two GCM-A03 twin mountings
Missile armament: two quadruple container-launchers for eight MM.40 Exocet anti-ship missiles, and (to be fitted) one Albatros octuple launcher for 16 Aspide SAMs
Torpedo armament: none
Anti-submarine armament: two Mk 32 triple 12·75-in (324-mm) mountings for Mk 46 torpedoes, and helicopter-launched weapons (see below)
Aircraft: one MBB BO105CB helicopter in a hangar aft
Electronics: one Sea Tiger II air/surface-search radar, one Castor IIB radar used in conjunction with the Vega II gun fire-control system, two Canopus optronic directors, one Krupp-Atlas ASO 4-2 active search and attack hull sonar, one TAVITAC action information system, one Phoenix ESM system with AC672 warning and Scimitar jamming elements, and two Dagaie chaff/flare launchers
Propulsion: four MTU 20V 1163 TB92 diesels delivering 20,800 kW (27,895 hp) to two shafts
Performance: maximum speed 27 kt on four diesels and 18 kt on two diesels; range 10,500 km (6,525 miles) at 18 kt
Complement: 94

The *Lekir* and her sistership carry a notably complete suite of multi-role weapons and electronics for the South-East Asia region.

Class

1. Colombia

Name	No.	Builder	Laid down	Com-missioned
Almirante Padilla	51	Howaldtswerke	Mar 1981	Oct 1983
Caldas	52	Howaldtswerke	Jun 1981	Feb 1984
Antioquia	53	Howaldtswerke	Jun 1981	Apr 1984
Independente	54	Howaldtswerke	Jun 1981	Jul 1984

(These are small but highly capable general-purpose frigates with automation to reduce manning requirements.)

2. Malaysia

Name	No.	Builder	Laid down	Com-missioned
Kasturi	25	Howaldtswerke	Jan 1983	Aug 1984
Lekir	26	Howaldtswerke	Jan 1983	Aug 1984

(The Malaysian ships differ quite considerably from the Colombian vessels in a number of important respects. At 97·3 m/319·2 ft and 3·5 m/11·5 ft the length and draught are slightly altered, modifying the standard and full-load displacements to 1,500 and 1,850 tons respectively. The gun armament is one 100-mm/3·94-in Creusot Loire L/55 DP in a Creusot Loire Compact single mounting, one 57-mm Bofors L/70 DP in a single mounting, and four 30-mm AA in two Emerlec twin mountings; the missile armament comprises two twin container-launchers for four MM.38 Exocet anti-ship missiles; the anti-submarine armament comprises one 375-mm/14·76-in twin-barrel rocket-launcher; and there is only provision for a Westland Wasp HAS.Mk 1 helicopter. The electronics fit is different, comprising one DA-08 air/surface-search radar, one TM1226C navigation radar, one radar used in conjunction with the WM-22 gun fire-control system, two LIOD optronic directors, one ASO 84-5 sonar, one ESM system with RAPIDS warning and Scimitar jamming elements, and two Dagaie chaff/flare launchers. The complement is 13 + 111. Malaysia hopes to buy another two of the class as soon as funding permits.)

'Ulsan' class FFG

(South Korea)
Type: anti-ship guided-missile frigate
Displacement: 1,600 tons standard and 2,180 tons full load
Dimensions: length 102·0 m (334·6 ft); beam 11·5 m (37·7 ft); draught 3·4 m (11·2 ft)
Gun armament: two 76-mm (3-in) OTO Melara L/62 DP in OTO Melara Compact single mountings, and eight 30-mm Oerlikon L/85 AA in four Emerlec twin mountings
Missile armament: two Mk 141 quadruple container-launchers for eight RGM-84 Harpoon anti-ship missiles
Torpedo armament: none
Anti-submarine armament: two Mk 32 triple 12·75-in (324-mm) mountings for Mk 46 torpedoes, and 12 depth charges
Aircraft: none
Electronics: one DA-05 air/surface-search radar, one ZW-06 surface-search and navigation radar, one radar used in conjunction with the WM-28 gun and SSM fire-control system, two LIROD optronic directors, one PHS 32 active search and attack hull sonar, one SLQ-25 Nixie towed torpedo-decoy system, one ESM system with warning and jamming elements, four Mk 36 Super RBOC chaff/flare launchers, and SRN-15 TACAN

Propulsion: CODOG arrangement, with two General Electric LM2500 gas turbines delivering 54,400 hp (40,560 kW) and two MTU 16V 538 diesels delivering 5000 kW (6,705 hp) to two shafts
Performance: maximum speed 34 kt on gas turbines or 18 kt on diesels; range 7400 km (4,600 miles) at 18 kt
Complement: 16 + 128

Class

1. South Korea

Name	No.	Builder	Laid down	Com-missioned
Ulsan	FF951	Hyundai Shipyards		Jan 1981
Seoul	FF952	Korea Shipbuilding		Jun 1985
Masan	FF955	Korean Tacoma		Jul 1985
Kyong Buk	FF956	Daewoo SY		1986
Chung Nam	FF957	Korea SEC		1986
Chon Nam	FF958	Hyundai Shipyards		Jun 1989
Che Ju	FF959	Daewoo SY		Jun 1989

Note: Despite a comparatively small size and displacement, these are powerful ships with modern sensors and weapons, admirably suited to the tactical needs of the South Korean navy for coastal operations.

'Van Speijk' class FFG

(Netherlands)

Type: anti-submarine and anti-ship guided-missile frigate
Displacement: 2,255 tons standard and 2,835 tons full load
Dimensions: length 113·4 m (372·0 ft); beam 12·5 m (41·0 ft); draught 5·5 m (18·0 ft)
Gun armament: one 76-mm (3-in) OTO Melara L/62 DP in an OTO Melara Compact single mounting
Missile armament: two Mk 141 quadruple container-launchers for eight RGM-84 Harpoon anti-ship missiles (351 and 352 only, with the possibility of an MM.40 Exocet fit for later ships), and two quadruple launchers for 32 Sea Cat SAMs
Torpedo armament: none
Anti-submarine armament: two Mk 32 triple 12·75-in (324-mm) mountings for Mk 46 torpedoes, and helicopter-launched weapons (see below)
Aircraft: one Westland Wasp HAS.Mk 1 helicopter in a hangar aft
Electronics: one LW-03 air-search radar, one DA-05 air/surface-search radar, one Type 1006 navigation radar, two radars used in conjunction with two WM-44 SAM fire-control systems, one radar used in conjunction with the WM-45 gun fire-control system, one LIROD optronic director, one CWE 610 active search and attack hull sonar, one SQR-18A passive towed-array sonar, one SEWACO II action information system, one Daisy data-handling system, Link 11 and 14 data-links, one ESM system with UA-13 warning element, and two Corvus chaff launchers
Propulsion: two Babcock & Wilcox boilers supplying steam to two sets of Werkspoor/English Electric geared turbines delivering 22,370 kW (30,000 hp) to two shafts
Performance: maximum speed 28·5 kt; range 8350 km (5,190 miles) at 12 kt
Complement: 180

Class

1. Indonesia

Name	No.	Builder	Laid down	Commissioned
Ahmed Yani	351	Nederlandse Dok	Jun 1964	Aug 1967
Slamet Riyadi	352	Nederlandse Dok	Oct 1963	Feb 1967
Yos Sudarso	353	Koninklijke Maatschappij	Jul 1963	Mar 1967
Oswald Siahaan	354	Koninklijke Maatschappij	Jul 1963	Aug 1967
ex-*Isaac Sweers*	355	Nederlandse Dok	May 1965	May 1968
ex-*Evertsen*	356	Koninklijke Maatschappij	Jul 1965	Dec 1967

Note: These Indonesian units were originally Dutch ships, the six-strong 'Van Speijk' class modelled very closely on the 'Leander Batch 2' class. The ships have a powerful anti-ship capability without serious detriment to short-range anti-aircraft and anti-submarine capability. The ships of the first pair

were bought early in 1986 for delivery late in the same year with a number of updating modifications such as replacement of the original two 4·5-in (114-mm) guns in a twin mounting by the current 76-mm (3-in) OTO Melara Compact mounting, the removal of the original Limbo Mk 10 mortar in favour of triple mountings for anti-submarine torpedoes, and the addition of WM-28 gun and SSM fire-control systems. The ships of the second pair were bought late in 1987 and early in 1988. The ships of the third pair were delivered in September 1989 and November 1989 respectively. The ships were delivered with all equipment and spares apart from their helicopters, the Indonesians buying Westland Wasp light helicopters in a separate deal.

The *Isaac Sweers* is one of six ex-Dutch 'Van Speijk' class frigates bought by Indonesia, the Westland Wasp HAS.Mk 1 helicopter providing limited but still useful medium-range surveillance and anti-submarine capability.

'Vosper Thornycroft Mk 5' class FFG

(UK/Iran)

Type: anti-ship and anti-submarine guided-missile frigate
Displacement: 1,100 tons standard and 1,350 tons full load
Dimensions: length 310·0 ft (94·4 m); beam 36·3 ft (11·1 m); draught 14·0 ft (4·3 m)
Gun armament: one 4·5-in (114-mm) Vickers L/55 DP in a Mk 8 single mounting, two 35-mm Oerlikon L/90 AA in a GDM-A twin mounting, two 23-mm L/80 AA in a twin mounting, and two 12·7-mm (0·5-in) machine-guns
Missile armament: one quintuple container-launcher for five Sea Killer anti-ship missiles
Torpedo armament: none
Anti-submarine armament: one Limbo Mk 10 three-barrel mortar
Aircraft: none
Electronics: one AWS 1 air/surface-search radar, one Decca 1226 surface-search radar, one Decca 629 navigation radar, two Sea Hunter radars used in conjunction with the SSM fire-control system, one Type 174 active search hull sonar, one Type 170 active attack hull sonar, one ESM system with RDL-2AC warning element, and two Mk 5 rocket flare launchers
Propulsion: CODOG arrangement, with two Rolls-Royce Olympus TM3B gas turbines delivering 46,000 hp (34,300 kW) or two Paxman Ventura die-

sels delivering 3,800 hp (2835 kW) to two shafts
Performance: maximum speed 39 kt on gas turbines or 18 kt on diesels; range 3,700 miles (5955 km) at 17 kt
Complement: 125 with a maximum of 146 possible

Class

1. Iran ('Saam' class)

Name	No.	Builder	Laid down	Commissioned
Alvand	71	Vosper Thornycroft	May 1967	May 1971
Alborz	72	Vickers	Mar 1968	Mar 1971
Sabalan	73	Vickers	Dec 1967	Jun 1972

Note: Members of a class that originally numbered four ships, these nicely balanced small combatants were designed to an imperial Iranian specification, and are air-conditioned throughout. The ships were originally called *Saam*, *Zaal* and *Rostam* respectively, and their current serviceability must be considered moderately doubtful as a result of the Western embargo on spares since the overthrow of the Shah in 1979. Their sistership *Sahand* (originally *Faramarz*) was sunk in action with US Navy forces during 1988, and in 1989 the *Sabalan* was undergoing major repairs after breaking her back in the same action.

'Vosper Thornycroft Mk 7' class FFG

(UK/Libya)

Type: anti-ship guided-missile frigate

Displacement: 1,360 tons standard and 1,780 tons full load

Dimensions: length 333·0 ft (101·5 m); beam 38·3 ft (11·7 m); draught 11·2 ft (3·4 m)

Gun armament: one 4·5-in (114-mm) Vickers L/55 DP in a Mk 8 single mounting, two 35-mm Oerlikon L/90 AA in a GDM-A twin mounting, and two 20-mm Oerlikon AA in two A41A single mountings

Missile armament: two twin container-launchers for four Otomat anti-ship missiles, and one Albatros quadruple launcher for 64 Aspide SAMs

Torpedo armament: none

Anti-submarine armament: two ILAS 3 triple 324-mm (12·75-in) mountings for A 244 torpedoes

Aircraft: none

Electronics: one RAN 12 air/surface-search radar, one RAN 10S surface-search radar, two RTN 10X radars used in conjunction with two Argo NA10 SAM and gun fire-control systems, one IPN 10 action information system, one TSM 2310 Diodon active search and attack hull sonar, and one ESM system with INS-1 warning and RDS-1 jamming elements

Propulsion: CODOG arrangement, with two Rolls-Royce Olympus TM2A gas turbines delivering 46,400 hp (34,600 kW) or two Paxman Ventura diesels delivering 3,500 hp (2610 kW) to two shafts

Performance: maximum speed 37·5 kt on gas turbines and 17 kt on diesels; range 6,550 miles (10,540 km) at 17 kt

Complement: 130

Class

1. Libya			Laid	Com-
Name	No.	Builder	down	missioned
Dat Assawari	F211	Vosper Thornycroft	Sep 1968	Feb 1973

Note: This is in essence an enlarged version of the 'Vosper Thornycroft Mk 5' class frigate with sensors and weapons largely of Italian origin.

A particular feature of the *Dat Assawari* (seen here with an old pennant number) is the incorporation of a 35-mm twin mounting on the extreme stern.

'Whitby' or 'Type 12' class FFG

(UK/India)

Type: anti-ship and anti-submarine guided-missile frigate

Displacement: 2,145 tons standard and 2,555 tons full load

Dimensions: length 369·8 ft (112·7 m); beam 41·0 ft (12·5 m); draught 17·8 ft (5·4 m)

Gun armament: four 30-mm L/65 DP in two twin mountings

Missile armament: one triple container-launcher for three SS-N-2B 'Styx' anti-ship missiles

Torpedo armament: none

Anti-submarine armament: one Limbo Mk 10 three-barrel mortar

Aircraft: one HAL Chetak helicopter in a hangar aft

Electronics: one DA-05 air/surface-search radar, one 'Square Tie' surface-search and SSM fire-control radar, one ZW-06 navigation radar, two 'Drum Tilt' 30-mm gun fire-control radars, one Type 177 active search hull sonar, one Type 170B active search and attack hull sonar, one Type 162M bottom classification hull sonar, one G738 towed torpedo-decoy system, one ESM system with Telegon IV warning element, and two Mk 5 chaff launchers

Propulsion: two Babcock & Wilcox boilers supplying steam to two sets of English Electric geared turbines delivering 30,000 hp (22,370 kW) to two shafts

Performance: maximum speed 30 kt; range 5,200 miles (8370 km) at 12 kt

Complement: 11 + 220

Class

1. India			Laid	Com-
Name	No.	Builder	down	missioned
Trishul	F42	Harland & Wolff	1957	Jan 1960

Note: Obsolete by any modern standards, this ship was at first indistinguishable from its British original but has since been heavily modified with Soviet weapons and a mix of British, Dutch and Soviet electronics. Its sister ship *Talwar* was deleted in 1988.

The original British standard *Tenby* differs considerably from the Indian unit.

'Wielingen' or 'E-71' class FFG

(Belgium)

Type: anti-ship and anti-submarine guided-missile frigate

Displacement: 1,880 tons standard and 2,430 tons full load

Dimensions: length 106·4 m (349·0 ft); beam 12·3 m (40·3 ft); draught 5·6 m (18·4 ft)

Gun armament: one 100-mm (3·94-in) Creusot Loire L/55 DP in a Modèle 1968 single mounting

Missile armament: two twin container-launchers for four MM.38 Exocet anti-ship missiles, and one Mk 29 octuple launcher for eight RIM-7 NATO Sea Sparrow SAMs

Torpedo armament: none

Anti-submarine armament: one 375-mm (14·76-in) Creusot-Loire six-barrel rocket-launcher, and two single 533-mm (21-in) mountings for 10 L5 torpedoes

Aircraft: none

Electronics: one DA-05 air/surface-search radar, one surface-search radar used in conjunction with the WM-25 fire-control system, one TM1645/9X navigation radar, two Panda optical directors, one SQS-505A active search and attack hull sonar, one SEWACO IV action information system, one SLQ-25 Nixie towed torpedo-decoy system, one ESM system with DR 2000 warning element, and two Mk 36 Super RBOC chaff/flare launchers

Propulsion: CODOG arrangement, with one Rolls-Royce Olympus TM3B gas turbine delivering 28,000 hp (20,880 kW) or two Cockerill CO-240 V12 2400 diesels delivering 4500 kW (6,035 hp) to two shafts

Performance: maximum speed 29·2 kt on gas turbine or 20 kt on diesels; range 8350 km (5,190 miles) at 18 kt

Complement: 15 + 145

The only major surface combatants ever operated by the Belgian navy, the *Wielingen* and her three sisterships are optimized for anti-submarine work.

Class				
1. Belgium			**Laid**	**Com-**
Name	**No.**	**Builder**	**down**	**missioned**
Wielingen	F910	Boelwerf	Mar 1974	Jan 1978
Westdiep	F911	Cockerill	Sep 1974	Jan 1978
Wandelaar	F912	Boelwerf	Mar 1975	Oct 1978
Westhinder	F913	Cockerill	Dec 1975	Oct 1978

Note: These Belgian-designed ships have only modest power and limited performance, but possess an attractive blend of sensors and weapons for the escort role. Plans to fit a 30-mm Goalkeeper CIWS mounting have been shelved for financial reasons.

'Yubari' or 'Type 227' class FFG

(Japan)

Type: anti-ship and anti-submarine guided-missile coastal frigate

Displacement: 1,470 tons standard and 1,690 tons full load

Dimensions: length 91·0 m (298·6 ft); beam 10·8 m (35·4 ft); draught 3·6 m (11·8 ft)

Gun armament: one 76-mm (3-in) OTO Melara L/62 DP in an OTO Melara Compact single mounting, and one 20-mm Phalanx Mk 15 CIWS mounting

Missile armament: two Mk 141 quadruple container-launchers for eight RGM-84 Harpoon anti-ship missiles

Torpedo armament: none

Anti-submarine armament: one 375-mm (14·76-in) Bofors Type 71 four-barrel rocket-launcher, and two Type 68 triple 12·75-in (324-mm) mountings for Mk 46 torpedoes

Aircraft: none

Electronics: one OPS-28C surface-search radar, one OPS-19 navigation radar, one radar used in conjunction with the Type 2-21 76-mm gun fire-control system, one OQS-4 active search and attack hull sonar, one ESM system with NOLQ-6C warning and OLT-3 jamming elements, and two Mk 36 Super RBOC chaff/flare launchers

Propulsion: CODOG arrangement, with one Rolls-Royce Olympus TM3B gas turbine delivering 22,500 hp (16,780 kW) or one Mitsubishi 6DRV 35/44 diesel delivering 3500 kW (4,695 hp) to two shafts

Performance: maximum speed 25 kt

Complement: 95

Class				
1. Japan			**Laid**	**Com-**
Name	**No.**	**Builder**	**down**	**missioned**
Yubari	DE227	Sumitomo	Feb 1981	Mar 1983
Yubetsu	DE228	Hitachi	Feb 1982	Mar 1984

Note: These two ships were developed as enlarged versions of the semi-experimental *Ishikari* with sensors and weapons optimized for the coastal anti-ship and anti-submarine roles under cover of land-based air strength.

'Alpino' class FF

(Italy)

Type: gun frigate

Displacement: 2,000 tons standard and 2,700 tons full load

Dimensions: length 113·3 m (371·7 ft); beam 13·3 m (43·6 ft); draught 3·9 m (12·7 ft)

Gun armament: six 76-mm (3-in) OTO Melara L/62 DP in OTO Melara single mountings

Missile armament: none

Torpedo armament: none

Anti-submarine armament: two Mk 32 triple 12·75-in (324-mm) mountings for Mk 46 torpedoes, one Mk 113 Menon single-barrel mortar, and helicopter-launched weapons (see below)

Aircraft: two Agusta (Bell) AB.212ASW helicopters in a hangar aft

Electronics: one SPS-12 air-search radar, one SPS 702 surface-search radar, one SPN 748 navigation radar, two RTN 10X radars used in conjunction with two Argo Orion gun fire-control systems, one Raytheon DE 1164 active search and attack sonar with hull and variable-depth elements, one Elettronica ESM system with warning and jamming elements, and two SCLAR chaff/flare launchers

Propulsion: CODAG arrangement, with two Tosi/Metrovick G.6 gas turbines delivering 15,000 hp (11,185 kW) and four Tosi OTV-320 diesels delivering 12,520 kW (16,790 hp) to two shafts

Performance: maximum speed 28 kt on diesels and gas turbines or 20 kt on diesels; range 6500 km (4,040 miles) at 18 kt

Complement: 13 + 150

Class				
1. Italy			**Laid**	**Com-**
Name	**No.**	**Builder**	**down**	**missioned**
Alpino	F580	CNR, Riva Trigoso	Feb 1963	Jan 1968
Carabiniere	F581	CNR, Riva Trigoso	Jan 1965	Apr 1968

Note: Though obsolescent, these ships have been upgraded with new sonar and retain a useful offensive capability against submarines through their two embarked helicopters.

Overleaf, top: The obsolescent *Carabiniere* is being maintained in overall capability by improvements in her anti-submarine sensor suite.

'Annapolis' class FF

(Canada)
Type: gun frigate
Displacement: 2,400 tons standard and 3,000 tons full load
Dimensions: length 371·0 ft (113·1 m); beam 42·0 ft (12·8 m); draught 14·4 ft (4·4 m)
Gun armament: two 3-in (76-mm) L/60 DP in a Mk 33 twin mounting
Missile armament: none
Torpedo armament: none
Anti-submarine armament: two Mk 32 triple 12·75-in (324-mm) mountings for Mk 46 torpedoes, and helicopter-launched weapons (see below)
Aircraft: one Sikorsky CH-124a Sea King helicopter in a hangar amidships
Electronics: one SPS-503 (CMR 1820) air/surface-search radar, one SPS-10 surface-search radar, one Sperry Mk II navigation radar, one SPG-48 radar used in conjunction with the Mk 69 (to be rebuilt as digital Mk 60) gun fire-control system, one SQS-505 active search and attack hull sonar, one SQR-501 passive search towed-array sonar, one SQS-501 bottom-classification hull sonar, one CCS-280 action information system with ADLIPS data-handling system, Link 11 and 14 data-links, one SLQ-25 Nixie towed torpedo-decoy system, one ESM system with CANEWS warning element, four Mk 36 Super RBOC chaff/flare launchers, and URN-22 TACAN
Propulsion: two Babcock & Wilcox boilers supplying steam to two sets of English Electric geared turbines delivering 30,000 hp (22,370 kW) to two shafts
Performance: maximum speed 28 kt; range 5,475 miles (8810 km) at 14 kt
Complement: 11 + 199

Class

| 1. Canada | | | Laid | Com- |
Name	No.	Builder	down	missioned
Annapolis	265	Halifax Shipyards	Jul 1960	Dec 1964
Nipigon	266	Marine Industries	Apr 1960	May 1964

Note: In the early 1980s these ships were extensively upgraded to reappear as capable anti-submarine ships with a large helicopter.

Despite her small displacement, the *Nipigon* carries a large embarked helicopter for effective long-range capability against submarines.

'Baptista de Andrade' class FF

(Portugal)
Type: gun frigate
Displacement: 1,250 tons standard and 1,380 tons full load
Dimensions: length 84·6 m (277·5 ft); beam 10·3 m (33·8 ft); draught 3·6 m (11·8 ft)
Gun armament: one 100-mm (3·94-in) Creusot Loire L/55 DP in a Modèle 1968 single mounting, and two 40-mm Bofors L/70 AA in single mountings
Missile armament: provision for the wartime shipping of two single container-launchers for two MM.38 Exocet anti-ship missiles
Torpedo armament: none
Anti-submarine armament: two Mk 32 triple 12·75-in (324-mm) mountings for Mk 46 torpedoes
Aircraft: provision for one helicopter on a platform aft
Electronics: one AWS 2 air/surface-search radar, one RM316P navigation radar, one Pollux radar used in conjunction with the Vega fire-control system, and one Diodon active search and attack hull sonar
Propulsion: two OEW/SEMT-Pielstick 12 PC2-V400 diesels delivering 8200 kW (11,000 hp) to two shafts
Performance: maximum speed 23·5 kt; range 11,000 km (6,835 miles) at 18 kt
Complement: 11 + 111 plus provision for a marine detachment

The *Baptista de Andrade* is small and, possessing only limited sensors and weapons, is of little operational value for NATO anti-submarine purposes.

Class
1. Portugal			Laid	Com-
Name	No.	Builder	down	missioned
Baptista de Andrade	F486	Bazan	1972	Nov 1974
Joao Roby	F487	Bazan	1972	Mar 1975
Afonso Cerqueira	F488	Bazan	1973	Jun 1975
Oliveira E. Carmo	F489	Bazan	1972	Feb 1975

Note: These obsolete ships are of use only for patrol and training tasks.

'Bergamini' class FF

(Italy)
Type: gun frigate
Displacement: 1,650 tons full load
Dimensions: length 95·0 m (311·7 ft); beam 11·4 m (37·4 ft); draught 3·2 m (10·5 ft)
Gun armament: two 76-mm (3-in) OTO Melara L/62 DP in OTO Melara single mountings
Missile armament: none
Torpedo armament: none
Anti-submarine armament: two Mk 32 triple 12·75-in (324-mm) mountings for Mk 46 torpedoes, one Mk 113 Menon single-barrel mortar, and helicopter-launched weapons (see below)
Aircraft: one Agusta (Bell) AB.204B helicopter in a hangar amidships
Electronics: one SPS-12 air-search radar, one SPQ 2A2 surface-search radar, one BX 732 navigation radar, one radar used in conjunction with the. Orion 3 gun fire-control system, one OG3 optical director, one SQS-40 active search and attack hull sonar, and one Elettronica ESM system with SPR-A warning element
Propulsion: four Fiat CB/LR diesels delivering 11,920 kW (15,985 hp) to two shafts
Performance: maximum speed 24 kt; range 5500 km (3,420 miles) at 18 kt
Complement: 13 + 150

Class
1. Italy			Laid	Com-
Name	No.	Builder	down	missioned
Virginio Fasan	F594	Navalmeccanica	Mar 1960	Oct 1962

Note: Despite the hangared accommodation for a single helicopter, this is an obsolete ship. Her sister ship *Carlo Margottini* was deleted in 1988.

The *Luigi Rizzo* is one of three 'Bergamini' class frigates that has already been discarded. Note the telescoping hangar of very lightweight construction, shielded at the rear only by a simple canvas screen.

'Berk' class FF

(Turkey)
Type: gun frigate
Displacement: 1,450 tons standard and 1,950 tons full load
Dimensions: length 95·2 m (312·2 ft); beam 11·8 m (37·8 ft); draught 4·4 m (14·4 ft)
Gun armament: two 3-in (76-mm) L/50 DP in a Mk 33 twin mounting
Missile armament: none
Torpedo armament: none
Anti-submarine armament: two Mk 32 triple 12·75-in (324-mm) mountings for Mk 46 torpedoes, two Hedgehog Mk 11 mortars, and one depth-charge rack
Aircraft: provision for one Agusta (Bell) AB.212ASW helicopter on a platform aft
Electronics: one SPS-40 air-search radar, one SPS-10 surface-search radar, one navigation radar, two Mk 34 radars used in conjunction with two Mk 63 gun fire-control systems, one SQS-29/31 active search and attack hull sonar, and one ESM system with WLR-1 warning element
Propulsion: four Fiat/Tosi 3-016-RSS diesels delivering 18,000 kW (24,140 hp) to one shaft
Performance: maximum speed 25 kt
Complement: not revealed

Class

1. Turkey Name	No.	Builder	Laid down	Com- missioned
Berk	D358	Golcuk Navy Yard	Mar 1967	Jul 1972
Peyk	D359	Golcuk Navy Yard	Jan 1968	Jul 1975

Note: The first major combatants built in Turkish yards, these ships are based on the US 'Claud Jones' design and are obsolescent.

'Bronstein' class FF

(USA)
Type: gun frigate
Displacement: 2,360 tons standard and 2,650 tons full load
Dimensions: length 371·5 ft (113·2 m); beam 40·5 ft (12·3 m); draught 23·0 ft (7·0 m)
Gun armament: two 3-in (76-mm) L/50 DP in a Mk 33 twin mounting
Missile armament: none
Torpedo armament: none
Anti-submarine armament: one Mk 16 octuple launcher for eight RUR-5A ASROC missiles, two Mk 32 triple 12·75-in (324-mm) mountings for Mk 46 torpedoes, and helicopter-launched weapons (see below)
Aircraft: provision for one Kaman SH-2F Seasprite helicopter on a platform aft
Electronics: one SPS-40 air-search radar, one SPS-10 surface-search radar, one LN-66 navigation radar, one Mk 35 radar used in conjunction with the Mk 56 gun fire-control system, one Mk 1 weapon direction system, one SQS-26AXR active search and attack bow sonar used in conjunction with the Mk 114 underwater weapons fire-control system, one T Mk 6 Fanfare torpedo decoy system, one ESM system with WLR-1 warning and ULQ-6 jamming elements, two Mk 36 Super RBOC chaff/flare launchers, one OE-82 satellite communications system, and one SRR-1 satellite communications receiver
Propulsion: two Foster-Wheeler boilers supplying steam to one set of De Laval geared turbines delivering 20,000 hp (14,915 kW) to one shaft
Performance: maximum speed 26 kt; range 3,685 miles (5930 km) at 20 kt
Complement: 14 + 202

Class

1. USA Name	No.	Builder	Laid down	Com- missioned
Bronstein	FF1037	Avondale	May 1961	Jun 1963
McCloy	FF1038	Avondale	Sep 1961	Oct 1963

Note: These were the first 'second-generation' frigates built by the USA after World War II, and pioneered the sonar and weapons that have become the standard for later American anti-submarine frigates.

'Cannon' class FF

(USA/Greece)
Type: gun frigate
Displacement: 1,240 tons standard and 1,900 tons full load
Dimensions: length 306·0 ft (93·3 m); beam 36·7 ft (11·2 m); draught 14·0 ft (4·3 m)
Gun armament: three 3-in (76-mm) L/50 DP in Mk 22 single mountings, four 40-mm Bofors L/60 AA in two Mk 1 twin mountings, and 14 20-mm Oerlikon L/70 AA in seven twin mountings
Missile armament: shoulder-launched FIM-43 Redeye SAMs
Torpedo armament: none
Anti-submarine armament: two Mk 32 single 12·75-in (324-mm) mountings for Mk 46 torpedoes, one Hedgehog Mk 10 mortar, eight depth-charge throwers, and one depth-charge rack
Aircraft: none
Electronics: one Decca surface-search and navigation radar, one Mk 26 radar used in conjunction with the Mk 52 3-in gun fire-control system, three Mk 51 40-mm gun fire-control systems, and one QCU-2 active search and attack hull sonar
Propulsion: diesel-electric arrangement, with four General Motors 16-278A diesels powering two electric motors delivering 6,000 hp (4475 kW) to two shafts
Performance: maximum speed 19·25 kt; range 10,350 miles (16,655 km) at 12 kt
Complement: 220

Class

1. Greece Name	No.	Builder	Laid down	Com- missioned
Aetos	D01	Tampa SB	Mar 1943	May 1944
Ierax	D31	Tampa SB	Apr 1943	Jul 1944
Leon	D54	Federal SB	Feb 1943	Aug 1943
Panthir	D67	Federal SB	Sep 1943	Jan 1944

(These elderly frigates are useful only for the patrol and training roles.)

2. Philippines			Laid	Com-
Name	**No.**	**Builder**	**down**	**missioned**
Datu Siratuna	PF77	Federal SB	Nov 1942	Jul 1943
Rajah Humabon	PF78	Norfolk NY	Jan 1943	Aug 1943

(The Filipino ships have SPS-5 surface-search and SPS-6C air-search radars, six rather than four 40-mm Bofors and six rather than 14 20-mm AA guns, no anti-submarine torpedoes, and a complement of about 165.)

Below left: The *Datu Kalantiaw* is a 'Cannon' class frigate (originally destroyer escort) which has now been deleted from Philippine service.

3. Thailand			Laid	Com-
Name	**No.**	**Builder**	**down**	**missioned**
Pin Klao	3	Western Pipe	1943	May 1944

(The Thai ship has three 3-in/76-mm and four 40-mm guns, two Mk 32 triple mountings for Mk 46 torpedoes, and SPS-5 surface-search radar.)

4. Uruguay			Laid	Com-
Name	**No.**	**Builder**	**down**	**missioned**
Uruguay	1	Federal SB	Dec 1942	Jul 1943

(The Uruguayan ship has three 3-in/76-mm and two 40-mm guns, no anti-submarine torpedoes, one SPS-6 air-search and one SPS-10 surface-search radar, and a complement of 160. Her sister ship *Artigas* was deleted in 1988.)

'Charles Lawrence' and 'Crosley' class FFs

(USA/Taiwan)
Type: gun frigate
Displacement: 1,680 tons standard and 2,130 tons full load
Dimensions: length 306·0 ft (93·3 m); beam 37·0 ft (11·3 m); draught 12·6 ft (3·8 m)
Gun armament: two 5-in (127-mm) L/38 DP in Mk 30 single mountings, six 40-mm Bofors L/60 AA in three twin mountings, and four or (833) eight 20-mm AA in two or four twin mountings
Missile armament: one Sea Chaparral quadruple launcher for 20 MIM-72 SAMs (in some ships only)
Torpedo armament: none
Anti-submarine armament: two Mk 32 triple 12·75-in (324-mm) mountings for Mk 46 torpedoes, and two depth-charge racks
Aircraft: none
Electronics: one SPS-5 surface-search radar, one Decca 707 navigation radar, one Mk 26 radar used in conjunction with the Mk 51 gun fire-control system, and one active search and attack hull sonar
Propulsion: two Foster-Wheeler boilers supplying steam to a General Electric turbo-electric drive delivering 12,000 hp (8950 kW) to two shafts
Performance: maximum speed 23·6 kt; range 5,750 miles (9255 km) at 15 kt
Complement: 200

Class

1. Ecuador			Laid	Com-
Name	**No.**	**Builder**	**down**	**missioned**
Moran Valverde	DD02	Philadelphia NY	1943	Sep 1943

(This Ecuadorean ship is an ex-'Charles Lawrence' class frigate/high-speed transport, and still serves in the latter role with a capacity for 162 troops that can be ferried in two LCUs. The armament is one 5-in/127-mm and four 40-mm AA guns, and the electronics include SPS-6 air-search and SPS-10 surface-search radars. The ship has a small helicopter platform aft.)

2. Mexico			Laid	Com-
Name	**No.**	**Builder**	**down**	**missioned**
Zacatecas	B05	Consolidated Steel	1943	Apr 1945
Usumacinta	B06	Consolidated Steel	1943	May 1945
*Coahuila**	B07	Bethlehem Steel	1944	Mar 1945
Chihuahua	B08	Norfolk NY	1943	Oct 1943

* 'Charles Lawrence' class
(These Mexican ships are similar to the Ecuadorean unit but have six 40-mm AA guns and SC air/surface-search radar.)

3. Taiwan			Laid	Com-
Name	**No.**	**Builder**	**down**	**missioned**
Tien Shan	815	Defoe SB	1944	Jun 1945
Yu Shan	832	Charleston NY	1943	Nov 1944
Hua Shan	833	Defoe SB	1944	Apr 1945
*Wen Shan**	834	Bethlehem Steel	1942	Jul 1943
Fu Shan	835	Charleston NY	1943	Jul 1944
*Lu Shan**	836	Defoe SB	1942	Aug 1943
Shou Shan	837	Bethlehem Steel	1944	Oct 1944
Tai Shan	838	Charleston NY	1943	Jan 1945
*Chung Shan**	843	Bethlehem Steel	1943	Sep 1943

* 'Charles Lawrence' class
(These Taiwanese ships comprise three ex-'Charles Lawrence' class and six ex-'Crosley' class units, and have vestigial fast-transport capability for 160 troops with one LVCP landing craft.)

'Chikugo' or 'Type 215' class FF

(Japan)
Type: gun frigate
Displacement: 1,470 tons, or (DE216 and 220) 1,500 tons or (DE222/225) 1,500 tons standard and 1,700 tons full load
Dimensions: length 93·0 m (305·1 ft); beam 10·8 m (35·5 ft); draught 3·5 m (11·5 ft)
Gun armament: two 3-in (76-mm) L/50 DP in a Mk 33 twin mounting, and two 40-mm Bofors L/60 AA in a Mk 1 twin mounting
Missile armament: none
Torpedo armament: none
Anti-submarine armament: one Mk 16 octuple launcher for eight RUR-5A ASROC missiles, and two Mk 32 triple 12·75-in (324-mm) mountings for Mk 46 torpedoes
Aircraft: none
Electronics: one OPS-14 air-search radar, one OPS-16 surface-search radar, one OPS-19 navigation radar, one Mk 33 radar used in conjunction with the Type 1B 3-in gun fire-control system, one Mk 51 40-mm gun fire-control system, one OQS-3 active search and attack hull sonar, one SQS-35J active search variable-depth sonar (in five ships), and one ESM system with NORL-5 warning element

Propulsion: four Mitsubishi/Burmeister & Wain UEV 30/40 (DE215, 217/219, 221, 223 and 225) or Mitsui 28VBC diesels delivering 12,000 kW (16,095 hp) to two shafts
Performance: maximum speed 25 kt; range 20,000 km (12,425 miles) at 12 kt
Complement: 12 + 148

Class

1. Japan			Laid	Com-
Name	**No.**	**Builder**	**down**	**missioned**
Chikugo	DE215	Mitsui	Dec 1968	Jul 1970
Ayase	DE216	Ishikawajima	Dec 1969	May 1971
Mikuma	DE217	Mitsui	Mar 1970	Aug 1971
Tokachi	DE218	Mitsui	Dec 1970	May 1972
Iwase	DE219	Mitsui	Aug 1971	Dec 1972
Chitose	DE220	Hitachi	Oct 1971	Aug 1973
Niyodo	DE221	Mitsui	Sep 1972	Feb 1974
Teshio	DE222	Hitachi	Jul 1973	Jan 1975
Yoshino	DE223	Mitsui	Sep 1973	Feb 1975
Kumano	DE224	Hitachi	May 1974	Nov 1975
Noshiro	DE225	Mitsui	Jan 1976	Aug 1977

Note: Designed for coastal operations, this class is notably quiet and is also the smallest type of warship to carry the ASROC system.

'Claud Jones' class FF

(USA/Indonesia)
Type: gun frigate
Displacement: 1,720 tons standard and 1,970 tons full load
Dimensions: length 310·0 ft (94·5 m); beam 38·7 ft (11·8 m); draught 18·0 ft (5·5 m)
Gun armament: one 3-in (76-mm) L/50 DP in a Mk 34 single mounting, two 37-mm L/63 AA in a twin mounting, and two 25-mm L/80 AA in a twin mounting
Missile armament: none
Torpedo armament: none
Anti-submarine armament: two Mk 32 triple 12·75-in (324-mm) mountings for Mk 44 torpedoes, and two Hedgehog mortars
Aircraft: none
Electronics: one SPS-6E air-search radar, one SPS-5D or (344) SPS-4 surface-search radar, one Decca 1226 navigation radar, one SPG-52 radar used in conjunction with the Mk 70 3-in gun fire-control system, one active search and attack hull sonar (SQS-44 in 341, SQS-45 in 342, SQS-39 in 343 and SQS-42

in 344) used in conjunction with the Mk 105 underwater weapons fire-control system, and one ESM system with WLR-1C warning element
Propulsion: four Fairbanks-Morse 38ND81/8 or (343) General Motors 16V-71 diesels delivering 9,200 hp (6860 kW) to one shaft
Performance: maximum speed 22 kt; range 3,450 miles (5550 km) at 18 kt
Complement: 12 + 159

Class

1. Indonesia

Name	No.	Builder	Laid down	Commissioned
Samadikun	341	Avondale	Oct 1957	May 1959
Martadinata	342	American SB	Oct 1958	Nov 1959
Monginsidi	343	Avondale	Jun 1957	Feb 1959
Ngurah Rai	344	American SB	Nov 1958	Mar 1960

Note: These are basic escorts whose utility is now limited to the patrol and training roles. The ships are being placed in reserve as the 'Van Speijk' class commissions into Indonesian service.

'Comandante Joao Belo' class FF

(Portugal)
Type: gun frigate
Displacement: 1,750 tons standard and 2,250 tons full load
Dimensions: length 102·7 m (336·9 ft); beam 11·7 m (38·4 ft); draught 4·8 m (15·7 ft)
Gun armament: three 100-mm (3·94-in) Creusot Loire L/55 DP in Modèle 1953 single mountings, and two 40-mm Bofors L/70 AA in single mountings
Missile armament: none
Torpedo armament: none
Anti-submarine armament: one 305-mm (12-in) Creusot Loire four-barrel mortar, and two triple 533-mm (21-in) mountings for L3 torpedoes
Aircraft: none
Electronics: one DRBV 22A air-search radar, one DRBV 50 surface-search radar, one RM316P navigation radar, one DRBC 31D gun fire-control radar, one DUBA 3 active search hull sonar, one SQS-17A active attack hull sonar, and one ESM system with ARBR 10 warning element
Propulsion: four SEMT-Pielstick 12 PC diesels delivering 11,920 kW

(15,985 hp) to two shafts
Performance: maximum speed 25 kt; range 13,900 km (8,635 miles) at 15 kt
Complement: 15 + 186

Class

1. Portugal

Name	No.	Builder	Laid down	Commissioned
Comandante Joao Belo	F480	A & C de Nantes	Sep 1965	Jul 1967
Comandante Hermenegildo Capelo	F81	A & C de Nantes	May 1966	Apr 1968
Comandante Roberto Ivens	F482	A & C de Nantes	Dec 1966	Nov 1968
Comandante Sacadura Cabral	F483	A & C de Nantes	Aug 1967	Jul 1969

Note: These lightly armed general-purpose frigates are based on the French 'Commandant Rivière' design. It was planned to replace the X and Y 100-mm (3·94-in) turrets with a helicopter platform and hangar or with anti-ship missiles, but this scheme now appears to have been shelved.

'Garcia' class FF

(USA)

Type: gun frigate

Displacement: 2,620 tons standard and 3,405 tons full load

Dimensions: length 414·5 ft (126·3 ft); beam 44·2 ft (13·5 m); draught 24·0 ft (7·3 m)

Gun armament: two 5-in (127-mm) L/38 DP in Mk 30 single mountings

Missile armament: none

Torpedo armament: none

Anti-submarine armament: one Mk 16 octuple launcher for eight or (last two vessels) 16 RUR-5A ASROC missiles, and two Mk 32 triple 12·75-in (324-mm) mountings for Mk 46 torpedoes

Aircraft: one Agusta (Sikorsky) ASH-3D Sea King in a hangar aft

Electronics: one SPS-40 air-search radar, one SPS-10 surface-search radar, one LN-66 navigation radar, one Mk 35 radar used in conjunction with the Mk 56 gun fire-control system, one Mk 1 weapon direction system, one SQS-26AXR or (last two ships) SQS-26BR active search and attack bow sonar used in conjunction with the Mk 114 underwater weapons fire-control system, one T Mk 6 Fanfare torpedo decoy system, one Prairie/Masker hull and propeller blade noise-suppression system, one ESM system with WLR-6 warning and ULQ-6 jamming elements, and SRN-15 TACAN

Propulsion: two Foster-Wheeler boilers supplying steam to two sets of Westinghouse or (last two ships) General Electric geared turbines delivering 35,000 hp (26,100 kW) to two shafts

Performance: maximum speed 27·5 kt; range 4,600 miles (7400 km) at 20 kt

Complement: 18 + 258

Below left: The US Navy's 'Garcia' class frigate *Voge* was to have been transferred to Turkey, but the arrangement was cancelled in 1989.

Class

1. Brazil Name	No.	Builder	Laid down	Com- missioned
Para		Bethlehem Steel	Jan 1963	May 1965
Paraiba		Avondale	Sep 1963	Dec 1965
Parana		Lockheed SB	Jul 1963	Mar 1968
Pernambuco		Lockheed SB	Apr 1963	Oct 1968

(These were the US Navy's *Bradley, Davidson, Sample* and *Albert David* [FF1041, 1045, 1048 and 1050], the first three decommissioned in 1988 and reactivated before transfer to Brazil in 1989, and the last handed over directly from active service in the same year.)

2. Pakistan Name	No.	Builder	Laid down	Com- missioned
Badr		Bethlehem Steel	Oct 1962	Dec 1964
Aslat		Defoe SB	Feb 1964	Jul 1968
Harbah		Avondale	Aug 1963	Aug 1965
Siqqat		Defoe SB	Feb 1964	Jun 1967

(These are the *Garcia, O'Callahan, Brumby* and *Koelsch* [FF1040, 1051, 1044 and 1049] decommissioned by the US Navy in 1988, and transferred to Pakistan in January, February, March and April 1989 respectively.)

Note: This 10-strong class was the US Navy successor to the 'Bronstein' class of development frigates, and are comparatively simple escort vessels optimized for the anti-submarine role with ASROC missiles and, in most cases, a light helicopter. In July 1989 Turkey decided not to proceed with its proposed lease from the US Navy of the ex-*Edward McDonnell* (FF1043) and ex-*Voge* (FF1047), built by Avondale and Defore Ship Building for commissioning in February 1965 and November 1966 respectively.

'Glover' class FF

(USA)

Type: gun frigate

Displacement: 2,645 tons standard and 3,425 tons full load

Dimensions: length 414·5 ft (126·3 m); beam 44·2 ft (13·5 m); draught 24·0 ft (7·3 m)

Gun armament: one 5-in (127-mm) L/38 DP in a Mk 30 single mounting

Missile armament: none

Torpedo armament: none

Anti-submarine armament: one Mk 16 octuple launcher for eight RUR-5A ASROC missiles, two Mk 32 triple 12·75-in (324-mm) mountings for Mk 46 torpedoes, and helicopter-launched weapons (see below)

Aircraft: provision for one Kaman SH-2F Seasprite helicopter on a platform aft

Electronics: one SPS-40 air-search radar, one SPS-10 surface-search radar, one LN-66 navigation radar, one Mk 35 radar used in conjunction with the Mk 56 gun fire-control system, one Mk 1 weapon designation system, one SQS-26AXR active/passive search and attack bow sonar and one SQS-35 active search variable-depth sonar used in conjunction with the Mk 114 underwater weapons fire-control system, one ESM system with WLR-1/3 warning and ULQ-6 jamming elements, one OE-82 satellite communications system, and one SRR-1 satellite communications receiver

Propulsion: two Foster-Wheeler boilers supplying steam to one set of Westinghouse geared turbines delivering 35,000 hp (26,100 kW) to one shaft

Performance: maximum speed 27 kt; range 4,600 miles (7400 km) at 20 kt

Complement: 18 + 262

Class

1. USA Name	No.	Builder	Laid down	Com- missioned
Glover	FF1098	Bath Iron Works	Jul 1963	Nov 1965

Note: This is a single-ship variation of the 'Garcia' class with pump-jet propulsion, the after gun of the 'Garcia' class being replaced by extra accommodation (initially for the research team).

'Isuzu' or 'Type 211' class FF

(Japan)
Type: gun frigate
Displacement: 1,490 tons standard and 1,700 tons full load
Dimensions: length 94·0 m (308·3 ft); beam 10·4 m (34·2 ft); draught 3·5 m (11·5 ft)
Gun armament: four 3-in (76-mm) L/50 DP in two Mk 33 twin mountings
Missile armament: none
Torpedo armament: none
Anti-submarine armament: one 375-mm (14·76-in) Bofors Type 71 four-barrel rocket-launcher, two Type 68 triple 12·75-in (324-mm) mountings for Mk 46 torpedoes, and (not in DE213) one Mk 1 Y-gun depth-charge thrower and one depth-charge rack
Electronics: one OPS-1 air-search radar, one OPS-16 surface-search radar, one ORD-1 navigation radar, two Mk 34 radars used in conjunction with two Mk 63 gun fire-control systems, one SQS-29 active search and attack hull sonar and (DE213) one OQA-1 active search variable-depth sonar used in conjunction with the Mk 105 underwater weapons fire-control system, and one ESM system with BLR-1 warning element

Propulsion: four Mitsubishi 12 UEV 30/40 or (DE214) Mitsui 1228V 3BU 38V diesels delivering 11,920 kW (15,985 hp) to two shafts
Performance: maximum speed 25 kt
Complement: 180

Class
1. Japan			Laid	Com-
Name	No.	Builder	down	missioned
Kitakami	DE213	Ishikawajima	Jun 1962	Feb 1964
Ooi	DE214	Maizuru	Jun 1962	Jan 1964

Note: This obsolete class is suitable only for the patrol and training roles, and the first and second ships of the class (*Isuzu* [DE211] and *Mogami* [DE212]) were converted into a support and a training ship during 1988 and 1987 respectively.

Previous page: The *Kitakami* in one of two survivors of the obsolete 'Isuzu' class, the other two ships having been converted into support units.

'Jiangnan' or 'Type 065' class FF

(China)
Type: gun frigate
Displacement: 1,350 tons standard and 1,600 tons full load
Dimensions: length 91·5 m (300·1 ft); beam 10·1 m (33·1 ft); draught 3·2 m (10·5 ft)
Gun armament: three 100-mm (3·94-in) L/56 DP in single mountings, eight 37-mm L/63 AA in four twin mountings, and four 14·5-mm (0·57-in) AA in two twin mountings
Missile armament: none
Torpedo armament: none
Anti-submarine armament: two RBU 1200 five-barrel rocket-launchers, four BMB-2 depth-charge throwers, and two depth-charge racks
Mines: 60
Aircraft: none
Electronics: one 'Ball End' surface-search radar, one 'Neptun' or 'Fin Curve' navigation radar, one 'Wok Won' 100-mm gun fire-control radar, one 'Twin Eyes' 37-mm gun fire-control radar, one 'Pegas-2M' active search and attack hull sonar, one 'Tamir' active search and attack hull sonar, and one 'High Pole-B' IFF system
Propulsion: two diesels delivering 17,900 kW (24,000 hp) to two shafts
Performance: maximum speed 28 kt; range 5200 km (3,230 miles) at 10 kt or 1675 km (1,040 miles) at 26 kt
Complement: 15 + 165

Class
1. China			Laid	Com-
Name	No.	Builder	down	missioned
Xiaguan	501	Tunglung, Guangzhou	1965	1967
Nanchong	502	Tunglung, Guangzhou	1966	1968
Kaiyuan	503	Tunglung, Guangzhou	1966	1968
Dongchuan	504	Tunglung, Guangzhou	1967	1969
Haikou	529	Tunglung, Guangzhou	1965	1967

Note: This is a Chinese development of the 'Chengdu' (Chinese version of the Soviet 'Riga' class) general-purpose frigate with larger dimensions and improved anti-submarine armament.

'Joao Coutinho' class FF

(Portugal)
Type: gun frigate
Displacement: 1,205 tons standard and 1,380 tons full load
Dimensions: length 84·6 m (277·5 ft); beam 10·3 m (33·8 ft); draught 3·6 m (11·8 ft)
Gun armament: two 3-in (76-mm) L/50 in a Mk 33 twin mounting, and two 40-mm Bofors L/70 AA in a twin mounting
Missile armament: none
Torpedo armament: none
Anti-submarine armament: one Hedgehog mortar, two depth-charge throwers, and two depth-charge racks
Aircraft: provision for one light helicopter on a platform aft
Electronics: one MLA-1B air-search radar, one RM1226C surface-search and navigation radar, one Mk 34 radar used in conjunction with the Mk 63 3-in gun fire-control system, one Mk 51 40-mm fire-control system, and one QCU-2 active search and attack hull sonar
Propulsion: two OEW/SEMT-Pielstick 12 PC2-V280 diesels delivering 7800 kW (10,460 hp) to two shafts
Performance: maximum speed 24·5 kt; range 10,925 km (6,790 miles) at 18 kt
Complement: 9 + 91 plus provision for a marine detachment of 34

Class
1. Portugal			Laid	Com-
Name	No.	Builder	down	missioned
Antonio Enes	F471	Bazan	Apr 1968	Jun 1971
Joao Coutinho	F475	Blohm und Voss	Sep 1968	Mar 1970
Jacinto Candido	F476	Blohm und Voss	Apr 1968	Jun 1970
General Pereira d'Eca	F477	Blohm und Voss	Oct 1968	Oct 1970
Augusto de Castilho	F484	Bazan	Aug 1968	Nov 1970
			Laid	Com-
Name	No.	Builder	down	missioned
Honorio Barreto	F485	Bazan	Jul 1968	Apr 1971

Note: These simple frigates are assigned to general-purpose tasks such as patrol and training. It had been planned to upgrade the class in a fashion similar to the 'Baptista de Andrade' class with anti-ship missiles and a point-defence missile system, but financial considerations have led to the abandonment of the idea. The ships are fitted with hull sonar, but it is believed that this equipment is not serviceable.

Though of comparatively recent construction, the *Joao Coutinho* and her three sisterships lack the weapons and electronics for modern high-intensity war.

'Köln' or 'Type 120' class FF

(West Germany)
Type: gun frigate
Displacement: 2,100 tons standard and 2,700 tons full load
Dimensions: length 109·9 m (360·5 ft); beam 11·0 m (36·1 ft); draught 5·1 m (16·7 ft)
Gun armament: two 100-mm (3·94-in) Creusot Loire L/55 DP in Modèle 1953 single mountings, and six 40-mm Bofors L/60 AA in two single and two twin Breda mountings
Missile armament: none
Torpedo armament: none
Anti-submarine armament: two 375-mm (14·76-in) Bofors Type 71 four-barrel rocket-launchers, four single 12·75-in (324-mm) mountings for Mk 46 torpedoes, two depth-charge throwers, and two depth-charge rails
Mines: 80
Aircraft: none
Electronics: one DA-02 air-search radar, one ZW-01 surface-search radar, two radars used in conjunction with two WM-44 100-mm gun fire-control systems, two radars used in conjunction with two WM-45 40-mm gun fire-control systems, one PAE/CWE active search and attack hull sonar used in conjunction with a Hollandse Signaalapparaten underwater weapons fire-control system, and one ESM system with warning element
Propulsion: CODAG arrangement, with two Brown-Boveri gas turbines delivering 17,900 kW (24,005 hp) and four MAN diesels delivering 8940 kW (11,990 hp) to two shafts
Performance: maximum speed 28 kt on gas turbines and diesels or 18 kt on diesels; range 1675 km (1,040 miles) at 28 kt
Complement: 17 + 193
Note: Though quite heavily armed, these general-purpose frigates are obsolete by the standards prevailing on NATO's northern theatre, and the class has been replaced in West German service by the 'Bremen' or 'Type 122' class FFGs, being transferred to Turkey as their replacements were worked into full West German service.

Name	No.	Builder	Laid down	Commissioned
Gelibolu	D360	H.C.Stulcken	Dec 1958	Dec 1962
Gemlik	D361	H.C.Stulcken	Apr 1958	Oct 1961
ex-*Lübeck*	D362	H.C.Stulcken	Oct 1959	Jun 1963
ex-*Braunschweig*	D363	H.C.Stulcken	Jul 1960	Jun 1964

West Germany's 'Köln' class frigate *Emden* has now become the Turkish navy's *Gemlik*, which retains a coastal anti-submarine utility.

'Leander Batch 1' class FF

(UK)
Type: gun frigate
Displacement: 2,450 tons standard and 2,860 tons full load
Dimensions: length 372·0 ft (113·4 m); beam 41·0 ft (12·5 m); draught 14·8 ft (4·5 m)
Gun armament: two 40-mm Bofors L/60 AA in Mk 9 single mountings
Missile armament: two quadruple launchers for Sea Cat SAMs
Torpedo armament: none
Anti-submarine armament: one launcher for Ikara missiles, one Limbo Mk 10 three-barrel mortar, and helicopter-launched weapons (see below)
Aircraft: one Westland Lynx HAS.Mk 2/3 helicopter in a hangar aft
Electronics: one Type 994 air/surface-search radar, one Type 975 navigation radar, two Type 903/904 radars used in conjunction with the GWS 22 SAM fire-control system, one Type 184P medium-range active search and attack hull sonar, one Type 170B short-range active search and attack hull sonar and one Type 162M bottom-classification hull sonar used in conjunction with the GWS 40 Ikara fire-control system, one ADAWS 5 action information system, one Type 182 towed torpedo-decoy system, one ESM system with UAA-8/9 warning and Type 668/669 jamming elements, and two Corvus chaff launchers

Propulsion: two Babcock & Wilcox boilers supplying steam to two sets of White/English Electric geared turbines delivering 30,000 hp (22,370 kW) to two shafts
Performance: maximum speed 28 kt; range 4,600 miles (7400 km) at 15 kt
Complement: 19 + 238

Class 1. UK Name	No.	Builder	Laid down	Conversion completed
Euryalus	F15	Scotts Engineering	Nov 1961	Mar 1976
Arethusa	F38	J.Samuel White	Sep 1962	Apr 1977

Note: Built as general-purpose frigates and commissioned in the mid-1960s, these ships were converted into specialist anti-submarine frigates in the mid-1970s, the 4·5-in (114-mm) gun mounting being replaced by the Ikara launcher. At the same time a second Sea Cat SAM launcher was added.

This early Batch 2 example now HMNZS *Waikato* has no external differences from the original Batch 1 vessels.

'Leopard' or 'Type 41' class FF

(UK/India)
Type: gun frigate
Displacement: 2,320 tons standard and 2,555 tons full load
Dimensions: length 339·8 ft (103·6 m); beam 40·0 ft (12·2 m); draught 16·0 ft (4·9 m)
Gun armament: two 4·5-in (114-mm) Vickers L/45 DP in a Mk 6 twin mounting, and two 40-mm Bofors L/60 AA in single mountings
Missile armament: none
Torpedo armament: none
Anti-submarine armament: one Limbo Mk 10 three-barrel mortar
Aircraft: none
Electronics: one Type 293Q surface-search radar, one Type 978 navigation radar, one Type 275 radar used in conjunction with the gun-control system, one Type 177 active search and attack hull sonar, one Type 162 bottom classification hull sonar, one ESM system with Telegon IV warning element, and two Mk 5 chaff launchers
Propulsion: eight Admiralty Standard Range Type 16 VVS ASR1 diesels delivering 12,380 hp (9230 kW) to two shafts

Performance: maximum speed 24 kt; range 8,625 miles (13,880 km) at 16 kt
Complement: 15 + 213

Class

1. Bangladesh

Name	No.	Builder	Laid down	Commissioned
Abu Bakr	F15	John Brown	Aug 1953	Mar 1957
Ali Haider	F17	William Denny	Nov 1953	Dec 1959

(These Bangladeshi ships are similar in essential respects to the Indian unit but each has two rather than one 4·5-in/114-mm twin mounting, one rather than two 40-mm AA guns, Type 965 air-search radar, Type 993 air/surface-search radar, and a complement of 15 + 220.)

2. India

Name	No.	Builder	Laid down	Commissioned
Betwa	F39	Vickers	1957	Dec 1960

(This Indian unit is used mainly in the training role, its after 4·5-in/114-mm gun mounting having been replaced by a large deckhouse. Her sister ship Beas was deleted in 1988.)

'Mackenzie' class FF

(Canada)
Type: gun frigate
Displacement: 2,380 tons standard and 2,880 tons full load
Dimensions: length 366·0 ft (111·6 m); beam 42·0 ft (12·8 m); draught 13·5 ft (4·1 m)
Gun armament: two 3-in (76-mm) L/70 DP in a Mk 6 twin mounting, and two 3-in (76-mm) L/50 DP in a Mk 33 twin mounting, or (264 only) four 3-in (76-mm) L/50 DP in two Mk 33 twin mountings
Missile armament: none
Torpedo armament: none
Anti-submarine armament: two Mk 32 triple 12·75-in (324-mm) mountings for Mk 46 torpedoes
Aircraft: none
Electronics: one SPS-12 air-search radar, one SPS-10 surface-search and navigation radar, one SPG-48 radar used in conjunction with the Mk 69 gun fire-control system, one SQS-505 active search and attack sonar with hull and variable-depth elements, one SQS-501 bottom classification hull sonar, one ADLIPS action information system, Link 11 and 14 data-links, one SLQ-25

Nixie towed torpedo-decoy system, and one ESM system with WLR-1 warning element
Propulsion: two Babcock & Wilcox boilers supplying steam to two sets of English Electric geared turbines delivering 30,000 hp (22,370 kW) to two shafts
Performance: maximum speed 28 kt; range 5,475 miles (8810 km) at 14 kt
Complement: 11 + 199

Class

1. Canada

Name	No.	Builder	Laid down	Commissioned
Mackenzie	261	Vickers	Dec 1958	Oct 1962
Saskatchewan	262	Victoria Machinery	Jul 1959	Feb 1963
Yukon	263	Burrard Dry Dock	Oct 1959	May 1963
Qu'Appelle	264	Davie SB	Jan 1960	Sep 1963

Note: These frigates were given a modest improvement by a refit in the early 1980s, but can be regarded only as obsolete.

'Makut Rajakumarn' class FF

(UK/Thailand)

Type: gun frigate
Displacement: 1,650 tons standard and 1,900 tons full load
Dimensions: length 320·0 ft (97·6 m); beam 36·0 ft (11·0 m); draught 18·1 ft (5·5 m)
Gun armament: two 4·5-in (114-mm) Vickers L/55 DP in Mk 8 single mountings
Missile armament: one Albatros octuple launcher for 24 Aspide SAMs
Torpedo armament: none
Anti-submarine armament: two STWS-2 triple 12·75-in (324-mm) mountings for Stingray torpedoes, and one depth-charge rack
Aircraft: none
Electronics: one DA-05 air/surface-search radar, one ZW-06 surface-search and navigation radar, one radar used in conjunction with WM-22 gun fire-control system, one Krupp-Atlas DSQS-21C active search and attack sonar, one Hollandse Signaalapparaten action information system, and one ESM system with warning element
Propulsion: CODOG arrangement, with one Rolls-Royce Olympus TM3B gas turbine delivering 23,125 hp (17,245 kW) or one Crossley/SEMT-Pielstick 12 PC2-V diesel delivering 4475 kW (6,000 hp) to two shafts

Performance: maximum speed 26 kt on gas turbine or 18 kt on diesel; range 5,750 miles (9250 km) at 18 kt on diesel or 1,380 miles (2220 km) at 26 kt on gas turbine
Complement: 16 + 124

Class

1. Thailand Name	No.	Builder	Laid down	Com-missioned
Makut Rajakumarn	7	Yarrow	Jan 1970	May 1973

Note: This most successful light frigate uses a high level of automation to reduce manning requirements. The ship has recently been upgraded in terms of its anti-submarine and anti-aircraft weapons, the former seeing the elimination of the Limbo mortar in favour of triple mountings for anti-submarine torpedoes, and the latter the replacement of the original Sea Cat launcher in favour of an Albatros system for Aspide SAMs. Plans to replace the after 4·5-in (114-mm) gun with anti-ship missiles, and thereby to convert the ship into an FFG, have been postponed.

Below left: The *Makut Rajakumarn* is seen in original configuration before the replacement of the Sea Cat SAM system by the Albatros system.

'Mirka I' and 'Mirka II' class FFs

(USSR)

Type: gun frigate
Displacement: 950 tons standard and 1,150 tons full load
Dimensions: length 82·4 m (270·3 ft); beam 9·1 m (29·9 ft); draught 3·0 m (9·8 ft)
Gun armament: four 76-mm (3-in) L/60 DP in two twin mountings
Missile armament: none
Torpedo armament: none
Anti-submarine armament: four or ('Mirka II' class ships) two RBU 6000 12-barrel rocket-launchers, one or ('Mirka II' class ships) two quintuple 406-mm (16-in) mountings for Type 40 torpedoes, and ('Mirka I' class ships only) one depth-charge rack
Aircraft: none
Electronics: one 'Slim Net' or (in some 'Mirka II' class ships) 'Strut Curve' air-search radar, one 'Don 2' surface-search and navigation radar, one 'Hawk Screech' gun fire-control radar, one high/medium-frequency active search and attack sonar, one high-frequency variable-depth sonar (in most ships), one ESM system with two 'Watch Dog' antennae/housings, two 'Square Head' and one 'High Pole-B' IFF systems
Propulsion: CODAG arrangement, with two gas turbines delivering 18,500 kW (24,810 hp) and two diesels delivering 9000 kW (12,070 shp) to two shafts
Performance: maximum speed 32 kt on gas turbines and diesels, and 20 kt on diesels; range 8900 km (5,530 miles) at 10 kt or 925 km (575 miles) at 30 kt
Complement: 96

A Royal Navy Wessex hovers near this Soviet Mirka I class corvette.

Class

1. USSR
9 'Mirka I' class ships
9 'Mirka II' class ships

Note: The 'Mirka I' class ships were built between 1964 and 1965 at Kaliningrad, the 'Mirka II' class ships following between 1965 and 1966 from the same yard. The basic vessel is derived from the 'Petya' class frigate with features to optimize it for the coastal anti-submarine role. In recent years the ships have been used mainly for patrol and training, and the obsolescence of the class as a whole is indicated by the recent removal into reserve of three 'Mirka I' class ships.

'Najin' class FF

(North Korea)

Type: gun frigate
Displacement: 1,500 tons full load
Dimensions: length 100·0 m (328·8 ft); beam 10·0 m (32·8 ft); draught 2·7 m (8·9 ft)
Gun armament: two 100-mm (3·94-in) L/56 DP in single mountings, four 57-mm L/80 AA in two twin mountings, four 25-mm L/60 AA in two twin mountings, and eight 14·5-mm (0.57-in) AA in four twin mountings
Missile armament: one twin container-launcher for two SS-N-2A 'Styx' anti-ship missiles (replacing the torpedo tube mounting on at least one ship)
Torpedo armament: one triple 533-mm (21-in) mounting for Type 53 torpedoes (on one ship only)
Anti-submarine armament: two RBU 1200 five-barrel rocket-launchers, two depth-charge throwers, two depth-charge racks, and torpedoes (see above)
Mines: about 30

Aircraft: none
Electronics: one 'Slim Net' air-search radar, one 'Skin Head' surface-search radar, one 'Pot Head' surface-search radar, one 'Pot Drum' gun fire-control radar, one active search and attack hull sonar, one active search variable-depth sonar, and one 'Ski Pole' IFF system
Propulsion: two diesels delivering 11,200 kW (15,020 hp) to two shafts
Performance: maximum speed 26 kt; range 7400 km (4,600 miles) at 14 kt
Complement: 180

Class

1. North Korea Name	No.	Builder	Laid down	Com-missioned
	3025		1971	1973
	3026			1975

Note: This is a simple frigate design optimized for coastal operations. The type is being converted into a limited-capability FFG with twin anti-ship missiles.

'Obuma' class FF

(Netherlands/Nigeria)
Type: gun frigate
Displacement: 1,725 tons standard and 2,000 tons full load
Dimensions: length 109·8 m (360·2 ft); beam 11·3 m (37·0 ft); draught 3·5 m (11·5 ft)
Gun armament: two 4-in (102-mm) Vickers L/45 DP in a Mk 19 twin mounting, two 40-mm Bofors AA in single mountings, and two 20-mm Oerlikon AA in single mountings
Missile armament: none
Torpedo armament: none
Anti-submarine armament: none
Aircraft: provision for a Westland Lynx Mk 89 helicopter on a platform aft

Electronics: one AWS 4 surface-search radar, and one Type 293 tactical radar
Propulsion: four MAN VV 24/30B diesels delivering 11,920 kW (15,985 hp) to two shafts
Performance: maximum speed 26 kt; range 6500 km (4,040 miles) at 15 kt
Complement: 216

Class

1. Nigeria			Laid	Com-
Name	No.	Builder	down	missioned
Obuma	F87	Wilton-Fijenoord	Apr 1964	Sep 1965

Note: This singleton unit is apparently in poor condition, the sonar having been removed and the Squid mortar being inoperative, and is used mainly for patrol and training.

'Petya I', 'Petya I (Modified)', 'Petya II' and 'Petya II (Modified)' class FFs

(USSR)
Type: gun frigate
Displacement: 950 tons standard and 1,150 tons or ('Petya II' classes) 1,180 tons full load
Dimensions: length 81·8 m (268·4 ft) or ('Petya II' classes) 82·5 m (270·7 ft); beam 9·1 m (29·9 ft); draught 2·9 m (9·5 ft)
Gun armament: four 76-mm (3-in) L/60 DP in two twin mountings
Missile armament: none
Torpedo armament: none
Anti-submarine armament: four ('Petya I' class) or two ('Petya I [Modified]' class) RBU 2500 16-barrel rocket-launchers, or ('Petya II' classes) two RBU 6000 12-barrel rocket-launchers, one ('Petya I' classes) or two ('Petya II' classes) quintuple 406-mm (16-in) mountings for Type 40 torpedoes, and two or ('Petya I [Modified]' class) one rack for 24 or 12 depth charges
Mines: 20/30 depending on type (not in 'Petya I [Modified]' class)
Aircraft: none
Electronics: one 'Slim Net' or ('Petya II' classes) 'Strut Curve' air/surface-search radar, one 'Neptun' or 'Don 2' or ('Petya II' classes) 'Don 2' navigation radar, one 'Hawk Screech' gun fire-control radar, one high/medium-frequency active search and attack hull sonar, one high-frequency active search variable-depth sonar (some ships only), one ESM system with two 'Watch Dog' antennae/housings, two 'Square Head' and one 'High Pole-B' IFF systems or ('Petya II' classes) one 'High Pole-B' IFF system
Propulsion: CODAG arrangement, with two gas turbines delivering 22,375 kW (30,010 hp) and one Type 61V-3 diesel delivering 4475 kW (6,000 hp) to three shafts
Performance: maximum speed 32 kt; range 9000 km (5,590 miles) at 10 kt or 850 km (530 miles) at 29 kt
Complement: 98

Class

1. Ethiopia

Name	No.	Builder
Zerai Deres	1616	Kaliningrad
	1617	Kaliningrad

The 'Petya II' class is identifiable by its two mountings for torpedoes, the after unit replacing two RBU 2500 anti-submarine rocket launchers. The ships are used mainly for training and patrol in coastal waters.

(These are 'Petya II' class ships transferred in July 1983 and March 1984 respectively.)

2. India ('Petya III' class)

Name	No.	Builder
Arnala	P68	Kaliningrad
Androth	P69	Kaliningrad
Anjadip	P73	Khabarovsk
Andaman	P74	Khabarovsk
Amini	P75	Khabarovsk
Kamorta	P77	Kaliningrad
Kadmath	P78	Kaliningrad
Katchal	P81	Khabarovsk

(These Indian ships are all of the 'Petya III' class, a variant of the 'Petya II' class with one triple 533-mm/21-in mounting for Type 53 torpedoes in place of the two 406-mm/16-in mountings for Type 40 torpedoes, and four RBU 2500 in place of two RBU 6000 rocket-launchers. Two of the original 10 units have been paid off.)

3. Syria ('Petya III' class)

Name	No.	Builder
	12	Kaliningrad
	14	Kaliningrad

(These Syrian ships are of the 'Petya III' class generally similar to the Indian ships.)

4. USSR
6 'Petya I' class ships
10 'Petya I (Modified)' class ships
15 'Petya II' class ships
1 'Petya II (Modified)' class ship
(The 'Petya I' class was built at Kaliningrad and Komsomolsk between 1961 and 1964, and followed by the 'Petya II' class between 1964 and 1969. The latter type differs mainly in having an additional torpedo tube mounting and improved anti-submarine rocket launchers. Both types were planned for the coastal anti-submarine role, and many were converted as trials vessels as later ships took over their primary role. Most are used now for patrol and training. Three ships have been deleted and about half the survivors are in reserve.)

5. Vietnam
3 'Petya II' class ships
2 'Petya III' class ships
(These units were transferred in December 1978 [two 'Petya III' class ships], December 1983 [two 'Petya II' class ships] and January 1984 [one 'Petya II' class ship].)

'PF103' class FF

(USA/Iran)

Type: gun frigate

Displacement: 900 tons standard and 1,135 tons full load

Dimensions: length 275·0 ft (83·8 m); beam 33·0 ft (10·1 m); draught 10·0 ft (3·0 m)

Gun armament: two 3-in (76-mm) L/50 DP in Mk 34 single mountings, two 40-mm Bofors L/60 AA in a twin mounting, two 23-mm L/80 AA in a twin mounting, and two 12·7-mm (0·5-in) machine-guns

Missile armament: none

Torpedo armament: none

Anti-submarine armament: four depth-charge throwers, and two Mk 9 racks for 24 depth charges

Aircraft: none

Electronics: one SPS-6C air-search radar, one Raytheon 1650 navigation radar, one Mk 34 radar used in conjunction with the Mk 63 gun fire-control system, one Mk 51 40-mm gun fire-control system, and one SQS-17 active search and attack hull sonar

Propulsion: two Fairbanks-Morse 38TD diesels delivering 5,600 hp (4175 kW) to two shafts

Performance: maximum speed 20 kt; range 3,500 miles (5635 km) at 15 kt

Complement: 140

Class

1. Iran

Name	No.	Builder	Laid down	Commissioned
Bayandor	81	Levingstone SB	Aug 1962	May 1964
Naghdi	82	Levingstone SB	Sep 1962	Jul 1964

(These are simple patrol frigates of limited performance and firepower. Two other units, *Khanamuie* and *Milanian*, were sunk in the Gulf War.)

2. Thailand

Name	No.	Builder	Laid down	Commissioned
Tapi	5	American SB	Apr 1970	Nov 1971
Khirirat	6	Norfolk SB	Feb 1972	Aug 1974

(The Thai ships differ from the Iranian units in having standard and full-load displacements of 885 and 1,170 tons respectively, an armament of one 76-mm/3-in OTO Melara L/62 DP in an OTO Melara Compact single mounting [with associated WM-25 radar fire-control system], one 40-mm Bofors L/70 AA, two 20-mm Oerlikon AA and two 0·5-in/12·7-mm machine-guns, and additional anti-submarine armament in the form of two Mk 32 triple 12·75-in/324-mm mountings for Mk 46 torpedoes used in conjunction with Krupp-Atlas DSQS-21C hull sonar. The ships have DA-05 air/surface-search radar.)

'President' class FF

(UK/South Africa)

Type: gun frigate

Displacement: 2,380 tons standard and 2,800 tons full load

Dimensions: length 370·0 ft (112·8 m); beam 41·1 ft (12·5 m); draught 17·3 ft (5·3 m)

Gun armament: two 4·5-in (114-mm) Vickers L/50 DP in a Mk 6 twin mounting, and two 40-mm Bofors L/70 AA in single mountings

Missile armament: none

Torpedo armament: none

Anti-submarine armament: two Mk 32 triple 12·75-in (324-mm) mountings for Mk 44 torpedoes, one Limbo Mk 10 three-barrel mortar, and helicopter-launched weapons (see below)

Aircraft: one Westland Wasp HAS.Mk 1 helicopter on a platform aft

Electronics: one Jupiter air-search radar, one Type 293 surface-search radar, one radar used in conjunction with the Argo NA9C gun fire-control system, one Type 177 active search hull sonar, one Type 170 active attack hull sonar, and one ESM system with UA-8/9 warning element

Propulsion: two Babcock & Wilcox boilers supplying steam to two sets of geared turbines delivering 30,000 hp (22,370 kW) to two shafts

Performance: maximum speed 29 kt; range 5,200 miles (8370 km) at 12 kt

Complement: 13 + 190

Class

1. South Africa

Name	No.	Builder	Laid down	Commissioned
President Pretorius	F145	Yarrow	Nov 1960	Mar 1964
President Steyn	F147	Alexander Stephens	May 1960	Apr 1963

Note: These are British 'Rothesay' or 'Type 12' class frigates revised to carry a light helicopter in a hangar made possible by the removal of one Limbo mortar. The ships are presently in reserve, though there are apparently plans to modernize the two ships thoroughly (with a hangar and platform aft for an Aérospatiale SA 330 Puma helicopter) and return them to full service.

'Rahmat' class FF

(UK/Malaysia)

Type: gun frigate
Displacement: 1,250 tons standard and 1,600 tons full load
Dimensions: length 308·0 ft (93·9 m); beam 34·1 ft (10·4 m); draught 14·8 ft (4·5 m)
Gun armament: one 4·5-in (114-mm) Vickers L/45 DP in a Mk 8 single mounting, and three 40-mm Bofors L/70 AA in single mountings
Missile armament: none
Torpedo armament: none
Anti-submarine armament: one Limbo Mk 10 three-barrel mortar
Aircraft: provision for a Westland Wasp HAS.Mk 1 helicopter on a hatch over the Limbo well
Electronics: one LW-02 air-search radar, one Decca 626 surface-search radar, one MS 32 navigation radar, one radar used in conjunction with the WM-22 gun fire-control system, one Type 174 active search hull sonar, one Type 170B active attack hull sonar, one ESM system with UA-3 warning and FH-4 jamming elements, and two Mk 1 chaff launchers

Propulsion: CODOG arrangement, with one Rolls-Royce Olympus TM1B gas turbine delivering 19,500 hp (14,545 kW) or one Crossley/SEMT-Pielstick SPC 2V diesel delivering 2870 kW (3,850 hp) to two shafts
Performance: maximum speed 26 kt on gas turbine or 16 kt on diesel; range 6,900 miles (11,105 km) at 16 kt
Complement: 140

Class

1. Malaysia			Laid	Com-
Name	No.	Builder	down	missioned
Rahmat	24	Yarrow	Feb 1966	Mar 1971

Note: This is a capable general-purpose frigate by South-East Asian standards, and the comparatively high level of automation allows a useful reduction in manning requirements. In 1983 the quadruple launcher for Sea Cat SAMs was replaced by a third 40-mm Bofors AA gun.

Previous page: The *Rahmat* is notable by South-East Asian standards for its good electronics and the low manning level made possible by automation.

'Restigouche (Improved)' class FF

(Canada)

Type: gun frigate
Displacement: 2,390 tons standard and 2,900 tons full load
Dimensions: length 371·0 ft (113·1 m); beam 42·0 ft (12·8 m); draught 14·1 ft (4·3 m)
Gun armament: two 3-in (76-mm) L/70 DP in a Mk 6 twin mounting
Missile armament: none
Torpedo armament: none
Anti-submarine armament: one Mk 16 octuple launcher for 16 RUR-5A ASROC missiles, two Mk 32 triple 12·75-in (324-mm) mountings for Mk 46 torpedoes, and one Limbo Mk 10 three-barrel mortar
Aircraft: none
Electronics: one SPS-503 (CMR 1820) air-search radar, one SPS-10 surface-search radar, one Decca 127E navigation radar, one SPG-48 radar used in conjunction with the Mk 69 gun fire-control system, one SQS-501 bottom-classification hull sonar and one SQS-505 active search and attack sonar (with hull and variable-depth elements) used in conjunction with a UCS 257 underwater weapons fire-control system, one ADLIPS action information system, Link 11 and 14 data-links, one SLQ-25 Nixie towed torpedo-decoy system,

one ESM system with CANEWS warning and ULQ-6 jamming elements, and four Mk 36 Super RBOC chaff/flare launchers
Propulsion: two Babcock & Wilcox boilers supplying steam to two sets of English Electric geared turbines delivering 30,000 hp (22,370 kW) to two shafts
Performance: maximum speed 28 kt; range 5,475 miles (8810 km) at 14 kt
Complement: 13 + 201

Class

1. Canada			Laid	Com-
Name	No.	Builder	down	missioned
Gatineau	236	Davie SB	Apr 1953	Feb 1959
Restigouche	257	Vickers	Jul 1953	Jun 1958
Kootenay	258	Burrard Dry Dock	Aug 1952	Mar 1959
Terra Nova	259	Victoria Machinery	Nov 1952	Jun 1959

Note: These elderly ships were modernized in the late 1960s, the second Limbo Mk 10 mortar being removed to make room for the ASROC launcher and variable-depth sonar that help provide the class with a continued though limited operational utility.

'Riga' class FF

(USSR)

Type: gun frigate
Displacement: 1,260 tons standard and 1,510 tons full load
Dimensions: length 91·5 m (300·1 ft); beam 10·1 m (33·1 ft); draught 3·2 m (10·5 ft)
Gun armament: three 100-mm (3·94-in) L/56 DP in single mountings, four 37-mm L/63 AA in two twin mountings, and (some ships) four 25-mm L/80 AA in two twin mountings
Missile armament: none
Torpedo armament: one twin or triple 533-mm (21-in) mounting for Type 53 dual-role torpedoes
Anti-submarine armament: two RBU 2500 16-barrel rocket-launchers, torpedoes (see above), and racks for 24 depth charges
Mines: 28
Aircraft: none
Electronics: one 'Slim Net' surface-search radar, one 'Neptun' or 'Don 2' navigation radar, one 'Sun Visor-B' 100-mm gun fire-control radar, one 'Wasp Head' 37-mm gun fire-control radar, one high-frequency active search and attack hull sonar, one active search variable-depth sonar (some ships only), one ESM system with two 'Watch Dog' antennae/housings, and two 'Square Head' and one 'High Pole' IFF systems
Propulsion: two boilers supplying steam to two sets of geared turbines delivering 14,900 kW (19,985 hp) to two shafts
Performance: maximum speed 30 kt; range 3700 km (2,300 miles) at 13 kt or 1300 km (810 miles) at 27 kt
Complement: 175

The 'Riga' class frigates were built in large numbers, but are obsolete and fast disappearing even from second-line patrol service.

Class

1. Bulgaria	
Name	No.
Druzki	11
Smeli	12
Bodri	13

(These are standard 'Riga' class frigates, the first pair being transferred in 1957 and 1958, and the last in 1985.)

2. USSR

40 ships (including 15 in reserve), known names being *Arkhangelsky Komsomolets, Astrakhansky Komsomolets, Bars, Barsuk, Bobr, Komsomolets Litvy, Kuguar, Kunitsa, Leopard, Rosomokha, Rys, Sovetsky Azerbaydzhan, Sovetsky Dagestan, Sovetsky Turkmenistan, Tuman, Volk* and *Voron*
(Production of some 64 'Riga' class coastal frigates was undertaken between 1955 and 1965 at Kaliningrad, Komsomolsk and Nikolayev. The class is now decidely obsolescent for anything but the simple patrol role.)

'River' class FF

(Australia)
Type: gun frigate
Displacement: 2,100 tons standard and 2,700 tons full load
Dimensions: length 370·0 ft (112·8 m); beam 41·0 ft (12·5 m); draught 17·3 ft (5·3 m)
Gun armament: two 4·5-in (114-mm) Vickers L/45 DP in a Mk 6 twin mounting
Missile armament: one quadruple launcher for 24 Sea Cat SAMs
Torpedo armament: none
Anti-submarine armament: one launcher for Ikara missiles, and two Mk 32 triple 12·75-in (324-mm) mountings for Mk 46 torpedoes
Aircraft: none
Electronics: one LW-02 air-search radar, one SPS-55 surface-search radar (in 46, 48 and 49 only), one Type 1006 navigation radar, one radar used in conjunction with the WM-22 gun fire-control system (45, 48 and 49) or WM-44 gun and SAM fire-control system (50 and 53) tied in with the Leander integrated fire-control system including the GWS 22 Sea Cat fire-control system, one GWS 20 SAM optical fire-control system (46, 48 and 49 only), one Mulloka active search and attack sonar, and one Type 162M side-looking classification hull sonar
Propulsion: two Babcock & Wilcox boilers supplying steam to two sets of geared turbines delivering 30,000 hp (22,370 kW) to two shafts
Performance: maximum speed 30 kt; range 3,900 miles (6275 km) at 12 kt
Complement: 15 + 217 (46, 48 and 49) or 15 + 226 (50 and 53)

As its layout reveals, the *Torrens* is one of two 'Leander' class variants sometimes known in Australian service as 'River (Improved)' class frigates.

Class				
1. Australia			**Laid**	**Com-**
Name	**No.**	**Builder**	**down**	**missioned**
Parramatta	46	Cockatoo Island DY	Jan 1957	Jul 1961
Stuart	48	Cockatoo Island DY	Mar 1959	Jun 1963
Derwent	49	HMA Naval Dockyard	Jun 1958	Apr 1964
Swan	50	HMA Naval Dockyard	Aug 1965	Jan 1970
Torrens	53	Cockatoo Island DY	Aug 1965	Jan 1971

Note: The first three ships are modelled on the British 'Type 12' class design, and the last two on the 'Leander Batch 1' class design. In the late 1970s and early 1980s the ships were modified with more advanced anti-submarine sensors and weapons.

'Salisbury' or 'Type 61' class FF

(UK/Bangladesh)
Type: gun frigate
Displacement: 2,170 tons standard and 2,410 tons full load
Dimensions: length 339·8 ft (103·6 m); beam 40·0 ft (12·2 m); draught 15·5 ft (4·7 m)
Gun armament: two 4·5-in (114-mm) Vickers L/45 DP in a Mk 6 twin mounting, and two 40-mm Bofors L/60 AA in Mk 9 single mountings
Missile armament: none
Torpedo armament: none
Anti-submarine armament: one Squid Mk 4 three-barrel mortar
Aircraft: none
Electronics: one Type 965 air-search radar, one Type 993 air/surface-search radar, one Type 975 surface-search radar, one Type 278M height-finding radar, one Type 978 navigation radar, one Mk 6M gun director, one Type 174 active search hull sonar, and one Type 170B active attack hull sonar

Propulsion: eight Admiralty Standard Range VVS ASR1 diesels delivering 14,400 hp (10,740 kW) to two shafts
Performance: maximum speed 24 kt; range 8,650 miles (13,920 km) at 16 kt or 2,650 miles (4265 km) at 24 kt
Complement: 14 + 223

Class				
1. Bangladesh			**Laid**	**Com-**
Name	**No.**	**Builder**	**down**	**missioned**
Umar Farooq	F16	Hawthorn Leslie	Aug 1953	Apr 1958

Note: Though obsolete by modern standards, this ship retains a patrol significance in the Bay of Bengal.

The *Lincoln* reveals the baseline British standard of the 'Salisbury' class from which the surviving Bangladeshi ship differs only modestly.

'Soho' class FF

(North Korea)

Type: gun frigate with secondary anti-ship missile capability
Displacement: 1,600 tons standard and 1,845 tons full load
Dimensions: length 75·0 m (246·1 ft); beam 15·0 m (49·2 ft); draught 3·8 m (12·5 ft)
Gun armament: one 100-mm (3·94-in) L/56 DP in a single mounting, two 37-mm L/63 AA in a twin mounting, and four 25-mm L/60 AA in a quadruple mounting
Missile armament: two twin container-launchers for four SS-N-2A 'Styx' anti-ship missiles
Torpedo armament: none
Anti-submarine armament: two RBU 1200 five-barrel rocket-launchers
Aircraft: none

Electronics: one 'Slim Net' air-search radar, one 'Skin Head' surface-search radar, one 'Pot Head' surface-search radar, one 'Pot Drum' gun fire-control radar, one active search and attack hull sonar, one active search variable-depth sonar, and one 'Ski Pole' IFF system
Propulsion: two diesels delivering unknown power to two shafts
Performance: maximum speed 27 kt
Complement: 190

Class

1. North Korea			Laid	Com-
Name	No.	Builder	down	missioned
		Najin	1980	1983

Note: This is a simple frigate design optimized for coastal operations. The type is in essence a 'short fat' version of the 'Najin' class and has limited anti-ship missile capability.

'Stanflex 2000' class FF

(Denmark)

Type: gun frigate
Displacement: 2,400 tons standard and 2,700 tons full load
Dimensions: length 104·0 m (341·2 ft); beam 14·4 m (47·2 ft); draught 6·0 m (19·7 ft)
Gun armament: one 76-mm (3-in) OTO Melara L/62 DP in an OTO Melara Super Rapid single mounting, and one or two 20-mm Oerlikon AA in one or two single mountings
Missile armament: none
Torpedo armament: none
Anti-submarine armament: none
Aircraft: one Westland Lynx Mk 80/91 in a hangar aft
Electronics: one AWS 6 air/surface-search radar, one navigation radar, one radar used with the NA10 fire-control system, and other systems as yet unrevealed
Propulsion: diesel-electric arrangement, with four diesel generators supplying current to one electric motor delivering 9000 kW (12,070 hp) to one shaft

Performance: maximum speed 20 kt; range 15,500 km (9,630 miles) at 18 kt
Complement: 60 with a maximum of 71 possible

Class

1. Denmark			Laid	Com-
Name	No.	Builder	down	missioned
		Svendborg Vaerft	1988	1990
		Svendborg Vaerft	1989	1991
		Svendborg Vaerft	1990	1992
		Svendborg Vaerft	1991	1993

Note: This class was ordered initially as replacement for the four-strong 'Hvidbjornen' class of fishery protection frigates. However, the inbuilt flexibility of the basic design makes it feasible that a fully armed version may follow in due course with a mix of weapons including anti-ship missiles, SAMs and anti-submarine weapons used with a more sophisticated electronic suite that would include an ESM system and chaff launchers.

'Tetal' class FF

(Romania)
Type: gun frigate
Displacement: 1,800 tons full load
Dimensions: length 95·0 m (311·6 ft); beam 11·5 m (37·7 ft); draught 3·0 m (9·8 ft)
Gun armament: four 76-mm (3-in) L/60 DP in two twin mountings, four 30-mm L/65 AA in two twin mountings, and two 14·5-mm (0·57-in) machine-guns
Missile armament: none
Torpedo armament: one twin 533-m (21-in) mounting for Type 53 dual-role torpedoes
Anti-submarine armament: two RBU 2500 16-barrel rocket-launchers, and torpedoes (see above)
Mines: probably fitted for minelaying
Aircraft: provision for one light helicopter on a platform aft
Electronics: one 'Strut Curve' air/surface-search radar, one 'Drum Tilt' gun fire-control radar, one medium-frequency active search and attack hull sonar, and one 'High Pole-B' IFF system
Propulsion: two diesels delivering unrevealed power to two shafts
Performance: not revealed
Complement: not revealed

Class 1. Romania Name	No.	Builder	Laid down	Com-missioned
	260	Mangalia		1983
	261	Mangalia		1984
	262	Mangalia		1985
	263	Mangalia		1987

Note: These simple patrol frigates are believed to be based on the Soviet 'Koni' design with narrower beam, less capable sensors and weapons, and a less powerful diesel propulsion system for inferior performance.

'Tribal' or 'Type 81' class FF

(UK/Indonesia)
Type: gun frigate
Displacement: 2,300 tons standard and 2,700 tons full load
Dimensions: length 360·0 ft (109·7 m); beam 42·5 ft (13·0 m); draught 18·0 ft (5·5 m)
Gun armament: two 4·5-in (114-mm) Vickers L/55 DP in Mk 5 single mountings, and two 20-mm Oerlikon AA in single mountings
Missile armament: two quadruple launchers for 32 Sea Cat SAMs
Torpedo armament: none
Anti-submarine armament: one Limbo Mk 10 three-barrel mortar, and helicopter-launched weapons (see below)
Aircraft: one Westland Wasp HAS.Mk 1 helicopter in a hangar aft
Electronics: one Type 965 air-search radar, one Type 993 surface-search radar, one Type 978 navigation radar, one Type 903 radar used in conjunction with the MRS 3 gun fire-control system, two Type 262 radars used in conjunction with two MRS 8 SAM fire-control systems, one Type 177 active search hull sonar, one Type 170B active attack hull sonar, one Type 162 side-looking classification hull sonar, one ESM system with warning element, and two Corvus chaff launchers
Propulsion: COSAG arrangement, with one boiler supplying steam to one Parsons Metrovick turbine delivering 12,500 hp (9320 kW) and two Yarrow AEI G.6 gas turbines delivering 7,500 hp (5595 kW) to one shaft
Performance: maximum speed 25 kt on steam and gas turbines or 17 kt on gas turbine; range 6,000 miles (9655 km) at 12 kt
Complement: 19 + 231

Class 1. Indonesia Name	No.	Builder	Laid down	Com-missioned
Martha Kristina Tiyahadu	331	Alex Stephens	Dec 1960	Apr 1964
Wilhelmus Zakarias Yohannes	332	Thornycroft	Nov 1958	Feb 1963
Hasanuddin	333	Devonport DY	Oct 1959	Feb 1962

Note: These general-purpose frigates were bought from the UK and refitted before being recommissioned in late 1985 and early 1986.

Opposite below: The canvas covering protects the starboard quadruple launcher for Sea Cat SAMs on the *Martha Kristina Tiyahadu*.

'Type 41/61' class FF

(UK/Malaysia)
Type: gun frigate
Displacement: 2,300 tons standard and 2,520 tons full load
Dimensions: length 339·3 ft (103·5 m); beam 40·0 ft (12·2 m); draught 16·0 ft (4·9 m)
Gun armament: two 4-in (102-mm) Vickers L/45 DP in a Mk 19 twin mounting, and two 40-mm Bofors L/70 AA in single mountings
Missile armament: none
Torpedo armament: none
Anti-submarine armament: one Limbo Mk 10 three-barrel mortar, and helicopter-launched weapons (see below)
Aircraft: provision for one Westland Wasp HAS.Mk 1 on a platform aft
Electronics: one AWS 1 air/surface-search radar, one Decca 45 navigation radar, one STD Mk 1 4-in gun director, one Type 174 active search hull sonar, and one Type 170B active attack hull sonar
Propulsion: eight Admiralty Standard Range VVS ASR1 diesels delivering 14,400 hp (10,740 kW) to two shafts
Performance: maximum speed 24 kt; range 5,525 miles (8890 km) at 15 kt
Complement: 210

Class 1. Malaysia Name	No.	Builder	Laid down	Com-missioned
Hang Tuah	F76	Yarrow	1965	May 1973

Note: Though rated officially as a frigate, this singleton hybrid of 'Leopard' and 'Salisbury' class features is a useful training ship with secondary patrol capability.

The ship now known as the *Hang Tuah* was the British *Mermaid* with the same pennant number, and the long after section accommodates the Limbo mortar.

'Albatros' class FFL

(Italy)
Type: gun corvette
Displacement: 800 tons standard and 950 tons full load
Dimensions: length 76·3 m (250·3 ft); beam 9·6 m (31·5 ft); draught 2·8 m (9·2 ft)
Gun armament: three 40-mm Bofors L/70 in Breda single mountings
Missile armament: none
Torpedo armament: none
Anti-submarine armament: two Mk 32 triple 12·75-in (324-mm) mountings for Mk 44 torpedoes, and (F542 and 545 only) two Hedgehog 24-tube mortars, two depth-charge throwers and one depth-charge rack
Aircraft: none
Electronics: one SPQ 2 surface-search radar, one BX 732 navigation radar, and one QCU 2 active search and attack hull sonar
Propulsion: two Fiat M409 diesels delivering 3900 kW (5,230 hp) to two shafts
Performance: maximum speed 19 kt; range 9250 km (5,750 miles) at 18 kt
Complement: 6 + 93

Class

1. Italy

Name	No.	Builder	Laid down	Com- missioned
Aquila	F542	Breda Marghera	Jul 1953	Oct 1956
Alcione	F544	Navalmeccanica	1953	Oct 1955
Airone	F545	Navalmeccanica	1953	Dec 1955

Note: These elderly ships are now completely obsolete, and useful only for patrol.

The *Aquila* was built in Italy for the Netherlands with US funding, and was returned to Italy in October 1961. The class is completely obsolete.

'Assad' class FFL(M)

(Italy/Libya)
Type: guided-missile corvette
Displacement: 670 tons full load
Dimensions: length 61·7 m (202·4 ft); beam 9·3 m (30·5 ft); draught 2·2 m (7·6 ft)
Gun armament: one 76-mm (3-in) OTO Melara L/62 DP in an OTO Melara Compact single mounting, and two 35-mm Oerlikon L/90 AA in a GDM-A twin mounting
Missile armament: four container-launchers for four Otomat anti-ship missiles
Torpedo armament: none
Anti-submarine armament: two ILAS 3 triple 324-mm (12·75-in) mountings for A 244 torpedoes
Mines: up to 16
Aircraft: none
Electronics: one RAN 11L/X air/surface-search radar, one TM1226C navigation radar, one RTN 10X radar used in conjunction with the Argo NA10 gun fire-control system, one Diodon active search and attack hull sonar, one IPN 10 action information system, and one ESM system with INS 1 warning element
Propulsion: four MTU 16V 956 TB91 diesels delivering 13,400 kW (17,970 hp) to four shafts
Performance: maximum speed 34 kt; range 8150 km (5,065 miles) at 14 kt
Complement: 58

Class

1. Iraq

Name	No.	Builder	Laid down	Com- missioned
*Mussa Ben Hussair**	F210	CNR, Muggiano	Jan 1982	Sep 1986
*Tariq Ibn Zyiad**	F212	CNR, Muggiano	May 1982	Oct 1986
Abdullah Ben Abi Sarh	F214	CNR, Breda, Mestre	Mar 1982	1987
Khalid Ibn al Walid	F216	CNR, Breda, Mestre	Jun 1982	1987
Saad Ibn Abi Waccade	F218	CNR, Breda, Marghera	Sep 1982	1988
Salah al Din al Ayuri	F215	CNR, Breda, Marghera	Sep 1982	1988

* equipped with helicopter

The *Assad el Touggour*, an 'Assad' class on trials off the Italian coast before the installation of her anti-ship missile armament.

(The Iraqi vessels are believed to be similar in all essential respects to the Libyan units, but have a missile armament of six Otomat anti-ship missiles [only two in each of the helicopter-carrying units] and one Albatros quadruple launcher for 16 Aspide SAMs, and a secondary gun armament of two 40-mm Bofors L/70 AA guns in a Breda twin mounting [not in helicopter-carrying units]. Two of the ships are fitted to carry an Agusta [Bell] AB.212ASW helicopter in a telescopic hangar aft. The electronic fit includes RAN 12L/X air-surface-search radar, 3RM 20 navigation radar, a Gamma ESM system and two SCLAR chaff/flare launchers. The basic complement is 51 without aircrew.)

2. Libya

Name	No.	Builder	Laid down	Com- missioned
Assad el Tadjer	412	CNR, Muggiano	May 1976	Sep 1979
Assad el Touggour	413	CNR, Muggiano	May 1976	Feb 1980
Assad al Khali	414	CNR, Muggiano	Oct 1977	Mar 1981
Assad al Hudud	415	CNR, Muggiano	May 1978	Mar 1981

(These are highly capable light combatants with potent anti-ship and useful anti-submarine capability.)

'Badr' class FFL(M)

(USA/Saudi Arabia)

Type: guided-missile corvette

Displacement: 870 tons standard and 1,040 tons full load

Dimensions: length 245·0 ft (74·7 m); beam 31·5 ft (9·6 m); draught 14·6 ft (4·5 m)

Gun armament: one 76-mm (3-in) OTO Melara Compact L/62 DP in a Mk 75 single mounting, one 20-mm Phalanx Mk 15 CIWS mounting, two 20-mm Oerlikon AA in single mountings, one 81-mm (3·2-in) mortar, and two 40-mm Mk 19 grenade-launchers

Missile armament: two Mk 141 quadruple container-launchers for eight RGM-84 Harpoon anti-ship missiles

Torpedo armament: none

Anti-submarine armament: two Mk 32 triple 12·75-in (324-mm) mountings for Mk 46 torpedoes

Aircraft: none

Electronics: one SPS-40B air-search radar, one SPS-55 surface-search and navigation radar, one radar used in conjunction with the Mk 92/95 (WM-25/28) gun and SAM fire-control system, one Mk 24 optical director, one Raytheon DE 1164 active search and attack hull sonar used in conjunction with the Mk 309 underwater weapons fire-control system, one SLQ-32(V)1 ESM system with warning element, and two Mk 36 Super RBOC chaff/flare launchers

Propulsion: CODOG arrangement, with one General Electric LM2500 gas turbine delivering 23,000 hp (17,150 kW) or two MTU 12V 692 TB91 diesels delivering 3000 kW (4,025 hp) to two shafts

Performance: maximum speed 30 kt on gas turbine or 16 kt on diesels; range 4,600 miles (7400 km) at 20 kt

Complement: 7 + 51

Class

1. Saudi Arabia			Laid	Com-
Name	No.	Builder	down	missioned
Badr	612	Tacoma BB	Oct 1979	Nov 1980
Al Yarmook	614	Tacoma BB	Jan 1980	May 1981
Hitteen	616	Tacoma BB	May 1980	Oct 1981
Tabuk	618	Tacoma BB	Sep 1980	Jan 1982

(These are highly capable anti-ship corvettes with good anti-submarine capability.)

2. Thailand			Laid	Com-
Name	No.	Builder	down	missioned
Rattanakosin	1	Tacoma BB	Feb 1984	Sep 1986
Sukhothai	2	Tacoma BB	Mar 1984	Jun 1987

(These units are similar to the Saudi ships with the exception of the details listed below. The full-load displacement is 960 tons. The secondary armament comprises two 40-mm Bofors L/70 AA in a Breda Compact twin mounting, the missile armament is eight RGM-84 Harpoon anti-ship missiles in two Mk 141 quadruple container-launchers and 24 Aspide SAMs for one Albatros octuple launcher, and the anti-submarine armament is Stingray torpedoes in two Mk 32 triple mountings. The electronic suite includes DA-05 air/surface-search radar, ZW-06 surface-search radar, Decca 1226 navigation radar, one radar used in conjunction with the WM-25 fire-control system, LIROD 8 optronic director, Krupp-Atlas DSQS-21C active search and attack hull sonar, Mini-SADOC action information system, Elettronica ESM system with warning element, and one Dagaie chaff/flare launcher. The propulsion arrangement of two MTU 20V 1163 TB83 diesels delivers 11,000 kW/14,755 hp to two shafts for a maximum speed of 26 kt and a range of 5550 km/3,450 miles at 16 kt. The complement is 15 + 72 excluding flag staff.)

The *Badr* and her Saudi sisterships have powerful offensive and defensive armament, the latter including the stern mounted Phalanx CIWS.

'Bulgarian' class FFL

(Algeria)

Type: gun corvette

Displacement: 500 tons standard

Dimensions: length 59·3 m (194·6 ft); beam 8·5 m (27·9 ft); draught 2·6 m (8·5 ft)

Gun armament: one 76-mm (3-in) OTO Melara L/62 DP in an OTO Melara Compact single mounting, and two 40-mm Bofors L/70 AA in a Breda Compact single mounting

Missile armament: none

Torpedo armament: none

Anti-submarine armament: none

Aircraft: none

Electronics: not revealed

Propulsion: three MTU 20V 538 diesels delivering 11,175 kW (14,990 hp) to three shafts

Performance: maximum speed 36 kt

Complement: not revealed

Class

1. Algeria			Laid	Com-
Name	No.	Builder	down	missioned
		Mers-el-Kebir	Jul 1983	1988

Note: This simple corvette was built with Bulgarian assistance, and the dimensional data suggests that it is a narrow-beam derivative of the 'Nanuchka' class design. It is thought that another two units will be built.

'Cassiopea' class FFL

(Italy)

Type: gun corvette
Displacement: 1,000 tons standard and 1,475 tons full load
Dimensions: length 79·8 m (261·8 ft); beam 11·8 m (38·7 ft); draught 3·5 m (11·5 ft)
Gun armament: one 76-mm (3-in) OTO Melara L/62 DP in an OTO Melara Compact single mounting, and two 20-mm Oerlikon AA in single mountings
Missile armament: none
Torpedo armament: none
Anti-submarine armament: helicopter-launched weapons (see below)
Aircraft: one Agusta (Bell) AB.212ASW helicopter in a hangar aft
Electronics: one surface-search radar, one navigation radar, one RTN 20X radar used in conjunction with the NA20 gun fire-control system, one ESM system with warning element, and other systems

Propulsion: two Fincantieri/GMT BL 230·16 diesels delivering 6550 kW (8,785 hp) to two shafts
Performance: maximum speed 20 kt; range 6115 km (3,800 miles) at 17 kt
Complement: 8 + 70

Class

| 1. Italy | | | | |
Name	No.	Builder	Laid down	Commissioned
Cassiopea	P401	CNR, Muggiano	Feb 1987	May 1989
Libra	P402	CNR, Muggiano	Feb 1987	Jul 1989
Spica	P403	CNR, Muggiano	Feb 1987	Nov 1989
Vega	P404	CNR, Muggiano	Sep 1987	Sep 1990
Orione	P405	CNR, Muggiano		

Note: This class of simple gun corvettes is designed mainly for the patrol role, and should eventually total eight ships.

'De Cristoforo' class FFL

(Italy)

Type: gun corvette
Displacement: 850 tons standard and 1,020 tons full load
Dimensions: length 80·2 m (263·2 ft); beam 10·3 m (33·7 ft); draught 2·7 m (9·0 ft)
Gun armament: two 76-mm (3-in) OTO Melara L/62 DP in OTO Melara single mountings
Missile armament: none
Torpedo armament: none
Anti-submarine armament: two Mk 32 triple 12·75-in (324-mm) mountings for Mk 46 torpedoes, and one Mk 113 Menon single-barrel mortar
Aircraft: none
Electronics: one SPQ 2B air/surface-search radar, one BX 732 navigation radar, one Orion 3 radar used in conjunction with the OG3 gun fire-control system, one SQS-36 active search and attack sonar (with hull and variable-depth elements) used in conjunction with the DLB 1 underwater weapons fire-control system, and one ESM system with SPR warning element

Propulsion: two Fiat 3012 RSS diesels delivering 6250 kW (8,380 hp) to two shafts
Performance: maximum speed 23 kt; range 7400 km (4,600 miles) at 16 kt
Complement: 8 + 123

Class

| 1. Italy | | | | |
Name	No.	Builder	Laid down	Commissioned
Pietro de Christofaro	F540	CNR, Riva Trigoso	Apr 1963	Dec 1965
Umberto Grosso	F541	Cantieri Ansaldo	Oct 1962	Apr 1965
Licio Visintini	F546	CRDA, Monfalcone	Sep 1963	Aug 1966
Salvatore Todaro	F550	Cantieri Ansaldo	Oct 1962	Apr 1966

Note: These four units were produced as improved versions of the 'Albatros' class design, and like their predecessors are now obsolete and useful only for the patrol role.

The *Licio Visintini* and her three sisterships are obsolete corvettes retaining only a vestigial utility even in second-line roles.

'Dong Hae' class FFL(M)

(South Korea)

Type: guided-missile corvette

Displacement: 1,180 tons full load

Dimensions: length 88·3 m (289·7 ft); beam 10·0 m (32·8 ft); draught 2·9 m (9·5 ft)

Gun armament: one or two 76-mm (3-in) OTO Melara L/62 DP in OTO Melara Compact single mountings, two or four 40-mm Bofors L/70 AA in one or two Breda twin mountings (in later ships only as replacement for the 30-mm twin mountings), two or four 30-mm Oerlikon L/85 AA in one or two Emerlec twin mountings, and one 20-mm Phalanx Mk 15 CIWS mounting (later ships only)

Missile armament: two container-launchers for two MM.38 Exocet anti-ship missiles (in some ships only)

Torpedo armament: none

Anti-submarine armament: two Mk 32 triple 12·75-in (324-mm) mountings for Mk 46 torpedoes, and 12 depth charges (in some ships only)

Aircraft: none

Electronics: one Marconi 1810 surface-search radar, one Marconi 1802 navigation radar, one radar used in conjunction with the WM-28 fire-control system integrated with one WSA 423 weapon automation system, one Radamec optronic director, one PHS 32 active search and attack hull sonar (not in all), one Mini-Combat action information system, one ESM system with warning and jamming elements, and two Mk 36 Super RBOC chaff/flare launchers

Propulsion: CODOG arrangement, with one General Electric LM2500 gas turbine delivering 27,200 hp (20,280 kW) or two SEMT-Pielstick 12 PA6-V280 diesels delivering 5000 kW (6,705 hp) to two shafts

Performance: maximum speed 32 kt on gas turbine; range 7400 km (4,600 miles) at 15 kt

Complement: 10 + 85

Class

1. South Korea Name	No.	Builder	Laid down	Com- missioned
Dong Hae	711	Korea SEC		1982
Su Won	712	Korea Tacoma		1983
An Yang	713	Daewoo		1983
Kang Reung	715	Hyundai		1983
Mok Po	756	Daewoo		1983
Kong Ju	757	Hyundai		1983
Po Hang	758	Korea SEC		1984
Kun San	759	Korea Tacoma		1984
Chung Ju	761	Korea Tacoma		1985
Kim Chon	762	Korea SEC		1985
Jin Ju	763	Hyundai		1986
Yo Su	765	Daewoo		1986
Sun Chon	766	Korea Tacoma		1987
Am Dong	767	Korea SEC		1987
Won Ju	768	Daewoo		1988
Yee Kee	769	Hyundai		1988
Chon Am		Korea Tacoma		1988
Je Chon		Korea SEC		1988
Song Nam		Daewoo		1988
Bu Chon		Hyundai		1988
Dae Chon		Korea Tacoma		1988
Jin Hae		Korea SEC		1988

Note: This is an an advanced corvette type admirably suited to Korean coastal operations. It is thought that the 22 current ships (out of a planned total of 26) fall into three subclasses: the first is optimized for the anti-submarine role (without Exocet), the second for the anti-ship role (without anti-submarine weapons) and the last for the higher-threat anti-ship role (with Exocet and the Phalanx CIWS mounting).

'Esmeraldas' class FFL(M)

(Italy/Ecuador)

Type: guided-missile corvette

Displacement: 620 tons standard and 685 tons full load

Dimensions: length 62·3 m (204·4 ft); beam 9·3 m (30·5 ft); draught 2·5 m (8·2 ft)

Gun armament: one 76-mm (3-in) OTO Melara L/62 DP in an OTO Melara Compact single mounting, and two 40-mm Bofors L/70 AA in one Dardo twin mounting

Missile armament: two triple container-launchers for six MM.40 Exocet anti-ship missiles, and one Albatros quadruple launcher for Aspide SAMs

Torpedo armament: none

Anti-submarine armament: two ILAS 3 triple 324-mm (12·75-in) mountings for A 244/S torpedoes

Aircraft: provision for a Bell Model 206B JetRanger helicopter on a platform amidships

Electronics: one RAN 10S air/surface-search radar, one 3RM 20 navigation radar, one RTN 10X radar used in conjunction with the Argo NA21 gun fire-control system and its C03 directors, one RTN 20X radar used in conjunction with the Dardo fire-control system, one Diodon active search and attack hull sonar, one IPN 20 action information system, one ESM system with Gamma warning and jamming elements, and one SCLAR chaff/decoy launcher

Propulsion: four MTU 20V 956 TB92 diesels delivering 18,200 kW (24,405 hp) to four shafts

Performance: maximum speed 37 kt; range 7900 km (4,910 miles) at 14 kt

Complement: 51

Class

1. Ecuador Name	No.	Builder	Laid down	Com- missioned
Esmeraldas	CM11	CNR, Muggiano	Sep 1979	Aug 1982
Manabi	CM12	CNR, Ancona	Feb 1980	Jun 1983
Los Rios	CM13	CNR, Muggiano	Dec 1979	Oct 1983
El Oro	CM14	CNR, Ancona	Mar 1980	Dec 1983
Galapagos	CM15	CNR, Muggiano	Dec 1980	May 1984
Loja	CM16	CNR, Ancona	Mar 1981	May 1984

The *Esmeraldas* reveals extensive electronics and armament including a 76-mm (3-in) gun, an Albatros quadruple SAM launcher, triple torpedo mountings, anti-ship missiles and, invisible at the stern, a 40-mm gun mounting.

Note: Developed from the 'Assad' class with more powerful engine and provision for a helicopter, these vessels offer an exceptional combination of sensors and weapons, and are little short of frigates in their overall capabilities.

'Grisha I', 'Grisha III' and 'Grisha V' class FFL(M)s

(USSR)

Type: guided-missile corvette

Displacement: 950 tons standard and 1,200 tons full load

Dimensions: length 72·0 m (236·2 ft); beam 10·0 m (32·8 ft); draught 3·7 m (12·1 ft)

Gun armament: two 57-mm L/80 DP in a twin mounting or ('Grisha V' class ships) one 76-mm (3-in) L/60 DP in a single mounting, and ('Grisha III' and 'Grisha V' class ships) one 30-mm ADGM-630 CIWS mounting

Missile armament: one twin launcher for 20 SA-N-4 'Gecko' SAMs

Torpedo armament: two twin 533-mm (21-in) mountings for Type 53 dual-role torpedoes

Anti-submarine armament: two RBU 6000 12-barrel rocket-launchers, torpedoes (see above), and two rails for 12 depth charges

Mines: 18 instead of depth charges

Aircraft: none

Electronics: one 'Strut Curve' or ('Grisha V' class ships) 'Strut Pair' air/surface-search radar, one 'Don 2' navigation radar, one 'Pop Group' SAM fire-control radar, one 'Muff Cob' ('Grisha I' class ships) or 'Bass Tilt' ('Grisha III' and 'Grisha V' class ships) gun fire-control radar, one high/medium-frequency active search and attack sonar, one high-frequency active search variable-depth sonar, one ESM system with two 'Watch Dog' antennae/housings, and one 'High Pole-B' IFF system

Propulsion: CODAG arrangement, with one gas turbine delivering 11,250 kW (15,090 hp) and two diesels delivering 12,000 kW (16,095 hp) to three shafts

Performance: maximum speed 30 kt; range 3700 km (2,300 miles) at 20 kt or 925 km (575 miles) at 30 kt

Complement: 60 ('Grisha I' class ships) or 70 ('Grisha III' and 'Grisha V' class ships)

In the 'Grisha II' class the SA-N-4 launcher on the foredeck is replaced by a second twin 57-mm mounting, here trained on the photographing aeroplane.

Class

1. USSR

15 'Grisha I' class ships

32 'Grisha III' class ships

12 'Grisha V' class ships with another 3 building

Note: Built between 1968 and 1975 at Kiev, Khabarovsk and Zelenodolsk, the 'Grisha I' class succeeded the 'Mirka' and 'Petya' classes as the USSR's primary anti-submarine corvette type for coastal and escort deployment. The improved 'Grisha III' class followed between 1973 and 1985 at the same yards, differing only in the addition of the CIWS mounting and its associated radar, which replaces the 'Muff Cob' radar for control of both gun systems. The 'Grisha V' class entered production in 1975, and features the same type of 76-mm/3-in single mounting as used in the 'Tarantul' class. There is also the **'Grisha II'** class, a maritime patrol type of which 12 are operated by the KGB security service. This has a second 57-mm twin mounting in place of the SA-N-4 'Gecko' self-protection SAM launcher, and known names (all gemstones) are *Ametyst, Brilliant, Izumrud, Rubin, Sapfir* and *Zhemchug*. Some 'Grisha II' and 'Grisha V' class ships may have two launchers for SA-N-5 'Grail' short-range SAMs.

'HDC 800' class FFL

(South Korea)

Type: gun corvette

Displacement: 950 tons full load

Dimensions: length 78·1 m (256·2 ft); beam 9·6 m (31·5 ft); draught 2·6 m (8·5 ft)

Gun armament: one 76-mm (3-in) OTO Melara L/62 DP in an OTO Melara Compact single mounting, four 30-mm Oerlikon L/85 AA in two Emerlec twin mountings, and two 20-mm Oerlikon AA in a twin mounting

Missile armament: none

Torpedo armament: none

Anti-submarine armament: two Mk 32 triple 12·75-in (324-mm) mountings for Mk 46 torpedoes, and 12 depth charges

Aircraft: none

Electronics: one Marconi 1810 surface-search and navigation radar, one radar used in conjunction with the WM-28 fire-control system, one Radamec optronic director, one PHS 32 active search and attack hull sonar, and one ESM system with warning element

Propulsion: CODOG arrangement, with one General Electric LM2500 gas turbine delivering 27,200 hp (20,280 kW) or two MTU 12V 956 TB82 diesels delivering 4600 kW (6,170 hp) to two shafts

Performance: maximum speed 31 kt on gas turbine; range 7400 km (4,600 miles) at 15 kt

Complement: 10 + 85

Class

1. South Korea			Laid	Com-
Name	No.	Builder	down	missioned
		Korea-Tacoma		
		Hyundai		

Note: Little is known of the two vessels of this class, which is essentially a scaled-down version of the 'Dong Hae' class without any missile armament. It is thought that both ships were commissioned in the second half of the 1980s.

'Kaszub' class FFL(M)

(Poland)

Type: guided-missile corvette

Displacement: about 1,200 tons

Dimensions: length 82·0 m (269·0 ft); beam 10·0 m (32·8 ft); draught 3·0 m (9·8 ft)

Gun armament: two 57-mm L/80 AA in a twin mounting, and four 23-mm L/70 AA in two twin mountings

Missile armament: one twin launcher for SA-N-4 'Gecko' SAMs

Torpedo armament: none

Anti-submarine armament: two RBU 6000 12-barrel rocket-launchers, four single 406-mm (16-in) launchers for Type 40 torpedoes, and two depth-charge rails

Aircraft: none

Electronics: one air/surface-search radar, one navigation radar, one 'Pop Group' SAM fire-control radar, one 'Muff Cob' 57-mm gun fire-control radar, one 'Bass Tilt' 23-mm gun fire-control radar, one ESM system with warning element, and one IFF system

Propulsion: probably CODOG arrangement

Performance: maximum speed 25 kt

Complement: not revealed

Class

1. Poland			
Name	No.	Builder	Commissioned
Kaszub	240	Stocznia Polnochnia	1987

Note: This is a simple corvette design apparently modelled on the Soviet 'Grisha' class with many alterations. There were many problems to be overcome before the ship could be commissioned, and it is thought that these difficulties may have led to the cancellation of the planned second unit.

'Khukri' class FFL(M)

(India)

Type: guided-missile corvette
Displacement: 1,200 tons
Dimensions: length 90·0 m (295·3 ft); beam not revealed; draught not revealed
Gun armament: two 57-mm L/70 DP in a twin mounting, and two 30-mm L/65 AA in a twin mounting
Missile armament: one or two twin container-launchers for two or four SS-N-2C 'Styx' anti-ship missiles, and one quadruple launcher for SA-N-5 'Grail' SAMs
Torpedo armament: none
Anti-submarine armament: none
Aircraft: provision for one HAL Chetak helicopter on a platform aft
Electronics: one 'Square Tie' air/surface-search radar, one navigation radar, one 'Bass Tilt' gun fire-control radar, one medium-frequency active search and attack hull sonar, IPN 10 action information system, and other systems
Propulsion: two Kirloskar/SEMT-Pielstick 18 PA6 diesels delivering 12,600 kW (16,900 hp) to two shafts
Performance: maximum speed 28 kt
Complement: not revealed

Class

1. India			Laid	Com-
Name	No.	Builder	down	missioned
Khukri		Mazagon DY	Sep 1985	1988
		Mazagon DY	1986	1989
Kirpan		Garden Reach SY	1987	1990
Khanjar		Garden Reach SY	1987	1990

Note: Little is known as yet about these Indian guided-missile corvettes, of which a total of 12 is planned. Indian sources suggest that the first four ships are optimized for the anti-submarine role and that the second four ships will be optimized for the anti-aircraft role, but details made available to date suggest that the present type is optimized for the anti-ship role. This leads to the speculation that there may be three subclasses: the first four optimized for anti-ship operations, and the two subsequent four-ship subclasses to be optimized for anti-submarine and anti-aircraft warfare.

'Lürssen FPB/MGB-62' class FFL(M)

(West Germany/Bahrain)

Type: guided-missile corvette
Displacement: 632 tons full load
Dimensions: length 62·95 m (206·5 ft); beam 9·3 m (30·5 ft); draught 2·9 m (9·5 ft)
Gun armament: one 76-mm (3-in) OTO Melara L/62 DP in an OTO Melara Compact single mounting, two 40-mm Bofors L/70 AA in a Breda Compact twin mounting, and two 20-mm Oerlikon L/93 AA in GAM-B01 single mountings
Missile armament: two twin container launchers for four MM.40 Exocet anti-ship missiles, and AS.15TT missiles carried by the embarked helicopter
Torpedo armament: none
Anti-submarine armament: none
Aircraft: provision for one Aérospatiale SA 365 Dauphin II helicopter on a platform amidships
Electronics: one Sea Giraffe air/surface-search radar, one Decca navigation radar, one 9LV 300 radar used in conjunction with one 9LV 331 fire-control system, one Philips optronic director, two Panda Mk 2 optical directors, one ESM system with Cutlass-E warning and Cygnus jamming elements, and two Dagaie chaff/flare launchers
Propulsion: four MTU 20V 538 TB93 diesels delivering 14,120 kW (18,940 hp) to four shafts
Performance: maximum speed 34·7 kt; range 7400 km (4,600 miles) at 16 kt
Complement: 7 + 36

Class

1. Bahrain ('FPB-62' class)			Laid	Com-
Name	No.	Builder	down	missioned
Bans al Manama		Lurssen		Dec 1987
Al Muharraq		Lurssen		Feb 1988

(This corvette is in essence an enlarged FAC[M], and the light helicopter adds considerably to anti-ship capability as it carries four AS.15TT anti-ship missiles, with four reloads.)

2. Singapore ('MGB-62' class)			Laid	Com-
Name	No.	Builder	down	missioned
Victory	P88	Lurssen		1989
Valour	P89	Singapore SBEC		1990
Vigilance	P90	Singapore SBEC		1990
Valiant	P91	Singapore SBEC		1990
Vigour	P92	Singapore SBEC		1990
Vengeance	P93	Singapore SBEC		1990

(These small but powerfully armed anti-ship and anti-submarine craft are genuinely of corvette capability, with the lead vessel built by the designer and the others under licence in Singapore. The full-load displacement is 600 tons, and the dimensions include a length of 63·0 m/206·7 ft, a beam of 9·3 m/30·5 ft and a draught of 5·4 m/17·7 ft. The armament comprises two Mk 141 quadruple container-launchers for eight RGM-84 Harpoon anti-ship missiles, one 76-mm/3-in OTO Melara L/62 DP in an OTO Melara Super Rapid mounting, two 40-mm Bofors L/70 AA in a Breda Compact twin mounting, two 20-mm Oerlikon AA in single mountings, and two ILAS 3 triple 324-mm/ 12·75-in mountings for A 244/S anti-submarine torpedoes. The comprehensive electronic fit includes one Hollandse Signaalapparaten surface-search radar, one navigation radar, one Philips Elektronikindustrier fire-control system, and one EDO 780 active search and attack variable-depth sonar. The propulsion arrangement is four MTU 20V 958 TB93 diesels delivering 14,000 kW/18,775 hp to four shafts for a maximum speed of 30 kt and a range of 7400 km/4,600 miles at 18 kt. The complement is 44. It is possible that improved anti-aircraft/anti-missile armament may be retrofitted in the form of a modular Naval Crotale SAM system or a 30-mm Goalkeeper CIWS mounting.)

3. United Arab Emirates/Abu Dhabi ('FPB-62' class)			Laid	Com-
Name	No.	Builder	down	missioned
	P6201	Lurssen		
	P6202	Lurssen		
	P6203	Lurssen		
	P6204	Lurssen		

(This version of the 'FPB-62' design has a full-load displacement of about 630 tons and should have been delivered in the late 1980s [first pair] and early 1990s [second pair]. The type lacks the helicopter of the Bahraini version, but has considerably more embarked firepower in the form of eight MM.40 Exocet anti-ship missiles, one 76-mm OTO Melara L/62 DP in an OTO Melara Compact single mounting, one Naval Crotale launcher for R.440 SAMs and one SANDRAL sextuple launcher for Mistral SAMs. The electronic suite [including a Naja optronic director, an ESM system with Cutlass warning and Cygnus jamming elements, and two Dagaie chaff launchers] is also highly capable, and the propulsion arrangement comprises four MTU diesels delivering 14,000 kW/18,775 hp for a maximum speed of 32 kt and a range of 7400 km/4,600 miles at 16 kt. The complement is 43.)

'Minerva' class FFL([M])

(Italy)

Type: gun (guided-missile) corvette
Displacement: 1,030 tons light and 1,285 tons full load
Dimensions: length 86·6 m (284·1 ft); beam 10·3 m (33·8 ft); draught 3·16 m (10·4 ft)
Gun armament: one 76-mm (3-in) OTO Melara L/62 DP in an OTO Melara Compact single mounting, and fitted for but not with four 40-mm Bofors L/70 AA in two Dardo twin mountings
Missile armament: one Albatros Mk 2 octuple launcher for eight Aspide SAMs (with capacity for a larger magazine), and fitted for but not with two or three twin Teseo 2 container-launchers for four or six Otomat Mk 2 anti-ship missiles
Torpedo armament: none
Anti-submarine armament: two B515 triple 324-mm (12·75-in) mountings for A 244/S torpedoes
Aircraft: none
Electronics: one RAN 10S/SP air/surface-search radar, one SPN 728 navigation radar, one RTN 20X radar used in conjunction with the NA30 Albatros and gun fire-control system, two RTN 10X radars used in conjunction with the Dardo fire-control system, one NA18L optronic director used in conjunc-

tion with the NA16 Pegaso back-up fire-control system, one Raytheon DE 1167 active search and attack hull sonar, one Mini-SADOC 2 action information system, one INS 3 ESM system with warning and jamming elements, two SCLAR chaff/decoy launchers, and two Barricade chaff launchers
Propulsion: two Fincantieri/GMT BM 230·20 DVM diesels delivering 8200 kW (11,000 hp) to two shafts
Performance: maximum speed 24 kt; range 6500 km (4,040 miles) at 18 kt
Complement: 10 + 113
Class
1. Italy

Name	No.	Builder	Laid down	Commissioned
Minerva	F551	CNR, Riva Trigoso	Mar 1985	Feb 1987
Urania	F552	CNR, Riva Trigoso	Apr 1985	Jun 1987
Danaide	F553	CNR, Muggiano	Jun 1985	Sep 1987
Sfinge	F554	CNR, Muggiano	Sep 1986	Jan 1988
Driade	F555	CNR, Riva Trigoso	Apr 1988	Apr 1990
Chimera	F556	CNR, Riva Trigoso	Jul 1988	Aug 1990
Fenice	F557	CNR, Muggiano	Sep 1988	Dec 1990
Sibilla	F558	CNR, Riva Trigoso	Apr 1989	Apr 1991

Note: Designed as a low-cost replacement for the 'Albatros' and 'De Cristoforo' classes, primarily in the offshore patrol, fishery protection and training roles, these ships can be transformed into useful missile-armed corvettes, when the secondary gun armament would also be shipped. A dedicated missile version is also proposed with six Otomat anti-ship missiles and an electronics fit optimized for the anti-ship and anti-aircraft roles (the Albatros missiles and 76-mm/3-in gun being complemented by two 40-mm Breda L/70 AA in a Breda Fast Forty twin mounting), and a helicopter-equipped anti-ship and anti-submarine version with a 76-mm (3-in) OTO Melara Super Rapid main gun, six Otomat anti-ship missiles and a platform aft for an Agusta (Bell) AB.212ASW helicopter.

'Nanuchka I', 'Nanuchka III' and 'Nanuchka IV' class FFL(M)s

(USSR)

Type: guided-missile corvette
Displacement: 560 tons standard and 660 tons full load
Dimensions: length 59·3 m (194·6 ft); beam 13·0 m (42·65 ft); draught 2·6 m (8·5 ft)
Gun armament: two 57-mm L/80 AA in a twin mounting, or ('Nanuchka III' and 'Nanuchka IV' class ships) one 76-mm (3-in) L/60 DP in a single mounting and one 30-mm ADGM-630 CIWS mounting
Missile armament: two triple container-launchers for six SS-N-9 'Siren' anti-ship missiles or ('Nanuchka IV' class ship) two sextuple container-launchers for 12 anti-ship missiles of an unknown type, and one twin launcher for 20 SA-N-4 'Gecko' SAMs
Torpedo armament: none
Anti-submarine armament: none
Aircraft: none
Electronics: one 'Band Stand' air/surface-search and SSM fire-control radar, one 'Peel Pair' surface-search radar, one 'Spar Stump' navigation radar, one 'Pop Group' SAM fire-control radar, one 'Muff Cob' or ('Nanuchka III' and 'Nanuchka IV' class ships) 'Bass Tilt' gun fire-control radar, two 'Fish Bowl' SSM data-links, one ESM system with one 'Bell Tap' antenna/housing, two chaff launchers, and one 'Square Head' and one 'High Pole-B' IFF systems
Propulsion: six M 504 diesels delivering 22,500 kW (30,175 hp) to three shafts
Performance: maximum speed 36 kt; range 8350 km (5,190 miles) at 15 kt or 1675 km (1,040 miles) at 31 kt
Complement: 10 + 50

Class
1. Algeria ('Nanuchka II' class)

Name	No.	Commissioned
Ras Hamidou	801	Jul 1980
Salah Reis	802	Feb 1981
Reis Ali	803	May 1982
	804	1989

(These Algerian ships are 'Nanuchka II' class units based on the 'Nanuchka I' class but fitted with two triple container-launchers for SS-N-2C 'Styx' anti-ship missiles and search radar limited to a single 'Square Tie' surface-search equipment supported by 'Don 2' navigation radar. The Algerians are reported to be unhappy with the Soviet diesels and are considering their replacement with West German MTU engines.)

2. India ('Nanuchka II' class)

Name	No.	Commissioned
Vijay Durg	K71	Apr 1977
Sindhu Durg	K72	Sep 1977
Hos Durg	K73	Apr 1978

(These Indian ships are standard 'Nanuchka II' class units similar in all essential respects to the Algerian units, and a total of five is planned.)

3. Libya ('Nanuchka II' class)

Name	No.	Commissioned
Ean Mara	416	Oct 1981
Ean el Gazala	417	Feb 1983
Ean Zara	418	Feb 1984

(These Libyan units are standard 'Nanuchka II' class units similar in all essential respects to the Algerian units. A fourth Libyan unit, *Ean Zarquit* [419], was sunk by US air attack in March 1986.)

4. USSR
17 'Nanuchka I' class ships
14 'Nanuchka III' class ships with 1 more building
1 'Nanuchka IV' class ship
(The 'Nanuchka' series has been built since 1969 at Petrovsky and Leningrad, and also ['Nanuchka III' class only] in Pacific yards, the last delivering their first ship in 1978. The type offers excellent anti-ship capability on a small and speedy hull, and at present it is unknown whether the single 'Nanuchka IV' class ship is a trials unit or the first of a new subclass.)

The 'Nanuchka I' class is identifiable by the 57-mm twin mounting at the stern, where 'Nanuchka III' units have a 76-mm (3-in) single mounting.

'Parchim I' and 'Parchim II' class FFL(G)s

(East Germany)

Type: gun corvette
Displacement: 960 tons standard and 1,200 tons full load
Dimensions: length 72·5 m (237·9 ft); beam 9·4 m (30·8 ft); draught 3·5 m (11·5 ft)
Gun armament: two 57-mm L/80 AA in a twin mounting or ('Parchim II' class ships) one 76-mm (3-in) L/60 DP, and two 30-mm AA in an AK-230 twin mounting or ('Parchim II' class ships) one 30-mm ADGM-630 CIWS mounting
Missile armament: two quadruple launchers for 32 SA-N-5 'Grail' SAMs

Torpedo armament: two twin 533-mm (21-in) mountings for Type 53 dual-role torpedoes ('Parchim II' class ships)
Anti-submarine armament: two RBU 6000 12-barrel rocket-launchers, four single 406-mm (16-in) mountings for Type 40 torpedoes or ('Parchim II' class ships) Type 53 torpedoes (see above), and two racks for 24 depth charges
Mines: 20/30 depending on type
Aircraft: none
Electronics: one 'Strut Curve' air-search radar, one TSR333 navigation radar, one 'Muff Cob' or ('Parchim II' class ships) 'Bass Tilt' gun fire-control radar, one high-frequency active search and attack hull sonar, one high-

frequency active search variable-depth sonar (some ships only), one ESM system with two 'Watch Dog' antennae/housings, two chaff launchers, and one 'High Pole-B' and one 'Cross Loop-B' IFF systems
Propulsion: two diesels delivering 9000 kW (12,070 hp) to two shafts
Performance: maximum speed 25 kt
Complement: 60

Class
1. East Germany ('Parchim I' class)

Name	No.	Builder	Commissioned
Parchim	242	Peenewerft	Apr 1981
Lübz	221	Peenewerft	Sep 1981
Bützow	241	Peenewerft	1981
Bad Doberan	222	Peenewerft	1981
Perleberg	243	Peenewerft	1981
Wismar	241	Peenewerft	1982
Waren	223	Peenewerft	1982
Güstrow	234	Peenewerft	1982
Ludwigslust	232	Peenewerft	1982
Ribnitz-Darmgarten	224	Peenewerft	1982
Grevesmühlen	233	Peenewerft	1984
Prenzlau	231	Peenewerft	1984
Angermunde	214	Peenewerft	1984
Sternberg	212	Peenewerft	1985
Gädebusch	211	Peenewerft	1985
Bergen	213	Peenewerft	1985

(This East German coastal defence corvette class is based on the hull of the Soviet 'Grisha' class but provided with higher freeboard and different armament. The vessels serve in four squadrons each containing four sequentially numbered vessels.)

2. USSR ('Parchim II' class)
7 ships with 5 more building
(Built at Peenewerft specially for the Soviet navy since 1985, with the first unit delivered in 1986, this is similar to the East German 'Parchim I' class in all but armament details. It is likely that 12 ships will be procured to replace the elderly 'Petya' class in the Baltic.)

The 'Parchim' class has a 30-mm twin mounting and rocket launchers forward, and a 57-mm twin mounting aft. The twin diesels exhaust through the sides.

'Pauk' class FFL(G)

(USSR)
Type: gun corvette
Displacement: 580 tons full load
Dimensions: length 58·0 m (190·3 ft); beam 10·5 m (34·4 ft); draught 2·5 m (8·2 ft)
Gun armament: one 76-mm (3-in) L/60 DP in a single mounting, and one 30-mm ADGM-630 CIWS mounting
Missile armament: one quadruple launcher for eight SA-N-5 'Grail' SAMs
Torpedo armament: none
Anti-submarine armament: two RBU 1200 five-barrel rocket-launchers, four single 406-mm (16-in) mountings for Type 40 torpedoes, and two racks for 12 depth charges
Aircraft: none
Electronics: one 'Peel Cone' air/surface-search radar, one 'Spin Trough' surface-search and navigation radar, one 'Bass Tilt' gun fire-control radar, one medium-frequency active search and attack hull sonar, one medium-frequency active search variable-depth sonar, one ESM system with warning element, two chaff launchers, and one 'Square Head' and one 'High Pole-B' IFF systems
Propulsion: four M 504 diesels delivering 12,000 kW (16,095 hp) to two shafts
Performance: maximum speed 34 kt
Complement: 40

Class
1. USSR
30 ships with more 3 more building and ? more planned
Note: Designed as replacement for the 'Poti' class, this useful patrol and anti-submarine type is derived from the 'Tarantul' class. The first unit was delivered in 1979 and the building programme continues.

The 'Pauk' class is in essence an anti-submarine derivative of the 'Tarantul' class, with an extended stern for variable-depth sonar.

'Poti' class FFL(G)

(USSR)
Type: gun corvette
Displacement: 500 tons standard and 580 tons full load
Dimensions: length 60·0 m (196·8 ft); beam 8·0 m (26·2 ft); draught 2·8 m (9·2 ft)
Armament: two 57-mm L/80 DP in a twin mounting
Missile armament: none
Torpedo armament: none
Anti-submarine armament: two RBU 6000 12-barrel rocket-launchers, and four single 406-mm (16-in) mountings for Type 40 torpedoes
Electronics: one 'Strut Curve' air-search radar, one 'Spin Trough' surface-search and navigation radar, one 'Muff Cob' gun fire-control radar, one high-frequency active search and attack variable-depth sonar, one ESM system with two 'Watch Dog' antennae/housings, and one 'High Pole-B' IFF system
Propulsion: CODOG arrangement, with two gas turbines delivering

22,400 kW (30,045 hp) or two M 503A diesels delivering 6000 kW (8,065 hp) to two shafts
Performance: maximum speed 38 kt; range 11,130 km (6,915 miles) at 10 kt or 925 km (575 miles) at 34 kt
Complement: 80

Class
1. Bulgaria
3 ships
(These were delivered in the mid-1970s.)

2. Romania
3 ships
(These were delivered in the late 1960s.)

3. USSR
55 ships
(Built between 1961 and 1968 at Khabarovsk and Zelenodolsk, this is an obsolescent coastal anti-submarine type.)

'Saar 5' or 'Lahav' class FFL(M)

(Israel)
Type: guided-missile corvette
Displacement: 985 tons standard and 1,200 tons full load
Dimensions: length 77·2 m (253·2 ft); beam 8·8 m (28·9 ft); draught 4·2 m (13·8 ft)
Gun armament: two 76-mm (3-in) OTO Melara Compact L/62 DP in Mk 75 single mountings, and (general-purpose version) four 30-mm AA in two TCM-30 twin mountings
Missile armament: two Mk 141 quadruple container-launchers for eight RGM-84 Harpoon anti-ship missiles or (anti-submarine variant) four container-launchers for four Gabriel Mk II anti-ship missiles, and one Barak 1 vertical-launch system for 32 Barak SAMs
Torpedo armament: none
Anti-submarine armament: (anti-submarine version only) one 375-mm (14·76-in) Bofors three-barrel rocket-launcher, two Mk 32 triple 12·75-in (324-mm) mountings for Mk 46 torpedoes, and helicopter-launched weapons (see below)
Aircraft: one Mata Hellstar remotely piloted helicopter or (anti-submarine version only) one Agusta (Bell) AB.212ASW helicopter in a hangar amidships

Electronics: an extensive radar, sonar and ESM fit including an Elbit action information system, a data-link, an Elbit ESM system with warning and jamming elements, and two chaff/flare launchers
Propulsion: CODAG arrangement, with one General Electric LM2500 gas turbine delivering 24,000 hp (17,895 kW) and two MTU diesels delivering 3000 kW (4,025 hp) to two shafts
Performance: maximum speed 42 kt on gas turbine or 25 kt on diesels; range 8350 km (5,190 miles) at 22 kt; endurance 20 days
Complement: 45

Class
1. Israel

Name	No.	Builder	Laid down	Commissioned
Lahav				

Note: Israel plans to procure four of this class (two in the general-purpose and two in the anti-submarine configurations) with US funding so that despite construction in Israel the prime contractor will be Litton. In some sources it is claimed that the Gabriel II missiles are intended for anti-submarine use, presumably with a depth charge or homing torpedo as payload.

'Sleipner' class FFL

(Norway)
Type: gun corvette
Displacement: 600 tons standard and 780 tons full load
Dimensions: length 69·4 m (227·7 ft); beam 8·3 m (27·2 ft); draught 2·7 m (9·0 ft)
Gun armament: one 3-in (76-mm) L/50 DP in a Mk 34 single mounting, and one 40-mm Bofors L/70 AA in a single mounting
Missile armament: none
Torpedo armament: none
Anti-submarine armament: one Terne III six-barrel rocket-launcher, and two Mk 32 triple 12·75-in (324-mm) mountings for Mk 46 torpedoes
Aircraft: none
Mines: provision for minelaying
Electronics: one TM1229 surface-search radar, one Decca 202 navigation radar, one fire-control system with two TVT-300 optronic directors, one

Spherion TSM 2633 active search and attack hull sonar, and one Terne III Mk 3 active attack hull sonar
Propulsion: four MTU diesels delivering 6700 kW (8,985 hp) to two shafts
Performance: maximum speed 20 + kt
Complement: 62

Class
1. Norway

Name	No.	Builder	Laid down	Commissioned
Sleipner	F310	Nylands Verksted	1963	Apr 1965
Aeger	F311	Akers	1964	Mar 1967

Note: Though the class was planned at a strength of five units, only these two ships were built. Despite a recent improvement in the main sonar, the ships can be regarded only as obsolescent.

The *Sleipner* and her sistership are attractively modelled corvettes, but are obsolescent even in the coastal protection role.

'Tarantul I', 'Tarantul II' and 'Tarantul III' class FFL(M)s

(USSR)
Type: guided-missile corvette
Displacement: 480 tons standard and 580 tons full load
Dimensions: length 56·0 m (183·7 ft); beam 10·5 m (34·4 ft); draught 2·5 m (8·2 ft)
Gun armament: one 76-mm (3-in) L/60 DP in a single mounting, and two

30-mm ADGM-630 CIWS mountings
Missile armament: two twin container-launchers for four SS-N-2C 'Styx' anti-ship missiles or ('Tarantul III' class ships) two or one twin container-launcher for four or two SS-N-22 'Sunburn' anti-ship missiles, and one quadruple launcher for 16 SA-N-5 'Grail' SAMs
Torpedo armament: none
Anti-submarine armament: none
Aircraft: none
Electronics: one 'Plank Shave' or ('Tarantul II' and 'Tarantul III' class ships) 'Light Bulb' air/surface-search and SSM fire-control radar, one 'Band Stand'

surface-search radar (not in 'Tarantul I' class ships), one 'Spin Trough' navigation radar, one 'Bass Tilt' gun fire-control radar, one ESM system with four antennae/housings, two chaff launchers, and one 'Square Head' and one 'High Pole-B' IFF systems

Propulsion: CODOG or COGOG arrangement, with two NK-12M gas turbines delivering 18,000 kW (24,140 hp) and/or two diesels or gas turbines delivering between 3000 and 4500 kW (4,025 and 6,035 hp) to two shafts

Performance: maximum speed 36 kt; range 3700 km (2,300 miles) at 20 kt or 740 km (460 miles) at 36 kt

Complement: 50

Class

1. East Germany

Name	No.	Builder	Commissioned
Albin Koebis	571	Petrovsky	Sep 1984
Rudolf Egelhofer	572	Petrovsky	Dec 1985
Fritz Globig	573	Petrovsky	Sep 1985
Paul Eisenschneider	574	Petrovsky	Jan 1986
Hans Beimler	575	Petrovsky	Nov 1986

(These are 'Tarantul I' class ships, and more are to be delivered as replacements for East Germany's 'Osa I' class FACs.)

2. India

Name	No.	Builder	Commissioned
Veer	K40	Petrovsky	May 1987
Nirbhik	K41	Petrovsky	Jan 1988
Nipat	K42	Petrovsky	Jan 1989

(These three Soviet-supplied 'Tarantul I' class ships are to be complemented by five more Soviet-supplied vessels and a possible 16 examples of an improved version to be built in India at Mazagon Docks.)

3. Poland

Name	No.	Builder	Commissioned
Gornik	434	Petrovsky	Dec 1983
Hutnik	435	Petrovsky	Apr 1984
Stozniowiec	436	Petrovsky	Jan 1988

(These 'Tarantul I' class ships are to be joined by at least one and possibly nine more units.)

4. USSR

2 'Tarantul I' class ships
20 'Tarantul II' class ships
10 'Tarantul III' class ships with 3 more building and ? more planned
(The 'Tarantul' classes use basically the same hull as the 'Pauk' class without the latter's extended transom for the accommodation of variable-depth sonar. The first 'Tarantul I' class ship was delivered from Petrovsky in 1978, with others from Kolpino and Pacific coast yards. The 'Tarantul II' class was built between 1980 and 1986, and the current variant is the 'Tarantul III'.)

'Thetis' or 'Type 420' class FFL

(West Germany)

Type: gun corvette

Displacement: 575 tons standard and 730 tons full load

Dimensions: length 70·0 m (229·7 ft); beam 8·2 m (26·9 ft); draught 2·7 m (8·6 ft)

Gun armament: two 40-mm Bofors L/70 AA in a Breda twin mounting

Missile armament: none

Torpedo armament: none

Anti-submarine armament: one 375-mm (14·76-in) Bofors four-barrel rocket-launcher, one quadruple 12·75-in (324-mm) mounting for Mk 46 torpedoes, and two depth-charge rails

Aircraft: none

Electronics: one TRS 3001 surface-search radar, one Kelvin Hughes 14/9 navigation radar, one Krupp-Atlas ELAC 1BV active search and attack hull sonar, one WM-9 gun fire-control system, and one ESM system with warning element

Propulsion: two MAN V84V diesels delivering 5100 kW (6,840 hp) to two shafts

Performance: maximum speed 19·5 kt; range 5100 km (3,170 miles) at 15 kt

Complement: 4 + 60

Class

1. West Germany

Name	No.	Builder	Laid down	Commissioned
Thetis	P6052	Rolandwerft		Jul 1961
Hermes	P6053	Rolandwerft		Dec 1961
Najade	P6054	Rolandwerft		May 1962
Triton	P6055	Rolandwerft		Nov 1962
Theseus	P6056	Rolandwerft		Aug 1963

Note: These are obsolete coastal corvettes used mainly for training.

'Turunmaa' class FFL

(Finland)

Type: gun corvette

Displacement: 660 tons standard and 770 tons full load

Dimensions: length 74·1 m (243·1 ft); beam 7·8 m (25·6 ft); draught 2·4 m (7·9 ft)

Gun armament: one 120-mm (4·7-in) Bofors L/46 DP in a Bofors single mounting, four 23-mm L/60 AA in two twin mountings, and two 12·7-mm (0·5-in) machine-guns

Missile armament: none

Torpedo armament: none

Anti-submarine armament: two RBU 1200 five-barrel rocket-launchers, and two depth-charge racks

Aircraft: none

Electronics: one WM-22 surface-search radar, one navigation radar, one 9LV 200 radar used with the 9LV 200 Mk 2 fire-control system, one EOS-400 optronic director, and one high-frequency active search and attack hull sonar

Propulsion: CODOG arrangement, with one Rolls-Royce Olympus TM1A gas turbine delivering 15,000 hp (11,185 kW) or three MTU diesels delivering 2235 kW (3,000 hp) to three shafts

Performance: maximum speed 35 kt on gas turbine or 17 kt on diesels; range 4600 km (2,860 miles) at 14 kt

Complement: 70

Class

1. Finland

Name	No.	Builder	Laid down	Commissioned
Turunmaa	03	Wartsila	Mar 1967	Aug 1968
Karjala	04	Wartsila	Mar 1967	Oct 1968

Note: These obsolescent ships were updated in the first half of the 1980s with new radar and sonar, and possibly with a SAM system, and remain useful in the peculiar waters of the Finnish archipelago.

For their small size the *Turunmaa* and her sistership carry a potent gun armament, including the substantial 120-mm (4·7-in) weapon on the foredeck.

'Vigilance' class FFL(M)

(UK/Brunei)
Type: guided-missile corvette
Displacement: 985 tons
Dimensions: not revealed
Gun armament: one 76-mm (3-in) OTO Melara L/62 DP in an OTO Melara Compact single mounting, two 40-mm Bofors L/70 AA in a Breda Compact twin mounting, and two 20-mm Oerlikon AA in single mountings
Missile armament: two quadruple container-launchers for eight MM.40 Exocet anti-ship missiles
Torpedo armament: none
Anti-submarine armament: none
Aircraft: provision for one helicopter (up to the size of the Sikorsky SH-60 Seahawk) on a platform aft
Electronics: one air/surface-search radar, one navigation radar, one fire-control system, one ESM system with warning element, chaff/flare launchers, and other systems
Propulsion: two diesels delivering unrevealed power to two shafts
Performance: maximum speed 30+ kt; range 6,350 miles (10,220 km) at 12 kt
Complement: 50/55 with provision for 24 marines

Class
1. Brunei

Name	No.	Builder	Laid down	Commissioned
		Vosper Thornycroft		
		Vosper Thornycroft		
		Vosper Thornycroft		

Note: Designed by Vosper Thornycroft and ordered in 1989, these are powerful corvettes with a genuine multi-role capability.

'Vosper Mk 1' class FFL

(UK/Ghana)
Type: gun corvette
Displacement: 440 tons standard and 500 tons full load
Dimensions: length 177·0 ft (53·9 m); beam 28·5 ft (8·7 m); draught 13·0 ft (4·0 m)
Gun armament: one 4-in (102-mm) Vickers L/33 DP in a Mk 52 single mounting, and one 40-mm Bofors L/70 AA in a single mounting
Missile armament: none
Torpedo armament: none
Anti-submarine armament: one Squid three-barrel mortar
Aircraft: none
Electronics: one AWS 1 air-search radar, one Type 978 navigation radar, and one Type 164 active search and attack hull sonar
Propulsion: two MTU diesels delivering 4250 kW (5,700 hp) to two shafts
Performance: maximum speed 20 kt; range 3,350 miles (5390 km) at 14 kt
Complement: 9 + 45

Class
1. Ghana

Name	No.	Builder	Laid down	Commissioned
Kromantse	F17	Vosper		Jul 1964
Keta	F18	Vickers		May 1965

(This is a light corvette suitable only for patrol and training.)

2. Libya

Name	No.	Builder	Laid down	Commissioned
Tobruk	C411	Vosper		Apr 1966

(This Libyan ship is similar to the two Ghanaian units, but has two rather than one 40-mm guns, two Paxman Ventura 16 YJCM diesels delivering 3,800 hp/2835 kW for a speed of 18 kt, and a complement of 5 + 58.)

As the *Kromantse* is very lightly armed and possesses only modest electronics, it is suited to patrol and training. Visible here are the type's guns, 4-in (102-mm) and 40-mm weapons fore and aft.

'Vosper Thornycroft Mk 3' class FFL

(UK/Nigeria)
Type: gun corvette
Displacement: 580 tons standard and 660 tons full load
Dimensions: length 202·0 ft (61·6 m); beam 31·0 ft (9·5 ft); draught 11·3 ft (3·5 m)
Gun armament: one 76-mm (3-in) OTO Melara L/62 DP in an OTO Melara Compact single mounting, and two 40-mm Bofors L/70 AA in single mountings
Missile armament: none
Torpedo armament: none
Anti-submarine armament: none
Aircraft: none
Electronics: one AWS 1 air/surface-search radar, one TM1626 navigation radar, one radar used with the WM-22 gun fire-control system, one Naja optronic director, and IPN 10 action information system
Propulsion: two MAN VSV 24·30-B diesels delivering 5960 kW (7,995 hp) to two shafts
Performance: maximum speed 22 kt; range 3,450 miles (5550 km) at 14 kt
Complement: 8 + 59

Class
1. Nigeria

Name	No.	Builder	Laid down	Commissioned
Otobo	F82	Vosper Thornycroft	Sep 1970	Nov 1972

Note: This ship was taken in hand by an Italian yard in 1988 for conversion into an offshore patrol vessel: the programme comprises a complete overhaul of the hull, replacement of the engines, revision of the armament and modification of the electronic suite to the standard described above. A sistership, *Dorina*, was deleted in 1987.

The *Otobo* is seen in her original configuration with two 4-in (102-mm) DP guns in a Mk 19 twin mounting located on the foredeck. In a recent overhaul this mounting has been replaced by a single 76-mm (3-in) gun.

'Vosper Thornycroft Mk 9' class FFL

(UK/Nigeria)
Type: gun corvette
Displacement: 680 tons standard and 780 tons full load
Dimensions: length 226·0 ft (69·0 m); beam 31·5 ft (9·6 m); draught 9·8 ft (3·0 m)
Gun armament: one 76-mm (3-in) OTO Melara L/62 DP in an OTO Melara Compact single mounting, one 40-mm Bofors L/70 AA in a Breda 350 single mounting, and two 20-mm Oerlikon AA in single mountings
Missile armament: one triple launcher for 12 Sea Cat SAMS
Torpedo armament: none
Anti-submarine armament: one 375-mm (14·76-in) Bofors two-barrel rocket-launcher
Aircraft: none
Electronics: one AWS 2 air/surface-search radar, one TM1226 navigation radar, one radar used in conjunction with the WM-24 SAM and gun fire-control system, one PMS 26 active search and attack hull sonar, and one ESM system with Cutlass warning element
Propulsion: two MTU 20V 956 TB92 diesels delivering 13,120 kW (17,595 hp) to two shafts
Performance: maximum speed 27 kt; range 2,550 miles (4105 km) at 14 kt
Complement: 90

Class
1. Nigeria

Name	No.	Builder	Laid down	Commissioned
Erinomi	F83	Vosper Thornycroft	Oct 1975	Jan 1980
Enyimiri	F84	Vosper Thornycroft	Feb 1977	Jul 1980

Note: By local standards these should be modestly capable vessels, but much of their sensor and armament fit is inoperative.

'Al Siddiq' class FAC(M)

(USA/Saudi Arabia)
Type: fast attack craft (missile)
Displacement: 425 tons standard and 480 tons full load
Dimensions: length 190·5 ft (58·1 m); beam 26·5 ft (8·1 m); draught 11·0 ft (3·4 m)
Gun armament: one 76-mm (3-in) OTO Melara Compact L/62 DP in a Mk 75 single mounting, one 20-mm Phalanx Mk 15 CIWS mounting, two 20-mm Oerlikon L/80 AA in single mountings, two 81-mm (3·2-in) mortars, and two Mk 19 40-mm grenade-launchers
Missile armament: two Mk 141 twin container-launchers for four RGM-84 Harpoon anti-ship missiles
Torpedo armament: none
Anti-submarine armament: none
Electronics: one SPS-55 surface-search radar, one radar used in conjunction with the Mk 92/94 (WM-25/28) gun and SSM fire-control system, one Mk 24 optical director, one SLQ-32(V)1 ESM system with warning element, and two Mk 36 Super RBOC chaff/flare launchers
Propulsion: CODOG arrangement, with one General Electric LM2500 gas turbine delivering 23,000 hp (17,150 kW) or two MTU 12V 652 TB91 diesels delivering 3000 kW (4,025 hp) to two shafts
Performance: maximum speed 38 kt on gas turbine or 15·5 kt on diesels; range 3,350 miles (5390 km) at 14 kt
Complement: 5 + 33

Class
1. Saudi Arabia

Name	No.	Builder	Commissioned
Al Siddiq	511	Peterson Builders	Dec 1980
Al Farouq	513	Peterson Builders	Jun 1981
Abdul Aziz	515	Peterson Builders	Aug 1981
Faisal	517	Peterson Builders	Nov 1981
Kahlid	519	Peterson Builders	Jan 1982
Amyr	521	Peterson Builders	Jun 1982
Tariq	523	Peterson Builders	Aug 1982
Oqbah	525	Peterson Builders	Oct 1982
Abu Obaidah	527	Peterson Builders	Dec 1982

Note: Though comparatively large, these craft are confined in offensive terms to anti-ship operations with a powerful missile and gun armament. The CIWS mounting provides a very useful defensive capability against anti-ship missiles.

Located on the stern of *Al Siddiq* is a Phalanx CIWS mounting and two twin containers for Harpoon anti-ship missiles, while just forward of them are two canvas-shrouded 20-mm cannon in single mountings on each beam.

'Balcom 10' class FAC(M)

(East Germany)
Type: fast attack craft (missile)
Displacement: about 500 tons full load
Dimensions: length 52·0 m (170·6 ft); beam 9·5 m (31·2 ft); draught 2·2 m (7·2 ft)
Gun armament: one 76-mm (3-in) L/60 DP in a single mounting, and one 30-mm ADGM-630 CIWS mounting
Missile armament: two quadruple container-launchers for eight SS-N-X anti-ship missiles
Torpedo armament: none
Anti-submarine armament: none
Electronics: one 'Plank Shave' air/surface-search radar, one navigation radar, one 'Bass Tilt' gun fire-control radar, one ESM system with warning element, two chaff launchers, and one 'Square Head-A' IFF and one 'Salt Pot' IFF systems
Propulsion: four diesels delivering unrevealed power to four shafts
Performance: maximum speed 38 kt
Complement: 45

Class
1. East Germany

Name	No.	Builder	Commissioned
	91		1989

Note: This new class of FAC(M) is being produced as replacement for the 'Osa I' class craft currently operated by East Germany, and a total of at least 12 is expected. The type appears to be a development of the 'Tarantul' class hull with diesel propulsion. The missile is a new type as yet undesignated in the West, and resembles the French Exocet to judge by the external appearance of the container-launchers.

'Brooke Marine 32·6-m' class FAC(M)

(UK/Kenya)
Type: fast attack craft (missile)
Displacement: 120 tons standard and 145 tons full load
Dimensions: length 107·0 ft (32·6 m); beam 20·0 ft (6·1 m); draught 5·6 ft (1·7 m)
Gun armament: two 30-mm Oerlikon L/85 AA in a GCM-A03 twin mounting
Missile armament: four container-launchers for four Gabriel II anti-ship missiles
Torpedo armament: none
Anti-submarine armament: none
Electronics: one AC1226 surface-search and navigation radar, one RTN 10X radar used with the Argo NA10 fire-control system, one optronic director, and other systems
Propulsion: two Paxman Valenta diesels delivering 5,400 hp (4025 kW) to two shafts
Performance: maximum speed 25·5 kt; range 2,875 miles (4625 km) at 12 kt
Complement: 3 + 18

Class
1. Kenya

Name	No.	Builder	Commissioned
Madaraka	P3121	Brooke Marine	Jun 1975
Jamhuri	P3122	Brooke Marine	Jun 1975
Harambe	P3123	Brooke Marine	Aug 1975

(These were built as patrol craft, and converted to FAC[M]s in 1981, 1983 and 1982 respectively.)

2. Nigeria

Name	No.	Builder	Commissioned
Makurdi	P167	Brooke Marine	Aug 1974
Hadejia	P168	Brooke Marine	Aug 1974
Jebba	P171	Brooke Marine	Apr 1977
Oguta	P172	Brooke Marine	Apr 1977

(With standard and full-load displacements of 115 and 143 tons respectively, these craft have a propulsion arrangement of two Paxman Ventura YCJM diesels delivering 3,000 hp/2235 kW to two shafts for a maximum speed of 20·5 kt. The armament comprises four 30-mm Oerlikon L/85 AA in two Emerlec twin mountings, and the electronic suite includes TM1226 surface-search and navigation radar. The complement is 4 + 17 in the patrol role.)

'Brooke Marine 37·5-m' class FAC(G)

(UK/Algeria)
Type: fast attack craft (gun)
Displacement: 166 tons standard and 200 tons full load
Dimensions: length 123·0 ft (37·5 m); beam 22·6 ft (6·9 m); draught 6·0 ft (1·8 m)
Gun armament: one 76-mm (3-in) OTO Melara L/62 DP in an OTO Melara Compact single mounting, and two 23-mm L/87 AA in a twin mounting
Missile armament: none
Torpedo armament: none
Anti-submarine armament: none
Electronics: one TM1226 surface-search and navigation radar, and other systems
Propulsion: two MTU 12V 538 TB92 diesels delivering 4500 kW (6,035 hp) to two shafts
Performance: maximum speed 27 kt; range 3,800 miles (6115 km) at 12 kt
Complement: 3 + 24

The Omani *Al Mujahid* is typical of the various 'Brooke Marine 37·5-m' classes in FAC(G) configuration with a 76-mm (3-in) OTO Melara dual-purpose gun on the foredeck and a single 20-mm cannon aft.

Class

1. Algeria ('Kebir' class)

Name	No.	Builder	Commissioned
El Yadekh	341	Brooke Marine	1982
El Mourakeb	342	Brooke Marine	1983
	343	Mers-el-Kebir	1988
	344	Mers-el-Kebir	1985
	345	Mers-el-Kebir	1985
	346	Mers-el-Kebir	Nov 1985
	347	Mers-el-Kebir	1988
	348	Mers-el-Kebir	1988
	349	Mers-el-Kebir	1988

(These Algerian craft are based on the standard 'Brooke 37·5-m' hull, but have been completed as FAC(G)s with a gun armament that includes a 76-mm/3-in OTO Melara L/62 DP in an OTO Melara Compact single mounting forward and a 20-mm Oerlikon AA in a single mounting aft, or in some craft two 30-mm L/65 AA in a twin mounting forward. Another three units may have been ordered in the late 1980s.)

2. Barbados

Name	No.	Builder	Commissioned
Trident	P01	Brooke Marine	1982

(This FAC[P] is similar to the Omani units but with standard and full-load displacements of 155·5 and 190 tons respectively. The armament comprises single 40-mm Bofors L/70 and 20-mm Oerlikon guns, and the 6,000 hp/4475 kW provided by two Paxman Valenta 12RP-200 diesels allows a maximum speed of 29 kt. The complement is 27.)

3. Oman ('Al Wafi' class)

Name	No.	Builder	Commissioned
Al Wafi	B4	Brooke Marine	Mar 1977
Al Fulk	B5	Brooke Marine	Mar 1977
Al Mujahid	B6	Brooke Marine	Jul 1977
Al Jabbar	B7	Brooke Marine	Oct 1977

(The 'Al Wafi' class is a variant of the now-deleted 'Al Mansur' FAC[M] class optimized for the FAC[M] role with standard and full-load displacements of 135 and 153 tons, dimensions that include a length of 123 ft/37·5 m, a beam of 22·5 ft/6·9 m and a draught of 6·0 ft/2·2m, a main armament of one 76-mm/3-in OTO Melara Compact L/62 DP and a secondary armament of one 20-mm AA used in conjunction with Decca 1226 surface-search radar, Decca 1229 navigation radar, a Sea Archer fire-control system and a Laurence Scott optical director. Propulsion is entrusted to two Paxman Ventura 16 RP200 diesels delivering 4,800 hp/3580 kW for a maximum speed of 25 kt, and the complement is 3 + 24.)

'Constitucion' class FAC(M/G)

(UK/Venezuela)

Type: fast attack craft (missile/gun)

Displacement: 170 tons full load

Dimensions: length 121·0 ft (36·9 m); beam 23·3 ft (7·1 m); draught 6·0 ft (1·8 m)

Gun armament: one 76-mm (3-in) OTO Melara L/62 DP in an OTO Melara Compact single mounting (PC11, 13 and 15 only) and one 40-mm Bofors L/70 AA in a Breda single mounting

Missile armament: two Teseo container-launchers for two Otomat anti-ship missiles (PC12, 14 and 16 only)

Torpedo armament: none

Anti-submarine armament: none

Electronics: one SPQ 2D surface-search radar, and (P11, 13 and 15 only) one RTN 10X radar used in conjunction with the Argo NA10 gun fire-control system

Propulsion: two MTU 16V 538 TB90 diesels delivering 5400 kW (7,240 hp) to two shafts

Performance: maximum speed 31 kt; range 2500 km (1,555 miles) at 16 kt

Complement: 3 + 14

Note: These are comparatively light FACs of which three are equipped with anti-ship missiles. All the craft are to be modernized in the near future, the three FAC(G)s being turned into FAC(M)s by the replacement of the 76-mm (3-in) gun with RGM-84 Harpoon anti-ship missiles. It is likely that the three current FAC(M)s will then receive the same missile type in place of their Otomat weapons.

Class

1. Venezuela

Name	No.	Builder	Commissioned
Constitucion	PC11	Vosper Thornycroft	Aug 1974
Federacion	PC12	Vosper Thornycroft	Mar 1975
Independencia	PC13	Vosper Thornycroft	Sep 1974
Libertad	PC14	Vosper Thornycroft	Jun 1975
Patria	PC15	Vosper Thornycroft	Jan 1975
Victoria	PC16	Vosper Thornycroft	Sep 1975

The *Constitucion* is seen in the baseline configuration of this class, with the forward 76-mm (3-in) gun that is to be replaced by missiles.

'Cormoran' class FAC(P)

(Spain/Morocco)

Type: fast attack craft (patrol)

Displacement: 425 tons full load

Dimensions: length 58·1 m (190·6 ft); beam 7·6 m (24·9 ft); draught 2·7 m (8·9 ft)

Gun armament: one 40-mm Bofors L/70 AA in a single mounting, and two 20-mm GIAT AA in single mountings

Missile armament: none

Torpedo armament: none

Anti-submarine armament: none

Electronics: one surface-search and navigation radar

Propulsion: two Bazan/MTU 16V 956 TB82 diesels delivering 2850 kW (3,820 hp) to two shafts

Performance: maximum speed 22 kt; range 11,300 km (7,020 miles) at 12 kt; endurance 10 days

Complement: 51

Class

1. Morocco

Name	No.	Builder	Commissioned
L. V. Rabhi	310	Bazan	Sep 1988
Errachiq	311	Bazan	1989
El Akid	312	Bazan	1989
El Maher	313	Bazan	1989
El Majid	314	Bazan	1989
El Bachir	315	Bazan	1989

(Retaining the same basic hull as the 'Lazaga' class [itself a low-powered derivative of the 'Lürssen FPB-57' class design] but using a lower-powered propulsion arrangement for reduced speed, these are long-endurance patrol and fishery protection duty vessels that clearly possess the potential for later conversion into more heavily armed FACs and even FAC[M]s.)

2. Venezuela

Name	No.	Builder	Commissioned
		Bazan	
		Bazan	
		Bazan	

(Ordered in 1987, these craft are to be similar to the Moroccan in dimensions except for a length of 55·0 m/180·4 ft but, with 9000 kW/12,070 hp delivered by three MTU 16V 956 TB91 diesels to three shafts, are capable of 35 kt. The craft have been completed as FAC[M]s with an armament of two Mk 141 twin container-launchers for four RGM-84 Harpoon anti-ship missiles, one 76-mm/3-in OTO Melara L/62 DP in an OTO Melara Compact single mounting and two 40-mm Bofors L/70 AA in a Breda twin mounting. The complement is 5 + 27. A fourth unit may later be built in Venezuela.)

'Dvora' class FAC(M)

(Israel)

Type: fast attack craft (missile)

Displacement: 47 tons full load

Dimensions: length 21·6 m (70·8 ft); beam 5·5 m (18·0 ft); draught 1·8 m (5·91 ft)

Gun armament: two 20-mm Oerlikon L/80 AA in single mountings, and two 0·5-in (12·7-mm) machine-guns

Missile armament: two container-launchers for two Gabriel anti-ship missiles

Torpedo armament: none

Anti-submarine armament: none

Electronics: one Decca 926 surface-search and navigation radar, one EL/M-2221 fire-control radar, and one DG fire-control system

Propulsion: two MTU 12V 331 TC81 diesels delivering 4050 kW (5,430 hp) to two shafts

Performance: maximum speed 36 kt; range 1300 km (810 miles) at 32 kt

Complement: 10

Class
1. Israel
8 craft

(These are based on the hull of the 'Dabur' class patrol craft with slight enlargement and considerably more power. The missile armament is notably heavy for so small a hull, in fact the world's smallest with missile armament. In 1987 Israel ordered another six units as **'Super Dvora' class** FAC[G]s, each 22·4 m/73·5 ft long, carrying an armament of two 20-mm AA in single mountings and two 0·5-in/12·7-mm machine-guns but capable of being retrofitted as FAC[M]s with Gabriel missiles, and possessing a more powerful propulsion arrangement for a maximum speed of 40 kt.)

2. Sri Lanka ('Super Dvora' class)

Name	No.	Builder	Commissioned
	P453	Israel Aircraft Industries	1984
	P454	Israel Aircraft Industries	1984
	P455	Israel Aircraft Industries	1986
	P456	Israel Aircraft Industries	1986
	P457	Israel Aircraft Industries	1986
	P458	Israel Aircraft Industries	1986
	P463	Israel Aircraft Industries	1987
	P463	Israel Aircraft Industries	1987
	P463	Israel Aircraft Industries	1988
	P463	Israel Aircraft Industries	1988
	P463	Israel Aircraft Industries	1988
	P463	Israel Aircraft Industries	1988

(These are FAC[G]s with an armament of two 20-mm Oerlikon cannon and two 0·5-in/12·7-mm machine-guns. The first six craft have two MTU 12V 331 diesels delivering 2000 kW/2,680 hp to two shafts for a maximum speed of 36 kt, and the craft of the second batch of six craft have greater power for improved speed.)

3. Taiwan ('Hai Ou' class)
50 craft

(This is a development of the 'Dvora' class by the Sun Yat-sen Scientific Research Institute built by the Tsoying Shipyard of the China Shipbuilding Corporation. The armament comprises two Hsiung Feng anti-ship missiles, one 20-mm Oerlikon AA gun and two 0·5-in/12·7-mm machine-guns, the propulsion arrangement features two MTU 12V 331 TC81 diesels delivering 2030 kW/2,725 hp to two shafts for a maximum speed of 36 kt, and the electronics include RCA R76 C5 surface-search and fire-control radar, a Kollmorgen Mk 35 optical director, and four AV2 chaff launchers.)

The units of the 'Dvora' class are the world's smallest missile craft. The area aft of the bridge is dominated by the container-launchers for two Gabriel anti-ship missiles.

'Flagstaff 2' FAH(M)

(USA/Israel)

Type: fast attack hydrofoil (missile)

Displacement: 91·5 tons standard and 105 tons full load

Dimensions: length 84·0 ft (25·6 m); beam 24·0 ft (7·3 m); draught 5·0 ft (1·6 m)

Gun armament: four 30-mm AA in two TCM-30 twin mountings

Missile armament: two twin container-launchers for four RGM-84 Harpoon and two single container-launchers for two Gabriel III anti-ship missiles

Torpedo armament: none

Anti-submarine armament: none

Electronics: surface-search and navigation radars, one EL/M-2221 fire-control radar, and one DG fire-control system

Propulsion: two diesels delivering unrevealed power for hullborne operation, and two Allison 501KF gas turbines delivering 5,400 hp (4025 kW) to four shafts for foilborne operation

Performance: maximum speed 48 kt; range 3,000 miles (4830 km) at 8 kt hullborne and 1,150 miles (1850 km) at 42 kt foilborne

Complement: 15

Class
1. Israel

Name	No.	Builder	Commissioned
Shimrit	M161	Grumman Lantana	1982
Livnit	M162	Grumman Lantana	1984
Snapirit	M163	Grumman Lantana	1985

Note: An advanced high-performance hydrofoil with two types of anti-ship missiles, the 'Flagstaff 2' class was originally to have numbered 12 units but has been curtailed at just these three, possibly reflecting the severe teething problems encountered with getting the craft into service.

Above and above right: The *Shimrit* is lead craft of the 'Flagstaff 2' class of FAH(M)s armed in the unusual but typical Israeli fashion with a mix of two anti-ship missile types, the Gabriel and the Harpoon.

'Flyvevisken' class FAC(G)

(Denmark)
Type: fast attack craft (gun)
Displacement: about 300 tons full load
Dimensions: length 54·0 m (177·2 ft); beam 9·0 m (29·5 ft); draught 2·5 m (8·2 ft)
Gun armament: one 76-mm (3-in) OTO Melara L/62 DP in an OTO Melara Super Rapid single mounting, and two 0·5-in (12·7-mm) machine-guns
Missile armament: none
Torpedo armament: none
Anti-submarine armament: none
Electronics: one AWS 6 surface-search radar, one Terma Pilot navigation radar, one radar used in conjunction with the 9LV 200 Mk 3 Sea Viking fire-control system (with TV, FLIR and laser sensors), one ESM system with Sabre warning and Cygnus jamming elements, and other systems as required
Propulsion: CODAG arrangement, with one General Electric LM2500 gas turbine delivering 6,000 hp (4475 kW) and two MTU 16V 396 TB94 diesels delivering 5200 kW (6,975 hp) to three shafts

Performance: maximum speed 30 kt on gas turbine and diesels, and 20 kt on diesels
Complement: 15/18 with a maximum of 28 possible

Class
1. Denmark

Name	No.	Builder	Commissioned
Flyvevisken	P550	Karlskrona/Aalborg	Oct 1987
Hajen	P551	Karlskrona/Aalborg	Dec 1989
Havkatten	P552	Karlskrona/Aalborg	1990
Laxen	P553	Karlskrona/Aalborg	1991
Makaelen	P554	Karlskrona/Aalborg	1991
Støren	P555	Karlskrona/Aalborg	1992
Svaerdvisken	P556	Karlskrona/Aalborg	1992

Note: A class of 16 such craft is planned, this 'Standard Flex 300' type being schemed as replacement for the 'Daphne' class of seaward defence vessels, 'Soloven' class of FAC(T)s, and 'Sund' class of mine countermeasures vessels. The design has thus been optimized for adaptability to several roles with 'plug-in' guns, missiles and electronics.

'Göteborg' class FAC(M)

(Sweden)
Type: fast attack craft (missile)
Displacement: 300 tons standard and 380 tons full load
Dimensions: length 57·0 m (187·0 ft); beam 8·0 m (26·2 ft); draught 2·0 m (6·6 ft)
Gun armament: one 57-mm L/70 SAK Mk 2 DP in a Bofors single mounting, and one 40-mm Bofors L/70 AA in a single mounting
Missile armament: four twin container-launchers for eight Rbs 15M anti-ship missiles
Torpedo armament: two single 533-mm (21-in) mountings for Tp 613 wire-guided dual-role torpedoes
Anti-submarine armament: one Elma grenade system with four LLS-920 nine-barrel launchers, and (in place of two 533-mm torpedo mountings) two twin 400-mm (15·75-in) mountings for Tp 431 wire-guided torpedoes
Mines: fitted for minelaying
Electronics: one Sea Giraffe 150 HC air/surface-search radar, one Terma PN 612 navigation radar, two radars used in conjunction with 9LV 400 gun fire-control systems (with TV, FLIR and laser sensors), one RCI-400 missile fire-control system, two 9LV 200 Mk 3 optronic directors, one TSM 2643

Salmon active search variable-depth sonar and one Simrad SS 304 active attack hull sonar used in conjunction with the 9AU 300 underwater weapons fire-control system, one ESM system with Carol warning and Argo jamming elements, and four Philax chaff/flare launchers
Propulsion: three MTU 16V 396 TB94 diesels delivering 6450 kW (8,650 hp) to KaMeWa waterjets
Performance: maximum speed 32 + kt
Complement: 7 + 29 with a maximum of 40 possible

Class
1. Sweden

Name	No.	Builder	Commissioned
Göteborg	K21	Karlskrona	1990
Gälve	K22	Karlskrona	1990
Kalmar	K23	Karlskrona	1991
Sundsvall	K24	Karlskrona	1991

Note: Heavily armed and propelled somewhat unusually amongst hullborne FACs by waterjets, these four craft are planned as replacements for the elderly 'Spica I' class FAC(T)s. Unlike earlier Swedish FACs, which are armed almost exclusively for the anti-ship role, the 'Göteborg' class has an effective dual capability against surface and underwater vessels.

'H3' class FAC(M)

(China)
Type: fast attack craft (missile)
Displacement: 239 tons
Dimensions: length 47·0 m (154·2 ft); beam 7·5 m (24·6 ft); draught 1·9 m (6·2 ft)
Gun armament: one 76-mm (3-in) OTO Melara Compact L/62 DP in a single Mk 75 mounting, and one 20-mm Phalanx Mk 15 CIWS mounting
Missile armament: eight container-launchers for eight C-801 anti-ship missiles
Torpedo armament: none
Anti-submarine armament: none

Electronics: one surface-search radar used in conjunction with the WM-25 fire-control system, one navigation radar, and other systems
Propulsion: three Allison 570KF gas turbines delivering 19,000 hp (14,165 kW) to KaMeWa waterjets
Performance: maximum speed 50 + kt
Complement: not revealed

Class
1. China
1 craft plus ? more building and ? more planned
Note: These boats are being built in the USA by Edward Heinemann and Nickum Spaulding Associates, and may eventually total 15 in number. The boats combine Chinese missiles with high-quality Western guns, electronics and engines.

'Hauk' class FAC(M)

(Norway)

Type: fast attack craft (missile)
Displacement: 120 tons standard and 148 tons full load
Dimensions: length 36·5 m (119·7 ft); beam 6·1 m (20·0 ft); draught 1·5 m (5·0 ft)
Gun armament: one 40-mm Bofors L/70 AA in a single mounting, and one 20-mm Rheinmetall AA in a single mounting
Missile armament: six container-launchers for six Penguin Mk II (possibly to be retrofitted with Penguin Mk III) anti-ship missiles
Torpedo armament: two single 533-mm (21-in) mountings for two Tp 61 wire-guided torpedoes
Anti-submarine armament: none
Electronics: two TM1226 surface-search and navigation radars, one MSI-80S fire-control system using one TVT-300 optonic tracker and one laser rangefinder, and one Simrad SQ-3D/QF active search hull sonar
Propulsion: two MTU 16V 538 TB91 diesels delivering 5400 kW (7,240 hp) to two shafts
Performance: maximum speed 34 kt; range 815 km (505 miles) at 34 kt
Complement: 20

Class
1. Norway

Name	No.	Builder	Commissioned
Hauk	P986	Bergens Mek	Aug 1977
Ørn	P987	Bergens Mek	Jan 1979
Terne	P988	Bergens Mek	Mar 1979
Tjeld	P989	Bergens Mek	May 1979
Skarv	P990	Bergens Mek	Jul 1979
Teist	P991	Bergens Mek	Sep 1979
Jo	P992	Bergens Mek	Nov 1979
Lom	P993	Bergens Mek	Jan 1980
Stegg	P994	Bergens Mek	Mar 1980
Falk	P995	Bergens Mek	Apr 1980
Ravn	P996	Westamarin	May 1980
Gribb	P997	Westamarin	Jul 1980
Geir	P998	Westamarin	Sep 1980
Erle	P999	Westamarin	Dec 1980

Note: These are in essence 'Snögg' class craft with a more capable fire-control system. They are particularly impressive small FAC(G)s with a large missile armament and a capability against closer-range targets with two powerful torpedoes.

'Helsinki' class FAC(M)

(Finland)

Type: fast attack craft (missile)
Displacement: 280 tons standard and 300 tons full load
Dimensions: length 45·0 m (147·6 ft); beam 8·9 m (29·2 ft); draught 3·0 m (9·9 ft)
Gun armament: one 57-mm SAK 57 L/70 DP in a Bofors single mounting, and four 23-mm L/60 AA in two twin mountings
Missile armament: four container-launchers for four Rbs 15M anti-ship missiles
Torpedo armament: none
Anti-submarine armament: none
Electronics: one 9LGA 208 surface-search radar, one radar used in conjunction with the 9LV 225 fire-control system, one EOS 40 optronic director, one Simrad SS 304 active search hull sonar, and one ESM system with Matilda warning element
Propulsion: three MTU 16V 538 TB92 diesels delivering 8175 kW (10,965 hp) to three shafts
Performance: maximum speed 30 kt
Complement: 30

Class
1. Finland

Name	No.	Builder	Commissioned
Helsinki	60	Wartsila	Sep 1981
Turku	61	Wartsila	Jun 1985
Oulu	62	Wartsila	Oct 1985
Kotka	63	Wartsila	Jun 1986

Note: This class has been designed for a 30-year life, with features to make possible the alteration of armament to suit specific roles.

'Helsinki 2' class FAC(M)

(Finland)

Type: fast attack craft (missile)
Displacement: 200 tons standard
Dimensions: length 48·0 m (157·5 ft); beam 8·0 m (26·2 ft); draught 2·7 m (8·6 ft)
Gun armament: one 57-mm Bofors SAK 57 L/70 DP in a single mounting
Missile armament: four or eight container-launchers for four or eight Rbs 15M anti-ship missiles
Torpedo armament: none
Anti-submarine armament: one Elma grenade system with four LLS-920 nine-barrel launchers
Electronics: one 9GA 208 surface-search radar, one navigation radar, one 9LV 25 radar used in conjunction with the 9LV 200 Mk 3 Sea Viking fire-control system (with TV, FLIR and laser sensors), one 9LW 300 ESM system with warning element, and decoy and chaff/flare launchers
Propulsion: two MTU 16V 538 TB92 diesels delivering 6000 kW (8,045 hp) to two waterjets
Performance: maximum speed 30 + kt
Complement: not revealed

Class
1. Finland

Name	No.	Builder	Commissioned
Luokka	64	Hollming SY	1990
	65	Hollming SY	1991
	66	Hollming SY	1991
	67	Hollming SY	1992

Note: Current plans call for a total of eight units in this class. The craft are to be built with only four anti-ship missiles, though there is deck space and electronic capacity for eight missiles to be shipped.

'Huchuan' class FAH(T)

(China)

Type: fast attack hydrofoil (torpedo)

Displacement: 39 tons standard and 46 tons full load

Dimensions: length 21·8 m (71·5 ft); beam 6·3 m (20·7 ft) over foils and 5·0 m (16·4 ft) over hull; draught 1·0 m (3·3 ft) foilborne and 3·6 m (11·8 ft) hullborne

Gun armament: four 14·5-mm (0·57-in) machine-guns in two twin mountings

Missile armament: none

Torpedo armament: two single 533-mm (21-in) mountings for two Type 53 torpedoes

Anti-submarine armament: depth charges

Electronics: one 'Skin Head' surface-search radar

Propulsion: three M 50F diesels delivering 2700 kW (3,620 hp) to three shafts

Performance: maximum speed 55 kt foilborne; range 925 km (575 miles) at cruising speed

Complement: 11

Class

1. Albania
32 craft
2. China
120+ craft
3. Pakistan
4 craft
4. Romania
3 craft plus 27 locally built craft
5. Tanzania
4 craft

Note: There is nothing exceptional about this useful FAH(T), which entered production at the Hutong yard at Shanghai in 1966. Production continues at the rate of about 10 craft per year. Older boats have one gun mounting amidships and the other aft, while newer boats have one mounting forward of the bridge and the other aft, plus a revised electronic fit.

Opposite page, bottom: In the 'Huchuan' class the forward hydrofoil set can be retracted into hull recesses for higher hullborne performance.

'Hugin' class FAC(M)

(Sweden)

Type: fast attack craft (missile)

Displacement: 120 tons standard and 150 tons full load

Dimensions: length 36·6 m (120·0 ft); beam 6·3 m (20·7 ft); draught 1·7 m (5·6 ft)

Gun armament: one 57-mm SAK 57 Mk 1 L/70 DP in a Bofors single mounting

Missile armament: six container-launchers for six Rb 12 (Penguin Mk II) anti-ship missiles (to be replaced by six Rbs 15M anti-ship missiles)

Torpedo armament: none

Anti-submarine armament: one Elma grenade system with four LLS-920 nine-barrel rocket-launchers, and two depth-charge racks

Mines: 24 on two rails in place of missiles

Electronics: one Skanter Mk 009 surface-search and navigation radar, one radar used in conjunction with the 9LV 200 Mk 2 fire-control system, one Simrad SQ 3D/SF active search and attack hull sonar, and one ESM system with EWS 905 warning element

Propulsion: two MTU 20V 672 TY90 diesels delivering 5350 kW (7,175 hp) to two shafts

Performance: maximum speed 36 kt

Complement: 3 + 19

Class

1. Sweden

Name	No.	Builder	Commissioned
Hugin	P151	Bergens Mek	Jul 1978
Munin	P152	Bergens Mek	Jul 1978
Magne	P153	Bergens Mek	Oct 1978
Mode	P154	Westamarin	Jan 1979
Vale	P155	Westamarin	Apr 1979
Vidar	P156	Westamarin	Aug 1979
Mjölner	P157	Westamarin	Oct 1979
Mysing	P158	Westamarin	Feb 1980
Kaparen	P159	Bergens Mek	Aug 1980
Väktaren	P160	Bergens Mek	Sep 1980
Snapphanen	P161	Bergens Mek	Jan 1980
Spejaren	P162	Bergens Mek	Mar 1980
Styrbjörn	P163	Bergens Mek	Jun 1980
Starkodder	P164	Bergens Mek	Aug 1981
Tordön	P165	Bergens Mek	Oct 1981
Tirfing	P166	Bergens Mek	Jan 1982

Note: This is a capable anti-ship class suited to coastal operations in the Swedish archipelago and in the Baltic. It is reported that some of the class are being retrofitted with variable-depth sonar, reflecting Sweden's increasing fears about Soviet submarine capability.

**Above: The SAK 57 Mk 1 is a powerful dual-role weapon on a FAC.
Below: The *Hugin* is seen in the original configuration for the class with six container-launchers for Penguin Mk II anti-ship missiles.**

'Komar' class FAC(M)

(USSR)

Type: fast attack craft (missile)

Displacement: 68 tons standard and 75 tons full load

Dimensions: length 26·8 m (87·9 ft); beam 6·2 m (20·3 ft); draught 1·5 m (4·9 ft)

Gun armament: two 25-mm AA in a twin mounting

Missile armament: two container-launchers for two SS-N-2A 'Styx' anti-ship missiles

Torpedo armament: none

Anti-submarine armament: none

Electronics: one 'Square Tie' surface-search radar, one 'Dead Duck' IFF, and one 'High Pole-A' IFF

Propulsion: four M 50F diesels delivering 3600 kW (4,830 shp) to four shafts

Performance: maximum speed 40 kt; range 740 km (460 miles) at 30 kt

Complement: 4 + 19

Class

1. Bangladesh ('Hegu' class)

Name	No.	Commissioned
Durbar	P8111	Apr 1983
Duranta	P8112	Apr 1983
Durvedya	P8113	Nov 1983
Durdam	P8114	Nov 1983

(These are standard ex-Chinese craft with two HY-2 anti-ship missiles.)

2. China

110 + locally-built **'Hegu' class** or **'Type 024' class** developments with four 25-mm L/60 AA in two twin mountings and, as a successive retrofit, four C-801 missiles in place of the original two HY-2 (SS-N-2 'Styx') missiles. There is also a single **'Hema' class** FAH(M) with a forward set of foils and an additional 2·0 m (6·6 ft) of length allowing the installation of a third twin 25-mm mounting aft of the missiles.

3. Egypt ('Hegu' class)

Name	No.	Commissioned
	611	Oct 1984
	612	Oct 1984
	613	Oct 1984
	614	Oct 1984
	615	Oct 1984
	616	Oct 1984

(These are standard ex-Chinese craft with two HY-2 anti-ship missiles.)

4. North Korea

8 craft, plus

8 locally built **'Sohung' class** developments with another 2 building

5. Pakistan ('Hegu' class)

Name	No.	Commissioned
Haibat	P1021	May 1981
Jalalat	P1022	May 1981
Jurat	P1023	Oct 1981
Shujaat	P1024	Oct 1981

(These are standard ex-Chinese craft with two HY-2 anti-ship missiles.)

Note: This elderly Soviet class is disappearing from service, Cuba, Egypt and Syria having disposed of their 'Komars'. However, the Chinese- and North Korean-built versions are still in production and comparatively widespread service.

Above: The 'Komar' class FAC(M) design is dominated by the container-launchers for its two large but obsolescent SS-N-2 anti-ship missiles.

'La Combattante II' class FAC(M)

(France/Greece)

Type: fast attack craft (missile)

Displacement: 234 tons standard and 275 tons full load

Dimensions: length 47·0 m (154·2 ft); beam 7·1 m (23·3 ft); draught 2·5 m (8·2 ft)

Gun armament: four 35-mm Oerlikon L/90 AA in two GDM-A twin mountings

Missile armament: two twin container-launchers for four MM.38 Exocet anti-ship missiles

Torpedo armament: two single 533-mm (21-in) mountings for two SST-4 wire-guided torpedoes

Anti-submarine armament: none

Electronics: one Triton surface-search radar, one Decca 1226C navigation radar, and one Pollux radar used in conjunction with the Vega fire-control system

Propulsion: four MTU 16V 538 diesels delivering 9000 kW (12,070 hp) to four shafts

Performance: maximum speed 36·5 kt; range 3700 km (2,300 miles) at 15 kt or 1575 km (980 miles) at 25 kt

Complement: 4 + 36

Class

1. Greece

Name	No.	Builder	Commissioned
Anthipoploiarhos Anninos	P14	CMN, Cherbourg	Jun 1972
Ipoploiarhos Arliotis	P15	CMN, Cherbourg	Apr 1972
Ipoploiarhos Konidis	P16	CMN, Cherbourg	Jul 1972
Ipoploiarhos Batsis	P17	CMN, Cherbourg	Dec 1971

(These craft are to be modernized by the early 1990s.)

2. Iran ('Kaman' class)

Name	No.	Builder	Commissioned
Kaman	P221	CMN, Cherbourg	Aug 1977
Zoubin	P222	CMN, Cherbourg	Sep 1977
Khadang	P223	CMN, Cherbourg	Mar 1978
Falakhon	P226	CMN, Cherbourg	Mar 1978
Shamshir	P227	CMN, Cherbourg	Mar 1978
Gorz	P228	CMN, Cherbourg	Aug 1978
Gardouneh	P229	CMN, Cherbourg	Sep 1978
Khanjar	P230	CMN, Cherbourg	Aug 1981
Heyzeh	P231	CMN, Cherbourg	Aug 1981
Tabarzin	P232	CMN, Cherbourg	Aug 1981

(These Iranian craft are similar in hull and machinery to the Greek units, but have a different armament and electronic fit. The armament comprises one 76-mm/3-in OTO Melara L/62 DP in an OTO Melara Compact single mounting, one 40-mm Bofors L/70 AA in a Breda single mounting and two twin container-launchers for four RGM-84 Harpoon anti-ship missiles used in conjunction with a WM-28 gun and SSM fire-control system. The Iranians lack Harpoon missiles because of a US embargo on the delivery of weapons to the country, and the last three were never fitted with Harpoon launchers. The propulsion comprises four MTU 16V 538 TB91 diesels delivering 10,740 kW/14,405 hp, but as the full-load displacement is 275 tons the maximum speed is 34·5 kt. A complement of 31 is carried. Eleventh and twelfth units, *Peykan* and *Joshan*, were sunk in combat, the former by the Iraqis during 1980 in the Gulf War, and the latter by the Americans during April 1988.)

3. Libya ('La Combattante IIG' class)

Name	No.	Builder	Commissioned
Sharara	518	CMN, Cherbourg	Feb 1982
Wahag	522	CMN, Cherbourg	May 1982
Shehab	524	CMN, Cherbourg	Apr 1982

Shouaiai	528	CMN, Cherbourg	Sep 1982
Shoula	532	CMN, Cherbourg	Oct 1982
Shafak	534	CMN, Cherbourg	Dec 1982
Bark	536	CMN, Cherbourg	Mar 1983
Rad	538	CMN, Cherbourg	May 1983
Laheeb	542	CMN, Cherbourg	Jul 1983

(These Libyan craft are to an enlarged 'La Combattante II' design with a full-load displacement of 311 tons on a length of 49·4 m/162·1 ft, a beam of 7·1 m/23·3 ft and a draught of 2·0 m/6·6 ft. The armament comprises one 76-mm/3-in OTO Melara L/62 DP in an OTO Melara Compact single mounting and two 40-mm Bofors L/70 AA in a Breda twin mounting plus four container-launchers for four Otomat anti-ship missiles. The electronics fit is one Triton surface-search radar, one Castor I radar used in conjunction with the Vega II fire-control system, and one Panda optical director. Four MTU 20V 538 TB91 diesels deliver 13,400 kW/17,970 hp to four shafts for a maximum speed of 39 kt and a range of 2960 km/1,840 miles at 15 kt. The complement is 27. A tenth unit, Waheed [526], was sunk by US forces in March 1986, and a second 'La Combattante IIG' class unit was severely damaged two days later.)

4. Malaysia ('La Combattante IID' or 'Perdana' class)

Name	No.	Builder	Commissioned
Perdana	3501	CMN, Cherbourg	Dec 1972
Serang	3502	CMN, Cherbourg	Jan 1973
Ganas	3503	CMN, Cherbourg	Feb 1973
Ganyang	3504	CMN, Cherbourg	Mar 1973

(These Malaysian craft are close to the norm in displacement and dimensions. The armament comprises one 57-mm SAK 57 Mk 1 L/70 DP in a Bofors single mounting and one 40-mm Bofors L/70 AA in a single mounting, plus two container-launchers for two MM.38 Exocet anti-ship missiles. The electronic suite includes Triton surface-search radar, Decca 616 navigation radar, Pollux radar used in conjunction with the Vega fire-control system, one ESM system with warning element, and four chaff/flare launchers. Four MTU 870 diesels deliver 10,400 kW/13,950 hp to four shafts for a maximum speed of 36·5 kt and a range of 1500 km/930 miles at 25 kt. The complement is 5 + 30.)

The *Antiploiarhos Laskos* is typical of the 'La Combattante' class.

5. West Germany ('Type 148' class)

Name	No.	Builder	Commissioned
Tiger	P6141	CMN, Cherbourg	Oct 1972
Iltis	P6142	CMN, Cherbourg	Jan 1973
Luchs	P6143	CMN, Cherbourg	Apr 1973
Marder	P6144	CMN, Cherbourg	Jun 1973
Leopard	P6145	CMN, Cherbourg	Aug 1973
Fuchs	P6146	Lürssen/CMN	Oct 1973
Jaguar	P6147	CMN, Cherbourg	Nov 1973
Löwe	P6148	Lürssen/CMN	Jan 1974
Wolf	P6149	CMN, Cherbourg	Feb 1974
Panther	P6150	Lürssen/CMN	Mar 1974
Häher	P6151	CMN, Cherbourg	Jun 1974
Storch	P6152	Lürssen/CMN	Jul 1974
Pelikan	P6153	CMN, Cherbourg	Sep 1974
Elster	P6154	Lürssen/CMN	Nov 1974
Alk	P6155	CMN, Cherbourg	Jan 1975
Dommel	P6156	Lürssen/CMN	Feb 1975
Weihe	P6157	CMN, Cherbourg	Apr 1975
Pinguin	P6158	Lürssen/CMN	May 1975
Reiher	P6159	CMN, Cherbourg	Jun 1975
Kranich	P6160	Lürssen/CMN	Aug 1975

(These West German craft are derivatives of the standard 'La Combattante II' class design with standard and full-load displacements of 234 and 265 tons on dimensions that include a length of 47·0 m/154·2 ft, a beam of 7·6 m/24·9 ft and a draught of 2·5 m/8·2 ft. The armament consists of one 76-mm/3-in OTO Melara L/62 DP in an OTO Melara Compact single mounting and one 40-mm Bofors L/70 AA in a single mounting, plus two twin container-launchers for four MM.38 Exocet anti-ship missiles and provision for minelaying; if the 40-mm gun is removed two minelaying rails can be installed. The radars include one Triton G air/surface-search, one 3RM 20 navigation and one Castor radar used in conjunction with the Vega fire-control system, and other features are the Panda optical director, the Link 11 data-link and an ESM system with warning element. The powerplant comprises four MTU 872 diesels delivering 10,800 kW/14,485 shp to four shafts for a maximum speed of 36 kt and a range of 1125 km/700 miles at 30 kt. The complement is 4 + 26.)

'La Combattante III' class FAC(M)

(France/Greece)

Type: fast attack craft (missile)

Displacement: 359 tons or (P24/29) 329 tons standard and 425 tons or (P24/29) 429 tons full load

Dimensions: length 56·2 m (184·0 ft); beam 8·0 m (26·2 ft); draught 2·1 m (7·0 ft)

Gun armament: two 76-mm (3-in) OTO Melara L/62 DP in OTO Melara Compact single mountings, and four 30-mm Oerlikon L/85 AA in two Emerlec twin mountings

Missile armament: four container-launchers for four MM.38 Exocet anti-ship missiles or (P24/29) six container-launchers for six Penguin Mk II anti-ship missiles

Torpedo armament: two single 533-mm (21-in) mountings for two SST-4 wire-guided torpedoes (P20/23 only)

Anti-submarine armament: none

Electronics: one Triton surface-search radar, one Decca 1226 navigation radar, one Castor II and one Pollux radar used in conjunction with the Vega I or II fire-control system, and two Panda optical directors

Propulsion: four MTU 20V 538 TB92 diesels delivering 15,500 kW (20,790 hp), or (P24/29) four MTU 20V 538 TB91 diesels delivering 11,200 kW (15,020 shp), in each case to four shafts

Performance: maximum speed 35·7 kt or (P24/29) 32·5 kt; range 3700 km (2,300 miles) at 15 kt or 1300 km (810 miles) at 32·6 kt

Complement: 5 + 37

Class

1. Greece

Name	No.	Builder	Commissioned
Antiploiarhos Laskos	P20	CMN, Cherbourg	Apr 1977
Plotarhis Blessas	P21	CMN, Cherbourg	Jul 1977
Ipoploiarhos Mikonios	P22	CMN, Cherbourg	Feb 1978
Ipoploiarhos Troupakis	P23	CMN, Cherbourg	Nov 1977
Simeoforos Kavaloudis	P24	Hellenic Shipyards	Jul 1980
Anthipoploiarhos Kostakos	P25	Hellenic Shipyards	Sep 1980
Ipoploiarhos Deyiannis	P26	Hellenic Shipyards	Dec 1980
Simeoforos Xenos	P27	Hellenic Shipyards	Mar 1981
Simeoforos Simitzopoulos	P28	Hellenic Shipyards	Jun 1981
Simeoforos Starakis	P29	Hellenic Shipyards	Oct 1981

(These craft fall into two subclasses, the four built in France having fewer anti-ship missiles but two anti-ship torpedoes and higher performance, while the six licence-built in Greece have more anti-ship missiles but no torpedoes and lower performance.)

2. Nigeria ('La Combattante IIIB' class)

Name	No.	Builder	Commissioned
Siri	P181	CMN, Cherbourg	Feb 1981
Ayam	P182	CMN, Cherbourg	Jun 1981
Ekun	P183	CMN, Cherbourg	Sep 1981

(These Nigerian craft have standard and full-load displacements of 385 and 430 tons on a length of 56·2 m/184·4 ft, a beam of 7·6 m/24·9 ft and a draught of 2·1 m/7·0 ft. The armament comprises one 76-mm/3-in OTO Melara L/62 DP in an OTO Melara Compact single mounting, two 40-mm Bofors L/70 AA in a Breda twin mounting, four 30-mm Oerlikon L/85 AA in two Emerlec twin mountings and four container-launchers for four MM.38 Exocet anti-ship missiles. The electronic suite includes Triton surface-search radar, Decca 1226 navigation radar and Castor II radar used in conjunction with the Vega fire-control system; other features are two Panda optical directors and an ESM system with RDL-2 warning element. Four MTU 16V 956 TB92 diesels deliver 15,000 kW/20,120 hp to four shafts for a maximum speed of 41 kt. The complement is 42.)

3. Qatar ('La Combattante IIIM' class)

Name	No.	Builder	Commissioned
Damsah	Q01	CMN, Cherbourg	Nov 1982
Al Ghariyah	Q02	CMN, Cherbourg	Feb 1983
Rbigah	Q03	CMN, Cherbourg	May 1983

(These Qatari craft are similar to the Tunisian units in all essential respects.)

4. Tunisia ('La Combattante IIIM' class)

Name	No.	Builder	Commissioned
La Galite	501	CMN, Cherbourg	Oct 1984
Tunis	502	CMN, Cherbourg	Nov 1984
Carthage	503	CMN, Cherbourg	Dec 1984

(Though similar to the Greek units, these Tunisian craft have a beam enlarged to 8·2 m/26·9 ft for standard and full-load displacements of 345 and 425 tons respectively. The armament comprises one 76-mm/3-in OTO Melara L/62 DP in an OTO Melara Compact single mounting, two 40-mm Bofors L/70 AA in a Breda twin mounting, two 30-mm Oerlikon L/75 AA in a GCM-A03 twin mounting and two quadruple container-launchers for eight MM.40 Exocet anti-ship missiles. Amongst the electronic fit are the standard Triton surface-search radar, Castor II radar used in conjunction with the Vega II fire-control system, a Sylosat satellite navigation system, two Naja optronic directors, an ESM system with warning element, and one Dagaie chaff/flare launcher. The propulsion system comprises four MTU 20V 538 TB93 diesels delivering 14,400 kW/19,315 hp to four shafts for a maximum speed of 38·5 kt and ranges of 5200 km/3,230 miles at 10 kt or 1300 km/810 miles at 33 kt. The complement is 35.)

'Lürssen FPB-36' class FAC(G)

(West Germany/Mauritania)

Type: fast attack craft (gun)

Displacement: 139 tons full load

Dimensions: length 36·2 m (118·7 ft); beam 5·8 m (19·0 ft); draught 1·9 m (6·2 ft)

Gun armament: one 40-mm Bofors L/70 AA in a single mounting, one 20-mm Oerlikon AA in a single mounting, and two 0·5-in (12·7-mm) machine-guns in single mountings

Missile armament: none

Torpedo armament: none

Anti-submarine armament: none

Electronics: one Raytheon RN 1220/6XB surface-search radar, and one Panda optical director

Propulsion: two MTU 16V 538 TB90 diesels delivering 4300 kW (5,765 hp) to two shafts

Performance: maximum speed 36 kt; range 2225 km (1,385 miles) at 17 kt

Complement: 3 + 16

Class

1. Chile ('Guacolda' class)

Name	No.	Builder	Commissioned
Guacolda	80	Bazan	Jul 1965
Fresia	81	Bazan	Dec 1965
Quidora	82	Bazan	1966
Tegualda	83	Bazan	1966

(These FAC[T]s may be regarded as the precursors of the 'FPB-36' type, with a full-load displacement of 134 tons on a length of 36·0 m/118·1, a beam of 5·6 m/18·4 ft and a draught of 2·2 m/7·2 ft. The armament is two 40-mm Bofors L/60 AA in single mountings and four single 533-mm/21-in mountings for heavyweight anti-ship torpedoes. Electronics are limited to a single Decca 505 surface-search and navigation radar, and propulsion is entrusted to two Mercedes-Benz 839 B6 diesels delivering 3600 kW/4,830 hp to two shafts for a maximum speed of 32 kt. The complement is 20.)

2. Ecuador ('Manta' class)

Name	No.	Builder	Commissioned
Manta	LM27	Lürssen	Jun 1971
Tulcan	LM28	Lürssen	Apr 1971
Nuevo Rocafuerte	LM29	Lürssen	Jun 1971

(This is a missile-armed variant of the 'Guacolda' class with standard and full-load displacements of 119 and 134 tons, and dimensions that include a length of 36·4 m/119·4 ft, a beam of 5·8 m/19·1 ft and a draught of 1·8 m/6·0 ft. The armament comprises four container-launchers for four Gabriel II anti-ship missiles and four 30-mm Oerlikon L/85 AA guns in two Emerlec twin mountings. The electronic suite comprises a navigation radar and a Pollux radar used in conjunction with the Vega fire-control system. The propulsion arrangement comprises three Mercedes-Benz diesels delivering 6750 kW/9,055 hp to three shafts for a maximum speed of 42 kt. The complement is 19.)

3. Mauritania

Name	No.	Builder	Commissioned
El Vaiz	P361	Bazan	Oct 1979
El Beig	P362	Bazan	May 1979
El Kinz	P363	Bazan	Aug 1982

(These are small and wholly unexceptional FAC[G]s limited in practical use to patrol and training.)

4. Spain ('Barcelo' class)

Name	No.	Builder	Commissioned
Barcelo	P11	Lürssen	Mar 1976

Name	No.	Builder	Commissioned
Laya	P12	Bazan	Dec 1976
Javier Quiroga	P13	Bazan	Apr 1977
Ordonez	P14	Bazan	Jun 1977
Acevedo	P15	Bazan	Jul 1977
Candido Perez	P16	Bazan	Nov 1977

(This is a simple FAC[G] type with a full-load displacement of 134 tons and dimensions that include a length of 36·2 m/118·7 ft, a beam of 5·8 m/19·0 ft and a draught of 1·9 m/6·2 ft. The armament comprises one 40-mm Bofors L/70 AA in a Breda single mounting, two 20-mm Oerlikon L/85 AA in two GAM-B01 single mountings and two 0·5-in/12·7-mm machine-guns in single mountings; the craft are also each fitted for but not with two single mountings for 533-mm/21-in torpedoes, and for but not with container-launchers for two or four anti-ship missiles in place of the torpedo tubes and 20-mm cannon. The electronic fit includes one Raytheon 1220/6XB surface-search radar and one CSEE optical director. The propulsion arrangement is based on two Bazan-built MTU 16V 538 TB90 diesels delivering 4300 kW/5,765 hp to two shafts for a maximum speed of 36 kt and a range of 2225 km/1,385 miles at 17 kt. The complement is 3 + 16.)

'Lürssen FPB-38' class FAC(G)

(West Germany/Bahrain)
Type: fast attack craft (gun)
Displacement: 188 tons standard and 205 tons full load
Dimensions: length 38·5 m (126·3 ft); beam 7·0 m (22·9 ft); draught 2·2 m (7·2 ft)
Gun armament: two 40-mm Bofors L/70 AA in a Breda Compact twin mounting, and two 7·62-mm (0·3-in) machine-guns in single mountings
Missile armament: none
Torpedo armament: none
Anti-submarine armament: none
Mines: two rails fitted for 14 mines
Electronics: one 9GR 600 surface-search and fire-control radar, one Decca 1226 navigation radar, one Lynx optronic director used in conjunction with the 9LV 100 fire-control system
Propulsion: two MTU diesels delivering 6700 kW (8,985 hp) to two shafts
Performance: maximum speed 33 kt; range 2000 km (1,245 miles) at 16 kt or 1100 km (685 miles) at 30·5 kt
Complement: 3 + 16 plus provision for 2 spare officers

Class
1. Bahrain

Name	No.	Builder	Commissioned
Al Riffa	10	Lürssen	Aug 1981
Hawar	11	Lürssen	Nov 1981

(This is a small FAC[G] type with only limited armament and capabilities.)
2. Malaysia

Name	No.	Builder	Commissioned
		Lürssen	

(This class of light FAC[G]s is eventually to total 18 in Malaysian service, and is designed mainly for the patrol role. The type has a full-load displacement of 221 tons, a length of 38·5 m/126·3 ft and a beam of 7·0 m/23·0 ft. The armament comprises two 20-mm Oerlikon cannon in GAM-B01 single mountings and two 7·62-mm/0·3-in machine-guns in single mountings, and the fire-control system is of the optical type. The propulsion arrangement comprises two MTU diesels delivering 7360 kW/9,870 hp to two shafts for a maximum speed of 34·7 kt and ranges of 2225 km/1,385 miles at 24 kt or 1760 km/1,095 miles at 32·5 kt. The crew is 7 + 30 plus provision for 1 spare officer.)
3. United Arab Emirates (Abu Dhabi)

Name	No.	Builder	Commissioned
		Lürssen	
		Lürssen	

(These two craft are in no way exceptions to the general configuration and capabilities of the class.)
4. West Germany

Name	No.	Builder	Commissioned
		Lürssen	

(Little has been revealed about West Germany's plan for this small FAC force, which will probably be used for the coastal patrol role.)

'Lürssen TNC-42' class FAC(T)

(West Germany/Greece)
Type: fast attack craft (torpedo)
Displacement: 160 tons standard and 190 tons full load
Dimensions: length 42·5 m (139·4 ft); beam 7·2 m (23·4 ft); draught 2·4 m (7·9 ft)
Gun armament: two 40-mm Bofors L/70 AA in single mountings
Missile armament: none
Torpedo armament: four single 533-mm (21-in) mountings for four SST-4 wire-guided torpedoes
Anti-submarine armament: none
Mines: up to eight in place of torpedo tubes
Electronics: surface-search and navigation radar
Propulsion: four MTU 16V 538 diesels delivering 10,700 kW (14,350 hp) to four shafts
Performance: maximum speed 42 kt; range 1850 km (1,150 miles) at 32 kt or 925 km (575 miles) at 40 kt
Complement: 39

Class
1. Greece

Name	No.	Builder	Commissioned
Hesperos	P50	Lürssen	Aug 1958
Kentauros	P52	Kroger	Nov 1958
Kyklon	P53	Lürssen	Mar 1959
Lelaps	P54	Lürssen	Feb 1959
Skorpios	P55	Kroger	Nov 1959
Tyfon	P56	Lürssen	Jun 1959

(These Greek craft were transferred from West Germany in 1976 and 1977, together with three others to be cannibalized for spares.)
2. Indonesia

Name	No.	Builder	Commissioned
Beruang	652	Lürssen	1959
Harimau	654	Lürssen	1960

(These Indonesian craft are the survivors of eight craft supplied from West Germany, and generally similar to the baseline configuration. The complement is 39.)

3. Saudi Arabia

Name	No.	Builder	Commissioned
Dammam		Lürssen	1969
Khabar		Lürssen	1969
Maccah		Lürssen	1969

(These craft were transferred in 1976 after extensive refitting in West Germany, and have a complement of 3 + 30. Though the craft have a capability against surface ships with their torpedoes, they are used mainly for patrol and training.)
4. Sweden ('Spica I' class)

Name	No.	Builder	Commissioned
Spica	T121	Gotaverken	Aug 1966
Capella	T123	Gotaverken	Mar 1966
Vega	T125	Karlskrona Varvet	Nov 1967
Virgo	T126	Karlskrona Varvet	Mar 1968

(This obsolescent class of six craft is now in the process of deletion despite its upgrade to an interim FAC[M] standard. The type has standard and full-load displacements of 185 and 215 tons, and the dimensions include a length of 42·7 m/140·1 ft, a beam of 7·1 m/23·3 ft and a draught of 2·6 m/8·5 ft. The armament consists of one 57-mm Bofors SAK 57 Mk 1 DP in a Bofors single mounting, six single 533-mm/21-in mountings for six Tp 61 wire-guided torpedoes and, if two or four torpedo-tube mountings are unshipped, four or eight container-launchers for four or eight Rbs 15M anti-ship missiles. The electronic fit includes one Skanter Mk 009 surface-search and navigation radar, and one radar used in conjunction with the WM-22 fire-control system. The propulsion arrangement of this licence-built series differs radically from the West German norm, however, being composed of three Rolls-Royce Proteus gas turbines delivering 12,720 hp/9485 kW to three shafts for a maximum speed of 40 kt. The complement is 7 + 21.)
5. Turkey

Name	No.	Builder	Commissioned
Tufan	P331	Lürssen	1962
Mizrak	P333	Lürssen	1962
Kalkan	P335	Lürssen	1959
Karayel	P336	Lürssen	1962

(These are the survivors of seven 'Jaguar' class craft transferred between late 1976 and early 1977 as operational craft together with another three non-operational craft for cannibalization as spares.)

6. Turkey ('Kartal' class)

Name	No.	Builder	Commissioned
Denizkusu	P321	Lürssen	1967
Atmaca	P322	Lürssen	1967
Sahin	P323	Lürssen	1967
Kartal	P324	Lürssen	1967
Pelikan	P326	Lürssen	1968
Albatros	P327	Lürssen	1968
Simsek	P328	Lürssen	1968
Kasirga	P329	Lürssen	1967

(The 'Kartal' class is a variant of the 'Jaguar' class produced for the Turkish navy in the FAC[M] role. The type has standard and full-load displacements of 160 and 190 tons, and dimensions that include a length of 42·8 m/140·5 ft, a beam of 7·1 m/23·5 ft and a draught of 2·2 m/7·2 ft. The armament is fairly impressive, comprising four container-launchers for four Penguin Mk II anti-ship missiles, two 40-mm Bofors L/70 AA in single mountings, and four single 533-mm/21-in mountings for heavyweight anti-ship torpedoes. The primary electronic systems are a Decca 1226 surface-search and navigation radar and a radar used in conjunction with the WM-28 fire-control system. The

'Lürssen FPB/TNC-45' class FAC(M)

(West Germany/United Arab Emirates)

Type: fast attack craft (missile)

Displacement: 235 tons standard and 260 tons full load

Dimensions: length 44·9 m (147·3 ft); beam 7·0 m (23·0 ft); draught 2·5 m (8·2 ft)

Gun armament: one 76-mm (3-in) OTO Melara L/62 DP in an OTO Melara Compact single mounting, two 40-mm Bofors L/70 AA in a Breda Compact twin mounting, and two 7·62-mm (0·3-in) machine-guns in single mountings

Missile armament: two twin container-launchers for four MM.40 Exocet anti-ship missiles

Torpedo armament: none

Anti-submarine armament: none

Electronics: one TM1226 surface-search and navigation radar, one 9LV 200 Mk 2 radar used with a 9LV 223 fire-control system, one USFA optronic director, one Panda optical director, one ESM system with Cutlass-E warning and Cygnus jamming elements, and one Dagaie chaff/flare launcher

Propulsion: four MTU 16V 538 TB92 diesels delivering 11,480 kW (15,395 hp) to four shafts

Performance: maximum speed 41·4 kt; range 2800 km (1,740 miles) at 16 kt on two engines or 925 km (575 miles) at 38·5 kt

Complement: 5 + 35 plus provision for 3 spare men

Class
1. Argentina

Name	No.	Builder	Commissioned
Intrepida	P85	Lürssen	Jul 1974
Indomita	P86	Lürssen	Dec 1974

(These Argentine craft are FAC[G]s. The design is modestly different from that of later 'FPB/TNC-45' craft, with slightly more length and beam. The full-load displacement is 268 tons and the dimensions include a length of 45·4 m/149·0 ft, a beam of 7·4 m/24·3 ft and a draught of 2·3 m/7·5 ft. The armament consists of one 76-mm/3-in OTO Melara L/62 DP in an OTO Melara Compact single mounting, and two 40-mm Bofors L/70 AA in single mountings, complemented by two single 533-mm/21-in mountings for SST-4 wire-guided torpedoes. The electronic fit includes one Decca 12 navigation radar, one WM-22 optronic gun fire-control system, one WM-11 torpedo fire-control system, and an ESM system with warning element. The propulsion arrangement comprises four MTU MD 872 diesels delivering 10,400 kW/13,950 hp to four shafts for a maximum speed of 40 kt and a range of 2700 km/1,680 miles at 20 kt. The complement is 2 + 37.)

2. Bahrain

Name	No.	Builder	Commissioned
Ahmed el Fateh	20	Lürssen	Feb 1983
Al Jabiri	21	Lürssen	May 1984
Abdul Rahman al Fadel	22	Lürssen	Sep 1986
Sabah	23	Lürssen	1988

(These Bahraini craft are standard FAC[M] basically similar to the UAE craft. The standard and full-load displacements are 228 and 259 tons respectively, and the dimensions include a length of 44·9 m/147·3 ft, a beam of 7·0 m/23·0 ft and a draught of 2·5 m/8·2 ft. The armament comprises two twin container-launchers for four MM.40 Exocet anti-ship missiles, one 76-mm/3-in OTO

propulsion arrangement of four MTU 16V 538 diesels delivers 8940 kW/ 11,990 hp to four shafts for a maximum speed of 42 kt. The complement is 39. A ninth unit, *Meltem*, sank after collision with a Soviet ship in 1985 and though salvaged was deemed too badly damaged for economical repair.)

7. West Germany ('Zobel' class)

Name	No.	Builder	Commissioned
Wiesel	P6093	Lürssen	Jun 1962
Dachs	P6094	Lürssen	Sep 1962
Hyäne	P6099	Kroger	May 1963
Frettchen	P6100	Lürssen	Jun 1963
Ozelot	P6101	Lürssen	Oct 1963

(These obsolete craft are the survivors of 40 **'Jaguar' class** FAC(T)s built by Lürssen [30 craft] and Kroger [10 craft], of which most have now been deleted or transferred to friendly navies. The type has a full-load displacement of 220 tons, and the dimensions include a length of 42·6 m/139·7 ft, a beam of 7·0 m/23·0 ft and a draught of 2·9 m/9·5 ft. The armament comprises two 40-mm Bofors L/70 AA in single mountings and two 533-mm/21-in mountings for two Seal wire-guided torpedoes. The electronic fit includes two radars used in conjunction with WM-20 fire-control systems. The propulsion arrangement comprises four MTU diesels delivering 8940 kW/11,990 hp to four shafts for a maximum speed of 35 + kt. The complement is 4 + 26.)

Melara L/62 DP in an OTO Melara Compact single mounting, two 40-mm Bofors L/70B AA in a Breda Compact twin mounting, and two 7·62-mm/0·3-in machine-guns in single mountings. The electronic fit includes a 9LV 200 surface-search radar used in conjunction with a 9LV 223 fire-control system, a Decca 1226 navigation radar, a Panda optical director, an ESM system with Cutlass-E warning and RDL-2ABC jamming elements, and a Dagaie chaff/flare launcher. The propulsion arrangement comprises four MTU diesels delivering 11,480 kW/15,395 hp to four shafts for a maximum speed of 41·5 kt and a range of 2800 km/1,740 miles at 16 kt on two engines. The craft of the second pair each have a beam of 7·3 m/23·9 ft and engines delivering 11,600 kW/15,560 hp for a maximum speed of 42 kt, and the third pair of boats ordered in 1986 will probably be to this revised pattern. The complement is 6 + 30 plus provision for 3 spare men.)

3. Chile

Name	No.	Builder	Commissioned
Iquique		CMN, Cherbourg	1969
Covadonga		CMN, Cherbourg	1969

(These Chilean craft are the ex-Israeli 'Saar 3' class boats *Hanit* and *Hetz* sold to Chile in December 1988. The armament comprises six container-launchers for six Gabriel Mk II anti-ship missiles, one 76-mm/3-in OTO Melara L/62 DP in an OTO Melara Compact single mounting, and two 20-mm Oerlikon AA in single mountings.)

4. Ecuador ('Quito' class)

Name	No.	Builder	Commissioned
Quito	LM24	Lürssen	Jul 1976
Guayaquil	LM25	Lürssen	Dec 1977
Cuenca	LM26	Lürssen	Jul 1977

The Ecuadorean *Quito* (here with old pennant number) is a good example of maximizing punch on a small hull: four MM/38 missiles are complemented by a 76-mm (3-in) gun forward and two 35-mm guns in a twin mounting aft.

(These Ecuadorean craft approximate closely to the norm at a full-load displacement of 255 tons and dimensions that include a length of 45·0 m/147·6 ft, a beam of 7·0 m/23·0 ft and a draught of 2·5 m/8·2 ft. The armament comprises four single container-launchers for four MM.38 Exocet anti-ship missiles, and the other armament consists of one 76-mm/3-in OTO Melara L/62 DP in an OTO Melara Compact single mounting and two 35-mm Oerlikon L/90 AA in a GDM-A twin mounting. The electronic fit includes one Triton air/surface-search radar, one Decca navigation radar, and one Pollux radar used in conjunction with the Vega fire-control system. The propulsion arrangement comprises four MTU 16V 538 diesels delivering 10,400 kW/13,950 hp to four shafts for a maximum speed of 40 kt and ranges of 3350 km/2,080 miles at 16 kt or 1300 km/810 miles at 40 kt. The complement is 35.)

5. Ghana

Name	No.	Builder	Commissioned
Dzata	P28	Lürssen	Jul 1980
Sebo	P29	Lürssen	Jul 1980

(These Ghanaian craft are FAC[G]s with a full-load displacement of 269 tons and dimensions that include a length of 44·9 m/147·3 ft, a beam of 7·0 m/23·0 ft and a draught of 2·7 m/8·9 ft. The armament, originally consisting of one 76-mm/3-in OTO Melara L/62 DP in an OTO Melara Compact single mounting and one 40-mm Bofors L/70 AA in a single mounting, has been revised to two 40-mm Bofors L/70 AA in single mountings to suit the craft better for their current fishery protection role. The electronic fit includes one surface-search radar used in conjunction with the Canopus A fire-control system, one Type 978 navigation radar, and one LIOD optronic director. The propulsion arrangement of two MTU 16V 538 TB91 diesels delivers 5300 kW/7,110 hp to two shafts for a maximum speed of 29·5 kt and ranges of 4450 km/3,320 miles at 15 kt or 2050 km/1,275 miles at 25 kt. The complement is 5 + 30 with a maximum of 55 possible.)

6. Israel ('Saar 2' class)

Name	No.	Builder	Commissioned
Mivtach	311	CMN, Cherbourg	1968
Miznag	312	CMN, Cherbourg	1968
Mifgav	313	CMN, Cherbourg	1968
Eilath	314	CMN, Cherbourg	1968
Haifa	315	CMN, Cherbourg	1968
Akko	316	CMN, Cherbourg	1968

(These Israeli FAC[M]s were built in France to avoid political problems with West Germany, and are exceptionally well equipped. The standard and full-load displacements are 220 and 250 tons, and the dimensions include a length of 45·0 m/147·6 ft, a beam of 7·0 m/23·0 ft and a draught of 2·5 m/8·2 ft. The armament comprises between two and eight container-launchers for Gabriel II anti-ship missiles [two trainable triple container-launchers being fitted on the after ring mountings if only one 40-mm gun is carried], between one and three 40-mm Bofors L/70 AA in Breda single mountings, two or four 0·5-in/12·7-mm machine-guns in single mountings, and two Mk 32 twin 12·75-in/324-mm mountings for Mk 46 anti-submarine torpedoes if no triple container-launcher units are shipped. The electronic fit includes one Neptune air/surface-search radar, one RTN 10X radar used in conjunction with the Argo NA10 fire-control system, one EDO 780 active search and attack variable-depth sonar [not in all craft], an ESM system with an Elta MN-53 warning element and a jamming element, and a combination of six 24-tube and four single-tube chaff launchers. The propulsion arrangement of four MTU MD 871 diesels delivers 10,000 kW/13,410 hp to four shafts for a maximum speed of 40+ kt and ranges of 4650 km/2,890 miles at 15 kt, 2950 km/1,835 miles at 20 kt or 1850 km/1,150 miles at 30 kt. The complement is 5 + 30/35.)

7. Israel ('Saar 3' class)

Name	No.	Builder	Commissioned
Saar	331	CMN, Cherbourg	1969
Soufa	332	CMN, Cherbourg	1969
Gaash	333	CMN, Cherbourg	1969
Herev	341	CMN, Cherbourg	1969

(These Israeli craft are very similar to the 'Saar 2' class units, but have no anti-submarine provision and a more powerful gun armament, centred on a forward-located 76-mm/3-in OTO Melara L/62 DP in an OTO Melara Compact single mounting with the option of two 40-mm Bofors L/70 AA or two triple container-launchers for Gabriel II anti-ship missiles aft.)

8. Kuwait

Name	No.	Builder	Commissioned
Al Boom	P4501	Lürssen	1983
Al Betteel	P4503	Lürssen	1983
Al Sanbouk	P4505	Lürssen	1983
Al Saadi	P4507	Lürssen	1983
Al Ahmadi	P4509	Lürssen	1984
Al Abdali	P4511	Lürssen	1984

(These Kuwaiti FAC[M]s have standard and full-load displacements of 255 and 275 tons respectively, and dimensions that include a length of 44·9 m/147·3 ft, a beam of 7·0 m/23·0 ft and a draught of 2·68 m/8·8 ft. The armament comprises two twin container-launchers for four MM.40 Exocet anti-ship missiles, one 76-mm/3-in OTO Melara L/62 DP in an OTO Melara Compact single mounting, two 40-mm Bofors L/70B AA in a Breda Compact twin mounting, and two 7·62-mm/0·3-in machine-guns in single mountings. The electronic fit is one S 810 surface-search radar, one TM1226C navigation radar, one 9LV 200 radar used with the 9LV 228 fire-control system, one Lynx optical director, one ESM system with Cutlass-E/Matilda warning element, and one Dagaie chaff/flare launcher. The propulsion arrangement comprises four MTU 16V 956 TB92 diesels delivering 11,600 kW/15,560 hp to four shafts for a maximum speed of 41·5 kt and a range of 3100 km/1,925 miles at 16 kt on two engines. The complement is 5 + 30 plus provision for 3 spare men.)

9. Malaysia ('Jerong' class)

Name	No.	Builder	Commissioned
Jerong	3505	Hong-Leong Lürssen	Mar 1976
Todak	3506	Hong-Leong Lürssen	Jun 1976
Paus	3507	Hong Leong Lürssen	Aug 1976
Yu	3508	Hong-Leong Lürssen	Nov 1976
Baung	3509	Hong-Leong Lürssen	Jan 1977
Pari	3510	Hong-Leong Lürssen	Mar 1977

(These Malaysian craft are FACs with a full-load displacement of 244 tons, and dimensions that include a length of 44·9 m/147·3 ft, a beam of 7·0 m/23·0 ft and a draught of 2·48 m/8·15 ft. The armament consists of one 57-mm Bofors SAK 57 Mk 1 L/70 DP in a Bofors single mounting, one 40-mm Bofors L/70 AA in a single mounting, and two 7·62-mm/0·3-in machine-guns in single mountings. The electronic fit includes one Decca 626 surface-search radar, one MS 32 navigation radar, one radar used in conjunction with the WM-28 fire-control system, one Naja optronic director and one Panda optical director. The propulsion arrangement of three MTU MD 872 diesels delivers 7950 kW/10,665 hp to three shafts for a maximum speed of 34 kt and ranges of 3700 km/2,300 miles at 15 kt or 1300 km/810 miles at 31·5 kt. The complement is 5 + 31.)

10. Singapore

Name	No.	Builder	Commissioned
Sea Wolf	P76	Lürssen	1972
Sea Lion	P77	Lürssen	1972
Sea Dragon	P78	Singapore SB & Eng	1974
Sea Tiger	P79	Singapore SB & Eng	1974
Sea Hawk	P80	Singapore SB & Eng	1975
Sea Scorpion	P81	Singapore SB & Eng	1975

(These Singapore craft have standard and full-load displacements of 226 and 254 tons respectively, and dimensions that include a length of 44·9 m/147·3 ft, a beam of 7·0 m/23·0 ft and a draught of 2·3 m/7·5 ft. The armament comprises two single and one triple container-launchers for five Gabriel I anti-ship missiles, or two twin container-launchers for four RGM-84 Harpoon anti-ship missiles and two single container-launchers for two Gabriel I anti-ship missiles, one 57-mm Bofors SAK 57 Mk 1 DP in a Bofors single mounting, and one 40-mm Bofors L/70 AA in a single mounting. The electronic fit includes a Kelvin Hughes 17 surface-search and navigation radar, one radar used in conjunction with the WM-28/5 fire-control system, and an ESM system with warning element. The propulsion arrangement of four MTU 16V 538 TB92 diesels delivers 10,740 kW/14,405 hp to four shafts for a maximum speed of 38 kt and a range of 3700 km/2,300 miles at cruising speed. The complement is 5 + 36.)

11. Thailand

Name	No.	Builder	Commissioned
Prabparapak	1	Singapore SB & Eng	Jul 1976
Hanhak Sattru	2	Singapore SB & Eng	Nov 1976
Suphairin	3	Singapore SB & Eng	Feb 1977

(These Thai craft are essentially similar to the Singapore units in dimensions, weapons, electronics, propulsion and performance.)

12. United Arab Emirates (Abu Dhabi)

Name	No.	Builder	Commissioned
Ban Yas	P4501	Lürssen	Nov 1980
Marban	P4502	Lürssen	Nov 1980
Rodqm	P4503	Lürssen	Jul 1981
Shaheen	P4504	Lürssen	Jul 1981
Sagar	P4505	Lürssen	Sep 1981
Tarif	P4506	Lürssen	Sep 1981

(These were the world's first operational craft with the MM.40 version of the Exocet, and it is believed that the UAE may order more of the type in the near future.)

Above: The *Ban Yas* is lead craft of Abu Dhabi's six-strong force of 'TNC-45' class FAC(M)s each carrying a main armament of four Harpoon missiles.

Below: The *Achimoto* is a typical 'PB-57' class FAC(G) with single 76-mm (3-in) OTO Melara and 40-mm Bofors guns located fore and aft respectively.

'Lürssen FPB/PB-57' class FAC(G[M])

(West Germany/Spain)
Type: fast attack craft (gun [missile])
Displacement: 275 tons standard and 393 tons full load
Dimensions: length 58·1 m (190·6 ft); beam 7·62 m (25·0 ft); draught 2·8 m (9·2 ft)
Gun armament: one 76-mm (3-in) OTO Melara L/62 DP in an OTO Melara Compact single mounting, one 40-mm Bofors L/70 AA in a Breda single mounting, and two 20-mm Oerlikon L/85 AA in GAM-B01 single mountings
Missile armament: provision for two twin container-launchers for four RGM-84 Harpoon anti-ship missiles
Torpedo armament: none
Anti-submarine armament: provision for two Mk 32 triple 12·75-in (324-mm) mountings for Mk 46 torpedoes, and two depth-charge racks
Electronics: one surface-search radar used in conjunction with the WM-22/41 fire-control system, one Raytheon TM 1620/6X navigation radar, one HSM Mk 22 optical director, fitted for but not with one ELAC active search and attack hull sonar, and one ESM system with warning element
Propulsion: two Bazan/MTU MA15 TB91 diesels delivering 6000 kW (8,045 hp) to two shafts
Performance: maximum speed 31 kt; range 12,050 km (7,490 miles) at 17 kt or 5000 km (3,105 miles) at 28 kt
Complement: 4 + 26 plus provision for 2 spare men

Class

1. Ghana

Name	No.	Builder	Commissioned
Achimota	P28	Lürssen	Dec 1979
Yogaga	P29	Lürssen	May 1980

(These Ghanaian craft are of the original 'PB-57' class of FAC[G]. The type has a full-load displacement of 389 tons and the dimensions include a length of 58·1 m/190·6 ft, a beam of 7·62 m/25·0 ft and a draught of 3·0 m/9·85 ft. The armament comprises one 76-mm/3-in OTO Melara L/62 DP in an OTO Melara Compact single mounting and one 40-mm Bofors L/70 AA in a single mounting. The electronic fit includes a surface-search and navigation radar used in conjunction with a Canopus A fire-control system, a Type 978 navigation radar, and a LIOD optronic director. The propulsion arrangement of three MTU 16V 538 TB91 diesels delivers 7950 kW/10,665 hp to three shafts for a maximum speed of 33 kt and ranges of 9635 km/5,985 miles at 17 kt or 3700 km/2,300 miles at 30 kt. The complement is 7 + 38 plus provision for 2 VIPs.)

2. Indonesia

Name	No.	Builder	Commissioned
Andau	650	Lürssen	Oct 1986
Singa	651	Lürssen	Oct 1987
Kakap	652	Lürssen	Apr 1988
Ajak	653	Lürssen	Oct 1988

(The Indonesian navy is procuring eight of these 'PB 57' class craft in two variants optimized for anti-submarine warfare [two craft], gun/torpedo-armed patrol [two craft] and combat search-and-rescue [four craft with the possibility of another eight under consideration], the last under control of the maritime security agency rather than the navy proper. Common features are a full-load displacement of 416 tons, and dimensions that include a length of 58·1 m/190·6 ft, a beam of 7·62 m/25·0 ft and a draught of 2·73 m/9·0 ft. The patrol version is a FAC[G] with a gun armament comprising one 57-mm Bofors SAK 57 Mk 2 L/70 DP in a Bofors single mounting, one 40-mm Bofors L/70 in a single mounting and two 20-mm Rheinmetall AA in single mountings; the electronic fit of this variant includes one Decca 2459 surface-search radar, one WM-22 fire-control system, one NA18 optronic director, one Thomson-CSF ESM system with warning element, and one Dagaie chaff/flare launcher; the propulsion arrangement comprises two MTU 16V 956 TB92 diesels delivering 6150 kW/8,250 hp to two shafts for a maximum speed of 30·5 kt and ranges of 11,300 km/7,020 miles at 15 kt or 4075 km/2,530 miles at 28·1 kt; and the complement is 9 + 31, plus provision for 2 VIPs, 6 spare officers and, in the secondary SAR role, 9 survivors. The ASW version has two single 533-mm/21-in launchers for SUT wire-guided torpedoes, PHS 32 active search and attack hull sonar and a LIOD optronic director. The SAR version has a platform for one MBB [Nurtanio] BO105 helicopter in place of the after guns and torpedo tubes. The first, third, fourth and fifth craft are of the SAR type, the second and sixth craft are of the ASW type, and the seventh and eighth craft are of the FAC[G] type.)

3. Kuwait

Name	No.	Builder	Commissioned
Istiqlal	P5702	Lürssen	Nov 1982
Sabhan	P5704	Lurssen	Mar 1983

(The Kuwaiti craft are standard 'FPB-57' class boats with a full-load displacement of 410 tons and dimensions that include a length of 58·1 m/190·6 ft, a beam of 7·62 m/25·0 ft and a draught of 2·78 m/9·1 ft. The armament comprises two twin container-launchers for four MM.40 Exocet anti-ship missiles, one 76-mm/3-in OTO Melara L/62 DP in an OTO Melara Compact single mounting, one 40-mm Bofors L/70 AA in a single mounting, and two 7·62-mm/0·3-in machine-guns in single mountings. The electronics fit includes one S 810 surface-search radar, one Decca 1226 navigation radar, one 9LV 200 radar used in conjunction with a 9LV 228 fire-control system, one Lynx optical director, one ESM system with Cutlass-E warning and Cygnus jamming elements, and one Dagaie chaff/flare launcher. The propulsion arrangement comprises three MTU 16V 956 TB91 diesels delivering 8280 kW/11,105 hp to three shafts for a maximum speed of 33·5 kt and ranges of 6675 km/4,150 miles at 15 kt or 2780 km/1,725 miles at 31·2 kt. The complement is 5 + 27, plus provision for 2 VIPs and 18 trainees [4 officers and 14 ratings].)

4. Morocco ('Lazaga [Modified]' class)

Name	No.	Builder	Commissioned
El Khattabi	304	Bazan	Jul 1981
Commandant Azouggargh	305	Bazan	Aug 1982
Commandant Boutouba	306	Bazan	Nov 1981
Commandant El Harty	307	Bazan	Feb 1982

(These Moroccan craft are derived from the Spanish vessels, and have a full-load displacement of 425 tons as well as dimensions that include a length of 58·1 m/190·6 ft, a beam of 7·6 m/24·9 m and a draught of 2·7 m/8·9 ft. The armament comprises two twin container-launchers for four MM.40 Exocet anti-ship missiles, one 76-mm/3-in OTO Melara L/62 DP in an OTO Melara Compact single mounting, one 40-mm Bofors L/70 AA in a single mounting, and two 20-mm Oerlikon L/90 AA in GAM-B01 single mountings; there is no torpedo or anti-submarine armament. The electronic fit includes one ZW-06 surface-search radar, one radar used in conjunction with the WM-25 fire-control system, and a Panda optical director. The propulsion arrangement comprises two MTU 16V 956 TB91 diesels delivering 6000 kW/8,050 hp to two shafts for a maximum speed of 30 kt, and the complement is 41.)

5. Nigeria

Name	No.	Builder	Commissioned
Ekpe	P178	Lürssen	Aug 1981
Damisa	P179	Lürssen	Apr 1981
Agu	P180	Lürssen	Apr 1981

(These Nigerian FAC[M]s are based on the standard 'FPB-57' hull with a full-load displacement of 444 tons and dimensions that include a length of 58·1 m/190·6 ft, a beam of 7·62 m/25·0 ft and a draught of 3·1 m/10·2 ft. The armament comprises four single container-launchers for four Otomat Mk 1 anti-ship missiles, one 76-mm/3-in OTO Melara L/62 DP in an OTO Melara Compact single mounting, two 40-mm Bofors L/70 AA in a Breda Compact twin mounting, and four 30-mm Oerlikon L/85 AA in two Emerlec twin mountings. The electronic fit includes one Triton air/surface-search radar, one radar used in conjunction with the WM-28/41 fire-control system, and one ESM system with warning and RDL-2ABC jamming elements. The propulsion arrangement comprises four MTU 16V 956 TB92 diesels delivering 15,000 kW/20,120 hp to four shafts for a maximum speed of 42 kt and ranges of 3700 km/2,300 miles at 16 kt or 1250 km/775 miles at 36 kt. The complement is 7 + 45 plus provision for 2 spare officers.)

The *Villamil* of the Spanish 'Lazaga' class is typical of the FAC(G) in that it can be upgraded to FAC(M) standard quickly and easily in time of crisis.

6. Spain ('Lazaga' class)

Name	No.	Builder	Commissioned
Lazaga	P01	Lürssen	Jul 1975
Alsedo	P02	Bazan	Feb 1977
Cadarso	P03	Bazan	Jul 1976
Villamil	P04	Bazan	Apr 1977
Bonifaz	P05	Bazan	Jul 1977
Recalde	P06	Bazan	Dec 1977

(These 'PB 57' class craft are used mainly for patrol and training, with provision for conversion in times of crisis into anti-ship and anti-submarine FAC[M]s with additional sensors and weapons.)

7. Turkey ('Dogan' class)

Name	No.	Builder	Commissioned
Dogan	P340	Lürssen	Jun 1977
Marti	P341	Taskizak NY	Jul 1978
Tayfun	P342	Taskizak NY	Jul 1979
Volkan	P343	Taskizak NY	Jul 1980
Ruzgar	P344	Taskizak NY	Dec 1984
Poyraz	P345	Taskizak NY	Feb 1984
Gurbet	P346	Tazkizak NY	Oct 1988
Firtina	P347	Tazkizak NY	1989

(These Turkish units are to the standard 'FPB-57' class specification with standard and full-load displacements of 398 tons and 436 tons respectively, and dimensions that include a length of 58·1 m/190·6 ft, a beam of 7·62 m/25·0 ft and a draught of 2·83 m/9·3 ft. The armament comprises two quadruple container-launchers for eight RGM-84 Harpoon anti-ship missiles, one 76-mm/3-in OTO Melara L/62 DP in an OTO Melara Compact single mounting, and two 35-mm Oerlikon L/90 AA in a GDM-A twin mounting. The electronic fit includes one Decca 1226 surface-search and navigation radar, one radar used in conjunction with the WM-28/41 fire-control system, one HSA optical director, one ESM system with Susie I warning element, and two chaff/flare launchers. The propulsion arrangement comprises four MTU 16V 956 TB91 diesels delivering 13,400 kW/17,970 hp to four shafts for a maximum speed of 38 kt and ranges of 2400 km/1,490 miles at 26 kt or 1850 km/1,1150 miles at 36 kt. The complement is 5 + 33, plus provision for 2 spare men.)

8. West Germany ('Type 143A' class)

Name	No.	Builder	Commissioned
Gepard	P6121	AEG/Lürssen	Dec 1982
Puma	P6122	AEG/Lürssen	Feb 1983
Hermelin	P6123	AEG/Kroger	May 1983
Nerz	P6124	AEG/Lürssen	Jul 1983
Zobel	P6125	AEG/Telefunken	Sep 1983
Frettchen	P6126	AEG/Telefunken	Dec 1983
Dachs	P6127	AEG/Telefunken	Mar 1984
Ozelot	P6128	AEG/Lürssen	May 1984
Wiesel	P6129	AEG/Kroger	Jul 1984
Hyäne	P6130	AEG/Kroger	Nov 1984

(These West German craft are to a modified 'FPB-57' class design, with standard and full-load displacements of 295 and 391 tons, and dimensions that include a length of 57·7 m/189·3 ft, a beam of 7·6 m/24·9 ft and a draught of 2·5 m/8·2 ft. The armament comprises two twin container-launchers for four MM.38 Exocet anti-ship missiles, one 76-mm/3-in OTO Melara L/62 DP in an OTO Melara Compact single mounting and [to be retrofitted] one EX-31 launcher for 24 RIM-116 RAM SAMs; the type can also be equipped for minelaying. The electronic suite includes one surface-search radar used in conjunction with the WM-27 fire-control system, one 3RM 20 navigation radar, one AGIS action information system, one ESM system with FL1800 warning element, and one Hot Dog/Silver Dog chaff/flare launcher. The propulsion arrangement of four MTU 16V 956 SB80 diesels delivers 13,400 kW/17,970 hp to four shafts for a maximum speed of 40 kt and a range of 4825 km/3,000 miles at 16 kt. The complement is 4 + 30.)

9. West Germany ('Type 143B' class)

Name	No.	Builder	Commissioned
Albatros	P6111	Lürssen	Nov 1976
Falke	P6112	Lürssen	Apr 1976
Geier	P6113	Lürssen	Jun 1976
Bussard	P6114	Lürssen	Aug 1976
Sperber	P6115	Kroger	Sep 1976
Greif	P6116	Lürssen	Nov 1976
Kondor	P6117	Kroger	Dec 1976
Seeadler	P6118	Lürssen	Mar 1977
Habicht	P6119	Kroger	Dec 1977
Kormoran	P6120	Lürssen	Jul 1977

(These West German craft were originally of the 'Type 143' class with an

The Turkish navy's *Dogan* reveals the full FAC(M) capability of the 'FPB-57' class with eight Harpoon anti-ship missiles to complement one 76-mm (3-in) dual-purpose and two 35-mm anti-aircraft guns located fore and aft.

armament of two twin container-launchers for four MM.38 Exocet anti-ship missiles, two 76-mm/3-in OTO Melara L/62 DP in two OTO Melara Compact single mountings, and two single 533-mm/21-in mountings for two wire-guided torpedoes. The after 76-mm/3-in mounting has been removed for installation on 'Type 143A' class craft, and an EX-31 launcher for 24 RIM-116 RAM SAMs is to be installed in what has now become the 'Type 143B' class. The displacement, dimensions and electronics are the same as those for the 'Type 143A' class, but the propulsion arrangement comprises four MTU 16V 956 TB91 diesels delivering 16,000 kW/21,460 hp to four shafts for a maximum speed of 40 kt and a range of 2400 km/1,490 miles at 30 kt. The complement is 4 + 36.)

'Matka' class FAH(M)

(USSR)

Type: fast attack hydrofoil (missile)

Displacement: 225 tons standard and 260 tons full load

Dimensions: length 39·6 m (129·9 ft); beam 12·5 m (41·0 ft) over foils and 7·6 m (24·9 ft) over hull; draught 4·0 m (13·1 ft) foilborne and 2·1 m (6·9 ft) hullborne

Gun armament: one 76-mm (3-in) L/60 DP in a single mounting, and one 30-mm ADGM-630 CIWS mounting

Missile armament: two container-launchers for two SS-N-2C 'Styx' anti-ship missiles

Torpedo armament: none

Anti-submarine armament: none

Electronics: one 'Plank Shave' air/surface-search and SSM fire-control radar, one 'Cheese Cake' navigation radar, one 'Bass Tilt' gun fire-control radar, two chaff launchers, and one 'Square Head' and one 'High Pole-B' or 'Salt Pot-B' IFF systems

Propulsion: three M 504 diesels delivering 11,250 kW (15,090 hp) to three shafts

Performance: maximum speed 40 kt; range 2775 km (1,725 miles) at 14 kt hullborne or 1110 km (690 miles) at 35 kt foilborne

Complement: 33

Class
1. USSR
16 craft

Note: This class was built at the Kolpino yard in Leningrad between 1977 and 1983, when the type was superseded in production by the 'Tarantul' class. The basic design appears to combine the hull of the 'Osa' class with the foil system of the 'Turya' class.

'MV 400' class FAC(G)

(Italy/Thailand)
Type: fast attack craft (gun)
Displacement: 450 tons full load
Dimensions: length 60·4 m (198·2 ft); beam 8·8 m (29·0 ft); draught 4·5 m (14·8 ft)
Gun armament: two 76-mm (3-in) OTO Melara L/62 DP in OTO Melara Compact single mountings, and two 40-mm Bofors L/70 AA in a Breda Compact twin mounting
Missile armament: provision for the retrofitting of anti-ship missiles
Torpedo armament: none
Anti-submarine armament: none
Electronics: one ZW-06 surface-search radar, one radar used in conjunction with the WM-25 fire-control system (with data provision for SSMs), one 3RM 20 navigation radar, one LIROD 8 optronic director, one ESM system with warning element, and four Mk 135 chaff launchers
Propulsion: three MTU 20V 538 TB92 diesels delivering 11,250 kW (15,090 hp) to three shafts
Performance: maximum speed 30 kt; range 4600 km (2,860 miles) at 18 kt or 1675 km (1,040 miles) at 30 kt
Complement: 6 + 35

Class
1. Thailand ('Chon Buri' class)

Name	No.	Builder	Commissioned
Chon Buri	1	CN Breda	Dec 1982
Songkhla	2	CN Breda	Jan 1983
Phuket	3	CN Breda	May 1983

Note: These are comparatively large FAC(G)s, but have the capability for easy conversion to FAC(M)s should the situation demand it.

'Nasty' class FAC(T)

(Norway)
Type: fast attack craft (torpedo)
Displacement: 70 tons standard and 82 tons full load
Dimensions: length 24·5 m (80·3 ft); beam 7·5 m (24·5 ft); draught 2·1 m (6·8 ft)
Gun armament: one 40-mm Bofors L/70 AA in a single mounting, and one 20-mm Rheinmetall AA in a single mounting
Missile armament: none
Torpedo armament: four single 533-mm (21-in) tubes for four heavyweight anti-ship torpedoes
Anti-submarine armament: none
Electronics: one surface-search and navigation radar
Propulsion: two Napier Deltic diesels delivering 6,200 hp (4625 kW) to two shafts
Performance: maximum speed 45 kt; range 1100 km (685 miles) at 25 kt or 835 km (520 miles) at 40 kt
Complement: 18

Class
1. Greece

Name	No.	Builder	Commissioned
Andromeda	P196	Batservice	Nov 1965
Kyknos	P198	Batservice	Feb 1967
Pigasos	P199	Batservice	Apr 1967
Toxotis	P228	Batservice	May 1967

(Five survivors of this originally six-strong class were placed in reserve during the early 1980s, but these four craft were refurbished and recommissioned in 1988. The craft have two MTU MI 312 V331 diesels delivering 2300 kW/3,085 hp to two shafts for a maximum speed of 40 kt and a range of 1250 km/775 miles at 17 kt. and the complement is 20.)

2. Norway ('Tjeld' class)

Name	No.	Builder	Commissioned
Sel	P343	Batservice	Jun 1960
Hval	P348	Batservice	Jun 1961
Laks	P349	Batservice	Jun 1961
Knurr	P357	Batservice	Dec 1961
Skrei	P380	Batservice	Jan 1966
Hai	P381	Batservice	Jul 1964
Lyr	P387	Batservice	Feb 1965
Delfin	P388	Batservice	Mar 1962

(These craft are now of only minimal utility except for training.)

'October' class FAC(M)

(Egypt)
Type: fast attack craft (missile)
Displacement: 82 tons full load
Dimensions: length 25·5 m (84·0 ft); beam 6·1 m (20·0 ft); draught 1·3 m (5·0 ft)
Gun armament: four 30-mm Oerlikon L/75 AA in two GCM-A03 twin mountings
Missile armament: two container-launchers for two Otomat anti-ship missiles
Torpedo armament: none
Anti-submarine armament: none
Electronics: one S 810 air/surface-search radar, one ST 802 radar used in conjunction with the Sapphire fire-control system, one optronic director, one ESM system with Matilda warning element, and two Protean chaff/flare launchers
Propulsion: four CRM 18V-12D/55 YE diesels delivering 4000 kW (5,365 hp) to four shafts
Performance: maximum speed 40 kt; range 750 km (465 miles) at 30 kt
Complement: 20

Class
1. Egypt
6 craft (nos 781, 783, 785, 787, 789 and 791)
Note: These craft were built in Alexandria in 1975 and 1976 using a hull identical with that of the Soviet 'Komar' class for a sensor and weapon fit of Western origins.

'Osa I' and 'Osa II' class FAC(M)

(USSR)
Type: fast attack craft (missile)
Displacement: 165 tons standard and 210 tons or ('Osa II' class craft) 245 tons full load
Dimensions: length 39·0 m (127·9 ft); beam 7·8 m (25·6 ft); draught 1·8 m (5·9 ft)
Gun armament: four 30-mm L/65 AA in two twin mountings
Missile armament: four container-launchers for four SS-N-2A 'Styx' or ('Osa II' class craft) SS-N-2C 'Styx' anti-ship missiles, and (in some 'Osa II' class craft) one quadruple launcher for four SA-N-5 'Grail' SAMs
Torpedo armament: none
Anti-submarine armament: none
Electronics: one 'Square Tie' surface-search and missile fire-control radar, one 'Drum Tilt' gun fire-control radar, and two 'Square Head' and one 'High Pole-A' or 'High Pole-B' IFF systems
Propulsion: three M 503A diesels delivering 9000 kW (12,070 hp) or ('Osa II' class craft) M 504 diesels delivering 11,250 kW (15,090 hp), in each case to three shafts
Performance: maximum speed 38 kt or ('Osa II' class craft) 40 kt; range 1500 km (930 miles) at 30 kt or 925 km (575 miles) at 35 kt
Complement: 5 + 25

Class
1. Algeria
3 'Osa I' class craft (nos 641, 642 and 643)
9 'Osa II' class craft (nos 644, 645, 646, 647, 648, 649, 650, 651 and 652)
2. Angola
6 'Osa II' class craft
3. Bulgaria
3 'Osa I' class craft (nos 103, 112 and 113)
3 'Osa II' class craft (nos 101, 102 and 111)
4. China
7 'Osa I' class
100 + **'Huangfen' class** craft built in China

The latter have a gun armament of four 25-mm L/60 or (in later craft and as a retrofit in earlier craft) four 30-mm L/65 in two twin mountings, and four HY-2 or (in later craft and as a retrofit in earlier craft) six or eight C-801 anti-ship missiles. The class is credited with a speed of 41 kts.

5. Cuba
5 'Osa I' class craft
13 'Osa II' class craft

6. East Germany
12 'Osa I' class craft
These are the *Max Reichspietsch* (711), *Heinrich Dorrenbach* (712), *Richard Sorge* (713), *Walter Kramer* (714), *Otto Tost* (731), *Karl Meseberg* (732), *August Lüttgens* (733), *Anton Saefkow* (734), *Josef Schares* (751), *Paul Schulz* (752), *Paul Wieczorek* (753) and *Fritz Gast* (754)

7. Egypt
7 'Osa I' class craft (nos 631, 633, 635, 637, 639, 641 and 643)

8. Ethiopia
7 'Osa II' class craft (nos FMB 160, 161, 162 and 163)

9. Finland
4 **'Tuima' class** craft of Soviet construction but fitted with Finnish electronics plus Western navigation radar
These are the *Tuima* (11), *Tuisku* (12), *Tuuli* (14) and *Tyrsky* (15)

10. India
6 'Osa I' class craft
8 'Osa II' class craft
The former are the *Vidyut* (K83), *Vijeta* (K84)*, *Vinash* (K85), *Nipat* (K86), *Nashat* (K87)* and *Nirghat* (K89)
The latter are the *Prachand* (K90), *Pralaya* (K91), *Pratapro (K92)*, *Prabal* (K93), *Chapal* (K94), *Chamak* (K95), *Chatak* (K96) and *Charag* (K97)
* patrol craft without missiles

11. Iraq
2 'Osa I' class craft
5 'Osa II' class craft
The former are the *Nisan* (R14) and *Hazirani* (R15)
The latter are the *Khalid Ibn Ali Walid* (R18), *Said* (R19), (R21), (R22) and (R23)

12. Libya
12 'Osa II' class craft
These are the *Al Katum* (511), *Al Zuara* (513), *Al Ruha* (515), *Al Baida* (517), *Al*

The 'Osa' class FAC(M) has four SS-N-2 missiles, but only limited defensive power in two twin 30-mm mountings.

Nabha (519), *Al Safhra* (521), *Al Fikah* (523), *Al Sakab* (525), *Al Mosha* (527), *Al Mathur* (529), *Al Bitar* (531) and *Al Sadad* (533)

13. North Korea
8 'Osa I' class craft
4 'Huangfen' class craft
10 locally built **'Soju' class** craft with another 2 building

14. Pakistan
4 'Huangfen' class craft (nos P1025, P1026, P1027 and P1028)

15. Poland
12 'Osa I' class craft (nos 422, 423, 424, 425, 426, 427, 428, 429, 430, 431, 432 and 433)

16. Romania
6 'Osa I' class craft (nos 194, 195, 196, 197, 198 and 199)

17. Somalia
2 'Osa II' class craft

18. South Yemen
6 'Osa II' class craft (nos 116, 117, 118, 119, 120 and 121)

19. Syria
6 'Osa I' class craft (nos 21, 22, 23, 24, 25 and 26)
6 'Osa II' class craft

20. USSR
50 'Osa I' class craft
30 'Osa II' class craft

21. Vietnam
8 'Osa II' class craft

22. Yugoslavia
10 'Osa I' class craft
These are the *Mitar Acev* (RC301), *Vlado Bagat* (RC302), *Petar Drapsin* (RC303), *Stevo Filipovic* (RC304), *Zikica Jovanovic Spanac* (RC305), *Nikola Martinovic* (RC306), *Josip Mazar Sosa* (RC307), *Karlo Rojc* (RC308), *Franc Rozman Stanec* (RC309) and *Velimir Skorpik* (RC310)

Note: The 'Osa I' class craft were built in the early 1960s, and the 'Osa II' class craft in the late 1960s. Many yards were involved. The type is now obsolescent but still in very widespread service.

'Osprey 55' class FAC(M)

(Denmark/Greece)

Type: fast attack craft (missile)

Displacement: 400 tons standard and 475 tons full load

Dimensions: length 54·8 m (179·8 ft); beam 10·3 m (33·8 ft); draught 2·6 m (8·5 ft)

Gun armament: one 76-mm (3-in) OTO Melara L/62 DP in an OTO Melara single mounting, and two 40-mm Bofors L/70 AA in a Breda Fast Forty twin mounting

Missile armament: two Mk 141 twin container-launchers for four RGM-84 Harpoon anti-ship missiles

Torpedo armament: none

Anti-submarine armament: none

Mines: fitted with two rails

Electronics: one Plessey surface-search and navigation radar, one fire-control system, one Plessey action information system, one ESM system, and chaff/flare launchers

Propulsion: two MTU 16V 396 diesels delivering unrevealed power to two shafts

Performance: maximum speed 24 + kt

Complement: about 20

Class

1. Greece

Name	No.	Builder	Commissioned
		Hellenic Shipyards	
		Hellenic Shipyards	

(The contract for the licensed production of these two craft was signed with Danyard in 1987, the object being the construction of two large FAC[M]s of limited performance but high capabilities in the anti-ship and patrol roles. The planned total is 10 units.)

2. Senegambia ('Osprey [Improved] class)

Name	No.	Builder	Commissioned
Fouta		Danyard	Jun 1987

(This craft is designed for patrol rather than offensive operations as a true FAC, and this is reflected in the armament and sensors. The former comprise two 30-mm Hispano-Suiza cannon, and the latter FR 1411 surface-search radar and FR 1221 navigation radar. The propulsion arrangement comprises two Burmeister & Wain/MAN Alpha 12V 23/30-DVO diesels delivering 3700 kW/4,960 hp to two shafts for a maximum speed of 20 kt. The complement is 4 + 34 with provision for 8 passengers.)

'P 48S' class FAC(M)

(France/Cameroun)

Type: fast attack craft (missile)

Displacement: 308 tons full load

Dimensions: length 52·6 m (172·5 ft); beam 7·2 m (23·6 ft); draught 2·4 m (7·9 ft)

Gun armament: two 40-mm Bofors L/70 AA in single mountings

Missile armament: two quadruple container-launchers for eight MM.40 Exocet anti-ship missiles

Torpedo armament: none

Anti-submarine armament: none

Electronics: two Decca 1226 surface-search and navigation radars, two Naja optronic directors, and one Decca Cane 100 action information system

Propulsion: two SACM/AGO 195 V16 CZSHR diesels delivering 4800 kW (6,440 hp) to two shafts

Performance: maximum speed 25 kt; range 3700 km (2,300 miles) at 16 kt

Complement: 6 + 33

Class

1. Cameroun

Name	No.	Builder	Commissioned
Bakassi	P104	SFCN	Jan 1984

Note: Though comparatively slow and possessing only limited electronic capability, this large FAC(M) has particularly potent anti-ship missile armament.

Eight MM-40 Exocet missiles provide the *Bakassi* with a major capability against ships, though the gun armament of two 40-mm weapons is light.

'P400' class FAC(M)

(France)

Type: fast attack craft (missile)

Displacement: 406 tons standard and 454 tons full load

Dimensions: length 54·5 m (178·6 ft); beam 8·0 m (26·2 ft); draught 2·5 m (8·3 ft)

Gun armament: one 40-mm Bofors L/60 AA in a single mounting, one 20-mm GIAT AA in a single mounting, and one 7·62-mm (0·3-in) machine-gun

Missile armament: fitted for but generally not with two container-launchers for two MM.38 Exocet anti-ship missiles, and (to replace 20-mm gun) one SADRAL sextuple launcher for Mistral SAMs

Torpedo armament: none

Anti-submarine armament: none

Electronics: one Decca 1226 surface-search and navigation radar

Propulsion: two SEMT-Pielstick 16 PA4-V200 VGDS diesels delivering 6000 kW (8,045 hp) to two shafts

Performance: maximum speed 24·5 kt; range 7800 km (4,845 miles) at 15 kt

Complement: 3 + 21 plus berthing and stores provision for the accommodation of 20 troops in the overseas transport role

Class
1. France

Name	No.	Builder	Commissioned
L'Audacieuse	P682	CMN, Cherbourg	Sep 1986
La Boudeuse	P683	CMN, Cherbourg	Jan 1987
La Capricieuse	P684	CMN, Cherbourg	Mar 1987
La Fougeuse	P685	CMN, Cherbourg	Mar 1987
La Glorieuse	P686	CMN, Cherbourg	Apr 1987
La Gracieuse	P687	CMN, Cherbourg	Jul 1987
La Moqueuse	P688	CMN, Cherbourg	Apr 1987
La Railleuse	P689	CMN, Cherbourg	May 1987
La Rieuse	P690	CMN, Cherbourg	Jun 1987
La Tapageuse	P691	CMN, Cherbourg	Jan 1988

(These simple FACs are generally disposed in pairs in four of France's overseas territories, the remaining pair being kept in home waters.)

2. Gabon

Name	No.	Builder	Commissioned
General B.A.Oumar	P07	CMN, Cherbourg	June 1988
	P08	CMN, Cherbourg	1990

(These two Gabonaise units are generally similar to the French craft, but the primary armament of each is a 57-mm Bofors SAK 57 Mk 2 L/70 DP, supported by one or two 20-mm Oerlikon AA in a single or twin mounting.)

***L'Audacieuse* looks curiously naked with armament restricted to two guns (a 40-mm weapon forward and a 20-mm cannon aft), but can be fitted with Exocet anti-ship and Mistral surface-to-air missiles as required.**

'Patra' class FAC(G)

(France)

Type: fast attack craft (gun)

Displacement: 115 tons standard and 147·5 tons full load

Dimensions: length 37·0 m (121·4 ft); beam 5·5 m (18·0 ft); draught 1·6 m (5·2 ft)

Gun armament: one 40-mm Bofors L/60 AA in a single mounting, and one or two 12·7-mm (0·5-in) machine-guns in single mountings

Missile armament: none

Torpedo armament: none

Anti-submarine armament: none

Electronics: one surface-search and navigation radar

Propulsion: two AGO 195 V12 CZSHR diesels delivering 3000 kW (4,025 hp) to two shafts

Performance: maximum speed 26 kt; range 3250 km (2,020 miles) at 10 kt or 1400 km (870 miles) at 20 kt

Complement: 1 + 17

Class
1. France

Name	No.	Builder	Commissioned
Trident	P670	Auroux	Dec 1976
Glaive	P671	Auroux	Apr 1977
Epee	P672	CMN, Cherbourg	Oct 1976
Pertuisane	P673	CMN, Cherbourg	Jan 1977

(These French craft are simple FACs whose low-powered engines and indifferent performance suit them to the patrol rather than combat role.)

2. Ivory Coast

Name	No.	Builder	Commissioned
L'Ardent		Auroux	Oct 1978
L'Intrepide		Auroux	Oct 1978

(These Ivory Coast units are similar to the French craft but with a missile armament of four SS.12 anti-ship missiles are only limited-capability FAC[M]s.)

3. Mauritania

Name	No.	Builder	Commissioned
Le Dix Juillet	P411	Auroux	May 1982

(This was the private-venture prototype for the 'Patra' class, subsequently bought by Mauritania and used as a basic FAC[G] with an armament of one 40-mm Bofors L/60 AA, one 20-mm Oerlikon AA and two 0·5-in/12·7-mm machine-guns.)

The *Glaive* is typical of this indifferent FAC(G) type produced by France for the patrol rather than combat role. Low installed power results in a speed of only 26 kt, which only just qualifies the 'Patra' class for the FAC designation.

'Pegasus' class FAH(M)

(USA)

Type: fast attack hydrofoil (missile)

Displacement: 240 tons full load

Dimensions: length 132·9 ft (40·5 m) with foils extended and 145·3 ft (44·3 m) with foils retracted; beam 47·5 ft (14·5 m) with foils extended and 28·2 ft (8·6 m) with foils retracted; draught 23·2 ft (7·1 m) with foils extended and 6·2 ft (1·9 m) with foils retracted

Gun armament: one 76-mm (3-in) OTO Melara Compact L/62 DP in a Mk 75 single mounting

Missile armament: two Mk 141 quadruple container-launchers for eight RGM-84 Harpoon anti-ship missiles

Torpedo armament: none

Anti-submarine armament: none

Electronics: one SPS-64 surface-search and navigation radar, one radar used in conjunction with the WM-28 (PHM-1) or Mk 92/94 (others) gun and SSM fire-control system, one SWG-1A(V)4 launch and control system, one ESM system with SLQ-650 warning and jamming element, two Mk 34 RBOC chaff/flare launchers, one OE-82 satellite communication system, one WSC-3 satellite communications transceiver, and one SRR-1 satellite communications receiver

Propulsion: two MTU 8V 331 TC81 diesels delivering 1220 kW (1,635 hp) to two waterjets for hullborne operation, and one General Electric LM2500 gas turbine delivering 18,000 hp (13,420 kW) to two waterjets for foilborne operation

Performance: maximum speed 48 kt foilborne or 12 kt hullborne; range 1,950 miles (3140 km) at 9 kt or 800 miles (1285 km) at 40 kt

Complement: 4 + 20

Class

1. USA

Name	No.	Builder	Commissioned
Pegasus	PHM1	Boeing	Jul 1977
Hercules	PHM2	Boeing	Jul 1982
Taurus	PHM3	Boeing	Oct 1981
Aquila	PHM4	Boeing	Dec 1981
Aries	PHM5	Boeing	Apr 1982
Gemini	PHM6	Boeing	Jun 1982

Note: These are capable FAH(M)s with advanced sensors and weapons, but do not really fit into the US Navy's operational scheme.

The *Taurus* and her sister craft are capable FAH(M)s, but are basically irrelevant to the US Navy's philosophy of deep-ocean operations.

'PR 72P' class FAC(M)

(France/Peru)

Type: fast attack craft (missile)

Displacement: 470 tons standard and 560 tons full load

Dimensions: length 64·0 m (210·0 ft); beam 8·35 m (27·4 ft); draught 1·6 m (5·2 ft)

Gun armament: one 76-mm (3-in) OTO Melara L/62 DP in an OTO Melara Compact single mounting, two 40-mm Bofors L/70 AA in a Breda Compact twin mounting, and two 20-mm AA in single mountings

Missile armament: two twin container-launchers for four MM.38 Exocet anti-ship missiles

Torpedo armament: none

Anti-submarine armament: none

Electronics: one Triton surface-search radar, one TM1226 navigation radar, one Castor II radar used in conjunction with the Vega fire-control system, and one Panda optical director

Propulsion: four SACM/AGO 240 V16 diesels delivering 16,400 kW (21,995 hp) to four shafts

Performance: maximum speed 34 kt; range 4625 km (2,875 miles) at 16 kt

Complement: 36 with a maximum of 46 possible

Class

1. Morocco ('PR 72M' class)

Name	No.	Builder	Commissioned
Okba	33	SFCN	Dec 1976
Triki	34	SFCN	Jul 1977

(These Moroccan craft are smaller than the Peruvian units, with standard and full-load displacements of 375 and 445 tons on dimensions that include a length of 57·5 m/188·8 ft, a beam of 7·6 m/24·9 ft and a draught of 2·1 m/7·1 ft. The craft are FAC[G]s, however, with an armament of one 76-mm/3-in OTO Melara L/62 DP in an OTO Melara Compact single mounting and one 40-mm Bofors L/70 AA in single mounting, but there is provision for the installation of two twin container-launchers for four MM.38 Exocet anti-ship missiles used in conjunction with the Vega fire-control system; each vessel has one navigation radar and two Panda optical directors. The powerplant comprises four AGO V16 ASHR diesels delivering 8200 kW/11,000 hp for a maximum speed of 28 kt. The complement is 5 + 48.)

2. Peru ('PR 72P' class)

Name	No.	Builder	Commissioned
Velarde	P21	SFCN	Jul 1980
Santillana	P22	SFCN	Jul 1980
De Los Heros	P23	SFCN	Nov 1980
Herrera	P24	SFCN	Feb 1981
Larrea	P25	SFCN	Jun 1981
Sanchez Carrion	P26	SFCN	Sep 1981

(By local standards these large FAC[M]s are powerful craft with good missile and gun armament.)

3. Senegambia ('PR 72S' class)

Name	No.	Builder	Commissioned
Njambuur	P773	SFCN	1982

(This Senegambian unit is similar to the Moroccan unit, and is a FAC[G] with a length of 58·7 m/192·5 ft, a beam of 7·6 m/24·9 ft and a draught of 2·2 m/7·2 ft for standard and full-load displacements of 375 and 450 tons. The gun armament comprises two 76-mm/3-in OTO Melara Compact L/62 DP in two OTO Melara Compact single mountings and two 20-mm AA in single mountings, and the electronic fit is more capable than that of the Moroccan craft with one Decca 1226 surface-search and navigation radar, plus two Naja optronic directors. The four AGO V16 RVR diesels deliver 9600 kW/12,875 hp to four shafts for a maximum speed of 29 kt. The complement is 39, with provision for 7 passengers.)

The Peruvian *Herrera* carries four MM·38 Exocet missiles, 76-mm (3-in) gun, two 40-mm Bofors guns, and two 20-mm cannon.

'Province' class FAC(M)

(UK/Oman)
Type: fast attack craft (missile)
Displacement: 310 tons standard and 395 tons full load
Dimensions: length 186·0 ft (56·7 m); beam 26·9 ft (8·2 m); draught 8·9 ft (2·7 m)
Gun armament: one 76-mm (3-in) OTO Melara L/62 DP in an OTO Melara Compact single mounting, and two 40-mm Bofors L/70 AA in a Breda Compact twin mounting
Missile armament: two triple or (B11, 12 and 14) quadruple container-launchers for six or eight MM.40 Exocet anti-ship missiles
Torpedo armament: none
Anti-submarine armament: none
Electronics: one AWS 4 or (B11, 12 and 14) TM1226C surface-search and tactical radar used in conjunction with a Sea Archer or (B11, 12 and 14) Philips 307 fire-control system, one optronic director, one ESM system with Cutlass warning and Scorpion jamming elements, and two Barricade chaff/flare launchers
Propulsion: four Paxman Valenta 18RP-200 diesels delivering 18,200 hp (13,570 kW) to four shafts
Performance: maximum speed 40 kt; range 2,300 miles (3700 km) at 18 kt
Complement: 5 + 40 plus provision for 14 trainees

Class
1. Kenya ('Nyayo' class)

Name	No.	Builder	Commissioned
Nyayo	P3126	Vosper Thornycroft	Jul 1987
Umoja	P3127	Vosper Thornycroft	Sep 1987

(These Kenyan boats were ordered late in 1984, and are FAC[M]s with a main armament of two twin container-launchers for four Otomat Mk 2 anti-ship missiles backed by a 76-mm/3-in OTO Melara L/62 DP gun in an OTO Melara Compact single mounting, two 30-mm Oerlikon L/85 AA in a GCM-A03-2 twin mounting, and two 20-mm Oerlikon AA in two A41A single mountings. The electronics include one AWS 4 surface-search radar, one AC1226 navigation radar, one ST 802 fire-control radar and one Signaal 423 fire-control radar, plus a CAAIS 450 action information system, an ESM system with warning element, and two Barricade chaff/flare launchers. With principal dimensions that include a length of 186·0 ft/56·7 m, a beam of 26·9 ft/8·2 m and a draught of 7·9 ft/2·4 m, the craft each have a full-load displacement of 400 tons, and the propulsion comprises four Paxman Valenta 18RP-200CM diesels delivering 18,200 hp/13,570 kW to four shafts for a maximum speed of 40 kt. The complement is 40.)

2. Oman

Name	No.	Builder	Commissioned
Dhofar	B10	Vosper Thornycroft	Aug 1982
Al Sharqiyah	B11	Vosper Thornycroft	Nov 1983
Al Bat'nah	B12	Vosper Thornycroft	Jan 1984
Musandam	B14	Vosper Thornycroft	Mar 1989

(These are large and powerful FAC[M]s with potent missile armament plus the barrelled weapons for effective operations against smaller craft in confined waters.)

Above: Senegambia's *Njambuur* is a FAC(G) version of the 'PR-72' class design with two 76-mm (3-in) OTO Melara guns in single mountings.

Below: The FAC(M)s of the Omani 'Province' class carry a variable number of MM.40 Exocet missiles in the cluttered area forward of the after deckhouse.

'PSMM Mk 5' class FAC(M)

(USA/South Korea)

Type: fast attack craft (missile)

Displacement: 240 tons standard and 268 tons full load

Dimensions: length 176·2 ft (53·7 m); beam 23·9 ft (7·3 m); draught 9·5 ft (2·9 m)

Gun armament: one 3-in (76-mm) OTO Melara L/62 DP in an OTO Melara Compact single mounting, two 30-mm Oerlikon L/85 AA in an Emerlec twin mounting, and two 0·5-in (12·7-mm) machine-guns in single mountings

Missile armament: (PGM352, 353 and 355) four Standard launchers for eight RIM-66 ARM anti-ship missiles or (others) or two twin container-launchers for four RGM-84 Harpoon anti-ship missiles

Torpedo armament: none

Anti-submarine armament: none

Electronics: one SPS-58 air-search radar, one HC-75 surface-search and navigation radar, one SPG-50 radar used in conjunction with the Mk 63 gun fire-control system or (PGM356 onwards) one Westinghouse W-120 radar used in conjunction with the H 930 fire-control system, one ESM system with warning element, and two Mk 33 RBOC chaff/flare launchers

Propulsion: six Avco Lycoming TF35 gas turbines delivering 16,800 hp (12,525 kW) to two shafts

Performance: maximum speed 40 + kt; range 2,750 miles (4425 km) at 18 kt

Complement: 5 + 27

Class

1. Indonesia ('Dagger' class)

Name	No.	Builder	Commissioned
Mandau	621	Korea-Tacoma	Oct 1979
Rencong	622	Korea-Tacoma	Oct 1979
Badik	623	Korea-Tacoma	Feb 1980
Keris	624	Korea-Tacoma	Feb 1980

(These Indonesian craft differ somewhat from the South Korean units, having a full-load displacement of 270 tons on a hull with a length of 50·2 m/164·7 ft, a beam of 7·3 m/23·9 ft and a draught of 2·3 m/7·5 ft. The armament comprises one 57-mm Bofors SAK 57 Mk 1 L/70 DP in a Bofors single mounting, one 40-mm Bofors L/70 AA in a single mounting and two 20-mm Rheinmetall AA in single mountings used in conjunction with the NA18 optronic director, plus two twin container-launchers for four MM.38 Exocet anti-ship missiles used in conjunction with the radar of the WM-28 fire-control system; each vessel also possesses a Decca 1226 surface-search and navigation radar. The powerplant is a CODOG arrangement with one General Electric LM2500 gas turbine or two MTU 12V 331 TC81 diesels delivering 25,000 hp/18,640 kW and 1670 kW/2,240 hp respectively to two shafts for maximum speeds of 41 kt on the gas turbine or 17 kt on the diesels. The complement is 7 + 36. Indonesia originally intended to procure eight of this class, but the plan seems to have been curtailed at the four current units.)

The Taiwanese *Lung Chiang* is seen on running trials before the installation of weapons and the suite of operational electronics.

2. South Korea

Name	No.	Builder	Commissioned
Paek Ku 52	PGM352	Tacoma BB	Mar 1975
Paek Ku 53	PGM353	Tacoma BB	Mar 1975
Paek Ku 55	PGM355	Tacoma BB	Feb 1976
Paek Ku 56	PGM356	Tacoma BB	Feb 1976
Paek Ku 57	PGM357	Korea-Tacoma	1977
Paek Ku 58	PGM358	Korea-Tacoma	1977
Paek Ku 59	PGM359	Korea-Tacoma	1977
Paek Ku 61	PGM361	Korea-Tacoma	1978

(The first three of this class are unusual in being armed with the radar-homing anti-ship version of the Standard SAM.)

3. Taiwan ('Lung Chiang' class)

Name	No.	Builder	Commissioned
Lung Chiang	PGG581	Tacoma BB	May 1978
Sui Chiang	PGG582	China SB	1982

(These Taiwanese craft are similar to the South Korean units, but at standard and full-load displacements of 220 and 250 tons their dimensions include a length of 164·5 ft/50·2 m, a beam of 23·9 ft/7·3 m and a draught of 7·5 ft/2·3 m. The craft are FAC[M]s with four container-launchers for four Hsiung Feng I anti-ship missiles, backed by a gun armament of one 76-mm/3-in OTO Melara L/62 DP in an OTO Melara Compact single mounting, two 30-mm Oerlikon L/85 AA in an Emerlec twin mounting, and two 0·5-in/12·7-mm machine-guns in single mountings. The electronics include one RAN 11L/X air/surface-search radar, one Argo NA10 fire-control system, one HR 76 radar used in conjunction with the H 930 missile fire-control system [PGG582 only], one IPN 10 action information system, and four chaff launchers. The CODOG powerplant has three Avco Lycoming TF35 gas turbines delivering 13,800 hp/10,290 kW or three General Motors 12V 149TI diesels delivering 2,880 hp/2145 kW to three shafts for maximum speeds of 40 or 20 kt respectively. The complement is 5 + 29. The Taiwanese had planned to produce a large class whose later units would have had RGM-84 Harpoon anti-ships missiles and the RCA R76 C5 fire-control system, but the USA's refusal of an export licence for the Harpoon led to cancellation of the plan as the type has suspect stability with the Hsiung Feng missiles.)

Note: The 'PSSM Mk 5' class design is the Patrol Ship Multi-Mission Mk 5 derivative of the **'Asheville' class** FAC(G). Seventeen of this patrol combatant type were built for the US Navy between 1966 and 1971 for coastal patrol and blockade, but were not extensively used: the class has a full-load displacement of 245 tons on dimensions that include a length of 164·5 ft (50·1 m), a beam of 23·8 ft (7·3 m) and a draught of 9·5 ft (2·9 m) for a speed of 38 kt on the CODOG arrangement of two Cummins diesels delivering 3,500 hp (2610 kW) or one General Electric gas turbine delivering 13,300 hp (9915 kW) to two shafts. The standard armament is one 3-in (76-mm) gun in a Mk 76 single mounting, one 40-mm Bofors AA in a Mk 3 single mounting, and two 0·5-in (12·7-mm) machine-guns in a twin mounting. The craft are now out of US service and either exported (one to South Korea as a FAC[M] with two Standard ARM anti-ship missiles, and two each to Colombia, Taiwan [now deleted] and Turkey as FAC[G]s) or awaiting transfer.

'Rade Koncar' or 'Type 211' class FAC(M)

(Yugoslavia)

Type: fast attack craft (missile)
Displacement: 240 tons full load
Dimensions: length 45·0 m (147·6 ft); beam 8·4 m (27·6 ft); draught 2·5 m (8·2 ft)
Gun armament: two 57-mm L/70 Bofors SAK 57 Mk 1 DP in Bofors single mountings
Missile armament: two twin container-launchers for four SS-N-2B 'Styx' anti-ship missiles
Torpedo armament: none
Anti-submarine armament: none
Electronics: one Decca 1226 surface-search and navigation radar, and one Philips TAB radar used in conjunction with the 9LV 200 fire-control system
Propulsion: two Rolls-Royce Proteus gas turbines delivering 11,600 hp (8650 kW) and two MTU 20V 538 TB92 diesels delivering 5400 kW (7,240 hp) to four shafts
Performance: maximum speed 40 kt; range 1850 km (1,150 miles) at 20 kt or 925 km (575 miles) at 35 kt
Complement: 5 + 25

Class
1. Libya

Name	No.	Builder	Commissioned
		Tito SY	
		Tito SY	
		Tito SY	
		Tito SY	

(These are unexceptional FAC[M]s ordered in 1985 and probably making use of weapons and sensors already available to Libya. The gun armament is one 76-mm/3-in OTO Melara L/62 DP in an OTO Melara Compact single mounting, one 40-mm Bofors L/70 AA in a Breda single mounting, two 30-mm AA in a twin mounting, and two 12·7-mm/0·5-in machine-guns. The missile armament comprises two twin container-launchers for four SS-N-2C 'Styx'

anti-ship missiles. The fact that the craft have not yet been delivered probably means that the programme is in abeyance, probably because of the Western embargo on the supply of military equipment [including engines] to Libya.)

2. Yugoslavia

Name	No.	Builder	Commissioned
Rade Koncar	RT401	Tito SY	Apr 1977
Vlado Cetkovic	RT402	Tito SY	Mar 1978
Ramiz Sadiko	RT403	Tito SY	Aug 1978
Hasan Zahirovic-Laca	RT404	Tito SY	Dec 1978
Orce Nikolov	RT405	Tito SY	Aug 1979
Ante Banina	RT406	Tito SY	Nov 1980

(These Yugoslav craft are based on the hull of the Swedish 'Spica II' class with the amidships bridge of the Malaysian 'Spica II-M' class, simple electronics of Western origins, a propulsion arrangement of Western origins, and a mix of Soviet and Swedish armament.)

The resemblance of the 'Rade Koncar' class to the Swedish 'Spica II' design is unmistakable despite the presence over the stern of two large containers for Soviet SS-N-2 anti-ship missiles.

'Ramadan' class FAC(M)

(UK/Egypt)

Type: fast attack craft (missile)
Displacement: 310 tons full load
Dimensions: length 170·6 ft (52·0 m); beam 25·0 ft (7·6 m); draught 6·6 ft (2·0 m)
Gun armament: one 76-mm (3-in) OTO Melara L/62 DP in an OTO Melara Compact single mounting, and two 40-mm Bofors L/70 AA in a Breda Compact twin mounting
Missile armament: two twin container-launchers for four Otomat Mk 1 anti-ship missiles
Torpedo armament: none
Anti-submarine armament: none
Electronics: one S 820 surface-search radar, one S 810 navigation radar, two ST 802 radars used in conjunction with the Sapphire fire-control system, two optronic directors, two optical directors, one CAAIS action information system, one ESM system with Cutlass warning and Cygnus jamming elements, and two Protean chaff/flare launchers
Propulsion: four MTU 20V 538 TB91 diesels delivering 12,800 kW (17,170 hp) to four shafts
Performance: maximum speed 40 kt; range 3700 km (2,300 miles) at 16 kt
Complement: 4 + 26

Class
1. Egypt

Name	No.	Builder	Commissioned
Ramadan	670	Vosper Thornycroft	Jul 1981
Khyber	672	Vosper Thornycroft	Sep 1981
El Kadesseya	674	Vosper Thornycroft	Apr 1982
El Yarmouk	676	Vosper Thornycroft	May 1982
Badr	678	Vosper Thornycroft	Jun 1982
Hettein	680	Vosper Thornycroft	Oct 1982

Note: This powerful FAC(M) class features a nicely balanced sensor and armament combination optimized for the anti-ship role.

The FAC(M)s of Egypt's 'Ramadan' class have effective sensors and anti-ship missiles balanced by a useful gun armament located fore and aft.

Above: The sensors of the 'Ramadan' class FAC(M) are based on one surveillance and two fire-control radars as well as two optronic directors.

Below: The Thai navy's *Ratcharit* is typical of the modern FAC(M) with a nice balance of sensors, missiles and gun armament.

'Ratcharit' class FAC(M)

(Italy/Thailand)

Type: fast attack craft (missile)

Displacement: 235 tons standard and 270 tons full load

Dimensions: length 49·8 m (163·4 ft); beam 7·5 m (24·6 ft); draught 2·3 m (7·5 ft)

Gun armament: one 76-mm (3-in) OTO Melara L/62 DP in an OTO Melara Compact single mounting, and one 40-mm Bofors L/70 AA in a Breda single mounting

Missile armament: two twin container-launchers for four MM.38 Exocet anti-ship missiles

Torpedo armament: none

Anti-submarine armament: none

Electronics: one Decca surface-search and navigation radar, one radar used in conjunction with the WM-25 fire-control system, and one ESM system with warning element

Propulsion: three MTU 20V 538 TB91 diesels delivering 10,050 kW (13,480 hp) to three shafts

Performance: maximum speed 37 kt; range 3700 km (2,300 miles) at 15 kt

Complement: 7 + 38

Class
1. Thailand

Name	No.	Builder	Commissioned
Ratcharit	4	CNR, Breda	Aug 1979
Witthayakhom	5	CNR, Breda	Nov 1979
Udomdet	6	CNR, Breda	Feb 1980

Note: These are medium-sized FAC(M)s with modest missile armament and the standard blend of one 76 mm (3-in) DP and one 40-mm AA gun.

'Saar 4' or 'Reshef' class FAC(M)

(Israel)

Type: fast attack craft (missile)

Displacement: 415 tons standard and 450 tons full load

Dimensions: length 58·0 m (190·6 ft); beam 7·8 m (25·6 ft); draught 2·4 m (8·0 ft)

Gun armament: one 76-mm (3-in) OTO Melara L/62 DP in an OTO Melara Compact single mounting (not in *Tarshish*), one 20-mm Phalanx Mk 15 CIWS mounting, two 20-mm Oerlikon AA in single mountings, and two 0·5-in (12·7-mm) machine-guns in single mountings

Missile armament: one Mk 141 twin or quadruple container-launcher for two or four RGM-84 Harpoon anti-ship missiles, or four or six container-launchers for four or six Gabriel II or III anti-ship missiles, or a mix of the two missile types

Torpedo armament: none

Anti-submarine armament: none

Aircraft: one Mata Hellstar light remotely piloted helicopter on a platform aft (*Tarshish* only)

Electronics: one Neptune air/surface-search radar, one RTN 10X radar used in conjunction with the Argo NA10 fire-control system, one ELAC active search and attack hull sonar (not in *Yaffo*), one ESM system with MN-53 warning and jamming elements, and chaff launchers (one 45-tube, four or six 24-tube and four 1-tube)

Propulsion: four MTU 16V 956 TB91 diesels delivering 10,400 kW (13,950 hp) to four shafts

Performance: maximum speed 32 kt; range 7400 km (4,600 miles) at 17·5 kt or 3075 km (1,910 miles) at 30 kt

Complement: 45

Class
1. Chile

Name	No.	Builder	Commissioned
Casma	30	Haifa Shipyard	May 1974
Chipana	31	Haifa Shipyard	Oct 1973

(These Chilean craft are similar to the original Israeli norm, but have a missile armament of four Gabriel anti-ship missiles, a barrelled armament of two 76-mm/3-in OTO Melara L/62 DP in OTO Melara Compact single mountings and two 20-mm Oerlikon AA in single mountings, and a less sophisticated sensor fit based on a Neptune surface-search and navigation radar used in conjunction with an EL/M 2221 fire-control system; each vessel also possesses four Israeli chaff launchers. The craft [ex-*Romat* and ex-*Keshet*] were transferred to Chile in 1979 and 1981 respectively. Chile planned to build more of the type under licence, but the normalization of relations with Argentina after the Vatican's settlement of the Beagle Channel dispute may have caused the cancellation of the notion, especially as the country bought two 'Saar 3' class FACs from Israel in 1989.)

2. Israel

Name	No.	Builder	Commissioned
Reshef		Haifa Shipyard	Apr 1973
Kidon		Haifa Shipyard	Sep 1974
Tarshish		Haifa Shipyard	Mar 1975
Yaffo		Haifa Shipyard	Apr 1975
Nitzhon		Haifa Shipyard	Sep 1978
Atsmout		Haifa Shipyard	Feb 1979
Moledet		Haifa Shipyard	May 1979
Komemiut		Haifa Shipyard	Aug 1980

(These are in every way exceptional FAC[M]s built to a basic design from Lürssen but adapted to Israeli requirements to produce long-range craft of very good sea-keeping qualities and devastating missile armament. The extension of this armament has led to the modification of the original gun armament, which is reflected in the fit carried by the Chilean craft. Israel plans to replace the CIWS mounting with a vertical-launch system for Barak 1 SAMs.)

3. South Africa ('Minister' class)

Name	No.	Builder	Commissioned
Jan Smuts	P1561	Haifa Shipyard	Sep 1977
P. W. Botha	P1562	Haifa Shipyard	Dec 1977
Frederic Cresswell	P1563	Haifa Shipyard	May 1978
Jim Fouche	P1564	Sandock Austral	Dec 1978
Frans Erasmus	P1565	Sandock Austral	Jul 1979
Oswald Pirow	P1566	Sandock Austral	Mar 1980
Hendrik Mentz	P1567	Sandock Austral	Sep 1982
Kobie Coetzee	P1568	Sandock Austral	Mar 1983
Magnus Malan	P1569	Sandock Austral	Jul 1986
	P1571	Sandock Austral	1989
	P1572	Sandock Austral	1990
	P1573	Sandock Austral	1990

(These South African craft are a variation on the Israeli norm, with a full-load displacement of 430 tons on dimensions that include a length of 62·2 m/204·0 ft, a beam of 7·8 m/25·6 ft and a draught of 2·4 m/8·0 ft. The armament comprises two 76-mm/3-in OTO Melara L/62 DP in OTO Melara Compact single mountings, two 20-mm Oerlikon AA in single mountings, two 0·5-in/12·7-mm machine-guns in single mountings, and six container-launchers for six Skorpioen [Gabriel II] anti-ship missiles. The electronics, propulsion and performance are similar to those of the Israeli craft, and the complement is 7 + 40. It is reported that another three units are to be built to an improved standard.)

The Israeli navy's *Reshef* is seen in its original form with two 76-mm (3-in) guns and containers for an impressive seven Gabriel anti-ship missiles.

'Saar 4·5' or 'Aliya/Romat' class FAC(M)

(Israel)
Type: fast attack craft (missile)
Displacement: 488 tons standard
Dimensions: length 61·7 m (202·4 ft); beam 7·6 m (24·9 ft); draught 2·5 m (8·2 ft)
Gun armament: one 76-mm (3-in) OTO Melara L/62 DP in an OTO Melara Compact single mounting (not *Alia* and *Geoula*), one 20-mm Phalanx Mk 15 CIWS mounting, two 20-mm Oerlikon AA in single mountings, and two or four 0·5-in (12·7-mm) machine-guns in a twin or quadruple mounting
Missile armament: one (*Aliya* and *Geoula*) or two (*Romat* and *Keshet*) Mk 141 quadruple container-launchers for four or eight RGM-84 Harpoon anti-ship missiles, and four (*Aliya* and *Geoula*) or eight (*Romat* and *Keshet*) container-launchers for four or eight Gabriel II or III anti-ship missiles
Torpedo armament: none
Anti-submarine armament: helicopter-launched weapons (see below)
Aircraft: one Agusta (Bell) AB.206 helicopter or Mata Hellstar light remotely piloted helicopter in a hangar amidships (*Alia* and *Geoula* only)
Electronics: one Neptune air/surface-search radar, one RTN 10X radar used in conjunction with the Argo NA10 fire-control system, one ELAC hull sonar, one Elta ESM system with MN-53 warning and jamming elements, and chaff/flare launchers (one 45-tube, one 24-tube and four 1-tube)
Propulsion: four MTU 16V 956 TB91 diesels delivering 10,400 kW (13,950 hp) to four shafts
Performance: maximum speed 31 kt; range 7400 km (4,600 miles) at 17 kt or 2800 km (1,740 miles) at 30 kt
Complement: 53 (*Aliya* and *Geoula*) or 45 (*Romat* and *Keshet*)

Class
1. Israel

Name	No.	Builder	Commissioned
Aliya		Haifa Shipyard	Aug 1980
Geoula		Haifa Shipyard	Dec 1980
Romat		Haifa Shipyard	Oct 1981
Keshet		Haifa Shipyard	1982

Note: These large FAC(M)s are designed as leaders for flotillas of smaller craft, and have quite exceptional missile firepower even in *Aliya* and *Geoula*, which have a small helicopter for the mid-course guidance update of long-range anti-ship missiles, and as a secondary task for anti-submarine defence.

'Shanghai II', 'Shanghai III' and 'Shanghai IV' class FAC(G)s

(China)
Type: fast attack craft (gun)
Displacement: 120 tons standard and 155 tons full load
Dimensions: length 39·0 m (128·0 ft); beam 5·5 m (18·0 ft); draught 1·7 m (5·5 ft)
Gun armament: four 37-mm L/63 AA in two twin mountings and four 25-mm AA in two twin mountings, or ('Shanghai III' and 'Shanghai IV' class craft) two 57-mm L/70 AA in a twin mounting and one 25-mm AA in a single mounting; some craft have two 75-mm (2·95-in) Type 56 recoilless rifles in a twin mounting
Missile armament: none
Torpedo armament: none
Anti-submarine armament: two throwers for eight depth charges
Mines: up to 10
Electronics: one 'Skin Head' or 'Pot Head' surface-search radar, one hull-mounted sonar, one variable-depth sonar (some craft only), and one 'High Pole-A' IFF system
Propulsion: two M 50F diesels delivering 1800 kW (2,415 hp) and two Type 12D6 diesels delivering 1350 kW (1,810 hp) to four shafts
Performance: maximum speed 30 kt; range 1500 km (930 miles) at 17 kt
Complement: 6 + 30

Class
1. Albania
6 'Shanghai II' class craft (nos 541, 542, 543. 544. 545 and 546)
2. Bangladesh
8 'Shanghai II' class craft
These are the *Shaheet Daulat* (P411), *Shaheed Farid* (P412), *Shaheed Mohobullah* (P413), *Shaheed Akhtarruddin* (P414), *Tahweed* (P611), *Tawfiq* (P612), *Tamjeed* (P613) and *Tanveer* (P614)
3. China
290 + 'Shanghai II, III and IV' class craft
4. Congo
3 'Shanghai II' class craft (nos 201, 202 and 203)
5. Egypt
4 'Shanghai II' class craft (nos 793, 795, 797 and 799)
6. Guinea
6 'Shanghai II' class craft (nos P733, P734, P735, P736, P737 and P738)
7. North Korea
15 'Shanghai II' class craft
8. Pakistan
12 'Shanghai II' class craft
These are the *Quetta* (P141), *Lahore* (P142), *Marden* (P143), *Gilgit* (P144), *Pishin* (P145), *Sukkur* (P146), *Sehwan* (P147), *Bahawalpur* (P149), *Banum* (P154), *Kalat* (P156), *Larkana* (P157) and *Sahiwal* (P160)
9. Romania
27 'Shanghai II' class craft
These are the *Saturn* and *Venus* for harbour security, the VP20 to VP40 for maritime border patrol, and the VS41 to VS44 for anti-submarine patrol with a high-frequency search and attack hull sonar and two racks of depth charges
10. Sri Lanka
6 'Shanghai II' class craft
These are known locally as the **'Sooraya' class** and are named *Sooraya* (P3140), *Weeraya* (P3141), *Ranakami* (P3142), *Balawatha* (P3144), *Jagatha* (P3145) and *Rakshaka* (P3146)
11. Tanzania
6 'Shanghai II' class craft (nos JW9841, JW9842, JW9843, JW9844, JW9845 and JW9846)
12. Tunisia
2 'Shanghai II' class craft
These are the *Gafsah* (P305) and *Amilcar* (P306)
13. Zaire
4 'Shanghai II' class craft

'Shershen' and 'Mol' class FAC(T)s

(USSR)
Type: fast attack craft (torpedo)
Displacement: ('Shershen' class) 145 tons standard and 175 tons full load, or ('Mol' class) 160 tons standard and 200 tons full load
Dimensions: ('Shershen' class) length 34·7 m (113·8 ft); beam 6·7 m (222·0 ft); draught 1·5 m (4·9 ft), or ('Mol' class) length 39·0 m (127·9 ft); beam 8·1 m (26·6 ft); draught 1·8 m (5·9 ft)
Gun armament: four 30-mm L/65 AA in two twin mountings
Missile armament: none
Torpedo armament: four single 533-mm (21-in) mountings for four Type 53 torpedoes
Anti-submarine armament: two racks for 12 depth charges
Electronics: one 'Pot Drum' surface-search radar, one 'Drum Tilt' gun-control radar, one 'Square Head' IFF system, and one 'High Pole-A' IFF system
Propulsion: ('Shershen' class) three M 503A diesels delivering 9000 kW (12,070 hp) or ('Mol' class) three M 504 diesels delivering 11,250 kW (15,090 hp), in each case to three shafts
Performance: maximum speed ('Shershen' class) 47 kt or ('Mol' class) 36 kt; range 1500 km (930 miles) at 30 kt
Complement: ('Shershen' class) 23 or ('Mol' class) 25

Class
1. Angola
4 'Shershen' class craft
2. Bulgaria
6 'Shershen' class craft (nos 104, 105, 106, 114, 115 and 116)
3. Cape Verde
2 'Shershen' class craft with torpedo armament (nos 451 and 452)
4. Congo
1 'Shershen' class craft without torpedo armament
5. East Germany
6 'Shershen' class craft
These are the *Wilhelm Florin*, *Fritz Behn*, *Willi Brezdel*, *Walte Huesman*, *Edgar André* and *Ernst Grube*

6. Egypt
6 'Shershen' class craft (nos 751, 753, 755, 757, 759 and 761)
7. Ethiopia
2 'Mol' class craft (nos FTB110 and FTB111)
8. Guinea
3 'Shershen' class craft
9. North Korea
3 'Shershen' class craft
10. Somalia
4 'Mol' class craft
11. USSR
7 'Shershen' class craft
13. Vietnam
16 'Shershen' class craft

With an armament of four torpedoes and four 30-mm cannon, the 'Shershen' class FAC(T) is obsolescent in most technical and operational respects.

14. Yugoslavia
14 'Shershen' class craft

These are the *Pionir* (TC211), *Partizan* (TC212), *Proleter* (TC213), *Topcider* (TC214), *Ivan* (TC215), *Jadran* (TC216), *Kornat* (TC217), *Biokovak* (TC218), *Streljko* (TC219), *Crvena Zvijezda* (TC220), *Partizan III* (TC221), *Partizan II* (TC222), *Napredak* (TC223) and *Pionir II* (TC224)

Note: These are obsolete FAC(T)s built from 1962 in a number of Soviet yards. The 'Mol' is essentially an enlarged version of the 'Shershen' specifically for export.

The 'Snögg' class *Rapp* is usefully armed with four Penguin missiles in addition to four 533-mm (21-in) torpedoes and a 40-mm Bofors gun.

'Snögg' class FAC(M/T)

(Norway)

Type: fast attack craft (missile and torpedo)
Displacement: 100 tons standard and 135 tons full load
Dimensions: length 36·5 m (119·8 ft); beam 6·1 m (20·0 ft); draught 1·5 m (5·0 ft)
Gun armament: one 40-mm Bofors L/70 AA in a single mounting
Missile armament: four container-launchers for four Penguin anti-ship missiles
Torpedo armament: four single 533-mm (21-in) mountings for four Tp 61 wire-guided torpedoes
Anti-submarine armament: none
Electronics: one TM626 surface-search and navigation radar, one TORC1 torpedo fire-control system and (being fitted) one MSI-80S fire-control system with one TVT-300 optronic tracker and one laser rangefinder

Propulsion: two MTU 16V 538 TB92 diesels delivering 5400 kW (7,240 hp) to two shafts
Performance: maximum speed 32 kt; range 1000 km (620 miles) at 32 kt
Complement: 3 + 16

Class
1. Norway

Name	No.	Builder	Commissioned
Snögg	P980	Batservice	1970
Rapp	P981	Batservice	1970
Snar	P982	Batservice	1970
Rask	P983	Batservice	1971
Kvikk	P984	Batservice	1971
Kjapp	P985	Batservice	1971

Note: These craft have been modernized with better electronics, but can be regarded only as obsolescent.

'Sparviero' class FAH(M)

(Italy)
Type: fast attack hydrofoil (missile)

Displacement: 60 tons standard and 62·5 tons full load

Dimensions: length 24·6 m (80·7 ft) with foils retracted and 23·0 m (75·4 ft) with foils extended; beam 12·0 m (39·4 ft) with foils retracted, 10·8 m (35·4 ft) with foils extended and 7·0 m (22·9 ft) hull; draught 4·3 m (14·1 ft) hullborne with foils extended and 1·8 m (5·9 ft) foilborne

Gun armament: one 76-mm (3-in) OTO Melara L/62 DP in an OTO Melara Compact single mounting

Missile armament: two container-launchers for two Otomat Mk 2 anti-ship missiles

Torpedo armament: none

Anti-submarine armament: none

Electronics: one 3RM 7-250 surface-search and navigation radar, one RTN 10X radar used in conjunction with the Argo NA10 fire-control system, and one Farad A ESM system with warning element

Propulsion: CODOG arrangement, with one Isotta Fraschini ID 38 N6V diesel delivering 120 kW (161 hp) to one retractable propeller for hullborne operation, or one Rolls-Royce Proteus 15M560 gas turbine delivering 5,000 hp (3,728 kW) to one waterjet for foilborne operation

Performance: maximum speed 50 kt foilborne or 8 kt hullborne; range 2225 km (1,385 miles) at 8 kt or 740 km (460 miles) at 45 kt

Complement: 2 + 8

Class
1. Italy

Name	No.	Builder	Commissioned
Sparviero	P420	Alinavi	Jul 1974
Nibbio	P421	CNR, Muggiano	Mar 1982
Falcone	P422	CNR, Muggiano	Mar 1982
Astore	P423	CNR, Muggiano	Feb 1983
Grifone	P424	CNR, Muggiano	Feb 1983
Gheppio	P425	CNR, Muggiano	Jan 1983
Condor	P426	CNR, Muggiano	Jan 1984

(These small daylight-only craft pack considerable firepower into a small hull, the two missiles being powerful types usable to best effect with the capable electronic system of these craft.)

2. Japan
(These three craft are to be built under licence in Japan to a standard generally similar to the Italian baseline configuration, but will have a primary armament of SSM-1B anti-ship missiles developed from the coast-launched SSM-1.)

Below left: Although packing only a comparatively small punch, the *Sparviero* and her sister craft are fast and agile, and also small targets.

Below: The bridge of the *Sparviero*.

'Spica II' class FAC(M/T)

(Sweden)

Type: fast attack craft (missile and torpedo)

Displacement: 190 tons standard and 230 tons full load

Dimensions: length 43·6 m (143·0 ft); beam 7·1 m (23·3 ft); draught 2·4 m (7·4 ft)

Gun armament: one 57-mm Bofors SAK 57 Mk 2 L/70 DP in a Bofors single mounting

Missile armament: eight container-launchers for eight Rbs 15M anti-ship missiles

Torpedo armament: up to six single 533-mm (21-in) mountings for up to six Tp 61 wire-guided torpedoes in place of the missiles

Anti-submarine armament: none

Mines: fitted for minelaying

Electronics: one Sea Giraffe air/surface-search radar, one 9LV 200 Mk 2 radar used in conjunction with the 9LV 228 fire-control system, one action information system, one ESM system with EWS 905 warning element, and two Philax chaff/flare launchers

Propulsion: three Rolls-Royce Proteus gas turbines delivering 12,900 hp (9620 kW) to three shafts

Performance: maximum speed 40·5 kt

Complement: 7 + 20

Class

1. Malaysia ('Spica-M' class)

Name	No.	Builder	Commissioned
Handalan	5311	Karlskrona Varvet	Aug 1979
Perkasa	5312	Karlskrona Varvet	Aug 1979
Pendekar	5313	Karlskrona Varvet	Aug 1979
Gempita	5314	Karlskrona Varvet	Aug 1979

(These Malaysian craft are essentially diesel-engined versions of the Swedish 'Spica II' class craft, with three MTU 16V 538 TB91 diesels delivering 8100 kW/10,865 hp to three shafts for a maximum speed of 34·5 kt and a range of 3425 km/2130 miles at 14 kt. The full-load displacement is 240 tons. The armament comprises one 57-mm Bofors SAK 57 Mk 2 L/70 DP and one 40-mm Bofors L/70 AA guns, each in a single mounting, and two twin container-launchers for four MM.38 Exocet anti-ship missiles. The electronics include one 9GR 600 surface-search radar, one Decca 616 navigation radar, one 9LV 212 radar used with the 9LV 228 Mk 2 fire-control system, an optronic AA fire-control system. and one ESM system with a Susie warning element. The propulsion arrangement comprises three MTU 16V 538 TB91 diesels delivering 8055 kW/10,805 hp to three shafts for a maximum speed of 34·5 kt and a range of 3400 km/2,115 miles at 14 kt. The complement is 6 + 34. The craft have provision for the installation of 12·75-in/324-mm tubes for Mk 46 or Stingray anti-submarine torpedoes, and there are plans to procure an additional four units when funding permits.)

2. Sweden

Name	No.	Builder	Commissioned
Norrköping	R131	Karlskrona Varvet	May 1973
Nynäshamn	R132	Karlskrona Varvet	Sep 1973
Norrtälje	R133	Karlskrona Varvet	Feb 1974
Varberg	R134	Karlskrona Varvet	Jun 1974
Västerås	R135	Karlskrona Varvet	Oct 1974
Västervik	R136	Karlskrona Varvet	Jan 1975
Umeå	R137	Karlskrona Varvet	May 1975
Piteå	R138	Karlskrona Varvet	Sep 1975
Luleå	R139	Karlskrona Varvet	Nov 1975
Halmstad	R140	Karlskrona Varvet	Apr 1976
Strömstad	R141	Karlskrona Varvet	Sep 1976
Ystad	R142	Karlskrona Varvet	Jan 1976

(This is an impressive FAC with missile and/or torpedo capability and a powerful DP gun.)

'Stockholm' class FAC(M)

(Sweden)

Type: fast attack craft (missile)

Displacement: 310 tons standard and 335 tons full load

Dimensions: length 50·0 m (164·0 ft); beam 6·8 m (22·3 ft); draught 1·9 m (6·2 ft)

Gun armament: one 57-mm L/70 Bofors SAK 57 Mk 2 DP in a Bofors single mounting, and one 40-mm Bofors L/70 AA in a single mounting

Missile armament: four twin container-launchers for eight Rbs 15M anti-ship missiles

Torpedo armament: two single 533-mm (21-in) mountings for two Tp 613 wire-guided torpedoes, or two twin 400-mm (15·75-in) mountings for four Tp 42 wire-guided torpedoes

Anti-submarine armament: four Elma LLS-920 nine-barrel rocket-launchers, Tp 42 torpedoes (see above), and two depth-charge racks

Mines: has laying capability

Electronics: one Sea Giraffe air/surface-search radar, one navigation radar, one 9LV 200 Mk 3 radar used in conjunction with the Maril fire-control system, one 9LV 300 gun fire-control system with one 9LV 100 optronic director, one TSM 2642 Salmon active search variable-depth sonar, one Simrad SS 304 active attack hull sonar, one ESM system with EWS 905 warning element, and two Philax chaff/flare launchers

Propulsion: CODAG arrangement, with one Allison 570KF gas turbine delivering 6,000 hp (4475 kW) and two MTU 16V 396 TB93 diesels delivering 3150 kW (4,225 hp) to three shafts

Performance: maximum speed 32 kt on gas turbine and diesels or 20 kt on diesels; range 1850 km (1,150 miles) at 20 kt

Complement: 30

Class
1. Sweden

Name	No.	Builder	Commissioned
Stockholm	K11	Karlskrona Varvet	Feb 1985
Malmö	K12	Karlskrona Varvet	May 1985

Note: These potent craft act as flotilla leaders for Sweden's smaller FAC types, and have also been trialled with Plessey variable-depth sonar to improve their already useful anti-submarine capability.

Below left: The *Stockholm* and her sister craft are both advanced multi-role FAC(M)s with the size and crew to act as flotilla leaders for smaller FACs.

'Stenka' class FAC(G/T)

(USSR)

Type: fast attack craft (gun and torpedo)

Displacement: 170 tons standard and 210 tons full load

Dimensions: length 39·0 m (127·9 ft); beam 7·8 m (25·6 ft); draught 1·8 m (5·9 ft)

Gun armament: four 30-mm L/65 AA in two twin mountings

Missile armament: none

Torpedo armament: none

Anti-submarine armament: four single 406-mm (16-in) mountings for four Type 40 torpedoes, and two depth-charge racks

Electronics: one 'Pot Drum' or 'Peel Cone' surface-search radar, one 'Drum Tilt' gun fire-control radar, one high-frequency active search variable-depth sonar, and two 'Square Head' and one 'High Pole' IFF systems

Propulsion: three M 503A diesels delivering 9000 kW (12,070 hp) to three shafts

Performance: maximum speed 36 kt; range 1500 km (930 miles) at 24 kt or 925 km (575 miles) at 35 kt

Complement: 30

Class
1. Cambodia
4 craft without sonar or torpedo armament
2. Cuba
3 craft without sonar or torpedo armament
3. USSR
114 craft with ? more building and ? more planned

Note: The 'Stenka' class is based on the hull of the 'Osa' class, and is now building at the rate of about five craft per year at Petrovsky, Leningrad and Vladivostok. The programme was launched in 1967.

'Storm' class FAC(M)

(Norway)

Type: fast attack craft (missile)

Displacement: 100 tons standard and 135 tons full load

Dimensions: length 36·5 m (119·8 ft); beam 6·1 m (20·0 ft); draught 1·5 m (4·9 ft)

Gun armament: one 76-mm (3-in) Bofors L/50 in a Bofors single mounting, and one 40-mm Bofors L/70 AA in a single mounting

Missile armament: six container-launchers for six Penguin Mk II anti-ship missiles

Torpedo armament: none

Anti-submarine armament: none

Electronics: one TM1226 surface-search and navigation radar, one radar used in conjunction with the WM-26 fire-control system, and (being fitted) one MSI-80S fire-control system with one TVT-300 optronic tracker and one laser rangefinder

Propulsion: two MTU 872A diesels delivering 5400 kW (7,240 hp) to two shafts

Performance: maximum speed 32 kt

Complement: 4 + 15

Class
1. Norway

Name	No.	Builder	Commissioned
Blink	P961	Bergens Mek	1965
Glimt	P962	Bergens Mek	1966
Skjold	P963	Westermoen	1966
Trygg	P964	Bergens Mek	1966
Kjekk	P965	Bergens Mek	1966
Djerv	P966	Westermoen	1966
Skudd	P967	Bergens Mek	1966
Arg	P968	Bergens Mek	1966
Steil	P969	Westermoen	1967
Brann	P970	Bergens Mek	1967
Tross	P971	Bergens Mek	1967
Hvass	P972	Westermoen	1967
Traust	P973	Bergens Mek	1967
Brott	P974	Bergens Mek	1967
Odd	P975	Westermoen	1967
Brask	P977	Bergens Mek	1967
Rokk	P978	Westermoen	1968
Gnist	P979	Bergens Mek	1968

Note: These are small but agile FAC(M)s designed specifically for the particular operational conditions faced by the Norwegian navy in countering maritime incursions along the country's very long coastline. The hull is basically that of the 'Snögg' class FAC.

Despite their age, the 'Storm' class craft are still capable FAC(M)s through their capable missiles. This is the *Skudd*.

'Turya' class FAH(T)

(USSR)

Type: fast attack hydrofoil (torpedo)

Displacement: 190 tons standard and 250 tons full load

Dimensions: length 39·6 m (129·9 ft); beam 12·5 m (41·0 ft) over foils and 7·6 m (25·0 ft) for hull; draught 4·0 m (13·1 ft) over foils and 1·8 m (5·9 ft) for hull

Gun armament: two 57-mm L/80 AA in a twin mounting, two 25-mm L/80 AA in a twin mounting, and one 14·5-mm (0·57-in) machine-gun

Missile armament: none

Torpedo armament: four single 533-mm (21-in) mountings for four Type 53 dual-role torpedoes

Anti-submarine armament: torpedoes (see above), and one depth-charge rack

Electronics: one 'Pot Drum' surface-search radar, one 'Muff Cob' gun fire-control radar, one high-frequency active search and attack variable-depth sonar, and one 'Square Head' and one 'High Pole' IFF systems

Propulsion: three M 504 diesels delivering 11,250 kW (15,090 hp) to three shafts

Performance: maximum speed 40 kt foilborne; range 2700 km (1,680 miles) at 14 kt hullborne or 1100 km (685 miles) at 35 kt foilborne

Complement: 30

Class

1. Cambodia
2 craft

2. Cuba
9 craft

3. Ethiopia
2 craft (nos HTB112 and HTB113)

4. Seychelles
1 craft (named *Zoroaster*) without sonar and torpedo armament

5. USSR
30 craft

6. Vietnam
5 craft

Note: Based on the hull of the 'Osa' class with a single forward hydrofoil, this class has been built since 1972 at Petrovsky, Leningrad and Vladivostok. Since 1978 production has been for export only.

'Vosper Thornycroft 110-ft' class FAC(G)

(UK/Singapore)

Type: fast attack craft (gun)

Displacement: 112 tons standard and 142 tons full load

Dimensions: length 109·6 ft (33·5 m); beam 21·0 ft (6·4 m); draught 5·6 ft (1·8 m)

Gun armament: one 76-mm (3-in) Bofors L/50 in a single mounting or ('Type A' craft) one 40-mm Bofors L/70 AA in a single mounting, and one 20-mm Oerlikon L/80 AA in a single mounting

Missile armament: none

Torpedo armament: none

Anti-submarine armament: none

Electronics: one MS 32 surface-search radar, one Decca 626 navigation radar, and ('Type B' craft) one radar used in conjunction with the WM-26 fire-control system

Propulsion: two MTU 16V 538 diesels delivering 5400 kW (7,240 hp) to two shafts

Performance: maximum speed 32 kt; range 1,275 miles (2050 km) at 14 kt

Complement: 3 + 19/22

Class

1. Singapore

Name	No.	Builder	Commissioned
Independence	P69	Vosper Thornycroft	Jul 1970
Freedom	P70	Vosper, Singapore	Jan 1971
Justice	P71	Vosper, Singapore	Apr 1971
*Sovereignty**	P72	Vosper Thornycroft	Feb 1971
*Daring**	P73	Vosper, Singapore	Sep 1971
*Dauntless**	P74	Vosper, Singapore	1971

* 'Vosper Thornycroft 110-ft Type B' class craft

(This is a simple FAC[G] type produced in two forms with the lead boat of each subclass from the UK and the other from Vosper Thornycroft's Singaporean subsidiary.)

2. United Arab Emirates

Name	No.	Builder	Commissioned
Ardhana	P1101	Vosper Thornycroft	Jun 1975
Zurara	P1102	Vosper Thornycroft	Aug 1975
Murban	P1103	Vosper Thornycroft	Sep 1975
Al Ghullan	P1104	Vosper Thornycroft	Sep 1975
Radoom	P1105	Vosper Thornycroft	Jul 1976
Ghanadhah	P1106	Vosper Thornycroft	Jul 1976

These craft are used mainly for patrol, but at a full-load displacement of 175 tons have a useful gun armament comprising two 30-mm Oerlikon L/65 AA in a GCM-A twin mounting and one 20-mm Oerlikon L/80 AA in an A41A single mounting. Electronics consist of a single TM1626 surface-search and navigation radar. The propulsion comprises two Paxman Valenta 16RP-200M diesels delivering 5,400 hp/4025 kW to two shafts for a maximum speed of 30 kt, and the range is 2,100 miles/3380 km at 14 kt. The complement is 26.)

'Waspada' class FAC(M)

(UK/Brunei)
Type: fast attack craft (missile)
Displacement: 206 tons full load
Dimensions: length 121·0 ft (36·9 m); beam 23·5 ft (7·2 m); draught 6·0 ft (1·8 m)
Gun armament: two 30-mm Oerlikon L/85 AA in a GCM-A03 single mounting, and two 7·62-mm (0·3-in) machine-guns
Missile armament: two single container-launchers for two MM.38 Exocet anti-ship missiles
Torpedo armament: none
Anti-submarine armament: none
Electronics: one TM1229 surface-search and navigation radar, one radar used with the Sea Archer fire-control system, and one ESM system with RDL warning element

Propulsion: two MTU 20V 538 TB91 diesels delivering 6700 kW (8,985 hp) to two shafts
Performance: maximum speed 32 kt; range 1,380 miles (2220 km) at 14 kt
Complement: 4 + 20

Class
1. Brunei

Name	No.	Builder	Commissioned
Waspada	P02	Vosper, Singapore	1978
Pejuang	P03	Vosper, Singapore	1979
Seteria	P04	Vosper, Singapore	1979

Note: These medium-size FAC(M)s are ideally suited to the coastal requirement of Brunei, and in 1988 were committed to an upgrade programme designed to improve the fire-control and ESM systems.

Below left: Though only lightly armed in missiles and guns, the *Waspada* and her two sisters are effective FAC(M)s in terms of the local threat.

'Wildcat' class FAC(M)

(South Korea)
Type: fast attack craft (missile)
Displacement: 140 tons full load
Dimensions: length 33·9 m (108·9 ft); beam 6·9 m (22·6 ft); draught 2·4 m (7·9 ft)
Gun armament: two 40-mm Bofors L/60 AA in single mountings, and two 0·5-in (12·7-mm) machine-guns
Missile armament: two container-launchers for two MM.38 Exocet anti-ship missiles
Torpedo armament: none
Anti-submarine armament: none
Electronics: one Raytheon 1645 surface-search and navigation radar

Propulsion: two MTU 518D diesels delivering 7400 kW (9,925 hp) to two shafts, or (PKM272) three MTU 16V 536 TB90 diesels delivering 8100 kW (10,865 hp) to three shafts
Performance: maximum speed 40 kt; range 1500 km (930 miles) at 17 kt
Complement: 5 + 24

Class
1. South Korea

Name	No.	Builder	Commissioned
	PKM271	Korea-Tacoma	1972
	PKM272	Korea-Tacoma	1972

Note: These are elderly and obsolescent FAC(M)s now useful mainly for training and patrol.

'Willemoes' class FAC(M/T)

(Denmark)
Type: fast attack craft (missile/torpedo)
Displacement: 260 tons full load
Dimensions: length 46·0 m (150·9 ft); beam 7·4 m (24·0 ft); draught 2·5 m (8·2 ft)
Gun armament: one 76-mm (3-in) OTO Melara L/62 DP in an OTO Melara Compact single mounting
Missile armament: two Mk 141 single or twin container-launchers for two or four RGM-84 Harpoon anti-ship missiles
Torpedo armament: two or four single 533-mm (21-in) mountings for two Tp 61 wire-guided torpedoes
Anti-submarine armament: none
Electronics: one 9GR 208 surface-search radar, one Terma 20T 48 Super navigation radar, one 9LV 200 radar used in conjunction with the 9LV 228 fire-control system, one EPLO action information system, and one ESM system with Cutlass warning element
Propulsion: CODOG arrangement, with three Rolls-Royce Proteus 52M/544 gas turbines delivering 12,750 hp (9510 kW) or two General Motors 8V-71 diesels delivering 1,600 hp (1195 kW) to three shafts
Performance: maximum speed 38 kt on gas turbines or 12 kt on diesels

Complement: 5 + 20

Class
1. Denmark

Name	No.	Builder	Commissioned
Bille	P540	Frederikshavn Vaerft	Oct 1976
Bredal	P541	Frederikshavn Vaerft	Jan 1977
Hammer	P542	Frederikshavn Vaerft	Apr 1977
Huitfeld	P543	Frederikshavn Vaerft	Jun 1977
Krieger	P544	Frederikshavn Vaerft	Sep 1977
Norby	P545	Frederikshavn Vaerft	Nov 1977
Rodsteen	P546	Frederikshavn Vaerft	Feb 1978
Sehested	P547	Frederikshavn Vaerft	May 1978
Suenson	P548	Frederikshavn Vaerft	Aug 1978
Willemoes	P549	Frederikshavn Vaerft	Jun 1976

Note: This class is similar to the Swedish 'Spica II' design, and was prepared by Lürssen in West Germany. The craft generally carry two missiles and two torpedoes.

Previous page: The _Bredal_ of the 'Willemoes' class reveals the type's original configuration with four torpedo tubes and a 76-mm (3-in) gun.

'Alligator' class LST

(USSR)
Type: landing ship tank
Displacement: 3,400 tons standard and 4,500 tons full load
Dimensions: length 111·0 m (364·1 ft); beam 15·5 m (50·9 ft); draught 4·5 m (14·8 ft)
Gun armament: two 57-mm L/80 AA in a twin mounting, four 25-mm L/80 AA in two twin mountings ('Alligator Type 4' class), and (last seven units only) two 122-mm (4·8-in) BM-21 40-tube rocket-launchers
Missile armament: three quadruple launchers for 24 SA-N-5 'Grail' SAMs
Torpedo armament: none
Anti-submarine armament: none
Aircraft: none
Capacity: 1,700 tons handled with the aid of two 5-ton cranes ('Alligator Type 1' class ships) or one 15-ton crane ('Alligator Type 2, 3 and 4' class ships); ramps are built into the bow and stern for roll-on/roll-off operations with up to 50 tanks; the Naval Infantry complement is about 120, though 250/300 can be accommodated for short voyages
Electronics: two 'Don-2' or one 'Don 2' and one 'Spin Trough' navigation radar, one 'Muff Cob' gun fire-control radar, and one 'High Pole-B' IFF system
Propulsion: two diesels delivering 6700 kW (8,985 hp) to two shafts
Performance: maximum speed 18 kt; range 20,000 km (12,425 miles) at 15 kt
Complement: 100

Class
1. USSR
4 'Alligator Type 1' class units named _Krimsky Komsomolets_, _Tomsky Komsomolets_, _Voronezhsky Komsomolets_ and _Komsomolets Karely_
2 'Alligator Type 2' class units named _Sergei Lazo_ and _Nikolai Obyekov_
6 'Alligator Type 3' class units named _Aleksandr Tortsev_, _Donetsky Shakhter_, _Krasnaya Presnya_, _Piotr Ilichev_, _50 Let Sheftsva VLKSM_ and _Ilya Azarov_
2 'Alligator Type 4' class units named _Nikolai Filchenkov_ and _Nikolai Vilkov_
Note: This class was built at Kaliningrad between 1964 and 1977, and provides the Soviet navy with a useful roll-on/roll-off medium-lift capability. The first two subclasses are optimized for transport and the latter two for over-the-beach assault, each ship being able to carry the equipment of a Naval Infantry battalion landing team.

'Anchorage' class LSD

(USA)
Type: landing ship dock
Displacement: 8,100 tons or (LSD36) 8,600 tons light and 13,700 tons or (LSD36) 13,600 tons full load
Dimensions: length 553·3 ft (168·8 m); beam 84·0 ft (25·6 m); draught 20·0 ft (6·1 m)
Gun armament: six 3-in (76-mm) L/50 DP in three Mk 33 twin mountings, and two 20-mm Phalanx Mk 15 CIWS mountings
Missile armament: none
Torpedo armament: none
Anti-submarine armament: none
Aircraft: provision for one helicopter on a platform aft
Capacity: the docking well in the stern measures 430 ft (131·1 m) in length and 50 ft (15·2 m) in width, and can accommodate three LCUs, or four LCACs, or 29 LCM(6)s or many LVTs; there is deck space for one LCM, and davits can take one LCPL and one LCVP; two 50-ton cranes are provided for the handling of freight; the troop accommodation is 18 + 348
Electronics: one SPS-40 air-search radar, one SPS-10 surface-search radar, one LN-66 navigation radar, one SLQ-32(V)1 ESM system with warning and jamming elements, four Mk 36 Super RBOC chaff/flare launchers, one OE-82 satellite communications system, one WSC-3 satellite communications transceiver, and one SRR-1 satellite communications receiver
Propulsion: two Foster-Wheeler or (LSD36) Combustion Engineering boilers supplying steam to two sets of De Laval geared turbines delivering 24,000 hp (17,895 kW) to two shafts
Performance: maximum speed 22 kt
Complement: 24 + 350

Class
1. USA

Name	No.	Builder	Laid down	Commissioned
Anchorage	LSD36	Ingalls SB	Mar 1967	Mar 1969
Portland	LSD37	General Dynamics	Sep 1967	Oct 1970
Pensacola	LSD38	General Dynamics	Mar 1969	Mar 1971
Mount Vernon	LSD39	General Dynamics	Jan 1970	May 1972
Fort Fisher	LSD40	General Dynamics	Jul 1970	Dec 1972

Note: This is virtually a repeat of the 'Thomaston' class with a tripod rather than pole mast as the major distinguishing feature. The removable helicopter platform covers virtually the whole docking well, which is larger than that of the 'Thomaston' class.

'Atsumi' class LST

(Japan)
Type: landing ship tank
Displacement: 1,480 tons or (LST4102/4103) 1,550 tons standard
Dimensions: length 89·0 m (291·9 ft); beam 13·0 m (42·6 ft); draught 2·7 m (8·9 ft)
Gun armament: four 40-mm Bofors L/70 AA in two Mk 1 twin mountings
Missile armament: none
Torpedo armament: none

Anti-submarine armament: none
Aircraft: none
Capacity: 400 tons including five battle tanks, or 130 troops; two LCVPs are carried in davits
Electronics: one OPS-9 surface-search and navigation radar, and two Mk 51 gun fire-control systems
Propulsion: two Kawasaki/MAN V8V 22/30 AMTL diesels delivering 6700 kW (8,985 hp) to two shafts
Performance: maximum speed 14 kt or (LST4102/4103) 13 kt; range 16,675 km (10,360 miles) at 12 kt

Complement: 100 or (LST4102/4103) 95

Class
1. Japan

Name	No.	Builder	Laid down	Commissioned
Atsumi	LST4101	Sasebo		Nov 1972
Motobu	LST4102	Sasebo		Dec 1973
Nemuro	LST4103	Sasebo		Oct 1977

Note: As with Japan's other LST type, the three 'Miura' class ships, the task of the 'Atsuma' class vessels is transport between the Japanese home islands.

'Austin' class LPD

USA
Type: amphibious transport dock
Displacement: 10,000 tons light and 15,900 tons (LPD4/6) or 16,550 tons (LPD7/10) or 16,900 tons (AGF11 and LPD12/13) or 17,000 tons (LPD14/15) full load
Dimensions: length 570·0 ft (173·8 m); beam 100·0 ft (30·5 m); draught 23·0 ft (7·0 m)
Gun armament: two 3-in (76-mm) L/50 DP in a Mk 33 twin mounting, and two 20-mm Phalanx Mk 15 CIWS mountings
Missile armament: none
Torpedo armament: none
Anti-submarine armament: none
Aircraft: up to six Boeing Vertol CH-46D/E Sea Knight helicopters on a platform aft (with a small telescopic hangar for one helicopter)
Capacity: the docking well measures 395 ft (120·4 m) in length and 50 ft (15·2 m) in width, and can accommodate one LCU and three LCM(6)s, or two LCACs, or nine LCM(6)s, or four LCM(8)s, or 28 LVTPs; freight is handled by two forklifts, six cranes and one elevator; the troop accommodation is 930 in LPD4/6 and LPD14/15 or 840 in LPD7/10, AGF11 and LPD12/13
Electronics: one SPS-40B air-search radar, one SPS-10F or SPS-67 surface-search radar, one LN-66 navigation radar, one SLQ-32(V)1 ESM system with warning and jamming elements, four Mk 36 Super RBOC chaff/flare launchers, one OE-82 satellite communications system, one WSC-3 satellite communications transceivers, one SRR-1 satellite communications receiver, and URN-25 TACAN
Propulsion: two Foster-Wheeler or (LPD5 and 12) Babcock & Wilcox boilers supplying steam to two sets of De Laval geared turbines delivering 24,000 hp (17,895 kW) to two shafts

Performance: maximum speed 21 kt; range 8,865 miles (14,265 km) at 20 kt
Complement: 24 + 396 plus accommodation for a flag staff of 90 in LPD7/13

Class
1. USA

Name	No.	Builder	Laid down	Commissioned
Austin	LPD4	New York NY	Feb 1963	Feb 1965
Ogden	LPD5	New York NY	Feb 1963	Jun 1965
Duluth	LPD6	New York NY	Dec 1963	Dec 1965
Cleveland	LPD7	Ingalls SB	Nov 1964	Apr 1967
Dubuque	LPD8	Ingalls SB	Jan 1965	Sep 1967
Denver	LPD9	Lockheed SB	Feb 1964	Oct 1968
Juneau	LPD10	Lockheed SB	Jan 1965	Jul 1969
Coronado	AGF11	Lockheed SB	May 1965	May 1970
Shreveport	LPD12	Lockheed SB	Dec 1965	Dec 1970
Nashville	LPD13	Lockheed SB	Mar 1966	Feb 1970
Trenton	LPD14	Lockheed SB	Aug 1966	Mar 1971
Ponce	LPD15	Lockheed SB	Oct 1966	Jul 1971

Note: This is an enlarged version of the 'Raleigh' class design, with the same size of docking well but lengthened by 12 m (39·4 ft) just forward of this to provide additional vehicle accommodation. The helicopter platform above the docking well is not removable, and is provided (except in LPD4) with a telescoping hangar to accommodate one of the six Boeing Vertol CH-46 helicopters that can be carried. LPD7/13 have an additional bridge and can serve as flagships. AGF11 is an 'Austin' class LPD converted into a command ship for the US 3rd Fleet.

The *Dubuque* is an amphibious transport dock of the 'Austin' class, a key element of the USA's capability to project its land-based power over global distances through the use of US Marine Corps' amphibious forces.

'Batral' class LSM

(France)
Type: landing ship medium
Displacement: 750 tons standard and 1,330 or (L9032, 9033 and 9034) 1,410 tons full load
Dimensions: length 80·0 m (262·4 ft); beam 13·0 m (42·6 ft); draught 2·4 m (7·9 ft)
Gun armament: two 40-mm Bofors L/60 AA in single mountings or (L9032, 9033 and 9034) two 20-mm GIAT AA in single mountings, one 81-mm (3·2-in) mortar, and two 12·7-mm (0·5-in) machine-guns in single mountings
Missile armament: none
Torpedo armament: none
Anti-submarine armament: none
Aircraft: provision for one Aérospatiale SA 319B Alouette III Astazou helicopter on a platform aft
Capacity: up to 380 tons, including troops and 12 vehicles, offloaded with the aid of a 10-ton derrick into one LCVP and one LCPS; troop accommodation is provided for 5 + 133 or (L9032, 9033 and 9034) 188
Electronics: one DRBN 32 navigation radar, and two active search hull-mounted sonars
Propulsion: two SACM V12 diesels delivering 2700 kW (3,620 hp) to two shafts
Performance: maximum speed 16 kt; range 8350 km (5,190 miles) at 13 kt
Complement: 3 + 36

Class
1. Chile
Name	No.	Builder	Laid down	Commissioned
Maipo	91	Asmar	1980	Jan 1982
Rancagua	92	Asmar	1980	Aug 1983
Chacabuco	93	Asmar	1982	Apr 1986

(These ships are identical in all essential respects to the baseline French units.)

2. France
Name	No.	Builder	Laid down	Commissioned
Champlain	L9030	Brest ND		Oct 1974
Francis Garnier	L9031	Brest ND		Jun 1974
Dumont d'Urville	L9032	CMN, Cherbourg		Feb 1983
Jacques Cartier	L9033	CMN, Cherbourg		Sep 1983
La Grandière	L9034	CMN, Cherbourg		Jan 1987

(The fifth unit was built for export but failed to find a buyer.)

3. Gabon
Name	No.	Builder	Laid down	Commissioned
President el Hadji Omar Bongo	L05	CMN, Cherbourg		Nov 1984

(Though similar to the French ships, this Gabonaise unit can accommodate a helicopter up to the Aérospatiale SA 330 Puma in size.)

4. Ivory Coast
Name	No.	Builder	Laid down	Commissioned
L'Eléphant		AFO	1975	Feb 1977

(This is identical to the French ships.)

5. Morocco
Name	No.	Builder	Laid down	Commissioned
Daoud Ben Aicha	402	Dubigeon		May 1977
Ahmed Es Sakali	403	Dubigeon		Sep 1977
Abou Abdallah el Ayachi	404	Dubigeon		Mar 1978

(These are identical to the French ships.)

The 'Batral' class *Francis Garnier* is seen in typical beaching mode with a stern anchor laid out to prevent the stern from swinging and to aid the process of unbeaching when required.

'Blue Ridge' class LCC

(USA)

Type: amphibious force command ship

Displacement: 16,790 tons or (LCC20) 16,100 tons light and 18,370 tons or (LCC20) 18,645 tons full load

Dimensions: length 620·0 ft (189·0 m); beam 82·0 ft (25·0 m); draught 29·0 ft (8·8 m)

Gun armament: four 3-in (76-mm) L/50 DP in two Mk 33 twin mountings, and two 20-mm Phalanx Mk 15 CIWS mountings

Missile armament: two Mk 25 octuple launchers for RIM-7 Sea Sparrow SAMs

Torpedo armament: none

Anti-submarine armament: none

Aircraft: provision for two utility helicopters on a platform aft

Capacity: three LCPs and two LCVPs

Electronics: one SPS-48C 3D radar, one SPS-40C air-search radar, one SPS-65 surface-search radar, one LN-66 navigation radar, two radars used in conjunction with two Mk 115 SAM fire-control systems, Naval Tactical Data System, Amphibious Command Information System, Naval Intelligence Processing System, Link 11 and 14 data-links, one SLQ-32(V)3 ESM system with warning and jamming elements, four Mk 36 Super RBOC chaff/flare launcher, one OE-82 satellite communications system, four WSC-3 satellite communications transceivers, one SRR-1 satellite communications receiver, and URN-25 TACAN

Propulsion: two Foster-Wheeler boilers supplying steam to one set of General Electric geared turbines delivering 22,000 hp (16,405 kW) to one shaft

Performance: maximum speed 23 kt; range 15,000 miles (24,140 km) at 16 kt

Complement: 43 + 778 plus command staff (see below)

Right: The *Mount Whitney* is extensively adapted as a command ship for major forces.

Below: The *Blue Ridge* and *Mount Whitney* are rarely seen together, as the ships are used to command widely separated fleets.

Class
1. USA

Name	No.	Builder	Laid down	Commissioned
Blue Ridge	LCC19	Philadelphia NY	Feb 1967	Nov 1970
Mount Whitney	LCC20	Newport News	Jan 1969	Jan 1971

Note: Based on the 'Iwo Jima' class design with the major hangar spaces adapted as offices, operations rooms and accommodation for the command staff (a maximum of 200 + 500), the two units of the 'Blue Ridge' class are the world's only custom-designed command ships, originally schemed as integrated air/land/sea amphibious control vessels but in fact used as fleet command vessels for the 7th Fleet (LCC19) and 2nd Fleet (LCC20).

'Bougainville' class LSD

(France)
Type: landing ship dock
Displacement: 4,875 tons standard and 5,600 tons full load
Dimensions: length 113·5 m (372·3 ft); beam 17·0 m (55·8 ft); draught 4·3 m (14·1 ft)
Gun armament: two 0·5-in (12·7-mm) machine-guns in single mountings
Missile armament: none
Torpedo armament: none
Anti-submarine armament: none
Aircraft: provision for two Aérospatiale AS 332B Super Puma helicopters on a platform amidships
Capacity: the docking well in the stern measures 78·0 m (255·9 ft) in length and 10·2 m (33·5 ft) in width, and has a docking capability of 394 tons including one EDIC or two LCMs; one fixed 36·4-ton fixed crane and one 24·6-ton travelling crane are provided for the handling of 1,180 tons of freight, and accommodation is provided for 500 troops for 8 days
Electronics: two Decca 1226 surface-search and navigation radars
Propulsion: two SACM/AGO 195/12 RVR diesels delivering 3600 kW (4,830 hp) to two shafts
Performance: maximum speed 14·6 kt; range 11,100 km (6,895 miles) at 12 kt
Complement: 6 + 47

Class
1. France

Name	No.	Builder	Laid down	Commissioned
Bougainville	L9077	Dubigeon	Jan 1986	Apr 1988

Note: This ship is used in association with the French nuclear weapons test programme in the Pacific, but has a useful troop transport capability as well as extensive workshop, spares and medical facilities.

'Cabildo' class LSD

(USA/Greece)
Type: landing ship dock
Displacement: 4,790 tons light and 9,355 tons full load
Dimensions: length 457·8 ft (139·6 m); beam 72·2 n (22·0 m); draught 18·0 ft (5·5 m)
Gun armament: eight 40-mm Bofors L/60 AA in two quadruple mountings, and four 20-mm Rheinmetall AA in two S20 twin mountings
Missile armament: none
Torpedo armament: none
Anti-submarine armament: none
Aircraft: provision for one helicopter on a platform aft
Capacity: the docking well in the stern measures 392·0 ft (119·5 m) in length and 44·0 ft (13·4 m) in width, and its docking capability includes three LCUs, or 18 LCMs or 32 LVTs; two fixed 35-ton fixed cranes are provided for the handling of freight
Electronics: one SPS-6 air-search radar, and one SPS-5 surface-search and navigation radar
Propulsion: two boilers supplying steam to two sets of geared turbines delivering 7,000 hp (5220 kW) to two shafts
Performance: maximum speed 15·4 kt; range 9,200 miles (14,805 km) at 12 kt
Complement: 250

Class
1. Greece

Name	No.	Builder	Laid down	Commissioned
Nafratoussa	L153	Boston NY	Jan 1945	Oct 1945

(This ship was leased from the USA in 1971 and bought in 1980. It can now be considered only obsolete.)

2. Taiwan

Name	No.	Builder	Laid down	Commissioned
Cheng Hai	618	Gulf SB		May 1945

(This ship was transferred in 1977, but was modernized in the 1960s with an armament of 12 40-mm Bofors L/60 AA in two quadruple and two twin mountings, SPS-5 surface-search and LN-66 navigation radars, and a complement of 316.)

'Capana' class LST

(South Korea/Venezuela)
Type: landing ship tank
Displacement: 4,070 tons full load
Dimensions: length 104·0 m (341·1 ft); beam 15·4 m (50·5 ft); draught 7·8 m (25·6 ft)
Gun armament: six 40-mm Bofors L/70 AA in three Breda twin mountings, and two 20-mm Oerlikon AA in GAM-B01 single mountings
Missile armament: none
Torpedo armament: none
Anti-submarine armament: none
Aircraft: provision for one helicopter on a platform aft
Capacity: 1,800 tons of cargo or 202 troops; four LCVPs are carried in davits
Electronics: one surface-search radar, one navigation radar, and one NA18/V optronic director
Propulsion: two diesels delivering 5400 kW (7,240 hp) to two shafts
Performance: maximum speed 15 kt; range 10,400 km (6,460 miles) at 11 kt
Complement: 13 + 104

Class
1. Indonesia

Name	No.	Builder	Laid down	Commissioned
Teluk Semangka	512	Korea-Tacoma		Jan 1981
Teluk Penju	513	Korea-Tacoma		Jan 1981
Teluk Mandar	514	Korea-Tacoma		Jul 1981
Teluk Sampit	515	Korea-Tacoma		Jun 1981
Teluk Banten	516	Korea-Tacoma		May 1982
Teluk Ende	517	Korea-Tacoma		Sep 1982

(These are similar to the Venezuelan ships in all essential respects, but the armament of each is two 40-mm Bofors L/70 AA in single mountings. The first four ships each have a small platform for the carriage of a single Westland Wasp HAS.Mk 1 helicopter, but the last two each have a larger platform able to accommodate three Nurtanio [Aérospatiale] NAS-332 Super Puma helicopters.)

2. Venezuela

Name	No.	Builder	Laid down	Commissioned
Capana	T61	Korea-Tacoma		Jul 1984
Esequibo	T62	Korea-Tacoma		Jul 1984
La Guajira	T63	Korea-Tacoma		Nov 1984
Los Llanos	T64	Korea-Tacoma		Nov 1984

(These are unexceptional LSTs.)

'De Soto County' class LST

(USA)
Type: landing ship tank
Displacement: 4,165 tons light and 7,100 tons full load
Dimensions: length 445·0 ft (135·6 m); beam 62·0 ft (18·9 m); draught 17·5 ft (5·3 m)
Gun armament: six 3-in (76-mm) L/50 DP in three Mk 33 twin mountings
Missile armament: none
Torpedo armament: none
Anti-submarine armament: none
Aircraft: none
Capacity: 23 tanks or other vehicles each weighing up to 75 tons, or 30 + 604 troops; four LCVPs are carried in davits
Electronics: one SPS-21 surface-search and navigation radar, and one Mk 51 fire-control system
Propulsion: six Cooper-Bessemer or (LST1173) Fairbanks-Morse diesels delivering 13,700 hp (10,215 kW) to two shafts
Performance: maximum speed 16·5 kt
Complement: 15 + 173

Above right: Now deleted by the Italian navy, the *Caorle* of the bow-loading LST 'De Soto' class was the US Navy's *York County*, built by Newport News and commissioned in September 1957.

Class

1. Argentina

Name	No.	Builder	Laid down	Commissioned
Cabo San Antonio	Q42	AFNE, Rio Santiago		1971

(This single LST was produced under licence, and differs from the US base-line ships in having 60-ton Stulcken heavy-lift gear, an armament of 12 40-mm Bofors L/60 AA in three quadruple mountings plus four 20-mm Oerlikon AA in two twin mountings, AWS 1 search radar and three Mk 5 optical fire-control systems, provision for a helicopter on a crossdeck, and accommodation for 700 troops [plus eight LCVPs] or 23 medium tanks.)

2. Brazil

Name	No.	Builder	Laid down	Commissioned
Duque de Caxais	G26	Avondale		Nov 1957

(This is similar to its original US configuration apart from its 60-ton Stulcken heavy-lift gear and provision for a helicopter on a crossdeck.)

3. USA

Name	No.	Builder	Laid down	Commissioned
Suffolk County	LST1173	Boston NY		Aug 1957
Lorrain County	LST1177	American SB		Oct 1959
Wood County	LST1178	American SB		Aug 1959

(These were the ultimate bow-door LSTs produced for the US Navy. All three ships are now in reserve, others of the class having been released for export to friendly countries.)

'Fearless' class LPD

(UK)

Type: amphibious assault ship

Displacement: 11,060 tons standard and 12,120 tons full load

Dimensions: length 520·0 ft (158·5 m); beam 80·0 ft (24·4 m); draught 20·5 ft (6·2 m)

Gun armament: two 40-mm Bofors L/70 AA in Mk 9 single mountings or (L11) four 30-mm Oerlikon L/75 AA in two GCM-A03 twin mountings and two 20-mm Oerlikon AA in two GAM-B01 single mountings

Missile armament: four or (L11) two quadruple launchers for Sea Cat SAMs

Torpedo armament: none

Anti-submarine armament: none

Aircraft: five Westland Sea King HC.Mk 4 helicopters on a platform aft

Capacity: the docking well can accommodate four LCM(9)s, and the capacity of these craft can be supplemented by four davit-borne LCVPs; a typical load is 15 MBTs, seven 3-ton trucks and 20 Land Rovers; the normal troop complement is 400, but 700/1,000 troops can be carried under austere conditions

Electronics: one Type 994 air/surface-search radar, one Type 1006 navigation radar, two or (L11) one GWS 20 SAM optical fire-control systems, one CAAIS action-information system, one ESM system with warning element, and two Corvus chaff launchers

Propulsion: two Babcock & Wilcox boilers supplying steam to two sets of English Electric geared turbines delivering 22,000 hp (16,405 kW) to two shafts

Performance: maximum speed 21 kt; range 5,750 miles (9250 km) at 20 kt

Complement: 50 + 500 plus 3 + 22 aircrew and 3 + 85 marines

Class
1. UK

Name	No.	Builder	Laid down	Commissioned
Fearless	L10	Harland & Wolff	Jul 1962	Nov 1965
Intrepid	L11	John Brown	Dec 1962	Mar 1967

The *Intrepid* is one of two 'Fearless' class assault ships operated by the Royal Navy, and is now obsolescent and due for replacement if the UK is to retain an ability for the projection of amphibious forces.

Note: Designed as the assault transport for an amphibious group, each of these ships has command accommodation for an integrated brigade staff for the control of air/land/sea operations.

'Frosch I' and 'Frosch II' class LSTs

(East Germany)
Type: landing ship tank
Displacement: 1,950 tons or ('Frosch II' class ships) 2,000 tons standard and 4,000 tons full load
Dimensions: length 91·0 m (298·4 ft); beam 11·0 m (36·1 ft); draught 2·8 m (9·2 ft)
Gun armament: four 57-mm L/70 AA in two twin mountings, four 30-mm L/65 or ('Frosch II' class ships) 25-mm L/80 AA in two twin mountings, and ('Frosch I' class ships only) two 122-mm (4·8-in) BM-21 40-tube rocket-launchers
Missile armament: none
Torpedo armament: none
Anti-submarine armament: none
Aircraft: none
Capacity: up to 800 tons including 12 tanks or 16 lighter AFVs; the troop accommodation is normally 60, though 260 can be carried for short periods
Electronics: one 'Strut Curve' air-search radar, one TSR 333 surface-search and navigation radar, two 'Muff Cob' 57-mm gun fire-control radars, two 'Drum Tilt' 30-mm gun fire-control radars, one ESM system, and one 'Square Head' and one 'High Pole' IFF systems
Propulsion: two Type 40D diesels delivering 3750 kW (5,030 hp) to two shafts
Performance: maximum speed 18 kt
Complement: 40

Class
1. East Germany
12 'Frosch I' class ships
2 'Frosch II' class ships
Note: Though based on the Soviet 'Ropucha' class, the 'Frosch I' type has considerably heavier armament and was built between 1975 and 1979 at Wolgast by the Peenewerft yard for assault landings covered by the rocket-launchers and guns; the type can also be used as a stern minelayer. Built in 1980, the two 'Frosch II' class units are thought to be assault cargo transports.

'Ivan Rogov' class LPD

(USSR)
Type: amphibious transport dock
Displacement: 14,000 tons full load
Dimensions: length 158·0 m (518·2 ft); beam 24·5 m (80·2 ft); draught 6·5 m (21·2 ft)
Gun armament: two 76-mm (3-in) L/60 DP in a twin mounting, four 30-mm ADGM-630 CIWS mountings, and one 122-mm (4·8-in) BM-21 40-tube rocket-launcher
Missile armament: one twin launcher for 20 SA-N-4 'Gecko' SAMs, and two quadruple launchers for SA-N-5 'Grail' SAMs
Torpedo armament: none
Anti-submarine armament: none
Aircraft: up to four Kamov Ka-25 'Hormone-C' or Ka-27 'Helix-C' helicopters on a platform forward and in a hangar aft
Capacity: the docking well measures some 79·0 m (259·2 ft) in length and 13·0 m (42·6 ft) in width, and can accommodate two 'Lebed' class hovercraft and one 'Ondatra' class LCM, or three 'Gus' class hovercraft; the normal troop accommodation is for a Naval Infantry battalion of 522 with 40 tanks carried on a tank deck 60·0 m (196·9 ft) long and 13·75 m (45·1 ft) wide, though the tank complement is halved when maximum landing craft/hovercraft are carried
Electronics: one 'Head Net-C' 3D radar, one 'Don Kay' or 'Palm Frond'

surface-search and navigation radar, one 'Owl Screech' 76-mm gun fire-control radar, two 'Bass Tilt' CIWS fire-control radars, one 'Pop Group' SAM fire-control radar, one ESM system with two 'Bell Shroud' and two 'Bell Squat' antennae/housings, two chaff launchers, and one 'High Pole' IFF system
Propulsion: two gas turbines delivering 29,800 kW (39,970 hp) to two shafts
Performance: maximum speed 25 kt; range 18,500 km (11,500 miles) at 12 kt or 7400 km (4,600 miles) at 18 kt
Complement: 400

Class
1. USSR

Name	Builder	Laid down	Commissioned
Ivan Rogov	Kaliningrad		1978
Aleksandr Nikolayev	Kaliningrad	1979	1983
	Kaliningrad	1985	

Note: These are the largest amphibious warfare vessels yet built by the Soviets, and are each designed to carry a reinforced Naval Infantry battalion landing team with all its equipment plus 10 PT-76 light amphibious tanks, or the tank battalion of a Naval Infantry regiment. It is thought that four of the class will be produced, one for each Soviet fleet.

Though small by US standards, the *Aleksandr Nikolayev* and her sistership show that the Soviets see the need for long-range amphibious capability.

'Iwo Jima' class LPH

(USA)
Type: amphibious assault ship
Displacement: 18,040 tons (LPH2), 18,155 tons (LPH3), 18,000 tons (LPH7), 18,300 tons (LPH9), 18,515 tons (LPH10), 18,240 tons (LPH11) and 18,825 tons (LPH12) full load

Dimensions: length 602·3 ft (183·7 m); beam 84·0 ft (25·6 m); draught 26·0 ft (7·9 m); flightdeck length 602·3 ft (183·7 m) and width 104·0 ft (31·7 m)
Gun armament: four 3-in (76-mm) L/50 DP in two Mk 33 twin mountings, and two 20-mm Phalanx Mk 16 CIWS mountings
Missile armament: two Mk 25 octuple launchers for RIM-7 Sea Sparrow SAMs
Torpedo armament: none

Anti-submarine armament: none

Aircraft: 20 Boeing Vertol CH-46D/E Sea Knight or 11 Sikorsky CH-53D/E Sea Stallion helicopters (or a mixture of the two), or a mix of 24 CH-46, CH-53, Bell AH-1 HueyCobra and Bell UH-1 'Huey' helicopters, and (with a reduced helicopter complement) four BAe/McDonnell Douglas AV-8B Harrier II STOVL aircraft

Capacity: accommodation is provided for a US Marine Corps battalion landing team of 144 + 1,602 plus its equipment, artillery and vehicles; the accommodation amounts to 4,300 sq ft (400 m²) for vehicles and 37,400 cu ft (3475 m³) for palletized stores plus bulk storage for 6,500 US gal (24,605 litres) of vehicle fuel and 405,000 US gal (1,533,090 litres) of turbine fuel

Electronics: one SPS-58 3D radar (not in LPD11), one SPS-40 air-search radar, one SPS-10 surface-search radar, one LN-66 navigation radar, one SPN-35 and one SPN-43 aircraft control radars, two Mk 71 directors used in conjunction with two Mk 63 gun fire-control systems, two radars used in conjunction with two Mk 115 SAM fire-control systems, one SLQ-36(V)3 ESM system with warning and jamming elements, four Mk 36 Super RBOC chaff/flare launchers, one OE-82 satellite communications system, four WSC-3 satellite communications transceivers, one SRR-1 satellite communications receiver, and URN-25 TACAN

Propulsion: two Combustion Engineering or (LPD9) Babcock & Wilcox boilers supplying steam to one set of Westinghouse or (LPD10) De Laval or (LPD12) General Electric geared turbines delivering 22,000 hp (16,405 kW) to one shaft

Performance: maximum speed 23 kt; range 11,500 miles (18,505 km) at 20 kt

Complement: 48 + 638

Class
1. USA

Name	No.	Builder	Laid down	Commissioned
Iwo Jima	LPH2	Puget Sound NY	Apr 1959	Aug 1961
Okinawa	LPH3	Puget Sound NY	Apr 1960	Apr 1962
Guadalcanal	LPH7	Philadelphia NY	Sep 1961	Jul 1963
Guam	LPH9	Philadelphia NY	Nov 1962	Jan 1965
Tripoli	LPH10	Ingalls SB	Jun 1964	Aug 1966
New Orleans	LPH11	Philadelphia NY	Mar 1966	Nov 1968
Inchon	LPH12	Ingalls SB	Apr 1968	Jun 1970

The *Iwo Jima* **and her sisterships are the primary means available to the USA for the large-scale movement of US Marine Corps units into regions where helicopter-carried assault is required.**

Note: Based on the modified design of the World War II type of escort carrier, these ships are each intended for the transport and helicopter-assault landing of a reinforced battalion landing team of the US Marine Corps.

The layout of the *Guadalcanal* **reveals clearly that the design of the 'Iwo Jima' class was based on an aircraft-carrier: in more precise terms, the escort carrier developed in World War II.**

'Jason' class LST

(Greece)
Type: landing ship tank
Displacement: 4,400 tons full load
Dimensions: length 115·9 m (380·2 ft); beam 15·3 m (50·2 ft); draught 3·3 m (10·8 ft)
Gun armament: one 76-mm (3-in) OTO Melara L/62 DP in an OTO Melara Compact single mounting, four 35-mm Oerlikon L/90 AA in two GDM-A twin mountings, and four 20-mm Rheinmetall AA in two twin mountings
Missile armament: none
Torpedo armament: none
Anti-submarine armament: none
Aircraft: provision for two helicopters on a platform aft
Capacity: not revealed; four LCVPs are carried in davits
Electronics: one surface-search and navigation radar
Propulsion: two diesels delivering 7750 kW (10,395 hp) to two shafts
Performance: maximum speed 17 kt
Complement: not revealed

Class
1. Greece

Name	No.	Builder	Laid down	Commissioned
		Eleusis Shipyard	Apr 1987	1988
		Eleusis Shipyard		
		Eleusis Shipyard		
		Eleusis Shipyard		
		Eleusis Shipyard		

Note: These are simple LSTs of a ro/ro design with stern and bow ramps.

'LSM 1' class LSM

(USA)
Type: landing ship medium
Displacement: 1,095 tons full load
Dimensions: length 203·5 ft (62·0 m); beam 34·6 ft (10·5 m); draught 8·5 ft (2·6 m)
Gun armament: (typical) two 40-mm Bofors AA in a twin mounting, and a varying number of 20-mm AA in single mounting
Missile armament: none
Torpedo armament: none
Anti-submarine armament: none
Aircraft: none
Capacity: up to 900 tons, though 740 tons is the maximum for beaching at a draught of 3·4 ft (1·0 m)
Electronics: one surface-search and navigation radar
Propulsion: two Fairbanks-Morse or General Motors diesels delivering 2,800 hp (2090 kW) to two shafts
Performance: maximum speed 12 kt
Complement: about 60

Class
1. China
14 ships
2. Greece
5 ships
3. Paraguay
1 ship
4. Philippines
4 ships
5. South Korea
7 ships
6. Taiwan
4 ships
7. Thailand
3 ships
8. Vietnam
3 ships
Note: These elderly vessels are of limited combat value except in low-intensity theatres, but have considerable value for local transport and the like.

The 'LSM 1' class is completely obsolete but still extant in considerable numbers. This is the Greek *Ipoploiarhos Grigoropoulos*.

'LST 1-1152' class LST

(USA)

Type: landing ship tank

Displacement: 1,655 tons standard and 3,640 tons full load

Dimensions: length 328·0 ft (100·0 m); beam 50·0 ft (15·2 m); draught 14·0 ft (4·3 m)

Gun armament: (typical) up to 10 40-mm Bofors AA in two twin and six single mountings, or two 3-in (76-mm) L/50 DP in a Mk 33 twin mounting and six 40-mm Bofors AA

Missile armament: none

Torpedo armament: none

Anti-submarine armament: none

Aircraft: none

Capacity: up to 1,875 tons, though 446 tons is the maximum for beaching at the designed draught

Electronics: one surface-search and navigation radar

Propulsion: two General Motors diesels delivering 1,700 hp (1270 kW) to two shafts

Performance: maximum speed 11·6 kt; range 6,900 miles (11,105 km) at 9 kt

Complement: 100/125

Class

1. Brazil
1 ship
2. China
13 ships
3. Ecuador
1 ship
4. Greece
5 ships
5. Indonesia
7 ships
6. Malaysia
2 ships
7. Philippines
24 ships
8. Singapore
5 ships
9. South Korea
8 ships
10. Taiwan
21 ships
11. Thailand
4 ships
12. Turkey
2 ships
13. Vietnam
3 ships

Note: These elderly vessels are of limited combat value except in low-intensity theatres, but are much used for local transport and communications.

'Magar' class LST

(India)

Type: landing ship tank

Displacement: 5,550 tons full load

Dimensions: length 125·6 m (412·1 ft); beam 18·2 m (59·8 ft); draught 4·0 m (13·1 ft)

Gun armament: not revealed

Missile armament: none

Torpedo armament: none

Anti-submarine armament: none

Aircraft: provision for one helicopter on a platform

Capacity: not revealed

Electronics: one surface-search and navigation radar

Propulsion: two SEMT-Pielstick diesels delivering 6200 kW (8,315 hp) to two shafts

Performance: maximum speed 16 kt

Complement: about 65

Class
1. India

Name	No.	Builder	Laid down	Commissioned
Magar	L11	Garden Reach, Calcutta		Jul 1987
Gharial	L12	Garden Reach, Calcutta		1989

Note: This Indian design is based on that of the British 'Sir Lancelot' class, and should eventually total eight ships.

'Miura' class LST

(Japan)

Type: landing ship tank

Displacement: 2,000 tons standard

Dimensions: length 98·0 m (321·4 ft); beam 14·0 m (45·9 ft); draught 3·0 m (9·9 ft)

Gun armament: two 3-in (76-mm) L/50 DP in a Mk 33 twin mounting, and (LST4151/4152) two 40-mm Bofors L/70 AA in a twin mounting

Missile armament: none

Torpedo armament: none

Anti-submarine armament: none

Aircraft: none

Capacity: 10 battle tanks, or 200 troops, or two LCMs; two LCVPs are carried in davits

Electronics: one OPS-14 air-search radar, one OPS-16 surface-search radar, one OPS-18 surface-search and navigation radar, one Type 1 3-in gun fire-control system, and one Mk 51 40-mm gun fire-control system

Propulsion: two Kawasaki/MAN V8V 22/30 AMTL diesels delivering 3300 kW (4,425 hp) to two shafts

Performance: maximum speed 14 kt

Complement: 115

Class
1. Japan

Name	No.	Builder	Laid down	Commissioned
Miura	LST4151	Ishikawajima-Harima		Jan 1975
Ojika	LST4152	Ishikawajima-Harima		Mar 1976
Satsuma	LST4153	Ishikawajima-Harima		Feb 1977

Note: These simple LSTs are used mainly for logistic support.

'Newport' class LST

(USA)

Type: landing ship tank

Displacement: 8,450 tons full load

Dimensions: length 522·3 ft (159·2 m); beam 69·5 ft (21·2 m); draught 17·5 ft (5·3 m)

Gun armament: four 3-in (76-mm) L/50 DP in two Mk 33 twin mountings, and one 20-mm Phalanx Mk 15 CIWS mounting

Missile armament: none

Torpedo armament: none

Anti-submarine armament: none

Aircraft: provision for one helicopter on a platform aft

Capacity: 500 tons of vehicles on a floor area of 19,000 sq ft (1765 m²), the vehicles exiting over a 75-ton capacity 112·0-ft (34·1-m) derrick-supported bow ramp or, if amphibious, through a stern gate; the parking area is sufficient for 25 LVTPs and 17 2·5-ton trucks, or for 21 MBTs and 17 2·5-ton trucks; each ship can also carry four sections of pontoon causeway; the troop accommodation is 20 + 380

Electronics: one SPS-10F (being replaced by SPS-67) surface-search radar, one LN-66 or (LST1188 and 1192/1194) CRP 3100 Pathfinder navigation radar, one SLQ-32 ESM system with warning and jamming elements, one Mk 36 Super RBOC chaff/flare launcher, one OE-82 satellite communications system, one WSC-3 satellite communications transceiver, and one SSR-1 satellite communications receiver

Propulsion: six General Motors or (LST1182/1198) Alco diesels delivering 16,000 hp (11,930 kW) to two shafts

Performance: maximum speed 20 kt; range 2,875 miles (4625 km) at 14 kt

Complement: 13 + 244

Above right: The *Cayuga* is typical of the 'Newport' class, and is seen as an aircraft transport with McDonnell Douglas F-4 Phantom IIs at the stern.

Class
1. USA

Name	No.	Builder	Laid down	Commissioned
Newport	LST1179	Philadelphia NY	Nov 1966	Jun 1969
Manitowoc	LST1180	Philadelphia NY	Feb 1967	Jan 1970
Sumter	LST1181	Philadelphia NY	Nov 1967	Jun 1970
Fresno	LST1182	National Steel & SB	Dec 1967	Nov 1969
Peoria	LST1183	National Steel & SB	Feb 1968	Feb 1970
Frederick	LST1184	National Steel & SB	Apr 1968	Apr 1970
Schenectady	LST1185	National Steel & SB	Aug 1968	Jun 1970
Cayuga	LST1186	National Steel & SB	Sep 1968	Aug 1970
Tuscaloosa	LST1187	National Steel & SB	Nov 1968	Oct 1970
Saginaw	LST1188	National Steel & SB	May 1969	Jan 1971
San Bernardino	LST1189	National Steel & SB	Jul 1969	Mar 1971
Boulder	LST1190	National Steel & SB	Sep 1969	Jun 1971
Racine	LST1191	National Steel & SB	Dec 1969	Jul 1971
Spartanburg County	LST1192	National Steel & SB	Feb 1970	Sep 1971
Fairfax County	LST1193	National Steel & SB	Mar 1970	Oct 1971
La Moure County	LST1194	National Steel & SB	May 1970	Dec 1971
Barbour County	LST1195	National Steel & SB	Aug 1970	Feb 1972
Harlan County	LST1196	National Steel & SB	Nov 1970	Apr 1972
Barnstable County	LST1197	National Steel & SB	Dec 1970	May 1972
Bristol County	LST1198	National Steel & SB	Feb 1971	Aug 1972

Note: This class was the culmination of US LSTs in World War II, with a pointed bow and dropping ramp to ensure a 20-kt cruising speed. The type has bow and stern gates for through loading and unloading.

'Normed' class LST

(France/Thailand)
Type: landing ship tank
Displacement: 3,540 tons standard and 4,235 tons full load
Dimensions: length 103·0 m (337·8 ft); beam 15·7 m (51·5 ft); draught 3·5 m (11·5 ft)
Gun armament: one 40-mm Bofors L/70 AA in a single mounting, two 20-mm Oerlikon in GAM-B01 single mountings, two 0·5-in (12·7-mm) machine-guns in single mountings, and one 81-mm (3·2-in) mortar
Missile armament: none
Torpedo armament: none
Anti-submarine armament: none
Aircraft: provision for two Agusta (Bell) AB.212 or Bell Model 214 helicopters on a platform aft
Capacity: 14 tanks, or 12 APCs, or 850 tons of cargo; three LCVPs and one LCPL are carried

The French navy's *Ouragan* is in no way exceptional, and therefore of typical configuration for a landing ship dock.

Electronics: one Decca surface-search and navigation radar, and two Sea Archer fire-control radars
Propulsion: two MTU 20V 1163 TB62 diesels delivering 7150 kW (9,590 hp) to two shafts
Performance: maximum speed 16 kt; range 13,000 km (8,080 miles) at 12 kt
Complement: 129

Class
1. Thailand

Name	No.	Builder	Laid down	Commissioned
Sichang	LST6	Ital Thai		Oct 1987
Surin	LST7	Bangkok Dock		Feb 1989

Note: These ships, which are eventually to total six units, are to a French design by Chantiers du Nord and have bow doors and 17-m (55·8-ft) ramps. The second unit is believed to be 9·5 m (31·2 ft) longer than the first ship and to be powered by MWM diesels, and if this is the case it is likely that the planned four additional units will be to this standard.

'Ouragan' class LSD

(France)
Type: landing ship dock
Displacement: 5,800 tons light and 8,500 tons full load
Dimensions: length 149·0 m (488·9 ft); beam 23·0 m (75·4 ft); draught 5·4 m (17·7 ft)
Gun armament: two 120-mm (4·7-in) mortars, and four 40-mm Bofors L/60 AA in single mountings
Missile armament: none
Torpedo armament: none
Anti-submarine armament: none
Aircraft: the main helicopter platform can accommodate three Aérospatiale SA 321 Super Frelon or 10 Aérospatiale SA 319B Alouette III Astazou helicopters, while the removable platform aft can accommodate one Super Frelon or three Alouette III helicopters
Capacity: the docking well measures 120·0 m (393·7 ft) in length and 14·0 m (45·9 ft) in width, and can accommodate two EDIC landing craft each carrying 11 tanks, or 18 LCM(6)s loaded for the direct-assault role, in which case troop accommodation is 343; in the logistic role a freight load of 1,500 tons can be carried, typical loads being one 400-ton craft, or 12 50-ton barges, or 120 AMX-13 light tanks, or 84 amphibious tractors, or 340 jeeps, or 18 Super Frelons, or 80 Alouette IIIs; there are two 35-ton cranes for the handling of freight
Electronics: one Decca 1229 navigation radar, and (in *Ouragan*) one SQS-17 active search hull sonar
Propulsion: two SEMT-Pielstick diesels delivering 6400 kW (8,585 hp) to two shafts
Performance: maximum speed 17 kt; range 16,675 km (10,360 miles) at 15 kt
Complement: 10 + 228

Class
1. France

Name	No.	Builder	Laid down	Commissioned
Ouragan	L9021	Brest ND	Jun 1962	Jun 1965
Orage	L9022	Brest ND	Jun 1966	Apr 1968

Note: Designed for logistic transport as well as amphibious assault, the two 'Ouragans' are now elderly and due for replacement.

'Polnochny' class LSM

(USSR)
Type: landing ship medium
Displacement: ('Polnochny Type A' class ships) 780 tons standard and 800 tons full load, or ('Polnochny Type B' class ships) 790 tons standard and 850 tons full load, or ('Polnochny Type C' class ships) 700 tons standard and 1,150 tons full load
Dimensions: ('Polnochny Type A' class ships) length 73·0 m (239·5 ft); beam 8·5 m (27·9 ft); draught 1·8 m (5·8 ft), or ('Polnochny Type B' class ships) length 74·0 m (242·7 ft); beam 8·5 m (27·9 ft); draught 1·8 m (5·8 ft), or ('Polnochny Type C' class ships) length 82·0 m (269·0 ft); beam 10·0 m (32·8 ft); draught 1·8 m (5·8 ft)
Gun armament: two 140-mm (5·5-in) 8-tube rocket-launchers, and ('Polnochny Type A' class ships) two 30-mm L/65 AA in a twin mounting (some ships only), or ('Polnochny Type B' class ships) two or four 30-mm L/65 AA in one or two twin mountings, or ('Polnochny Type C' class ships) four 30-mm L/65 AA in two twin mountings
Missile armament: two or ('Polnochny Type B and C' class ships) four quadruple launchers for 16 or 32 SA-N-5 'Grail' SAMs
Torpedo armament: none
Anti-submarine armament: none
Aircraft: none
Capacity: up to 350 tons including six tanks, or 180 troops
Electronics: one 'Spin Trough' or surface-search and navigation radar, one 'Drum Tilt' fire-control radar, and one 'Square Head' and one 'High Pole-A' IFF systems
Propulsion: two diesels delivering 3750 kW (5,030 hp) to two shafts
Performance: maximum speed 19 kt or ('Polnochny Type C' class ships) 18 kt; range 1850 km (1,150 miles) or ('Polnochny Type C' class ships) 1675 km (1,040 miles) at 17 kt
Complement: 40

Class
1. Algeria
1 'Polnochny Type A' class ship
2. Angola
3 'Polnochny Type B' class ships
3. Cuba
2 'Polnochny Type B' class ships
4. Egypt
3 'Polnochny Type A' class ships
5. Ethiopia
2 'Polnochny Type C' class ships
6. India
9 'Polnochny Type C' class ships
7. Iraq
3 'Polnochny Type C' class ships
8. Libya
3 'Polnochny Type C' class ships
9. Poland
11 'Polnochny Type A' class ships
11 'Polnochny Type B' class ships
1 'Polnochny Type C' class ship
10. Somalia
1 'Polnochny Type B' class ship
11. South Yemen
3 'Polnochny Type B' class ships
12. Syria
3 'Polnochny Type B' ships
13. USSR
35 'Polnochny Type A and B' class ships
8 'Polnochny Type C' class ships
14. Vietnam
3 'Polnochny Type B' class ships
Note: These ships were all built at the Polnochny yard at Gdansk in Poland between 1961 and 1973.

'PS700' class LST

(France/Libya)
Type: landing ship tank
Displacement: 2,800 tons full load
Dimensions: length 99·5 m (326·4 ft); beam 15·5 m (51·2 ft); draught 2·4 m (7·9 ft)
Gun armament: six 40-mm Bofors L/70 AA in three Breda twin mountings, and one 81-mm (3·2-in) mortar
Missile armament: none
Torpedo armament: none
Anti-submarine armament: none
Aircraft: provision for one Aérospatiale SA 316B Alouette III helicopter on a platform aft
Capacity: 11 battle tanks or 240 troops

Electronics: one surface-search and navigation radar, and one Panda optical director
Propulsion: two SEMT-Pielstick diesels delivering 4000 kW (5,365 hp) to two shafts
Performance: maximum speed 15·4 kt; range 7400 km (4,600 miles) at 14 kt
Complement: 35

Class
1. Libya

Name	No.	Builder	Laid down	Commissioned
Ibn Ouf	132	CNI Mediterranée	Apr 1976	Mar 1977
Ibn Harissa	134	CNI Mediterranée	Apr 1977	Mar 1978

Note: These are simple yet effective LSTs with good AA armament.

Previous page: The *Ibn Ouf* (seen with an old pennant number) is one of two 'PS700' class landing ship tanks operated by the Libyan navy.

'Raleigh' class LPD

(USA)
Type: amphibious transport dock
Displacement: 8,040 tons light and 13,600 tons or (LPD2) 14,665 tons full load
Dimensions: length 521·8 ft (159·1 m); beam 100·0 ft (30·5 m); draught 22·0 ft (6·7 m)
Gun armament: four or six 3-in (76-mm) L/50 DP in two or three Mk 33 twin mountings, and two 20-mm Phalanx Mk 15 CIWS mountings
Missile armament: none
Torpedo armament: none
Anti-submarine armament: none
Aircraft: six Boeing Vertol CH-46D/E Sea Knight helicopters on a platform aft
Capacity: the docking well measures 168·0 ft (51·2 m) in length and 50·0 ft (15·2 m) in width, and can accommodate one LCAC, or one LCU and three LCM(6)s, or four LCM(8)s or 20 LVTs; further ship-to-shore capability is provided by two LCM(6)s or four LCPLs launched by crane; the troop capacity is 143 + 996
Electronics: one SPS-40 air-search radar, one SPS-10 surface-search radar, one LN-66 navigation radar, one Mk 56 gun fire-control system, two Mk 51 gun fire-control systems, one SLQ-32(V)1 ESM system with warning and jamming elements, four Mk 36 Super RBOC chaff/flare launchers, one OE-02 satellite communications system, one WSC-3 satellite communications transceiver, one SRR-1 satellite communications receiver, and URN-25 TACAN
Propulsion: two Babcock & Wilcox boilers supplying steam to two sets of De Laval geared turbines delivering 24,000 hp (17,895 kW) to two shafts
Performance: maximum speed 21 kt; range 11,050 miles (17,785 km) at 16 kt
Complement: 29 + 400

Class
1. USA

Name	No.	Builder	Laid down	Commissioned
Raleigh	LPD1	New York NY	Jun 1960	Sep 1962
Vancouver	LPD2	New York NY	Nov 1960	May 1963
La Salle	AGF3	New York NY	Apr 1962	Feb 1964

Note: These are to a concept developed from that of the LSD, with increased troop/vehicle accommodation at the expense of well deck area. The *La Salle* is used as a command ship in the Indian Ocean and Persian Gulf areas.

The 'Raleigh' class amphibious transport dock *La Salle* has been revised to serve as command ship for US Navy forces in the Persian Gulf region.

'Ropucha' class LST

(USSR)

Type: landing ship tank
Displacement: 3,450 tons standard and 4,400 tons full load
Dimensions: length 113·0 m (370·7 ft); beam 14·5 m (47·6 ft); draught 3·6 m (11·5 ft)
Gun armament: four 57-mm L/80 AA in two twin mountings
Missile armament: four quadruple launchers for 32 SA-N-5 'Grail' SAMs (in some ships only)
Torpedo armament: none
Anti-submarine armament: none
Aircraft: none
Capacity: 230 troops plus 24 tanks, or 450 tons of stores
Electronics: one 'Strut Curve' air/surface-search radar, one 'Don-2' naviga-tion radar, one 'Muff Cob' gun fire-control radar, and two 'High Pole-A' or 'Salt Pot-A' IFF systems
Propulsion: two diesels delivering 6700 kW (8,985 hp) to two shafts
Performance: maximum speed 18 kt; range 11,100 km (6,900 miles) at 12 kt or 6500 km (4,040 miles) at 16 kt
Complement: 95

Class

1. South Yemen
1 ship
2. USSR
24 ships

Note: Built at the Polnochny yard at Gdansk in Poland in two batches (1974-1978 and 1980-1988), these LSTs provide the USSR with a useful AFV lift capability in a roll-on/roll-off design.

'San Giorgio' class LPD

(Italy)

Type: amphibious transport dock
Displacement: 6,685 tons standard and 7,665 tons full load
Dimensions: length 133·3 m (437·2 ft); beam 20·5 m (67·3 ft); draught 5·3 m (17·4 ft)
Gun armament: one 76-mm (3-in) OTO Melara L/62 DP in an OTO Melara Compact single mounting, two 20-mm AA in single mountings, and two 0·5-in (12·7-mm) machine-guns
Missile armament: none
Torpedo armament: none
Anti-submarine armament: none
Aircraft: the flightdeck can accommodate five helicopters up to the Boeing Vertol CH-47 Chinook in size
Capacity: the docking well of unspecified size can accommodate an unspecified number of landing craft; the troop accommodation is a 516-man battalion with 36 APCs, and on the flightdeck can be stowed either 30 medium tanks or a combination of 3 LCMs and 3 LCVPs
Electronics: one RAN 10S surface-search radar, one SPN 748 navigation radar, one RTN 10X radar used in conjunction with the Argo NA21 fire-control system, one ESM system with warning element, and two SCLAR chaff/flare launchers
Propulsion: two GMT A 420·12 diesels delivering 12,500 kW (16,765 hp) to two shafts
Performance: maximum speed 21 kt; range 13,900 km (8,635 miles) at 16 kt or 8350 km (5,190 miles) at 20 kt
Complement: 170

Class

1. Italy

Name	No.	Builder	Laid down	Commissioned
San Giorgio	L9892	CNR, Riva Trigoso	Jun 1985	Oct 1987
San Marco	L9893	CNR, Riva Trigoso	Jun 1986	Dec 1988

Note: These are comparatively simple yet highly effective LSDs with bow doors for assault operations.

'Sarucabey' class LST

(Turkey)

Type: landing ship tank
Displacement: 2,600 tons full load
Dimensions: length 92·0 m (301·8 ft); beam 14·0 m (45·9 ft); draught 2·3 m (7·5 ft)
Gun armament: three 40-mm Bofors L/70 AA in single mountings, and four 20-mm Oerlikon AA in two twin mountings
Missile armament: none
Torpedo armament: none
Anti-submarine armament: none
Aircraft: provision for one helicopter on a platform aft
Mines: up to 150 in place of amphibious lift capability
Capacity: 11 battle tanks, or 12 jeeps, or 600 troops; two LCVPs are carried in davits
Electronics: one surface-search radar, and one navigation radar
Propulsion: three diesels delivering 3225 kW (4,325 hp) to three shafts
Performance: maximum speed 14 kt
Complement: not revealed

Class

1. Turkey

Name	No.	Builder	Laid down	Commissioned
Sarucabey	NL123	Taskizak NY		Jul 1984
Karamurselbey	NL124	Taskizak NY		Jul 1985

Note: These are wholly unexceptional LSTs with a useful secondary capabi-lity as minelayers. It is planned that another three units should be procured.

'Tarawa' class LHA

(USA)

Type: multi-role amphibious assault ship
Displacement: 39,300 tons full load
Dimensions: length 820·0 ft (249·9 m); beam 106·6 ft (32·5 m); draught 26·0 ft (7·9 m); flightdeck length 820·0 ft (249·9 m) and width 118·1 ft (36·0 m)
Gun armament: three 5-in (127-mm) L/54 DP in Mk 45 single mountings, six 20-mm L/80 AA in Mk 67 single mountings, and two 20-mm Phalanx Mk 16 CIWS mountings
Missile armament: none
Torpedo armament: none
Anti-submarine armament: none
Aircraft: up to 26 Boeing Vertol CH-46D/E Sea Knight or 19 Sikorsky CH-53D/E Sea Stallion helicopters, and (by a reduction of embarked heli-copter strength) a varying number of BAe/McDonnell Douglas AV-8B Har-rier II STOVL aircraft
Capacity: apart from two full-length hangar decks under the flightdeck, there is a docking well measuring 268·0 ft (81·7 m) in length and 78·0 ft (23·8 m) in width, and this is able to accommodate four LCUs; other landing capacity is provided by six LCM(6)s; vehicle accommodation amounts to 33,730 sq ft (3135 m²), and palletized stores to a volume of 116,900 cu ft (3310 m³) can also be carried; liquid storage is provided for 10,000 US gal (37,855 litres) of vehicle fuel and 400,000 US gal (1,514,160 litres) of turbine fuel; the troop accommodation can take one US Marine Corps reinforced battalion of 172 + 1,731 men
Electronics: one SPS-52C 3D radar, one SPS-40B air-search radar, one SPS-10F surface-search radar, one LN-66 navigation radar, one SPG-60 search-and-track radar and one SPQ-9A track-while-scan radar used in con-junction with four Mk 86 gun fire-control systems, Integrated Tactical Amphibious Warfare Data System, one SLQ-32(V)3 ESM system with warn-ing and jamming elements, four Mk 36 Super RBOC chaff/flare launchers, one OE-82 satellite communications system, one WSC-3 satellite communi-cations transceiver, one SRR-1 satellite communications receiver, and URN-25 TACAN
Propulsion: two Combustion Engineering boilers supplying steam to two sets of Westinghouse geared turbines delivering 70,000 hp (52,190 kW) to two shafts
Performance: maximum speed 24 kt; range 11,500 miles (18,505 km) at 20 kt
Complement: 56 + 879

Above: A view of the *Saipan's* stern reveals the main means available to 'Tarawa' class ships to deliver their load, namely landing craft (or hovercraft) from the docking well or helicopters from the flightdeck.

Below: The *Tarawa* reveals part of her original defensive armament, which comprised three 5-in (127-mm) guns and two MK 25 Sea Sparrow launchers.

Class
1. USA

Name	No.	Builder	Laid down	Commissioned
Tarawa	LHA1	Ingalls SB	Nov 1971	May 1976
Saipan	LHA2	Ingalls SB	Jul 1972	Oct 1977
Belleau Wood	LHA3	Ingalls SB	Mar 1973	Sep 1978
Nassau	LHA4	Ingalls SB	Aug 1973	Jul 1979
Peleliu	LHA5	Ingalls SB	Nov 1976	May 1980

Note: These were the world's largest amphibious warfare ships until overtaken by the 'Wasp' class, and combine in a single hull the capabilities of the LPH, LPD, amphibious command ship and amphibious cargo ship. Each ship carries a reinforced battalion landing team of the US Marine Corps, and has facilities such as a 300-bed hospital. The RIM-116 RAM short-range SAM system may be fitted in the early 1990s.

'TCD 90' class LSD

(France)

Type: landing ship dock

Displacement: 9,300 tons light and 11,800 tons full load

Dimensions: length 168·0 m (551·2 ft); beam 23·5 m (77·1 ft); draught 5·2 m (17·1 ft)

Gun armament: two 40-mm Bofors AA in a twin mounting, and four 20-mm GIAT AA in single mountings

Missile armament: two SADRAL sextuple launchers for Mistral SAMs

Torpedo armament: none

Anti-submarine armament: none

Aircraft: four Aérospatiale AS 332F Super Puma helicopters in a hangar amidships

Capacity: the docking well measures 120·0 m (393·7 ft) in length and 14·0 m (45·9 ft) in width, and can accommodate 10 CTM LCMs, or one EDIC landing craft tank and four CTMs, or two EDICs, plus two LCVPs; there is a removable vehicle deck, and when this is used the stores area increases from 970 m² (10,440 sq ft) to 1360 m² (14,640 sq ft); the cargo payload is 1,810 tons and the troop accommodation is 470

Electronics: one DRBV 51 air-search radar, two surface-search radars, one RM1229 navigation radar, and one Syracuse satellite communications system

Propulsion: two SEMT-Pielstick 16 PC2·5-V400 diesels delivering 14,900 kW (19,980 hp) to two shafts

Performance: maximum speed 21 kt; range 20,400 km (12,675 miles) at 15 kt

Complement: 210

Right and below: Two views of a model of the *Foudre*, lead ship of the 'TCD90' class, reveal the type's very capacious hull.

Class
1. France

Name	No.	Builder	Laid down	Commissioned
Foudre	L9011	Brest ND	Mar 1986	1991
	L9012	Brest ND		
	L9013	Brest ND		

Note: These three ships are being produced as replacements for the 'Ouragan' class, and their rationale is that the three ships should between them be able to lift a complete mechanized regiment with all its vehicles and heavy equipment. Each ship has two operating theatres and a 30-bed hospital, and in an emergency could lift 1,600 troops under austere conditions.

'Terrebonne Parish' class LST

(USA/Peru)
Type: landing ship tank
Displacement: 2,950 tons standard and 5,800 tons full load
Dimensions: length 384·0 ft (117·1 m); beam 55·0 ft (16·8 m); draught 17·0 ft (5·2 m)
Gun armament: six 20-mm Oerlikon AA in single mountings
Missile armament: none
Torpedo armament: none
Anti-submarine armament: none
Aircraft: provision for one helicopter on a platform forward
Capacity: 2,200 tons of cargo including 10 battle tanks, or 395 troops; four LCVPs are carried in davits
Electronics: one SPS-10 surface-search radar, and one navigation radar
Propulsion: four General Motors 15-278A diesels delivering 6,000 hp (4475 kW) to two shafts
Performance: maximum speed 15 kt; range 17,275 miles (24,580 km) at 9 kt
Complement: 116

Class
1. Greece

Name	No.	Builder	Laid down	Commissioned
Inouse	L104	Bath Iron Works		Mar 1953
Kos	L116	Christy Corporation		Sep 1954

(The original class of 16 ships is no longer in US service, most having been transferred to friendly countries. Greece acquired these two units in 1977, and they approximate to the original American standard with an armament of six 3-in/76-mm L/50 DP guns in three Mk 21 twin mountings used in association with two Mk 63 fire-control systems and their Mk 34 radars, and supported by two 20-mm Rheinmetall AA in single mountings.)

2. Peru

Name	No.	Builder	Laid down	Commissioned
Paita	DT141	Ingalls SB		Oct 1953
Pisco	DT142	Ingalls SB		Sep 1953
Callao	DT143	Ingalls SB		Nov 1953
Eten	DT144	Bath Iron Works		Dec 1953

(These obsolescent LSTs were transferred in 1974 and commissioned into the Peruvian navy in 1985.)

3. Spain

Name	No.	Builder	Laid down	Commissioned
Velasco	L11	Bath Iron Works		Nov 1952
Martina Alvarez	L12	Christy Corporation		Jun 1954
Conde del Venadito	L13	Bath Iron Works		Sep 1953

(These vessels were transferred in the early 1970s, and bought by Spain in 1978. The armament and electronics are similar to those of the Greek ships, and the lift capability includes 395 troops, or 10 M48 battle tanks or 17 LVTPs. Each ship carries three LCVPs and one LCP.)

4. Turkey

Name	No.	Builder	Laid down	Commissioned
Ertugrul	L401	Christy Corporation		1954
Serdar	L402	Christy Corporation		1954

(These vessels were transferred in 1973 and 1974 respectively, and are similar to the Greek ships other than in having SPS-21 surface-search radar.)

5. Venezuela

Name	No.	Builder	Laid down	Commissioned
Amazonas	T51	Ingalls SB		1953

(Transferred in 1973 and bought in 1977, this ship is similar to the Greek units and is to be modernized.)

'Thomaston' class LSD

(USA)
Type: landing ship dock
Displacement: 6,880 tons light and 12,150 tons full load
Dimensions: length 510·0 ft (155·5 m); beam 84·0 ft (25·6 m); draught 19·0 ft (5·8 m)
Gun armament: six 3-in (76-mm) L/50 DP in three Mk 33 twin mountings, and (LSD34) one 20-mm Phalanx Mk 15 CIWS mounting
Missile armament: none
Torpedo armament: none
Anti-submarine armament: none
Aircraft: provision for helicopters on a platform over the docking well
Capacity: the docking well measures 391·0 ft (119·2 m) in length and 48·0 ft (14·6 m) in width, and can accommodate 21 LCM(6)s, or three LCUs and six LCM(6)s, or 50 LVTs with another 30 LVTs housed on the mezzanine and upper decks; the troop accommodation is 340
Electronics: one SPS-6 air-search radar, one SPS-10 surface-search radar, one LN-66 or (Brazilian ship) CRP 3100 Pathfinder navigation radar, one Mk

The lines of the *Fort Snelling* indicate that the basic design of the 'Thomaston' class is elderly, and for this reason the class is being replaced by the 'Whidbey Island' class. The original armament comprised 16 3-in (76-mm) AA in eight twin mountings.

36 Super RBOC chaff/flare launcher, one OE-82 satellite communications system, one WSC-3 satellite communications transceiver, and one SRR-1 satellite communications receiver

Propulsion: two Babcock & Wilcox boilers supplying steam to two sets of General Electric geared turbines delivering 24,000 hp (17,895 kW) to two shafts

Performance: maximum speed 22·5 kt; range 11,500 miles (18,505 km) at 8 kt

Complement: 20 + 380

Class
1. Brazil

Name	No.	Builder	Laid down	Commissioned
Ceara		Ingalls SB	Oct 1954	Aug 1956

(This was the US Navy's *Alamo* [LSD33] transferred in 1989.)

2. USA

Name	No.	Builder	Laid down	Commissioned
Thomaston	LSD28	Ingalls SB	Mar 1953	Sep 1954
Plymouth Rock	LSD29	Ingalls SB	May 1953	Nov 1954
Fort Snelling	LSD30	Ingalls SB	Aug 1953	Jan 1955
Point Defiance	LSD31	Ingalls SB	Nov 1953	Mar 1955
Spiegel Grove	LSD32	Ingalls SB	Sep 1954	Jun 1956
Hermitage	LSD34	Ingalls SB	Apr 1955	Dec 1956
Monticello	LSD35	Ingalls SB	Jun 1955	Mar 1957

(These were the USA's first LSDs of post-World War II construction, and incorporated lessons from the Korean War. The class is being phased out of front-line service as the 'Whidbey Island' class enters service, and five of the ships have already been placed in reserve.)

'Type Ro-Ro 1300' class LST

(West Germany/Nigeria)
Type: landing ship tank
Displacement: 1,470 tons standard and 1,860 tons full load
Dimensions: length 87·0 m (285·4 ft); beam 14·0 m (45·9 ft); draught 2·3 m (7·5 ft)
Gun armament: one 40-mm Bofors L/70 AA in a Breda single mounting, and two 20-mm Oerlikon AA in single mountings
Missile armament: none
Torpedo armament: none
Anti-submarine armament: none
Aircraft: provision for one helicopter on a platform amidships
Capacity: 460 tons of cargo including five 40-ton tanks and 220 troops on long-haul trips, or between 540 and 1,000 troops on short-haul trips
Electronics: one Decca 1226 surface-search and navigation radar
Propulsion: two MTU 16V 956 TB92 diesels delivering 5000 kW (6,705 hp) to two shafts
Performance: maximum speed 17 kt; range 9250 km (5,750 miles) at 10 kt
Complement: 6 + 50

Class
1. Nigeria

Name	No.	Builder	Laid down	Commissioned
Ambe	LST1312	Howaldtswerke		Apr 1979
Ofiom	LST1313	Howaldtswerke		Jul 1979

Note: These are ro/ro vessels each with a 4-m (13·1-ft) stern ramp and a 19-m (62·3-ft) bow ramp.

'Wasp' class LHD

(USA)

Type: multi-role amphibious assault ship
Displacement: 28,235 tons light and 40,530 tons full load
Dimensions: length 844·0 ft (257·3 m); beam 106·0 ft (32·3 m); draught 26·0 ft (7·9 m); flightdeck length 820·0 ft (250·0 m) and width 106·0 ft (32·3 m)
Gun armament: three 20-mm Phalanx Mk 15 CIWS mountings, and eight 0·5-in (12·7-mm) machine-guns
Missile armament: two Mk 29 octuple launchers for RIM-7 Sea Sparrow SAMs
Torpedo armament: none
Anti-submarine armament: none
Aircraft: 42 Boeing Vertol CH-46D/E Sea Knight helicopters (36 in the hangar and 6 on deck), with the capability to support other types such as the Bell UH-1N 'Huey' and AH-1T/W SeaCobra, Sikorsky CH-53D/E Sea Stallion/Super Stallion and Sikorsky SH-60b Sea Hawk helicopters, plus the Bell/Boeing MV-22 Osprey tilt-rotor aircraft and between 6/8 (normal) and 20 (maximum) McDonnell Douglas/BAe AV-8B Harrier II STOVL aircraft; the ships are designed to serve as secondary sea-control ships with an alternative complement of 20 McDonnell Douglas/BAe AV-8B STOVL aircraft
Capacity: the docking well is of unrevealed length and 50 ft (15·2 m) width, and can accommodate three LCAC air-cushion vehicles or varying numbers of LCUs, LCMs and LVTs; the vehicle accommodation extends to 22,000 sq ft (2044 m²), and that for stores to 100,900 cu ft (2857 m³); troop accommodation is provided for 1,873 men
Electronics: one SPS-48E or (LHD1) one SPS-52C 3D radar, one SPS-49(V)5 air-search radar, one SPS-67 surface-search radar, one SPS-64 navigation radar, two Mk 23 target-acquisition radars used with the Mk 91 SAM fire-control system, one SYS-2(V)3 weapon-control system, one SPN-35 and one SPN-42 aircraft control radars, Integrated Tactical Amphibious Warfare System, one SLQ-25 Nixie towed torpedo-decoy system, one SLQ-32(V)3 ESM system with warning and jamming elements, four or eight Mk 36 Super RBOC chaff/flare launchers, one OE-82 satellite communications system, one WSC-3 satellite communications transceiver, one SRR-1 satellite communications receiver, and TACAN
Propulsion: two Combustion Engineering boilers supplying steam to two sets of Westinghouse geared turbines delivering 70,000 hp (52,200 kW) to two shafts
Performance: maximum speed 20 kt; range 11,000 miles (17,700 km) at 18 kt
Complement: 98 + 982

Class
1. USA

Name	No.	Builder	Laid down	Commissioned
Wasp	LHD1	Ingalls SB	Aug 1985	Mar 1989
Essex	LHD2	Ingalls SB	May 1988	Apr 1992
Kearsage	LHD3	Ingalls SB	Dec 1989	Jan 1993
Boxer	LHD4	Ingalls SB		Feb 1994
	LHD5			

Note: This new class is designed to become the cornerstone of US amphibious capability in the late 1990s and beyond, and while resembling the LHA it incorporates features of the LPD for greater operational capability with more helicopters than the LHA plus a useful landing craft/hovercraft capacity. The type is slated to replace the 'Iwo Jima' class, and 11 or 12 units are planned though only five are currently projected. The type resembles the 'Tarawa' class in capability, though it has advantages in more modern design, improved weapons and systems, and the relocation of the command, control and communications facilities to an under-deck location providing greater protection from enemy fire and also allowing the bridge structure to be reduced by two decks in height.

Previous page: The *Wasp* is lead ship of an important new class that will become the mainstay of the US Navy's ability to deliver US Marine Corps amphibious forces in the first part of the next century.

'Whidbey Island' class LSD

(USA)

Type: landing ship dock
Displacement: 11,125 tons light and 15,725 tons full load
Dimensions: length 609·6 ft (185·9 m); beam 84·0 ft (25·6 m); draught 20·5 ft (6·3 m)
Gun armament: two 20-mm Phalanx Mk 15 CIWS mountings, two 20-mm AA in Mk 67 single mountings, and eight 0·5-in (12·7-mm) machine-guns
Missile armament: none
Torpedo armament: none
Anti-submarine armament: none
Aircraft: two Sikorsky CH-53D/E Sea Stallion helicopters or BAe/McDonnell Douglas AV-8B Harrier II STOVL aircraft on a flightdeck aft
Capacity: the docking well measures 440·0 ft (134·1 m) in length and 50·0 ft (15·2 m) in width, and can accommodate four LCAC hovercraft, or three LCUs, or 21 LCM(6)s, or 64 LVTPs; including four loaded LCACs in the dock, the vehicle area amounts to 12,500 sq ft (1161·25 m²), and up to 5,000 cu ft (141·6 m³) of palletized freight can also be carried; the troop capacity is 450
Electronics: one SPS-49(V) air-search radar, one SPS-67(V) surface-search radar, one SPS-64 navigation radar, one SLQ-32(V)1 ESM system with warning and jamming elements, four Mk 36 Super RBOC chaff/flare launchers, one OE-82 satellite communications system, one WSC-3 satellite communications transceiver, one SRR-1 satellite communications receiver, and URN-25 TACAN
Propulsion: four Colt-Pielstick 16 PC2V-V400 diesels delivering 41,600 hp (31,020 kW) to two shafts
Performance: maximum speed 22 kt; range 20,750 miles (33,400 km) at 18 kt
Complement: 21 + 319

Class
1. USA

Name	No.	Builder	Laid down	Commissioned
Whidbey Island	LSD41	Lockheed SB	Aug 1981	Feb 1985
Germantown	LSD42	Lockheed SB	Aug 1982	Feb 1986
Fort McHenry	LSD43	Lockheed SB	Jun 1983	Aug 1987
Gunston Hall	LSD44	Avondale	May 1986	Jan 1989
Comstock	LSD45	Avondale	Oct 1986	Jun 1989
Tortuga	LSD46	Avondale	Mar 1987	Nov 1989
Rushmore	LSD47	Avondale	Nov 1987	Apr 1990
Ashland	LSD48	Avondale	Apr 1988	Aug 1990
Harpers Ferry	LSD49	Avondale	Apr 1991	Nov 1993
	LSD50			

Note: This class (planned to a total of eight units) is designed to replace the 'Thomaston' class, and is in essence an improved 'Anchorage' class design. Another five units, beginning with LSD49, constitute the **'Whidbey Island (Modified)' class** to a design optimized for the assault cargo-carrying rather than assault troop-delivery role with two rather than four LCAC hovercraft to permit the carriage of more vehicles and stores.

'Yukan' class LST

(China)

Type: landing ship tank
Displacement: 3,110 tons standard
Dimensions: length 120·0 m (393·6 ft); beam 15·3 m (50·2 ft); draught 8·0 m (26·25 ft)
Gun armament: eight 57-mm L/50 DP in four twin mountings, or four 57-mm L/50 DP in two twin mountings and four 25-mm L/60 AA in two twin mountings, and (in some ships) four 25-mm L/60 AA in two twin mountings
Missile armament: none
Torpedo armament: none
Anti-submarine armament: none
Aircraft: none
Capacity: 10 tanks and 200 troops; two LCVPs are carried in davits
Electronics: one 'Neptun' surface-search and navigation radar
Propulsion: two SEMT-Pielstick 12 PA6-V280 diesels delivering unrevealed power to two shafts
Performance: maximum speed 13 kt
Complement: not revealed

Class
1. China
3 ships (nos 927, 928 and 929) plus ? more building and ? more planned

Note: These ships are building at the rate of about one every two years, and have stern and bow ramps for ro/ro operation. It is thought that a total of 14 is likely.

The *Fort McHenry* is the third unit of the new 'Whidbey Island' class, which is to partner the 'Wasp' class as core transport for the US Marine Corps.

Following page: Typical of the modern surface-to-air missile is the Standard Missile as epitomized by this RIM-66B Standard SM-1 MR on the MK 13 Mod 4 single-arm launcher of the *Nicholas*.

'Yuliang' class LSM

(China)
Type: landing ship medium
Displacement: 800 tons standard and 1,600 tons full load
Dimensions: length 72·0 m (236·2 ft); beam 13·8 m (45·3 ft); draught 3·3 m (10·8 ft)
Gun armament: four 37-mm L/63 AA in two twin mountings, four 25-mm L/60 AA in two twin mountings, and two 122-mm (4·8-in) BM-21 40-tube rocket-launchers
Missile armament: none
Torpedo armament: none
Anti-submarine armament: none

Aircraft: none
Capacity: 3 tanks
Electronics: one surface-search and navigation radar
Propulsion: two diesels delivering unrevealed power to two shafts
Performance: not revealed
Complement: not revealed

Class
1. China
31 ships plus 5 more building
Note: This useful class started in 1971 with the single **'Yuliang' class** prototype, which is numbered in the total above, the definitive **'Yuliang' class** entering production in 1980 at three or four comparatively small yards.

Hai Ying-1 (CSS-N-2)

(China)
Type: single-stage submarine-launched ballistic missile
Dimensions: diameter 1·50 m (4·92 ft); length 10·00 m (32·81 ft)
Weights: total round 14,000 kg (30,864 lb); post-boost vehicle not revealed
Warhead: one 1-megaton thermonuclear RV
Propulsion: one storable liquid-propellant rocket delivering unrevealed thrust
Range: 2700 km (1,678 miles)
CEP: 2800 m (3,062 yards)
Launch: submarine tube
Guidance: inertial

Variant
Hai Ying-1: designated **CSS-N-2** in the US terminology for Chinese weapons, this is a limited-service interim SLBM pending the widespread adoption of the JL-1

Ju Lang-2 (CCS-N-4)

(China)
Type: two-stage submarine-launched ballistic missile
Dimensions: diameter 2·30 m (7·54 ft); length 12·80 m (41·99 ft)
Weights: total round 20,000 kg (44,092 lb); post-boost vehicle not revealed
Warhead: one 2-megaton thermonuclear RV
Propulsion: (first stage) one solid-propellant rocket delivering unrevealed thrust, and (second stage) one solid-propellant rocket delivering unrevealed thrust
Range: 3200 km (1,988 miles)
CEP: 1850 m (2,023 yards)
Launch: submarine tube
Guidance: inertial

Variants
Ju Lang-1: designated **CSS-N-3** in the US terminology for Chinese weapons, the JL-1 (giant wave-1) missile has undergone a lengthy development programme on the basis of the DF-2's technology and design, and began to enter service in 1983 on board China's very slowly increasing number of missile submarines; it is believed that the JL-1 has a 20/200-kiloton or 1-megaton warhead, a diameter of about 1·5 m (4·92 ft), a length of about 10·0 m (32·81 ft), a weight of 13,800 kg (30,423 lb) and a range of 2800 km (1,740 miles)
Ju Lang-2: much improved and enlarged **CSS-N-4** version with a larger 2-megaton warhead and longer range, currently under development for retrofitting in China's 'Xia' class of SSBNs

Aérospatiale MSBS M-4

(France)
Type: three-stage submarine-launched ballistic missile
Dimensions: diameter 1·93 m (6·33 ft); length 11·05 m (36·25 ft)
Weights: total round 35,073 kg (77,323 lb); post-boost vehicle not revealed
Warhead: six 150-kiloton TN-70 or miniaturized TN-71 thermonuclear MIRVs
Propulsion: (first stage) one SEP 401 (P10) solid-propellant rocket delivering 71,000-kg (156,526-lb) thrust, (second stage) one SEP 402 (P6) solid-propellant rocket delivering 30,000-kg (66,138-lb) thrust and (third stage) one SEP 403 solid-propellant rocket delivering 7000-kg (15,432-lb) thrust
Range: 4500 km (2,796 miles) with TN-70 warheads and 5000+ km (3,105+ miles) with TN-71 warheads
CEP: 460 m (503 yards)
Launch: submarine tube
Guidance: Sagem/EMD inertial

Variants
M-4: becoming operational in 1985, the M-4 is of a wholly new French SLBM generation design of considerably greater weight and dimensions for significantly deeper underwater launch depth and improved range with a MIRV bus hardened against electro-magnetic pulse and carrying penetration aids; range is improved with the miniaturized TN-71 warheads, and each system is designed to cover a target area 350 km (217·5 miles) long by 150 km (93·2 miles) wide
M-4C: due to enter service in 1994 on the new SSBN *Le Triomphant*, this is an advanced development of the M-4 with longer range, anti-AMB features and, probably, the new TN-75 warhead

Aérospatiale MSBS M-20

(France)
Type: two-stage submarine-launched ballistic missile
Dimensions: diameter 1·50 m (4·92 ft); length 10·40 m (34·12 ft)
Weights: total round 20,055 kg (44,213 lb); post-boost vehicle not revealed
Warhead: one 1·2-megaton TN-60 thermonuclear in an MR-60 RV
Propulsion: (first stage) one SEP 904 (P10) solid-propellant rocket delivering 45,000-kg (99,206-lb) thrust for 50 seconds and (second stage) one SEP Rita 11 (P6) solid-propellant rocket delivering 32,000 kg (70,547-lb) thrust for 52 seconds
Range: 3000 km (1,864 miles)
CEP: 930 m (1,017 yards)
Launch: submarine tube
Guidance: Sagem/EMD Sagittaire inertial

Variant
MSBS M-20: this medium-weight SLBM entered service in 1977 as successor to the first-generation M-2, which itself entered service in 1974 as an updated version of the M-1 that entered service in 1971; the warhead is carried in a modified Rita 11/P6 second stage and is supported by penetration aids; the TN-60 warhead is hardened against the effects of high-altitude nuclear explosions

SS-N-5 'Sark'

(USSR)
Type: two-stage submarine-launched ballistic missile
Dimensions: diameter 1·42 m (4·66 ft); length 12·90 m (42·32 ft)
Weights: total round 17,000 kg (37,477 lb); post-boost vehicle not revealed
Warhead: one 1-megaton thermonuclear RV
Propulsion: (first stage) one solid-propellant rocket delivering unrevealed thrust and (second stage) one solid-propellant rocket delivering unrevealed thrust
Range: 1400 km (870 miles)
CEP: 2800 m (3,060 yards)
Launch: submarine tube
Guidance: inertial

Variant
SS-N-5 'Sark': now serving in the theatre nuclear role on board 13 'Golf II' class missile submarines, the SS-N-5 missile is comparable in many respects to the original version of the US Polaris SLBM and began to enter service in 1964 as the Soviets' first submarine-launched ballistic missile with a genuine capability for underwater launch; data on the weapon are still scanty, and it is not known with certainty if the type uses solid-propellant or storable liquid-propellant rockets for a range that some sources put as high as 2400 km (1,490 miles); by current standards the range and accuracy are poor; the missile was produced as the **D-4** and is known in Soviet military terminology as the **R-21**; there exists a certain confusion as to the proper NATO reporting name for this missile, for right into the mid- and late 1980s the name 'Serb' has been associated with this weapon; however, some reports of the mid-1980s suggest that the NATO appellation is in fact not 'Serb' but 'Sark', the reporting name generally associated with the world's first operational submarine-launched ballistic missile, known in American terminology as the SS-N-4; this has opened the possibility of the NATO reporting name sequence being pushed forward by one missile to allocate the name 'Serb' to the SS-N-7 (previously 'Sawfly') and the name 'Sawfly' to the previously unnamed SS-N-8

SS-N-6 'Serb'

(USSR)
Type: two-stage submarine-launched ballistic missile
Dimensions: diameter 1·80 m (5·91 ft); length 10·00 m (32·81 ft)
Weights: total round 18,900 kg (41,667 lb); post-boost vehicle 680 kg (1,499 lb)
Warhead: (Model 1) one 700-kiloton nuclear RV, (Model 2) one 650-kiloton nuclear RV, or (Model 3) two 350-kiloton nuclear MRVs
Propulsion: (first stage) one storable liquid-propellant rocket delivering unrevealed thrust, and (second stage) one storable liquid-propellant rocket delivering unrevealed thrust
Range: (Model 1) 2400 km (1,490 miles) or (Models 2 and 3) 3000 km (1,865 miles)
CEP: 1850 m (2,023 yards)
Launch: submarine tube
Guidance: inertial

SS-N-6 'Serb' Model 1: introduced in 1970, this is a hybrid second/third-generation SLBM using technology and components derived from the SS-11 'Sego'; the warhead size and comparatively poor CEP dictate the weapon's targeting against area targets; for many years it was thought that this missile had the NATO reporting name 'Sawfly', but this is apparently not the case; the type has the Soviet designation **R-21**

SS-N-6 'Serb' Model 2: introduced in 1973, this version trades throw-weight for range, the reduction of 50 kilotons in warhead yield providing an additional 600 km (373 miles) of range to provide the launch submarines with greater operating area

SS-N-6 'Serb' Model 3: introduced in 1974, this variant combines the range of the Model 2 with a double warhead configuration for maximum effect against cities and other area targets

SS-N-8 'Sawfly'

(USSR)

Type: two-stage submarine-launched ballistic missile
Dimensions: diameter 1·65 m (5·41 ft); length 12·90 m (42·32 ft)
Weights: total round 20,400 kg (44,974 lb); post-boost vehicle 680 kg (1,499 lb)
Warhead: (Model 1) one 1·2-megaton nuclear RV or (Model 2) one or two 800-kiloton nuclear MRVs
Propulsion: (first stage) one storable liquid-propellant rocket delivering unrevealed thrust, and (second stage) one storable liquid-propellant rocket delivering unrevealed thrust
Range: (Model 1) 7800 km (4,845 miles) or (Model 2) 9100 km (5,655 miles)
CEP: (Model 1) 1410 m (1,540 yards) or (Model 2) 1550 m (1,695 yards)
Launch: submarine tube
Guidance: stellar-inertial

Variants

SS-N-8 'Sawfly' Model 1: introduced in 1971 on board 'Delta I' class SSBNs, the SS-N-8 is a fourth-generation SLBM with good range but only moderate CEP despite the use of two stellar fixes to update the inertial guidance

SS-N-8 'Sawfly' Model 2: introduced in 1977, this variant is a developed version carrying the same weight of warhead over greater range

SS-N-17 'Snipe'

(USSR)

Type: two-stage submarine-launched ballistic missile
Dimensions: diameter 1·65 m (5·41 ft); length 11·06 m (36·29 ft)
Weights: total round not revealed; post-boost vehicle 1135 kg (2,502 lb)
Warhead: one 500-kiloton or 1-megaton thermonuclear RV
Propulsion: (first stage) one solid-propellant rocket delivering unrevealed thrust and (second stage) one solid-propellant rocket delivering unrevealed thrust
Range: 3900 km (2,425 miles)
CEP: 1400 m (1,530 yards)
Launch: submarine tube
Guidance: stellar-inertial

Variant

SS-N-17 'Snipe': introduced in 1977 on the sole 'Yankee II' class SSBN, the SS-N-17 is the first Soviet SLBM known definitely to have solid-propellant rockets; it is also believed that the type has post-boost propulsion for manoeuvring in space, yet the CEP is still too great for the missile's use in anything but the countervalue role

SS-N-18 'Stingray'

(USSR)

Type: two-stage submarine-launched ballistic missile
Dimensions: diameter 1·80 m (5·91 ft); length 14·10 m (46·26 ft)
Weights: total round 25,000 kg (55,115 lb); post-boost vehicle not revealed
Warhead: (Model 1) three 200-kiloton nuclear MIRVs, (Model 2) one 450-kiloton nuclear RV, or (Model 3) seven 200-kiloton nuclear MIRVs
Propulsion: (first stage) one storable liquid-propellant rocket delivering unrevealed thrust, and (second stage) one storable liquid-propellant rocket delivering unrevealed thrust
Range: (Models 1 and 3) 6500 km (4,040 miles) or (Model 2) 8000 km (4,970 miles)
CEP: (Models 1 and 3) 1410 m (1,540 yards) or (Model 2) 1550 m (1,695 yards)
Launch: submarine tube
Guidance: stellar-inertial

Variants

SS-N-18 'Stingray' Model 1: designated **RSM-50** by the Soviets, this fourth-generation SLBM entered service in 1976 aboard 'Delta III' class SSBNs and was the first Soviet SLBM with a MIRVed warhead

SS-N-18 'Stingray' Model 2: introduced in 1979, this variant offers greater range with a payload reduced to one RV

SS-N-18 'Stingray' Model 3: introduced in 1979, this variant took over from the Model 1 with a load of seven smaller MIRVs

SS-N-20 'Sturgeon'

(USSR)

Type: three-stage submarine-launched ballistic missile
Dimensions: diameter 2·00 m (6·56 ft); length 15·00 m (49·2 ft)
Weights: total round not revealed; post-boost vehicle not revealed
Warhead: between six and nine 100/200-kiloton nuclear MIRVs
Propulsion: (first stage) one solid-propellant rocket delivering unrevealed thrust, (second stage) one solid-propellant rocket delivering unrevealed thrust) and (third stage) one solid-propellant rocket delivering unrevealed thrust)
Range: 8300 km (5,160 miles)
CEP: better than 500 m (547 yards)
Launch: submarine tube
Guidance: stellar-inertial

Variant

SS-N-20 'Sturgeon': introduced in 1981 as the primary armament of the huge 'Typhoon' class SSBN, the SS-N-20 entered development in 1973 as a fifth-generation SLBM of good range and advanced capabilities; the range of the missile allows launch submarines to operate from Soviet sanctuary areas and under the Arctic ice cap and still hit targets anywhere in the USA; the type is known to the Soviets as the **RSM-52**

SS-N-23 'Skiff'

(USSR)

Type: two-stage submarine-launched ballistic missile
Dimensions: diameter 2·00 m (6·56 ft); length 13·60 m (44·62 ft)
Weights: total round not revealed; post-boost vehicle not revealed
Warhead: seven 150-kiloton nuclear MIRVs
Propulsion: (first stage) one storable liquid-propellant rocket delivering unrevealed thrust, and (second stage) one storable liquid-propellant rocket delivering unrevealed thrust
Range: 8300 km (5,160 miles)
CEP: 560 m (612 yards)
Launch: submarine tube
Guidance: stellar-inertial

Variant

SS-N-23 'Skiff': introduced in 1985 aboard the 'Delta IV' class SSBN, this is a capable fifth-generation SLBM notable for its good range and low CEP; some estimates put the number of MIRVs as high as 10, and it is possible that the type will be retrofitted in the 'Delta III' class SSBNs as replacement for the shorter-ranged SS-N-18 series

Lockheed UGM-27C Polaris A3TK Chevaline

(USA/UK)

Type: two-stage submarine-launched ballistic missile
Dimensions: diameter 4·50 ft (1·372 m); length 32·29 ft (9·84 m)
Weights: total round 35,000 lb (15,876 kg); post-boost vehicle 1,500 lb (680 kg)
Warhead: three 200-kiloton W58 nuclear warheads carried in three MRVs plus an unknown number of decoys and penetration aids on the basic Penetration Air Carrier (post-boost bus)
Propulsion: (first stage) one Aerojet A3P solid-propellant rocket delivering 80,000-lb (36,288-kg) thrust, and (second stage) one Hercules solid-propellant rocket delivering unrevealed thrust
Range: 2,950 miles (4750 km)
CEP: 1,015 yards (930 m)
Launch: submarine tube
Guidance: General Electric/MIT/Hughes/Raytheon Mk 2 inertial

Variant

UGM-27C Polaris A3TK Chevaline: this is now the only version of the Polaris SLBM left in service, the missiles having been updated in the 'Chevaline' programme of the 1970s to carry, instead of the original three British 200-kiloton warheads, several (but generally assumed to be three) British MRVs capable of a 45-mile (72-km) lateral separation; the warheads are hardened against electro-magnetic pulse and fast radiation, and the warhead bus also contains chaff penetration aids and several (perhaps three) decoys

Lockheed UGM-73A Poseidon C3

(USA)

Type: two-stage submarine-launched ballistic missile
Dimensions: diameter 6·17 ft (1·88 m); length 34·00 ft (10·36 m)
Weights: total round 65,000 lb (29,484 kg); post-boost vehicle 3,300 lb (1497 kg)
Warhead: 10 40/50-kiloton W68 nuclear warheads carried in 10 Mk 3 MIRVs, or 14 W76 100-kiloton nuclear warheads carried in 14 Mk 3 MIRVs
Propulsion: (first stage) two Thiokol/Hercules solid-propellant rockets each delivering unrevealed thrust, and (second stage) two Hercules solid-propellant rockets each delivering unrevealed thrust
Range: 2,485 miles (4000 km) with 14 MIRVs or 3,230 miles (5200 km) with 10 MIRVs
CEP: 605 yards (553 m)
Launch: submarine tube
Guidance: General Electric/MIT/Hughes/Raytheon Mk 4 inertial

Variant

UGM-73A Poseidon C3: introduced in 1970 as successor to the Polaris SLBM, the Poseidon marked an eightfold increase in target-devastation capability at the same range as its predecessor, the Poseidon's real advantages being much improved CEP and a MIRVed payload (the first in a US SLBM)

Lockheed UGM-96A Trident I C4

(USA)

Type: three-stage submarine-launched ballistic missile
Dimensions: diameter 74·00 in (1·88 m); length 34·00 ft (10·36 m)
Weights: total round 73,000 lb (33,113 kg); post-boost vehicle 3,000 + lb (1361 + kg)
Warhead: eight 100-kiloton W76 nuclear warheads carried in eight Mk 4 MIRVs
Propulsion: (first stage) one Thiokol/Hercules solid-propellant rocket delivering unrevealed thrust, (second stage) one Hercules solid-propellant rocket delivering unrevealed thrust, and (third stage) one UTC-CSD solid-propellant rocket delivering unrevealed thrust; there is also a powered post-boost bus
Range: 4,230 miles (6810 km)
CEP: 500 yards (547 m)
Launch: submarine tube
Guidance: Mk 5 stellar-inertial

Variants

UGM-96A Trident I C4: introduced in 1979 as the primary armament of the 'Ohio' class SSBNs and also carried in a number of converted 'Benjamin Franklin' and 'Lafayette' class SSBNs, the Trident I is essentially the Poseidon SLBM with a third stage for much increased range and a very much more advanced warhead based on the Mk 4 MIRV, the bus being manoeuvrable in space for maximum accuracy; should the Soviets upgrade their SLBM capabilities to a marked degree, the USA plans to develop the Mk 5 Evader MARV for installation on the Trident I; this payload can be manoeuvred independently in space and during re-entry to offer maximum target scope while adversely affecting the defence's ability to achieve interceptions
UGM-133A Trident II D5: entering flight test in 1987, this is a much improved development for use in the 'Ohio' class SSBN; the type has a diameter of 6 ft 10·66 in (2·10 m), a length of 44 ft 6·6 in (13·58 m), a launch weight of about 130,000 lb (58,968 kg) and a range of 7,500 miles (12,070 km); the first two stages have graphite-epoxy rather than Kevlar casings but contain the same basic motors as the Trident I with a burn time of about 65 seconds each, while the third stage has a United Technologies motor with a burn time of about 40 seconds for a burn-out speed of about 13,635 mph (21,943 km/h); the payload comprises 10 to 15 Mk 5 RVs each with one 335-kiloton W78 warhead; guidance is entrusted to the Mk 6 stellar-inertial system offering a CEP as low as 130 yards (120 m); the Royal Navy's version will probably have eight British-designed warheads in a US-provided manoeuvring bus

General Dynamics BGM-109B Tomahawk

(USA)

Type: ship/submarine-launched tactical anti-ship cruise missile
Dimensions: diameter 21·00 in (0·533 m); length 20·17 ft (6·15 m); span 8·33 ft (2·54 m)
Weight: total round 3,200 lb (1451·5 kg)
Warhead: 1,000-lb (454-kg) impact-fused HE
Powerplant: one Atlantic Research solid-propellant booster rocket delivering 7,050-lb (3198-kg) thrust, and one Williams Research F107-WR-400 turbofan delivering 600-lb (272-kg) thrust
Performance: speed 500 mph (805 km/h); range 290 + miles (467 km)
CEP: 65 ft (20 m)
Guidance: Litton inertial plus active radar terminal homing

Variants

BGM-109A Tomahawk: the BGM-109 series is the land- and ship/submarine-launched equivalent to the AGM-86B, and the type began to enter service in 1983; the BGM-109A naval variant is known as the **TLAM-N** (Tactical Land Attack Missile - Nuclear), a ship- and submarine-launched encapsulated version with the selectable-yield 200-kiloton W80 Mod 0 warhead, a range of 1,555 miles (2502 km) and a CEP of 305 yards (280 m) with inertial and TERCOM guidance
BGM-109B Tomahawk: also known as the **TASM** (Tactical Anti-Ship Missile), this was designed for ship and submarine launch, and carries a conventional warhead derived from that of the AGM-12 Bullpup air-to-surface missile; terminal guidance is provided by an active radar seeker derived from that of the RGM-84A Harpoon anti-ship missile, and this commands the missile into a pop-up/dive attack to strike the target on its vulnerable upper surfaces
BGM-109C Tomahawk: also known as the **TLAM-C** (Tactical Land Attack Missile - Conventional), and this is essentially the airframe of the BGM-109A with the warhead of the BGM-109B and DSW-15(V) DSMAC terminal guidance for great accuracy over a range of 925 miles (1490 km)

SS-N-21 'Sampson'

(USSR)

Type: submarine-launched tactical/strategic cruise missile
Dimensions: diameter 0·533 m (21·00 in); length 6·90 m (22·64 ft); span 3·45 m (11·32 ft)
Weights: total round 1500 kg (3,307 lb); warhead 150/250-kiloton thermonuclear or HE
Propulsion: one turbojet or turbofan delivering unrevealed thrust
Performance: speed not known; range 2750 or 3000 km (1,710 or 1,865 miles)
CEP: 45 m (150 ft)
Guidance: inertial with terrain-following update

Variant

SS-N-21 'Sampson': entering service in the second half of the 1980s, this is the encapsulated tube-launched submarine variant of the USSR's equivalent of the BGM-109 as a type with air-launched (AS-15 'Kent') and coast-launched (SS-C-4) versions; it presumably offers a choice of targeting and warhead options to provide Soviet attack submarines with a wide variety of attack choices

SS-NX-24

(USSR)

Type: ship- and submarine-launched cruise missile
Dimensions: (estimated) diameter 1·25 m (49·2 in); length 12·0 m (39·37 ft); span 5·9 m (19·36 ft)
Weights: not known
Propulsion: not known
Performance: speed supersonic; range not known
CEP: not known
Guidance: not known

Variant

SS-NX-24: little is known of this new Soviet cruise missile, which is probably designed for the delivery of a nuclear warhead against high-value naval targets; the type is variously estimated to have a range between 1800 and 3600 km (1,118 and 2,237 miles) and is also being developed for a land-based application

CPMIEC C-801

(China)

Type: ship-launched medium-range anti-ship missile
Dimensions: diameter 0·36 m (14·17 in); length 5·814 m (19·075 ft); span 1·118 m (3·68 ft)
Weight: total round about 815 kg (1,797 lb)
Warhead: 165-kg (364-lb) semi-armour piercing HE
Propulsion: one solid-propellant booster rocket delivering unrevealed thrust, and one solid-propellant sustainer rocket delivering unrevealed thrust
Performance: speed 1110 km/h (684 mph); range 50 km (31 miles)
Guidance: strapdown inertial for the cruise phase, and monopulse active radar for the terminal phase

Variant

C-801: introduced to Chinese service in 1983, the C-801 is an advanced anti-ship missile of which little is known with certainty; the type is said to be compatible with the fire-control system used with the Chinese HY-2 and FL-1 derivatives of the Soviet SS-N-2 'Styx' missile; this is certainly an advanced anti-ship cruise missile, and can also be launched from aircraft, shore batteries and surfaced submarines; the type cruises at a preset altitude of 20 or 30 m (66 or 98 ft); the type is also known as the **YJ-6**, YJ standing for Ying Ji (eagle strike)

CPMIEC HY-4

(China)

Type: ship-launched medium/long-range anti-ship missile
Dimensions: diameter 0·76 m (29·92 in); length 7·36 m (24·15 ft); span 2·75 m (9·02 ft)
Weight: total round 2000 kg (4,409 lb)
Warhead: 500-kg (1,102-lb) semi-armour-piercing HE
Propulsion: one solid-propellant booster rocket delivering unrevealed thrust, and one sustainer turbojet delivering unrevealed thrust
Performance: speed between 980 and 1040 km/h (609 and 646 mph); range 150 km (93 miles)
Guidance: strapdown inertial for the cruise phase, and monopulse active radar for the terminal phase

Variants

HY-2: this is the major Chinese version of the Soviet SS-N-2 'Styx' heavyweight anti-ship missile, using solid-propellant rocket propulsion with (in the coast-launched version) a strap-on solid-propellant booster rocket; this basic weapon comes in three forms as the HY-2 with active radar homing and a cruise altitude of 100 m (330 ft), the **HY-2A** with passive IR homing and a cruise altitude of 30 m (100 ft), and the **HY-2G** with active radar homing and a radar altimeter for constant cruising height to a range of 95 km (59 miles)
HY-4: longer-range version of the HY-2 with the fuselage lengthened to allow the insertion of a turbojet engine and its fuel together with a ventral air inlet; there are air- and ship-launched versions of this model, which cruises at an altitude between 70 and 200 m (230 and 655 ft) to a maximum effective range of 135 km (84 miles)

Aérospatiale MM.38 Exocet

(France)

Type: ship-launched medium-range anti-ship missile
Dimensions: diameter 0·45 m (13·75 in); length 5·21 m (17·09 ft); span 1·004 m (3·29 ft)
Weight: total round 750 kg (1,653 lb)
Warhead: 165-kg (364-lb) GP1 blast fragmentation HE
Propulsion: one SEP Epervier solid-propellant booster rocket delivering unrevealed thrust, and one SEP Eole V solid-propellant sustainer rocket delivering unrevealed thrust
Performance: speed Mach 0·93; range 4·5/45 km (2·8/28 miles)
Guidance: inertial plus TRT RAM.01 radar altimeter for the cruise phase, and EMD ADAC active radar for the terminal phase

Variants

MM.38 Exocet: the most widely produced anti-ship missile of Western origins, the Exocet was designed in the late 1960s and began to enter service in 1974; since that date the missile has seen extensive operational use (notably in the Falklands war of 1982 and in the current war between Iraq and Iran); the missile is launched towards the target on data provided by the launch ship's sensors and fire-control system, and cruises at low altitude until some 10 km (6·2 miles) from the anticipated target position, when the monopulse active seeker head is turned on, the target acquired and the terminal phase initiated at the one of three heights preselected at launch with sea state in mind; residual fuel adds to the effects of the warhead detonation, which has in itself proved somewhat troublesome and unreliable; late-production rounds have the Super ADAC radar with greater resistance to electronic countermeasures
SM.39 Exocet: submarine-launched version of the MM.38 fired from a torpedo tube in a 5·80-m (19·03-ft) powered and guided VSM capsule weighing 1350 kg (2,976 lb) complete with missile; the capsule is driven to the surface at a shallow angle by its own solid-propellant booster, and on breaking the surface blows off its nose cap before initiating a gas generator to eject the missile for an otherwise conventional attack profile
MM.40 Exocet: much improved version of the ship-launched missile; the rocket engines have been improved, and the use of a lightweight container/launcher allows the type (despite the greater missile weight of 850 kg/1,874 lb) to be carried by smaller vessels, or alternatively in larger numbers by larger launch platforms; the dimensions of the MM.40 version include a length of 5·78 m (18·96 ft) and a span of 1·135 m (3·72 ft); the range is 70 km (43·5 miles)

IMI Gabriel I and II

(Israel)

Type: ship-launched medium-range anti-ship missile
Dimensions: diameter 0·34 m (13·4 in); length 3·35 m (11·00 ft) or (Gabriel II) 3·42 m (11·22 ft); span 1·38 m (4·53 ft) or (Gabriel II) 1·34 m (4·40 ft)
Weight: total round 431 kg (950 lb) or (Gabriel II) 522 kg (1,151 lb)
Warhead: 100-kg (220-lb) blast fragmentation HE
Propulsion: one solid-propellant booster rocket delivering unrevealed thrust, and one solid-propellant sustainer rocket delivering unrevealed thrust
Performance: speed Mach 0·65 or (Gabriel II) Mach 0·7: range 21 km (13 miles) or (Gabriel II) 36 km (22·4 miles)
Guidance: inertial plus radar altimeter for the cruise phase, and optical or semi-active radar for the terminal phase

Variants

Gabriel I: developed in the 1960s, this somewhat short-ranged anti-ship missile nevertheless has good capabilities (especially in terms of its resistance to electronic countermeasures), the cruise and approach phases of its flight being akin to those of the Gabriel Mk III, though the sea-skimming attack is made under optical or semi-active radar control
Gabriel II: extended-range version of the Mk I with a longer body and more propellant
Chungshan Institute of Science and Technology Hsiung Feng I: this is the Taiwanese version of the Gabriel Mk II incorporating a number of local modifications and components, including a new guidance system designed by the Sun Yat-sen Institute; it is believed that the dimensions and primary operational data of the Hsiung Feng I (male bee I) are very similar to those of the Israeli original; the weapon is produced for coastal and shipborne applications, the former on a triple launcher carried on a semi-trailer, and the latter on triple or single launchers for installation on destroyers or fast attack craft respectively
Atlas Skorpioen: South African version of the Gabriel incorporating local components

IMI Gabriel III

(Israel)

Type: ship-launched medium-range anti-ship missile
Dimensions: diameter 0·34 m (13·4 in); length 3·81 m (12·50 ft); span 1·34 m (4·40 ft)
Weight: total round 600 kg (1,323 lb)
Warhead: 150-kg (331-lb) blast fragmentation HE
Propulsion: one solid-propellant rocket delivering 3600-kg (7,937-lb) thrust
Performance: speed Mach 0·73; range 60+ km (37·3+ miles)
Guidance: inertial plus radar altimeter for the cruise phase, and active radar for the terminal phase

Variants

Gabriel III: derived from the earlier Gabriel anti-ship missiles, the ship-launched Gabriel III introduces a frequency-agile active radar seeker, though the optical and semi-active radar homing systems of the Gabriel I and II can also be used; the weapon can thus have three guidance modes, namely fire-and-forget, fire and update via a data-link from a targeting helicopter or similar, and fire and command using the launch vessel's radar for better targeting data; the missile cruises at 100 m (330 ft) and then descends to 20 m

The Gabriel I is still a modestly effective anti-ship weapon, and amongst its advantages is a choice of terminal guidance modes to suit conditions.

(66 ft) for the approach to the target, the actual attack being made at a preset height of 1·5, 2·5 or 4 m (4·9, 8·25 or 13·1 ft) depending on the sea state

Gabriel IV: updated version with a length of 4·7 m (15·42 ft) and powered by a small turbojet for a range of 200 km (124 miles); there will doubtless be provision for mid-course update of the inertial navigation system of this variant, whose development is anticipated for the early 1990s

OTO Melara/Matra Otomat

(Italy/France)

Type: ship-launched medium-range anti-ship missile
Dimensions: diameter 0·46 m (18·1 in); length 4·82 m (15·81 ft); span 1·19 m (3·9 ft)
Weight: total round 770 kg (1,698 lb)
Warhead: 210-kg (463-lb) semi-armour-piercing HE comprising 65 kg (143 lb) of HE and 145 kg (320 lb) of incendiary material, plus any residual fuel
Propulsion: two jettisonable Hotchkiss-Brandt/SNPE solid-propellant booster rockets each delivering 3500-kg (7,717-lb) thrust, and one Turboméca TR 281 Arbizon sustainer turbojet delivering 400-kg (882-lb) thrust
Performance: speed Mach 0·9; range 6/60 + km (3·7/37·3 + miles) when fired as a singleton, or 6/80 + km (3·7/49·7 + miles) when fired in salvo
Guidance: autopilot plus radar altimeter for the cruise phase, and (Otomat) Thomson-CSF 'Col Vert' two-axis active radar or (Otomat 2) SMA single-axis active radar for the terminal phase

Variants

Otomat: developed for shipboard or coastal operation from a self-contained container-launcher, the Otomat is a capable air-breathing anti-ship missile; the weapon cruises at 250 m (820 ft) before descending to 20 m (66 ft) in the closing stages of the attack, when the active radar system is turned on; the Thomson-CSF 'Col Vert' system causes the missile to climb to 175 m (575 ft) and then dive on the vulnerable upper surfaces of the target

Otomat 2 Teseo: version of the basic Otomat fitted with SMA active radar terminal homing and the TG-2 command guidance system so that a mid-course update can be fed into the missile guidance package from a helicopter or other source; this allows the missile to operate effectively to a maximum-fuel range of 180 + km (112 miles) followed by a sea-skimming terminal attack

Otomach 2: supersonic version projected for development in the late 1980s with a version of the Alfa-Romeo AR318 turbojet, a range of 100 + km (62·1 + miles) and a 100-kg (220-lb) warhead; the type will also have a more advanced seeker

Kongsberg Penguin III

(Norway)

Type: ship-launched medium-range anti-ship missile
Dimensions: diameter 0·28 m (11·02 in); length 3·17 m (10·40 ft); span 1·00 m (3·28 ft)
Weight: total round 360 kg (794 lb)
Warhead: 121-kg (267-lb) semi-armour-piercing HE
Propulsion: one Raufoss Ammunisjons solid-propellant rocket delivering unrevealed thrust
Performance: speed Mach 0·9; range 40 km (25 miles) from a surface launch and 60 km (37·3 miles) from an air launch
Guidance: Kongsberg Vapenfabrikk inertial for the cruise phase, and Kongsberg Vapenfabrikk IR for the terminal phase

Variants

Penguin I: the Western world's first anti-ship missile, the Penguin Mk I was conceived in the early 1960s and entered service in 1972 as part of Norway's defence against maritime invasion, and as such was optimized for good performance in the country's peculiar coastal waters after launch from fast attack craft; the result is a missile with IR terminal homing, treated as a round of ammunition and launched on information supplied by the launch platform's sensors and fire-control system; this ship-launched version has a two-stage rocket and height control by a pulsed-laser altimeter; the weight is 340 kg (750 lb), the dimensions include a length of 2·96 m (9·71 ft) and a span of 1·40 m (4·59 ft), and the performance figures include a speed of Mach 0·8 and a range of 20 km (12·4 miles); the missiles still in service are being upgraded to **Penguin I Mod 7** standard with the seeker of the Penguin II Mod 3

Penguin II: improved Penguin I with range boosted to 30 km (18·6 miles) and a weight of 340 kg (750 lb) in the ship-launched **Penguin II Mod 3** (also used by Sweden with the designation **Rb 12**), which has a length of 2·95 m (9·68 ft) and a span of 1·40 m (4·59 ft); the type entered service in the early 1980s, and surviving rounds are being upgraded to **Penguin II Mod 5** standard with enhanced seeker performance

Penguin III: air-launched development (also capable of ship launch) with a longer body, shorter-span wings, a single-stage rocket and a radar altimeter; the type is a highly capable weapon programmed to fly a circuitous approach to the target via a waypoint; as with the earlier versions of the missile, the use of infra-red terminal homing gives the target virtually no warning of the missile's imminent arrival, so reducing the time available for countermeasures

Saab Rb 08A

(Sweden)
Type: ship-launched medium/long-range anti-ship missile
Dimensions: diameter 0·66 m (25·98 in); length 5·72 m (18·77 ft); span 3·01 m (9·88 ft)
Weight: total round 1215 kg (2,679 lb)
Warhead: 250-kg (551-lb) blast fragmentation HE
Propulsion: two jettisonable solid-propellant booster rockets each delivering unrevealed thrust, and one Turboméca Marboré IID turbojet delivering 400-kg (882-lb) thrust
Performance: speed Mach 0·85; range 250 km (155 miles)
Guidance: autopilot plus TRT radar altimeter for the cruise phase, and Thomson-CSF active radar for the terminal phase

Variant
Rb 08A: developed by French and Swedish interests on the basis of the Nord CT-20 target drone and introduced in 1967, the Rb 08A is a large and powerful anti-ship missile whose considerable range capability requires the use of active radar terminal homing

Saab Rbs 15M

(Sweden)
Type: ship-launched medium/long-range anti-ship missile
Dimensions: diameter 0·50 m (19·7 in); length 4·35 m (14·27 ft); span 1·40 m (4·59 ft)
Weight: total round 780 kg (1,720 lb)
Warhead: blast fragmentation HE
Propulsion: two jettisonable Saab solid-propellant booster rockets each delivering unrevealed thrust, and one Microturbo TRI 60-2 sustainer turbojet delivering 377-kg (831-lb) thrust
Performance: speed high subsonic; range 100 km (62 miles)
Guidance: autopilot plus radar altimeter for the cruise phase, and Philips Elektronikindustrier/Bofors Electronics active radar for the terminal phase

Variant
Rbs 15M: entering service in the second half of the 1980s, this is a potent ship-launched anti-ship missile fired (after onboard programming using data derived from the ship's sensors and fire-control system) with the aid of two jettisonable solid-propellant rockets to fly at medium or low altitude (the former capability being essential in the Swedish archipelago) to the point at which the active seeker is turned on, whereupon the missile drops to sea-skimming height for the attack

Chungshan Institute of Science and Technology Hsiung Feng II

(Taiwan)
Type: ship-launched medium/long-range anti-ship missile
Dimensions: not revealed
Weight: total round not revealed

Warhead: blast fragmentation HE
Propulsion: one jettisonable solid-propellant booster rocket delivering unrevealed thrust, and one sustainer turbojet delivering unrevealed thrust
Performance: speed high subsonic; range 80 km (50 miles)
Guidance: autopilot for the cruise phase (with provision for midcourse update by data-link), and active radar for the terminal phase

Variant
Hsiung Feng II: this is a Taiwanese long-range development of the baseline Hsiung Feng I resembling the McDonnell Douglas RGM-84 Harpoon rather than the Gabriel; details are signally lacking, though it is thought that Taiwan pressed ahead with this development using an air-breathing engine after the USA refused to allow a Taiwanese purchase of the RGM-84; the type was originally developed for ship- and shore-based launchers, though it seems likely that submarine- and air-launched versions will follow

SS-N-2A/B 'Styx'

(USSR)
Type: ship-launched medium-range anti-ship missile
Dimensions: diameter 0·75 m (29·53 in); length 6·30 m (20·67 ft); span 2·75 m (9·02 ft)
Weight: total round 3000 kg (9,843 lb)
Warhead: 500-kg (1,102-lb) blast fragmentation HE
Propulsion: one jettisonable solid-propellant booster rocket delivering unrevealed thrust, and one storable liquid-propellant sustainer rocket delivering unrevealed thrust
Performance: speed Mach 0·9; range 37 km (23·0 miles) or 85 km (52·8 miles) without or with midcourse update
Guidance: autopilot for the cruise phase (with provision for midcourse update from a helicopter), and active radar terminal or radio command for the terminal phase

Variants
SS-N-2A 'Styx': entering service in 1958, this seminal but large anti-ship missile is obsolescent but still in widespread service, despite its limitations when faced by electronic countermeasures or effective point defences; the type has a preset cruise altitude of up to 300 m (985 ft); the missile has the Soviet military designation **P-15** and the production designation **4K40**
SS-N-2B 'Styx': entering service in 1965, this updated missile has folding wings for better shipboard stowage, and may also have infra-red terminal homing
SS-N-2C 'Styx': entering service in the early 1970s, this version of the SS-N-2B has longer range (80 km/50 miles) and updated avionics, the latter allowing a sea-skimming approach to the target; the extended range of this weapon makes mid-course guidance by a helicopter all but essential if the type's full range capability is to be used; the variant is sometimes known as the **SS-N-2 (Mod)**

SS-N-3B/C 'Shaddock'

(USSR)
Type: ship- and surfaced submarine-launched long-range anti-ship missile
Dimensions: diameter 0·86 m (33·86 in); length 19·90 m (65·29 ft); span 2·10 m (6·89 ft)
Weight: total round 4500 kg (9,921 lb)
Warhead: 350-kiloton nuclear or 1000-kg (2,205-lb) blast fragmentation HE
Propulsion: two jettisonable solid-propellant booster rockets each delivering unrevealed thrust, and one sustainer turbojet or ramjet delivering unrevealed thrust
Performance: speed Mach 1·4; range 75 km (46·6 miles) or 250 km (59·0 miles) for SS-N-3B or 465 km (288·9 miles) for SS-N-3C without or with midcourse update
Guidance: autopilot for the cruise phase (with provision for midcourse update from a helicopter or aeroplane) and active radar for the terminal phase

Variants
SS-N-3A 'Shaddock': introduced in 1962 as a successor to the NATO-designated SS-N-3C strategic missile, the SS-N-3A is the 'Shaddock' variant designed for launch from surfaced submarines, its primary targets being US carrier battle groups with the nuclear warhead; the long range of the weapon makes midcourse guidance update a key necessity on ranges of more than 75 km (46·6 miles), provision of such a capability increasing maximum effective range to 250 km (155·3 miles); alternative estimates give nuclear warhead yields of 800 kilotons and 1 megaton; the missile has the Soviet military designation **P-7,** though its production designation remains unknown

SS-N-3B 'Shaddock': this is the surface vessel companion to the SS-N-3A, and was introduced at the same time; the variant is associated with 'Scoop Pair' radar

SS-N-3C 'Shaddock': introduced in 1960, this was the initial member of the 'Shaddock' series, and designed as an area-attack weapon against US strategic targets with autopilot control but no terminal homing system; the missile has the Soviet military designation **P-6**, though its production designation remains unknown

SS-N-7 'Starbright'

(USSR)
Type: submarine-launched medium-range anti-ship missile
Dimensions: diameter 0·55 m (21·66 in); length 6·70 m (21·98 ft); span not revealed
Weight: total round 3375 kg (7,441 lb)
Warhead: 200-kiloton nuclear or 500-kg (1,102-lb) blast fragmentation HE
Propulsion: one solid-propellant rocket delivering unrevealed thrust
Performance: speed Mach 0·95; range 55 km (34 miles)
Guidance: autopilot for the cruise phase, and active radar for the terminal phase

Variant
SS-N-7 'Starbright': designed for underwater launch through the tubes of a submarine, the SS-N-7 was designed as a weapon against US carrier battle groups, and began to enter service in 1968; the type cruises at a height of some 30 m (100 ft)

SS-N-9 'Siren'

(USSR)
Type: ship- and submarine-launched medium/long-range anti-ship missile
Dimensions: diameter 0·55 m (21·66 in); length 9·20 m (30·18 ft); span 2·50 m (8·20 ft)
Weight: total round 3000 kg (6,614 lb)
Warhead: 200-kiloton nuclear or 500-kg (1,102-lb) blast fragmentation HE
Propulsion: one solid-propellant rocket delivering unrevealed thrust
Performance: speed Mach 0·9; range 65 km (40·4 miles) or 130 km (80·8 miles) without or with midcourse update
Guidance: autopilot for the cruise phase (with provision for midcourse update from a helicopter), and combined active radar and IR for the terminal phase

Variant
SS-N-9 'Siren': introduced in 1969 on board light missile corvettes, and then developed for encapsulated launch from the tubes of submerged submarines, the SS-N-9 is similar to the SS-N-7 in concept and operation, though its range makes necessary the use of third-party targeting for effective maximum-range accuracy; the use of two terminal homing modes dictates a cruise altitude of 75 m (245 ft)

SS-N-12 'Sandbox'

(USSR)
Type: ship- and submarine-launched long-range anti-ship missile
Dimensions: diameter 0·86 m (33·86 in); length 10·70 m (35·10 ft); span 2·50 m (8·20 ft)
Weight: total round 5000 kg (11,023 lb)
Warhead: 350-kiloton nuclear or 1000-kg (2,205-lb) blast fragmentation HE
Propulsion: two jettisonable solid-propellant booster rockets each delivering unrevealed thrust, and one sustainer turbojet or ramjet delivering unrevealed thrust
Performance: speed Mach 2·5; range 110 km (68·4 miles) or 300 km (186·4 miles) without or with midcourse update
Guidance: autopilot for the cruise phase (with provision for midcourse update from a helicopter, aeroplane or radar ocean surveillance satellite), and active radar for the terminal phase

Variant
SS-N-12 'Sandbox': this potent missile is believed to be an updated version of the SS-N-3 series, with longer range and more advanced avionics so that a sea-skimming attack profile can be flown; like the 'Shaddock' series, the SS-N-12 is of aeroplane configuration with folding wings for shipboard stowage, and requires mid-course updating for effective use over its maximum range; the type is associated with 'Trap Door' or 'Front Door' radar

SS-N-19 'Shipwreck'

(USSR)
Type: ship- and submarine-launched long-range anti-ship missile
Dimensions: diameter not revealed; length about 10·0 m (32·8 ft); span not revealed
Weight: total round not revealed
Warhead: 500-kiloton thermonuclear
Propulsion: one turbojet delivering unrevealed thrust
Performance: speed Mach 2·5; range 110 km (68·4 miles) or 465 km (288·9 miles) without or with midcourse update
Guidance: inertial for the cruise phase (with provision for midcourse update from an aeroplane or radar ocean surveillance satellite), and unrevealed guidance for the terminal phase

Variant
SS-N-19 'Shipwreck': very little is known of this weapon, which entered service in 1980 and is carried by the 'Kirov' class battle-cruisers and the 'Oscar I and II' classes of nuclear-powered cruise missile submarines; the high speed is clearly a very strong tactical advantage, but the full range of the weapon can only be exploited with the aid of mid-course guidance update from a specialist air platform such as the Tupolev Tu-95 'Bear-D' fixed-wing aeroplane

SS-N-22 'Sunburn'

(USSR)
Type: ship-launched short/medium-range anti-ship missile
Dimensions: not revealed
Weight: total round not revealed
Warhead: blast fragmentation HE
Propulsion: one solid-propellant rocket delivering unrevealed thrust
Performance: speed supersonic; range 55 km (34·2 miles) or 115 km (71·5 miles) without or with midcourse guidance update
Guidance: inertial for the cruise phase (with provision for midcourse update from a helicopter), and combined radar and IR for the terminal phase

Variant
SS-N-22 'Sunburn': very little is known of this weapon; it is thought that the missile is in essence an improved version of the SS-N-9 introduced in 1982 for use on board the Soviet 'Sovremenny' class destroyers and later on 'Tarantul III' class corvettes; the advanced avionics are believed to confer a true sea-skimming capability as well as a 'home-on-jam' terminal mode in conditions of electronic countermeasures; like the SS-N-9, the SS-N-22 is associated with 'Band Stand' radar

BAe Sea Eagle

(UK)
Type: air-launched medium/long-range anti-ship missile
Dimensions: diameter 15·75 in (0·40 m); length 13·58 ft (4·14 m); span 3·94 ft (1·20 m)
Weight: total round 1,300 lb (590 kg)
Warhead: blast fragmentation HE
Propulsion: one Microturbo TRI 60-1 turbojet delivering 367-kg (787-lb) thrust
Performance: speed Mach 0·9 + ; range 30/60 miles (48·3/96·6 km) depending on launch altitude
Guidance: autopilot plus radar altimeter for the cruise phase, and Marconi active radar for the terminal phase

Variant
Sea Eagle SL: currently under development, this ship-launched derivative of the Sea Eagle air-launched missile is fitted with boost rockets and carried in a lightweight container/launcher

McDonnell Douglas RGM-84A Harpoon

(USA)
Type: ship-launched medium/long-range anti-ship missile
Dimensions: diameter 13·5 in (0·343 m); length 15·06 ft (4·58 m); span 3·00 ft (0·914 m)
Weight: total round 1,498 lb (679 kg)
Warhead: 500-lb (227-kg) proximity and impact delayed-action penetrating blast HE
Propulsion: one Aerojet solid-propellant booster rocket delivering 14,550-lb (6600-kg) thrust, and one Teledyne CAE J402-CA-400 sustainer turbojet delivering 680-lb (308-kg) thrust
Performance: speed Mach 0·85; range 68 miles (110 km)
Guidance: Lear-Siegler or Northrop strap-down inertial plus Honeywell

An RGM-84 Harpoon anti-ship missile emerges from a Mk 141 container-launcher on board a 'Spruance' class guided-missile destroyer.

APN-194 radar altimeter for the cruise phase and Texas Instruments PR-53/DSQ-28 two-axis active radar for the terminal phase

Variants

RGM-84A Harpoon: the Western world's most important ship-launched anti-ship missile, the Harpoon was conceived in the late 1960s as a capable but comparatively cheap weapon emphasizing reliability rather than outright performance in all respects but electronic capability and range, where the use of a turbojet rather than a rocket in the sustainer role pays handsome dividends; the missile can be fired in range and bearing mode, allowing the late activation of the active radar as a means of reducing the chances of the missile being detected through its own emissions, or in the bearing-only mode for earlier activation of the radar where the precise location of the target is not available at missile launch time; if no target is found after the low-level approach, the missile undertakes a preprogrammed search pattern, and acquisition of the target is followed in the 60-mile (97-km) range Block I initial-production missiles by a steep pop-up climb and dive onto the target's more vulnerable upper surfaces; later Block IB and Block IC missiles have greater range and the capability for a sea-skimming rather than pop-up attack, and the Block IC type has enhanced electronic counter-countermeasures capability plus the ability to fly a dog-leg course via three preprogrammed waypoints; currently under development is the Block II type with range increased to more than 120 miles (193 km), plus variable flight profiles and increased capability against electronic countermeasures; the **UGM-84A Sub-Harpoon** is the submarine-launched version installed in a capsule for tube firing in a manner similar to that of the SM.39 version of the Exocet

RGM-84B Harpoon: version of the RGM-84A with improved electronics, more flexible tactical flight profiles and a 570-lb (258·6-kg) warhead; there is also a **UGM-84B Sub-Harpoon** tube-launched encapsulated version for use by submarines

RGM-84C Harpoon: much improved model incorporating the flight profile capabilities of the RGM-84A Blocks IB, IC and II missiles, and entering service in the second half of the 1980s; the type is also available in a submarine-launched version as the **UGM-84C Sub-Harpoon**

DDS Ikara

(Australia)

Type: ship-launched anti-submarine weapon system
Dimensions: span 5·00 ft (1·52 m); length 11·22 ft (3·42 m); height 5·15 ft (1·57 m)
Weight: total round varies according to payload
Warhead: typically 507-lb (230-kg) Mk 46 lightweight torpedo
Propulsion: one Murawa two-stage solid-propellant rocket delivering unrevealed thrust
Performance: speed Mach 0·8; range 15 miles (24 km)
Guidance: autopilot plus radar altimeter, and radio command

Variants

Ikara: developed in Australia as a major anti-submarine weapon, the Ikara is a small aircraft-configured missile launched (on data provided by the ship's sonar systems via the fire-control system) towards the anticipated position of the target, the missile being fed with upgraded information in flight so that it can paradrop its homing torpedo payload (initially the US Mk 44, then the Mk 46 and recently a number of European weapons such as the

Marconi Stingray and Whitehead A 244/S) over the target for autonomous continuance of the attack while the missile clears the area and crashes

Ikara GWS 40: British version of the system with target data provided through the ship's Action Data Automation Weapons System

Branik: version for Brazil with a dedicated missile tracking and guidance system

Super Ikara: under development by the Australian Department of Defence Support and BAe (but currently at a very low priority), the Super Ikara is a much updated and improved version of the basic concept matched to the performance of modern sonar detection systems; the launch vehicle has folding wings to facilitate shipboard stowage, and is boosted by a solid-propellant rocket before an air-breathing sustainer engine takes over for flight to a range of 60 miles (96 km), a range that will almost certainly dictate the provision of mid-course update; the payload can comprise any of the modern generation of acoustic-homing lightweight torpedoes such as the British Sting Ray, the French Murene and the US Mk 50 Barracuda

Latécoère Malafon Mk 2

(France)

Type: ship-launched anti-submarine weapon system
Dimensions: diameter 0·65 m (25·6 in); span 3·30 m (10·83 ft); length 6·15 m (20·18 ft)
Weight: total round 1500 kg (3,307 lb)
Warhead: 540-kg (1,190-lb) L4 homing torpedo
Propulsion: two SNPE Venus solid-propellant booster rockets each delivering unrevealed thrust
Performance: speed 830 km/h (516 mph); range 13,000 m (14,215 yards)
Guidance: autopilot plus radar altimeter, and radio command

Variant

Malafon Mk 2: introduced in 1966, the production Malafon Mk 2 operates in a manner similar to the Ikara, but glides under radio control after the initial boost phase of the flight, dropping its nose-mounted torpedo payload some 800 m (875 yards) from the target's anticipated position by decelerating the airframe with a braking parachute; the torpedo then falls into the water and continues the attack autonomously

FRAS-1

(USSR)

Type: ship-launched anti-submarine weapon system
Dimensions: diameter 0·70 m (27·56 in); length 6·20 m (20·34 ft); span 1·30 m (51·2 in)
Weight: total round 800 kg (1,764 lb)
Warhead: 5-kiloton nuclear (fission) or 450-mm (17·7-in) homing torpedo
Propulsion: one solid-propellant rocket delivering unrevealed thrust
Performance: speed Mach 1 + ; range 30 km (18·6 miles)
Guidance: none

Variant

FRAS-1: associated with the SUW-N-1 twin launcher (with 20-round magazine) found on many large Soviet surface vessels, the FRAS-1 rocket entered service in 1967 and is believed to be derived from the FROG series of artillery rockets; the weapon is launched on data supplied by the launch ship's sonar via the appropriate fire-control system, and operates in a manner similar to that of the American ASROC system

SS-N-14 'Silex'

(USSR)

Type: ship-launched anti-submarine weapon system
Dimensions: diameter 0·55 m (21·65 in); length 7·60 m (24·93 ft); span 1·10 m (43·3 in)
Weight: total round 1000 kg (2,205 lb)
Warhead: 1/5-kiloton nuclear or 450-mm (17·7-in) homing torpedo
Propulsion: one solid-propellant rocket delivering unrevealed thrust
Performance: speed Mach 0·95; range 7·4/55 km (4·6/34·2 miles)
Guidance: radio command

Variant

SS-N-14 'Silex': though now rightly appreciated as an anti-submarine weapon in the mould of the Ikara and Malafon (though of considerably superior performance), the 'Silex' was at first thought by the West to be a surface-to-surface tactical missile, the Soviets having waged a subtle but convincing disinformation campaign between 1968 (when the first launchers went to sea) and 1974 (when the missile was introduced); the weapons are

carried in quadruple launchers, though the 'Kirov' class battle-cruisers each have a twin launcher with 26 rounds, and guidance is effected with the aid of 'Head Light' or 'Eye Bowl' radars after the missile has been launched on information provided by the ship's sonar system

SS-N-15 'Starfish'

(USSR)

Type: submarine-launched anti-submarine weapon system
Dimensions: diameter 0·533 m (21·00 in); length 6·50 m (21·33 ft)
Weight: total round 1900 kg (4,189 lb)
Warhead: 5-kiloton nuclear depth charge
Propulsion: one solid-propellant rocket delivering unrevealed thrust
Performance: speed Mach 1·5; range 37 km (23 miles)
Guidance: none

Variant

SS-N-15 'Starfish': introduced in 1972, the SS-N-15 is believed to be based on the American SUBROC system and is very similar in its concept and method of operation; the type is deployed aboard most Soviet nuclear attack submarines, and on the 'Tango' class patrol submarine

SS-N-16 'Stallion'

(USSR)

Type: submarine-launched anti-submarine weapon system
Dimensions: diameter 0·65 m (25·6 in); length 6·50 m (21·33 ft)
Weight: total round 2150 kg (4,740 lb)
Warhead: 450-mm (17·7-in) homing torpedo or (possibly) one nuclear depth charge of unrevealed yield
Propulsion: one solid-propellant rocket delivering unrevealed thrust
Performance: speed Mach 1·5; range 55 km (34·2 miles)
Guidance: inertial

Variant

SS-N-16 'Stallion': introduced in the mid-1970s as an updated, inertially guided and longer-ranged development of the SS-N-15 concept, the SS-N-16 is of greater diameter than its precursor, and paradrops its homing torpedo payload into the water over the anticipated target position; most Soviet nuclear-powered attack and modern conventionally-powered patrol submarines carry the weapon

Boeing/Gould Sea Lance

(USA)

Type: ship- and submarine-launched anti-submarine weapon system
Dimensions: diameter 21·00 in (0·533 m); length 21·00 ft (6·40 m)
Weight: total round 2,700 lb (1224·7 kg)
Warhead: 800-lb (363-kg) Mk 50 Barracuda homing torpedo or one nuclear depth charge of unrevealed yield
Propulsion: one Hercules solid-propellant rocket delivering unrevealed thrust
Performance: speed Mach 1·5 + ; range 63·3/103·6 miles (101·9/166·7 km)
Guidance: none

Variant

Sea Lance: due to enter service in the 1990s after development as the **ASW-SOW** (Anti-Submarine Warfare - Stand-Off Weapon), the Sea Lance is the successor to SUBROC, offering greater range and full compatibility with the latest digital Mk 117 fire-control system, which programmes the weapon and fires it towards the target area; the encapsulated missile is launched through a standard torpedo tube, and its rocket motor is ignited only after the weapon has reached the surface, wrap-round fins unfolding as the missile leaves the capsule to fly a ballistic trajectory, probably discarding its burned-out rocket and leaving the warhead to continue into the anticipated target area

Honeywell RUR-5A ASROC

(USA)

Type: ship-launched anti-submarine weapon system
Dimensions: diameter 12·75 in (0·324 m); length (Mk 44 payload) 15·00 ft (4·57 m) or (Mk 46 payload) 14·79 ft (4·51 m); span 33·25 in (0·845 m)
Weight: total round (Mk 44 payload) 957 lb (434 kg), (Mk 46 payload) 1,073 lb (487 kg) or (Mk 17 payload) 825 lb (374 kg)
Warhead: 425-lb (192·8-kg) Mk 44 torpedo, or 508-lb (230·4-kg) Mk 46 torpedo, or 1·5-kiloton W44 nuclear in a 260-lb (117·9-kg) in a Mk 17 depth charge

Propulsion: one Naval Propellant Plant solid-propellant rocket delivering 11,000-lb (4990-kg) thrust
Performance: speed Mach 0·8; range 2,025/11,600 yards (1850/10,605 m)
Guidance: none
Variants
RUR-5A ASROC: introduced in 1962 aboard surface units of the US Navy, the Anti-Submarine ROCket is a ballistic weapon aimed and launched from the Mk 16 octuple dedicated launcher or Mks 10 and 26 twin SAM/ASROC launchers on information supplied by the ship's sonar system via the underwater weapons fire-control system; the weapon flies ballistically, the rocket being jettisoned when exhausted to leave the payload to continue alone to the target's anticipated position for an autonomous attack; only the US Navy has the Mk 17 depth charge with the W44 nuclear warhead
ASROC (VL): updated version currently under development for service in the 1990s for vertical launch from the Mk 41 launcher unit able to accommodate ASROC, BGM-109 Tomahawk, RGM-84 Harpoon and RIM-66/67 Standard missiles; the weapon is boosted vertically, aligned onto the correct trajectory and then flies ballistically after the booster has been discarded

Goodyear UUM-44A SUBROC

(USA)
Type: submarine-launched anti-submarine weapon system
Dimensions: diameter 21·00 in (0·533 m); length 22·00 ft (6·71 m)
Weight: total round 4,000 lb (1814 kg)
Warhead: 650-lb (294·8-kg) 1/5-kiloton W55 nuclear
Propulsion: one Thiokol TE-260G solid-propellant rocket delivering unrevealed thrust
Performance: speed Mach 1·5; range 35 miles (56·3 km)
Guidance: Singer-Kearfott SD-510 inertial
Variant
UUM-44A SUBROC: introduced in 1965 as part of the anti-submarine weapon inventory of US nuclear-powered attack submarines (which generally carry four or six of these SUBmarine ROCkets), the UUM-44A is a tube-launched weapon fired on the data supplied by the boat's BQQ-2 sonar suite via the analog Mk 113 fire-control system; the rocket is ignited under the water, forcing the missile up and out of the water to fly towards the target's anticipated position, above which the nuclear warhead is released (by explosive bolts and retro-thrust deceleration of the missile) to fall into the water and detonate at the preset depth with a lethal radius of 5,300/7,000 yards (4845/6400 m); the type is being phased out of service as older boats retire, for the system is incompatible with the newer boats' digital Mk 117 fire-control system

CPMIEC HQ-61

(China)
Type: ship-launched short-range surface-to-air missile
Dimensions: diameter 0·286 m (11·26 in); length 3·99 m (13·09 ft); span 1·166 m (45·9 in)
Weight: total round 300 kg (661 lb)
Warhead: blast fragmentation HE
Propulsion: one solid-propellant rocket delivering unrevealed thrust
Performance: speed Mach 3; range limits 3000/10,000 m (3,280/10,935 yards); altitude limits 0/8000 m (0/26,245 ft)
Guidance: strapdown inertial for the midcourse phase and CW semi-active radar for the terminal phase
Variant
HQ-61: this Chinese-developed SAM bears a resemblance to the American Sparrow series, but is larger and heavier than the US weapon; in both services the weapon is associated with a twin launcher, that on ships being located above the below-decks rotary magazine, and both types are used in conjunction with a Chinese radar based on the Soviet 'Flat Face'

Aérospatiale/Thomson-CSF SAN 90

(France)
Type: ship-launched medium-range surface-to-air missile
Dimensions: not revealed
Weight: total round not revealed
Warhead: blast fragmentation HE
Propulsion: one solid-propellant booster rocket delivering unrevealed thrust, and one solid-propellant sustainer rocket delivering unrevealed thrust
Performance: speed high supersonic; range limits not revealed/25 km (not revealed/15·53 miles) altitude limits not revealed

Guidance: strapdown inertial for the midcourse phase, and active radar for the terminal phase

Variant
SAN 90: this is the designation of the navalized version of the SA 90 land-based missile, and is designed for use with the **SAAM** ship-borne system; the particular emphasis of naval operations will probably make the missile somewhat different from the land-based SA 90, but there will nonetheless be sufficient commonality of design features and components to create considerable financial and operational savings; the SAN 90 is designed to provide French warships with an effective counter to all-azimuth aircraft, radiation-homing missile and anti-ship cruise missile attacks out to a range of 10,000 m (10,935 yards); the missile will probably be fired from a multiple vertical launcher, be fitted with a high-precision terminal guidance system to ensure minimum miss distance, and have rocket propulsion rather than the mixed rocket/ramjet propulsion of the SA 90 land-based model; the radar antenna will be located as high up the launch vessel's superstructure as possible to secure the farthest possible radar horizon as a means of early detection of sea-skimmers.

DTCN/Matra Masurca Mk 2 Mod 3

(France)
Type: ship-launched medium-range area-defence surface-to-air missile
Dimensions: diameter (missile) 0·406 m (16·00 in) and (booster) 0·57 m (22·44 in); length (missile) 5·38 m (17·65 ft) and (booster) 3·32 m (10·89 ft); span (missile) 0·77 m (30·31 in) and (booster) 1·50 m (59·06 in)
Weight: total round 2098 kg (4,625 lb)
Warhead: 100-kg (220-lb) blast fragmentation HE
Propulsion: one SNPE Polka solid-propellant booster rocket delivering 34,780-kg (76,675-lb) thrust, and one SNPE Jacee solid-propellant sustainer rocket delivering 2423-kg (5,342-lb) thrust
Performance: speed Mach 3; range limits not revealed/50 km (not revealed/31 miles); altitude limits 30/2300 m (100/75,460 ft)
Guidance: semi-active radar homing

Variant
Masurca Mk 2 Mod 3: the only version of this French area-defence weapon now in service, the Masurca Mk 2 Mod 3 introduced semi-active radar rather than radar beam-riding guidance; the type is used on a twin-rail launcher and fed from a 48-round magazine; a 3D surveillance radar provides target detection and acquisition, whereupon two weapon-direction systems (each fitted with a Thomson-CSF DRBC 51 tracking and target illuminating radar) take over; the DRBC 51 follows the target aircraft continuously, and also controls the pointing of the target-illuminating antenna

Matra R.440

(France)
Type: ship-launched point defence surface-to-air missile
Dimensions: diameter 0·15 m (5·9 in); length 2·89 m (9·48 ft); span 0·54 m (21·25 in)
Weight: total round 85 kg (187·4 lb)
Warhead: 15-kg (33-lb) blast fragmentation HE
Propulsion: one SNPE Lens solid-propellant rocket delivering 4850-kg (10,962-lb) thrust
Performance: speed Mach 2·30; range limits 500/13,000 m (545/14,215 yards) against helicopters and non-manoeuvring targets, or 500/8500 m (545/9,295 yards) against manoeuvring targets, or 500/6500 m (545/7,110 yards) against low-altitude and sea-skimming targets; altitude limits 15/5000 m (50/16,405 ft)
Guidance: Thomson-CSF radar command with IR/radar gathering and tracking

Variant
R.440: entering service in 1971 after development from 1964, the R.440 SAM is designed for use in the Cactus and Crotale land-based SAM systems, and is designed for all-weather close-range engagement of aircraft flying at up to Mach 1·2; the same basic missile is used in the Naval Crotale system; the missile has canard configuration, a powder propulsion rocket and a capable infra-red fuse designed to initiate warhead detonation according to intercept geometry calculations or by impact; the lethal radius of the warhead is 8 m (26·25 ft), which is apparently less by a considerable margin than the likely miss distance; single-shot kill probability is thus claimed as 80%, rising to 96% for a salvo; the missile accelerates to its maximum speed of Mach 2·3 in 2·3 seconds, and reaches 8000 m (8,750 yards) in 20 seconds; the

naval system is designated Naval Crotale, and uses a four- or eight-round launcher (respectively **Naval Crotale 4B** or **Naval Crotale 8B**) for the short-range air defence of warships against medium-altitude, low-altitude and sea-skimming attacks; the Naval Crotale system uses Thomson-CSF Ku-band radar acquisition of targets out to a range of 18,000 m (19,685 yards), though any such threats below an altitude of 50 m (165 ft) are handled by an electro-optical tracking system; for adverse-weather operations there is also the **Naval Crotale EDIR** system (also known as **Naval Crotale 8S**) with SAT SEID passive IR tracking of the target and the missile; the IR tracker has a maximum range of 20,000 m (21,875 yards); there is also a **Naval Crotale 8MS** modular system for installation on craft down to a displacement of 200 tons and featuring a lightweight eight-round launcher and fire-director turret that can also be used for gunfire control

Matra Mistral

(France)

Type: ship-launched point defence surface-to-air missile
Dimensions: diameter 0·90 m (3·54 in); length 1·80 m (5·91 ft); span 0·19 m (7·48 in)
Weight: total round 17 kg (37·5 lb)
Warhead: 3-kg (6·6-lb) blast fragmentation HE
Propulsion: SEP solid-propellant booster and sustainer rockets delivering unrevealed thrust
Performance: speed Mach 2·6; range limits 500/6000 m (545/6,560 yards); altitude limits not revealed
Guidance: SAT passive IR homing

Variant

Mistral: entering service in 1986, this lightweight SAM is designed for land and naval use, the latter primarily in the **SADRAL** (Système d'Auto-Défense Rapprochée Anti-aérienne Léger, or light close-range self-defence AA system) designed as for the point defence of larger warships with the Mistral missile; the SADRAL system uses a remotely-controlled six-round launcher also mounting the target-acquisition TV camera, though longer-range acquisition is undertaken by the parent ship's radar, with an optronic system as back-up for the two main acquisition channels; the weight of the mount and six missiles is 900 kg (1,984 lb), plus another 600 kg (1,323 lb) of associated control equipment etc; the **LAMA** is a lightweight point defence missile system developed by CSEE and comprising an optical director/operator's seat flanked by three missile tubes on each side; the type is generally offered with the Mistral missile, but other types (FIM-92 Stinger or RBS 70 Rayrider) can be fitted; the weight of the whole system is in the order of 1000 kg (2,205 lb); the **SIMBAD** (Système Intégré de Mistral Bi-tube d'Auto-Défense, or two-tube Mistral integrated self-defence system) is designed for use on smaller warships; the two missile tubes can be attached to any 20-mm cannon mounting, the gunner using the cannon sight to designate the target.

IMI Barak 1

(Israel)

Type: ship-launched point defence surface-to-air missile
Dimensions: diameter 0·17 m (6·7 in); length 2·17 m (7·12 ft); span 0·68 m (26·77 in)
Weight: total round 86 kg (189·6 lb)
Warhead: 22-kg (48·5-lb) blast fragmentation HE
Propulsion: one solid-propellant triple-thrust rocket delivering unrevealed thrust
Performance: speed Mach 1·7; range limits 500/10,000 m (550/10,935 yards); altitude limits not revealed
Guidance: Elta AMDRS radar command with optical back-up

Variant

Barak 1: developed for the point defence of small warships, the Barak 1 can be carried in an eight-round 2500-kg (5,511-lb) launcher on a mounting derived from that of the TCM-20 AA gun mounting, or in a 1300-kg (2,866-lb) eight-round vertical launcher with 24 reloads in an underdeck magazine; as the missile is of the radar command type, all-weather operation is ensured, and the automatic operation of the system gives capability against multiple attack by aircraft or sea-skimming missiles; the launcher systems offer 360° engagement capability at any elevation between − 25° and + 85°.

Selenia Aspide 1A

(Italy)

Type: ship-launched medium-range surface-to-air missile
Dimensions: diameter 0·203 m (8·0 in); length 3·70 m (12·14 ft); span 0·80 m (31·5 in)

Weight: total round 220 kg (485 lb)
Warhead: 35-kg (77-lb) blast fragmentation HE
Propulsion: one SNIA-Viscosa solid-propellant rocket delivering unrevealed thrust
Performance: speed Mach 4; range limits not revealed/15,000 m (not revealed/16,405 yards); altitude limits not revealed/5000 m (not revealed/16,405 ft)
Guidance: Selenia semi-active radar homing

Variant

Aspide 1A: this is basically similar to the Aspide air-to-air missile, in this instance differing only in the cropping of the wings to fit the surface system's quadruple or octuple launcher; a single-shot kill probability of more than 70% is claimed; the **Albatros** is the ship-borne system using the Aspide missile fired from an OTO Melara launcher with four or eight cells (reloaded in the case of the eight-cell launcher from an optional Riva-Calzoni 16-round underdeck magazine); the Albatros system works in conjunction with the RTN 10X tracking radar and RTN 12X target-illuminating radar; the **Albatros Tipo 1/1** system uses a single director, and the **Albatros Tipo 2/1** system two directors

Bofors Rbs 70 Rayrider

(Sweden)

Type: ship-launched point defence tactical surface-to-air missile
Dimensions: (without booster) diameter 0·106 m (4·17 in); length 1·32 m (4·33 ft); span 0·32 m (12·6 in)
Weight: total round 15 kg (33·07 lb)
Warhead: 1-kg (2·2-lb) blast fragmentation HE
Propulsion: one Bofors solid-propellant booster rocket delivering unrevealed thrust, and one IMI solid-propellant sustainer rocket delivering unrevealed thrust
Performance: speed supersonic; range limits not revealed/5000 m (not revealed/5,470 yards); altitude limits 0/3000 m (0/9,845 ft)
Guidance: laser beam-riding

Variants

Rbs 70 Rayrider: developed in the late 1960s and early 1970s, the Rbs 70 system comprises a stand (a post with tripod legs), a sight unit and 24-kg (52·9-lb) container with preloaded missile; once fired, the missile is gathered into the sight unit's field of vision and then rides the sight's laser straight to the target, where the detonating warhead fills its lethal volume with heavy metal pellets; the empty container can then be replaced by a full one for another engagement; a time of 6 seconds is claimed as the minimum from target detection to missile launch; the naval version is the **Rbs 70 SLM** with a special stand and gyro-stabilized optics; the type can be fitted on the smallest naval vessels, and into-action times of 5 seconds are not uncommon, with a reload time of 20 seconds standard; target designation can also be provided by the vessel's surveillance radar, allowing the operator to slew his mounting to the correct bearing before the target comes into sight.
Rbs 70M Nightrider: night-capable version using the same basic technology as the Rbs 70 Rayrider, but featuring an updated missile with a larger sustainer rocket and heavier warhead used on a remotely-controlled launcher complete with TV and IR cameras and the laser transmitter

Shorts Sea Cat

(UK)

Type: ship-launched point defence surface-to-air missile
Dimensions: diameter 7·5 in (0·191 m); length 4·86 ft (1·48 m); span 25·6 in (0·65 m)
Weight: total round 150 lb (68 kg)
Warhead: 22-lb (10-kg) blast fragmentation HE
Propulsion: one IMI dual-thrust solid-propellant rocket delivering unrevealed thrust
Performance: speed Mach 0·9; range limits not revealed/6,000 yards (not revealed/5485 m); altitude limits 100/3,000 ft (30/915 m)
Guidance: radio command to line of sight with optical gathering and tracking

Variants

Sea Cat GWS 20: introduced to service in the early 1960s, the Sea Cat is a lightweight optically controlled point-defence missile well-suited to the requirements of small ships and small navies; the missile is generally carried on quadruple launchers, though a lightweight triple mounting is available for smaller vessels, and the operator acquires his target through binoculars before firing the missile, acquiring it visually and guiding it to the target; the latest version of the Sea Cat is being developed with anti-radiation homing, though it is unclear whether this is intended for anti-ship or anti-aircraft use

Sea Cat GWS 21: Sea Cat system linked with a radar fire-control system for blind-fire capability; the radar fire-control systems used include the Type 262, Contraves Sea Hunter, San Giorgio NA9 and Hollandse Signaalapparaten WM-40 series

Sea Cat GWS 22: Sea Cat system linked with the MRS3/GWS 22 gun/missile fire-control system with Types 903 and 904 radars for blind-fire capability

Sea Cat GWS 24: Sea Cat system linked with a Marconi closed-circuit TV fire-control system, as well as WSA-4 and Type 912 radar

BAe Sea Dart

(UK)

Type: ship-launched medium-range area-defence surface-to-air missile
Dimensions: diameter 16·5 in (0·42 m); length 14·44 ft (4·40 m); span 36·0 in (0·914 m)
Weight: total round 1,210 lb (549 kg)
Warhead: blast fragmentation HE
Propulsion: one jettisonable IMI solid-propellant booster rocket delivering 35,275-lb (16,000-kg) thrust, and one Rolls-Royce Odin sustainer ramjet delivering variable thrust
Performance: speed Mach 3·5; range limits not revealed/50 + miles (not revealed/80 + km); altitude limits 100/82,000 ft (30/24,995 m)
Guidance: GEC/Sperry semi-active radar homing

Variants

Sea Dart GWS 30: this is a highly capable third-generation naval surface-to-air missile designed for all-altitude engagements at long range, and also for limited surface-to-surface use at ranges out to 18 miles (29 km); the GWS 30 fire-control system is associated with the Type 909 missile-guidance radar after the ship's Type 965 radar has provided long-range warning and the designation of the target in three dimensions to the twin-rail launcher and Type 909 radars; the proximity-fused warhead is capable of dealing with all aerial targets; the launcher is automatically reloaded from an underdeck magazine holding 22 rounds; an abandoned variant was the Sea Dart Mk2 GWS 31 with greater range and Type 1030 STIR radar, and some of the capabilities expected from this development are to be retrofitted on existing systems in a programme announced in 1986; these include the Type 996 3D radar (with automatic rather than manual transfer of data from the surveillance to the tracker radars) and a new warhead

Lightweight Sea Dart: this proposed version is suitable for smaller warships, and comprises a fixed launcher (for containerized Sea Dart rounds), a small fire-control system and Marconi 805SD tracking/illuminating radar

BAe Sea Slug Mk 2

(UK)

Type: ship-launched medium-range area-defence surface-to-air missile
Dimensions: diameter 16·1 in (0·409 m); length 20·0 ft (6·096 m); span 56·6 in (1·438 m)
Weight: total round not revealed
Warhead: 297-lb (135-kg) blast fragmentation HE
Propulsion: four jettisonable solid-propellant Bristol Aerojet rockets each delivering unrevealed thrust, and one ICI solid-propellant sustainer rocket delivering unrevealed thrust
Performance: speed high supersonic; range limits not revealed/36 miles (not revealed/58 km); altitude limits not revealed/50,000 + ft (not revealed/15,240 + m)
Guidance: radar beam-riding

Variant

Sea Slug Mk 2: now obsolete but still found on a few 'County' class destroyers, the Sea Slug was the UK's first operational naval SAM, and the initial Sea Slug Mk 1 was superseded by the Mk 2 with greater range and a capability against low-flying aircraft as well as surface vessels out to the radar horizon; this system is particularly massive, and is associated with a large twin launcher, Type 965 surveillance radar, Type 277 height-finding radar and Type 901 tracking and missile-guidance radar

BAe Sea Wolf

(UK)

Type: ship-launched point defence surface-to-air missile

Dimensions: diameter 7·1 in (0·18 m); length 6·25 ft (1·91 m); span 22·00 in (0·56 m)
Weight: total round 176 lb (79·8 kg)
Warhead: 29·5-lb (13·4-kg) blast fragmentation HE
Propulsion: one Bristol/RPE Blackcap solid-propellant rocket delivering unrevealed thrust
Performance: speed Mach 2+; range limits ?/7,000 yards (?/6400 m); altitude limits 15/10,000 ft (5/3050 m)
Guidance: Marconi radio semi-automatic command to line of sight with radar and/or IR missile and target tracking

Variants

Sea Wolf GWS 25: designed during the 1960s and introduced in 1979, the Sea Wolf is a highly capable point-defence system capable of dealing with aircraft, missiles and even shells; the complete **Sea Wolf GWS 25 Mod 0** equipment (sextuple launcher, automatic reloader, 30-round magazine, fire-control system, Marconi-Elliott TV tracker, Type 910 tracking radar, etc) is both bulky and weighty (making it difficult to install the system on ships of less than 2,500-ton displacement), and the desire to install two such systems on the double-ended 'Type 22' class frigates dictated the eventual dimensions and displacement of the ships; the later **Sea Wolf GWS 25 Mod 3** makes use of the Type 911 (Marconi 805SW with the millimetric-wavelength DN181 Blindfire) radar for a considerably lighter installation, suitable for ships down to 1,000-ton displacement

Lightweight Sea Wolf or Sea Wolf VM40: this is a lightweight system devised by BAe and Hollandse Signaalapparaten using the HSA STIR tracking radar and a converted four-round Sea Cat launcher with automatic reloading or (considerably lighter) four disposable plastic or long-life metal launch tubes

Vertical-Launch Sea Wolf GWS 26 Mod 1: this system is being developed for the British 'Type 23e' class frigate and for export, the type offering faster response time, greater range (11,00 yards/10,060 m) and reduced system weight; a 32-cell launcher designed by IMI or developed by Vickers from the Martin-Marietta VLS for the US Navy is used with this system

Vertical-Launch Sea Wolf GWS 27: private-venture development by BAe and Marconi for autonomous fire-and-forget capability with enhanced electronic counter-countermeasures capability (through the installation of an active radar seeker operating in conjunction with SACLOS or inertial midcourse guidance) over an increased maximum range of 6·2 miles (10 km)

SA-N-1 'Goa'

(USSR)

Type: ship-launched medium-range area-defence surface-to-air missile
Dimensions: diameter (missile) 0·46 m (18·1 in) and (booster) 0·701 m (27·6 in); length overall 6·70 m (21·98 ft); span (missile) 1·22 m (4·00 ft) and (booster) 1·50 m (4·92 ft)
Weight: total round (SA-N-1A) 946 kg (2,805·5 lb) or (SA-N-1B) 950 kg (2,094·4 lb)
Warhead: 10-kiloton nuclear or 60-kg (132-lb) blast fragmentation HE
Propulsion: one jettisonable solid-propellant booster rocket delivering unrevealed thrust, and one solid-propellant sustainer rocket delivering unrevealed thrust
Performance: speed Mach 2·1; range limits 6000/22,000 m (6,560/24,060 yards); altitude limits 50/15,250 m (165/50,030 ft)
Guidance: radio command or (SA-N-1B) semi-active radar terminal homing

Variants

SA-N-1A 'Goa': navalized version of the land-based SA-3A, the SA-N-1A was introduced in 1961 as the USSR's first fully-deployed surface-to-air missile; the type is used on a twin launcher stabilized in one axis and supplied from a 16-round magazine, and is controlled with the aid of 'Peel Group' radar; the missile has the service designation **M-1**

SA-N-2B 'Goa': improved version with the 'Peel Group' radar modified to provide semi-active radar guidance

SA-N-3 'Goblet'

(USSR)

Type: ship-launched medium-range area-defence surface-to-air missile
Dimensions: diameter 0·70 m (27·6 in); length 6·40 m (21·00 ft); span 1·70 m (5·58 ft)
Weight: total round 540 kg (1,190 lb)
Warhead: 25-kiloton nuclear or 150-kg (331-lb) blast fragmentation HE
Propulsion: one solid-propellant rocket delivering unrevealed thrust
Performance: speed Mach 2·8; range limits (early version) 6/30 km (3·7/18·6

miles) or (later version) 6/55 km (3·7/37 miles); altitude limits 90/24,500 m (295/80,380 ft)
Guidance: radar command

Variant
SA-N-3 'Goblet': at first thought to be the naval derivative of the SA-6 'Gainful', this powerful SAM entered Soviet service in 1967 as a partial successor to the SA-N-1 'Goa' system; the type is fired from a twin launcher, and the radar fire-control system is the 'Head Light' outfit; the missile can also be used in the surface-to-surface role over ranges as far as the radar horizon

SA-N-4 'Gecko'

(USSR)
Type: ship-launched point defence tactical surface-to-air missile
Dimensions: diameter 0·21 m (8·25 in); length 3·20 m (10·50 ft); span 0·64 m (25·2 in)
Weight: total round 190 kg (419 lb)
Warhead: 40- to 50-kg (88- to 110-lb) blast fragmentation HE
Propulsion: one solid-propellant dual-thrust rocket delivering unrevealed thrust
Performance: speed Mach 2; range limits 1600/12,000 m (1,750/13,125 yards); altitude limits 50/13,000 m (165/42,650 ft)
Guidance: radar or optical command plus semi-active radar and/or IR terminal homing

Variant
SA-N-4 'Gecko': naval version of the SA-8B land-based SAM, the SA-N-4 entered service in the early 1970s and is associated with a retractable twin launcher (fed by an 18- or 20-round magazine) and the 'Pop Group' radar fire-control system; the missile can also be used in the surface-to-surface role over any range to the radar horizon

SA-N-5 'Grail'

(USSR)
Type: ship-launched point defence surface-to-air missile
Dimensions: diameter 0·07 m (2·75 in); length 1·30 m (4·27 ft); span not revealed
Weight: total round 9·2 kg (20·3 lb)
Warhead: 2·5-kg (5·5-lb) blast fragmentation HE
Propulsion: one solid-propellant booster rocket delivering unrevealed thrust, and one solid-propellant sustainer rocket delivering unrevealed thrust
Performance: speed Mach 1·5; range limits not revealed/3600 m (not revealed/3,935 yards); altitude limits 45/1500 m (150/4,920 ft)
Guidance: IR homing

Variant
SA-N-5 'Grail': naval version of the SA-7B, the improved model of the basic SA-7A man-portable SAM with an IFF system and a more powerful motor, increasing speed to Mach 1·7 and ceiling to 4800 m (15,750 ft); this point-defence weapon is used in a four-round pedestal mount (with lockers containing four or eight reloads) on small surface combatants, auxiliaries and amphibious warfare ships

SA-N-6 'Grumble'

(USSR)
Type: ship-launched medium-range area-defence surface-to-air missile
Dimensions: diameter 0·45 m (17·72 in); length 7·00 m (22·97 ft); span 1·20 m (3·94 ft)
Weight: total round 1500 kg (3,307 lb)
Warhead: 100-kg (220-lb) blast fragmentation HE or (possibly) nuclear with an unrevealed yield
Propulsion: one solid-propellant rocket delivering unrevealed thrust
Performance: speed Mach 6; range limits 9·5/65 km (5·9/40·4 miles); altitude limits 10/30,500 m (33/100,065 ft)
Guidance: semi-active radar for the cruise phase and active radar terminal homing

Variant
SA-N-6 'Grumble': entering service in 1978, this is the naval version of the SA-10, designed for vertical launch from underdeck silos each fed by an eight-round rotary magazine; mid-course target illumination is provided by the launch ship's 'Top Dome' radar

SA-N-7 'Gadfly'

(USSR)
Type: ship-launched short/medium-range area-defence surface-to-air missile
Dimensions: diameter 0·40 m (15·75 in); length 5·60 m (18·37 ft); span 1·20 m (3·94 ft)
Weight: total round 650 kg (1,433 lb)
Warhead: 90-kg (198-lb) blast fragmentation HE
Propulsion: one jettisonable solid-propellant booster rocket delivering unrevealed thrust, and one solid-propellant sustainer rocket delivering unrevealed thrust
Performance: speed Mach 3; range limits 3/30 km (1·86/18·6 miles); altitude limits 30/15,000 m (100/49,213 ft)
Guidance: radio command plus semi-active monopulse radar terminal homing

Variant
SA-N-7 'Gadfly': naval version of the SA-11 land-based SAM, the SA-N-7 was introduced in 1981 and is intended to replace the SA-N-1 'Goa' series, and the standard fit is two single launchers with six to eight 'Front Dome' target-illuminating radars for the engagement of multiple targets

SA-N-9

(USSR)
Type: ship-launched short/medium-range surface-to-air missile
Dimensions: (estimated) 0·60 m (23·6 in); length 3·50 m (11·48 ft); span not known
Weight: total round not revealed
Warhead: blast fragmentation HE
Propulsion: solid-propellant rocket delivering unrevealed thrust
Performance: speed not revealed; range limits not revealed/16,000 m (not revealed/17,500 yards); altitude limits 18/18,000 m (60/59,055 ft)
Guidance: radar command

Variant
SA-N-9: ship-launched missile first seen in the form of the vertical launchers carried on the 'Udaloy' class, *Novorossiysk* ('Kiev' class) and *Frunze* ('Kirov' class) ships, which were initially thought to be for the SA-NX-8 missile; the SA-N-9 is designed as successor to the SA-N-4 'Goa' series, and is matched to the 'Top Mesh/Top Plate' 3D surveillance and 'Cross Sword' guidance radars; the missiles are accommodated in an eight-round underdeck magazine that rotates to bring a missile into the single launch position under a deck hatch

General Dynamics RIM-2D(N) Terrier

(USA)
Type: ship-launched medium-range area-defence surface-to-air missile
Dimensions: diameter (missile) 13·5 in (0·343 m) and (booster) 18·0 in (0·457 m); length (missile) 13·5 ft (4·115 m) and (booster) 25·83 ft (7·874 m); span (missile) 3·5 ft (1·07 m)
Weight: missile 1,180 lb (535·2 kg) and booster 1,820 lb (825·5 kg)
Warhead: 1-kiloton W45 nuclear
Propulsion: one Allegany Ballistics solid-propellant booster rocket delivering unrevealed thrust, and one Allegany Ballistics solid-propellant sustainer rocket delivering unrevealed thrust
Performance: speed Mach 3; range limits not revealed/23 miles (not revealed/37 km); altitude limits 500/80,000 ft (150/24,385 m)
Guidance: radar beam-riding

Variants
RIM-2D(N) Terrier: introduced in 1958, this nuclear-armed version of the RIM-2D dedicated air-defence SAM was developed to provide US surface combatants with a nuclear-armed surface-to-air missile with powerful surface-to-surface capability out to the radar horizon; most other variants of the extensive Terrier family have been or are being replaced in the surface-to-air role by the RIM-66/RIM-67 Standard Series; associated with the Terrier is the Mk 10 twin launcher and magazines holding 40, 60, or 80 reload rounds
RIM-2F Terrier: introduced in 1963, this conventionally-armed SAM has an overall length of 26·17 ft (7·98 m), a weight of 3,090 lb (1402 kg) and propulsion comprising an Atlantic Research Mk 30 Mod 2 solid-propellant booster rocket and a Naval Ordnance Station Indian Head Mk 12 Mod 1 (later Thiokol Mk 70 Mod 1) solid-propellant sustainer rocket; the variant uses semi-active radar homing

Raytheon RIM-7M Sea Sparrow

(USA)

Type: ship-launched point defence surface-to-air missile
Dimensions: diameter 8·0 in (0·203 m); length 13·08 ft (3·99 m); span 40·0 in (1·02 m)
Weight: total round 503 lb (228·2 kg)
Warhead: 88-lb (40-kg) blast fragmentation HE
Propulsion: one Hercules Mk 58 Mod 4 two-stage solid-propellant rocket delivering unrevealed thrust
Performance: speed Mach 3 + ; range limits not revealed/24,250 yards (not revealed/22,175 m); altitude limits 25/50,000 ft (8/15,240 m)
Guidance: semi-active radar homing

Variants

RIM-7E5 Sea Sparrow: developed in the early 1960s from the AIM-7E Sparrow air-to-air missile, the RIM-7E5 is powered by the Mk 38 solid-propellant rocket and was adopted in 1969 as the US Navy's **Basic Point Defense Missile System** together with the Mk 25 octuple launcher located on a converted 3-in (76-mm) gun mounting; associated with this system are the analog Mk 115 fire-control system and the Mk 51 manually-controlled director and illuminator; a version of the same missile, the AIM-7E2 air-to-air missile with reduced minimum engagement range plus enhanced manoeuvrability, was adopted for the **Canadian Sea Sparrow System**, which uses a four-round launcher associated with the Hollandse Signaalapparaten WM-22/6 fire-control system with monopulse track while scan, moving target indication search, pulse-Doppler tracking, continuous-wave target illumination and electronic counter-countermeasures capabilities
RIM-7F Sea Sparrow: the missile is derived from the AIM-9F with the Mk 58 or Mk 65 solid-propellant rocket and improved capabilities against low-flying targets, and is compatible with the **NATO Sea Sparrow System** and its Mk 29 octuple launcher, digital fire-control system, and powered tracker and illuminator
RIM-7H5 Sea Sparrow: RIM-7E5 reconfigured for compatability with the Mk 29 launcher and its associated electronics including the Mk 91 fire-control system
RIM-7M Sea Sparrow: improved missile based on the AIM-7M with its monopulse seeker, and adopted in 1983; the type has folding fins for less bulky naval installation
RIM-7P Sea Sparrow: under development in the late 1980s in parallel with the AIM-9P Sparrow air-to-air missile, this is a Raytheon project whose details have not been revealed; it is likely that the improvement under consideration is electronic rather than aerodynamic or propulsive

General Dynamics RIM-24B Improved Tartar

(USA)

Type: ship-launched medium-range area-defence surface-to-air missile
Dimensions: diameter 13·5 in (0·343 m); length 15·5 ft (4·724 m); span 24·0 in (0·609 m)
Weight: total round 1,325 lb (601 kg)
Warhead: blast fragmentation HE
Propulsion: one Aerojet Mk 27 Mod 2/3 dual-thrust solid-propellant rocket delivering unrevealed thrust
Performance: speed Mach 1·8; range limits not revealed/20 miles (not revealed/32·2 km); altitude limits 50/70,000 ft (15/21,335 m)
Guidance: semi-active radar homing

Variant

RIM-24B Improved Tartar: introduced in 1963, this is the only production version of the RIM-24 Tartar series remaining in service; it is a comparatively light medium-range weapon (with a dual-thrust rocket to obviate the need for a booster) designed for use as the primary weapon of destroyers and lighter vessels, and as the secondary armament of cruisers; the basic role is the interception of low- and medium-level attackers with a FRAG-HE warhead, though the type can engage high-altitude attackers and has a surface-to-surface capability out to the radar horizon; the type is associated with the Mk 11 twin launcher (plus a magazine for 42 reload rounds) and Mks 13 and 22 single launchers (40 and 16 reload rounds respectively), and with the SPG-51 missile-guidance radar, the combination generally being operated in conjunction with the SPS-52 search radar for early warning
RIM-24C Improved Tartar: upgraded RIM-24B

General Dynamics RIM-66A/B Standard SM-1 MR

(USA)

Type: ship-launched medium-range area-defence surface-to-air missile
Dimensions: diameter 13·5 in (0·343 m); length (RIM-66A) 14·67 ft (4·47 m) or (RIM-66B) 15·5 ft (4·724 m); span 36·0 in (0·914 m)
Weight: total round (RIM-66A) 1,276 lb (578·8 kg) or (RIM-66B) 1,342 lb (608·7 kg)
Warhead: blast fragmentation HE
Propulsion: one Aerojet/Hercules MK 56 Mod 0 dual-thrust solid-propellant rocket delivering unrevealed thrust
Performance: speed Mach 2 + ; range limits (RIM-66A) not revealed/28·75 miles (not revealed/46·25 km) or (RIM-66B) not revealed/41·6 miles) (not revealed/67 km); altitude limits (RIM-66A) not revealed/50,000 ft (not revealed/15,240 m) or (RIM-66B) not revealed/62,500 ft (not revealed/19,050 m)
Guidance: semi-active radar homing

Variants

RIM-66A Standard SM-1 MR: designed from the early 1960s as replacement for the Tartar short/medium-range area-defence SAM, the Standard SM-1 MR series reflected a growing realization in the US Navy that the primary threat faced in Soviet air attack was saturation of the American warships' target-illumination capabilities as the Terrier and Tartar systems require a dedicated illuminator for each missile; the RIM-66A (notable as the first US Navy missile with all-solid-state electronics, though still of the analog type), entered service in 1968 with the Mk 27 Mod 0 solid-propellant rocket, and is generally associated with the Mk 11/12 twin launcher (42 missiles), Mk 13 single launcher (40 missiles), Mk 22 single launcher (16 missiles) and Mk 26 single launcher (24, 44, or 64 missiles); the type has a horizon-limited surface-to-surface capability, and a proximity- and impact-fused HE warhead
RIM-66B Standard SM-1 MR: improved RIM-66A with upgraded motor for increases of 45% in range and 25% in maximum engagement altitude, but otherwise having the capabilities of the RIM-66A

General Dynamics RIM-67A Standard SM-1 ER

(USA)

Type: ship-launched medium/long-range area-defence surface-to-air missile
Dimensions: diameter 13·5 in (0·343 m); length 26·17 ft (7·98 m); span 36·0 in (0·914 m)
Weight: total round 1,360 lb (616·9 kg)
Warhead: blast fragmentation HE
Propulsion: one jettisonable Naval Propellant Plant Mk 12 Mod 1 solid-propellant booster rocket delivering unrevealed thrust, and one Atlantic Research Mk 30 Mod 2 solid-propellant sustainer rocket delivering unrevealed thrust
Performance: speed Mach 2·5 + ; range limits not revealed/46 miles (not revealed/74 km); altitude limits not revealed/80,000 ft (not revealed/24,385 m)
Guidance: semi-active radar homing

Variant

RIM-67A Standard SM-1 ER: produced in parallel with the RIM-66A and RIM-66B as a longer-range weapon to replace the Terrier and Talos systems of the previous generation, the RIM-67A has a different propulsion arrangement (a booster stage being appended to the base of the missile power) for greater range and a higher altitude limit; the ER (Extended Range) versions of the Standard missile are associated with the Mk 10 twin launcher and a magazine for 40, 60, or 80 missiles depending on the size of the parent ship

General Dynamics RIM-66C Standard SM-2 MR

(USA)

Type: ship-launched medium-range area-defence surface-to-air missile
Dimensions: diameter 13·5 in (0·343 m); length 15·5 ft (4·724 m); span 36·0 in (0·914 m)
Weight: total round 1,342 lb (608·7 kg)
Warhead: blast fragmentation HE

Propulsion: one Aerojet/Hercules Mk 56 Mod 0 dual-thrust solid-propellant rocket delivering unrevealed thrust
Performance: speed Mach 2+; range limits not revealed/56 miles (not revealed/74 km); altitude limits not revealed/80,000 ft (not revealed/24,385 m)
Guidance: semi-active radar homing

Variants

RIM-66C Standard SM-2 MR: introduced to match the AEGIS weapon system (SPY-1A phased-array radar, Mk 99 fire-control system, Mk 1 weapons-control system and Mk 1 command and decision system), the SM-2 series is an electronic development of the SM-1 type with digital electronics including a monopulse homing receiver (instead of the SM-1's conical-scan semi-active homing) with greater resistance to electronic countermeasures, an inertial reference unit for mid-course guidance, and a data-link for mid-course updating and thus optimization of the flight profile by making possible a more energy-efficient trajectory to increase range; in the SM-2 MR model this produces a 60% increase in range compared with that of the SM-1 MR

Standard SM-2 MR(N): version under development with a W81 low-yield nuclear warhead, providing the US Navy with a capable tactical/operational weapon against high-threat attacks on major units (together with a powerful surface-to-surface capability out to the radar horizon, or beyond it with the aid of mid-course update from a targeting helicopter)

General Dynamics RIM-67B Standard SM-2 ER

(USA)

Type: ship-launched long-range area-defence surface-to-air missile
Dimensions: diameter 13·5 in (0·343 m); length 27·0 ft (8·23 m); span 36·0 in (0·914 m)
Weight: total round 3,058 lb (1387·1 kg)
Warhead: blast fragmentation HE
Propulsion: one jettisonable Naval Propellant Plant Mk 12 Mod 1 solid-propellant booster rocket delivering unrevealed thrust, and one Atlantic Research Mk 30 Mod 2 solid-propellant sustainer rocket delivering unrevealed thrust
Performance: speed Mach 2.5+; range limits not revealed/92 miles (not revealed/148 km); altitude limits not revealed/100,000 ft (not revealed/30,480 m)
Guidance: semi-active radar homing

Variants

RIM-67B Standard SM-2 ER: this is the extended-range equivalent of the RIM-66B, and has the same electronic improvements for optimum trajectory, in this case boosting range by 100%
Standard SM-2 ER(N): version under development with a W81 low-yield nuclear warhead, and offering the same type of capabilities as the SM-2 MR(N) though having greater need of mid-course guidance if the full range capability of the missile is to be used in the surface-to-surface role

Ford MIM-72C Sea Chaparral

(USA)

Type: ship-launched point defence surface-to-air missile
Dimensions: 5·12 in (0·13 m); length 9·54 ft (2·91 m); span 24·76 in (0·629 m)
Weight: total round 190 lb (86·3 kg)
Warhead: 24·7 lb (11·2-kg) M250 blast fragmentation HE
Propulsion: one Bermite Mk 50 Mod 0 solid-propellant rocket delivering unrevealed thrust
Performance: speed supersonic; range limits not revealed/6,500 yards (not revealed/5945 m); altitude limits 1,150/10,000 ft (350/3050 m)
Guidance: Ford Aerospace IR homing

Variant

MIM-72C Sea Chaparral: this is the naval version of the Chaparral system, used only by the Taiwanese navy for the point defence of major units; the missile is identical to the land-based MIM-72C/R weapon, and the launcher incorporates a minimum of change; there is also a naval version of the MIM-72F missile for use in the Sea Chaparral system

General Dynamics RIM-116A RAM

(USA)

Type: ship-launched point defence surface-to-air missile
Dimensions: diameter 5·0 in (0·127 m); length 9·17 ft (2·79 m); span 17·25 in (0·438 m)
Weight: total round 159 lb (72·1 kg)
Warhead: 22·4-lb (10·2-kg) WDU-17/B blast fragmentation HE
Propulsion: one Bermite/Hercules Mk 36 Mod 7 solid-propellant rocket delivering 3,000-lb (1361-kg) thrust
Performance: speed Mach 2+; range limits not revealed/10,300 yards (not revealed/9420 m); altitude limits not revealed
Guidance: General Dynamics semi-active radar and IR terminal homing

Variant

RIM-116A RAM: designed as a missile counterpart to the Phalanx 20-mm close-in gun system, the Rolling Airframe Missile is intended as a point-defence system for frigates and attack craft faced with missile as well as aircraft attack; the missile uses proved components wherever possible (the warhead, fuse and motor of the AIM-9 Sidewinder, and the infra-red seeker of the FIM-92 Stinger for example), together with a rolling airframe and passive radar seeker for mid-course guidance and to ensure that the terminal homing system is accurately aligned towards the end of the flight; current launcher options are the EX-31 with 24 tubes on a Phalanx gun mounting for training and elevation (West German and Danish vessels), and five-round inserts fitted into the two central lower cells of the Mk 16 octuple ASROC launcher or of the Mks 25 and 29 Sea Sparrow octuple launchers (US vessels)